CW01338758

THE COMPLETE SONGS OF HUGO WOLF

by the same author

THE BOOK OF LIEDER, chosen, translated and introduced by Richard Stokes
BOULEZ ON CONDUCTING – PIERRE BOULEZ, translated by Richard Stokes
CURSING BAGELS – ALFRED BRENDEL, translated by Richard Stokes
THE VEIL OF ORDER – ALFRED BRENDEL, translated by Richard Stokes
ONE FINGER TOO MANY – ALFRED BRENDEL, translated by Richard Stokes

also by Richard Stokes

J. S. BACH – THE COMPLETE CANTATAS, translated by Richard Stokes, Scarecrow Press
THE PENGUIN BOOK OF ENGLISH SONG: SEVEN CENTURIES OF POETRY FROM CHAUCER TO AUDEN, edited with an introduction and notes by Richard Stokes, Penguin Classics
A FRENCH SONG COMPANION (with Graham Johnson) OUP
THE SPANISH SONG COMPANION (with Jacqueline Cockburn and Graham Johnson) Gollancz
MEMOIRS OF AN ACCOMPANIST – HELMUT DEUTSCH, translated by Richard Stokes, Kahn & Averill

DEAREST FATHER – FRANZ KAFKA, translated by Hannah and Richard Stokes, Alma Classics
METAMORPHOSIS – FRANZ KAFKA, translated by Richard Stokes, Hesperus Press
THE TRIAL – FRANZ KAFKA, translated by Richard Stokes, Alma Classics
THE MARQUISE OF O – HEINRICH VON KLEIST, translated by Richard Stokes, Alma Classics
HISTOIRES NATURELLES – JULES RENARD, translated by Richard Stokes, Alma Classics

THE COMPLETE SONGS
OF
HUGO WOLF
LIFE, LETTERS, LIEDER

RICHARD STOKES

WITH A FOREWORD BY IAN BOSTRIDGE

faber

First published in 2021
by Faber & Faber Ltd
Bloomsbury House
74–77 Great Russell Street
London WC1B 3DA

Typeset by Agnesi Text, Hadleigh, Suffolk
Printed and bound by CPI Group (UK) Ltd, Croydon, CR0 4YY

All rights reserved
English translation, Introduction and editorial matter © Richard Stokes, 2021
Foreword © Ian Bostridge, 2021

The right of Richard Stokes to be identified as translator of this work has been asserted in accordance with Section 77 of the Copyright, Designs and Patents Act 1988

A CIP record for this book
is available from the British Library

ISBN 978–0–571–36069–7

2 4 6 8 10 9 7 5 3 1

FOR GRAHAM JOHNSON

HW to Josef Strasser, Perchtoldsdorf, 23 March 1888

Was ich jetzt aufschreibe, das, lieber Freund, schreibe ich auch schon für die Nachwelt. Es sind Meisterwerke [. . .] darüber es unter Musikverständigen nur eine Stimme gibt, dass seit Schubert und Schumann nichts ähnliches da war.

What I now write, dear friend, I write for posterity also. They are masterpieces [. . .] about which there is only one opinion among those of musical discernment – namely that there has been nothing like them since Schubert and Schumann.

HW to Emil Kauffmann, Traunkirchen, 12 October 1891

Wahrlich, mir graut schon vor meinen Liedern. Die schmeichelhafte Anerkennung als „Liederkomponist" betrübt mich in die innerste Seele. Was anders will es denn bedeuten, als eben einen Vorwurf, daß ich immer nur Lieder componire, daß ich doch nur ein kleines genre beherrsche u. dieses nicht einmal vollkommen.

Truly, I have come to dread my songs. The flattering recognition I've gained as a 'song composer' makes me sick at heart. What else does it mean, other than a reproach that I only ever write songs, that I am only master of a small genre, & do not even have complete mastery of that.

Contents

Foreword *Ian Bostridge* xi

Introduction xv
Acknowledgements xxii
How to Use This Book xxv
Translator's Note xxvi

Chronology: Life xxix
Chronology: Letters xxxvii
Chronology: Lieder xlv

THE POETS

Anonymous 3
Lord Byron 8
Adelbert von Chamisso 13
Joseph von Eichendorff 16
Emanuel Geibel (*Spanisches Liederbuch*) 52
Johann Wolfgang von Goethe 107
Friedrich Hebbel 174
Heinrich Heine 181
Karl Herloßsohn 205
Paul Heyse (*Italienisches Liederbuch*) 207
Edmund Hoefer 259
August Heinrich Hoffmann von Fallersleben 261
Henrik Ibsen 266
Johann Georg Jacobi 274
Gottfried Keller 276
Justinus Kerner 290
Theodor Körner 295
Nikolaus Lenau 298
Lenz Lorenzi 314
August Mahlmann 315
Friedrich von Matthisson 316

Michelangelo Buonarroti 320
Eduard Mörike 330
Paul Peitl 419
Ludwig Pfau 422
August von Platen 424
Robert Reinick 430
Otto Roquette 448
Friedrich Rückert 450
Joseph Victor von Scheffel 457
William Shakespeare 463
Julius Sturm 469
Heinrich Zschokke 471
Vincenz Zusner 473

Correspondents 475

Appendix 1   Detlev von Liliencron's 'An Hugo Wolf' 525
Appendix 2   Michael Haberlandt's Funeral Oration 530
Appendix 3   Orchestrated Songs 532
Appendix 4   Opera 534
Appendix 5   Sketches and Fragments 541

Bibliography 545
Index of Titles and First Lines 549
General Index 564

Foreword

IAN BOSTRIDGE

I owe my love for the Lied to the author of this book, Richard Stokes, my German teacher at my London school, who enthused whole classes of awkward adolescents with the rare joys of experiencing great poetry through the transformative apparatus of Romantic song. We sang songs together in class and we went to concerts, notably the Songmakers Almanac evenings which the pianist Graham Johnson was hosting down the road at Wigmore Hall.

What an extraordinary moment in London's musical life it was for song lovers, around 1980; a felicitous fusion of one audience (elderly German expatriates) steeped in the culture of their upbringing, and another excited by the notion of London as a capital of European culture. It all came together in a hall that opened less than two years before the death of Hugo Wolf, the Bechstein Hall, now the Wigmore, a perfect space for song, which embodies in bricks, mortar and marble the words that open Wolf's *Italienisches Liederbuch* – *Auch kleine Dinge können uns entzücken* – small things can also delight us.

And so London ended up being the European centre not just of capital markets but also of the Lied. A hundred years after the death of Hugo Wolf, song recitals and song audiences were flourishing in London in a way unimaginable in Paris, Amsterdam or even Vienna and Berlin. And, twenty years on from that, the Wigmore is still at the forefront of keeping song alive in the midst of a phenomenon with a very early twentieth-century feel, a global pandemic.

Schubert was for us schoolboys the beginning of it all – the drama of 'Erlkönig' to set out with, but then the whole gamut from the ravishment of 'Gretchen am Spinnrade' to the sly charm of 'Heidenröslein', and finally a first encounter with the Everest of the genre, *Winterreise*. For adolescent boys of a certain tragic disposition, *Die schöne Müllerin* was, of course, indispensable. With all this wonderful musical experience at hand, we learned some of the first lessons of the Lied: bad poems can make great songs; melody is not everything.

Schubert was misunderstood, even by his friends, as a melodist. It is true that in the mysterious business of creating memorable, satisfying melodies (as opposed to catchy, insistent tunes) he was a master. But what made the Romantic Lied new was the symbiosis between voice and piano. This relationship is intensified in the songs of Robert Schumann, and by the time we get to Hugo Wolf and the late nineteenth century, any idea of the piano part of a song as mere accompaniment is absurd.

My very first encounter with Hugo Wolf predated my schoolboy love affair with the Lied and feels sort of accidental. In the 1970s, Leonard Bernstein persuaded Barbra Streisand to record an album of classical song, *Classical Barbra*, which included among its tracks the delicate yearning of Wolf's setting of Eichendorff's 'Verschwiegene Liebe'. My brother owned the album and so, secretly, Wolf must have entered my bloodstream.

As a fragile teenage tenor I was impressed by the mighty side of Wolf: for instance, the fury and terror of 'Der Feuerreiter' from the Mörike songbook, a song I didn't dare sing in public until I was well into my thirties. For an idea of how simply gripping a Wolf song can be, watch Dietrich Fischer-Dieskau and Sviatoslav Richter rehearsing it, on YouTube, F-D simply astonished by Richter's casual virtuosity – he seems to be sight reading – and relishing every feverish moment. Late at night as an undernourished adolescent I would grapple with the titanic defiance of a song which I will never sing in public, Wolf's setting of Goethe's 'Prometheus', a bass-baritone song if ever there was one, but a masterful rendering of a great, great poem.

Here is one issue with Wolf that singers must deal with, the issue of transposition. While Schubert seems to have been quite relaxed about which keys his songs should be sung in, Wolf was apparently more picky. It has been common over the years for baritones to transpose Wolf's songs down; less common for tenors, for example, to transpose them up. 'Prometheus' does have a low resonance grandeur, in piano and voice, which it is difficult to ignore; but over the years the very different grandeur of another Goethe setting, 'Grenzen der Menschheit', has drawn me back to it again and again. There can be no greater example in the whole song literature of a piece that binds together metaphysical poetry and metaphysical music to give us a vision of the infinite. If I transpose it, I feel guilty, but I can't give it up.

There are songs of Wolf that I continue to find refractory – the percussive clatter of some of the drinking songs from the Goethe set is challenging for performers and audience alike, and it's difficult to avoid a hint of unwanted aggression. But what I take away overall from my experience with Hugo Wolf is his wonderful way with melody, when it suits the poem – a poem like 'Der Gärtner', or 'Verborgenheit', or the peerless 'Nun wandre, Maria' from the *Spanisches Liederbuch* – and his ability in other songs to create such extraordinary intensity that lack of obvious melody, as the voice traces the movements of the mind, is both appropriate and unnoticed. In my early twenties, the Mörike settings of 'Peregrina I and II' were often with me in concert and masterclass, and one cannot live more fully as a singer than by singing these burning, brief masterpieces.

I've performed a lot of Wolf over the past quarter-century, but two experiences stand out. First, a series of concerts, in Europe and the US, with close colleagues (Angelika Kirchschlager and Julius Drake) performing the *Spanisches*

Liederbuch. As a concert piece, the set is unwieldy, though every song is to treasure. The religious songs are just right for one half of a recital; the secular songs are simply too many. The whole cycle is really one and a half evenings' worth, an awkward length to be sure. We ruthlessly decided to perform only a selection of the secular songs, and it was liberating.

Second (and, again, with Julius Drake), I remember some early recitals of the *Eichendorff-Lieder*. Wolf's most famous achievement, his Mörike songbook, shines musical light on every aspect of the poet's output. But again there are too many songs to be given in one recital, fifty-three in all. The Eichendorff set, much smaller, is wide-ranging, engaging with the Romantic mystery of the poet – famously brought to life by Schumann in his Op. 39 *Liederkreis* – but also with his witty, youthful braggadocio. They make a wonderful recital half.

There could be no better starting point for understanding these songs than Richard Stokes's detailed and engaging book.

March 2021

Introduction

Audiences still find Wolf difficult. They flock to Liederabende devoted to the songs of Beethoven, Brahms, Mahler, Mendelssohn, Schubert, Schumann or Strauss – but Wolf, one of the greatest of all Lieder composers, they find difficult. Touring north Germany with the *Italienisches Liederbuch*, Helmut Deutsch found the songs described by the press on one occasion as „fast vergessene Lieder" ('almost forgotten songs'), and although complete performances of the *Italian Songbook* are relatively common in Great Britain, entire recitals devoted to Wolf's other songs are rare. Dietrich Fischer-Dieskau relates in *Hugo Wolf. Leben und Werk* how George Szell asked him after a Mörike-Abend in Lucerne, „Weshalb singen Sie so etwas überhaupt? Das ist doch gar keine Musik!" ('But why do you even sing such stuff? It's simply not music!')

Melody is the stumbling block. The melodic line of most nineteenth-century Lieder composers is essentially *cantabile*. It's possible – though scarcely recommended – to perform many songs by Brahms, Mendelssohn, Schubert and Schumann without the words, without a singer, but with an instrumental obbligato. Or as vocalises. The full meaning of each song would, of course, go out of the window, but it would be possible – even pleasant. Think of the many wonderful transcriptions of Schubert Lieder by Liszt. Not just *Schwanengesang* and selections from *Die schöne Müllerin* and *Winterreise* but such gems as 'Auf dem Wasser zu singen', 'Du bist die Ruh', 'Ave Maria', 'Erlkönig', 'Die Forelle', 'Frühlingsglaube', 'Gretchen am Spinnrade', 'Die junge Nonne', 'Meeres Stille' and 'Rastlose Liebe'. Schubert's melodies lend themselves to such treatment.

With Wolf's Lieder this is generally not the case. Exceptions such as 'Fußreise', 'Verborgenheit' or 'Der Gärtner' merely prove the rule, and it's significant that it was precisely these songs that Wolf began to criticise with some bitterness when they were so frequently performed. He wrote to Karl Mayr (15 March 1897) that he considered 'Verborgenheit' to be „abgedroschen" – hackneyed (see HW to Karl Mayr, 15 March 1897, p. 285). In a letter to Paul Müller of 16 May 1898, he referred to it, along with 'Fußreise' and 'Der Gärtner', as „Vorspeise leichtere[r] Kost" – a rather light hors d'œuvre. And Oskar Grohe, in a letter of 26 September 1904 to Wolf's first biographer Ernst Decsey, described Wolf's fury at the way singers programmed 'Verborgenheit' rather than other songs of his: „Immer singen's, als wenn ich nix Anderes geschrieben hätte. Einstampfen laß ich das Lied noch." ('They always sing it, as though I had written nothing else. I shall have the song pulped.') These wonderful Lieder became popular because of their melodic immediacy, but they were not, in Wolf's view, typical of his art.

Wolf's greatest Lieder are different. Take the Harper's songs from *Wilhelm Meister*, for example. Schubert, Schumann and Wolf all approached these poems – the loneliest in all Goethe – in different ways. The pathological nature of the Harper's character in 'Wer nie sein Brot mit Tränen aß' is painted by Schumann with the help of manic splashes of sound, frenzied repetitions and virtuoso pianistic flourishes; Schubert's way in his *Gesänge des Harfners* is simpler: plaintive, heart-rending melodies all in A minor, his key of disenchantment and derangement, which he was also to use in 'Der Leiermann'. Wolf, on the other hand, portrays the Harper's madness through intense chromaticism, daring dissonances and a seeming absence of tonality – not easy for the listener used to the *cantabile* quality of Schubert's melodies. The main focus in Wolf's songs, as he explains in a letter to Karl Mayr of 22 April 1897 (p. 285), is the piano, not the vocal line; it is for this reason that the title pages of his songbooks state that the songs were not written for 'voice with pianoforte accompaniment' but rather for 'voice *and* pianoforte'. The influence of Wagner is unmistakable, not only in the quasi-orchestral piano writing, but also in the often tortuously chromatic harmonies that so disturbed some of his contemporaries, and that some audiences still find difficult today. Discussing the way in which Wagner and Wolf treat text, Ernest Newman writes in his biography of Wolf: 'The vocal music of Wagner and Wolf is "unvocal" only for those who cannot understand it. They do not understand it because, whatever their musical culture may be, they are deficient in poetic culture; they can sing but they cannot think; they are musical instruments, not human beings.' Put more gently: only through active engagement with the poem is it possible to appreciate the power and beauty of Wolf's songs.

Time and again Wolf allows the piano (as in 'Im Frühling' and 'Auf einer Wanderung') to weave its way in and out of the vocal line to highlight details of the poem. Vocal line and accompaniment both have their own *raison d'être* – the miracle is the way in which he fuses the two. And to express this lyrico-dramatic style, he preferred singers who did not sing too beautifully but also sought to interpret the poem. The baritone Theodor Reichmann, for example, is taken to task in two of Wolf's reviews (13 February and 13 March 1887) for his bland renderings of Loewe's 'Edward' and 'Heinrich der Vogler'. „Eine Löwesche Ballade verlangt ebensowohl Auffassung als Stimme," he writes. ('A Loewe ballad requires interpretation as much as a [good] voice.')

Wolf was not the first composer to designate his songs *Gedichte* (*Poems*) instead of *Lieder* or *Gesänge* – important precedents include Schumann's *Zwölf Gedichte von Justinus Kerner*, Op. 35 (1840), *Zwölf Gedichte aus F. Rückert's Liebesfrühling für Gesang und Pianoforte*, Op. 37 (1841) and *Sechs Gedichte von N. Lenau*, Op. 90 (1850); Wagner's *Fünf Gedichte für eine Frauenstimme* (1857–8); Brahms's *Fünf Gedichte*, Op. 19 (1858–9); and Richard Strauss's *Acht Gedichte aus* Letzte Blätter *von Hermann von Gilm*, which date from 1885, three years before

Wolf's *Mörike-Lieder*. But Wolf was the first Lieder composer who consistently designated his great song collections *Gedichte* instead of *Lieder*; and Detlev von Liliencron tells us in his poem 'An Hugo Wolf' (see APPENDIX 1), that Wolf also, out of admiration for Mörike, 'set the poet's portrait on the first page'.

He was well aware that audiences might find his songs difficult. Describing a private recital of some of the *Goethe-Lieder* that he gave in October 1890 to a select group of friends, Wolf wrote a letter to Melanie Köchert (12 October 1890, p. 120) that gives vent to his despair at ever being properly understood as a composer:

> Im Ganzen gewann ich den Eindruck, daß ich nicht verstanden wurde, daß man zu sehr mit dem musikalischen sich beschäftigte u. darüber das Neue u. eigenartige meiner musikalisch-dichterischen Auffassung vergaß.

> On the whole I gained the impression that I had not been understood, that people were concerned too much with the musical element & had thus lost sight of what is new & original in my musico-poetic conception.

There is, however, nothing forbidding about Wolf's songs – he was capable of writing melodies that were as memorable as Schubert's and there are, especially in the *Mörike-Lieder*, many passages of great diatonic beauty when he finds a remarkable number of ways to deploy simple triadic progressions, as in the chiming bells of 'Auf einer Wanderung' and 'In der Frühe', the harp-like arpeggios of 'An eine Äolsharfe' or the devout harmonies of 'Gebet' and 'An die Geliebte'. And although in a letter to Oskar Grohe of 22 February 1896 he writes that he detests programme music („Ich hasse alle Programme"), his songs abound in the most delightful tonal analogues, every bit as beguiling as Schubert's: birdsong in 'Karwoche', lutes in 'Nachruf', gunfire in 'Unfall', a donkey's bray in 'Schweig' einmal still', a spinning-wheel in 'Die Spinnerin', bees in 'Der Knabe und das Immlein', cuckoos in 'Lied des transferierten Zettel', a violin in 'Wie lange schon', alpine bells in 'Abendbilder', a guitar in 'Deine Mutter, süßes Kind', a tambourine in 'Klinge, klinge, mein Pandero', a harp in 'Gesang Weylas', a carillon in 'Zum neuen Jahr', gusting winds in 'Begegnung', cantering horses in 'Der Soldat I', thunder in 'Der Jäger', a river in 'Heimweh' (Mörike), the hiss of a snake in 'Verschling' der Abgrund' and so on.

In other ways too, Wolf has much in common with the great Lieder composers who preceded him. Like them, he repeats text. Although there are only two examples of word repetitions in the *Italienisches Liederbuch* and five in the *Spanisches Liederbuch*, his songs abound in repetition – of single words, of phrases and occasionally of whole stanzas. Repetition as a means of highlighting emotion is something that all the great Lieder composers employ and Wolf is no exception. Many of the songs in the *Mörike-Lieder* repeat phrases to memorable emotional effect. Consider the swooning repetition of „wie süß bedrängt ihr dies Herz" in 'An eine Äolsharfe'; the manner in which the repeated „Doch in der

Mitten" in 'Gebet' mirrors the poet's sudden realisation that there *is* a solution to his emotional problem; or in 'Der Gärtner' the repeat of „Nimm tausend für Eine/Nimm alle dafür!" – to an altered dynamic – that speaks volumes about the gardener's lascivious intentions. And like other Lieder composers, Wolf will sometimes use inauthentic versions of a poem ('Das verlassene Mägdlein'), omit verses ('Geh, Geliebter, geh jetzt'), or add interjections of his own ('Die Zigeunerin', 'Lied des transferierten Zettel'). Nor is his prosody always faultless; like all Lieder composers he can on occasion be 'guilty' of false accentuation – the *Mörike-Lieder*, in particular, reveal a number of prepositions set as strong downbeats. When the shape of the melody demands it, as in the delectable curveting of the horse in 'Der Gärtner', he will sacrifice correct accentuation: „Auf ihrem Leibrößlein" instead of „Auf ihrem *Leibrößlein*" and „*durch* die Allee" instead of „durch die Al*lee*" – with wonderfully expressive results. See also notes to 'Auch kleine Dinge' (p. 232), 'Nachtzauber' (p. 42) and 'Auf einer Wanderung' (p. 381).

It is strange that some audiences should still find Wolf so inaccessible, when in the realm of comic song he (and Carl Loewe) hold such indisputable sway. Wolf's admiration for Loewe is well known: Gustav Schur in *Erinnerungen an Hugo Wolf* tells us that Wolf preferred Loewe's setting of 'Erlkönig' to Schubert's, and Heinrich Werner in *Hugo Wolf in Maierling* describes how Wolf would sing Loewe's 'Archibald Douglas' over and over again. Wolf was only nine years old when Loewe died, and he was quite clearly influenced by the older composer, especially in his comic songs. There is an abundance of humour in almost all of Wolf's great collections: the *Eichendorff-Lieder* are full of memorably earthy portraits of students, scholars, sailors, soldiers; the *Italienisches Liederbuch* bristles with weirdos, lascivious would-be monks, a dwarf lover, an impoverished lover, a nymphomaniac with twenty-one lovers; in the *Mörike-Lieder* Wolf gives full rein to his imagination to present us with cackling storks, a hungover poet, a critic who's booted downstairs to the strains of a Viennese waltz, a nubile young girl holding a phallus-like fish in her hands, and a withered old woman dispensing didactic advice; while the *Goethe-Lieder* brim with witty bibulous songs.

The Complete Songs of Hugo Wolf has been written in an attempt to make his Lieder more accessible. There are books on Beethoven, Brahms and Schubert that contain the texts and English translations of all their piano-accompanied Lieder: Paul Reid's *The Beethoven Song Companion* (Manchester University Press, 2007), Eric Sams's *The Songs of Johannes Brahms* (Yale University Press, 2000) and Graham Johnson's encyclopaedic *Franz Schubert: The Complete Songs* (Yale University Press, 2014) with translations by Richard Wigmore. No such book exists on Wolf – only Eric Sams's pioneering *The Songs of Hugo Wolf* (Methuen, 1961) which, despite illuminating comments on the music, merely prints English paraphrases of the German songs that were published in Wolf's lifetime.

The volume is also designed to give us a better understanding of Wolf the man. Rosa Mayreder writes in her *Erinnerungen an Hugo Wolf* how the composer, when asked by a music magazine to supply a portrait and a biographical sketch, answered: „Ich heiße Hugo Wolf, bin am 13. März 1860 geboren und derzeit noch am Leben. Soviel genügt Biographie." ('My name is Hugo Wolf, I was born on 13 March 1860 and am still alive. That's enough biography.') And elsewhere in the same essay she recalls how he once told her: „Wenn jemand bloß mich, meine Person, liebt und schätzt, so pfeif' ich darauf. Meine Werke, meine Musik muß er lieben und schätzen, für die muß er sich über alles interessieren – meine Person ist dabei ganz Nebensache." ('I could not care less if people just love and appreciate me as a person. It's my work, my music that they must above all be interested in – my person is irrelevant.') Although *The Complete Songs of Hugo Wolf* contains no essay on his life, extensive biographical details can be found in the CHRONOLOGIES (pp. xxix–lvii) and CORRESPONDENTS (pp. 475–524), in the numerous notes and the many quotations from Wolf's letters.

Wolf was one of the most gifted and prolific letter-writers in the history of music – for which reason all extracts are given in both German and English. Many of his letters were written in a rush. Writing two or even three letters a day was as common as composing two or three songs a day and he would sometimes write over thirty letters a month, to friends, relatives, lovers, publishers, patrons, singers, critics and impresarios. The year 1896 was the most prolific with over three hundred letters or cards. By liberal quotations from his correspondence a picture emerges of a man full of contradictions: arrogant, domineering, uncompromising, vulnerable, eccentric, loving, loyal, disloyal, witty, scatological, child-loving, childish, manic depressive, euphoric, inconsistent, well read, cruel, kind, grateful, selfish, unpractical, impetuous, megalomanic, irascible – and, at the end of his life, insane.

The Complete Songs of Hugo Wolf means exactly that: this volume contains the texts and translations of all the poems he set to music: piano-accompanied Lieder, a cappella songs, and songs with choral and orchestral accompaniment, such as 'Elfenlied' from Shakespeare's *A Midsummer Night's Dream* and 'Christnacht', a setting of August von Platen's poem about Christmas Eve. Fragments are listed under each poet but those poems are not included. Wolf's rate of composition was erratic. When inspired, songs flowed from his pen at a rate that was almost unprecedented in the history of Lieder, comparable only to Schubert's outpouring in 1815 and Schumann's in 1840 – see HW to Josef Strasser, 23 March 1888, p. 351, for Wolf's own description of this heightened state of creativity. Most of his great song collections were characterised by such frenzied bursts of activity, but when the mood was not upon him, he fell prey to a creative paralysis that caused him untold suffering, which he described in countless letters to friends, such as this outburst to Oskar Grohe on 12 June 1891:

> Mit dem Komponieren ist es rein aus. Ich glaube, daß ich wohl nie mehr eine Note aufschreiben werde.
>
> I have finished composing. I think I shall probably never write another note.

The first period of extended creative inertia lasted from 1883 (after his failure to interest a succession of publishers in his songs) to February 1888, when suddenly the floodgates opened with the composition of the *Mörike-Lieder*. It was during these barren years that he worked as music critic for the *Wiener Salonblatt*, a post procured for him by Heinrich Köchert, the husband of his mistress Melanie. The second period ran from the end of 1891 (after he had finished Book I of the *Italienisches Liederbuch*) to March 1895, when he began the composition of his first opera, *Der Corregidor* – three years during which he composed hardly a note of original music. When suffering from writer's block, Wolf would often orchestrate already existing songs – see APPENDIX 3: he wished to reach a wider audience and harboured megalomanic ambitions of becoming a great orchestral and operatic composer.

For Wolf was not content to remain a mere song composer all his life. The Austrian novelist Adalbert Stifter opens his Preface to *Bunte Steine* (1853) with this statement:

> Es ist einmal gegen mich bemerkt worden, daß ich nur das Kleine bilde, und daß meine Menschen stets gewöhnliche Menschen seien.
>
> It has been held against me that I depict only what is small-scale, and that my characters are always ordinary human beings.

He then proceeds proudly to defend his philosophy. Unlike Stifter, Wolf became increasingly disillusioned by the small-scale format of his works, despite the perfection of his final songbook. The title of 'songwriter' became anathema to him. In a letter to his friend Kauffmann of 1 June 1891, he complains that he cannot continue to write songs for another thirty years:

> Unmöglich kann ich doch 30 Jahre hindurch noch Lieder od. Musiken zu Ibsen'schen Dramen schreiben. Und doch wird es nie zur heissersehnten Oper kommen. Ich bin eben am Ende. Möge es bald ein vollständiges sein – ich wünsche nichts sehnlicher.
>
> There's no way that I can spend the next 30 years writing songs or incidental music to Ibsen's plays. The fervently longed-for opera will never materialise. I've reached the end. May it come soon and completely – that is my most ardent wish.

Instead of being flattered by the increasing success of his Lieder, he saw in the public's praise an implied reproach that he was master of what was only a minor genre.

After *Der Corregidor*, he planned a second opera – *Manuel Venegas* – but by 1897 tertiary syphilis had set in and his mind gave way. When Mahler, a friend of long standing, proved unable to stage *Der Corregidor*, Wolf claimed to have been appointed Director of the Vienna Hofoper in his stead. He was eventually removed to an asylum. The letters of this period describe plans to tour the world with his own operas, as we read in this unhinged letter from the asylum to Heinrich Potpeschnigg, dated Vienna, 6 December 1897:

> Nach meiner Freilassung (vermutlich am 15. d. M.) übersiedle ich sofort nach Luzern, wo ich mein ständiges Quartier aufschlagen werde. Von dort aus will ich mich umsehen, um ein Opernpersonal samt Orchester zusammenzutrommeln, das unter meiner Fahne alle Staaten (ausgenommen Österreich) bereisen soll, und zwar zum Behufe von Opernvorstellungen und Konzerten, wobei natürlich nur meine Werke, die Opern: Corregidor, Venegas und Penthesilea, Fest auf Solhaug, Prinz von Homburg etc. aufgeführt werden.

> After my release (presumably on the 15th of this month), I shall move at once to Lucerne, where I shall set up my permanent headquarters. From there I shall take steps to drum up an opera company, with orchestra, that shall under my banner tour every country (except Austria), giving concerts and operatic performances devoted exclusively of course to my works: the operas *Der Corregidor, Manuel Venegas, Penthesilea, Das Fest auf Solhaug, Prinz von Homburg*, etc.

Delusions of grandeur were followed by periods of calm. He attempted to drown himself in the Traunsee. The final years of mental and physical suffering in the asylum were alleviated by the regular visits of Melanie Köchert, to whom all his songs are dedicated. He died, horribly wasted and shrunken, in the arms of his nurse Johann Scheibner in 1903, and was buried in the Zentralfriedhof alongside Beethoven and Schubert.

RICHARD STOKES
London, 2021

ACKNOWLEDGEMENTS

The Complete Songs of Hugo Wolf could not have been written without the work of these eminent scholars:

ERNST DECSEY (1870–1941) was an Austrian music critic who studied harmony, counterpoint and composition at the Vienna Conservatoire under Bruckner and Robert Fuchs. He was later active as music critic first for the *Grazer Tagespost* and then for the *Neues Wiener Tagblatt*, a position he held until 1938. While Wolf was still alive, he published a number of pieces on the composer and his music, including an article in the October 1901 edition of *Die Musik* titled 'Aus Hugo Wolfs letzten Jahren'; this was followed shortly after Wolf's death by 'Hugo-Wolf-Miszellen', which appeared in the *Musikbuch aus Österreich* of 1904. His magnum opus, *Hugo Wolf*, was published by Schuster & Loeffler in four volumes between 1903 and 1906: *Hugo Wolfs Leben. 1860–1887* appeared in 1903; *Hugo Wolfs Schaffen. 1888–1891* in 1904; *Der Künstler und die Welt. 1892–1895* in 1904; and *Höhe und Ende. 1896–1903* in 1906. By interviewing countless individuals who had known Wolf intimately, and through access to their correspondence, Decsey was able to paint a detailed portrait of the composer to which all subsequent Wolf scholars have referred.

WALTER LEGGE (1906–1979). A turning point in Legge's life occurred when he read Ernest Newman's pioneering *Hugo Wolf*, a biography published in 1907. It was Newman (1868–1959) who first aired the idea of a Hugo Wolf Society in his *Sunday Times* article of 13 September 1931 in which he urged the formation of a Hugo Wolf Gramophone Record Society, and suggested that Elena Gerhardt should be approached. Fred Gaisberg, head of the Artistes Department of the Gramophone Company, and Compton Mackenzie, founder-editor of *The Gramophone*, also played an important part in the creation of the Hugo Wolf Society, but it was Legge who was 'the prime mover', as Gaisberg put it in a letter of 14 October 1931. There were eventually 500 members who financed the venture by subscription, thus enabling Legge to invite a galaxy of celebrated singers and pianists to record some 140 of Wolf's Lieder for the Hugo Wolf Society: Karl Erb, Marta Fuchs, Elena Gerhardt, Ria Ginster, Gerhard Hüsch, Herbert Janssen, Alexander Kipnis, Tiana Lemnitz, John McCormack, Elisabeth Rethberg, Helge Roswaenge, Friedrich Schorr, Ludwig Weber, Coenraad van Bos, Gerald Moore, Hans Udo Müller and Michael Raucheisen. In 1932 Legge founded the London Lieder Club and began to write for the *Manchester Guardian*, and during 1938–9 he was Thomas Beecham's assistant artistic director at Covent Garden. As a record producer, he helped to create a huge number of first-rate recordings of operas, orchestral and chamber works. He founded the Philharmonia Chorus in 1957.

Having set out with Frank Walker to write the definitive Wolf biography, Legge eventually left that task to his colleague. He had, however, collected a vast amount of material, which he continued to expand and which he bequeathed to his wife, Elisabeth Schwarzkopf. She handed the material – a priceless gift – to DIETRICH FISCHER-DIESKAU (1925–2012), who included many letters, that still today remain unpublished in their entirety, in his *Hugo Wolf. Leben und Werk*.

FRANK WALKER (1907–1962) was educated at Portsmouth Grammar School and earned a living as an official in the General Post Office, and in his free time as a musicologist. Fluent in German and Italian, he had two main areas of interest: Giuseppe Verdi and Hugo Wolf. His articles on Wolf began to appear in the mid-1930s in *Music & Letters*, *The Musical Times*, *The Music Review*, *The Monthly Musical Record* and elsewhere. His life's work, *Hugo Wolf: A Biography*, was first published in 1951 and then translated into German by Witold Schey in 1953. The idea of a book on Wolf came from Walter Legge, the co-founder of the Gramophone Company's Hugo Wolf Society. Most of the initial research was carried out by Legge, who interviewed such important Wolf figures as his siblings Käthe and Gilbert; the publisher Emil Heckel; one of Wolf's closest friends, Friedrich Eckstein; and the tenor Ferdinand Jäger jnr who sang Wolf songs from the *Italienisches Liederbuch* and the *Goethe-Lieder* at the opening of Vienna's Hugo-Wolf-Verein on 14 May 1897. The Legge–Walker collaboration was not a success, principally because, as Walker wrote, 'My colleague's numerous other activities seemed to leave him less and less time for his work with me.' Walker acknowledged Legge's contribution, and continued the work on his own, collecting original material during nine months in Austria from August 1945 to the end of April 1946, following in Wolf's footsteps, visiting correspondents and spending a week at Traunkirchen as the guest of Frau Hilde Wittgenstein, one of the Köchert children, who showed him Wolf's correspondence – since destroyed – with her mother Melanie Köchert. The second edition of *Hugo Wolf: A Biography* contained a chapter (XIII) and a few shorter passages that had not appeared in the first edition, 'out of regard for the feelings of then living people' – details of Wolf's love affairs with Melanie Köchert and Frieda Zerny.

ERNST HILMAR (1938–2016), whose *Hugo Wolf Enzyklopädie* contains 518 entries on every aspect of Wolf's life and works – an indispensable source of information.

LEOPOLD SPITZER (1942–2020), whose *Hugo Wolf: Briefe* was published between 2010 and 2011 by the Internationale Hugo Wolf-Gesellschaft, Vienna. The first three volumes reproduce Wolf's letters from the periods 1873–91, 1892–5 and

1896–1901, while the fourth provides commentaries and extensive indexes. This remarkable editorial achievement contains over 2,200 letters and cards that Wolf wrote between 1873 and 1901, and they appear in their original form without any editorial embellishment.

MARGRET JESTREMSKI, whose *Hugo-Wolf-Werkverzeichnis* discusses every work by Wolf chronologically, giving factual information, not found elsewhere, on sources, dating, gestation, handwriting, sketches, autographs, proofs, publication details, first performances, etc., etc. What Köchel did for Mozart and Deutsch for Schubert, Jestremski has done for Wolf – and much more.

I am also indebted to:

ERIC SAMS (1926–2004) whose *The Songs of Hugo Wolf* first kindled my interest in Wolf.

GRAHAM JOHNSON, to whom this book is dedicated, whose conversations, publications, lectures and performances of art song have been a constant source of illumination.

SUSAN YOUENS, whose writing on Lieder in general and her two books on Wolf in particular, have been an inspiration: *Hugo Wolf: The Vocal Music* and *Hugo Wolf and his Mörike Songs*.

I am most grateful to everyone at Faber and Faber, especially Belinda Matthews for her belief in the book, and Jill Burrows, whose flair for fixing layout tangles, detecting stylistic infelicities and providing imaginative solutions has been without compare – I could not have been more fortunate. I am indebted to Maria Majno, Barry Ife, Thormod Rønning Kvam and Martin Schøyen for their advice on assembling the Italian, Spanish and Norwegian poems; and finally, I should like to thank David Harman for his eagle-eyed checking of the typescript, and a multitude of German-speaking friends who have helped me solve thorny linguistic problems.

RICHARD STOKES
London, 2020

HOW TO USE THIS BOOK

The Complete Songs of Hugo Wolf gathers together for the first time the texts and translations of all the songs – piano accompanied, orchestral and choral – of Hugo Wolf. The book is arranged alphabetically, according to poet, and each chapter follows the same format. Listed after the poet's name are the poems set by Wolf (both published and unpublished in his lifetime) in order of composition – thus allowing the reader to see how many songs were composed on a particular day. Four sections then follow: POET, COMPOSER, LETTERS, LIEDER. The POET section gives a biographical account of the writer; COMPOSER explores Wolf's association with each poet; LETTERS contains numerous quotations from Wolf's correspondence that throw light on the songs and his life; and the final LIEDER section presents all the poems (with parallel translations) that Wolf set, printed with their authentic punctuation and versification. Other composers who have set the same poem are listed below the texts.

Notes elucidate difficult syntax and arcane meanings, and give biographical details relevant to either composer or poet. Further biographical detail is given in the INTRODUCTION, the CHRONOLOGIES and the section on CORRESPONDENTS.

TRANSLATOR'S NOTE

My past translations of these poems have been revised for this volume. The aim has been to convey the full sense and as much as possible the tone of each poem, without any slavish adherence to the rhyme and rhythm of the originals.

Most music publishers adopt a cavalier attitude to a poet's punctuation and versification. Some, it's true, print the poems at the front or back of the score, and the first edition of Schumann's 'Belsatzar' printed Heine's poem separately – the only instance of such a practice in his Lieder. But, in general, the punctuation of the poem as presented in the score varies significantly from that of the poet's first or subsequent editions. Every effort has been made in *The Complete Songs of Hugo Wolf* to respect the authentic shape of each German poem: versification, punctuation, indentations, italics and orthography have all been carefully reproduced. Not just for aesthetic reasons. Francis Turner Palgrave, in his Introduction to a volume of poems by Robert Herrick (Macmillan and Co, 1892), writes perceptively, 'The poet's own spelling and punctuation bear, or may bear, a gleam of his personality.' And a poet's use of punctuation and italics can significantly alter the meaning of a poem. Let this example from Mörike's 'Der Gärtner' suffice. The final strophe runs:

Und willst du dagegen	And if you in exchange
Eine Blüte von mir,	Want a flower from me,
Nimm tausend für Eine,	Take a thousand for *one*,
Nimm alle dafür!	Take all in return!

The italic in line three, here represented by a capital letter („Eine"), suggests that the *Lady Chatterley*-like gardener will give the princess all his flowers, if she in return will reward him with her maidenhead. All depends on that italicised indefinite article for the lubricious innuendo to be grasped. That not a single modern edition of the song prints this italic is deplorable.

Composers down the ages have tweaked original poems to suit their own settings, and *The Complete Songs of Hugo Wolf* prints the text as it appears in the songs – minus the many repetitions. Notes indicate the poet's original wording and an asterisk all those occasions on which Wolf repeats words and phrases. Wolf's predilection for repetition is not always realised: over a quarter of the songs in the *Mörike-Lieder*, for example, repeat words or phrases. It was only in Wolf's final great songbook, the *Italienisches Liederbuch*, that he dispensed with repetition almost entirely – two examples in forty-six songs, one in 'Du denkst mit einem Fädchen mich zu fangen' and one in 'Benedeit die sel'ge Mutter'.

TRANSLATOR'S NOTE

I have attempted to date all the poems by Eichendorff, Goethe, Heine and Mörike to enable the reader to engage with matters of autobiographical interest. Eichendorff's 'Lieber alles', for example, was written in 1809 at a time when he was pondering what career path to follow; Goethe's 'Phänomen', which states that old men too can fall in love, was penned by the sixty-four-year-old poet on 25 July 1814 on his way to Wiesbaden where he was to meet Marianne von Willemer for the first time; Heine's 'Sie haben heut' abend Gesellschaft' dates from the autumn of 1823, a month after he had written that traumatic letter to Moses Moser (see note 1 to 'Sie haben heut' abend Gesellschaft', p. 197) expressing his anguish at visiting Hamburg for the first time since his break with Amalie; and Mörike's despairing 'Wo find' ich Trost?' was written in 1827 when the twenty-three-year-old curate, full of doubts about his vocation and distraught at the terminal illness of his older sister Luise, was still reeling from the Maria Meyer episode.

As D. H. Lawrence put it in his introductory Note to *The Collected Poems* (1928):

> It seems to me that no poetry, not even the best, should be judged as if it existed in the absolute, in the vacuum of the absolute. Even the best poetry, when it is at all personal, needs the penumbra of its own time and place and circumstances to make it full and whole.

A word on Wolf's voluminous correspondence. He wrote so many letters, often with such great speed, that he attached little importance to formal correctness. Such impetuosity often resulted in wayward grammar, syntax, orthography, inconsistent use of apostrophes, commas, umlauts, capitals, 'ß' and 's'. No attempt has been made, however, to tidy up his style – although absent quotation marks in song titles have been restored in the English translation by using the English convention: 'Gebet' instead of „Gebet".

Three proper nouns, one a cumbersome compound, defy elegant translation. They appear as Niederösterreichische Landesirrenanstalt (Lower Austrian Provincial Mental Asylum), Zentraler Friedhof (Central Cemetery) and Hofoper (Vienna Opera House).

Chronology: Life

1860

Hugo Philipp Jakob Wolf born to Philipp and Katharina Wolf on 13 March in Windischgraz (Steiermark), today's Slovenj Gradec in Slovenia.

1865

Father teaches Wolf piano and violin.

1868

The eight-year-old Wolf attends his first opera, Donizetti's *Belisario*, in Klagenfurt, and is entranced.

1870

Attends the Gymnasium in Graz and expelled six months later for 'utterly unsatisfactory work' („ganz ungenügend").

1871

Student at the Konvikt of Sankt Paul in Carinthia. Plays the organ at Mass and makes chamber music.

1872

Wolf's school reports from St Paul's indicate that he excelled in only two subjects: singing and gymnastics.

1873

Leaves St Paul's in June due to unsatisfactory progress in Latin and Slovenian; enters the Gymnasium in Marburg (today's Maribor) in the autumn. Acquires the nickname Wölferl. Plays in the school orchestra. Discovers Haydn, Mozart and especially Beethoven, whose symphonies he plays in piano reductions with fanatical zeal. Poor reports.

1875

Composes 5 songs, his first attempts at composition. Dedicates his Piano Sonata to his father. Leaves school and from September is a fellow student of Mahler at the

Konservatorium der Gesellschaft der Musikfreunde, the Vienna Conservatoire. Hears Wagner's *Tannhäuser* and *Lohengrin* and is smitten. Aged fifteen, he visits Wagner on 12 December at the Hotel Imperial in Vienna and describes the encounter in detail in a letter to his parents, after which he becomes, in his own words, a 'Wagnerianer'.

1876

Composes *c.* 15 songs and choruses. Takes some of his compositions to Hans Richter, who gives him advice. Begins his Symphony in B major.

1877

Composes 7 songs. Expelled from the Conservatoire for impertinence and lack of discipline (he had informed the director that he was forgetting more than he was learning). Wolf returns to his parents' house, composes songs, piano pieces, choruses. Meets the composer Adalbert von Goldschmidt, who enables him to earn money as an accompanist and introduces him to his influential friends; meets Felix Mottl; attends the premiere of Bruckner's Third Symphony in Vienna's Musikverein, conducted by the composer. Syphilitic infection at the end of the year. According to Alma Mahler in *Erinnerungen an Gustav Mahler*, it was Goldschmidt who took Wolf to a brothel, the so-called „Lehmgruben", where he contracted „die Wunde, die nie sich schließen will" ('the wound that will never heal').

1878

Composes 26 songs and 7 fragments, including his first important collection, the Heine *Liederstrauß*. Wolf later called 1878 his 'Lodi in song', when he would usually compose at least 'one, sometimes two, good songs a day'. Plays dance music in a Gasthaus in Meidling to earn much needed money. Falls in love in the spring with Valentine (Vally) Franck, his first sweetheart. Approaches Joh. André in Offenbach and Breitkopf & Härtel in Leipzig with the intention of publishing some of his songs. Unsuccessfully. Begins his String Quartet in D minor, the *Grave* introduction of which is prefaced by Goethe's words from Faust: „Entbehren sollst du, sollst entbehren" ('You must renounce, renounce'), spoken by Faust when sealing his pact with Mephistopheles the Devil (Part I, line 1549). This invocation to renounce comments obliquely, perhaps, on the events that led to him contracting syphilis.

1879

Composes only 4 songs, perhaps because he was busy writing his String Quartet and the Symphony in F minor, to which he refers in a letter to his father of 10 May. Shares accommodation with Gustav Mahler. Disappointing visit to Brahms, who gives him little encouragement – his subsequent vilification of Brahms in his *Wiener Salonblatt* reviews did much to sour his relationship with Vienna's musical establishment, thus impeding his own recognition as a composer. Meets Melanie Köchert at the Goldschmidts and gives her piano lessons – she was soon to become his clandestine mistress. Meets Edmund Lang.

1880

Composes 6 songs, including his first Mörike setting, 'Suschens Vogel'. Summer in Maierling with Vally Franck (see Heinrich Werner, *Hugo Wolf in Maierling: Eine Idylle*). Composes piano paraphrases of Wagner's *Die Meistersinger von Nürnberg* and *Die Walküre*, the latter owing much to the piano reduction of the opera by Karl Klindworth. Continues writing his String Quartet. Meets the Werner family.

1881

Annus horribilis. Writes in *Daten aus meinem Leben*: 'Breach. Misery. Despair. Only one piano-accompanied song composed. Summer in Windischgraz. Winter in Salzburg, Kapellmeister at the theatre. Horrendous time.' Vally Franck breaks off their relationship and Wolf suffers emotional trauma. Composes the cathartic *Sechs geistliche Lieder* to poems by Eichendorff for unaccompanied mixed choir. Tries in vain to interest another publisher (Kistner Verlag) in his Heine *Liederstrauß*. Appointed second Kapellmeister at the Königliches Nationaltheater in Salzburg, but leaves after a disastrous three months. Turns vegetarian in emulation of Wagner.

1882

Composes 3 songs: 'Wiegenlied im Sommer', 'Wiegenlied im Winter' (both Reinick) and 'Mausfallen-Sprüchlein' (Mörike). In *Daten aus meinem Leben* for 1882, Wolf writes „Greulichen moralischen Katzenjammer" ('frightful moral hangover') – a possible reference to his syphilis. Yet he seems to recover his emotional equilibrium, writing to Henriette Lang on 25 May, „Zukunft und Vergangenheit sind mir fern; ich lebe nur in der Gegenwart und das macht mich so froh und glücklich." ('The future and the past are far distant; I live only in the present and that makes me so happy.') Short period of military service. First visit to Bayreuth (*Parsifal*). Friendship with Friedrich Eckstein who puts his vast library at Wolf's disposal. Spends summer in Maierling with the Werner family who would soon provide Wolf with accommodation in Perchtoldsdorf, where he composed some 120 Lieder and much of *Der Corregidor*.

1883

Composes 10 songs, including 'Zur Ruh, zur Ruh!' (Kerner). Despite Hanslick's letter of recommendation, B. Schott's Söhne declines to publish *Sechs Lieder für eine Frauenstimme*. A meeting with Franz Liszt inspires him to write *Penthesilea*. Deeply distressed by Wagner's death. Spends summer in Rinnbach as guest of the Köchert family.

1884

Composes only one song: 'Die Tochter der Heide' (Mörike). Heinrich Köchert arranges for Wolf to start work as a music critic for the *Wiener Salonblatt* at a monthly salary of 60 florins. Wolf publishes his first article in January. Incidental music to Kleist's *Prinz Friedrich von Homburg*. Shares a house with Hermann Bahr and Edmund Lang in Vienna. Composes fourth movement of his String Quartet.

1885

No songs composed. First meeting with Anton Bruckner. Lives on and off with the Köchert family in Vienna's Mehlmarkt, and from September in their villa in Döbling. The Rosé-Quartett declines to perform his String Quartet.

1886

Composes 3 songs: 'Der König bei der Krönung' (Mörike), 'Der Soldat II' (Eichendorff) and 'Biterolf' (Scheffel). Spends the summer with sister Modesta and brother-in-law Josef Strasser in Murau. *Penthesilea* refused by the Wiener Philharmoniker. Starts 'Christnacht'.

1887

Composes 8 songs, including 'Wanderers Nachtlied' (Goethe). *Serenade* for string quartet. Writes his final piece in April for the *Wiener Salonblatt*. Between 10 January 1884 and 24 April 1887 Wolf wrote more than 110 reviews. Death of Philipp Wolf, Hugo's father, on 9 May.

1888

Annus mirabilis that sees the composition of 53 Mörike, 25 Goethe and 13 Eichendorff Lieder. Moves to Perchtoldsdorf at the invitation of the Werner family and composes the first of the *Mörike-Lieder* ('Der Tambour') on 16 February. Rosa Papier gives the first public performance of Wolf songs ('Morgentau' and 'Zur Ruh, zur Ruh!'). *Sechs Lieder für eine Frauenstimme* and *Sechs Gedichte von Scheffel, Mörike, Goethe und Just. Kerner* published in Vienna by Emil Wetzler, after Friedrich Eckstein had generously prepared the ground. After his third visit to Bayreuth, Wolf lives with Eckstein in Vienna and Unterach, where he composes 12 Eichendorff and 10 Mörike Lieder. Recital at the Vienna Wagner-Verein devoted to the music of Beethoven and Wolf. Wolf accompanies Ferdinand Jäger (his first public appearance as an accompanist) and is delighted with the reception. Moves in December to Döbling where he works on the *Goethe-Lieder*: 25 Goethe songs composed between late October and late December.

1889

Composes 26 more *Goethe-Lieder* and 26 of the *Spanisches Liederbuch*. Wetzler publishes the *Mörike-Lieder*; Wolf orchestrates 'Elfenlied' (Shakespeare); 'Christnacht' completed. Hears *Tristan und Isolde* and *Die Meistersinger von Nürnberg* in Bayreuth. Lacom publishes the *Eichendorff-Lieder* and *Goethe-Lieder* in Vienna.

1890

Composes a further 18 of the *Spanisches Liederbuch*, 7 of the *Italienisches Liederbuch* and the 6 *Alte Weisen* (Keller). Ground-breaking article on Wolf as a Lieder composer by Joseph Schalk: 'Neue Lieder, neues Leben' appears on 22 January in Munich's *Allgemeine*

Zeitung. Rejects Rosa Mayreder's libretto of *Der Corregidor*. The Burgtheater commissions Wolf to write incidental music to Ibsen's *Das Fest auf Solhaug*. Considers Shakespeare's *The Tempest* as an opera. Extensive tour of Germany in late autumn. He meets Detlev von Liliencron in Munich at the house of Michael Georg Conrad where he performs the 53 songs of the *Mörike-Lieder* and the 51 of the *Goethe-Lieder* (see APPENDIX 1). Also meets Emil Kauffmann in Tübingen and Ludwig Strecker in Mainz. Contract with Schott's. First meeting with Heinrich Potpeschnigg.

1891

Composes 15 songs in December from the *Italienisches Liederbuch*. Tours Germany again, visiting Frankfurt, Karlsruhe, Mainz, Mannheim, Philippsburg, Stuttgart and Tübingen. Premiere of 'Christnacht' in Mannheim. Lukewarm reception of *Das Fest auf Solhaug* in the Burgtheater. Schott's publish *6 Alte Weisen* and the *Spanisches Liederbuch*.

1892

Composes no songs. Beginning of a long creative crisis. Concerts featuring his songs in Berlin. Meets Baron and Baroness von Lipperheide, Richard Sternfeld and Paul Müller. Plans *Manuel Venegas*. Schott's publish Book I of the *Italienisches Liederbuch* in December. Wolf orchestrates the *Italienische Serenade für kleines Orchester*.

1893

Composes no songs but orchestrates 2 *Goethe-Lieder*. Plans an opera on Grillparzer's *Weh dem, der lügt!* Shakespeare's 'Elfenlied' premiered in Graz.

1894

Composes no songs. Frosty meeting with Richard Strauss. Meets Hugo Faisst in Stuttgart. Stormy love affair with the singer Frieda Zerny – which complicates his relationship with Melanie Köchert. Liederabende with Zerny. Despairing search for an opera libretto. Travels to Berlin with Bruckner to attend premiere of his orchestral 'Elfenlied' and 'Der Feuerreiter'. Lives as a guest with the von Lipperheides in Berlin (Potsdamer Straße) and Schloss Matzen.

1895

Composes no songs. Accepts Rosa Mayreder's libretto to *Der Corregidor* and begins the opera in April–May in Perchtoldsdorf, finishing it at Schloss Matzen. Breaks off his affair with Frieda Zerny. Changes publisher, leaving Schott's for Heckel.

1896

Composes 24 songs for Book II of the *Italienisches Liederbuch* in Perchtoldsdorf. Also 3 Lieder to poems by Byron and Reinick. Successful premiere of *Der Corregidor* in

Mannheim on 7 July. Stays with the Köcherts in Traunkirchen. He lives for the first time in an apartment of his own: Schwindgasse 3 in Vienna. Revises *Der Corregidor*. On 28 August, a doctor diagnoses symptoms of paralysis. Heckel publishes Book II of the *Italienisches Liederbuch*. Paul Müller founds the Hugo-Wolf-Verein in Berlin.

1897

Composes his 3 last songs in March: the *Drei Gedichte von Michelangelo*. Act IV of *Der Corregidor* revised. *Vier Gedichte nach H. Heine, Shakespeare und Lord Byron* published. Begins work in the summer on the opera *Manuel Venegas*. Michael Haberlandt founds the Hugo-Wolf-Verein in Vienna. Gustav Mahler decides not to stage *Der Corregidor* at the Vienna Hofoper (though he will conduct the first performance in 1904). On 19 September, outbreak of madness. Wolf claims that he has been appointed Intendant of the Vienna Hofoper in Mahler's stead; plans to tour the world with his own operas. Wolf is taken to Dr Svetlin's mental asylum, where he reworks *Penthesilea*, orchestrates 'Wer sein holdes Lieb verloren' and 'Wenn du zu den Blumen gehst' from the *Spanisches Liederbuch*, and arranges Reinick's 'Morgenstimmung' for chorus and orchestra, changing the title to 'Morgenhymnus'.

1898

Discharged from Dr Svetlin's asylum on 24 January. Travels with Melanie Köchert and his sister Käthe to Trieste, Duino and the Adriatic. On their return, Melanie furnishes a home for him in the Mühlgasse (No. 22). Wolf busies himself with the revised second edition of the *Eichendorff-Lieder*. Hugo Faisst founds the Hugo-Wolf-Verein in Stuttgart. Periods of depression. Revised version of *Der Corregidor* performed in Strasbourg. Suicide attempt in the Traunsee. Committed on 4 October to the Niederösterreichische Landesirrenanstalt.

1899

A piano is placed at Wolf's disposal in his asylum room. He performs his own songs and plays over and over again the second movement of Beethoven's Piano Sonata Op. 90. Writes a despairing letter on 15 July to his sister Modesta which ends: „Kurz rette mich, wenn ich noch zu retten bin." ('In short, save me, if I can still be saved.') Tries to flee the asylum. Makes the occasional excursion to Perchtoldsdorf, under supervision.

1900

Paralysis sets in; he finds it increasingly difficult to talk.

1901

Visited by his seventy-seven-year-old mother, who later describes the occasion in a letter to Käthe Wolf, published in volume 4 of Spitzer's edition, p. 674. Wolf's health deteriorates and from August 1901, due to paralytic spasms, he has to sleep in a bed with high rails.

1899–1902

The horror of Wolf's situation, comparable to Schumann's in Endenich, can be gauged from this heartrending letter received by Edmund Lang during the second half of 1899:

> Hier ist es schrecklich einsam u. die Leute, die mich umgeben nehmen immer mehr eine drohende Haltung gegen mich ein. Meine Lage ist wahrlich nicht beneidenswerth u. z. um so weniger, als es mir gar nicht gelingt mich irgendwie verständlich zu machen. <u>Man will mich einfach nicht verstehn</u> und das macht mich dann ungeduldig u. so verschlimmere ich mir noch meine Situation. Was mir geschehen [sic], die schrecklichsten Marten stehn mir bevor. Ach, wenn Du mich doch von hier wegbringen könntest, aber das ist ja fast ganz ausgeschlossen. Kurz ich bin verdammt <u>ewig</u> u. ununterbrochen zu leiden. Was das zu bedeuten wirst Du am besten verstehn. Wäre ich doch nie hierher gekommen. Man hätte mich überhaupt in kein Irrenhaus bringen sollen u. Alles wäre anders geworden. Wie sich meine Zukunft gestalten wird? ich darf daran gar nicht denken. Kein Wasser, kein Getränk, überhaupt vielleicht gar keine Flüßigkeit wird mir zukommen u. ich werde jammervoll verschmachten müssen, abgesehen von den andern Qualen die mir zugedacht sind.
>
> Gott im Himmel möge mir's vergeben, wenn ich je wissentlich gegen ihn gesündigt.

> It is dreadfully lonely here & the people around me adopt an increasingly threatening attitude towards me. My situation is truly not to be envied, especially because I simply cannot make myself understood. <u>They simply refuse to understand me</u>, and that makes me impatient & so I aggravate my own situation. The most dreadful torments await me. Ah, if only you could take me away from here, but that of course is almost wholly out of the question. In short, I am condemned to suffer <u>eternally</u> & without respite. You will best understand what that means. If only I had not come here. They should never have brought me to a lunatic asylum – everything then would have turned out differently. What of my future? It doesn't bear thinking about. No water, nothing to drink, perhaps no fluids at all will be my lot & I shall have to languish in misery – quite apart from the other torments in store for me.
>
> God in Heaven forgive me if I have ever consciously sinned against Him.

1903

Dies on 22 February. Funeral service two days later in the Votivkirche. Burial in the Zentralfriedhof, beside Beethoven and Schubert. Michael Haberlandt in his funeral oration (see APPENDIX 2) recites the first verse of Wolf's Kerner song 'Zur Ruh, zur Ruh!', movingly adapted for the occasion.

Chronology: Letters

Of Wolf's 2,200 or so published letters and cards, over 800 were written in Vienna – at a variety of addresses. Unable to tolerate noise, and fastidious by nature, Wolf was constantly on the move: between 1875 and the summer of 1885, for example, he changed apartment in the capital some thirty times. His nomadic nature also led him further afield, partly because friends, sponsors and well-wishers invited him to stay, and partly because he wished to promote his songs and further his reputation with publishers and audiences outside Vienna. Over 200 letters were written in towns across Austria and Germany: Bayreuth, Berlin, Cologne, Frankfurt, Graz, Heidelberg, Karlsruhe, Mainz, Mannheim, Munich, Philippsburg, Salzburg, Stuttgart and Tübingen.

Brief notes on the places that appear at the head of each letter in this volume:

Döbling

Döbling was a suburb of Vienna much prized by the aristocracy. The Köchert family owned a villa in the Hirschengasse (now Billrothstraße 68) with a beautiful garden and classical temple. It was there that Wolf composed 37 of the *Goethe-Lieder* and most of Book I of the *Italienisches Liederbuch*. Wolf wrote some 130 letters during his many visits to Döbling.

Maierling

Within a stone's throw of Baden, some 30 kilometres to the south-west of Vienna, Maierling was a small village that consisted of a few farmhouses, a church and an inn. Wolf spent the summers of 1880 and 1882 in Maierling as a guest of Joseph Reitzes in the Marienhof. It was there that he met the Werner family and enjoyed an idyllic few weeks with Vally Franck (see p. 483). He composed his first masterpiece in Maierling – Mörike's 'Mausfallen-Sprüchlein' on 18 June 1882. And two months later he commemorated the little village in a 37-line poem: 'Bilder aus und um Maierling'

Matzen

Matzen, a small town near Brixlegg in the Tyrol, was where Wolf spent some of his happiest days (see pp. 497–8) as the guest of Baron Franz Josef von Lipperheide and his wife Baronin Frida von Lipperheide. Wolf lived in the „Jägerhäusl" ('hunting lodge') attached to their castle at Matzen while working on *Der Corregidor*. Over 200 of Wolf's letters bear the Matzen postmark.

Perchtoldsdorf

Perchtoldsdorf (or Petersdorf), 16 kilometres to the south-west of Vienna, is a small market town, a mere thirty-minute train-ride from the capital and some four hours on foot from Maierling. Here Wolf composed most of the *Mörike-Lieder*, Book II of the *Italienisches Liederbuch*, all the *Spanisches Liederbuch* and Act I and much of Act II of *Der Corregidor*. Some of his most euphoric letters (see entry for MÖRIKE) were penned at Brunnergasse 26, which belonged to the Werner family and is now the Hugo-Wolf-Haus. Opened in 1973, this museum, and especially the garden with the „Häuslein Windebang", is the most atmospheric of all the Wolf locations. Friedrich Eckstein was born in Perchtoldsdorf and Michael Haberlandt lived in Brunnergasse 7. Wolf wrote some 190 letters from Perchtoldsdorf.

Traunkirchen

Traunkirchen, where Wolf orchestrated 'Elfenlied' (Shakespeare), is a little town on the Traunsee in the Salzkammergut where he attempted suicide in 1898. In August 1891 he stayed at the Pfarrhof in a room that the local priest had put at his disposal. It was from Traunkirchen that Wolf penned some of his most despairing letters, describing his creative inertia.

Unterach

Unterach, at the southern end of the Attersee, was where Friedrich Eckstein owned a villa with a view of the lake and the Höllengebirge. It was there (and not in today's 'Hugo-Wolf-Weg') that Wolf composed half of the *Eichendorff-Lieder*, a few of the *Mörike-Lieder*, including 'Der Feuerreiter', most of the *Alte Weisen* and the first few songs of the *Italienisches Liederbuch*.

Waidhofen an der Ybbs

Waidhofen an der Ybbs in Lower Austria was where Wolf planned to compose *Dichterleben*, a song-cycle to poems by Hoffmann von Fallersleben. 'Liebesfrühling', 'Auf der Wanderung' and 'Ja, die Schönst'! ich sagt es offen' were composed on successive days. It was also there that he wrote 'Gretchen vor dem Andachtsbild der Mater Dolorosa'. Wolf had been invited to Waidhofen an der Ybbs by the Breuer family, and stayed in the Gasthaus Zum goldenen Pflug. After work, he would usually join his hosts in their villa and give the Breuer children piano lessons.

Windischgraz

Windischgraz, today's Slovenj Gradec in Slovenia, was where Wolf spent the first decade of his life, attending the Volksschule. It was in Windischgraz that he wrote the earliest of his letters to survive. He returned intermittently to his home town, mostly in the summer months, but the family atmosphere was strained (see pp. 517–19) and he could never find the peace he needed for composition. He also felt cut off and lonely, as we read at the start of this letter to Friedrich Umlauft of 17 August 1881: „Ich lebe hier so abgeschieden u. gottverlassen von der Welt" ('I feel so solitary here & godforsaken').

1875

			page
August	Windischgraz	Alexander Pöch	117
23 November	Vienna	Philipp and Katharina Wolf	536

1876

15 March	Vienna	Philipp and Katharina Wolf	118, 302
28 July	Windischgraz	Anna Vinzenzberg	296

1877

24 November	Vienna	Philipp Wolf	419
18 December	Vienna	Philipp Wolf	473
18 December	Vienna	Philipp and Katharina Wolf	304
22 December	Vienna	Philipp and Katharina Wolf	4

1878

2 January	Vienna	Philipp Wolf	10
17 February	Vienna	Philipp and Katharina Wolf	304
10 April	Vienna	Philipp and Katharina Wolf	4, 176, 305, 452
20 April	Vienna	Philipp and Katharina Wolf	176
Easter Sunday (21 April)	Vienna	Philipp and Katharina Wolf	118
29 April	Vienna	Philipp and Katharina Wolf	119
12 May	Vienna	Philipp and Katharina Wolf	177
27 August	Waidhofen a. d. Ybbs	Philipp Wolf	119, 263
16 October	Vienna	Philipp Wolf	191

1880

5 September	Maierling	Philipp Wolf	191

1881

26 January	Vienna	Henriette Lang	192
3 April	Vienna	Max Wolf	25

1882

21 October	Vienna	Bertha von Lackhner	345

1883

18 February	Vienna	Ludwig Strecker, B. Schott's Söhne	452

26 February	Vienna	Felix Mottl	453
late June/ early July	Vienna	Philipp and Katharina Wolf	453

1888

15 February	Perchtoldsdorf	Edmund Lang	292
22 February	Perchtoldsdorf	Edmund Lang	345
22 February	Perchtoldsdorf	Edmund Lang	346
24 February	Perchtoldsdorf	Friedrich Eckstein	347
24 February	Perchtoldsdorf	Edmund Lang	347
24 February	Perchtoldsdorf	Franz Schalk	348
25 February	Perchtoldsdorf	Marie Lang	348
March	Perchtoldsdorf	Theodor Helm	292
14 March	Perchtoldsdorf	Franz Schalk	349
17 March	Perchtoldsdorf	Bertha von Lackhner	349
20 March	Perchtoldsdorf	Edmund Lang	349
21 March	Perchtoldsdorf	Edmund Lang	350
21 March	Perchtoldsdorf	Franz Schalk	350
23 March	Perchtoldsdorf	Josef Strasser	351
27 March	Perchtoldsdorf	Friedrich Eckstein	351
31 March	Perchtoldsdorf	Modesta and Josef Strasser	293
14 April	Perchtoldsdorf	Edmund Lang	352
4 October	Unterach	Marie Lang	25
8 October	Unterach	Friedrich Eckstein	353
19 December	Döbling	Rudolf von Larisch	120
27 December	Döbling	Katharina Wolf	354

1889

8 February	Döbling	Joseph Schalk	25
7 September	Windischgraz	Joseph Schalk	26
5 November	Perchtoldsdorf	Friedrich Eckstein	59

1890

31 March	Perchtoldsdorf	Melanie Köchert	59
15 April	Perchtoldsdorf	Josef Strasser	59, 537
16 April	Perchtoldsdorf	Oskar Grohe	59, 425
19 April	Perchtoldsdorf	Katharina Wolf	354
13 May	Perchtoldsdorf	Melanie Köchert	433
21 May	Perchtoldsdorf	Emil Kauffmann	433
28 May	Unterach	Gustav Schur	279, 465
3 June	Unterach	Ilse Köchert	280
5 June	Unterach	Emil Kauffmann	355, 434
5 June	Unterach	Rudolf von Larisch	280

CHRONOLOGY: LETTERS   xli

16 June	Unterach	Melanie Köchert	60
24 June	Unterach	Melanie Köchert	280
24 June	Unterach	Gustav Schur	280
18 August	Döbling	Joseph von Schey	537
20 August	Ober-Döbling	Melanie Köchert	281
18 September	Döbling	B. Schott's Söhne	60
24 September	Unterach	Gustav Schur	215
25 September	Unterach	Oskar Grohe	355
27 September	Unterach	Gustav Schur	216
5 October	Rinnbach	Gustav Schur	216
12 October	Munich	Melanie Köchert	120
15 October	Stuttgart	Melanie Köchert	355
19 October	Mannheim	Melanie Köchert	60
22 October	Mainz	Melanie Köchert	282
22 October	Mainz	Gustav Schur	61
4 November	Vienna	Oskar Grohe	537
8 November	Vienna	Wilhelm Schmid	268
8 November	Vienna	Katharina Wolf	268
11 November	Döbling	Engelbert Humperdinck	269
13 November	Döbling	Melanie Köchert	216
14 November	Döbling	Oskar Grohe	217, 269
18 December	Döbling	Oskar Grohe	269
22 December	Ober-Döbling	Emil Kauffmann	121
23 December	Döbling	Katharina Wolf	357
30 December	Döbling	Oskar Grohe	217, 459

1891

7 January	Döbling	Käthe Wolf	61
26 February	Döbling	Oskar Grohe	426
12 March	Ober-Döbling	Engelbert Humperdinck	27
1 June	Unterach	Emil Kauffmann	538
1 August	Ebensee	Detlev von Liliencron	218, 283
12 October	Traunkirchen	Emil Kauffmann	218, 466
14 November	Döbling	Engelbert Humperdinck	61
27 November	Döbling	Katharina Wolf	270
2 December	Döbling	Melanie Köchert	219
15 December	Döbling	Emil Kauffmann	219
17 December	Döbling	Katharina Wolf	220
29 December	Döbling	Katharina Wolf	220

1892

9 January	Döbling	Oskar Grohe	538
6 March	Berlin	Melanie Köchert	62
2 April	Döbling	Emil Kauffmann	27, 221, 357

20 April	Döbling	B. Schott's Söhne	221
10 May	Döbling	B. Schott's Söhne	221
7 June	Döbling	B. Schott's Söhne	222
20 July	Traunkirchen	Jeanette Grohe	223
10 August	Traunkirchen	Oskar Grohe	223
16 October	Döbling	Siegfried Ochs	223, 358
18 October	Döbling	B. Schott's Söhne	224
20 October	Döbling	Richard Sternfeld	358
22 November	Döbling	Emil Kauffmann	225
7 December	Ober-Döbling	Käthe Wolf	225, 421
20 December	Döbling	B. Schott's Söhne	226
22 December	Döbling	Oskar Grohe	538
23 December	Döbling	Emil Kauffmann	227

1893

13 May	Döbling	Oskar Grohe	192
8 June	Traunkirchen	Oskar Grohe	193, 434
8 July	Traunkirchen	Oskar Grohe	122

1894

9 January	Berlin	Melanie Köchert	466
7 March	Vienna	Emil Kauffmann	28
16 March	Vienna	Oskar Grohe	177
24 March	Vienna	Katharina Wolf	283
24 April	Vienna	Frieda Zerny	194
21 June	Vienna	Frieda Zerny	459
26 June	Vienna	Melanie Köchert	283
3 July	Vienna	Melanie Köchert	284
14 July	Vienna	Richard Sternfeld	460
16 July	Vienna	Emil Kauffmann	29, 460
23 July	Vienna	Melanie Köchert	359
23 September	Matzen	Melanie Köchert	360
25 September	Matzen	Melanie Köchert	360
26 September	Matzen	Emil Kauffmann	360
16 November	Perchtoldsdorf	Melanie Köchert	361
16 December	Vienna	Heinrich Potpeschnigg	228
31 December	Vienna	B. Schott's Söhne	435

1895

18 January	Vienna	Oskar Grohe	539
26 February	Vienna	B. Schott's Söhne	62
17 May	Matzen	Melanie Köchert	361

CHRONOLOGY: LETTERS

1896

24 February	Vienna	Paul Müller	63, 122
31 March	Perchtoldsdorf	Paul Müller	228
3 April	Perchtoldsdorf	Melanie Köchert	228
8 April	Perchtoldsdorf	Emil Kauffmann	228
13 April	Perchtoldsdorf	Hugo Faisst	229
15 April	Perchtoldsdorf	Heinrich Potpeschnigg	229
23 April	Perchtoldsdorf	Melanie Köchert	229
27 April	Perchtoldsdorf	Frida von Lipperheide	230
28 April	Perchtoldsdorf	Katharina Wolf	230
14 May	Stuttgart	Melanie Köchert	230
17 July	Vienna	Friedrich Eckstein	362
21 July	Vienna	Oskar Grohe	362
24 July	Vienna	Hugo Faisst	362
25 July	Vienna	Hugo Faisst	231
22 October	Vienna	Paul Müller	435
25 October	Vienna	Hugo Faisst	436
17 December	Vienna	Heinrich Potpeschnigg	284
25 December	Vienna	Paul Müller	322
28 December	Vienna	Oskar Grohe	194
28 December	Vienna	Heinrich Potpeschnigg	10

1897

1 January	Vienna	Oskar Grohe	10
19 January	Vienna	Karl Heckel	10
27 January	Vienna	Karl Mayr	11
15 March	Vienna	Karl Mayr	285, 436
18 March	Vienna	Paul Müller	323
19 March	Vienna	Karl Heckel	323
24 March	Vienna	Oskar Grohe	323
29 March	Vienna	Hugo Faisst	325
6 April	Vienna	Paul Müller	325
8 April	Vienna	Hugo Faisst	363
10 April	Vienna	Emil Kauffmann	326
14 April	Vienna	Hugo Faisst	195
22 April	Vienna	Karl Mayr	285
13 May	Vienna	Oskar Grohe	326
1 June	Vienna	Edwin Mayser	363
10 July	Vienna	Karl Mayr	63
31 July	Vienna	Melanie Köchert	270
6 December	Vienna	Heinrich Potpeschnigg	64, 539

1898

9 September   Traunkirchen   Heinrich Potpeschnigg   326

Chronology: Lieder

The following table, based on Margret Jestremski's *Hugo-Wolf-Werkverzeichnis* (HWW), enables the reader to appreciate at a glance the erratic nature of Wolf's Lieder composition: weeks of sustained inspiration followed by months and sometimes years of creative inertia.

We sense in the Goethe, Heine and Lenau settings of 1875 and 1876 Wolf's wish to explore in depth the verse of a single poet. The year 1877 yielded a mere 7 songs – the consequence, perhaps, of his work on two symphonies, in B major and G minor, both of which remain fragments. The 26 songs of 1878 reflect his ambition to become known to a wider audience, although Breitkopf & Härtel and Johann André both declined to publish his Lieder. It was also the year in which he met Vally Franck, his first sweetheart, and the 12 settings of Heine's predominantly bitter poetry were composed in the midst of that tempestuous relationship.

The meagre output (4 songs) of 1879 can be partially explained by Brahms's harsh criticism of his Lieder, and Wolf's immersion in his String Quartet in D minor. The year 1880, during which he continued work on his String Quartet and composed piano paraphrases of *Die Meistersinger von Nürnberg* and *Die Walküre*, yielded a mere 6 songs, including his first Eichendorff settings ('Erwartung' and 'Die Nacht') and his first song to a text by Mörike ('Suschens Vogel'). Wolf described 1881 as his *annus horribilis* – the year in which Vally broke off their relationship. The *Sechs geistliche Lieder nach Gedichten von Eichendorff* were his attempt to exorcise that trauma. The year 1882 marks the composition of his first masterpiece, a setting of Mörike's 'Mausfallen-Sprüchlein', and the first songs to poems by Robert Reinick. And 1883 sees him exploring further poems by Eichendorff, striving to find his own style and break free from the influence of Robert Schumann. From January 1884 to April 1887 Wolf was busy earning a living by writing over a hundred concert and opera reviews for the *Wiener Salonblatt*. The death of his father on 9 May plunged him into deep despair. The twelve Lieder, however, that he did compose during these three years include such masterpieces as 'Der Soldat I', 'Der Soldat II' and 'Nachtzauber'.

If 1881 had been Wolf's *annus horribilis*, 1888 turned out to be his *annus mirabilis*: over ninety songs, most of them masterpieces. The floodgates opened with the composition of 'Der Tambour' (16 February). Songs now flowed from his pen, and Wolf's feeling of rapture is conveyed by a flurry of hyperbolic letters to his closest friends. Such was his heightened state of inspiration that in the course of this one year he turned his attention, occasionally simultaneously, to no fewer than three of his favourite poets: Eichendorff, Goethe and Mörike. The following year, 1889, continued the trend with over 60 settings: Eichendorff and Goethe again, but also the early songs of the *Spanisches Liederbuch* – the first time that Wolf set German translations from a different language. Translations from English, Italian and Norwegian were to follow in the next decade. Then 1890 saw him complete the *Spanisches Liederbuch*, start the *Italienisches Liederbuch* and compose the 6 *Keller-Lieder*. It was also the year in which he began to orchestrate some of his piano-accompanied songs. In early 1891 he composed his three *Ibsen-Lieder* and by the end of the year he had finished Book I of the *Italienisches Liederbuch*.

No songs were completed between 1892 and 1894. Instead, he orchestrated a number of already existing piano-accompanied Lieder ('Der Feuerreiter', 'Mignon' and 'Anakreons Grab') – often a sign with Wolf of creative inertia. Although there are no songs from 1895, he completed the first version of his opera *Der Corregidor*. But 1896 marked his return, after a barren four years, to Lieder composition, and the remaining 24 songs of the *Italienisches Liederbuch* were completed in little over a month. In March 1897, buoyed perhaps by the successful premiere of *Der Corregidor* in June 1896, he composed, despite alarming signs of incipient insanity, the *Drei Gedichte von Michelangelo*, which were destined, he thought, „mich populär zu machen" ('to make me popular') – see HW to Heinrich Potpeschnigg, 9 September 1898, p. 326.

Less than a month after that letter, following a suicide attempt in the Traunsee, Wolf was committed to the Niederösterreichische Landesirrenanstalt. While confined in the asylum for the last five years of his life, he wrote no songs, although he sketched the opening bars of an SATB setting of Eichendorff's 'Dein Wille, Herr, geschehe' ('May Thy will, O Lord, be done') in a heartrending, scarcely legible scrawl.

1875

by August	Nacht und Grab (Zschokke)	HWW 3
by August	Sehnsucht (Goethe)	HWW 4
by August	Der Fischer (Goethe)	HWW 5
by August	Auf dem See (Goethe)	HWW 7

1876

January	Meeresstille (Lenau)	HWW 14
3 January	Frühlingsgrüße (Lenau)	HWW 11
29 January	Liebesfrühling (Lenau)	HWW 15
30 January	Erster Verlust (Goethe)	HWW 16
February	Die Stimme des Kindes (Lenau)	HWW 20
28 February–3 April	Im Sommer (Jacobi)	HWW 22/1
28 February–3 April	Geistesgruß (Goethe)	HWW 22/2
28 February–3 April	Mailied (Goethe)	HWW 22/3
18 March–24 April	Abendglöcklein (Zusner)	HWW 23
1 May	Der goldene Morgen (Anon.)	HWW 25
3 May	Perlenfischer (Roquette)	HWW 26
6–7 May	Fröhliche Fahrt (Hoefer)	HWW 27
10–28 May	Im stillen Friedhof (Pfau)	HWW 28
by early September	Grablied (Lorenzi)	HWW 32
September	Gottvertrauen (Mahlmann)	HWW 33

autumn	Scheideblick (Lenau)	HWW 35
autumn	Stille Sicherheit (Lenau)	HWW 36
8–10 December	Ein Grab (Peitl)	HWW 37
17 December	Mädchen mit dem roten Mündchen (Heine)	HWW 38
18 December	Du bist wie eine Blume (Heine)	HWW 39
21 December	Wenn ich in deine Augen seh (Heine)	HWW 40

1877

4 January–24 February	Abendbilder (Lenau)	HWW 43
25 March–12 April	Ständchen (Körner)	HWW 44
23–25 April	Andenken (Matthisson)	HWW 45
27 April–8 May	An* (Lenau)	HWW 46
6–19 June	Morgentau (Anon.)	HWW 101/1
14–15 June	Wanderlied (Anon.)	HWW 48
August–29 December	Der Schwalben Heimkehr (Herloßsohn)	HWW 55
November	Bescheidene Liebe (Anon.)	HWW 53

1878

22–25 January	Traurige Wege (Lenau)	HWW 56
8 February	So wahr die Sonne scheinet (Rückert)	HWW 57
19–21 February and 11 March	Nächtliche Wanderung (Lenau)	HWW 58
20–23 March	Auf der Wanderschaft (Chamisso)	HWW 59
5–12 April	Die Spinnerin (Rückert)	HWW 101/3
16–27 April	Das Kind am Brunnen (Hebbel)	HWW 62
2–23 May	Das Vöglein (Hebbel)	HWW 101/2
3–6 May	Knabentod (Hebbel)	HWW 64
18–25 May	Sie haben heut' abend Gesellschaft (Heine)	HWW 69/1
23–24 May	Über Nacht (Sturm)	HWW 67
26–29 May	Ich stand in dunkeln Träumen (Heine)	HWW 69/2
31 May	Das ist ein Brausen und Heulen (Heine)	HWW 69/3
3–4 June	Wo ich bin, mich rings umdunkelt (Heine)	HWW 68
5 June	Aus meinen großen Schmerzen (Heine)	HWW 69/4
16 June	Mir träumte von einem Königskind (Heine)	HWW 69/5
June	Mein Liebchen, wir saßen beisammen (Heine)	HWW 69/6
22 June	Es blasen die blauen Husaren (Heine)	HWW 69/7
9 August	Liebesfrühling (Hoffmann von Fallersleben)	HWW 72
10 August	Auf der Wanderung (Hoffmann von Fallersleben)	HWW 73
11 August	Ja, die Schönst'! ich sagt' es offen (Hoffmann von Fallersleben)	HWW 74
22 August–9 September	Gretchen vor dem Andachtsbild der Mater Dolorosa (Goethe)	HWW 76

31 August– 1 September	Nach dem Abschiede (Hoffmann von Fallersleben)	HWW 75
4 October	Es war ein alter König (Heine)	HWW 79
6 October	Mit schwarzen Segeln (Heine)	HWW 80
7 October	Spätherbstnebel, kalte Träume (Heine)	HWW 81
13–17 October	Ernst ist der Frühling (Heine)	HWW 82

1879

8 July	Herbstentschluß (Lenau)	HWW 84
21 July	Frage nicht (Lenau)	HWW 85
24 July	Herbst (Lenau)	HWW 86
11 September	Herbstklage (Lenau)	HWW 87

1880

26 January	Erwartung (*Eichendorff-Lieder*)	HWW 88
3 February	Die Nacht (*Eichendorff-Lieder*)	HWW 89
13 February	Wie des Mondes Abbild zittert (Heine)	HWW 90
7 June	Nachruf (Eichendorff)	HWW 92
26 November	Sterne mit den goldnen Füßchen (Heine)	HWW 94
24 December	Suschens Vogel (Mörike)	HWW 96

1881

31 March–30 April	Aufblick (Eichendorff)	HWW 98/1
31 March–30 April	Einkehr (Eichendorff)	HWW 98/2
31 March–30 April	Resignation (Eichendorff)	HWW 98/3
31 March–30 April	Letzte Bitte (Eichendorff)	HWW 98/4
31 March–30 April	Ergebung (Eichendorff)	HWW 98/5
31 March–30 April	Erhebung (Eichendorff)	HWW 98/6
27 June	In der Fremde I (Eichendorff)	HWW 99

1882

18 June	Mausfallen-Sprüchlein (Mörike)	HWW 101/6
7–17 December	Wiegenlied im Sommer (Reinick)	HWW 101/4
20 December	Wiegenlied im Winter (Reinick)	HWW 101/5
31 December	Wohin mit der Freud'? (Reinick)	HWW 104/1

1883

12 January	Rückkehr (Eichendorff)	HWW 102
19 January	Ständchen (Reinick)	HWW 104/5
24 January	Nachtgruß (Reinick)	HWW 104/3
30 January	In der Fremde VI (Eichendorff)	HWW 103

19 February	Frühlingsglocken (Reinick)	HWW 104/4
18 March	Liebesbotschaft (Reinick)	HWW 104/6
12 April	Liebchen, wo bist du? (Reinick)	HWW 104/2
3 May	In der Fremde II (Eichendorff)	HWW 105
16 June	Zur Ruh, zur Ruh! (Kerner)	HWW 114/6
?1883	Wohin mit der Freud'? (Reinick); second version	HWW 107

1884

1 July	Die Tochter der Heide (Mörike)	HWW 109

1886

13 March	Der König bei der Krönung (Mörike)	HWW 114/2
14 December	Der Soldat II (*Eichendorff-Lieder*)	HWW 118/6
26 December	Biterolf (Scheffel)	HWW 114/3

1887

24 January	Wächterlied auf der Wartburg (Scheffel)	HWW 114/1
30 January	Wanderers Nachtlied (Goethe)	HWW 114/5
1 March	Beherzigung (Goethe)	HWW 114/4
7 March	Der Soldat I (*Eichendorff-Lieder*)	HWW 118/5
8 March	Die Kleine (Eichendorff)	HWW 115
19 March–16 April	Die Zigeunerin (*Eichendorff-Lieder*)	HWW 118/7
20 April	Waldmädchen (*Eichendorff-Lieder*)	HWW 116
24 May	Nachtzauber (*Eichendorff-Lieder*)	HWW 118/8

1888

24 January	Gesellenlied (Reinick)	HWW 160/1
24 January	Wo wird einst (Heine)	HWW 161/1
16 February	Der Tambour (*Mörike-Lieder*)	HWW 119/5
22 February	Der Knabe und das Immlein (*Mörike-Lieder*)	HWW 119/2
22 February	Ein Stündlein wohl vor Tag (*Mörike-Lieder*)	HWW 119/3
22 February	Jägerlied (*Mörike-Lieder*)	HWW 119/4
23 February	Der Jäger (*Mörike-Lieder*)	HWW 119/40
24 February	Nimmersatte Liebe (*Mörike-Lieder*)	HWW 119/9
25 February	Zur Warnung (*Mörike-Lieder*)	HWW 119/49
25 February	Auftrag (*Mörike-Lieder*)	HWW 119/50
29 February	Lied vom Winde (*Mörike-Lieder*)	HWW 119/38
1 March	Bei einer Trauung (*Mörike-Lieder*)	HWW 119/51
6 March	Der Genesene an die Hoffnung (*Mörike-Lieder*)	HWW 119/1
6 March	Zitronenfalter im April (*Mörike-Lieder*)	HWW 119/18
7 March	Elfenlied (*Mörike-Lieder*)	HWW 119/16
7 March	Der Gärtner (*Mörike-Lieder*)	HWW 119/17

8 March	Abschied (*Mörike-Lieder*)	HWW 119/53
10 March	Denk' es, o Seele! (*Mörike-Lieder*)	HWW 119/39
11 March	Auf einer Wanderung (*Mörike-Lieder*)	HWW 119/15
13 March	Verborgenheit (*Mörike-Lieder*)	HWW 119/12
13 March	Gebet (*Mörike-Lieder*)	HWW 119/28
14 March	Lied eines Verliebten (*Mörike-Lieder*)	HWW 119/43
17 March	Selbstgeständnis (*Mörike-Lieder*)	HWW 119/52
20 March	Erstes Liebeslied eines Mädchens (*Mörike-Lieder*)	HWW 119/42
21 March	Fußreise (*Mörike-Lieder*)	HWW 119/10
22 March	Begegnung (*Mörike-Lieder*)	HWW 119/8
22 March	Rat einer Alten (*Mörike-Lieder*)	HWW 119/41
24 March	Das verlassene Mägdlein (*Mörike-Lieder*)	HWW 119/7
27 March	Storchenbotschaft (*Mörike-Lieder*)	HWW 119/48
29 March	Frage und Antwort (*Mörike-Lieder*)	HWW 119/35
31 March	Lebe wohl (*Mörike-Lieder*)	HWW 119/36
1 April	Heimweh (*Mörike-Lieder*)	HWW 119/37
12 April	Seufzer (*Mörike-Lieder*)	HWW 119/22
14 April	Auf ein altes Bild (*Mörike-Lieder*)	HWW 119/23
15 April	An eine Äolsharfe (*Mörike-Lieder*)	HWW 119/11
20 April	Um Mitternacht (*Mörike-Lieder*)	HWW 119/19
21 April	Auf eine Christblume II (*Mörike-Lieder*)	HWW 119/21
28 April	Peregrina I (*Mörike-Lieder*)	HWW 119/33
30 April	Peregrina II (*Mörike-Lieder*)	HWW 119/34
3 May	Agnes (*Mörike-Lieder*)	HWW 119/14
5 May	Er ist's (*Mörike-Lieder*)	HWW 119/6
5 May	In der Frühe (*Mörike-Lieder*)	HWW 119/24
8 May	Im Frühling (*Mörike-Lieder*)	HWW 119/13
13 May	Nixe Binsefuß (*Mörike-Lieder*)	HWW 119/45
18 May	Die Geister am Mummelsee (*Mörike-Lieder*)	HWW 119/47
31 August	Verschwiegene Liebe (*Eichendorff-Lieder*)	HWW 118/3
14 September	Der Schreckenberger (*Eichendorff-Lieder*)	HWW 118/9
16 September	Der Glücksritter (*Eichendorff-Lieder*)	HWW 118/10
21 September	Seemanns Abschied (*Eichendorff-Lieder*)	HWW 118/17
22 September	Der Musikant (*Eichendorff-Lieder*)	HWW 118/2
22 September	Der Scholar (*Eichendorff-Lieder*)	HWW 118/13
23 September	Der verzweifelte Liebhaber (*Eichendorff-Lieder*)	HWW 118/14
25 September	Unfall (*Eichendorff-Lieder*)	HWW 118/15
26 September	Der Freund (*Eichendorff-Lieder*)	HWW 118/1
27 September	Liebesglück (*Eichendorff-Lieder*)	HWW 118/16
28 September	Das Ständchen (*Eichendorff-Lieder*)	HWW 118/4
29 September	Lieber alles (*Eichendorff-Lieder*)	HWW 118/11
29 September	Heimweh (*Eichendorff-Lieder*)	HWW 118/12
4 October	An den Schlaf (*Mörike-Lieder*)	HWW 119/29
4 October	Neue Liebe (*Mörike-Lieder*)	HWW 119/30
5 October	Zum neuen Jahr (*Mörike-Lieder*)	HWW 119/27
6 October	Schlafendes Jesuskind (*Mörike-Lieder*)	HWW 119/25

CHRONOLOGY: LIEDER   li

6 October	Wo find' ich Trost? (*Mörike-Lieder*)	HWW 119/31
8 October	Karwoche (*Mörike-Lieder*)	HWW 119/26
9 October	Gesang Weylas (*Mörike-Lieder*)	HWW 119/46
10 October	Der Feuerreiter (*Mörike-Lieder*)	HWW 119/44
11 October	An die Geliebte (*Mörike-Lieder*)	HWW 119/32
27 October	Harfenspieler I (*Goethe-Lieder*)	HWW 120/1
29 October	Harfenspieler II (*Goethe-Lieder*)	HWW 120/2
30 October	Harfenspieler III (*Goethe-Lieder*)	HWW 120/3
30 October	Philine (*Goethe-Lieder*)	HWW 120/8
2 November	Spottlied aus *Wilhelm Meister* (*Goethe-Lieder*)	HWW 120/4
4 November	Der Schäfer (*Goethe-Lieder*)	HWW 120/22
4 November	Anakreons Grab (*Goethe-Lieder*)	HWW 120/29
6 November	Der Rattenfänger (*Goethe-Lieder*)	HWW 120/11
6 November	Gleich und gleich (*Goethe-Lieder*)	HWW 120/25
9 November	Dank des Paria (*Goethe-Lieder*)	HWW 120/30
14 November	Frech und froh I (*Goethe-Lieder*)	HWW 120/16
15 November	St. Nepomuks Vorabend (*Goethe-Lieder*)	HWW 120/20
26 November	Auf eine Christblume I (*Mörike-Lieder*)	HWW 119/20
28 November	Gutmann und Gutweib (*Goethe-Lieder*)	HWW 120/13
9 December	Ritter Kurts Brautfahrt (*Goethe-Lieder*)	HWW 120/12
14 December	Der Sänger (*Goethe-Lieder*)	HWW 120/10
17 December	Mignon (*Goethe-Lieder*)	HWW 120/9
18 December	Mignon II (*Goethe-Lieder*)	HWW 120/6
19 December	Mignon I (*Goethe-Lieder*)	HWW 120/5
21 December	Frühling übers Jahr (*Goethe-Lieder*)	HWW 120/28
22 December	Mignon III (*Goethe-Lieder*)	HWW 120/7
27 December	Epiphanias (*Goethe-Lieder*)	HWW 120/19
28 December	Cophtisches Lied I (*Goethe-Lieder*)	HWW 120/14
28 December	Cophtisches Lied II (*Goethe-Lieder*)	HWW 120/15
30 December	Beherzigung (*Goethe-Lieder*)	HWW 120/18
31 December	Blumengruß (*Goethe-Lieder*)	HWW 120/24

1889

2 January	Prometheus (*Goethe-Lieder*)	HWW 120/49
7 January	Königlich Gebet (*Goethe-Lieder*)	HWW 120/31
9 January	Grenzen der Menschheit (*Goethe-Lieder*)	HWW 120/51
11 January	Ganymed (*Goethe-Lieder*)	HWW 120/50
16 January	So lang man nüchtern ist (*Goethe-Lieder*)	HWW 120/36
16 January	Was in der Schenke waren heute (*Goethe-Lieder*)	HWW 120/38
17 January	Ob der Koran von Ewigkeit sei? (*Goethe-Lieder*)	HWW 120/34
18 January	Trunken müssen wir alle sein! (*Goethe-Lieder*)	HWW 120/35
18 January	Sie haben wegen der Trunkenheit (*Goethe-Lieder*)	HWW 120/37
19 January	Phänomen (*Goethe-Lieder*)	HWW 120/32
21 January	Erschaffen und Beleben (*Goethe-Lieder*)	HWW 120/33
21 January	Nicht Gelegenheit macht Diebe (*Goethe-Lieder*)	HWW 120/39

23 January	Hochbeglückt in deiner Liebe (*Goethe-Lieder*)	HWW 120/40
23 January	Wie sollt' ich heiter bleiben (*Goethe-Lieder*)	HWW 120/45
24 January	Als ich auf dem Euphrat schiffte (*Goethe-Lieder*)	HWW 120/41
24 January	Dies zu deuten bin erbötig! (*Goethe-Lieder*)	HWW 120/42
25 January	Komm, Liebchen, komm! (*Goethe-Lieder*)	HWW 120/44
25 January	Wenn ich dein gedenke (*Goethe-Lieder*)	HWW 120/46
26 January	Hätt ich irgend wohl Bedenken (*Goethe-Lieder*)	HWW 120/43
29 January	Locken, haltet mich gefangen (*Goethe-Lieder*)	HWW 120/47
30 January	Nimmer will ich dich verlieren! (*Goethe-Lieder*)	HWW 120/48
2 February	Frech und froh II (*Goethe-Lieder*)	HWW 120/17
5 February	Der neue Amadis (*Goethe-Lieder*)	HWW 120/23
10 February	Genialisch Treiben (*Goethe-Lieder*)	HWW 120/21
12 February	Die Bekehrte (*Goethe-Lieder*)	HWW 120/27
24 December 1886– May 1889	Christnacht (Platen)	HWW 121
11 May	Elfenlied (Shakespeare)	HWW 148
11 May	Lied des transferierten Zettel (Shakespeare)	HWW 161/2
28 May	Seufzer (Mörike); orchestration	HWW 122
29 May	Karwoche (Mörike); orchestration	HWW 123
?May	Auf ein altes Bild (Mörike); orchestration	HWW 124
?May	Schlafendes Jesuskind (Mörike); orchestration	HWW 125
1 August	Skolie (Reinick)	HWW 160/3
21 October	Die Spröde (*Goethe-Lieder*)	HWW 120/26
28 October	Wer sein holdes Lieb verloren (*Spanisches Liederbuch*)	HWW 129/17
31 October	Ich fuhr über Meer (*Spanisches Liederbuch*)	HWW 129/18
31 October	Preciosas Sprüchlein gegen Kopfweh (*Spanisches Liederbuch*)	HWW 129/24
1/2 November	Wenn du zu den Blumen gehst (*Spanisches Liederbuch*)	HWW 129/16
2 November	Alle gingen, Herz, zur Ruh (*Spanisches Liederbuch*)	HWW 129/31
4 November	Nun wandre, Maria (*Spanisches Liederbuch*)	HWW 129/3
5 November	Die du Gott gebarst, du Reine (*Spanisches Liederbuch*)	HWW 129/2
5 November	Die ihr schwebet (*Spanisches Liederbuch*)	HWW 129/4
10 November	Bedeckt mich mit Blumen (*Spanisches Liederbuch*)	HWW 129/36
14 November	Seltsam ist Juanas Weise (*Spanisches Liederbuch*)	HWW 129/13
15 November	Treibe nur mit Lieben Spott (*Spanisches Liederbuch*)	HWW 129/14
17 November	In dem Schatten meiner Locken (*Spanisches Liederbuch*)	HWW 129/12
17 November	Und schläfst du, mein Mädchen (*Spanisches Liederbuch*)	HWW 129/37
19 November	Herz, verzage nicht geschwind (*Spanisches Liederbuch*)	HWW 129/21
19 November	Sagt, seid Ihr es, feiner Herr (*Spanisches Liederbuch*)	HWW 129/22

20 November	Klinge, klinge, mein Pandero (*Spanisches Liederbuch*)	HWW 129/11
24 November	Herr, was trägt der Boden hier (*Spanisches Liederbuch*)	HWW 129/9
26 November	Blindes Schauen, dunkle Leuchte (*Spanisches Liederbuch*)	HWW 129/19
26 November	Bitt' ihn, o Mutter (*Spanisches Liederbuch*)	HWW 129/26
5 December	„Wer tat deinem Füßlein Weh?" (*Spanisches Liederbuch*)	HWW 129/40
12 December	Auf dem grünen Balkon (*Spanisches Liederbuch*)	HWW 129/15
13 December	Sie blasen zum Abmarsch (*Spanisches Liederbuch*)	HWW 129/38
15 December	Führ mich, Kind, nach Bethlehem! (*Spanisches Liederbuch*)	HWW 129/5
16 December	Wunden trägst du, mein Geliebter (*Spanisches Liederbuch*)	HWW 129/10
19 December	Ach, wie lang die Seele schlummert! (*Spanisches Liederbuch*)	HWW 129/8
21 December	Ach, des Knaben Augen (*Spanisches Liederbuch*)	HWW 129/6
22 December	Mühvoll komm' ich und beladen (*Spanisches Liederbuch*)	HWW 129/7

1890

15 January	Nun bin ich dein (*Spanisches Liederbuch*)	HWW 129/1
5 February	Der Rattenfänger (Goethe); orchestration	HWW 126
20 February	Er ist's (Mörike); orchestration	HWW 127
21 February	Gesang Weylas (Mörike); orchestration	HWW 128
12 March	Prometheus (Goethe); orchestration	HWW 130
28 March	Trau nicht der Liebe (*Spanisches Liederbuch*)	HWW 129/29
29 March	Schmerzliche Wonnen und wonnige Schmerzen (*Spanisches Liederbuch*)	HWW 129/28
29 March	Weint nicht, ihr Äuglein! (*Spanisches Liederbuch*)	HWW 129/39
30 March	Ach im Maien war's, im Maien (*Spanisches Liederbuch*)	HWW 129/30
31 March	Eide, so die Liebe schwur (*Spanisches Liederbuch*)	HWW 129/20
1 April	Geh, Geliebter, geh jetzt! (*Spanisches Liederbuch*)	HWW 129/44
2 April	Liebe mir im Busen zündet (*Spanisches Liederbuch*)	HWW 129/27
2 April	Deine Mutter, süßes Kind (*Spanisches Liederbuch*)	HWW 129/41
3 April	Mögen alle bösen Zungen (*Spanisches Liederbuch*)	HWW 129/23
4 April	Sagt ihm, daß er zu mir komme (*Spanisches Liederbuch*)	HWW 129/25
by mid-April	Anakreons Grab (Goethe); orchestration	HWW 131
by mid-April	Ganymed (Goethe); orchestration	HWW 132
by mid-April	Mignon (Goethe); orchestration	HWW 133
11 April	Dereinst, dereinst, Gedanke mein (*Spanisches Liederbuch*)	HWW 129/32

12 April	Tief im Herzen trag' ich Pein (*Spanisches Liederbuch*)	HWW 129/33
14 April	Komm, o Tod, von Nacht umgeben (*Spanisches Liederbuch*)	HWW 129/34
16 April	Ob auch finstre Blicke glitten (*Spanisches Liederbuch*)	HWW 129/35
20 April	Da nur Leid und Leidenschaft (*Spanisches Liederbuch*)	HWW 129/42
27 April	Wehe der, die mir verstrickte (*Spanisches Liederbuch*)	HWW 129/43
6 May	In der Frühe (Mörike); orchestration	HWW 134
12 May	Dem Vaterland (Reinick)	HWW 135
May–4 June	Dem Vaterland (Reinick); orchestration	HWW 136
25 May	Tretet ein, hoher Krieger (*Keller-Lieder*)	HWW 137/1
2 June	Singt mein Schatz wie ein Fink (*Keller-Lieder*)	HWW 137/2
8–23 June	Wandl' ich in dem Morgentau (*Keller-Lieder*)	HWW 137/4
5–24 June	Wie glänzt der helle Mond (*Keller-Lieder*)	HWW 137/6
7–24 June	Das Köhlerweib ist trunken (*Keller-Lieder*)	HWW 137/5
16 June	Du milchjunger Knabe (*Keller-Lieder*)	HWW 137/3
25 June	Frohe Botschaft (Reinick)	HWW 138
4 September	Gebet (Mörike); orchestration	HWW 139
4 September	An den Schlaf (Mörike); orchestration	HWW 140
5 September	Neue Liebe (Mörike); orchestration	HWW 141
6 September	Wo find' ich Trost? (Mörike); orchestration	HWW 142
25 September	Auf eine Christblume I (Mörike); orchestration	HWW 143
25 September	Mir ward gesagt, du reisest in die Ferne (*Italienisches Liederbuch*)	HWW 159/2
2 October	Ihr seid die Allerschönste weit und breit (*Italienisches Liederbuch*)	HWW 159/3
3 October	Gesegnet sei, durch den die Welt entstund (*Italienisches Liederbuch*)	HWW 159/4
4 October	Selig, ihr Blinden (*Italienisches Liederbuch*)	HWW 159/5
13 November	Wer rief dich denn? Wer hat dich herbestellt? (*Italienisches Liederbuch*)	HWW 159/6
13 November	Der Mond hat eine schwere Klag' erhoben (*Italienisches Liederbuch*)	HWW 159/7
14 November	Nun laß uns Frieden schließen, liebstes Leben (*Italienisches Liederbuch*)	HWW 159/8
2 December	Harfenspieler I (Goethe); orchestration	HWW 144
4 December	Harfenspieler II (Goethe); orchestration	HWW 145
4 December	Harfenspieler III (Goethe); orchestration	HWW 146

1891

7–23 January	Ballade. Gesang Margits (*Ibsen-Lieder*)	HWW 150/1
7 March	Gudmunds zweiter Gesang (*Ibsen-Lieder*)	HWW 150/3

CHRONOLOGY: LIEDER

4 May	Denk' es, o Seele (Mörike); orchestration	HWW 147
October	Elfenlied (Shakespeare); orchestration	HWW 148
30 October	Gudmunds erster Gesang (*Ibsen-Lieder*)	HWW 150/2
29 November	Daß doch gemalt all deine Reize wären (*Italienisches Liederbuch*)	HWW 159/9
2 December	Du denkst mit einem Fädchen mich zu fangen (*Italienisches Liederbuch*)	HWW 159/10
3 December	Mein Liebster ist so klein (*Italienisches Liederbuch*)	HWW 159/15
4 December	Wie lange schon war immer mein Verlangen (*Italienisches Liederbuch*)	HWW 159/11
4 December	Und willst du deinen Liebsten sterben sehen? (*Italienisches Liederbuch*)	HWW 159/17
5 December	Geselle, woll'n wir uns in Kutten hüllen (*Italienisches Liederbuch*)	HWW 159/14
7 December	Nein, junger Herr, so treibt man's nicht fürwahr (*Italienisches Liederbuch*)	HWW 159/12
8 December	Hoffärtig seid Ihr, schönes Kind (*Italienisches Liederbuch*)	HWW 159/13
9 December	Auch kleine Dinge können uns entzücken (*Italienisches Liederbuch*)	HWW 159/1
10 December	Ein Ständchen Euch zu bringen kam ich her (*Italienisches Liederbuch*)	HWW 159/22
11 December	Ihr jungen Leute, die ihr zieht ins Feld (*Italienisches Liederbuch*)	HWW 159/16
12 December	Heb' auf dein blondes Haupt und schlafe nicht (*Italienisches Liederbuch*)	HWW 159/18
12 December	Mein Liebster singt am Haus im Mondenscheine (*Italienisches Liederbuch*)	HWW 159/20
16 December	Wir haben beide lange Zeit geschwiegen (*Italienisches Liederbuch*)	HWW 159/19
23 December	Man sagt mir, deine Mutter woll' es nicht (*Italienisches Liederbuch*)	HWW 159/21

1892

October–November	Der Feuerreiter (Mörike); orchestration	HWW 151

1893

31 October	Mignon (Goethe); orchestration (second version)	HWW 153
13 November	Anakreons Grab (Goethe); orchestration (second version)	HWW 154

1894

June–November	Wächterlied auf der Wartburg (Scheffel); arranged for men's chorus and orchestra (unfinished)	HWW 157

1896

25 March	Ich esse nun mein Brot nicht trocken mehr (*Italienisches Liederbuch*)	HWW 159/24
26 March	Mein Liebster hat zu Tische mich geladen (*Italienisches Liederbuch*)	HWW 159/25
28 March	Ich ließ mir sagen und mir ward erzählt (*Italienisches Liederbuch*)	HWW 159/26
29 March	Schon streckt' ich aus im Bett die müden Glieder (*Italienisches Liederbuch*)	HWW 159/27
30 March	Du sagst mir, daß ich keine Fürstin sei (*Italienisches Liederbuch*)	HWW 159/28
30–31 March	Laß sie nur gehn, die so die Stolze spielt (*Italienisches Liederbuch*)	HWW 159/30
2 April	Wie viele Zeit verlor ich, dich zu lieben! (*Italienisches Liederbuch*)	HWW 159/37
3–4 April	Und steht Ihr früh am Morgen auf vom Bette (*Italienisches Liederbuch*)	HWW 159/34
9 April	Wohl kenn' ich Euren Stand, der nicht gering (*Italienisches Liederbuch*)	HWW 159/29
12 April	Wie soll ich fröhlich sein und lachen gar? (*Italienisches Liederbuch*)	HWW 159/31
12 April	O wär dein Haus durchsichtig wie ein Glas (*Italienisches Liederbuch*)	HWW 159/40
13 April	Sterb' ich, so hüllt in Blumen meine Glieder (*Italienisches Liederbuch*)	HWW 159/33
13–17 April	Gesegnet sei das Grün und wer es trägt! (*Italienisches Liederbuch*)	HWW 159/39
by 19 April	Wenn du mich mit den Augen streifst und lachst (*Italienisches Liederbuch*)	HWW 159/38
20 April	Was soll der Zorn, mein Schatz, der dich erhitzt? (*Italienisches Liederbuch*)	HWW 159/32
21 April	Benedeit die sel'ge Mutter (*Italienisches Liederbuch*)	HWW 159/35
23 April	Nicht länger kann ich singen (*Italienisches Liederbuch*)	HWW 159/42
23 April	Schweig' einmal still, du garst'ger Schwätzer dort! (*Italienisches Liederbuch*)	HWW 159/43
24 April	Wenn du, mein Liebster, steigst zum Himmel auf (*Italienisches Liederbuch*)	HWW 159/36

25 April	Heut Nacht erhob ich mich um Mitternacht (*Italienisches Liederbuch*)	HWW 159/41
25 April	Ich hab' in Penna einen Liebsten wohnen (*Italienisches Liederbuch*)	HWW 159/46
26 April	O wüßtest du, wie viel ich deinetwegen (*Italienisches Liederbuch*)	HWW 159/44
29 April	Verschling' der Abgrund meines Liebsten Hütte (*Italienisches Liederbuch*)	HWW 159/45
30 April	Was für ein Lied soll dir gesungen werden (*Italienisches Liederbuch*)	HWW 159/23
8 September–23 October	Morgenstimmung (Reinick)	HWW 160/2
18–24/25 December	Keine gleicht von allen Schönen (Byron)	HWW 161/4
29–31 December	Sonne der Schlummerlosen (Byron)	HWW161/3

1897

18 March	Wohl denk' ich oft an mein vergang'nes Leben (*Michelangelo-Lieder*)	HWW 162/1
20 March	Alles endet, was entstehet (*Michelangelo-Lieder*)	HWW 162/2
22–28 March	Fühlt meine Seele (*Michelangelo-Lieder*)	HWW 162/3
1–4 December	Wer sein holdes Lieb verloren (*Spanisches Liederbuch*); orchestration (*Manuel Venegas*)	HWW 166
5–6 December	Wenn du zu den Blumen gehst (*Spanisches Liederbuch*); orchestration (*Manuel Venegas*)	HWW 167
12–17 December	Morgenhymnus (Reinick); version of 'Morgenstimmung' for chorus and orchestra	HWW 168

The Poets

Songs published during Wolf's lifetime are listed in **black type**; those unpublished during his lifetime in a paler typeface.

Anonymous

		page
Der goldene Morgen	1 May 1876	5
Bescheidene Liebe	November 1877	5
Morgentau	6–19 June 1877	6
Wanderlied	14–15 June 1877	6
Die Verlassene	19 June 1877	fragment
Poem possibly by Hans Schmidt		
Das Lied der Waise	10 October 1877	fragment
Poem possibly by Friedrich Steinebach		
Der schwere Traum	27 October 1878	fragment
Wahlspruch	?1883	TTBB

Not included here are the anonymous Spanish and Italian texts from the *Spanisches Liederbuch* and the *Italienisches Liederbuch* – which are listed under GEIBEL and HEYSE respectively. The earliest of Wolf's anonymous songs, according to Margret Jestremski, is 'Bescheidene Liebe' – see HW to his parents, 22 December 1877, p. 4. Mystery surrounds the provenance of 'Wanderlied' and 'Morgentau'. Dietrich Fischer-Dieskau (*Hugo Wolf. Leben und Werk*) maintains that the texts were taken from an old book of poetry that Wolf's father 'copied out in his own hand and gave to his fiancée Katharina'; Frank Walker (*Hugo Wolf: A Biography*) states that the poems were 'taken from an old song book – likely enough a volume of poems copied out by the hand of his father'. On one of the manuscripts of 'Wanderlied' Wolf wrote the name Albert Reinhold, which he later changed to „Aus einem alten Liederbuche".

COMPOSER

Wolf hoped (in vain) that not only 'Morgentau' and 'Wanderlied' but also 'An*' and 'Traurige Wege' (both Lenau, pp. 313, 310) would be published by Joh. André, a well-known publishing house in Offenbach-am-Rhein. When André declined, Wolf sent the songs to the revered musicologist Friedrich von Hausegger who, though not unimpressed by what he called the Mendelssohnian style, found the songs superficial. Wolf's fury knew no bounds – see the letter to his parents,

10 April 1878, below. He then offered the same songs, with the addition of 'Nächtliche Wanderung' (Lenau, p. 311), to Breitkopf & Härtel. He told his parents that Breitkopf & Härtel was much better known than André, and that his songs would be published within two months. 'Morgentau', in particular, he felt was a masterpiece (letter of 10 April), although he admitted that his setting of 'Nächtliche Wanderung' was not entirely successful. When Breitkopf also declined to publish, Wolf seems to have renounced all efforts to get into print. This suddenly changed with the publication in 1888 of *Sechs Lieder für eine Frauenstimme*, comprising 'Morgentau', 'Das Vöglein' (Hebbel, p. 179), 'Die Spinnerin' (Rückert, p. 455), 'Wiegenlied im Sommer', 'Wiegenlied im Winter' (both Reinick, pp. 437, 438) and 'Mausfallen-Sprüchlein' (Mörike, p. 365). One reason for this was the kindness and generosity of Friedrich Eckstein, a friend of independent means who was always ready to help the composer in times of emotional and financial need. He had already persuaded the small Viennese firm of Emil Wetzler to publish some of Bruckner's choral works, and was confident that it would now come to Wolf's rescue. Wolf selected six songs that he had composed between 1877 and 1882, defrayed the bulk of the costs from the legacy left him by his father, and dedicated the set to his mother. 'Morgentau' was one of the first Wolf songs to be sung in public: the celebrated contralto Rosa Papier performed it with 'Zur Ruh, zur Ruh!' in a recital she gave at the Saal Bösendorfer on 2 March 1888.

Wolf included 'Morgentau' and 'Wanderlied' in a volume of songs with the title: LIEDER und GESÆNGE. *1tes Heft. In Musik gesetzt von* HUGO WOLF that he sent in the summer of 1877 to the Ministry of Culture and Education. The other songs, which he hoped would earn him a bursary, were: 'Andenken' (Matthisson, p. 318), 'An*' (Lenau, p. 313), 'Ständchen' (Körner, p. 297) and 'Ein Grab' (Peitl, p. 421). He was unsuccessful and the manuscripts were returned.

LETTERS

HW to his parents, Vienna, 22 December 1877

Beiliegendes Lied[1] von mir ist sehr gelungen u. stammt schon vom November her.

The enclosed song has come out very well & was already composed back in November.

HW to his parents, Vienna, 10 April 1878

Wahrscheinlich hat er sie vorm Schlafengehen, nachdem nicht allein schon seine physischen, sondern auch psychischen Kräfte sehr erschlafft waren,

---

1 'Bescheidene Liebe'.

durchgesehen, denn sonst könnte er niemals zu diesem Fazit gelangen. Sogar ein starker Schumannscher Zug geht durch die Lieder, am meisten in den „Traurigen Wegen", aber Mendelssohn nimmermehr. [. . .] Als vollkommen gelungen, wo man mir nicht im geringsten Unreife vorwerfen kann, betrachte ich das in Windischgraz komponierte einfache Liedchen „Morgentau", über welches sich alle, denen ich es gezeigt, in dem Satz einigen, es fließe als wie ein ruhiger Bach hin.

He probably looked through the songs just before going to bed, when not only his physical but also his mental powers were relaxed, for otherwise he could never have arrived at this conclusion. A strong Schumannian trait runs through the songs, especially in 'Traurige Wege', but Mendelssohn? Never. [. . .] I consider the simple little song that I composed in Windischgraz, 'Morgentau', to be perfect, and which no one could criticise as being the slightest bit immature; everyone here I've shown it to agrees that it purls away like a quiet brook.

LIEDER

Der goldene Morgen

Golden lacht und glüht der Morgen
Über maiengrünen Höh'n,
Und die Seele bricht voll Sorgen
Und die Welt ist doch so schön.

Vöglein singen, Glocken schlagen,
Blütenduft durchzieht das Land.
Wirf dein Klagen und dein Zagen
Ganz in diesen Freudenbrand!

Bescheidene Liebe[1]

Ich bin wie and're Mädchen nicht,
Die, wenn sie lieben, schweigen,
Und, ihr Geheimnis hütend,
Stumm das kranke Köpfchen neigen.
Ja, meine Liebe ist nicht stumm,
Mein Plaudern geb' ich nicht darum,
Ich liebe doch ganz eigen.*

Ich bin wie and're Mädchen nicht,
Die, wenn sie lieben, hoffen;

The golden morning

The morning glows golden and laughs
Above the may-green hills,
And the heart breaks with sorrow
And yet the world is so fair.

Little birds sing, bells ring out,
A scent of blossom pervades the land.
Cast your grievances and fear
Into this great blaze of joy!

Modest love

I am not like other girls
Who keep silent when they love,
And, guarding their secret,
Bow their lovelorn little head.
Yes, my love is not silent.
I shall not stop my chatter,
For I love in my own special way.*

I am not like other girls
Who harbour hope when they love;

---

1 The song's popularity increased soon after Wolf's death, when Bote & Bock published a French version entitled 'Amour modeste' in March 1910.

Ich trage meine Lieb' zur Schau
Vor aller Welt ganz offen.
Oft hat mich schon lieb' Mütterlein
Mit dem Herzallerliebsten mein
Beim Kosen angetroffen.*

Ich bin wie and're Mädchen nicht,
Doch glücklich, wie ich glaube;
Denn meine Liebe richtet sich
Auf Trauring nicht und Haube.[1]
Er bleibt mein trauter Bräutigam,
Er girrt so süß, er ist so zahm,
Mein Lieb' ist meine Taube.*

I show my love quite openly
So that everyone might see.
My dear mother has often
Caught my lover and me
Red-handed as we cuddled.*

I am not like other girls,
But am, I believe, content;
For my love demands
Neither wedding-ring nor bonnet.
He will remain my dear fiancé,
He coos so sweetly, he is so tame,
My love is my own dove.*

* Wolf repeats these lines.

Wanderlied

Es segeln die Wolken, weiß niemand
    wohin?
Die Lüfte, sie rauschen, wohin wohl, wohin?
Sie wandern zusammen, sie kommen
    und flieh'n,
Mag keiner mir künden, wohin wohl,
    wohin?

So zieh' ich ins Leben mit fröhlichem Sinn,
Doch frage mich niemand, wohin wohl,
    wohin?
Noch duften die Blüten, noch locket
    das Grün,
Glück auf zu dem Wandern, weiß selbst
    nicht wohin!*

Wanderer's song

The clouds scud by, does no one know
    whither?
The breezes murmur, whither, whither?
They journey together, they come
    and they flee,
Can no one tell me, whither,
    whither?

Thus I set out into life, happy in mind,
But let no one ask me, whither,
    whither?
The blossom's still fragrant, the verdure
    still beckons,
Good luck with wandering, though I know
    not whither!*

* Wolf repeats the final line.

Morgentau[2]

Der Frühhauch hat gefächelt
Hinweg die schwüle Nacht,
Die Flur holdselig lächelt
In ihrer Lenzespracht;
Mild singt vom dunklen Baume
Ein Vöglein in der Früh,

Morning dew

The breath of dawn has fanned
Away the sultry night,
The meadow smiles blissfully
In its springtime splendour;
From the dark tree a little bird
Gently sings at dawn,

1 'Haube' = bonnet. „Unter die Haube kommen" = to get married. Wives used to wear bonnets as a sign of their marital status.
2 See HW to his parents, 10 April 1878, p. 4.

Es singt noch halb im Traume
Gar süße Melodie.

Die Rosenknospe hebet
Empor ihr Köpfchen bang,
Denn wundersam durchbebet
Hat sie der süße Sang;
Und mehr und mehr enthüllet
Sich ihrer Blätter Füll',
Und eine Träne quillet
Hervor so heimlich still.

Still half dreaming, it sings
A most sweet melody.

The rosebud fearfully
Raises its head aloft,
For the sweet song
Has magically thrilled her through;
Her abundant petals
Unfold more and more,
And a tear wells up
Most secretly and silently.

Lord Byron
(1788–1824)

		page
Keine gleicht von allen Schönen	18–24/25 December 1896	11
Sonne der Schlummerlosen	29–31 December 1896	12

POET

The son of an admiral and his second wife, a Scottish noblewoman, George Gordon Byron, 6th Baron Byron, grew up in Aberdeen. His childhood was unhappy; he suffered at the hands of a 'diabolical' mother and a vicious nurse. His club foot strengthened his resolve to excel at physical activities, and he was by all accounts a prodigious swimmer. In 1798, on the death of his great uncle, Byron inherited his title and the family estate at Newstead Abbey. He was educated at Harrow where, aged fifteen, he fell passionately in love with Mary Chaworth, one of his early erotic liaisons. From Harrow he went to Trinity College, Cambridge, where in 1807 *Hours of Idleness* was published. It was in Cambridge that he experienced the most intense of his homosexual relationships – with the fifteen-year-old chorister John Edleston whose death was to trigger the series of elegies known as the 'Thyrza' cycle, six of which were added to the first and second editions of *Childe Harold*.

From 1809 to 1811 Byron undertook a Mediterranean Grand Tour. His amorous private life resembled, if not quite rivalled, that of Casanova. He married Annabella Milbanke in 1812 but left her after a year. Next, his relationship with his half-sister Augusta, who became his constant companion, was to cause public outrage. Having left England in 1816, Byron sailed up the Rhine to Switzerland, where he joined Mary and Percy Bysshe Shelley. In January 1817 Claire Clairmont, Mary Shelley's stepsister, bore Byron a daughter, Allegra. He agreed to support mother and daughter but left them later in the year when the Shelleys returned to England. He then embarked on a number of relationships before settling down for a time in Italy with Teresa Guiccioli, who left her husband for Byron in 1821. Together they became involved with the Carbonari, a militant nationalist movement that Byron supported financially.

When the Carbonari's struggle foundered, Byron embraced another cause – that of Greek liberation from Turkish oppression. He set sail from Leghorn in the *Hercules*, which he had armed at his own expense, and arrived ten days later in Cephalonia. He was joined in January 1824 by the Greek leader Alexander

Mavrocordato, whose plan was to attack the Turkish stronghold at Lepanto. In April 1824 Byron caught a severe chill, which led to the rheumatic fever from which he died on the 19th of that month. Memorial services were held throughout Greece, where his heart and lungs were buried, but the rest of his body was returned to England. When the Deans of both St Paul's and Westminster Abbey refused to bury the poet, his friend John Cam Hobhouse arranged for the body to lie in state for a few days in London. He was finally interred in the family vault in the church of Hucknall Torkard, near Newstead Abbey.

Bryan N. S. Gooch and David Thatcher, in *Musical Settings of British Romantic Literature*, list almost 1,300 musical works based on Byron's poems. Pushkin evoked the Byronic hero in *Eugene Onegin*, and there were many composers, other than Tchaikovsky, who were inspired by his poems. Byron-based operas include Donizetti's *Parisina* (1833) and *Marino Faliero* (1835), Verdi's *I due Foscari* (1844) and *Il Corsaro* (1848). Berlioz, a great admirer, turned to Byron for *Le Corsaire* and *Harold en Italie*; *Manfred* influenced Schumann and Nietzsche (the *Manfred-Meditation* for piano), and Liszt based his *Tasso* on *The Lament of Tasso*. Byron's poems have proved less popular with song composers, apart from Isaac Nathan (30 settings – the complete *Hebrew Melodies*), Loewe (24), Schumann (6), Busoni (3), Mendelssohn (2), Wolf (2), and Balakirev, Goldmark, Ives, Mussorgsky and Rimsky-Korsakov (one each).

COMPOSER

Byron was one of Wolf's favourite authors. He sketched an overture to *The Corsair* for large orchestra in December 1877 (see the letter to his father of 2 January 1878, p. 10); turned to him again in the summer of 1880; read a biography of the poet in 1891, and set two poems in December 1896. 'Keine gleicht von allen Schönen' and 'Sonne der Schlummerlosen' form part of the *Vier Gedichte nach H. Heine, Shakespeare und Lord Byron*, of which only the Byron settings were freshly composed – see HW to Karl Mayr, 27 January 1897, p. 11. It seems that Wolf considered setting another Byron poem to music; he copied in his own hand Gildemeister's translation of 'I saw thee weep' – 'Ich sah dich weinen' – onto the same sheet of paper as 'Sonne der Schlummerlosen' and 'Keine gleicht von allen Schönen'.

LETTERS

HW to his father, Vienna, 2 January 1878

So komponierte ich am 27. Dezember [1877] die Skizzen zu einer Ouvertüre für großes Orchester, u. z. zur Lord Byronschen Erzählung „Der Korsar".[1] Es soll dieses mein erstes reiferes Werk sein, welches ich auch ohne Zagen dem Publikum darzubieten mir getraue.

On 27 December [1877] I sketched an overture for large orchestra to Byron's *The Corsair*. This is my first truly mature work which I feel confident to offer without hesitation to the public.

HW to Heinrich Potpeschnigg, Vienna, 28 December 1896

Das schönste Christkindl aber habe ich mir mit dem neuen Lied[2] gemacht. Hoffentlich gefällts Dir auch. Da ich sehr oft beim Arbeiten gestört wurde brauchte es eine ganze Woche, um mit der Composition in's Reine zu kommen.

My finest Christmas present is a new song. I hope you will like it too. Because of constant interruptions it took me a whole week to finish.

HW to Oskar Grohe, Vienna, 1 January 1897

Gestern in später Abendstunde – ich habe den Sylvester ganz allein d. h. in Gesellschaft von Lord Byron – kein übler Geselle – ein schönes Gedicht von ihm componirend – zugebracht.[3]

Late yesterday evening – I spent New Year's Eve quite alone, i.e. in the company of Lord Byron (not a bad companion) – I set to music a beautiful poem of his.

HW to Karl Heckel, Vienna, 19 January 1897

Mit heutigem sende ich Ihnen per Kreuzband 4 Lieder Manuskripte zu mit der ergeb. Bitte, falls Sie dieselben in Ihren Verlag nehmen wollen für deren baldige Drucklegung zu sorgen. Diese 4 Lieder bedeuten einen vorläufigen Abschluß meiner Thätigkeit als Liedercomponist.

Today I am posting you by special delivery the manuscripts of 4 songs and respectfully request you, should you wish to publish them, that they be printed

---

1 Although the overture was mentioned in two other letters to his family, no sketches have survived.
2 'Keine gleicht von allen Schönen'.   3 'Sonne der Schlummerlosen'.

HW to Karl Mayr, Vienna, 27 January 1897

Demnächst werden 4 Lieder von mir erscheinen 2 nach Heine u. Shakespeare ältern Datums u. 2 nach Lord Byron, ganz frisch gebacken.

soon. These 4 songs mark for the time being the end of my career as a Lieder composer.

4 songs of mine will be published soon – 2 settings respectively of Heine & Shakespeare that were composed a while ago, & 2 of Lord Byron, hot off the press.

LIEDER

Keine gleicht von allen Schönen

Keine gleicht von allen Schönen,
    Zauberhafte, dir!
Wie Musik auf Wassern tönen
    Deine Worte mir.
Wann das Meer vergißt zu rauschen,
    Um entzückt zu lauschen,
Lichte Wellen leise schäumen,
Eingelullte Winde träumen,

Wann der Mond die Silberkette
    Über Fluten spinnt,
Deren Brust im stillen Bette
    Atmet, wie ein Kind:
Also liegt mein Herz versunken,
Lauschend, wonnetrunken,
Sanft gewiegt und voll sich labend,
Wie des Meeres Sommerabend!

Translated by Otto Gildemeister

There be none of Beauty's daughters[1]

There be none of Beauty's daughters
    With a magic like thee;
And like music on the waters
    Is thy sweet voice to me:
When, as if its sound were causing
The charmed ocean's pausing,
The waves lie still and gleaming
And the lull'd winds seem dreaming:

And the midnight moon is weaving
    Her bright chain o'er the deep;
Whose breast is gently heaving,
    As an infant's asleep:
So the spirit bows before thee,
To listen and adore thee;
With a full but soft emotion,
Like the swell of Summer's ocean.

Also set by Mario Castelnuovo-Tedesco, John Foulds, Armstrong Gibbs, Fanny Mendelssohn Hensel, Joseph Holbrooke, Carl Loewe, Hamish MacCunn, Felix Mendelssohn, Hubert Parry, Roger Quilter, Charles Villiers Stanford and Maude Valérie White

---

1 Byron's manuscript reads 'Stanzas' – another hand added 'for Music' in pencil. The poem was first published in 1816, the year in which Byron's relationship with Claire Clairmont began, and she is possibly the subject of the poem; we know from Shelley's 'To Constantia singing' that she possessed a beautiful voice. Leslie A. Marchant suggests that the poem is associated with John Edleston, the beauty of whose voice was a constant theme in the 'Thyrza' poems. The poem was written six months

Sonne der Schlummerlosen

Sonne der Schlummerlosen,[1] bleicher Stern!
Wie Tränen zittern, schimmerst du von fern;
Du zeigst die Nacht, doch scheuchst sie nicht zurück,
Wie ähnlich bist du dem entschwundnen[2] Glück,

Dem Licht vergang'ner Tage, das fortan
Nur leuchten, aber nimmer wärmen kann!

Die Trauer wacht, wie es durchs Dunkel wallt,
Deutlich, doch fern, hell, aber o wie kalt!

Translated by Otto Gildemeister

Sun of the sleepless![3]

Sun of the sleepless! melancholy star!
Whose tearful beam glows tremulously far,
That show'st the darkness thou canst not dispel,
How like art thou to joy remembered well!

So gleams the past, the light of other days,
Which shines, but warms not with its powerless rays;

A night-beam Sorrow watcheth to behold,
Distinct, but distant – clear – but, oh how cold!

Also set by Sigfrid Karg-Elert, Loewe, Mendelssohn,[4] Nathan, Friedrich Nietzsche, Nikolai Rimsky-Korsakov, Ned Rorem and Robert Schumann

---

after the death of Edleston, who perished from consumption on 16 May 1811. In a letter to Elizabeth Pigot, dated 5 July 1807, Byron had written of Edleston, 'his *voice* first attracted my notice, his *countenance* fixed it, & his *manners* attached me to him forever'. A facsimile of Gildemeister's translation in Wolf's own hand is reproduced in Dietrich Fischer-Dieskau's *Hugo Wolf. Leben und Werk* (p. 355).
1   Wolf suffered throughout his life from insomnia. As a young composer, he resented sleep as something that curtailed the creative process; and as he grew older he became addicted to coffee which he prepared himself with a 'Non plus ultra' machine. At the height of his coffee mania he preferred to drink it hot, black, unadulterated and sweet but he confessed to Edmund Hellmer (*Hugo Wolf. Erlebtes und Erlauschtes*) that later in his life he tended to add water to reduce its strength.
2   Gildemeister: verschwundnen.
3   From *Hebrew Melodies*. Byron wrote these lines as part of the unfinished poem 'Harmodia'. When asked by Nathan whether the poem addressed the moon or the evening star, Byron replied facetiously, 'I see, Nathan, you have been *star* gazing, and are now in the *clouds*; I shall therefore leave the *Astronomer Royal* to direct you in that matter.'
4   Byron's poem was translated numerous times by a variety of different poets. Mendelssohn knew Loewe's 'Die Sonne der Schlaflosen', translated by Franz Theremin, but when he came to compose his own song, he decided to use his own version ('Schlafloser Augen Leuchte').

Adelbert von Chamisso
(1781–1838)

			page
Auf der Wanderschaft	20–23 March 1878		15
Was soll ich sagen?	between 1 April and 4 May 1878	fragment	

POET

Chamisso, in full Louis Charles Adelaïde de Chamisso de Boncourt, was a Frenchman who at the age of nine fled the Revolution with his family to the Netherlands, and subsequently to Würzburg and Bayreuth. He spent an idyllic childhood in Boncourt, a period he later recalled in a celebrated poem, 'Das Schloß Boncourt', which generations of German schoolchildren used to learn by heart. The years 1792–96 were spent fleeing from the armies of the Revolution. With the break-up of the family estate, the Chamisso children worked hard – with great financial success – at painting miniatures, a skill that would eventually secure Chamisso's entry into the Prussian court. He wrote his first poems in French during 1793–4: *Les yeux de mon imagination rédigés par une verve encore dans l'enfance. Chevalier de Chamisso âgé de 13–14 ans. A Liège, Dusseldorf et autres lieux 1793–94*. He finally settled in Berlin, became a page at the Prussian court, enrolled in the Prussian army and, as a Frenchman fighting against Napoleon, found life increasingly difficult. The German language, however, was quickly learned and it was not long before he found his niche in the literary life of Berlin, where he formed friendships with August von Schlegel and Varnhagen von Ense. An offshoot of these literary soirées was the creation of a *Musenalmanac* (1804), the first issue of which was printed at Chamisso's expense in 1804. It contained some of his own poems, and further editions featured works by Achim von Arnim, August von Schlegel and Johann Gottlieb Fichte.

In 1806 his regiment was put on a war footing and he was taken prisoner by the French in Hamelin. Released on parole, he went to France for a short time, returning to Germany in 1807. When Schlegel accompanied him to France in 1810, Chamisso was introduced to Madame de Staël in Paris, and followed her to Switzerland, where, at the age of thirty-two, he became obsessed with botany, returning to Berlin to study the subject in depth. He was unable to settle in Germany and moved to Kunersdorf, where he spent some time in voluntary exile.

It was there that he wrote his most famous work, the Novelle *Peter Schlemihls wundersame Geschichte*, the story of a man who sells his shadow to the Devil – an allegorical autobiography published in 1814.

In 1815, possibly to escape the interminable Napoleonic Wars, he joined a Russian-sponsored voyage round the world under Otto von Kotzebue as expedition scientist, the literary result of which was *Reise um die Welt in den Jahren 1815–1818* (1836), a travelogue culled from his expedition diaries that has stood the test of time. On his return to Germany, he was appointed to the staff of the Botanical Gardens in Berlin. From 1832 he was co-editor, with Gustav Schwab, of the *Deutscher Musenalmanac*. The *Frauen-Liebe und Leben* poems (Chamisso's punctuation), immortalised by Loewe and Schumann, to which he gave pride of place in his *Collected Works*, were started in 1829 and completed in January 1830 – a retrospective reimagining, perhaps, of the adoration felt for him by Antonie Piaste, the eighteen-year-old middle-class young woman he had married in 1819.

Following the success of his first volume of poetry, Chamisso wrote with pride: „Das Volk singt meine Lieder, man singt sie in den Salons, die Componisten reißen sich danach, die Jungen declamiren sie in den Schulen, mein Portrait erscheint nach Goethe, Tieck und Schlegel als das vierte in der Reihe der gleichzeitigen deutschen Dichter und schöne Damen drücken mir fromm die Hand." ('The people sing my songs, they are sung in salons, composers vie with each other to set them, boys recite them in school, my portrait appears after those of Goethe, Tieck and Schlegel as the fourth in the ranks of contemporary poets, and beautiful ladies squeeze my hand with devotion.') No less a figure than Heinrich Heine described Chamisso in his survey of German Romantic poetry (*Die romantische Schule*, 1836) as one of the „eigentümlichsten und bedeutendsten modernen Dichter" ('one of the most original and significant of modern poets'). And Thomas Mann wrote an essay on Chamisso in 1911, praising such poems as 'Schloß Boncourt', 'Die alte Waschfrau', 'Das Vermächtnis', 'Traum und Erwachen', 'Tragische Geschichte' (perhaps Mann knew Pfitzner's setting of 1907), 'Salas y Gomez' and 'Was soll ich sagen?', the poem that Wolf attempted to set in 1878. Mann also recalls how his mother used to sing *Frauenliebe und -leben* in the evenings.

COMPOSER

Wolf composed some hundred songs before the eruption of the *Mörike-Lieder* in 1888 – and as with the forty or so early Lieder of his contemporary Richard Strauss, there are some gems among them. Several give a tantalising glimpse of the mature Wolf and none of them, despite his own self-deprecating remarks, is insignificant. 'Auf der Wanderschaft', to a poem by Chamisso first published in the 1827 edition of *Peter Schlemihls wundersame Geschichte*, was composed on 20 March 1878, when Wolf had just turned eighteen. He was clearly dissatisfied, for at the foot of the page he wrote „Schlecht!" ('Bad!'). Three days later, he composed a second version, only to write „Noch schlechter!" ('Even worse!') on the manuscript. Neither song is as bad as he professed, but it was probably his inability to respond to the Heine-like humour of the poem that resulted in his pejorative remarks. On 1 April 1878 he also attempted another Chamisso setting, 'Was soll ich sagen?', which he then put aside, only to tackle it again on 4 May 1878 – to no avail. In despair he scribbled across the manuscript: „Zu viel Schumannisch, – deshalb nicht vollendet." ('Too much like Schumann – therefore not finished.') Wolf had a horror of imitation and plagiarism – see his letter to his parents of 10 April 1878, p. 305. As he put it in a letter to his mother of 19 September 1891: „Welch ein schreckliches Los für einen Künstler, der nichts Neues mehr zu sagen weiß!" ('What a terrible fate for an artist who has nothing new to say!')

LIED

Auf der Wanderschaft I and II[1]

Wohl wandert' ich aus in trauriger Stund',
    Es weinte die Liebe so sehr.
Der Fuß ist mir lahm, die Schulter mir wund,
    Das Herz, das ist mir so schwer.

Was singt ihr, ihr Vögel, im Morgenlicht?
    Ihr wißt nicht, wie scheiden thut!
Es drücken euch Sorgen und Schuhe nicht;

    Ihr Vögel, ihr habt es gut!

On the road I and II

I set out in a sad hour,
    Love was weeping so much,
My foot was sore, my shoulder hurt,
    My heart is so heavy.

Birds, why are you singing in the dawn?
    You don't know the pain of parting!
Worries don't depress you, shoes don't
    pinch you;
    How fortunate, birds, you are!

---

[1] It is clear from the two extant manuscripts of 'Auf der Wanderschaft' that Wolf intended to set all three poems of Chamisso's cycle: 'Wohl wandert' ich aus in trauriger Stund'', 'Der Regen strömt, die Sonne scheint' and 'Noch hallt nur aus der Ferne'. He gave each version of 'Auf der Wanderschaft' the same title: *Auf der Wanderschaft. 3 Gedichte von Chamisso in Musik gesetzt von Hugo Wolf.*

Joseph von Eichendorff
(1788–1857)

			page
Der Kehraus	?1880	lost	
Das zerbrochene Ringlein	?1880	lost	
Der traurige Jäger	?1880	lost	
Verschwiegene Liebe, first setting	1880	fragment	
Erwartung	26 January 1880		49
Die Nacht	3 February 1880		50
Nachruf	7 June 1880		29
Nachtgruß	2 November 1880	fragment	
Sechs geistliche Lieder nach Gedichten von Joseph von Eichendorff für vierstimmigen gemischten Chor a cappella	31 March – 30 April 1881; revised 1894?		
Aufblick			31
Einkehr			31
Resignation			31
Letzte Bitte			32
Ergebung			32
Erhebung			33
In der Fremde I	27 June 1881		33
In der Fremde II, first setting	3 February 1882 – 1 January 1883	fragment	
Rückkehr	12 January 1883		34
In der Fremde VI	30 January 1883		34
In der Fremde II, second setting	3 May 1883		35
Der Soldat II	14 December 1886		41
Der Soldat I	7 March 1887		40
Die Kleine	8 March 1887		36
Die Zigeunerin	19 March–16 April 1887		41
Waldmädchen	20 April 1887		50
Nachtzauber	24 May 1887		42
Verschwiegene Liebe, second setting	31 August 1888		38
Der Schreckenberger	14 September 1888		43
Der Glücksritter	16 September 1888		43
Seemanns Abschied	21 September 1888		48
Der Musikant	22 September 1888		38

Der Scholar	22 September 1888	46
Der verzweifelte Liebhaber	23 September 1888	46
Unfall	25 September 1888	47
Der Freund	26 September 1888	37
Liebesglück	27 September 1888	47
Das Ständchen	28 September 1888	39
Lieber alles	29 September 1888	44
Heimweh	29 September 1888	45

POET

Joseph, Freiherr von Eichendorff, grew up on the family estate in Silesia; the family also owned properties in Bohemia and Moravia. He spent an idyllic childhood at Schloß Lubowitz, surrounded by wooded mountains high above the Oder valley, and was educated by private tutors, speaking German and Polish and immersing himself in the folk songs of both languages. In 1801 he started boarding at a Catholic school in Breslau, where he fell in love with the operas of Mozart. In 1805, Joseph, aged seventeen, and his devoted brother Wilhelm went to Halle University to study law. During the vacation they took a walking tour through the Harz, making a detour to visit the poet Matthias Claudius. After three terms in Halle they returned home to Silesia for the summer of 1806. In 1807 Joseph moved to Heidelberg University, where he attended lectures by Joseph Görres on the Volksbücher, and was much influenced by Achim von Arnim and Clemens Brentano's *Des Knaben Wunderhorn*, a rich source of mostly anonymous German Romantic folk poems, published between 1805 and 1808, and dedicated to Goethe.

While he was in Heidelberg Eichendorff met the nineteen-year-old Katharina Barbara Förster, with whom he had a short-lived but passionate relationship. She was one of eleven children and worked for her elder brother, a master baker in Heidelberg; the family lived in Rohrbach, a short distance from the university town. Eichendorff's diaries chart the course of their affair. On 19 March 1808 he wrote her name in the snow but on 3 April, after Katharina's father had sold the family home, she left Rohrbach for good: „K. umschlungen u. sehr lieb. An der wohlbekannten Heke am Bache langer herzlicher Abschied." ('K. and I embraced; very loving. A long heartfelt leave-taking by the hedgerow alongside the brook that we knew so well.') Eichendorff and Katharina were never to meet again, but she lived on in his poetry. The sudden and traumatic end of their relationship almost certainly inspired some of Eichendorff's most celebrated poems, including 'Das zerbrochene Ringlein', later set to poignant music by Friedrich Glück. (Wolf's setting, which has not survived, was probably composed at the time of his break with Vally Franck.) The poems written between 1808 and 1810 are characterised by such key words as love, (in)fidelity, pain, parting, loneliness and death, as can be seen in the little cycle entitled *Der verliebte Reisende*, four of which were set by Wolf as 'In der Fremde I', 'In der Fremde II', 'In der Fremde VI' and 'Rückkehr'.

It was also in Heidelberg that in 1808 Eichendorff came under the influence of the poet Otto Heinrich, Graf von Loeben (see note 1, p. 37), who helped him to publish his first poems under the name Florens. Several appeared later in the *Deutscher Dichterwald*, after Loeben had written a letter of recommendation to Justinus Kerner, one of the editors:

> Ich werde meinen sanft gefühlvollen Freund Florens [...] veranlassen, Ihnen gleichfalls einiges zu senden, ist es Ihnen recht? Ich habe einige himmlische milde Lieder von ihm, die ich in den Almanach hineinwünschte.

> I'll persuade my gentle and sensitive friend Florens [...] likewise to send you some poems, if that is acceptable. I have some heavenly tender songs he has written, which I'd love to be included in the almanac.

Having left university, the brothers embarked on a Grand Tour, which took in Paris, Nuremberg and Vienna, before they returned home to help manage the declining family estate. Joseph's relationship with Aloysia (Louise) von Larisch, the daughter of a neighbouring landowner, deepened, and they became engaged in the spring of 1809. In the same year, Eichendorff visited Berlin, where he met Arnim, Brentano and Heinrich von Kleist. In 1810 he moved to Vienna to study for his law exams and came into frequent contact with Friedrich and Dorothea Schlegel, and the painter Philipp Veit, who was soon to become his closest friend. By this time Eichendorff had written many more poems – including 'O Täler weit, o Höhen' – that were soon to feature in every anthology of German poetry. In 1813, fired by Friedrich Wilhelm's appeal to the Prussian people, he enlisted as a volunteer in the War of Liberation and joined the Lützowsches Freikorps on 29 April. His poem 'An die Lützowschen Jäger', a fine song by Othmar Schoeck, describes retrospectively his military experiences – a romanticised account that contrasts starkly with his own prose version:

> Hier von *allen* befreundeten Truppen, selbst von dem größten Teile unseres Korps getrennt und verlassen, ohne Geld, Reiterei und Kanonen, trieb sich unser Bataillon [...] bei Tag und Nacht in Wäldern und Sümpfen umher, mit Hunger und unbeschreiblichem Elend unaufhörlich kämpfend.

> Here, separated from *all* friendly troops and even abandoned by the majority of our corps, without money, cavalry and cannon, our battalion drifted along [...] by day and night through forests and swamps, struggling with constant hunger and indescribable misery.

His battalion, commanded by Ludwig Jahn, consisted for the most part of intellectuals with very little military training – probably the reason they saw no action, although they were allowed to take part in the allied victory celebrations in Paris. Jakob Riedl, first lieutenant in the Tiroler Jägerkompagnie of the Lützowsches Freikorps, gives this convincing vignette of the dreamy poet:

> Heute lernte ich den Lützower Jäger Freiherrn von Eichendorff kennen – ein lieber Kamerad, der aber nach seiner träumerischen, sanften Art für das rauhe Kriegshandwerk nicht geschaffen scheint.
>
> Today I met one of the Lützow soldiers, Baron von Eichendorff – a dear comrade who, with his gentle and dreamy nature, does not seem cut out for the military profession.

Eichendorff left the Freikorps in August 1813, and was finally discharged from the army on 2 December 1814. He returned to Lubowitz and, with his brother, inherited 12,000 Reichstaler. By October he had finished the manuscript of *Ahnung und Gegenwart* and several poems about his war experiences, including 'Der Soldat I' and 'Der Soldat II', written in *c.* 1814 but not published until 1826 and 1837 respectively. It is not known whether Eichendorff knew fellow soldier-poet Theodor Körner, greatly admired by Schubert, who set fourteen of his poems. The full title of Körner's posthumously published poems reads: *Leyer und Schwert von Theodor Körner, Lieutenant im Lützow'scher Freykorps*. Körner himself can be seen in Georg Friedrich Kersting's patriotic painting *At the Sentry Post* (1815) which hangs in Berlin's Nationalgalerie – see p. 295.

The year 1815 saw the publication of Eichendorff's first novel, *Ahnung und Gegenwart*, and his marriage to Aloysia, who was to bear him four children and live with him until her death in 1855. From 1816 he held a number of positions in the Prussian Civil Service before his early retirement in 1844.

He met Clara and Robert Schumann in Vienna in January 1847, the occasion being a matinee at the Schumanns' apartment, where the *Liederkreis*, Op. 39, settings were performed. Clara wrote that Eichendorff had told her that Schumann had given life to his poems, and she – in a fit of mutual congratulation – replied that his poems gave life to her husband's music. Eichendorff, however, never mentioned the songs in his correspondence, and instead praised 'the beautiful settings by [Josef] Dessauer', a Bohemian composer, whose songs and operas once enjoyed great popularity and whom Wagner, in a letter to Schumann, described as a 'hypochondriacal eccentric'. Perhaps Eichendorff resented the numerous alterations that Schumann made to the poetry – some seventeen instances in all, including, in 'Die Stille', the omission of an entire verse, and in 'Intermezzo' the change of a title. None of the alterations is substantial, but it is conceivable that they would have irked a perfectionist such as Eichendorff.

Eichendorff took little part in the 1848 Revolution, although he wrote, according to his son, many poems on the conflict which he later destroyed. During his long career, he tried his hand at a number of literary genres: the novel (*Ahnung und Gegenwart, Dichter und ihre Gesellen*); Novellen (*Aus dem Leben eines Taugenichts, Das Marmorbild, Das Schloß Dürande*); drama (tragedies such as *Ezelin von Romano, Der letzte Held von Marienburg* and comedies including *Krieg den Philistern!* and *Die Freier*); verse epics (*Robert und Guiscard, Julian*), and of course poetry. When his wife's health deteriorated, the couple moved to Neisse to live with their daughter's family. After Aloysia's death, he began to write his memoirs, but fell ill with a cold in early November 1857, which finally led to pneumonia. He died on 26 November at about five in the morning and was buried four days later beside his wife.

Eichendorff's verse is to a quite unusual degree musical, which probably accounts for the frequency with which composers have set his poetry. According to Dietrich Fischer-Dieskau in *Töne sprechen, Worte klingen*, the final sixty-seven years of the nineteenth century produced well over five thousand Eichendorff settings. His poems – unlike Goethe's, Goethe being more an Augenmensch – are peppered with references to horns, bells, lutes, mandolins and other musical instruments. No other German poet wrote so many poems about minstrels, musicians or the sounds of nature, and his novels and Novellen are studded with lyrical poems in the manner of Goethe's *Wilhelm Meister* and Mörike's *Maler Nolten*.

Two themes predominate: beauty of landscape and religious faith. The beauty of God is manifested in nature, and Eichendorff – although, unlike the early Romantic writers, he never theorised about his ideas – attempted in much of his verse to free man's spirit from the tedium of everyday life. Many of his five hundred or so poems are variations on these themes, but his range is wider than is usually believed. He gathered his poems into eight genres: *Wanderlieder, Sängerleben, Zeitlieder, Frühling und Liebe, Totenopfer, Geistliche Gedichte, Romanzen* and *Aus dem Spanischen*. Wolf, with a predilection for the picaresque and vignettes of eccentrics, chose poems from each group, with the exceptions of *Geistliche Gedichte* and *Aus dem Spanischen*.

Eichendorff's dual existence as Romantic poet par excellence and efficient bureaucrat is as incongruous a combination as Franz Kafka the insurance man or Gottfried Keller the clerk to the canton of Zurich. His best-known Novelle, *Aus dem Leben eines Taugenichts* (*From the Life of a Good-for-nothing*), published in 1826, can be interpreted as the wishful dream of a conscientious civil servant, and a gentle satire on philistines' love of bureaucracy and worship of power and success. Many of his finest poems were written in towns, such as Berlin, Breslau, Danzig and Königsberg, where he longed for the countryside he loved so dearly. But Eichendorff was also aware of the darker side of life, and many of his poems, particularly those chosen by Schumann for his *Liederkreis*, Op. 39, express fear at isolation and distrust of other human beings. His bleakest poetry was written shortly after the death of his youngest daughter Anna, who died, aged seventeen months, on 24 March 1832. The Eichendorffs had lost another daughter, Agnes, a decade previously, aged fifteen months. Now, from this most recent catastrophe, he fashioned a cycle of five poems (extended to ten in 1837) that he titled *Auf meines Kindes Tod*. Othmar Schoeck set 'Von fern die Uhren schlagen' as part of his Op. 20, and Aribert Reimann concluded his *Nachtstück II* (1978) with 'Was ist mir denn so wehe?', but on the whole these wonderful poems, which shift in mood from bitterness and sadness to acceptance and, finally, a tentative hope, have been sadly ignored by Lieder composers.

Theodor Storm, in a letter to his father of 24 February 1854, gives this affectionate and convincing description of Eichendorff:

> Er ist ein Mann von mildem, liebenswürdigem Wesen, viel zu innerlich, um, was man gewöhnlich vornehm nennt, an sich zu haben; in seinen *stillen blauen Augen* liegt noch die ganze Romantik seiner wunderbaren poetischen Welt.

> He is a gentle and charming soul, and much too introspective to have anything about him that might be called distinguished; in his *quiet blue eyes* lies the entire romantic nature of his wonderful poetic world.

COMPOSER

Wolf's Eichendorff songs have never enjoyed the popularity of his more substantial collections: the *Mörike-Lieder*, the *Italienisches Liederbuch*, the *Goethe-Lieder* and the *Spanisches Liederbuch*. Critics have made the mistake of asserting that the *Eichendorff-Lieder* lack the emotional and musical weight of his other volumes, that there are only two acknowledged masterpieces ('Verschwiegene Liebe' and 'Das Ständchen'), that the songs represent the lighter side of Wolf's work, and that they were not composed in the state of feverish creativity that characterised his other collections. Even more damning was the opinion of the chief editor of Breitkopf & Härtel, to whom Wolf had sent the songs originally:

> Die Lieder von Wolf gehören zu dem Ungereimtesten, das die äußerste Linke der neudeutschen Schule wohl bisher gezeitigt haben mag, und haben nach meinem Begriffe der Tonkunst nichts weiter mit ihr gemein, als etwa das Elementare des Klanges und des Rhythmus.

> Wolf's lieder are amongst the most absurd things so far produced by the extreme left wing of the New German School [the followers of Wagner], and

have nothing in common with what I understand by 'music' except for the basic elements of sound and rhythm.

Eichendorff had always been one of Wolf's favourite poets. There is a title page in the Vienna City Library, probably dating from 1878, when Wolf was eighteen, that lists three *Romanzen von J. von Eichendorff* ('Der Kehraus', 'Das zerbrochene Ringlein' and 'Der traurige Jäger'), none of which has survived. Other early settings of his verse include a sketch for 'Verschwiegene Liebe', dating from 1880, whose vocal line bears no resemblance to that of the celebrated second version; and, also from 1880, three songs: 'Erwartung', 'Die Nacht' and 'Nachruf', the first two of which were included in the original *Eichendorff-Lieder*, but omitted from the second edition. All three songs were dedicated originally to Vally Franck as part of a group entitled *Lieder und Gesänge von N. Lenau und J. Eichendorff. Fräulein V ... F ... geweiht, von Hugo Wolf*. Composed at the height of his relationship with Vally, they are the most beautiful of his early Lieder. 'Die Nacht', with its hypnotic accompaniment, anticipates Wolf's later mastery in songs such as 'Nachtzauber' (1887), but his obvious debt to Schumann, most noticeably in the 'Zwielicht'-like prelude, perhaps explains why he decided to omit the song from the second edition of the *Gedichte von Joseph v. Eichendorff* – he had, after all, scribbled over the unfinished score of an early Chamisso setting of 1878, 'too much like Schumann'!

Wolf next turned to Eichendorff's poetry in April 1881 when, in the throes of his rejection by Vally Franck (see pp. 480–83), he composed the six beautiful *Geistliche Lieder* for unaccompanied mixed chorus to poems dealing with death, farewell and resignation to God's will, among them 'Resignation' ('Komm, Trost der Welt, du stille Nacht'), which Schumann had set so expressively as 'Der Einsiedler'. He began the work on 31 March 1881, and three days later wrote to his brother Max (see p. 25) describing how Vally had left him. Max was not the only recipient of doom-laden letters: his parents and his sister Katharina (Käthe) were also bombarded. Käthe recommended travel, while his father philosophised about the generally unhappy lot of mortals. Wolf, by changing the titles of the first three poems, and supplying the last three with a title where Eichendorff had given none ('Letzte Bitte', 'Ergebung', 'Erhebung'), created a nocturnal cycle that moves from despair to final affirmation. The first three Eichendorff poems were originally called 'Mittag' ('Aufblick'), 'Nachtgruß' ('Einkehr'), 'Der Einsiedler' ('Resignation'). The final two titles, in particular, ('Ergebung' and 'Erhebung') point sententiously, by the change of a mere letter, to the journey from dark to light. In the summer of the same year, Wolf wrote 'In der Fremde I' ('Da fahr' ich still im Wagen'), the first of three songs with the same title that he, as a struggling Kapellmeister in Salzburg, composed in that barren year, described in *Daten aus meinem Leben*[1]

[1] Hilde Wittgenstein-Köchert's copy of *Dates from my Life* was published by the Österreichische Musikzeitschrift.

as „Bruch. Elend. Jammer" ('Break-up. Misery. Distress'). Once again, the influence of Schumann is evident.

'In der Fremde II' was begun in February 1882 and finished in 1883, a year that saw the composition of ten Lieder, including 'In der Fremde VI' and 'Rückkehr'. The theme of all these songs is the one familiar from Schumann's celebrated Eichendorff *Liederkreis*, Op. 39: the isolation and loneliness of a traveller returning home, unrecognised and unknown. At this early stage in his career, Wolf was still tempted to select the type of Eichendorff poem that Schumann had set with such insight – the result, however, is hardly satisfactory, for though all these three poems have lines almost identical with those in Schumann's two 'In der Fremde' songs, Wolf's music, despite much beautiful detail, fails to crystallise and convince. Small wonder, then, that when, four years later, in 1888, he decided to compose a complete Eichendorff cycle, he for the most part turned his back on the themes of nostalgia and loneliness, and concentrated instead on the picaresque gallery of soldiers, students, sailors and minstrels that had, until then, been ignored by all composers setting Eichendorff's poetry.

After the end of January 1883, there followed a fallow period of almost four and a half years, which began with the death of his idol Wagner in February 1883, and the rejection by Breitkopf & Härtel of a proposed volume of Lieder. Compelled to eke out a living as a music critic, which left little time for composition, he was deeply depressed. Between 1884 and 1886, only four songs were written, including 'Der Soldat II' (14 December 1886), a theatrical tour de force that counsels a carpe diem attitude to life and depicts the onset of death in a succession of repeated phrases, whispered sepulchrally, as the song – Wolf's shortest in duration? – pants to an ominous close. Nibelung's anvils can be heard in the prelude, and the whole atmosphere is reminiscent of Wagner. Yet it is also wholly Wolfian in feel, and a wonderful example of what great Lieder can accomplish – here, the reducing of an operatic idea to its essence: a hint of the astonishing things to come.

The five songs he composed to Eichendorff texts between March and May 1887 are of the same high artistic order. In 'Der Soldat I', composed on 7 March, Wolf is clearly captivated by the prancing of the little horse that takes him to his beloved's castle and, when she becomes too possessive and demanding, away into the open countryside and freedom. It's remarkable how the little motif undergoes subtle changes: *staccato* and self-confident at the outset, lilting and tender at 'die mir besser gefällt', and then robust and arrogant in the final verse, as he abandons his fawning sweetheart. There is a striking resemblance between this music and Wolf's *Italian Serenade* for string quartet, composed two months later, which also owes its conception partly to Eichendorff, whose Novelle *Aus dem Leben eines Taugenichts* not only contains an Italian serenade, but also a poem ('Wer in die Fremde will wandern') that Wolf was to set in 1888 as 'Heimweh'. Wolf's source was Eichendorff's *Gedichte* published in 1878, but he would have known *Aus dem Leben eines Taugenichts* and appreciated the similarities between the hero and himself: a young musician who leaves his home and a fault-finding father to seek his fortune.

Having completed 'Der Soldat I', Wolf set three more Eichendorff poems, 'Die Kleine' (8 March), 'Die Zigeunerin' (19 March–16 April) and 'Waldmädchen' (20 April), all of which depict women as independent beings, in charge of their own destiny. 'Die Zigeunerin', with its deliciously flirtatious melismatic triplets, was included in the first edition of the *Eichendorff-Lieder*, which Wolf chose to end with 'Waldmädchen', whose virtuosic postlude, marked *sehr schnell* and, in the final bars, *diminuendo* (*pp* to *pppp* within four bars), he presumably regarded as a brilliant climax to his volume. 'Die Zigeunerin' was retained in the second edition of 1898, while 'Waldmädchen' was omitted by the composer, who by that time had written, in the Mörike volume, fairy music of incomparable delicacy. 'Die Kleine' was not published during Wolf's lifetime, perhaps because he felt that the slightly lubricious text might offend. The other Eichendorff setting of 1887 is 'Nachtzauber'; marked *sanft fliessend* and steeped in the sort of romantic enchantment that had so appealed to Schumann. The whole song flows along hypnotically, with a swaying accompaniment that seems almost to anticipate Debussy.

'Nachtzauber', written on 24 May, was virtually the last work composed by Wolf that year. His father had died a fortnight earlier, and he now fell prey to a creative paralysis that was broken only the following year by the eruption of the first Mörike songs. Having embarked on the *Mörike-Lieder*, he decided instead to complete the Eichendorff volume that he had begun in 1880 with the composition of 'Erwartung' and 'Die Nacht'. The rate of composition was, once again, remarkable: in quick succession, he wrote thirteen new songs between 31 August and 29 September 1888, and no fewer than nine in the week of 22–29 September. In a letter to Engelbert Humperdinck, dated 12 March 1891 (see p. 27), he made it clear that, following the current trend of realism he wished to 'abandon almost entirely the romantic element in Eichendorff's poetry, and turn instead to the comparatively unknown, the saucily humorous and robustly sensual side of the poet'. And a glance at Challier's *Großer Lieder-Katalog* of 1885 tells us that he was the first Lieder composer to have attended to this aspect of Eichendorff's poetry.

At the head of the published volume he placed 'Der Freund', a tribute to his friends who had helped defray the cost of publication (Friedrich Eckstein) and had encouraged him through his depression (Edmund Lang and the Schalk brothers, Joseph and Franz, to whom the volume was dedicated). To make even clearer his indebtedness to such friends, he followed the opening song with 'Der Musikant', a sort of humorous self-portrait, with lute arpeggios in the accompaniment, and a delicious modulation to a remote key at 'Weiß nicht, wo ich abends ruh", which conveys the minstrel's fear of spending the night without a roof over his head.

Wolf turned to Eichendorff again in March 1894 during his search for an opera libretto – see HW to Emil Kauffmann, 7 March 1894, p. 28.

LETTERS

HW to Max Wolf, Vienna, 3 April 1881

Der April ist für mich recht verhängnissvoll geworden –, ob's zum Guten od. Schlimmen ausschlägt weiß ich noch nicht; ich bin blind; blind, weil ich nur alles schwarz sehe u. den Ausweg aus diesem Schmerzenslabyrinth nie zu finden fürchte. Indessen fühle ich mich jetzt so weit erleichtert, daß ich Dir wenigstens für Deinen Brief danken kann. Die Ursache meines Kummers brauche ich Dir wohl kaum zu sagen – ich weiß es – Du verstehst mich schon u. nur so viel sage ich Dir, daß „Wally" schon seit 6. Oktb. 80 in Paris bei ihren Angehörigen ist, die in sie dringen daß sie sich verheirathe u. sie – ist schwach genug diesem Drängen nachzugeben.

April has proved to be a most fateful month for me – I don't yet know whether it will turn out well or bad; I am blind; blind, because I see everything wreathed in black, & I fear I shall never find a way out of this labyrinth of pain. Now that things have eased a little, I can at least thank you for your letter. I guess I don't need to tell you the cause of my grief – I know that you understand me, & all that I shall say is this: from 6 October 1880 'Wally' has been with her family in Paris; they are urging her to marry & she is weak enough to give in to their pressure.

HW to Marie Lang, Unterach, 4 October 1888

Auch 12 Eichendorffische Lieder sind mir schon gelungen. Sie sehen, die Mühle klappert.

12 Eichendorff Lieder have been completed. You see: the mill wheels are turning.

HW to Joseph Schalk, Döbling, 8 February 1889

Ich will mit der Öffentlichkeit nichts mehr zu thun haben; die Öffentlichkeit ist eine infame Canaille.[1] Ich will nur Privatmann sein. O wär' ich ein Schuster

---

1 Wolf's letter was triggered by the reaction from a section of the audience during a concert of Beethoven and Wolf Lieder in the Wagner-Verein on 7 February 1889 – see note 5 to 'Heimweh', p. 45.

gleich dem unvergleichlichen Sachs. Wie froh, wie glücklich könnte sich mein Leben gestalten! An Werktagen geschustert u. Sonntag im Feiertagsgewand componirt u. das nur aus „liebem Zeitvertreib" ganz intim nur für mich u. ein paar Freunde z. B. Dich, Löwe u. Hirsch.[1] Ja, das wäre eine Existenz! Du sagst, lieber Freund, daß es nur darauf ankommt Philosoph zu sein. Ich bin nicht genug Philosoph, um mich über den Neid u. die Machinationen meiner Feinde hinwegzusetzen, aber gerade genug Philosoph um nur für mich allein zu leben u. die Öffentlichkeit gänzlich zu ignoriren. Wollte ich nicht Dir u. Franziskus[2] vor der Öffentlichkeit – da ihr doch in derselben für mich eingestanden – meine Dankbarkeit bezeugen, keine Macht brächte mich dazu die Eichendorff'schen zu publiziren.

I shall have nothing more to do with the public; the public are scoundrels. I shall live exclusively for myself. If only I were a cobbler like the incomparable Sachs. How happy my life would then be! Weekdays: cobbling; Sundays: composing in my best clothes – as a 'cherished hobby', and only for myself & a few close friends, such as you, Löwe & Hirsch. What a life that would be! You tell me, dear friend, that it's just a question of being philosophical. I am not sufficiently philosophical to disregard the envy & machinations of my enemies, but am just about philosophical enough to live alone for myself & to wholly ignore the public. Were it not for the fact that I want to thank you and Franziskus publicly for your support, nothing on earth could persuade me to publish the Eichendorff Lieder.

HW to Joseph Schalk, Windischgraz, 7 September 1889

Endlich bin ich in der angenehmen Lage Dir die Eichendorff'schen, an deren Erscheinen ich nachgerade verzweifelt, zuzusenden. Auch wirst Du mir die Wiederholungen: wie stolz u. glücklich mich die Idee machte, diese Arbeit Dir u. Deinem Bruder zu widmen, freundlichst erlassen. Bleibe immer mein treuer Schiffmann,[3] wie ich mich willig Deiner Führung überlasse. –

I'm finally in the pleasant position of being able to send you the Eichendorff songs – I was in utter despair they would ever be published. And please allow me to repeat: how proud & happy the idea made me to dedicate this work to you & your brother. Always be my helmsman – I shall always be gladly guided by you.

---

1   Ferdinand Löwe (1863–1925), conductor and pianist in Vienna. It was he who conducted the *Adagio* from Bruckner's Seventh Symphony at Wolf's funeral. Richard Hirsch (dates unknown), official in a government finance department. Wolf often addressed him affectionately as 'Hirschlein'.
2   Franz Schalk, brother of Joseph.   3   See 'Der Freund', p. 37.

JOSEPH VON EICHENDORFF

HW to Engelbert Humperdinck, Ober-Döbling, 12 March 1891

Soeben schreibt mir Dr. Strecker,[1] daß Du [...] die Absicht habest zu Ostern eine Besprechung meiner sämmtlichen Lieder in der Frankfurter Zeitung einzurücken. [...] Ich bitte Dich so ausführlich, als es der Raum nur immer gestatten mag, Dein Thema zu behandeln. Gieb vor allem eine historische Darstellung der Entwicklung des Liedes, die ja, in ihrer Art, eine merkwürdige Verwandtschaft mit der Entwicklung der Oper aufweist. [...] Vergiß nicht hervorzuheben, daß jeder Band seine besondere Physiognomie trägt, wie dieß ja schon durch die Natur der poetischen Unterlage bedingt ist. Bei Eichendorff z. B. magst Du ein Gewicht darauf legen, wie, übereinstimmend mit unserer mehr realistischen Kunstanschauung, das romantische Element in meinen Eichendorffliedern fast ganz zurücktritt hingegen der Componist mit Vorliebe der keck humoristischen, derb sinnlichen Seite des Dichters, als welche so ziemlich unbekannt, sich zuwendet u. ihr einige gelungene Züge abdlauscht. Beispiel: der Schreckenberger, Glücksritter, Unfall, Scholar, Soldat I, Seemanns Abschied etc.

Dr Strecker has just written to me with the news that you [...] intend at Easter to review all my songs for the Frankfurt newspaper. [...] I beg you to do so in as much detail as space permits. Above all, trace the historical development of the Lied, which, in its own way, bears a remarkable resemblance to the development of opera. [...] Don't forget to stress that each volume has its own particular character, necessitated of course by the different characteristics of each poet. With Eichendorff, for example, you can emphasise how, following our current trend to greater realism in art, I have abandoned almost entirely the romantic element in Eichendorff's poetry, & turned instead to the comparatively unknown, the saucily humorous and robustly sensual side of the poet – with some success: 'Der Schreckenberger', 'Der Glücksritter', 'Unfall', 'Der Scholar', 'Der Soldat I', 'Seemanns Abschied', etc.

HW to Emil Kauffmann, Döbling, 2 April 1892

Sehr erstaunt auch bin ich über die Vorliebe Ihrer verehrten Frau für meine Zigeunerin. Dieses wild exotische Stück, eine seltsame Mischung von Übermuth u. Melancholie, u. die milde, ausgeglichene Art Ihrer Frau – wie passt das zueinander? Oder wäre es gerade der Contrast? Wie dem auch sei, zum mindesten ist es tolerant von Ihrer Frau, daß sie ihre Gunst Zigeunerinnen zuwendet, für die auch ich in poesie (u. Prosa) immer noch erglühen könnte.

---

1   Ludwig Strecker (1853–1943), head of Schott's publishing house. See p. 509.

I'm also most astonished at your esteemed wife's liking for my 'Zigeunerin'. This wildly exotic piece, a strange mixture of bravado & melancholy, & the gentle harmonious nature of your wife make for strange bedfellows! Or maybe opposites attract? Whatever – it's at least tolerant of your wife to favour gypsies, who are always capable of inspiring me too in poetry (and prose).

HW to Emil Kauffmann, Vienna, 7 March 1894

Auf Ihre Anregung hin habe ich die Eichendorff'sche Erzählung das Schloß Dürande neuerdings durchgelesen, um sie neuerdings wiederum ad acta zu legen. Das charakteristische clair-obscur der Eichendorff'schen Stimmung verträgt sich nun einmal nicht mit dem grellen Lampenlicht der Bühne. Ich möchte seine Erzählungen gedichtete Landschaftsbilder nennen, darin die hineingemalten Figuren nur eine ganz sekundäre Rolle spielen, das ungefähr, was die Maler als Staffage bezeichnen. Umgekehrt aber ist auf der Bühne die Scene Staffage u. die Personen haben in den Vordergrund zu treten u. z. in größt möglichster Deutlichkeit. Nun aber sehen Sie sich so eine Eichendorff'sche Figur mal an. Außer dem Kostüme u. ein bischen Farbe ist nichts charakteristisches an ihnen zu bemerken. Von Zeichnung u. psychologischer Ausgestaltung auch keine Spur. Nur vage schattenhafte Umrisse, ohne Phisiognomie, ohne Persönlichkeit, wie Traumgespenster tauchen sie plötzlich auf – man weiß nicht von woher, verduften wiederum, man weiß nicht, wohin. Sie ziehen wie Wolken am Himmel od. um ein Eichendorff'sches Bild zu gebrauchen, wie stille Träume vorüber, bald diese bald jene Form u. Gestalt annehmend. Das Alles mag ja sehr schön u. hoch poetisch sein u. die Phantasie angenehm beschäftigen, aber auf die Bühne taugt es nicht.

Following your suggestion, I have recently re-read Eichendorff's Novelle *Dürande Castle*, only to put it aside once more. Eichendorff's characteristic chiaroscuro atmosphere is simply not compatible with the bright lights of the stage. I would call his stories literary landscapes, in which all the delineated characters play a merely secondary role, resembling what painters call staffage. The reverse is true of the theatre: the decor is staffage & the characters must be placed in the foreground with the greatest possible clarity. Consider now a typical Eichendorff character. There's hardly anything but his costume & a bit of make-up. Not a trace of portrayal or psychological perspective. Only vague shadowy silhouettes, without faces or personality; they suddenly appear like dreamy ghosts – no one knows from where – then vanish, no one knows where to. They drift along like clouds in the sky or, to use an Eichendorff image, like silent dreams, assuming now this form, now that. That's all very well & highly poetic & agreeable for the imagination – but of no use at all in the theatre.

HW to Emil Kauffmann, Vienna, 16 July 1894

Auch gedenke ich ein Heft geistlicher Lieder von Eichendorff für gemischten Chor ohne Klavierbegleitung demnächst zu veröffentlichen. Dieselben sind allerdings schon im Jahre 1881 entstanden, tragen aber durchweg schon ein ganz modernes Gepräge, also, daß ich mich meiner Vaterschaft nicht zu schämen brauche.

I intend to publish in the near future a volume of spiritual songs – settings of Eichendorff – for a cappella mixed chorus. Although these were composed in 1881, they have such a modern feel about them that I have no need to be ashamed of having fathered them.

LIEDER

Wolf's source for his *Gedichte von Joseph v. Eichendorff* was probably the eleventh edition of *Gedichte von Joseph Freiherrn von Eichendorff* (Leipzig: C. F. Amelang's Verlag, 1878). This was based on the posthumously published *Joseph von Eichendorff's sämmtliche Werke* (1869), edited by Eichendorff's son Hermann. Wolf would not have been aware that Hermann retitled and sometimes even emended his father's poems, in much the same way that Johann Heinrich Voss tampered with Ludwig Hölty's verse in his edition of 1804. Wolf unwittingly used six inauthentic titles in his collection. In the following list the authentic title is given first: 'Der wandernde Musikant' ('Der Musikant'), 'Der wandernde Student' ('Der Scholar'), 'Der Glückliche' ('Liebesglück'), 'Steckbrief' ('Erwartung'), 'Die Nachtblume' ('Die Nacht'), 'Der verliebte Reisende' ('In der Fremde').

Nachruf[1]

Du liebe, treue Laute,
Wie manche Sommernacht,
Bis daß der Morgen graute,
Hab' ich mit dir durchwacht!

Die Täler wieder nachten,
Schon sinkt das Abendrot,[2]
Doch die sonst mit uns wachten,
Die liegen lange tot.

In memoriam

Dear faithful lute,
How many a summer night
Till daybreak
Have I kept watch with you!

Again the valleys darken,
The twilight now is fading,
But they who once kept watch with us
Perished long ago.

[1] This song and two others composed at the same time ('Erwartung' and 'Die Nacht') were clearly inspired by Wolf's attachment to Vally Franck, since they appear on a sheet of paper, once used as a cover for a sheaf of manuscripts that bore the following inscription: „Lieder und Gesänge von N. Lenau and J. v. Eichendorff. Fräulein V . . . F . . . geweiht, von Hugo Wolf". (Her full name on the dedication has been erased and replaced by dots.)
[2] Eichendorff: Kaum spielt noch Abendrot.

Was wollen wir nun singen	Why should we want to sing
Hier in der Einsamkeit,	Here in solitude,
Wenn alle von uns gingen,	When all have departed
Die unser Lied erfreut?	Who delighted in our song?
Wir wollen dennoch singen!	Nonetheless, we shall sing!
So still ist's auf der Welt;	The world is so still;
Wer weiß, die Lieder dringen	Who knows, songs may reach
Vielleicht zum Sternenzelt.	As far as the stars.
Wer weiß, die da gestorben,	Who knows, those who died
Sie hören droben mich,	May hear me up there,
Und öffnen leis die Pforten	And quietly open the gates,
Und nehmen uns zu sich.	And take us to them.

Poem first published 1838
Also set by Othmar Schoeck

Sechs geistliche Lieder nach Gedichten von Joseph von Eichendorff
für vierstimmigen gemischten Chor a cappella

Six Spiritual Songs after Poems by Joseph von Eichendorff
for mixed choir, unaccompanied

Composed soon after Vally Franck had ended her relationship with Wolf, and reflecting the trauma he felt at being abandoned, these six sacred songs never appeared in Wolf's lifetime, despite his attempts to interest a publisher. Towards the end of 1891 he sent the manuscripts of all six songs and 'Elfenlied' (Shakespeare) to Ludwig Strecker, the head of Schott's, who replied on 5 February 1892:

> Was die Quartette betrifft, so finde ich diese technisch so unverhältnissmässig schwer, dass ich nicht dazu rathen kann, sie herauszugeben.

> As for the quartets, I find them technically so disproportionately difficult that I cannot be persuaded to publish them.

They were eventually published by Lauterbach & Kuhn of Leipzig in 1903, both in Wolf's original version for a cappella mixed choir, edited by Eugen Thomas, and in the arrangement for male voice choir by Max Reger. Wolf toyed with the idea of giving the songs an organ accompaniment but decided against it, writing to Kauffmann on 19 March 1895: „A cappella klingen die Sachen doch weit vornehmer." ('The pieces will sound much nobler performed a cappella.') By the time the songs were first performed Wolf was confined to a mental home.

1 Aufblick[1]

Vergeht mir der Himmel
Vor Staube schier,
Herr, im Getümmel
Zeig' Dein Panier!

Wie schwank' ich sündlich,
Läßt Du von mir!
Unüberwindlich
Bin ich mit Dir!

Poem first published 1837

Gazing up

If I can no longer see Heaven
For so much dust,
Lord, show me Thy banner
Amidst the tumult!

How sinfully I falter,
If Thou dost abandon me!
I am invincible
When by Thy side!

2 Einkehr[2]

Weil jetzo alles stille ist
Und alle Menschen schlafen,
Mein' Seel' das ew'ge Licht begrüßt,
Ruht wie ein Schiff im Hafen.

Der falsche Fleiß, die Eitelkeit,
Was Keinen mag erlaben,
Darin der Tag das Herz zerstreut,
Liegt alles tief begraben.

Ein andrer König wundergleich[3]
Mit königlichen Sinnen,
Zieht herrlich ein im stillen Reich,
Besteigt die ew'gen Zinnen.

Poem first published 1837
Also set by Wilhelm Petersen and Schoeck

Harmony

Because everything now is silent
And everyone is sleeping,
My soul greets the eternal light,
At rest like a ship in harbour.

False diligence and vanity,
Which daily entertain the heart
And can delight no one,
Now lie in a deep grave.

Another king, miracle-like,
With regal thoughts,
Enters in splendour the silent realm,
Ascends the eternal battlements.

3 Resignation[4]

Komm, Trost der Welt, du stille Nacht![5]
Wie steigst du von den Bergen sacht,
Die Lüfte alle schlafen,
Ein Schiffer nur noch, wandermüd,
Singt über's Meer sein Abendlied
Zu Gottes Lob im Hafen.

Resignation

Come, comfort of the world, quiet night!
How softly from the hills you climb,
The breezes all are sleeping,
One sailor still, travel-wearied,
Sings across the sea his evening song
In praise of God in the harbour.

---

1 Eichendorff: 'Mittag'. 2 Eichendorff: 'Nachtgruß'. 3 Eichendorff: wunderreich.
4 Eichendorff called the poem 'Der Einsiedler'. It appears in his Novelle *Eine Meerfahrt*, where it is sung by Alma the Hermit.
5 An echo of the Grimmelshausen poem in the celebrated barock novel *Der abentheuerliche Simplicissimus* (1669), Book I, Chapter 7, which begins „Komm, Trost der Nacht, o Nachtigall"; and the first volume of *Des Knaben Wunderhorn* contains a poem, entitled 'Schall der Nacht', identical with the Grimmelshausen.

Die Jahre wie die Wolken gehn	The years, like the clouds, go by
Und lassen mich hier einsam stehn,	And leave me here in solitude,
Die Welt hat mich vergessen,	Forgotten by the world,
Da tratst du wunderbar zu mir,	Then wondrously you came to me,
Wenn ich beim Waldesrauschen hier	As I sat here lost in thought
Gedankenvoll gesessen.	By the murmuring forest.
O Trost der Welt, du stille Nacht!	O comfort of the world, quiet night!
Der Tag hat mich so müd gemacht,	The day has wearied me so,
Das weite Meer schon dunkelt,	The wide sea darkens now,
Laß ausruhn mich von Lust und Not,	Let me rest from joy and pain,
Bis daß das ew'ge Morgenrot	Until eternal dawn
Den stillen Wald durchfunkelt.	Flashes through the silent wood.

Poem first published 1837
Also set by Schoeck, Robert Schumann and Hermann Zilcher

4 Letzte Bitte[1]   A final plea

Wie ein todeswunder Streiter,	Like a mortally wounded warrior
Der den Weg verloren hat,	Who has lost his way,
Schwank' ich nun und kann nicht weiter,	I now falter, can walk no further,
Von dem Leben sterbensmatt.	Wearied of life unto death.
Nacht schon decket alle Müden	Night now covers all who are weary,
Und so still ist's um mich her,	Such silence now surrounds me,
Herr, auch mir gib endlich Frieden,	Lord, finally grant peace to me as well,
Denn ich wünsch' und hoff' nichts mehr.	For I wish and hope for nothing more.

Poem first published 1837

5 Ergebung[2]   Surrender

Dein Wille, Herr, geschehe!	May Thy will, O Lord, be done!
Verdunkelt schweigt das Land,	The darkened land is silent,
Im Zug der Wetter sehe	In the threatening storm
Ich schauernd deine Hand.	I tremble to see Thy hand.
O mit uns Sündern gehe	O be merciful
Erbarmend ins Gericht!	To us sinners!
Ich beug' im tiefsten Wehe	In deepest torment I bow
Zum Staub mein Angesicht!	My head to the dust!

Poem first published 1837
Also set by Max Reger

1   Eichendorff gave no title to the poem.
2   This chorus was sung at Wolf's funeral from behind the altar by the Wiener a cappella Chorverein, followed by an arrangement for brass band of the 'Trauermusik' from Bruckner's Seventh Symphony, inspired by the death of Wagner. While in the Niederösterreichische Landesirrenanstalt,

JOSEPH VON EICHENDORFF

6 Erhebung[1]

So laß herein nun brechen
Die Brandung, wie sie will,
Du darfst ein Wort nur sprechen,
So wird der Abgrund still;
Und bricht die letzte Brücke,
Zu Dir, der treulich steht,
Hebt über Not und Glücke
Mich einsam das Gebet.

Poem first published 1837

In der Fremde I[2]

Da fahr' ich still im Wagen,
Du bist so weit von mir,
Wohin er mich mag tragen,
Ich bleibe doch bei dir.

Da fliegen Wälder, Klüfte
Und schöne Täler tief,
Und Lerchen hoch in Lüften,
Als ob dein' Stimme rief'.

Die Sonne lustig scheinet
Weit über das Revier,
Ich bin so froh verweinet
Und singe still in mir.

Vom Berge geht's hinunter,
Das Posthorn schallt im Grund,
Mein' Seel' wird mir so munter,
Grüß' dich aus Herzensgrund!

Poem written before November 1810
Also set by Schoeck and Richard Trunk

The soul uplifted

Let the breakers pound
The shore as they will,
Thou hast only to speak a word,
And the abyss falls silent;
And should the last bridge collapse,
The lonely prayers of Thy loyal servant
Shall raise me
Above peril and fate.

In a foreign land I

Silent I ride in the coach,
You are so far from me,
Wherever it may bear me,
I shall remain with you.

Woods, gorges fly past,
And valleys lovely and deep,
And larks high in the air,
As if your voice were calling.

The sun shines brightly
Far across the countryside,
I weep such tears of joy,
And my heart sings within me.

Down from the mountain I come,
The posthorn rings out below,
My soul becomes so joyful,
I greet you from my heart!

Wolf sketched the opening bars of a setting for SATB and solo voice – possibly the last piece of music he composed. See Dietrich Fischer-Dieskau, *Hugo Wolf*, p. 390, for a facsimile of the fragment. Eichendorff gave no title to the poem.

1 Eichendorff gave no title to the poem.
2 Wolf's song was composed immediately after his relationship with Vally Franck had come to an end. The day before he had written Henriette Lang a tormented letter of lovelorn grief. Although she had abandoned him, he exclaimed, „Ja ich liebe die Wally [. . .] Ich werde sie immer und ewig lieben." ('Yes, I love Wally [. . .] I shall love her for evermore.') And documents from the estate of Walter Legge relate how Wolf, when his relationship with Frieda Zerny had foundered, sang 'In der Fremde' passionately and with exaggerated rubato, until he reached the line „Du bist so weit von mir" ('You are so far from me'), when he suddenly burst into tears and uttered a despairing laugh. The song was the first of a projected cycle of Eichendorff settings that came to nothing. Eichendorff's poem, which

Rückkehr[1]

Mit meinem Saitenspiele,
Das schön geklungen hat,
Komm' ich durch Länder viele
Zurück in diese Stadt.

Ich ziehe durch die Gassen,
So finster ist die Nacht
Und alles so verlassen,
Hatt's anders mir gedacht.

Am Brunnen steh ich lange,
Der rauscht fort, wie vorher,
Kommt mancher wohl gegangen,
Es kennt mich keiner mehr.

Da hört' ich geigen, pfeifen,
Die Fenster glänzten weit,
Dazwischen drehn und schleifen
Viel' fremde, fröhliche Leut'.

Und Herz und Sinn[2] mir brannten,
Mich trieb's in die weite Welt,
Es spielten die Musikanten,
Da fiel ich hin im Feld.

Poem written c. 1810

Homecoming

As I pluck the strings
That have made such lovely music,
I pass through many lands,
Returning to this town.

I make my way through its streets,
The night is so dark
And all is so deserted,
Unlike what I expected.

Long I stand by the fountain
That purls away as in the past,
Many people drift by me,
None know me any more.

Then I heard fiddling, piping,
Windows gleamed from afar,
While many happy strangers
Glide and whirl.

My heart and mind burned within me,
Out into the wide world I went,
The fiddlers played their music,
In the field I fell to the ground.

In der Fremde VI[3]

Wolken, wälderwärts gegangen,
Wolken, fliegend übers Haus,
Könnte ich an euch mich hangen,[4]
Mit euch fliegen weit hinaus!*

Taglang durch die Wälder schweif' ich,
Voll Gedanken sitz' ich still,
In die Saiten flüchtig greif' ich,
Wieder dann auf einmal still.

In a foreign land VI

Clouds that drift towards the woods,
Clouds that scud above the house,
Could I but cling to you
And with you fly far away.*

I roam the forest through the day,
Sit quietly, deep in thought,
My fingers pluck the strings,
Then all is silent once more.

---

* has no title, is the first of seven that appear in a group called, aptly for Wolf, *Der verliebte Reisende* (*The lovelorn traveller*).

1 The poem is the last of Eichendorff's *Der verliebte Reisende* collection. Serenades always seemed to bring out the best in Wolf, and 'Rückkehr' anticipates 'Das Ständchen', composed five years later – in both songs the singer listens to a serenade played by another. Wolf's other serenades include 'Mein Liebster singt am Haus im Mondenscheine', 'Heut' Nacht erhob ich mich', 'Nicht länger kann ich singen', 'Schweig' einmal still', 'Ein Ständchen Euch zu bringen', 'Ständchen' (Körner) and 'Ständchen' (Reinick).
2 Eichendorff: Sinne.   3 The sixth poem in the *Der verliebte Reisende* sequence.
4 Eichendorff: Könnt' ich an euch fest mich hangen.

JOSEPH VON EICHENDORFF

Schöne, rührende Geschichten
Fallen ein mir, wo ich steh,
Lustig muß ich schreiben, dichten,
Ist mir selber gleich so weh.*

Manches Lied, das ich geschrieben
Wohl vor manchem langen Jahr,
Da die Welt von treuem[1] Lieben
Schön mir überglänzet war,

Find ich's wieder jetzt voll Bangen:
Werd' ich wunderbar gerührt,
Denn so lange ist vergangen,[2]
Was mich zu dem Lied verführt.

Diese Wolken ziehen weiter,
Alle Vögel sind erweckt,
Und die Gegend glänzet heiter,
Weit und fröhlich aufgedeckt.

Regen flüchtig abwärts gehen,
Scheint die Sonne zwischendrein,
Und dein Haus, dein Garten stehen
Überm Wald im stillen Schein.

Doch du harrst nicht mehr mit Schmerzen,
Wo so lang' dein Liebster sei –
Und mich tötet noch im Herzen
Dieser Schmerzen Zauberei.

Poem written c. 1810
* Wolf repeats this line.

Beautiful and moving tales
I think of standing there,
I must write happy verses,
Though I myself am full of woe.*

Many a song that I once wrote,
Many a long year ago,
When the world shone fair for me
Radiantly from true love,

I find now fills me with disquiet:
I am wondrously affected,
For those times have long since gone,
Which once inspired the song.

The clouds drift past,
All the birds have woken,
And the countryside shines brightly,
Revealed in all its joyous breadth.

Rainshowers swiftly pass,
The sun shines in their stead,
And your house and your garden
Quietly glow above the wood.

But no more do you wait in grief,
Wondering where your love tarries so long –
And the spell of this grief
Still breaks my heart.

In der Fremde II[3]

Ich geh' durch die dunklen[4] Gassen
Und wandre von Haus zu Haus,
Ich kann mich noch immer nicht fassen,
Sieht alles so trübe aus.

Da gehen viel Männer und Frauen,
Die alle so lustig sehn,
Die fahren und lachen und bauen,
Daß mir die Sinne vergehn.

In a foreign land II

I walk through the dark streets
And wander from house to house,
I still cannot compose myself,
Everything looks so mournful.

Many men and women pass by,
Who look so happy, every one,
Who travel, laugh and farm the land,
That I quite lose my senses.

---

1 Eichendorff: vom treuen.   2 Eichendorff: Denn so lang ist das vergangen.
3 The song is the second poem of Eichendorff's *Der verliebte Reisende*. There is another version from 3 February 1882 – a single verse fragment.
4 Eichendorff: dunkeln.

Oft wenn ich bläuliche Streifen
Seh' über die Dächer fliehn,
Sonnenschein draußen schweifen,
Wolken am Himmel ziehn:

Da treten mitten im Scherze
Die Tränen ins Auge mir,
Denn die mich lieben von Herzen
Sind alle so weit von hier.

Poem written *c.* 1810

Often when I see bluish streaks
Drifting over roof-tops,
And sunshine everywhere outside,
And scudding clouds in the sky –

Then, amid all the gaiety,
Tears well into my eyes,
Since they who loved me dearly
Are all so far away.

Die Kleine[1]

Zwischen Bergen, liebe Mutter,
Weit den Wald entlang,
Reiten da drei junge Jäger
Auf drei Rößlein blank,
    lieb' Mutter,
Auf drei Rößlein blank.

Ihr könnt fröhlich sein, lieb' Mutter,
Wird es draußen still:
Kommt der Vater heim vom Walde,
Küßt Euch, wie er will,
    lieb' Mutter,
Küßt Euch, wie er will.

Und *ich* werfe mich im Bettchen
Nachts ohn' Unterlaß,
Kehr' mich links und kehr' mich rechts hin,
Nirgends hab' ich was,
    lieb' Mutter,
Nirgends hab' ich was.

Bin ich eine Frau erst einmal,
In der Nacht dann still,
Wend' ich mich nach allen Seiten,
Küß', so viel ich will,
    lieb' Mutter,
Küß', so viel ich will.

Poem written *c.* 1815

The young girl

Along the alpine valley, mother,
By the woodland ways,
Three young hunters come riding by
On three young gleaming steeds,
    dear mother,
On three young gleaming steeds.

You, dear mother, can be happy,
When outside all falls quiet:
When father returns from the forest,
He'll kiss you to his heart's content,
    dear mother,
Kiss you to his heart's content.

And *I* toss and turn in bed
All night long without respite,
Roll to the left and roll to the right,
I've nothing to call my own,
    dear mother,
Nothing to call my own.

When once I become a woman,
In the night I'll quietly turn
Whichever way I wish,
Kiss to my heart's content,
    dear mother,
Kiss to my heart's content.

---

1 Eichendorff's poem appeared first in *Ahnung und Gegenwart* (1815) where it is sung, according to Friedrich, by a beautiful Italian girl as she plaits her hair; when the grown-ups forbid her to sing it, she derives even greater pleasure from performing it 'heimlich' (secretly). It was reprinted as 'Die Fröhliche' in *Aus dem Leben eines Taugenichts und das Marmorbild. Zwei Novellen nebst einem Anhange von Liedern und Romanzen* (1826); and then as 'Die Kleine' in *Gedichte von Joseph Freiherrn*

Gedichte von Joseph v. Eichendorff für eine Singstimme und Klavier
Poems by Joseph v. Eichendorff for voice and piano

The first edition was published by C. Lacom in September 1889. When Wolf was preparing the revised second edition in 1898 for Verlag K. Ferd. Heckel, he decided to omit three of the songs that had appeared in the first edition: 'Erwartung', 'Die Nacht' and 'Waldmädchen'. These were now published by Heckel in the Anhang (Supplement) of the second edition.

1 Der Freund[1]

Wer auf den Wogen schliefe,
Ein sanft gewiegtes Kind,
Kennt nicht des Lebens Tiefe,
Vor süßem Träumen blind.

Doch wen die Stürme fassen
Zu wildem Tanz und Fest,
Wen hoch auf dunklen Straßen
Die falsche Welt verläßt:

Der lernt sich wacker rühren,
Durch Nacht und Klippen hin
Lernt der das Steuer führen
Mit sichrem, ernstem Sinn.[2]

Der ist vom echten Kerne,[3]
Erprobt zu Lust und Pein,
Der glaubt an Gott und Sterne,
Der soll mein Schiffmann sein![4]

Poem written *c.* 1809

The friend

Whoever would sleep on the waves,
A gently cradled child,
Knows not the depths of life,
Blinded by sweet dreams.

But he whom the storms seize
For wild dances and feasts,
Whom, high on dark straits,
The false world abandons –

He learns to bear himself bravely,
Through night and past reefs
He learns to steer a course
With a staunch and earnest heart.

He is a man of true worth,
Proven in joy and pain,
He believes in God and the stars,
My helmsman shall he be!

---

von Eichendorff (1837). Wolf's song was excluded from his *Gedichte von Joseph v. Eichendorff*, due, perhaps, to the faintly lubricious nature of the poem.
1   A tribute to Franz and Joseph Schalk, to whom the *Eichendorff-Lieder* are dedicated, and Friedrich Eckstein who helped defray the cost of publication – see HW to Joseph Schalk, 8 February 1889, p. 25. Eichendorff's poem, which has no title, is the first of a four-poem cycle called *Die Freunde*, addressed to a number of friends, including (in nos. 2 and 3) the poet Otto Heinrich, Graf von Loeben, two years older than Eichendorff, who helped him through his religious and creative crises and encouraged him to publish his poems – see p. 18. At a recital given by Ferdinand Jäger the Elder and Wolf at the Saal Bösendorfer on 9 March 1889, 'Der Freund' had to be encored twice – see Theodor Helm's review in the *Deutsche Zeitung*, 12 March 1899.
2   Eichendorff: Mit sichrem, ernsten Sinn.   3   Eichendorff: von echtem Kerne.
4   See HW to Joseph Schalk, 7 September 1889, p. 26.

2 Der Musikant[1]

Wandern lieb' ich für mein Leben,
Lebe eben wie ich kann,
Wollt' ich mir auch Mühe geben,
Paßt' es mir doch gar nicht an.

Schöne alte Lieder weiß ich,
In der Kälte, ohne Schuh',
Draußen in die Saiten reiß' ich,
Weiß nicht, wo ich abends ruh'.[2]

Manche Schöne macht wohl Augen,
Meinet, ich gefiel' ihr sehr,
Wenn ich nur was wollte taugen,[3]
So ein armer Lump nicht wär'. –

Mag dir Gott ein'n Mann bescheren,
Wohl mit Haus und Hof versehn!
Wenn wir zwei zusammen wären,
Möcht' mein Singen mir vergehn.[4]

Poem first published 1826
Also set by Reinhard Schwarz-Schilling

The minstrel

I simply love to wander,
And live as best I can,
And even were I to exert myself,
It wouldn't suit me at all.

Beautiful old songs I know,
Barefoot, out in the cold,
I pluck my strings in the street,
Not knowing where I'll rest at night.

Many a beauty gives me looks,
Fancying I would please her well,
If I'd only make something of myself,
Were not such a beggar wretch.

May God give you a husband,
Well provided with house and home!
If we two were together,
My singing might fade away.

3 Verschwiegene Liebe[5]

Über Wipfel und Saaten
In den Glanz hinein –
Wer mag sie erraten,
Wer holte sie ein? –

Secret love

Over treetops and cornfields
Into the gleaming light –
Who may guess them,
Who retrieve them?

---

1   Eichendorff's poem, which has no title, was first published in 1826 as the first of a five-poem sequence with the title *Der zufriedene Musikant*, which was changed in 1837 to *Der wandernde Musikant* – the name of Reinhard Schwarz-Schilling's Eichendorff cycle, a charming work comprising 'Wandern lieb' ich für mein Leben', 'Wenn die Sonne lieblich schiene', 'Bist du manchmal auch verstimmt' and 'Durch Feld und Buchenhallen'.
2   Like Eichendorff's minstrel, Wolf led a nomadic domestic existence – see HW to Friedrich Eckstein, 17 July 1896, p. 362, note 1.
3   An echo of the title of Eichendorff's most celebrated Novelle: *Aus dem Leben eines Taugenichts* (1826).
4   'Musikant' can have a slightly derogatory connotation in German, as we see in Wolf's letter to his parents of 29 June 1875: „Da Sie aber durchaus nicht wollen, dass ich ein Musikus – nicht wie Sie der Meinung sind Musikant – werde, so will ich gehorchen u. mich einem anderen Fache widmen." ('As you clearly do not wish me to become a musician – not minstrel, as you think – I shall obey and devote myself to another profession.') 'Musikus' can also be used playfully, as in 'Wie lange schon war immer mein Verlangen' from the *Italienisches Liederbuch*.
5   The poem, titled 'Gruß' by Eichendorff, was later incorporated into his verse narrative *Robert und Guiscard* (1855), where it is sung by Guiscard who, standing at his open window in the moonlight, breathes in the scent of lilac, senses (erroneously) his sweetheart Marie nearby, and sings the song 'from the depths of his heart'. The verse before Guiscard's song runs:

Gedanken sich wiegen,	Thoughts go floating,
Die Nacht ist verschwiegen,	The night is silent,
Gedanken sind frei.[1]	Thoughts are free.
Errät' es nur *Eine*,[2]	If only *she* could guess
Wer an sie gedacht	Who has been thinking of her
Beim Rauschen der Haine,	Amid the rustling groves,
Wenn niemand mehr wacht,	When no one else is awake
Als die Wolken, die fliegen,	But the scudding clouds –
Mein Lieb ist verschwiegen	My love is silent
Und schön wie die Nacht.	And lovely as night.

Poem first published 1855

4 Das Ständchen[3]

The serenade

Auf die Dächer zwischen blassen	Between pale clouds
Wolken schaut der Mond herfür,	The moon peers onto rooftops,
Ein Student dort auf der Gassen	There in the street a student sings
Singt vor seiner Liebsten Tür.	Before his sweetheart's door.

Schon schliefen Alle, Garten, Schloß und Lüfte,	Already all were asleep, garden, castle and breezes,
Nur Guiscard und die Nachtigallen nicht,	All except Guiscard and the nightingales,
Er stand am offnen Fenster, Fliederdüfte	He stood at the open window, the scent of lilac
Atmet' die Nacht herauf im Mondenlicht;	Was wafted up by the night in the moonlight;
Da war's, als hört' er gehn – zu solcher Stunde	Then he thought he heard footsteps – at this hour
Schweift' oft Marie – er sang aus Herzensgrunde:	Marie would often rove – and he sang from the depths of his heart:

1 Cf. 'Lied des Verfolgten im Turm' from *Des Knaben Wunderhorn*, set by Gustav Mahler.
2 „Errät' es nur Eine,/Wer an sie gedacht" clearly refers to Marie, but Wolf was probably thinking of Melanie Köchert, with whom he was already emotionally and clandestinely involved. It's a shame that modern scores fail to honour Wolf's italicised 'Eine', especially since he sets the word as a dotted minim on both syllables, implying that the word should be stressed by the singer. The song, according to Wolf's first biographer Ernst Decsey, was composed in a single flash of inspiration. Wolf, with a book of Eichendorff poems in his hand, was walking up and down Friedrich Eckstein's garden, immersing himself in the mood of the poem. Unable to bear the noise from the nearby factory, disturbed by whistling in the courtyard and the persistent sound of carpet-beating from another building, he turned on his heel, entered the house, went up to Eckstein's room, sat down at the piano, put the book of poems aside, and wrote out the complete song with hardly a pause for breath.
3 'Das Ständchen' is a serenade quite unlike any other. The title refers to the song sung by a young student outside his sweetheart's door, but we hear his serenade only as a lute accompaniment in the piano part, as it plays snatches of melody and pizzicato notes in the right hand. *Dolce* is the crucial marking, for the young student is happy and in love. This contrasts with the sad utterances in the vocal line of the old man who looks on distraught, as he is reminded of the happiness that he used to enjoy before his sweetheart died. He sings a sort of recitative, often on repeated notes, that never really coalesces into song, so that the contrast with the blithe serenader is made even more poignant; never really coalesces, that is, until at 'So in meinen jungen Tagen', when the vocal line

Und die Brunnen rauschen wieder	And again the fountains plash
Durch die stille Einsamkeit,	Through the silent solitude,
Und der Wald vom Berge nieder,	And the forest rustles down from the hills
Wie in alter schöner Zeit.	As in the good old days.
So in meinen jungen Tagen	Likewise in my young days,
Hab' ich manche Sommernacht	On many a summer's night
Auch die Laute hier geschlagen	I too plucked my lute here,
Und manch lust'ges Lied erdacht.	And composed many a merry song.
Aber von der stillen Schwelle	But from that silent threshold
Trugen sie mein Lieb' zur Ruh –	My love's been taken to rest.
Und du, fröhlicher Geselle,	I beg you, my blithe friend,
Singe, sing' nur immer zu!*	Sing on, sing ever on!*

Poem first published 1833
Also set by Erich Korngold and Trunk
* Wolf repeats words from the final line.

5 Der Soldat I

The soldier I

Ist auch schmuck nicht mein Rößlein,	Though my little horse is not well groomed,
So ist's doch recht klug,	He's really rather clever,
Trägt im Finstern zu 'nem Schlößlein	He carries me to a little chateau
Mich rasch noch genug.	Quickly enough in the dark.
Ist das Schloß auch nicht prächtig,	Though the chateau's not palatial,
Zum Garten aus der Tür	From the gate into the garden
Tritt ein Mädchen doch allnächtig	A girl steps every night
Dort freundlich herfür.	In friendly fashion.
Und ist auch die Kleine	And though the little creature's
Nicht die schönst' auf der Welt,	Not the prettiest in the world,
So gibt's doch just Keine,	There's simply no one else
Die mir besser gefällt.*	I like better.*
Und spricht sie vom Freien:[1]	But if she speaks of marriage,
So schwing' ich mich auf mein Roß –	I leap onto my horse –
Ich bleibe im Freien,	I'll remain outside in the open,
Und sie auf dem Schloß.*	And she in the chateau.*

Poem written c. 1814
Also set by Bruno Walter
* Wolf twice repeats these lines.

---

heart-breakingly echoes the lute-like accompaniment, reminding the old man of his own past happiness – an unforgettable moment that strikes to the heart.
1 Eichendorff puns on the word 'Freien', which means both 'wooing', 'marriage' and 'out in the open'.

JOSEPH VON EICHENDORFF   41

6 Der Soldat II[1]

Wagen mußt du und flüchtig erbeuten,

Hinter uns schon durch die Nacht
　hör' ich's schreiten,
Schwing' auf mein Roß dich nur schnell
Und küß' noch im Flug mich, wildschönes
　Kind,
Geschwind,
Denn der Tod ist ein rascher Gesell.*

The soldier II

You must be bold and quick to catch
　your prey,
Already I hear footsteps behind us
　in the night,
Quickly leap up onto my horse
And kiss me as we flee, my wild lovely
　child,
Make haste,
For Death is fleet of foot.*

Poem written c. 1814
Also set by Peter Cornelius
* Wolf repeats the final line several times to sepulchral effect.

7 Die Zigeunerin[2]

Am Kreuzweg, da lausche ich, wenn
　die Stern'
Und die Feuer im Walde verglommen,
Und wo der erste Hund bellt von fern,
Da wird mein Bräut'gam herkommen.
La, la, la ...

„Und als der Tag graut' durch das Gehölz,
Sah ich eine Katze sich schlingen,
Ich schoß ihr auf den nußbraunen Pelz,
Wie tat die weit überspringen! –[3]
Ha, ha, ha! ..."

Schad'[4] nur ums Pelzlein, du kriegst
　mich nit!
Mein Schatz muß sein wie die andern:
Braun und ein Stutzbart auf ungrischen
　Schnitt

The gypsy girl

At the crossroads I listen, when the stars

And camp fires in the wood have faded,
And where, afar, the first dog barks,
From there will my intended come.
La, la, la ...

'And when day dawned through the copse,
I saw a cat slinking,
I fired a shot at her nut-brown pelt,
How that made her jump! –
Ha, ha, ha! ...'

A pity about the pelt, but you won't
　catch me!
My sweetheart must be like the others!
Swarthy, with a beard of Hungarian
　trim,

1　Both poems 'Der Soldat I' and 'II' were published under the same title ('Der Soldat') in *Gedichte von Joseph Freiherrn von Eichendorff* (Berlin, 1837).
2　See HW to Emil Kauffmann, 2 April 1892, p. 27. Wolf's song is characterised by a plethora of 'La, la, la' and 'Ha, ha, ha' exclamations that do not appear in the original Eichendorff poem from the Novelle *Dichter und ihre Gesellen* (1834), where the first and third verses are sung by the actress Kordelchen, and the second by Baron Fortunat. She flirts with him but is in love with Guido the painter. The relevant passage runs: „[Kordelchen] schwang plötzlich ein Tamburin, daß es schwirrte, tanzte mit ihren roten, polnischen Stiefeln auf zigeunerisch und sang dazu." ('Kordelchen suddenly brandished a tambourine whose sound filled the air, sang and danced like a gypsy to it in her red, Polish boots.')
3　The line in the Novelle runs: „Die macht' einmal weite Sprünge!"
4　Wolf omits Eichendorff's "'S ist' before 'Schad'.

Und ein fröhliches Herze zum Wandern.
La, la, la ...

And a happy heart for wandering.
La, la, la ...

Poem first published 1834

8 Nachtzauber[1]

Hörst Du nicht die Quellen gehen[2]
Zwischen Stein und Blumen weit
Nach den stillen Waldes-Seen,
Wo die Marmorbilder stehen
In der schönen Einsamkeit?
Von den Bergen sacht hernieder,
Weckend die uralten Lieder,
Steigt die wunderbare Nacht,
Und die Gründe glänzen wieder,
Wie du's oft im Traum gedacht.*

Kennst die Blume Du, entsprossen
In dem mondbeglänzten Grund?
Aus der Knospe, halb erschlossen,
Junge Glieder blühend sprossen.
Weiße Arme, roter Mund,
Und die Nachtigallen schlagen,
Und rings hebt es an zu klagen,
Ach, vor Liebe todeswund,
Von versunk'nen schönen Tagen –
Komm', o komm'[§] zum stillen Grund!

Night magic

Do you not hear the distant springs
Flowing between rocks and flowers
Towards the silent woodland lakes
Where the marble statues stand
In lovely solitude?
Softly from the mountains,
Awakening age-old songs,
Wondrous night descends,
And the valleys gleam again,
As you often imagined in dreams.*

Do you know the flower that blossomed
In the moonlit valley?
From its half-open bud
Young limbs have flowered forth,
White arms, red lips,
And the nightingales are singing,
And all around a lament is raised,
Ah, wounded to death with love,
For the lovely days now lost –
Come, ah come[§] to the silent valley!

Poem written c. 1852
Also set by Trunk
* Wolf repeats the line.
[§] 'komm" is repeated by Wolf a further twice.

[1] The poem, which Eichendorff later called 'Zauberei der Nacht', first appeared without a title in the narrative poem *Julian* (1853) where it is sung in Canto XI by the beautiful Faustina. The final two strophes of the canto describe how Octavian has been bewitched by Faustina's sweet voice („süße Stimme"):

Und fort tönt's, die Nacht rauscht leise
Und der Mond so zaubrisch scheint,
Er erkannte Fausta's Weise,
Wußt' wohl, wen das Singen meint.

And the song rang on, night murmured softly
And magically the moon appeared,
He recognised Fausta's melody,
Knew well for whom it was meant.

Hat dem Klange folgen müssen
In den duftberauschten Grund –
Dort seitdem vor glüh'nden Küssen
War verstummt der Liedermund.

Was forced to follow the sound
Into the scent-drenched valley –
Where his glowing kisses
Silenced the mouth that had sung the song.

[2] Wolf's long-flighted melody takes precedence here over prosody: he stresses 'gehen' instead of 'Quellen'.

9 Der Schreckenberger[1]

Auf's Wohlsein meiner Dame,
Eine Windfahn' ist ihr Panier,
Fortuna ist ihr Name,
Das Lager ihr Quartier!

Und wendet sie sich weiter,
Ich kümmre mich nicht drum,
Da draußen ohne Reiter,
Da geht die Welt so dumm.

Statt Pulverblitz und Knattern
Aus jedem wüsten Haus
Gevattern sehn und schnattern[2]
Alle Lust zum Land hinaus.

Fortuna weint vor Ärger,
Es rinnet Perl' auf Perl':
„Wo ist der Schreckenberger?[3]
Das war ein andrer Kerl!"

Sie tut den Arm mir reichen,
Fama bläst das Geleit,
So zu dem Tempel steigen
Wir der Unsterblichkeit.

Poem first published 1841

The swashbuckler

Let's drink to my lady!
A weathervane's her banner,
Fortune's her name,
The camp's her billet!

And if she goes on her way,
It won't bother me,
For life in the outside world
Is dull without cavalrymen.

Instead of gunpowder and rattling muskets,
Gossips peer out of every drab house
And prattle
All pleasure from life.

Fortune sheds tears of vexation,
Trickling pearl on pearl:
'Where's my swashbuckling fellow?
He was a real man!'

She offers me her arm,
Fame sounds the advance,
Thus do we ascend
The Temple of Immortality.

10 Der Glücksritter[4]

Wenn Fortuna spröde tut,
Lass' ich sie in Ruh,
Singe recht und trinke gut,
Und Fortuna kriegt auch Mut,
Setzt sich mit dazu.

The soldier of fortune

When Fortune acts coyly,
I ignore her,
Sing out and drink my fill,
And Fortune cheers up too
And sits down beside me.

---

1 The poem occurs in Chapter 5 („Fortunas Schildknappen"/'Fortune's shield-bearers') of Eichendorff's Novelle *Die Glücksritter* (*Soldiers of Fortune*) (1840), where it is sung by a swashbuckling character to Fortuna. When he has finished, his comrades wave their hats and cry: „Vivat das hohe Brautpaar!" ('Long live the noble pair!').
2 Wolf indicates that the line should be sung *näselnd* ('nasally').
3 Helmut Deutsch in *Gesang auf Händen tragen* relates an amusing anecdote: when Hermann Prey during a Wolf Eichendorff recital in Rolandseck sang „Wo ist der Schreckenberger?/Das war ein andrer Kerl!", a ripple of laughter ran through the audience. It was only after the concert that they discovered the reason for such hilarity: Waldemar Schreckenberger was a leading politician in the Helmut Kohl government.
4 Wolf clearly conceived 'Der Schreckenberger' and 'Der Glücksritter' as a pair, since the processional theme at the end of the first song, marked *pompös* and *fff*, is repeated in the postlude of the second. 'Der Schreckenberger', which appeared in Eichendorff's Novelle *Die Glücksritter*, was

Doch ich geb' mir keine Müh':	But I remain aloof:
„He, noch eine her!"	'Hey, another glass!'
Kehr' den Rücken gegen sie,	I turn my back on her,
Lass' hoch leben die und die –	Drink the health of this or that lass –
Das verdrießt sie sehr.	Which makes her very cross.
Und bald rückt sie sacht zu mir:	And soon she sidles up to me:
„Hast Du deren mehr?"	'Any more of them?'
Wie Sie sehn. – „Drei Kannen schier,	As you see – 'Three tankards full
Und das lauter Klebebier!" –	Of pure malt beer!'
'S wird mir gar nicht schwer.	Not a problem for me!
Drauf sie zu mir lächelt fein:	Then she smiles at me slyly:
„Bist ein ganzer Kerl!"	'You're a real man!'
Ruft den Kellner, schreit nach Wein,	She summons the waiter, shouts for wine,
Trinkt mir zu und schenkt mir ein,	Drinks my health and pours my glass –
Echte Blum' und Perl.	Real bouquet and sparkle.
Sie bezahlet Wein und Bier,	She pays for the wine and beer,
Und ich, wieder gut,	And I, good-humoured once more,
Führe sie am Arm mit mir	Lead her out of the inn
Aus dem Haus wie 'n Kavalier,	On my arm, like a cavalier,
Alles zieht den Hut.	Everyone doffs his hat.

Poem written 1837

11 Lieber alles[1] — I'd sooner be all three

Soldat sein ist gefährlich,	Soldiering's dangerous,
Studieren sehr beschwerlich,	Studying's very arduous,
Das Dichten süß und zierlich,	Versifying's sweet and graceful,
Der Dichter gar possierlich	A poet's a figure of fun
In diesen wilden Zeiten.	In these wild times.
Ich möcht' am liebsten reiten,	Most of all I'd like to ride,
Ein gutes Schwert zur Seiten,	A good sword at my side,
Die Laute in der Rechten,	A lute in my right hand,
Studentenherz zum Fechten.	With a student's heart for the fight.
Ein wildes Roß ist's Leben,	Life's an untamed steed,
Die Hufe Funken geben,	Its hooves strike sparks,
Wer's ehrlich wagt, bezwingt es,	The truly bold man will tame it,
Und wo es tritt, da klingt es!	And where it treads it resounds!

Poem written 1809

---

inspired by the wildness of the Rettenbach region around Ischl, and 'Der Glücksritter' was actually committed to manuscript paper as Wolf rode in a mail coach from Ischl to Weißenbach.
1   The poem reviews the possibility of becoming a soldier, a student or a poet. Each profession is rejected in turn, for he wants to combine elements of all three – hence the title, which states that

12 Heimweh[1]

Wer in die Fremde will wandern,
Der muß mit der Liebsten gehn,
Es jubeln und lassen die Andern
Den Fremden alleine stehn.

Was wisset ihr, dunkle Wipfel,[2]
Von der alten, schönen Zeit?
Ach, die Heimat hinter den Gipfeln,
Wie liegt sie von hier so weit!

Am liebsten betracht' ich die Sterne,
Die schienen, wie[3] ich ging zu ihr,
Die Nachtigall hör' ich so gerne,
Sie sang vor der Liebsten Tür.

Der Morgen, das ist meine Freude!
Da steig' ich in stiller Stund'
Auf den höchsten Berg[4] in die Weite,
Grüß dich, Deutschland,
        aus Herzensgrund![5]

Homesickness

He who would journey abroad
Must go with his beloved,
For there people make merry
And leave the stranger alone.

What do you know, dark tree-tops,
Of the happy days now past?
Ah, my homeland beyond the mountains,
How far it lies from here!

I love best to watch the stars
That shone as I went to her,
I love to hear the nightingale
That sang at my beloved's door.

Morning is my delight!
At that peaceful hour I climb
The highest mountain for miles around,
And greet you, Germany,
        from the depths of my heart!

Poem first published 1826

---

he'd 'rather have them all'. Written in 1809, the poem reflects Eichendorff's uncertainty about his future. His studies had recently ended, he was making a name for himself as a poet, and a few years later would join the Lützowisches Freikorps in the fight against Napoleon. Perhaps 'Lieber alles' was written partly as a response to Napoleon's first defeat by Austria at Aspern in 1809. It was also in 1809 that Eichendorff wrote his celebrated patriotic poem 'Der Tiroler Nachtwache'. Wolf dedicated an autograph copy of 'Lieber alles' to his friend and benefactor Oskar Grohe (Nachlaß Hugo Wolf, Wienbibliothek, Musiksammlung).

1   The poem first appeared in Eichendorff's *Aus dem Leben eines Taugenichts* (*From the Life of a Good-for-nothing*), published in 1826, before appearing in the 1837 and 1841 editions of his poetry. It is sung by the hero far away from home in Italy, and we are told that he had learned it from a travelling apprentice miller. The poem expresses the hero's longing for his beloved Aurelie back in Germany, and as he sings it he hears the sound of an approaching posthorn. When the song is finished, he receives a letter from Aurelie which ends: „Es ist so öde hier, und ich kann kaum mehr leben, seit Sie von uns fort sind." ('It is so desolate here, and I can hardly live any longer, since you have been away.')
2   Eichendorff: dunkele.   3   Eichendorff: wenn.
4   Wolf's letter to August Halm, dated 4 November 1891, refers to the particularly high tessitura at the end of 'Heimweh': „Ich danke Ihnen für Ihre freundlichen Grüße „von dem höchsten Berg in die Weite", dessen Besteigung Ihnen vermuthlich nicht soviel Beschwer verursacht haben dürfte, als manchem Sänger das Erklimmern jener angeführten hohen Stelle, die sozusagen bereits im Gebiete der gesanglichen Schneeregion liegt." ('Thank you for your friendly greetings from "the highest mountain for miles around", to climb which was presumably not as difficult as many singers find climbing that high peak you mention which lies, as it were, in the snowy regions of the human voice.')
5   At one of the first performances of the *Eichendorff-Lieder*, on 7 February 1889, Wolf was accompanying Ferdinand Jäger in a performance of 'Heimweh' in the Wagner-Verein when, after the phrase „Grüß dich, Deutschland, aus Herzensgrund!", a roar of applause broke out among the Großdeutschen in the audience, drowning the postlude. Wolf was furious. He slammed down the piano lid and shouted vitriolically at the offending audience: „Und das im Wagner-Verein!" ('And

13 Der Scholar[1]

Bei dem angenehmsten Wetter
Singen alle Vögelein,
Klatscht der Regen auf die Blätter,
Sing ich so für mich allein.

Denn mein Aug' kann nichts entdecken,
Wenn der Blitz auch grausam glüht,
Was im Wandern könnt' erschrecken
Ein zufriedenes Gemüt.

Frei vom Mammon will ich schreiten
Auf dem Feld der Wissenschaft,
Sinne ernst und nehm' zu Zeiten
Einen Mund voll Rebensaft.

Bin ich müde vom Studieren,
Wann der Mond tritt sanft herfür,
Pfleg' ich dann zu musizieren
Vor der Allerschönsten Tür.

Poem first published 1834

The scholar

In the most pleasant of weathers
All the little birds are singing,
When raindrops rattle on the leaves,
I sing for myself alone.

For however fiercely the lightning blaze,
My eyes can see nothing
That could frighten a contented soul
In his wanderings.

Free from Mammon I shall traverse
The field of knowledge,
Thinking deeply, and at times
Quaffing the juice of the grape.

Whenever I tire of studying,
When gently the moon ascends the sky,
I am wont to make music
Before my sweetheart's door.

14 Der verzweifelte Liebhaber

Studieren will nichts bringen,
Mein Rock hält keinen Stich,
Meine Zither will nicht klingen,
Mein Schatz, der mag mich nicht.

Ich wollt', im Grün spazierte
Die allerschönste Frau,
Ich wär' ein Drach' und führte
Sie mit mir fort durch's Blau.

Ich wollt', ich jagt' gerüstet
Und legt' die Lanze aus,

The despairing lover

Studying's unprofitable,
My coat's all unstitched,
My zither won't sound,
My sweetheart doesn't love me.

I wish the fairest of women
Were walking in the fields,
And I were a dragon to bear her
Off into the blue.

I wish I were armed for the chase
And with couched lance

---

in the Wagner-Verein of all places!') The concert was interrupted and the Großdeutschen walked out. Alfred Brendel tells the story of a performance of Wolf's *Eichendorff-Lieder* in Wiesbaden with Hermann Prey, which in the first half seemed to send the audience to sleep; during the interval he offered Prey DM 50 if he would sing „Grüß' dich, SARA, aus Herzensgrund!" instead of „Grüß dich, Deutschland, aus Herzensgrund!" to rouse them from their torpor. Prey declined.

1 Eichendorff called his poem 'Der Student' or in some editions 'Der wandernde Student'. It was first printed in his Novelle *Dichter und ihre Gesellen* (1834) where there is no title. The song is heard at the beginning of Book 1, Chapter 6, by the hero Fortunat. The first two verses are sung by a Literatus (scholar), one of a strolling group of players who has been surprised by a thunderstorm. The same scholar, who (we are told) has 'eine schöne Männerstimme', also sings the last two verses after the group has found shelter in the town.

JOSEPH VON EICHENDORFF 47

Und jagte alle[1] Philister
Zur schönen Welt hinaus.

Ich wollt', ich läg'[2] jetzunder
Im Himmel still und weit
Und fragt'[3] nach all' dem Plunder
Nichts vor Zufriedenheit.

Chase all the philistines
Out of this lovely world.

I wish I were now lying
In the calm, broad heavens,
Enquiring nothing of the trivial world,
Simply filled with content.

Poem written *c.* 1830

15 Unfall[4]

Ich ging bei Nacht einst über Land,
Ein Bürschlein traf ich draußen,
Das hat 'nen Stutzen in der Hand
Und zielt auf mich voll Grausen.
Ich renne, da ich mich erbos',
Auf ihn in vollem Rasen,
Da drückt das kecke Bürschlein los
Und ich stürzt' auf die Nasen.
Er aber lacht mir in's Gesicht,
Daß er mich angeschossen,
Cupido war der kleine Wicht –
Das hat mich sehr verdrossen.

Mishap

Walking one night in the country,
I met a little boy,
In his hand he held a gun
And took grim aim at me.
Provoked, I rush at him
In a mighty rage,
The impish boy fires,
I fall flat on my nose.
But he laughs in my face
For having shot at me.
Cupid was the little brat's name –
I was greatly vexed.

Poem written *c.* 1828

16 Liebesglück[5]

Ich hab' ein Liebchen lieb recht von Herzen.
Hellfrische Augen hat's wie zwei Kerzen,
Und wo sie spielend streifen das Feld,
Ach wie so lustig glänzet die Welt!

Wie in der Waldnacht zwischen
    den Schlüften
Plötzlich die Täler sonnig sich klüften,
Funkeln die Ströme, rauscht himmelwärts
Blühende Wildnis – so ist mein Herz!

Love's happiness

I've a sweetheart I love with all my heart.
Her bright eyes sparkle like two candles,
And wherever they lightly fall,
Ah, how joyously the world shines!

As in dark forests between ravines

Suddenly the valleys emerge in sunlight,
The streams sparkle, and heavenwards
The blossoming wilderness rustles –
    so it is with my heart!

---

1 Eichendorff: all.   2 Eichendorff: säß.   3 Eichendorff: früg'.
4 Eichendorff's original title was 'Der Landreuter', modernised in later editions to 'Der Landreiter'. A 'Landreiter' is a mounted gendarme – which gives the poem a more macho feel than is evident in Mozart's 'Dans un bois solitaire', another song featuring Cupid. The poem forms part of Eichendorff's historical drama *Der letzte Held von Marienburg* (1830) in which Baysen sings the song to his own lute accompaniment. Eichendorff sent a copy of the play to Goethe, who did not reply.
5 Eichendorff: 'Der Glückliche'.

Wie vom Gebirge ins Meer zu schauen,	Like gazing from summits into the sea,
Wie wann[1] der Seefalk, hangend im Blauen,	Like a sea-falcon hovering in the blue
Zuruft der dämmernden Erd', wo sie blieb –	Asking the twilit earth where she has been –
So unermeßlich ist rechte Lieb'!	So immeasurable is true love!

Poem first published 1837
Also set by Felix Mendelssohn

17 Seemanns Abschied[2]   Sailor's farewell

Ade, mein Schatz, du mocht'st mich nicht,	Farewell, my sweet, you never loved me,
Ich war dir zu geringe.	I was too lowly for you.
Einst wandelst du bei Mondenlicht	One night you'll wander by moonlight
Und hörst ein süßes Klingen:	And hear sweet music.
Ein Meerweib singt, die Nacht ist lau,	A mermaid is singing, the night is mild,
Die stillen Wolken wandern,	The silent clouds drift by.
Da denk' an mich, 's ist meine Frau,	Then think of me and my mermaid wife,
Nun such' dir einen andern!	And find yourself another!
Ade, ihr Landsknecht', Musketier'!	Farewell, you troopers, musketeers!
Wir ziehn auf wildem Rosse,	We ride on wild horses
Das bäumt und überschlägt sich schier	That rear and nearly somersault
Vor manchem Felsenschlosse,	Before many a rocky fortress,
Der Wassermann bei Blitzesschein	The merman, lit by lightning,
Taucht auf in dunklen Nächten,	Looms up on dark nights,
Der Haifisch schnappt, die Möwen schrein –	The shark snaps, the gull shrieks –
Das ist ein lustig[3] Fechten!	What a merry skirmish!
Streckt nur auf eurer Bärenhaut	Just stretch out your lazy limbs
Daheim die faulen Glieder,	On your bearskin rug at home,
Gott Vater aus dem Fenster schaut,	God the Father looks out of his window
Schickt seine Sündflut wieder,	And sends a second Flood,
Feldwebel, Reiter, Musketier,	Sergeants, troopers, musketeers,
Sie müssen all' ersaufen,	All will have to drown,
Derweil mit frischem Winde wir	While we, before a brisk wind,
Im Paradies einlaufen.	Sail into Paradise.

Poem first published 1837

1   Eichendorff: wenn.
2   The song, in a slightly different form, is sung in the posthumously published Novelle *Eine Meerfahrt* by Leutnant Sanchez after a drinking bout and a duel at dawn. 'Seemanns Abschied' is yet another song that allows Wolf to display his gift for pictorial touches, such as the pounding waves (bass octaves), the snapping of shark jaws, the scream of seagulls, and also his remarkable ability to conjure up atmosphere, here a seascape reeking of tang and spray, and redolent of lashing winds, as we hear in the very first bar of the boisterous prelude that caused Bruckner, when Wolf showed him the song, to cry out in amazement: „Teufel! woher haben Sie den Akkord!" ('Where the devil did you get *that* chord from?')
3   Eichendorff: lust'ges.

JOSEPH VON EICHENDORFF

ANHANG	SUPPLEMENT

1 Erwartung[1]

Grüß' euch aus Herzensgrund:
Zwei Augen hell und rein,
Zwei Röslein auf dem Mund,
Kleid blank aus Sonnenschein!

Nachtigall klagt und weint,
Wollüstig rauscht der Hain,
Alles die Liebste meint:
Wo weilt sie so allein?

Weil's draußen finster war,
Sah ich viel hellern Schein,
Jetzt ist es licht und klar,
Ich muß im Dunkeln sein.

Sonne nicht steigen mag,
Sieht so verschlafen drein,
Wünschet den ganzen Tag,
Daß wieder Nacht möcht' sein.

Liebe geht durch die Luft,
Holt fern die Liebste ein;
Fort über Berg und Kluft!
Und sie wird doch noch mein!

Poem first published 1815

Anticipation

I greet you from the depths of my heart:
Two eyes bright and clear,
Two small roses on your lips,
A gleaming dress of sunlight!

The nightingale laments and weeps,
The grove rustles voluptuously,
Everything speaks of my sweetheart –
Where does she linger so alone?

Because it was dark outside,
I saw a much brighter glow,
Now it is light and clear,
I must dwell in darkness.

The sun, reluctant to rise,
Looks down so sleepily,
Wishing all day long
Night could come again.

Love moves through the air,
Goes to meet my distant beloved;
Off, over mountain and chasm!
And she will yet be mine!

---

1   See note 1 to 'Nachruf', p. 29. The poem forms part of Eichendorff's novel *Ahnung und Gegenwart* (1815) where it is sung in Book I, Chapter 2, by Graf Friedrich on horseback. Before he sings the song, we read:

> Das Bild der schönen Rosa stand wieder ganz lebendig in ihm auf, mit aller Farbenpracht des Morgens gemalt und geschmückt. Der Sonnenschein, der laue Wind und Lerchengesang verwirrte sich in das Bild, und so entstand in seinem glücklichen Herzen folgendes Liedchen, das er immerfort laut vor sich hersang.

> The picture of the beautiful Rosa rose again vividly within him, painted and adorned with all the glowing colours of the morning. The sunshine, the warm breeze and the larks' song wove themselves into the picture, and thus arose in his happy heart the following ditty which he sang aloud to himself as he rode away.

The ironic title of the poem is 'Steckbrief' ('Wanted!').

2 Die Nacht[1]

Nacht ist wie ein stilles Meer,
Lust und Leid und Liebesklagen
Kommen so verworren her
In dem linden Wellenschlagen.

Wünsche wie die Wolken sind,
Schiffen durch die stillen Räume,
Wer erkennt im lauen Wind,
Ob's Gedanken oder Träume? –

Schließ' ich nun auch Herz und Mund,
Die so gern den Sternen klagen:
Leise doch im Herzensgrund
Bleibt das linde Wellenschlagen.

Poem written *c.* 1833
Also set by Fanny Mendelssohn Hensel and Josef Gabriel Rheinberger

Night

Night is like a silent sea,
Joy and pain and lovers' laments
Mingle in such confusion
Among the gently lapping waves.

Wishes are like clouds,
Floating through silent space,
Who can tell in the warm breeze
If they be thoughts or dreams? –

Though I now close heart and lips
That so love lamenting to the stars:
Still in the depths of my heart,
The waves pulse gently on.

3 Waldmädchen[2]

Bin ein Feuer hell, das lodert
Von dem grünen Felsenkranz,
Seewind ist mein Buhl' und fordert[3]
Mich zum lust'gen Wirbeltanz,

Kommt und wechselt unbeständig:
Steigend wild,
Neigend mild,
Meine schlanken Lohen wend' ich:
Komm nicht nah mir, ich verbrenn' dich!

Wo die wilden Bäche rauschen
Und die hohen Palmen stehn,
Wenn die Jäger heimlich lauschen,
Viele Rehe einsam gehn.
Bin ein Reh, flieg' durch die Trümmer,
Über die Höh',

Forest nymph

I'm a bright fire that blazes
From the green-garlanded cliff,
The sea wind's my lover,
Who, summoning me to the joyous
    whirling dance,

Comes in his inconstant way,
Madly rising,
Gently falling,
I turn on him my tongue of flame:
Come not near me, or I'll burn you up!

Where the wild streams roar,
And the palm trees soar up,
When the hidden huntsmen listen,
Many a deer goes lonely by.
I'm a deer, leaping over rubble,
Over mountains,

---

1 See note 1 to 'Nachruf', p. 29. Eichendorff's original title was 'Die Nachtblume'. According to Hilda Schulhof, the poem, with an additional strophe between verses 2 and 3, featured in an early sketch of the novel *Dichter und ihre Gesellen*.
2 The poem, first printed in *Gedichte von Joseph Freiherrn von Eichendorff* (Berlin, 1837), was later included by the poet in his posthumously published Novelle *Eine Meerfahrt*, where it is sung by Alma. Thinking herself unobserved, she has put on Antonio's clothes. She wishes to enter his service, and he agrees to look after her.
3 Eichendorff: fodert.

JOSEPH VON EICHENDORFF

Wo im Schnee
Still die letzten Gipfel schimmern,
Folg' mir nicht, erjagst mich nimmer!

Bin ein Vöglein in den Lüften,
Schwing mich übers blaue Meer,
Durch die Wolken von den Klüften
Fliegt kein Pfeil mehr bis hieher,
Und die Au'n und Felsenbogen,
Waldeseinsamkeit
Weit, wie weit,
Sind versunken in die Wogen –
Ach, ich habe mich verflogen!

Poem first published 1837
Also set by Schumann

Where in the snow
The farthest peaks shimmer quietly,
Do not follow, you'll never catch me!

I'm a little bird in the air,
Soaring over the blue sea,
Here no arrow, shot from chasms,
Can reach me through the clouds;
And the meadows and arching cliffs,
Lonely woods
Far, far around,
Have vanished beneath the waves –
Ah, I have lost my way!

Emanuel Geibel
(1815–1884)

and Paul Heyse (1830–1914)

                                                                                                       page

Spanisches Liederbuch
nach Heyse und Geibel für eine Singstimme und Klavier

		page
Wer sein holdes Lieb verloren	28 October 1889, orchestrated 1–4 December 1897	80
Ich fuhr über Meer	31 October 1889, a.m.	81
Preciosas Sprüchlein gegen Kopfweh	31 October 1889, p.m.	87
Wenn du zu den Blumen gehst	1/2 November 1889, orchestrated 5–6 December 1897	79
Alle gingen, Herz, zur Ruh	2 November 1889	94
Nun wandre, Maria	4 November 1889	67
Die ihr schwebet	5 November 1889, afternoon	68
Die du Gott gebarst, du Reine	5 November 1889, evening	66
Bedeckt mich mit Blumen	10 November 1889	97
Seltsam ist Juanas Weise	14 November 1889	76
Treibe nur mit Lieben Spott	15 November 1889	78
In dem Schatten meiner Locken	17 November 1889, p.m., orchestrated summer 1895	75
Und schläfst du, mein Mädchen	17 November 1889	98
Herz, verzage nicht geschwind	19 November 1889, orchestrated autumn 1895	84
Sagt, seid Ihr es, feiner Herr	19 November 1889, afternoon	85
Klinge, klinge, mein Pandero	20 November 1889	75
Herr, was trägt der Boden hier	24 November 1889	73
Blindes Schauen, dunkle Leuchte	26 November 1889, a.m.	82
Bitt' ihn, o Mutter	26 November 1889, p.m.	89
„Wer tat deinem Füßlein weh?"	5 December 1889	101
Auf dem grünen Balkon	12 December 1889	78
Sie blasen zum Abmarsch	13 December 1889	99
Führ mich, Kind, nach Bethlehem!	15 December 1889	70
Wunden trägst du, mein Geliebter	16 December 1889	74
Ach, wie lang die Seele schlummert!	19 December 1889	72

Ach, des Knaben Augen	21 December 1889	70
Mühvoll komm' ich und beladen	22 December 1889	71
Nun bin ich dein	15 January 1890	65
Trau nicht der Liebe	28 March 1890	92
Weint nicht, ihr Äuglein	29 March 1890, a.m.	100
Schmerzliche Wonnen und wonnige Schmerzen	29 March 1890, p.m.	91
Ach im Maien war's, im Maien	30 March 1890	93
Eide, so die Liebe schwur	31 March 1890	83
Geh, Geliebter, geh jetzt!	1 April 1890	105
Liebe mir im Busen zündet	2 April 1890, noon	90
Deine Mutter, süßes Kind	2 April 1890, p.m.	102
Mögen alle bösen Zungen	3 April 1890	86
Sagt ihm, daß er zu mir komme	4 April 1890	88
Dereinst, dereinst, Gedanke mein	11 April 1890	94
Tief im Herzen trag' ich Pein	12 April 1890	95
Komm, o Tod, von Nacht umgeben	14 April 1890	96
Ob auch finstre Blicke glitten	16 April 1890	96
Da nur Leid und Leidenschaft	20 April 1890	103
Wehe der, die mir verstrickte	27 April 1890	104

POET

The immense popularity of Emanuel Geibel's poetry in the second half of the nineteenth century is reflected in the frequency with which Lieder composers turned to his verse for their songs. Ernst Challier in his *Großer Lieder-Katalog* lists over three and a half thousand settings. Geibel was one of the most popular poets of his day and made the acquaintance of several established members of the Romantic movement in Berlin, including Joseph von Eichendorff and Adelbert von Chamisso, who was influential in getting his first poems published. At the age of twenty-four Geibel visited Greece, thanks to the support of Bettina von Arnim, and became a lifelong devotee of the south. „Der Süden hat mich, wie in einem Zaubernetze, gefangen," ('The south has ensnared me as though in a magic web,') he wrote ecstatically from Athens to his friend Carl Conrad Theodor Litzmann. On his return, he started to learn Spanish and published his first volume of original poetry in 1840, from which Schumann selected 'Der Hidalgo' and 'Der Page' for his Op. 30, two of the first poems to put Spain on the Lieder map. In 1841 he was invited by Kammerherr von der Malsburg to catalogue the library of his late brother, Ernst Otto von der Malsburg, a celebrated translator of Calderón, who possessed a vast collection of Spanish books. The library was situated in secluded woodland and Geibel immersed himself in Spanish literature, writing to Henriette Nölting on 4 September 1841 about the visions he was conjuring up of Spain – a tapestry of „Orangenbäume, Cypressen, Mönche und braune Guerillas, und duftende Mondnächte voll Liebesabendtheuer, Citherspiel und blinkender Dolche" ('orange trees, cypresses, monks and swarthy guerrillas, and fragrant moonlit nights full of amorous adventures, the playing of zithers and the flashing of daggers'). From 1842 King Friedrich Wilhelm IV of Prussia granted him an annual stipend, which gave him financial independence. He travelled to Marburg to study the manuscripts of Spanish literature in the possession of Victor Aimé Huber, professor of medieval Spanish literature at Marburg University. In a letter to Paul Heidelbach of 17 April 1842, Geibel describes how he and Huber would discuss his translations, which were published the following year in Berlin as *Volkslieder und Romanzen der Spanier im Versmaße des Originals verdeutscht*. According to the latest research, it seems that Huber played a not inconsiderable part in the fashioning of the translations, many of which were reproduced in the *Spanisches Liederbuch*.

Geibel was fifteen years older than Heyse, and together they published their *Spanisches Liederbuch* in 1852, with a frontispiece by Heyse's friend Adolph von Menzel depicting a pair of lovers in Spanish dress. Geibel and Heyse translated about a third of the *Floresta de Rimas Antiguas Castellanas*, edited by Juan Nicolás Böhl de Faber, which had appeared between 1821 and 1825. Geibel soon received an honorary professorship in Munich and became the leading figure of the Münchner Dichterkreis, a group of poets that also included Heyse ('Auf die Nacht in der Spinnstub'n'), Hermann Lingg ('Immer leiser wird mein Schlummer'), Adolf Friedrich, Graf von Schack ('Mach auf, mach auf! doch leise, mein Kind'), Felix Dahn ('Du meines Herzens Krönelein') and Friedrich von Bodenstedt ('Mir träumte einst ein schöner Traum'). Geibel was also at the centre of a literary circle known as 'Die Krokodile' ('The Crocodiles'), which took its name from a poem by Lingg. Geibel, as the senior member, was known as the 'Ur-Krokodil', Lingg as the 'Teichkrokodil' (pond crocodile) and Heyse as the 'Eidechse' (lizard). Their poetry tended to shun contact with the political and social questions of the day, and was characterised by a love of nature, an espousal of formal beauty and a rejection of ugliness – qualities that commended the poetry of Geibel, in particular, to a huge number of Lieder composers, as diverse as Berg, Brahms, Bruch, Bruckner, Franz, Grieg, Griffes, Hensel, Jensen, Lassen, Liszt, Marx, Mendelssohn, Nietzsche, Pfitzner, Reger, Rubinstein, Clara and Robert Schumann, Silcher, Spohr, Richard Strauss and Wolf. In addition to his own verse, Geibel published numerous translations of French, Portuguese and Spanish poetry.

For a biography of Paul Heyse, see p. 209.

COMPOSER

Hugo Wolf was the only great Lieder composer to select verse written almost exclusively by the finest poets of the past. Unlike Schubert, Schumann, Brahms and Strauss, he ignored most contemporary poetry. If we exclude the juvenilia, composed before he turned twenty, unpublished during his lifetime and featuring such ephemeral figures as Heinrich Zschokke, Vincenz Zusner, Otto Roquette and Karl Herloßsohn, we find that from February 1888 – with the exception of three poems by Robert Reinick – he set in his songbooks only German poets of indisputable pedigree: 53 by Mörike, 20 by Eichendorff and 51 by Goethe. Having composed his final Goethe setting, however, in January 1889, he performed the most extraordinary volte-face, ignored the vast untapped wealth of German poetry, and turned to translations.

Why? Partly because he felt that he had exhausted contemporary German verse of the necessary quality, as we see from this outburst in a letter to Oskar Grohe of 11 August 1890: „Diese verfluchte Tendenzpoesie heutzutage!" ('This cursed didactic modern poetry!') But there is another reason, namely his lifelong interest in Spain and the south. Friedrich Eckstein tells us in „*Alte unnennbare Tage!*" that Wolf not only read Calderón and the Spanish mystics with enthusiasm, but possessed a great love of the literature of the Golden Age. Eckstein's own passion for the music of Tomás Luis de Victoria and the Jewish mystical poets of medieval Spain must also have rubbed off on the composer, and it was Eckstein who was instrumental in bringing Wolf's attention to the *Spanisches Liederbuch*. It was while working on the libretto for his first opera, *Der Corregidor*, collecting information about Spain and Spanish music, that Wolf first came across Geibel's and Heyse's translations. The introduction came through the writer Franz Zweybrück, who remembers the occasion in a letter he wrote to Ernst Decsey, Wolf's first biographer:

> Eines Nachmittages trat Eckstein mit Wolf auf mich zu und sagte: Herr Doktor, wüßten Sie vielleicht schöne Lyrik, die noch nicht komponiert ist? Wolf sucht und sucht und findet so wenig, was ihm paßt. Ich antwortete Eckstein nach einigem Nachdenken mit der Frage, ob er denn das Spanische Liederbuch von Heyse und die italienischen Übersetzungen von Geibel, Heyse und Leuthold kenne. Vor allem das zuerst genannte Büchlein! [. . .] Am anderen Tage brachte ich Wolf mein Exemplar von Heyses spanischem Liederbuch mit, und das Buch ist sicherlich einige Monate, wenn nicht länger, bei ihm geblieben.

> One afternoon Eckstein and Wolf came up to me, and Eckstein asked, 'Herr Doktor, do you by any chance know of a collection of really good lyrics which have not yet been set to music? Wolf has been searching and searching

and has found so little that is suitable.' I thought for a short while, and then asked whether he knew Heyse's *Spanish Songbook*, and the translations by Geibel, Heyse and [Heinrich] Leuthold from the Italian. I recommended the first little book in particular! [. . .] On the following day, I brought my copy of Heyse's *Spanish Songbook* for Wolf, and he certainly kept the book for several months, if not longer.

The German Romantic movement had a voracious appetite for poetry in all languages – the reason, perhaps, why James Macpherson had been able to hoodwink the literary establishment in 1760 with the publication of his *Fragments of Ancient Poetry collected in the Highlands of Scotland and translated from the Gaelic or Erse Language*, claiming that they were based on the authentic writings of the Celtic harpist Ossian. Herder's *Stimmen der Völker in Liedern*, a collection of poems translated from ancient literature from many lands (1778–1807), proved to be treasure trove for a number of Lieder composers. Between 1821 and 1825 Juan Nicolás Böhl de Faber (1770–1836) edited a three-volume anthology of poetry in Spanish entitled *Floresta de Rimas Antiguas Castellanas*, with notes for German readers. This became the chief source for poems selected by Geibel and Heyse for their *Spanisches Liederbuch*, published in 1852. In Zwickau, Schumann's father had published a sixteen-volume edition of Cervantes in German between 1825 and 1829, and Schumann himself continued the hispanophilia with his *Spanisches Liederspiel*, Op. 74, and *Spanische Liebeslieder*, Op. 138. Wolf would have been familiar with most of these works; Spain was in the air.

Wolf's passion for Spain was boundless. His Serbian friend, Prince Božidar Karadjordjević (see HW to B. Schott's Söhne, 26 February 1895, p. 62), would often sing him habaneras, cubanitas and madrilenas to guitar accompaniment. Wolf's correspondence is peppered with references to Spain; to Melanie Köchert, for example, he wrote on 10 July 1896 that he had greatly enjoyed a translation of Tirso de Molina's *Marta la piadosa* and relished its wit and humour, informing her also that Tirso's most famous play, *El burlador de Sevilla*, was the source of Da Ponte's libretto for *Don Giovanni*. And so it goes on. It was entirely logical that such an aficionado should wish to write 'Spanish' music – not just the *Spanisches Liederbuch*, but the opera *Der Corregidor* into which he incorporated two songs from the *Liederbuch*: 'In dem Schatten meiner Locken' and 'Herz, verzage nicht geschwind'. He also started work on another Spanish opera, *Manuel Venegas*, based on the novel by Alarcón y Ariza, *El niño de la bola* (1880), in which he intended to include 'Wer sein holdes Lieb verloren' and 'Wenn du zu den Blumen gehst'. In a letter to Oskar Grohe written in either March or April 1892 Wolf described the novel in the most glowing terms, praising its wonderful plot, characterisation, local colour and tragic outcome, and describing it as „echt spanisch u. doch dabei menschlich – ein wundersames

Gemälde, auf dem purpurschwarzen Untergrund des Mystischen" ('genuinely Spanish and also truly human – a glorious picture painted on the dark purple ground of mysticism').

Mysticism and deepest religious feeling is precisely what characterises the ten 'Sacred Songs' that open the *Spanisches Liederbuch*. Wolf followed Geibel and Heyse closely in this section, setting the opening ten poems of their collection and omitting only the final three, including the wonderful 'En una noche oscura' by St John of the Cross, which was too long for his purposes. The 'Sacred Songs' open with two hymns to the Virgin Mary and are followed by four poems that centre on the Nativity. All six are set by Wolf to music of great gentleness and affection. The pianist is instructed to play *langsam* in four of them, including, incidentally, 'Nun wandre, Maria', in many performances of which Mary seems to be bounding to Bethlehem. 'Ach, des Knaben Augen' and 'Nun bin ich dein' both radiate devotion, but 'Die ihr schwebet' expresses Mary's anxiety at the storm, as she shelters beneath the palm trees. Whereas in Brahms's setting of Lope de Vega's poem (Op. 91/2) it was the idea of peace that predominated, which he expressed with a seamless succession of parallel thirds, Wolf was clearly at pains to illustrate the impending danger that threatened both Mother and Child: plenty of dynamic contrast, surging bass octaves at „Ihr Palmen von Bethlehem", and chilling *sforzandi* at „Grimmige Kälte sauset hernieder". The winds sough throughout until, in the miraculous postlude, they abate and finally vanish, as Wolf rounds off the song with the opening motif in the opening key – but this time marked not *ziemlich bewegt* but *verklingend* or 'dying away'.

If the opening six sacred songs of the *Spanisches Liederbuch* focus on the Virgin and offer us glimpses into the life of the Holy Family, the final four deal with pathological remorse. In all four Wolf uses an almost identical piano figure to convey the sinner's obsessive guilt. The *legato* of the opening song gives way to *marcato*, dissonance and a veiling of tonality. The obsessive repetition of the same rhythmic figure throughout 'Mühvoll komm' ich und beladen' speaks of enormous spiritual distress and a masochism that brings to mind the agonised expressions in the sculptures of Juan Martínez Montañés (1568–1649) and other seventeenth-century Spanish artists.

The secular songs of the *Spanisches Liederbuch* are free from such morbidity and concentrate instead on the pain and rapture of erotic love. Wolf chose 34 of the 99 secular translations, and these vignettes of couples at peace and war are given a faintly Spanish flavour by the composer's simulations of guitars, mandolins, tambourines and dances, as in 'Deine Mutter, süßes Kind', 'Auf dem grünen Balkon', 'Seltsam ist Juanas Weise', 'Treibe nur mit Lieben Spott', 'Klinge, klinge, mein Pandero' and 'Ach, im Maien war's, im Maien'. However, in many of the songs Wolf makes no attempt at Spanish authenticity, and gems such as 'Wenn du zu den Blumen gehst', arguably the only one of the 34 secular songs to speak of unalloyed happiness, could equally well have appeared in the *Italienisches Liederbuch* or the Mörike volume.

Doubt, humiliation, scorn, despair, torment and the pain of parting and rejection are the principal themes of the *Spanisches Liederbuch*, and it is the men who suffer more. There are a dozen exclusively female songs, but many are not gender specific. Perhaps the most beautiful are the deeply felt songs that recall in their intensity the tortured, introspective outpouring of the sacred section. 'Komm, o Tod, von Nacht umgeben', for example, shares a similar chromaticism and uncertain tonality. Songs such as 'Alle gingen, Herz, zur Ruh', 'Dereinst, dereinst, Gedanke mein', 'Komm, o Tod, von Nacht umgeben' and 'Bedeckt mich mit Blumen' are all masterpieces of economy, and compress into sometimes no more than 20 bars a whole world of suffering and sorrow.

Wolf chose about a third of Geibel's and Heyse's translations of mostly sixteenth- and seventeenth-century poems from the *Spanisches Liederbuch*, and set about composing them in the typical bouts of frenetic inspiration that had characterised the Eichendorff, Mörike and Goethe volumes. Once again – as with the Mörike songbook – it was in the house of the Werner family at Perchtoldsdorf that the creative urge was unleashed; in a mere eight weeks, from 28 October to 22 December 1889, he composed no fewer than 27 songs. He spent Christmas with the Köcherts in Vienna, and on his return to Perchtoldsdorf in January composed a further song ('Nun bin ich dein'), before the influenza epidemic that was raging throughout Europe laid him low. For two and a half months he was silent, apart from orchestrating a few Mörike and Goethe songs. Inspiration returned with spring, and he finished the remaining 16 songs within a month.

As usual, he was thrilled by what he had achieved and promised that the songbook would show him 'von einer ganz neuen Seite' (HW to Oskar Grohe, 16 April 1890, p. 59). Two aspects of this 'new style' spring to mind. Firstly, the eschewal of verbal repetition: the *Spanisches Liederbuch* contains only five examples of Wolf repeating a word or phrase – whereas in the Mörike volume there had been multiple repetitions. Secondly, there is none of the variety in mood and theme of the earlier volumes, no ballads, no Weltanschauungslyrik, no nature songs and little humour. He seems now to be less inspired by details of the poem itself than the mood and ideas expressed in it. The vocal line tends to be less declamatory, less intent on responding in detail to verbal magic, while the accompaniment approximates more to a piano solo.

Schott's did not consider all the songs to be of equal merit, the reason perhaps for the original proposal to publish a selection of a mere twelve songs (HW to Melanie Köchert, 16 June 1890, p. 60) for a fee of 600 marks. Only when 300 copies had been sold would Schott's publish a complete edition. Eventually, to Wolf's irritation, the songs were published in six booklets in January 1891, and it was not until January 1892 that the one-volume edition appeared.

LETTERS

HW to Friedrich Eckstein, Perchtoldsdorf, 5 November 1889

Soeben habe ich ein Lied vollendet, das zu hören allein schon der Mühe verlohnte mich baldigst zu besuchen. Das Gedicht (aus dem spanischen Liederbuch) hat zum Gegenstand den hl. Joseph, Maria auf der Flucht nach Egypten geleitend.[1] Wenn Sie dieses Ereigniß <u>erleben</u> wollen müßen Sie meine Musik dazu hören. Sie werden Augen machen.

I have just finished composing a song, to hear which is worth all the trouble of visiting me as soon as possible. The subject of the poem (from the *Spanish Songbook*) is Joseph escorting Mary on the Flight into Egypt. If you want to <u>re-live</u> this journey, you must hear my music. You will be amazed.

HW to Melanie Köchert, Perchtoldsdorf, 31 March 1890

Soeben die <u>Krone</u> aller Spanischen componirt. Bin rasend bei Laune. Gott! wenn nur Niemand zu mir käme! Das Gedicht: „Eide, so die Liebe schwur" – Allerhöchster Hidalgo.[2] Werden Augen machen!

I have just composed the <u>crown</u> of the Spanish songs. My mood is euphoric. God! If only I'm not interrupted! The poem is called 'Eide, so die Liebe schwur' – Holy Hidalgo. You'll be amazed.

HW to Josef Strasser, Perchtoldsdorf, 15 April 1890

Ich bin jetzt wieder fleissig. Habe bereits 41 Spanische am Lager. 44 müssen's werden. Dann wird noch wie bisher in Liedern „gemacht" und dann . . . ja dann . . . ja dann will's gar hoch hinaus! Dann schreib' ich nur mehr Tetralogien.

I am now working hard again. 41 Spanish songs finished. The total must reach 44. That will then be once again the end of song composition, and then . . . then . . . then the sky will be the limit! Then I shall write only tetralogies.

HW to Oskar Grohe, Perchtoldsdorf, 16 April 1890

Auch habe ich einstweilen genug zu tun, mir die „Spanier" (ein großer Zyklus nach Heyse und Geibel) vom Halse zu schaffen. Sie werden in diesen Gesängen

---

1 'Nun wandre, Maria'.
2 An idiosyncratic cry of delight. Wolf is possibly referring to Schumann's song 'Der Hidalgo', a setting of a Geibel poem that he much admired.

mich von einer ganz neuen Seite kennen lernen; dürfte auch das beste sein, was bis jetzt meiner Feder entflossen.

Meanwhile I have my work cut out to complete the Spanish songs (a large cycle to translations by Heyse and Geibel). These songs will show me in a completely new light; they are probably the best I have composed till now.

HW to Melanie Köchert, Unterach, 16 June 1890

Er erweitert seinen ersten Vorschlag dahin, daß er erbötig wäre, nach Verkauf von 300 Exemplaren der 12 „Ausgewählten" die übrigen auch zu drucken. Ich werde ihm heute antworten [. . .], daß eine vollständige Bandausgabe veranstaltet werden müsse, falls wir Handeleins werden sollten.

He's enlarged on his first proposal, saying that he's willing to publish the remaining songs after 300 copies of the 12 selected songs have been sold. I shall reply to him today [. . .] that a complete edition in one volume must be published, if we are to do business.

HW to B. Schott's Söhne, Döbling, 18 September 1890

Um nun keine Zeit zu verlieren u. das Erscheinen meines spanischen Liederbuches bis zu Weihnachten zu ermöglichen, bitte ich den Stich dieses Werkes alsbald in Angriff zu nehmen. Gleichzeitig erlaube ich mir ein Heft meiner Lieder als Vorlage für den Stecher abzusenden, der sich in jeder Hinsicht genau an das Muster halten möge. Durchschnittlich sollen nur vier Systeme die Seiten füllen; zu Anfang auch oft nur drei; aber nur in den allernothwendigsten Fällen fünf.

To lose no time & to ensure that my *Spanisches Liederbuch* appears before Christmas, I beg you to start engraving the work as soon as possible. At the same time, I'm taking the liberty of sending the engraver a volume of my songs as a template – which he must follow exactly in every respect. There should on average be only four systems per page; at the beginning often only three; and only five where it is absolutely necessary.

HW to Melanie Köchert, Mannheim, 19 October 1890

Beide [Weingartner[1] and Grohe] waren voll der Bewunderung für meine Spanischen u. Keller'schen, namentlich war Weingartner entzückt von dem

---

1   Although Wolf admired Weingartner as a choral conductor, he had little time for his compositions. It is not known whether Wolf knew Weingartner's settings of Mörike that included 'Ein Stündlein wohl vor Tag', 'Er ist's', 'Gebet', 'An die Geliebte', 'Zum neuen Jahr' and 'Jägerlied'.

heiligen: „die ihr schwebet" etc., das ich immer u. immer wieder vorspielen mußte.

Both [Felix Weingartner and Oskar Grohe] were full of admiration for my Spanish & the Keller songs; Weingartner was especially delighted with the sacred 'Die ihr schwebet', etc., that I had to play for him over & over again.

HW to Gustav Schur, Mainz, 22 October 1890

Im Großen Ganzen versteht er [Ludwig Strecker, Director of Schott's Söhne] die „Spanischen" noch sehr schlecht, doch zeigt er guten Willen und Eifer für die Sache. Das Beste ist, daß ich seine Frau auf meine Seite gebracht, wobei ich es an den raffiniertesten Künsten, um mir diese wichtige Bundesgenossin zu sichern, nicht fehlen ließ.

He [Ludwig Strecker, Director of Schott's Söhne] has still on the whole a very poor grasp of the 'Spanish songs', but is full of enthusiasm and good intentions for the project. Fortunately, I've managed to get his wife on my side. It cost me a great deal of ingenuity to win her as an important ally.

HW to Käthe Wolf, Döbling, 7 January 1891

Jäger wurde das Lied „Wer sein holdes Lieb verloren" (aus dem Span. Liederbuch) von der Zensur gestrichen, weil man den Passus: „in die Blumen sank sie hin" zu anstößig fand. Wir haben uns darüber zu Tode gelacht. Die Grazer scheinen aber ganz besondere Tugendbolde zu sein.

Because of the censors, Jäger was unable to sing 'Wer sein holdes Lieb verloren' (from the *Span. Liederbuch*), as they found the line 'She sank down among the flowers' too shocking. We all died laughing. Graz folk seem to be especially puritanical.

HW to Engelbert Humperdinck, Döbling, 14 November 1891

Nun wimmelt das spanische Liederbuch von Fehlern, auch habe ich einige Aenderungen zu machen für gut befunden, die in die neue Ausgabe aufgenommen werden sollen.

The *Spanish Songbook* teems with errors, and I've also felt it wise to make a few other changes to be incorporated in the new edition.

HW to Melanie Köchert, Berlin, 6 March 1892

Mit Frl. Mayer[1] hatte ich ein kleines rencontre. Bei den Proben machte ich sie aufmerksam auf die falsche Ausdrucksweise des zuletzt wiederholten „ach nein!"[2] u. bedeutete ihr, wie sie es zu machen habe. Sie versprach meine Anweisung zu befolgen. Im Conzert aber kam's anders. Sie dachte wohl, wenn ich einmal am Podium bin, dann kann ich singen wie ich will, dann kann mir niemand was dreinreden. So mußte ich denn zu meinem Grimm u. zum Entsetzen aller Musikverständigen (daunter Siegfried Ochs, Weingartner, Genée[3]) den Schluß in der abgeschmackten, aufdringlichen, affenartigen Weise hören. [. . .] Aber die Strafe folgte auf dem Fusse nach. Die Composition hatte derart eingeschlagen, daß stürmisch eine Wiederholung verlangt wurde. Mayer bat mich, zu wiederholen. Ich schlug es ihr ab. Und da ich schließlich ohne die Sängerin am Podium erschien, brach ein tosender Applaus über mich herein zum größten Ärger der Gans, die durchaus noch einmal das Stück verschandeln wollte.

I had a little scene with Frl. Mayer. During rehearsals I drew her attention to her wrong interpretation of the final repeat of 'ach nein!' and demonstrated how it should be done. She promised to follow my instructions. But in the concert she did not. She probably thought that once I'm on stage there's no one to stop me singing it how I wish. So it was that, to my fury & the horror of all intelligent music lovers (including Siegfried Ochs, Weingartner, Genée) I had to hear the final phrase performed in a tasteless, offensive, asinine manner. [. . .] But her punishment was swift to follow. The song was such a success that there was tempestuous applause for it to be encored. Mayer asked me to perform it again. I refused. And when I eventually went out onto the stage without the singer, the applause I received was deafening – to the great irritation of the silly goose who wanted to ruin the piece a second time.

HW to B. Schott's Söhne, Vienna, 26 February 1895

Mein Freund, der Fürst Karageorgiewitsch, der meine Spanischen in französischer Sprache in den Pariser Salons singt, mußte zum Beispiel 3 Monate – sage drei Monate warten, ehe ihm der Band des spanischen Liederbuches zugeschickt wurde. Und auch dann erhielt er kein completes Exemplar, wie er wollte, sondern nur die „weltlichen" Spanischen. Beiläufig gesagt, war die Theilung gegen meinen Willen geschehen, denn nach meinem Dafürhalten

---

1 Friederike Mayer (1870–) was a soprano who, despite this incident, continued to promote Wolf's Lieder.
2 From 'In dem Schatten meiner Locken'.
3 Richard Genée (1823–1895), librettist, composer and conductor. It was probably Genée who introduced Wolf to Pedro de Alarcón y Ariza's *The Three-cornered Hat*, which led to the composition of *Der Corregidor*.

sollte es nur einen Band des spanischen Liederbuches geben. Hat je ein Mensch die geistlichen Lieder speziell bei Ihnen bestellt? Ich zweifle.

My friend, Prince Karageorgiewitsch, who sings my Spanish songs in French in Parisian salons, had to wait 3 months – I repeat, three months – before receiving a copy of the *Spanisches Liederbuch*. And even then he did not receive the complete work that he wanted but only the 'secular' songs. By the way, I was against dividing the songs into two sections – in my opinion, the *Spanish Songbook* should only be published as a single volume. Has anyone ever ordered just the sacred songs from you? I doubt it.

HW to Paul Müller, Vienna, 24 February 1896

Etwas anders verhält es sich mit dem Lied „wenn du zu den Blumen gehst"; man kann doch keinen Augenblick im Zweifel sein, ob dieses Stück von einer Frauen od. Männerstimme vorzutragen sei, u. wäre es nur des Textes halber. Frl. Lange wird deshalb gut thun, eine bessere Wahl zu treffen.[1]

It's somewhat different with the song 'Wenn du zu den Blumen gehst'; there can be absolutely no doubt as to whether this should be sung by a man or a woman – if only because of the text. Miss Lange would be advised to make a better choice.

HW to Karl Mayr, Vienna, 10 July 1897

Die in Ihren Volksliedersammlungen stehenden Processionslieder waren nicht zu gebrauchen. Hoernes[2] hat aus meinem spanischen Liederbuch eines der geistlichen Lieder für unsern Zweck ausgewählt [. . .]. Es ist das Lied „führ mich Kind, nach Bethlehem", dessen Klavierbegleitung sozusagen eigentlich schon der geborene Chorsatz ist. Die darüber gehaltene Singstimme wird von einem Vorbeter (Tenor) gesungen. Das muß eine herrliche Wirkung, obenan mit Orgelbegleitung (Positiv) geben.[3]

The processional songs in your folksong collections are not usable. Hoernes has chosen one of the spiritual songs from my *Spanisches Liederbuch* for our purpose [. . .]. It is 'Führ mich, Kind, nach Bethlehem!' whose piano accompaniment is, as it were, made for choral music. The vocal line will be sung by a prayer leader (tenor). The effect will be wonderful, accompanied above by a small chamber organ.

---

1 A purist view in this age of female *Winterreisen*. There are only about a dozen exclusively female songs in the secular part of the *Spanisches Liederbuch* as opposed to some 22 in the *Italienisches Liederbuch*.
2 Moriz Hoernes (1852–1917), librettist of *Manuel Venegas*.
3 The song features in Wolf's handwritten libretto of *Manuel Venegas* but was never set.

HW to Heinrich Potpeschnigg, Vienna, 6 December 1897

Gegenwärtig arbeite ich an der Instrumentation von zehn Liedern aus dem spanischen Liederbuch, die größtenteils zu Beginn des ersten Aktes Venegas vorkommen.[1]

I am at present orchestrating ten songs from the *Spanisches Liederbuch*, which mostly occur at the beginning of the first act of *Venegas*.

LIEDER

Spanisches Liederbuch
nach Heyse und Geibel für eine Singstimme und Klavier

Spanish Songbook
after Heyse and Geibel, for voice and piano

The German texts reproduce the orthography of Geibel and Heyse's first editions.

GEISTLICHE LIEDER[2]	SACRED SONGS
Quiero seguir [1]	
Quiero seguir	Estrella del mar,
á tí, flor de las flores,	puerto de folgura,
siempre decir	remedio de pesar
cantar á tus loores:	é de tristura:
non me partir	venme librar
de te servir,	é confortar,
mejor de las mejores!	Señora de altura!
Grand fianza	Nunca fallece
he yo en tí, Señora,	la tu merced cumplida,
la mi esperanza	siempre guarece
en tí es toda hora:	de cuitas é caida:
de tribulanza	nunca perece
sin tardanza	nin entristece
venme librar agora.	quien á tí non olvida.

---

1   Only two orchestrated songs from the *Spanisches Liederbuch* feature in *Manuel Venegas*: 'Wer sein holdes Lieb verloren' and 'Wenn du zu den Blumen gehst'. 'Führ mich, Kind, nach Bethlehem!' appears in the handwritten libretto, and Wolf also considered using 'Bedeckt mich mit Blumen', but these were never orchestrated.
2   All ten sacred songs were arranged by Max Reger for voice and organ.

EMANUEL GEIBEL

Sufro grand mal
sin merecer á tuerto,
me quejo tal
porque cuido ser muerto:
mas tu me val,

non veo ál
que me saque á puerto.

Juan Ruiz (*fl.* fourteenth century)
(Juan Nicolás Böhl de Faber (ed.), *Floresta de Rimas Antiguas Castellanas*, vol. I, p. 1)

1 Nun bin ich dein

Nun bin ich dein,
Du aller Blumen Blume,
Und sing' allein
Allstund zu deinem Ruhme;
Will eifrig sein,
Mich dir zu weihn
Und deinem Dulderthume.

Frau auserlesen,
Zu dir steht all mein Hoffen,
Mein innerst Wesen
Ist allezeit dir offen.
Komm, mich zu lösen
Vom Fluch des Bösen,
Der mich so hart betroffen!

Du Stern der See,
Du Port der Wonnen,
Von der im Weh
Die Wunden Heil gewonnen,
Eh' ich vergeh,
Blick' aus der Höh,
Du Königin der Sonnen!

Nie kann versiegen
Die Fülle deiner Gnaden;
Du hilfst zum Siegen
Dem, der mit Schmach beladen.
An dich sich schmiegen,
Zu deinen Füßen liegen
Heilt allen Harm und Schaden.

Ich leide schwer
Und wohl verdiente Strafen.
Mir bangt so sehr,
Bald Todesschlaf zu schlafen.
Tritt du einher,
Und durch das Meer
O führe mich zum Hafen!

Translated by Paul Heyse

Now I am thine

Now I am thine,
Thou flower of all flowers,
And shall sing solely
In thy praise always;
I shall zealously
Devote myself to thee
And thy suffering.

O chosen lady,
In thee is all my hope,
My innermost being
To thee is ever open.
Come, deliver me
From the curse of the Evil One
That has so sorely afflicted me!

Thou star of the sea,
Thou haven of delights,
Through whom the afflicted
Can find healing for their wounds,
Before I perish,
Look down on me,
Thou queen of suns!

Never can the abundance
Of thy mercy run dry;
Thou dost help him to victory
Who is laden with shame.
To cling to thee,
To lie at thy feet
Heals all grief and harm.

I suffer heavy
And richly deserved punishments.
I am in such dread
Of sleeping soon the sleep of death.
O draw near to me,
And through the ocean
Bring me, ah, to harbour!

O Vírgen que á Dios pariste [2]

O Vírgen que á Dios pariste,
y nos diste
á todos tan gran victoria;
tórname alegre de triste,
pues podiste
tornar nuestra pena en gloria.

Señora, á tí me convierte
de tal suerte,
que destruyendo mi mal
yo nada tema la muerte,
y pueda verte
en tu trono angelical.

Pues no manchada naciste,
y mereciste
alcanzar tan gran memoria;
torname alegre de triste,
pues podiste
tornar nuestra pena en gloria.

?Nicolás Nuñez (*fl.* fifteenth century)
(Böhl, vol. I, p. 7)

2 Die du Gott gebarst, du Reine

Die du Gott gebarst, du Reine,
Und alleine
Uns gelös't aus unsern Ketten,
Mach mich fröhlich, der ich weine,
Denn nur deine
Huld und Gnade mag uns retten.

Herrin, ganz zu dir mich wende,
Daß sich ende
Diese Qual und dieses Grauen,
Daß der Tod mich furchtlos fände,
Und nicht blende
Mich das Licht der Himmelsauen.

Weil du unbefleckt geboren,
Auserkoren
Zu des ew'gen Ruhmes Stätten –
Wie mich Leiden auch umfloren,

Unverloren
Bin ich doch, willst du mich retten.

Translated by Heyse

Thou who didst bear God, O pure one

Thou who didst bear God, O pure one,
And who alone
Delivered us from our chains,
Make me glad, I who weep,
For only thy
Grace and mercy can save us.

Lady, turn me to thee entirely,
That they might end,
This torment and this dread,
That death might find me unafraid,
And I be not blinded
By the light of the heavenly pastures.

Because thou wert born immaculate,
Chosen
To dwell in eternal glory –
However much sorrow dims my eyes
    with tears,
I am still not lost
If *thou* wilt save me.

Caminad esposa [3]

Caminad esposa,
Vírgen singular,
que los gallos cantan,
cerca está el lugar.

Caminad Señora
bien de todo bien,
que antes de una hora
somos en Belen:

EMANUEL GEIBEL

allá muy bien
podreis reposar,
que los gallos cantan,
cerca está el lugar.

Yo Señora siento
que vais fatigada,
y paso tormento
por veros cansada:
presto habrá posada
do podreis holgar:
que los gallos cantan,
cerca está el lugar.

[Señora, en Belen
ya presto seremos,
que allí habrá bien
dó nos alverguemos:
parientes tenemos
con quien descansar,
que los gallos cantan,
cerca está el lugar.]¹

Ay! Señora mia,
si parida os viese,
de albricias daría
cuanto yo tuviese:
este asno que fuese
holgaria dar,
que los gallos cantan,
cerca está el lugar.

Ocaña (*fl. c.* 1600)
(Böhl, vol. 1, p. 16)

3 Nun wandre, Maria
*Der h. Joseph singt.*²

Nun wandre, Maria,
Nun wandre nur fort.
Schon krähen die Hähne,
Und nah ist der Ort.

Nun wandre, Geliebte,
Du Kleinod mein,
Und balde wir werden
In Bethlehem sein.
Dann ruhest du fein
Und schlummerst dort.
Schon krähen die Hähne
Und nah ist der Ort.

Wohl seh ich, Herrin,
Die Kraft dir schwinden;
Kann deine Schmerzen

Journey on, Mary
Saint Joseph sings.

Journey on, Mary,
Keep journeying.
The cocks are crowing,
And the place is near.

Journey on, beloved,
You, my jewel,
And soon we shall
Be in Bethlehem.
Then shall you rest well
And slumber there.
The cocks are crowing,
And the place is near.

I well see, my lady,
That your strength is failing,
I can hardly, alas,

---

1 Heyse did not translate this stanza: 'My Lady, we shall soon/be in Bethlehem,/where there will be/somewhere we can stay:/we have relatives/we can rest with,/for the cocks are crowing/and the place is near.'
2 See HW to Friedrich Eckstein, 5 November 1889, p. 59. And Luke 2:1–5. The arduousness of the journey is beautifully caught by Wolf's incessant quaver thirds moving up and down the scale in the piano's right hand, expressing the close intimacy of the couple's relationship. Such sequences of thirds also feature in two other songs from the sacred section of the *Spanisches Liederbuch*: 'Ach, des Knaben Augen', in which the Virgin holds the Christ-child on her knee; and 'Führ' mich, Kind, nach Bethlehem!', where there is also a hint of journeying. The solicitous Joseph's anxiety, when he fears that his wife's strength is failing, is touchingly expressed by the troubled harmonies and dislocated rhythm at „Wohl seh ich, Herrin,/Die Kraft dir schwinden".

Ach, kaum verwinden.	Bear your agony.
Getrost! Wohl finden	Courage! We shall find
Wir Herberg dort.	Some shelter there.
Schon krähen die Hähne,	The cocks are crowing,
Und nah ist der Ort.[1]	And the place is near.
Wär' erst bestanden	If only your hour of pain
Dein Stündlein, Marie,	Were over, Mary,
Die gute Botschaft	I should handsomely reward
Gut lohnt' ich sie.	The happy tidings.
Das Eselein hie	This little ass here
Gäb' ich drum fort!	I'd gladly give away!
Schon krähen die Hähne,	The cocks are crowing,
Komm! Nah ist der Ort.	Come! The place is near.

Translated by Heyse

Pues andais en las palmas [4]

Pues andais en las palmas,
Ángeles santos,
que se duerme mi niño,
tened los ramos.

Palmas de Belen,
que mueven airados
los furiosos vientos
que suenan tanto,
no le hagais ruido,
corred mas paso:
que se duerme mi niño,
tened los ramos.

El niño divino
que está cansado
de llorar en la tierra,
por su descanso
sosegar quiere un poco
del tierno llanto:
que se duerme mi niño,
tened los ramos.

Rigurosos hielos
le estan cercando,
ya veis que no tengo
con que guardarlo:
Ángeles divinos
que vais volando,
que se duerme mi niño,
tened los ramos.

Lope de Vega (1562–1613)
(Böhl, vol. III, p. 13)

4 Die ihr schwebet[2,3]

Die ihr schwebet	Ye who hover
Um diese Palmen	About these palms
In Nacht und Wind,	In night and wind,
Ihr heil'gen Engel,	Ye holy angels,
Stillet die Wipfel!	Silence the treetops!
Es schlummert mein Kind.	My child is sleeping.

1 Heyse does not translate Ocaña's penultimate stanza (not included here).
2 See HW to Melanie Köchert, 19 October 1890, p. 60.
3 The song is sung as a lullaby in the pastoral novel *Los Pastores de Bélen* (1612).

Ihr Palmen von Bethlehem	You palms of Bethlehem
Im Windesbrausen,	In the raging wind,
Wie mögt ihr heute	Why do you bluster
So zornig sausen!	So angrily today?
O rauscht nicht also!	Oh roar not so!
Schweiget, neiget	Be still, lean
Euch leis' und lind;	Calmly and gently over us;
Stillet die Wipfel!	Silence the treetops!
Es schlummert mein Kind.	My child is sleeping.
Der Himmelsknabe	The heavenly babe
Duldet Beschwerde,	Bears many burdens,
Ach, wie so müd' er ward	Ah, how weary he has grown
Vom Leid der Erde.	With the sorrows of this world.
Ach nun im Schlaf ihm	Ah, now that in sleep
Leise gesänftigt	His pains
Die Qual zerrinnt,	Are gently eased,
Stillet die Wipfel!	Silence the treetops!
Es schlummert mein Kind.	My child is sleeping.
Grimmige Kälte	Bitter cold winds
Sauset hernieder,	Blow down on us,
Womit nur deck' ich	With what shall I cover
Des Kindleins Glieder!	My little child's limbs?
O all ihr Engel,	O all ye angels
Die ihr geflügelt	Who wing your way
Wandelt im Wind,	On the winds,
Stillet die Wipfel!	Silence the treetops!
Es schlummert mein Kind.	My child is sleeping.

Translated by Emanuel Geibel
Also set by Johannes Brahms

Llevadme, niño, á Belen [5]

Llevadme, niño, á Belen,
que os deseo ver, mi Dios,
y no hay quien
pueda ir á vos sin vos.

Movedme porque despierte,
para que vaya llamadme,
dadme la mano y guiadme
porque á caminar acierte:
asi llegaré á Belen
donde os quiero ver, mi Dios,
que no hay quien
pueda ir á vos sin vos.

La enfermedad del pecado
tan torpe me tiene hecho,
que no doy paso derecho
sin ser de vos ayudado:
llevadme pues á Belen
donde os contemple, mi Dios,
pues no hay quien
pueda ir á vos sin vos.

Anon.
(Böhl, vol. II, p. 37)

5 Führ mich, Kind, nach Bethlehem![1]

Führ mich, Kind, nach Bethlehem!
Dich, mein Gott, dich will ich sehn.
Wem geläng' es, wem,
Ohne dich zu dir zu gehn!

Rüttle mich, daß ich erwache,
Rufe mich, so will ich schreiten;
Gieb die Hand mir, mich zu leiten,
Daß ich auf den Weg mich mache.
Daß ich schaue Bethlehem,
Dorten meinen Gott zu sehn.
Wem geläng' es, wem,
Ohne dich zu dir zu gehn!

Von der Sünde schwerem Kranken
Bin ich träg' und dumpf beklommen.
Willst du nicht zu Hülfe kommen,
Muß ich straucheln, muß ich schwanken.
Leite mich nach Bethlehem,
Dich, mein Gott, dich will ich sehn.
Wem geläng' es, wem,
Ohne dich zu dir zu gehn!

Translated by Heyse

Lead me, child, to Bethlehem!

Lead me, child, to Bethlehem!
Thee, my God, thee will I see.
Who could ever come to thee,
Without thy help!

Shake me that I might wake,
Call me, and I shall come;
Stretch forth thy hand to guide me,
That I might set out,
That I might gaze on Bethlehem,
There to see my God.
Who could ever come to thee,
Without thy help!

I am sorely oppressed and weighed down
With the grievous sickness of sin.
If thou wilt not come to my aid,
I must stumble, I must falter.
Lead me to Bethlehem!
Thee, my God, thee will I see.
Who could ever come to thee,
Without thy help!

Los ojos del niño [6]

Los ojos del niño son
graciosos lindos y bellos,
y tiene un no sé qué en ellos
que me roba el corazon.

Pídole quiera mirarme
porque viéndose él en mí,
el mirar y amarse allí
es mirar por mi y amarme:
mis ojos van con razon
tras los del niño tan bellos,
pues tiene un no sé qué en ellos
que me roba el corazon.

Juan López de Ubeda (*fl.* fourteenth century)
(Böhl, vol. II, p. 40)

6 Ach, des Knaben Augen

Ach, des Knaben Augen sind
Mir so schön und klar erschienen,
Und ein Etwas strahlt aus ihnen,
Das mein ganzes Herz gewinnt.

Ah, the Infant's eyes

Ah, the Infant's eyes seem
So beautiful and clear to me,
And a radiance streams from them
That captures my whole heart.

---

1 See HW to Karl Mayr, 10 July 1897, and to Heinrich Potpeschnigg, 6 December 1897, pp. 63 and 64.

EMANUEL GEIBEL

Blickt' er doch mit diesen süßen
Augen nach den meinen hin!
Säh' er dann sein Bild darin,
Würd' er wohl mich liebend grüßen.
Und so geb' ich ganz mich hin,
Seinen Augen nur zu dienen,
Denn ein Etwas strahlt aus ihnen,
Das mein ganzes Herz gewinnt.

Translated by Heyse

If only he would turn
Those sweet eyes on mine!
If then he saw his image reflected there,
He would surely greet me lovingly.
So I surrender myself
To the sole service of his eyes,
For a radiance shines from them
That captures my whole heart.

7 Mühvoll komm' ich und beladen

In toil I come and heavy laden

Mühvoll komm' ich und beladen,
Nimm mich an, du Hort der Gnaden!

Sieh, ich komm' in Thränen heiß
Mit demüthiger Geberde,
Dunkel ganz vom Staub der Erde.
Du nur schaffest, daß ich weiß
Wie das Vließ der Lämmer werde.
Tilgen willst du ja den Schaden
Dem, der reuig dich umfaßt;
Nimm denn, Herr, von mir die Last,
Mühvoll komm' ich und beladen.

Laß mich flehend vor dir knie'n,
Daß ich über deine Füße
Nardenduft und Thränen gieße,
Gleich dem Weib, dem du verziehn,
Bis die Schuld wie Rauch zerfließe.
Der den Schächer du geladen:
„Heute noch in Edens Bann
Wirst du sein!" o nimm mich an,
Nimm mich an, du Hort der Gnaden!

Don Manuel del Rio[1]

In toil I come and heavy laden,
Receive me, O haven of mercy!

See, I come with burning tears
And humble mien,
All blackened with the dust of earth.
Thou alone canst make me white
As the fleece of lambs.
Thou shalt eradicate the wrongs
Of the penitent who embraces thee;
Take, then, Lord, the burden from me,
In toil I come and heavy laden.

Let me kneel before thee, pleading,
That I might anoint thy feet
With scented spikenard and tears,
Like that woman thou didst forgive,
Until my guilt disperses like smoke.
Thou who didst once tell the thief,
'Today shalt thou be with me
In Paradise!' – O take me,
Receive me, O haven of mercy!

---

1 Margaret G. Sleeman and Gareth A. Davies in 'The *Spanisches Liederbuch* of Emanuel Geibel and Paul Heyse and Its Reflection in the Songs of Hugo Wolf' argue convincingly that Don Manuel (Emanuel!) del Rio is none other than Emanuel Geibel. There is therefore no Spanish text.

Mucho ha que el alma duerme [8]

Mucho ha que el alma duerme,
bien será que recuerde.

Duerme sueño tan pesado
que como muerta cayó
luego que la adormeció
el veneno del pecado:
y pues el sol deseado
en los ojos ya le hiere,
bien será que recuerde.

Si ángeles no han podido
despertarla con cantar,
despierte, oyendo llorar
á Dios por ella nacido:
muy larga noche ha dormido,
y pues tal dia le viene,
bien será que recuerde.

Anon.
(Böhl, vol. I, p. 25)

8 Ach, wie lang die Seele schlummert! Ah, how long the soul has slumbered!

Ach, wie lang die Seele schlummert!
Zeit ist's, daß sie sich ermuntre.

Daß man todt sie wähnen dürfte,
Also schläft sie schwer und bang,
Seit sie jener Rausch bezwang,
Den im Sündengift sie schlürfte.
Doch nun ihrer Sehnsucht Licht
Blendend ihr ins Auge bricht:
Zeit ist's, daß sie sich ermuntre.

Mochte sie gleich taub erscheinen
Bei der Engel süßem Chor:
Lauscht sie doch wohl zag empor,
Hört sie Gott als Kindlein weinen.
Da nach langer Schlummernacht
Solch ein Tag der Gnad' ihr lacht,
Zeit ist's, daß sie sich ermuntre.

Translated by Geibel

Ah, how long the soul has slumbered!
It is time it roused itself.

Though it might be considered dead,
It has sunk into deep and fearful sleep,
Since overcome by that intoxication
Which it quaffed from the cup of sin.
But now the longed-for light
Breaks through and dazzles its eyes:
It is time it roused itself.

Though the soul seemed deaf
To the sweet angelic choirs,
If it timidly hearkens,
It will hear God weep like a little child.
After a long night of sleep,
Such a day of mercy now smiles on it,
That it is time it roused itself.

Qué producirá mi Dios [9]

Qué producirá mi Dios
tierra que regais asi?
'Las espinas para mí,
'y las flores para vos.'

Regada con tales fuentes
jardin se habrá de hacer!
'Sí, mas de él se han de coger
'guirnaldas muy diferentes.'

Cuyas han de ser, mi Dios,
esas guirnaldas, decí?
'Las de espinas para mí,
'las de flores para vos.'

Anon.
(Böhl, vol. I, p. 31)

9 Herr, was trägt der Boden hier[1,2]

Herr, was trägt der Boden hier,
Den du tränkst so bitterlich?
„Dornen, liebes Herz, für mich,
Und für dich der Blumen Zier."

Ach, wo solche Bäche rinnen,
Wird ein Garten da gedeihn?
„Ja, und wisse! Kränzelein,
Gar verschiedne, flicht man drinnen."
O mein Herr, zu wessen Zier
Windet man die Kränze? sprich!
„Die von Dornen sind für mich,
Die von Blumen reich' ich dir."

Translated by Geibel

Lord, what will the earth bring forth

Lord, what will the earth bring forth,
That you water with such bitter tears?
'Thorns, dear heart, for me,
And for you exquisite flowers.'

Ah, where such streams flow,
Can a garden flourish there?
'Yes, and know! Wreaths in great variety
Will be woven there.'
O my Lord, for whose adornment
Will the wreaths be woven, say?
'Those of thorns are for me,
Those of flowers I give to you.'

Feridas teneis mi vida [10]

Feridas teneis mi vida
y duélenvos:
tuviéralas yo y no vos!

Quien os puso de esa suerte,
mi Jesus enamorado?
'Ay que caro me ha costado,
'alma, buscarte y quererte:
'mis heridas son de muerte
'aunque dadas por tu amor.'
Feridas teneis mi vida
y duélenvos:
tuviéralas yo y no vos!

Fuera yo, Señor, la herida,
si son de muerte las vuestras.
'Pues que dolor de ellas muestras
'alma, llámalas de vida,

'que no veras en mi herida
'donde vida no te doy.'
Feridas teneis mi vida
y duélenvos:
tuviéralas yo y no vos!

Ay! como me han lastimado
las heridas que en vos veo!
'Para las que yo deseo
'pocas son las que me han dado,
'que no es buen enamorado
'el que no muere de amor.'
Feridas teneis mi vida
y duélenvos:
tuviéralas yo y no vos!

José de Valdivielso (1560–1638)
(Böhl, vol. 1, p. 37)

---

1   The scene is the Garden of Gethsemane where Christ keeps his lonely vigil. Geibel and Heyse had placed the poem after 'Wunden trägst du, mein Geliebter'; Wolf, by placing it before that poem, anticipates the Crucifixion – to memorable effect.
2   Stravinsky made an orchestral arrangement of the song, published by Boosey & Hawkes in 1969.

10 Wunden trägst du, mein Geliebter[1]

Wunden trägst du, mein Geliebter,
Und sie schmerzen dich;
Trüg' ich sie statt deiner, ich!

Herr, wer wagt' es, so zu färben
Deine Stirn mit Blut und Schweiß?
   „Diese Male sind der Preis,
Dich, o Seele, zu erwerben.
An den Wunden muß ich sterben,
Weil ich dich geliebt so heiß."

Könnt' ich, Herr, für dich sie tragen,
Da es Todeswunden sind.
   „Wenn dies Leid dich rührt, mein Kind,
Magst du Lebenswunden sagen:
Ihrer keine ward geschlagen,
Draus für dich nicht Leben rinnt."

Ach, wie mir in Herz und Sinnen
Deine Qual so wehe thut!
   „Härtres noch mit treuem Muth
Trüg' ich froh, dich zu gewinnen;
Denn nur der weiß recht zu minnen,
Der da stirbt vor Liebesglut."

Wunden trägst du, mein Geliebter,
Und sie schmerzen dich;
Trüg' ich sie statt deiner, ich!

Translated by Geibel

Thou art wounded, my beloved

Thou art wounded, my beloved,
And dost suffer pain;
Would I could bear it for thee!

Lord, who dares so to stain
Thy brow with blood and sweat?
   'These marks are the price
Of redeeming you, O soul.
From these wounds I must die
For my great love of you.'

O could I bear them, Lord, for thee,
For they are mortal wounds.
   'If this suffering moves thee, child,
You may call them living wounds;
Not one of them was made, from which
Life does not flow for you.'

Ah, how my heart and mind
Ache with thy anguish!
   'Harsher yet with true courage,
I'd gladly endure to redeem you;
For he alone knows how to love
Who has died for ardent love.'

Thou art wounded, my beloved,
And dost suffer pain;
Would I could bear it for thee!

WELTLICHE LIEDER

Tango vos, el mi pandero [1]

Tango vos, el mi pandero,
tango vos y pienso en al.

Si tu, pandero, supieses
mi dolor y le sintieses,
el sonido que hicieses
seria llorar mi mal.

Cuando taño este instrumento
es con fuerza de tormento,

SECULAR SONGS

por quitar del pensamiento
la memoria de este mal.

En mi corazon, Señores,
son continos los dolores,
los cantares son clamores:
tango vos y pienso en al.

Alvaro Fernandez de Almeida
(*fl.* sixteenth century)
(Böhl, vol. I, p. 289)

---

1 Stravinsky made an orchestral arrangement of the song, published by Boosey & Hawkes in 1969.

1 Klinge, klinge, mein Pandero

Klinge, klinge, mein Pandero,
Doch an andres denkt mein Herz.

Wenn du, muntres Ding, verständest
Meine Qual und sie empfändest,
Jeder Ton, den du entsendest,
Würde klagen meinen Schmerz.

Bei des Tanzes Drehn und Neigen
Schlag' ich wild den Takt zum Reigen,
Daß nur die Gedanken schweigen,
Die mich mahnen an den Schmerz.

Ach, ihr Herrn, dann will im Schwingen
Oftmals mir die Brust zerspringen,
Und zum Angstschrei wird mein Singen,
Denn an andres denkt mein Herz.

Translated by Geibel
Also set by Ferdinand Hiller, Adolf Jensen, Franz Lachner, Anton Rubinstein and Robert Schumann[1]

Ring out, ring out, my tambourine

Ring out, ring out, my tambourine,
Though my heart thinks of other things.

If you, blithe instrument, could understand
And feel my torment,
Each one of your sounds
Would bewail my grief.

As the dance whirls and dips,
I beat out wildly the dancers' rhythm,
Simply in order to silence the thoughts
That remind me of my grief.

Ah, good sirs, while I whirl around,
My heart often feels like breaking,
And my song becomes a cry of anguish,
For my heart thinks of other things.

Á la sombra de mis cabellos [2]

Á la sombra de mis cabellos
mi querido se adurmió:
si le recordaré ó no?

Peinaba yo mis cabellos
con cuidado cada dia,
y el viento los esparcia
revolviéndose con ellos,
y á su soplo y sombra de ellos
mi querido se adurmió:
si le recordaré ó no?

Diceme que le da pena
el ser en extremo ingrata,
que le da vida y le mata
esta mi color morena,
y llamándome sirena
él junto á mí se adurmió:
si le recordaré ó no?

Anon.
(Böhl, vol. 1, p. 283)

2 In dem Schatten meiner Locken[2]

In dem Schatten meiner Locken
Schlief mir mein Geliebter ein.
Weck' ich ihn nun auf? – Ach nein!

In the shadow of my tresses

In the shadow of my tresses
My lover has fallen asleep.
Shall I wake him now? – Ah no!

---

1 In his SSAA setting from Op. 69 ('Tamburinschlägerin') Schumann uses Eichendorff's translation of the poem.
2 Wolf incorporated 'In dem Schatten meiner Locken' into Act I of *Der Corregidor* (1895): Frasquita sings it to the amorous magistrate, to trick him into believing that her husband Lukas is asleep. The ploy works, and Frasquita begins to flirt with the Corregidor in the hope that he will find her nephew

Sorglich strählt' ich meine krausen
Locken täglich in der Frühe,
Doch umsonst ist meine Mühe,
Weil die Winde sie zerzausen.[1]
Lockenschatten, Windessausen
Schläferten den Liebsten ein.
Weck' ich ihn nun auf? – Ach nein!

Hören muß ich, wie ihn gräme,
Daß er schmachtet schon so lange,
Daß ihm Leben geb' und nehme
Diese meine braune Wange.
Und er nennt mich seine Schlange,
Und doch schlief er bei mir ein.
Weck' ich ihn nun auf? – Ach nein![2]

Translated by Heyse
Also set by Brahms and Jensen

Carefully I combed my curly tresses
Early each morning,
But my efforts are in vain,
For the winds tousle them.
Shadowing tresses, sighing breezes
Have lulled my lover to sleep.
Shall I wake him now? – Ah no!

I shall have to hear how he grieves,
How he has languished so long,
How his whole life depends
On these my dusky cheeks.
And he calls me his snake,
And yet he fell asleep at my side.
Shall I wake him now? – Ah no!

Estraño humor tiene Iuana [3]

Estraño humor tiene Iuana,
que quando mas triste estoy,
si suspiro, y digo oy,
ella responde Mañana.

Si me alegro, se entristece,
y canta, si ve que lloro,
y si digo que la adoro,
responde que me aborrece,
y en vella tan inhumana,
forçoso a morir estoy,
si suspiro, y digo oy,
ella responde Mañana.

Si alço mis ojos por vella,
baxa los suyos al suelo,
y presto los sube al cielo,
si los baxo como ella:
si digo que es soberana,
dize, que demonio soy,
si suspiro, y digo oy,
ella responde Mañana.

Por vencido me condena,
quando pretendo vitoria,
y si pido al cielo gloria,
me promete infierno y pena:
y es tan cruel y tyrana,
que si vee que a morir voy,
y suspirando digo oy,
ella responde mañana.

Anon.
(Not in Böhl)

3 Seltsam ist Juanas Weise

Seltsam ist Juanas Weise.
Wenn ich steh' in Traurigkeit,
Wenn ich seufz' und sage: heut,
„Morgen" spricht sie leise.

Juana's ways are strange

Juana's ways are strange.
When I am sad,
When I sigh and say, 'Today',
She murmurs, 'Tomorrow.'

---

a job. When the Corregidor attempts to kiss her, Frasquita eludes his embrace, trips and falls to the ground. Lukas pretends to have been awoken by the noise.
1 Wolf's first edition has 'zersausen'.   2 See HW to Melanie Köchert, 6 March 1892, p. 62.

EMANUEL GEIBEL

Trüb' ist sie, wenn ich mich freue; | She is gloomy when I am glad;
Lustig singt sie, wenn ich weine; | She sings merrily when I weep;
Sag' ich, daß sie hold mir scheine, | When I say I think her beautiful,
Spricht sie, daß sie stets mich scheue. | She says I always fill her with dread.
Solcher Grausamkeit Beweise | Such tokens of cruelty
Brechen mir das Herz in Leid – | Crush my heart in grief –
Wenn ich seufz' und sage: heut, | When I sigh and say, 'Today',
„Morgen" spricht sie leise. | She murmurs, 'Tomorrow.'

Heb' ich meine Augenlider,[1] | Whenever I raise my gaze,
Weiß sie stets den Blick zu senken; | She always contrives to lower hers;
Um ihn gleich emporzulenken, | Only to look up at me
Schlag' ich auch den meinen nieder. | As soon as I look down.
Wenn ich sie als Heil'ge preise, | When I call her a saint,
Nennt sie Dämon mich im Streit – | She, to be contrary, calls me a devil.
Wenn ich seufz' und sage: heut, | When I sigh and say, 'Today',
„Morgen" spricht sie leise. | She murmurs, 'Tomorrow.'

Sieglos heiß' ich auf der Stelle, | She calls me a failure on the spot,
Rühm' ich meinen Sieg bescheiden; | If modestly I claim a victory;
Hoff' ich auf des Himmels Freuden, | If I hope for heaven's joy,
Prophezeit sie mir die Hölle. | She prophesies me hell.
Ja, so ist ihr Herz von Eise, | Yes, so icy is her heart,
Säh' sie sterben mich vor Leid, | That if she saw me dying of grief
Hörte mich noch seufzen: heut, | And heard me sigh, 'Today',
„Morgen" spräch' sie leise. | She would murmur, 'Tomorrow.'

Translated by Geibel

Burla bien con desamor [4]

Burla bien con desamor
senyora ya
pues algun dia la mor
te burlara.

Burla bien quanto quisieres
y mandares
que la muger da plazeres
y pesares
burla bien del amor
senyora ya
pues algun dia la mor
te burlara.

Mira que si estas liberta
algun dia
Cupido te hara desierta

de alegria,
si burlas de mi dolor
señor[a] ya
pues algun dia la mor
te burlara.

Sepa el que carne vistiere
tenga auiso
que Cupido calla y hiere
de improuiso
burlate con disfauor
senyora ya
pues algun dia la mor
te burlara.

Anon.
(Not in Böhl)

---

1 Geibel: Augenlieder.

4 Treibe nur mit Lieben Spott

Treibe nur mit Lieben Spott,
Geliebte mein;
Spottet doch der Liebesgott
Dereinst auch dein!

Magst an Spotten nach Gefallen
Du dich weiden;
Von dem Weibe kommt uns Allen
Lust und Leiden.
Treibe nur mit Lieben Spott,
Geliebte mein;
Spottet doch der Liebesgott
Dereinst auch dein!

Bist auch jetzt zu stolz zum Minnen,
Glaub', o glaube:
Liebe wird dich doch gewinnen
Sich zum Raube,
Wenn du spottest meiner Noth,
Geliebte mein;
Spottet doch der Liebesgott
Dereinst auch dein!

Wer da lebt im Fleisch, erwäge
Alle Stunden:
Amor schläft und plötzlich rege
Schlägt er Wunden.
Treibe nur mit Lieben Spott,
Geliebte mein;
Spottet doch der Liebesgott
Dereinst auch dein!

Translated by Heyse

Just keep on mocking love

Just keep on mocking love,
My beloved;
But the god of love will mock
You one day too!

You can mock away
To your heart's content;
Women bring us all
Pleasure and pain.
Just keep on mocking love,
My beloved;
But the god of love will mock
You one day too!

Though you are now too proud to love,
You may rest assured:
Love will yet seize you
As its prey,
If you mock at my distress,
My beloved;
The god of love will mock
You one day too!

Let he who lives in the flesh
Always ponder this:
Cupid sleeps and will suddenly wake
And wound you.
Just keep on mocking love,
My beloved;
But the god of love will mock
You one day too!

5 Auf dem grünen Balkon[1]

Auf dem grünen Balkon mein Mädchen
Schaut nach mir durchs Gitterlein.
Mit den Augen blinzelt sie freundlich,
Mit dem Finger sagt sie mir: Nein!

Glück, das nimmer ohne Wanken
Junger Liebe folgt hienieden,
Hat mir Eine Lust beschieden,
Und auch da noch muß ich schwanken.

From her green balcony

From her green balcony my love
Peeps at me through the trellis.
Her eyes wink invitingly,
But her finger says: No!

Fortune, that never here on earth
Lets the course of young love run smooth,
Has granted me *one* joy,
But even so I am still in doubt.

---

1   No Spanish source can be traced. Sleeman and Davies suggest that the poem could be by Heyse. Heyse has 'Balcon' throughout.

NO STANZA BREAK

Schmeicheln hör' ich oder Zanken,	Sometimes I hear flattery, sometimes petulance
Komm' ich an ihr Fensterlädchen.	When I come to her shuttered window.
Immer nach dem Brauch der Mädchen	That is always the way with women,
Träuft ins Glück ein bischen Pein:	Mixing a drop of sadness into pleasure:
Mit den Augen blinzelt sie freundlich,	Her eyes wink invitingly,
Mit dem Finger sagt sie mir: Nein!	But her finger says: No!
Wie sich nur in ihr vertragen	How can she reconcile
Ihre Kälte, meine Glut?	Her coldness, my fire?
Weil in ihr mein Himmel ruht,	Because she is my heaven,
Seh' ich Trüb und Hell sich jagen.	I see darkness vie with light.
In den Wind gehn meine Klagen,	The wind bears away my lament
Daß noch nie die süße Kleine	That my little sweet
Ihre Arme schlang um meine;	Has never yet embraced me.
Doch sie hält mich hin so fein, –	Yet she puts me off so neatly –
Mit den Augen blinzelt sie freundlich,	Her eyes wink invitingly,
Mit dem Finger sagt sie mir: Nein!	But her finger says: No!

Niña si a la huerta vas [6]

Niña si a la huerta vas,	Tus labios le quitarán
coge las flores mas bellas,	a la rosa su belleza,
aunque si tu estás entre ellas,	pues donde tu gracia empieça
a ti misma escogeras.	las de otras acabarán.
	Y si ya dispuesta estás
Conociendo tu valor,	de yr a coger flores bellas,
tu grandeza, y excelencia,	si tu estuuieres entre ellas
qualquier flor en tu presencia	a ti misma escogeras.
perderá de su color.	
Y assi si a la huerta vas,	
y has de coger flores bellas,	
por ser tu la mejor dellas,	Anon.
a ti misma escogeras.	(Not in Böhl)

6 Wenn du zu den Blumen gehst [1,2]   When you go to the flowers

Wenn du zu den Blumen gehst,	When you go to the flowers,
Pflücke die schönsten, dich zu schmücken.	Pluck the loveliest to adorn yourself.
Ach, wenn d u in dem Gärtlein stehst,	Ah, if *you* grew in the garden,
Müßtest du dich selber pflücken.	You would have to pluck yourself.
Alle Blumen wissen ja,	All the flowers know well
Daß du hold bist ohne gleichen.	That you are lovely beyond compare.
Und die Blume, die dich sah –	And the flower that saw you

---

1 The song was orchestrated for inclusion in Wolf's *Manuel Venegas*.
2 See HW to Paul Müller, 24 February 1896, p. 63.

Farb' und Schmuck muß ihr erbleichen.
Wenn du zu den Blumen gehst,
Pflücke die schönsten, dich zu schmücken.
Ach, wenn d u in dem Gärtlein stehst,
Müßtest du dich selber pflücken.

Lieblicher als Rosen sind
Küsse, die dein Mund verschwendet,
Weil der Reiz der Blumen endet,
Wo d e i n Liebreiz erst beginnt.
Wenn du zu den Blumen gehst,
Pflücke die schönsten, dich zu schmücken.
Ach, wenn d u in dem Gärtlein stehst,
Müßtest du dich selber pflücken.

Translated by Heyse
Also set by Jensen and Karl Taubert

Would fade in colour and splendour.
When you go to the flowers,
Pluck the loveliest to adorn yourself.
Ah, if *you* grew in the garden,
You would have to pluck yourself.

Lovelier than roses are
The kisses your lips bestow,
For the charm of flowers ceases
Where *your* fair charms begin.
When you go to the flowers,
Pluck the loveliest to adorn yourself.
Ah, if *you* grew in the garden,
You would have to pluck yourself.

Quien gentil señora pierde [7]

Quien gentil señora pierde
por falta de conocer,
nunca debiera nacer.

Perdíla dentro de un huerto
cogiendo rosas y flores,
su lindo rostro cubierto
de vergonzosos colores:
ella me habló de amores,
no le supe responder:
nunca debiera nacer!

Perdíla dentro de un huerto
hablando de sus amores,
y yo simplon inexperto
callábale mis dolores:
desmayóse entre las flores,
no me supe valer:
nunca debiera nacer!

Anon.
(Böhl, vol. I, p. 280)

7 Wer sein holdes Lieb verloren[1]

Wer sein holdes Lieb verloren,
Weil er Liebe nicht versteht,
Besser wär' er nie geboren.

Ich verlor sie dort im Garten,
Da sie Rosen brach und Blüten.
Hell auf ihren Wangen glühten
Scham und Lust in holder Zier.
Und von Liebe sprach sie mir;
Doch ich größter aller Thoren
Wußte keine Antwort ihr –
Wär' ich nimmermehr geboren.

Whoever has lost his loved one

Whoever has lost his loved one
Through not understanding love –
Better he had never been born.

I lost her in the garden there,
As she was picking rosès and blossoms.
Her cheeks were glowing brightly,
Graced by modesty and joy.
And she spoke to me of love;
But I, the greatest of fools,
Knew not how to answer her –
Better I had never been born!

1 The song was orchestrated for inclusion in *Manuel Venegas*.

Ich verlor sie dort im Garten,
Da sie sprach von Liebesplagen,
Denn ich wagte nicht zu sagen,
Wie ich ganz ihr eigen bin.
In die Blumen sank sie hin,[1]
Doch ich größter aller Thoren
Zog auch davon nicht Gewinn –
Wär' ich nimmermehr geboren!

I lost her in the garden there,
As she spoke of the pangs of love,
For I dared not tell her
How utterly I was hers.
She sank down among the flowers,
But I, the greatest of fools,
Gained nothing from that either –
Better I had never been born!

Translated by Geibel

Las tierras corrí [8]

Las tierras corrí,
los mares pasé,
ventura busqué,
no la hay para mí:
todos cuantos ví
salen con ventura,
para mí ninguna.

La pena sufria
por mi pasatiempo;
pensaba que un tiempo
tras otro venia:
la ventura mia
trocóse en fortuna,
para mí ninguna.

Ventura buscaba,
fortuna tenia,
razon pedia,
amor la negaba:
mi fe firme estaba,
mas no mi ventura,
pues no veo ninguna.

Anon.
(Not in Böhl)

8 Ich fuhr über Meer

I sailed the seas

Ich fuhr über Meer,
Ich zog über Land,
Das Glück das fand
Ich nimmermehr.
Die Andern umher
Wie jubelten sie! –
Ich jubelte nie![2]

I sailed the seas,
I marched over land,
Without ever
Finding happiness.
How all the others
Rejoiced all around! –
I never rejoiced!

Nach Glück ich jagte,
An Leiden krankt' ich;
Als Recht verlangt' ich
Was Liebe versagte.
Ich hofft' und wagte –
Kein Glück mir gedieh,
Und so schaut' ich es nie!

I hunted fortune,
I fell ill with grief;
I demanded as a right
What love denied.
I hoped and dared –
No fortune favoured me,
And so I never glimpsed it!

---

1   See HW to Käthe Wolf, 7 January 1891, p. 61.   2   Heyse: Und ich jubelte nie.

Trug ohne Klage	I bore uncomplaining
Die Leiden, die bösen,	The terrible pain,
Und dacht', es lösen	And thought the bad
Sich ab die Tage.	Days would pass by.
Die fröhlichen Tage	But it's the happy days
Wie eilen sie! –	That speed past! –
Ich ereilte sie nie!	I never caught them up!

Translated by Heyse

Vista ciega, luz oscura [9]

Vista ciega, luz oscura,
gloria triste, vida muerta,
ventura de desventura,
lloro alegre, risa incierta:
hiel sabrosa, dulce agrura,
paz con ira y saña presta

es amor, con vestidura
de gloria que pena cuesta.

Rodrigo de Cota (*fl.* 1510)
(Böhl, vol. I, p. 301)

9 Blindes Schauen, dunkle Leuchte[1]

Blindes Schauen, dunkle Leuchte,	Blind seeing, dark light,
Ruhm voll Weh, erstorbnes Leben,	Sad glory, dead life,
Unheil, das ein Heil mir däuchte,	Disaster that seemed salvation,
Freud'ges Weinen, Lust voll Beben,	Joyful weeping, fearful pleasure,
Süße Galle, durst'ge Feuchte,	Sweet gall, parched moisture,
Krieg in Frieden allerwegen,	War in peace, everywhere, always –
Liebe, falsch versprachst du Segen,	False, O Love, was your promise of bliss,
Da dein Fluch den Schlaf mir scheuchte.	For your curse has deprived me of sleep.

Translated by Heyse

Iuramentos por amores [10]

Iuramentos por amores
amor no son valedores.

En las cortes de la mor
haueys de saber señor
que ay juyzios de fauor
y tambien de disfauores:
juramentos por amores
amor no son valedores.

Vereys alli descontentos
hazer dos mil juramentos
y como no ay fundamentos
van se con mayo y sus flores:
juramentos por amores
amor no son valedores.

Vereys pues los escriuanos
que son pensiamentos vanos

---

1 Geibel's translation ('Dunkler Sichtglanz') from 1843, set by Schumann as Op. 138/10, was replaced by Heyse's version.

tener tan ligeras manos
que scriuen dos mil errores:
juramentos por amores
amor no son valedores.

Y quando tienen audiencia
en presencia, o en ausencia

si pronuncian la sentencia
no executan sus rigores:
juramentos por amores
amor no son valedores.

Anon.
(Not in Böhl)

10 Eide, so die Liebe schwur[1]

Eide, so die Liebe schwur,
Schwache Bürgen sind sie nur.

Sitzt die Liebe zu Gericht,
Dann, Señor, vergesset nicht,
Daß sie nie nach Recht und Pflicht,
Immer nur nach Gunst verfuhr.
Eide, so die Liebe schwur,
Schwache Bürgen sind sie nur.

Werdet dort Betrübte finden,
Die mit Schwüren sich verbinden,
Die verschwinden mit den Winden,
Wie die Blumen auf der Flur.
Eide, so die Liebe schwur,
Schwache Bürgen sind sie nur.

Und als Schreiber an den Schranken
Seht ihr nichtige Gedanken.
Weil die leichten Händlein schwanken,
Schreibt euch keiner nach der Schnur.
Eide, so die Liebe schwur,
Schwache Bürgen sind sie nur.

Sind die Bürgen gegenwärtig,
Allesammt des Spruchs gewärtig,
Machen sie das Urtheil fertig; –
Von Vollziehen keine Spur!
Eide, so die Liebe schwur,
Schwache Bürgen sind sie nur.

Translated by Heyse

Oaths that love has sworn

Oaths that love has sworn
Are but feeble sureties.

When Love sits in judgment,
Then, Señor, do not forget,
That she proceeds not by right or duty,
But always by favour.
Oaths that love has sworn
Are but feeble sureties.

There you will find the distressed,
Binding themselves with vows,
Which vanish with the wind
Like flowers on the meadow.
Oaths that love has sworn
Are but feeble sureties.

And as clerks of the court
You'll find empty thoughts.
Because their feeble hands tremble,
They will not record you accurately.
Oaths that love has sworn
Are but feeble sureties.

When the evidence is given
And all await a verdict,
They will prepare the judgment; –
But never execute it!
Oaths that love has sworn
Are but feeble sureties.

---

[1] Wolf considered this song to be the 'crown' of the *Spanisches Liederbuch*. See HW to Melanie Köchert, 31 March 1890, p. 59.

Coraçon no desesperes [11]

Coraçon no desesperes
que mugeres son mugeres.

No te fies mucho en ellas
porque parescen estrellas
y son de fuego centellas
por tanto no desesperes
que mugeres son mugeres.

No fies de sus razones
que canten dulces canciones
y tienen mil inuenciones
y otros tantos paresceres
que mugeres son mugeres.

Ellas conellas conuienen
de palabras se mantienen
dessean lo que no tienen
prueuante por si las quieres
que mugeres son mugeres.

Tienen el seso tan vario
que si hablays lo necessario
ella quieren lo contrario
aunque quieren lo que quieres
que mugeres son mugeres.

Anon.
(Not in Böhl)

11 Herz, verzage nicht geschwind[1]

Herz, verzage nicht geschwind,
Weil die Weiber Weiber sind.[2]

Argwohn lehre sie dich kennen,
Die sich lichte Sterne nennen
Und wie Feuerfunken brennen.
Drum verzage nicht geschwind,
Weil die Weiber Weiber sind.

Laß dir nicht den Sinn verwirren,
Wenn sie süße Weisen girren;
Möchten dich mit Listen kirren,
Machen dich mit Ränken blind;
Weil die Weiber Weiber sind.

Sind einander stets im Bunde,
Fechten tapfer mit dem Munde,
Wünschen, was versagt die Stunde,
Bauen Schlösser in den Wind;
Weil die Weiber Weiber sind.

Und so ist ihr Sinn verschroben,
Daß sie, lobst du, was zu loben,
Mit dem Mund dagegen toben,
Ob ihr Herz auch Gleiches sinnt;
Weil die Weiber Weiber sind.

Heart, do not despair too soon

Heart, do not despair too soon,
Because women are women.

Learn to treat them with suspicion,
They who call themselves bright stars
And burn like sparks of fire.
Do not, therefore, despair too soon,
Because women are women.

Do not let your wits be confused
When they coo their wheedling words;
They would tame you with their cunning,
Blind you with their wiles;
Because women are women.

They are always in league with each other,
Fighting boldly with their tongues,
Wanting what the moment forbids,
Building castles in the air;
Because women are women.

And their minds are so perverse
That if you praise what merits praise,
They will rant against it,
Though in their hearts they think the same;
Because women are women.

Translated by Heyse

---

[1] Wolf incorporated the song into *Der Corregidor*, where it is sung in Act II by the eponymous magistrate to express his exasperation that the lovely Frasquita will not give herself to him.
[2] Wolf never felt comfortable in high society. On one occasion his friends had arranged for a

Dezi si soys vos galan [12]

Dezi si soys vos galan
el que lotro dia baylastes
y baylastes y cantastes.

Soys vos el que con canciones
a todas enmudescistes
en verdad que las truxistes
de lindas entonaciones:
vos soys segun la razones
a tan lindas apuntastes
y baylastes y cantastes.

Soys vos el que no sabia
baylar ni menos cantar
soys vos quien no sabia amar
y de mugeres huya:
vos soys mas yo juraria
que muy bien os requebrastes
y baylastes y cantastes.

Soys vos el que blazonaua
del baylar y la cancion
soys vos el quen vn rincon
se metia y no assomaua:
vos soys pienso y no soñaua
el que a todas nos cansastes
y baylastes y cantastes.

Anon.
(Not in Böhl)

12 Sagt, seid Ihr es, feiner Herr

Sagt, seid Ihr es, feiner Herr,
Der da jüngst so hübsch gesprungen
Und gesprungen und gesungen?

Seid Ihr der, vor dessen Kehle
Keiner mehr zu Wort gekommen?
Habt die Backen voll genommen,
Sangt gar artig, ohne Fehle.
Ja, Ihr seid's, bei meiner Seele,
Der so mit uns umgesprungen
Und gesprungen und gesungen.

Seid Ihr's, der auf Castagnetten
Und Gesang sich nicht verstand,
Der die Liebe nie gekannt,
Der da floh vor Weiberketten?
Ja Ihr seid's; doch möcht' ich wetten,
Manch ein Lieb habt Ihr umschlungen
Und gesprungen und gesungen.

Seid Ihr der, der Tanz und Lieder
So herausstrich ohne Maß?
Seid Ihr's, der im Winkel saß
Und nicht regte seine Glieder?
Ja Ihr seid's, ich kenn' Euch wieder,

Say, was it you, dear sir

Say, was it you, dear sir,
Who recently danced so nicely,
And danced and sang?

Was it you, whose voice
Stopped all from getting a word in?
Who talked so big,
Who sang so sweetly, without a slip?
Yes, upon my soul, it was you
Who capered with us like this,
And danced and sang.

Was it you who claimed to know
Nothing of castanets and song,
Who had never known love
And fled from female fetters?
Yes, it was you; but I'll wager
That you've embraced many a sweetheart
And danced and sung.

Was it you who praised
Dance and song to the skies?
Was it you who sat in the corner
And wouldn't stir a limb?
Yes, it was you, I recognise you now,

---

society lady to be present at a musical soirée and Wolf, taking an instant dislike to her, sat down at the piano, grinned mischievously, and sang 'Herz, verzage nicht geschwind', relishing the phrase: „Weil die Weiber Weiber sind"!

Der zum Gähnen uns gezwungen
Und gesprungen und gesungen!

Translated by Heyse

Dirá cuanto digere [13]

Dirá cuanto digere
la gente deslenguada,
que quiero á quien me quiere,
y amo y soy amada.

Malas nuevas suenen
de estos maldicientes,
que siempre se mantienen
de sangre de inocentes:
que digan las gentes
no se me da nada,
que quiero á quien me quiere,
y amo y soy amada.

Son difamadores
los desventurados,
por irles mal de amores

Who made us yawn
The way you danced and sang!

y ser despreciados:
todos mis pecados
son de puro honrada,
que quiero á quien me quiere,
y amo y soy amada.

Si yo de piedra fuese
seria razon
que no me comoviese
á sentir pasion:
mas es mi corazon
de carne y delicada,
que quiero á quien me quiere,
y amo y soy amada.

Anon.
(Böhl, vol. I, p. 298)

13 Mögen alle bösen Zungen

Mögen alle bösen Zungen
Immer sprechen, was beliebt;
Wer mich liebt, den lieb' ich wieder,
Und ich lieb' und bin geliebt.

Schlimme, schlimme Reden flüstern
Eure Zungen schonungslos;
Doch ich weiß es, sie sind lüstern
Nach unschuld'gem Blute bloß.
Nimmer soll es mich bekümmern,
Schwatzt so viel es euch beliebt;
Wer mich liebt, den lieb' ich wieder,
Und ich lieb' und bin geliebt.

Zur Verläumdung sich verstehet
Nur, wem Lieb' und Gunst gebrach,
Weil's ihm selber elend gehet,
Und ihn niemand minnt und mag.
Darum denk' ich, daß die Liebe
Drum sie schmähn, mir Ehre giebt;
Wer mich liebt, den lieb' ich wieder,
Und ich lieb' und bin geliebt.

Let all the spiteful tongues

Let all the spiteful tongues
Keep on saying what they please;
He who loves me, I love back,
And I love and am loved.

Your tongues whisper relentlessly
Wicked, wicked slanders;
But I know, they merely thirst
For innocent blood.
It will never bother me,
You may gossip to your heart's content;
He who loves me, I love back,
And I love and am loved.

Only those enjoy slander
Who lack affection and kindness,
Because they fare so wretchedly
And no one loves or wants them.
Therefore I think that the love
They revile is to my honour;
He who loves me, I love back,
And I love and am loved.

EMANUEL GEIBEL

Wenn ich wär' aus Stein und Eisen,	If I were made of stone and iron,
Möchtet ihr darauf bestehn,	You might well insist
Daß ich sollte von mir weisen	That I should reject
Liebesgruß und Liebesflehn.	Love's greetings, love's entreaties.
Doch mein Herzlein ist nun leider	But my little heart is, I fear, soft,
Weich, wie's Gott uns Mädchen gibt;	As God has fashioned it for us girls;
Wer mich liebt, den lieb' ich wieder,	He who loves me, I love back,
Und ich lieb' und bin geliebt.	And I love and am loved.

Translated by Geibel
Also set by Schumann

Cabecita, cabecita [14]

Cabecita, cabecita,
tente en tí, no te resbales;
y apareja dos puntales
de la paciencia bendita.
Solicita
la bonita
confiancita,
no te inclines
a pensamientos ruines:
verás cosas
que toquen en milagrosas,
Dios delante
y San Cristóbal gigante.

Miguel de Cervantes (1546–1616)
(Not in Böhl)

14 Preciosas[1] Sprüchlein gegen Kopfweh — Preciosa's prescription for headache

Köpfchen, Köpfchen, nicht gewimmert,	Don't whimper, hold your little head up high,
Halt dich wacker, halt dich munter,	Be brave, be of good cheer,
Stütz' zwei gute Säulchen unter,	Prop yourself up on two pillars,
Heilsam aus Geduld gezimmert!	Fashioned wholesomely of patience!
Hoffnung schimmert,	Hope now glimmers,

---

[1] The heroine in Cervantes's short story *La Gitanilla* from which this poem is taken. The tale makes no explicit mention of a headache, which is presumably Heyse's invention. In the story, the almost-fifteen-year-old Preciosa has just told her admirer Andrés Caballero that she has another suitor, the poet Clemente, alias Alonso Hurtado, who has written a love poem to her. Andrés almost faints at the news – and Preciosa whispers (not sings) 'Cabecita, cabecita' to him to quell his jealousy. Having recited the poem, she announces to the assembled company that if you repeat but half of the poem and make six signs of the cross over the heart of the person who feels giddy, he will be 'como una manzana' – as fresh as an apple. *La Gitanilla*, which Cervantes placed at the head of his twelve *Novelas ejemplares* (*Exemplary Short Novels*), is a story in the Romance tradition, telling of restored identities. Preciosa, who is described as being beautiful, courteous, chaste, well spoken, blonde, is anything but a gypsy, even though she sings and dances better than anyone else in the story. Abducted from her home at the age of two, Costanza (her real name) was brought up by the gypsies as Preciosa. She is actually the daughter of Doña Guiomar de Meneses and Don Fernando de Azevedo, a knight of the Order of Calatrava. And Andrés, far from being a commoner, turns out to be Don Juan de Cárcamo, a knight of the Order of Santiago. All ends happily, and after a series of adventures they are married at the end of the story. Like many of Eichendorff's Novellen, *La Gitanilla* contains a number of poems that are either sung or recited: five by Preciosa, two by the poet, and a duet shared by Andrés and Clemente.

Wie sich's auch verschlimmert	However bad things get,
Und dich kümmert.	However you are vexed.
Mußt mit Grämen	You must take nothing
Dir nichts zu Herzen nehmen,[1]	Grievously to heart,
Ja kein Märchen,	Especially stories
Daß zu Berg dir stehn die Härchen;	That make your hair stand on end;
Da sei Gott davor	To avoid that, pray to God
Und der Riese Christophor!*[2]	And the giant Christopher!*

Translated by Heyse
Also set by Peter Cornelius
* Wolf repeats this line.

Decidle que me venga á ver [15]

Decidle que me venga á ver,	y no han podido
que cuanto mas me riñen	mi amor tan firme mover:
tanto mas crece el querer.	que cuanto mas me riñen
	tanto mas crece el querer.
Al amor firme	
no vence ninguna fuerza,	Con mil ronces
y el reñirme	que os aborrezca me ruegan,
mas me le dobla y esfuerza:	mas entonces
que se destuerza	mucho mas amor me pegan,
cuidado podeis perder,	y si á mí llegan
que cuanto mas me riñen	en ser por vos es placer:
tanto mas crece el querer.	que cuanto mas me riñen
	tanto mas crece el querer.
Encerrada	
dos veces ya me han tenido,	
castigada	Anon.
y aun ásperamente he sido,	(Böhl, vol. I, p. 283)

15 Sagt ihm, daß er zu mir komme — Tell him to come to me

Sagt ihm, daß er zu mir komme,	Tell him to come to me,
Denn je mehr sie mich drum schelten,	For the more they scold me for it,
Ach, je mehr wächst meine Glut!	Ah, the more my passion grows!
O zum Wanken	Oh, Love can be shaken
Bringt die Liebe nichts auf Erden;	By nothing on earth;
Durch ihr Zanken	Their chiding
Wird sie nur gedoppelt werden.	Will only double its power.
Sie gefährden	It is not imperilled
Mag nicht aller Neider Wut;	By the fury of its enviers,

1 Heyse: Dir nur nichts zu Herzen nehmen.
2 The giant St Christopher was blessed with powers to ward off harm and distress. This is the first example of repetition in the *Spanisches Liederbuch*.

EMANUEL GEIBEL

Denn je mehr sie mich drum schelten,
Ach, je mehr wächst meine Glut!
Eingeschlossen
Haben sie mich lange Tage,
Unverdrossen
Mich gestraft mit schlimmer Plage.
Doch ich trage
Jede Pein mit Liebesmuth,
Und je mehr sie mich drum schelten,
Ach, je mehr wächst meine Glut!

Meine Peiniger
Sagen oft, ich soll dich lassen,
Doch nur einiger
Wolln wir uns ins Herze fassen.
Muß ich drum erblassen,
Tod um Liebe lieblich tut,
Und je mehr sie mich drum schelten,
Ach, je mehr wächst meine Glut!

Translated by Heyse

For the more they scold me for it,
Ah, the more my passion grows!
They've locked me in
For days on end,
Have persistently
Punished me severely.
But I bear every pain
With the fortitude of love,
And the more they scold me for it,
Ah, the more my passion grows!

My tormentors
Often say I should leave you,
But this only makes us
Cleave to each other more.
And if I must fade away and die,
To die for love will be sweet,
And the more they scold me for it,
Ah, the more my passion grows!

Rogaselo madre [16]

Rogaselo madre
rogaselo al niño,
que no tire mas,
que matan sus tiros.

Madre la mi madre
el amor esquiuo
me ofende, y agrada,
me dexa, y le sigo.
Viera yo vnos ojos
el otro Domingo,
del cielo milagro,

del suelo peligro.
Lo que cuentan madre
de los Basiliscos,
por mi alma passa
la vez que los miro.
Rogaselo madre
rogaselo al niño,
que no tire mas,
que matan sus tiros.

Anon.
(Not in Böhl)

16 Bitt' ihn, o Mutter

Bitt' ihn, o Mutter,
Bitte den Knaben,
Nicht mehr zu zielen,
Weil er mich tödtet.

Mutter, o Mutter,
Die launische Liebe
Höhnt und versöhnt mich,
Flieht mich und zieht mich.

Tell him, O mother

Tell him, O mother,
Tell Cupid
Not to aim at me any more,
For he's killing me.

Mother, O mother,
Capricious love
Mocks and soothes me,
Shuns me and entices me.

NO STANZA BREAK

Ich sah zwei Augen	I saw two eyes
Am letzten Sonntag,	Last Sunday,
Wunder des Himmels,	The wonder of Heaven,
Unheil der Erde.	The bane of the world.
Was man sagt, o Mutter,	What is said, O mother,
Von Basilisken,[1]	Of basilisks,
Erfuhr mein Herze,	My heart discovered
Da ich sie sah.	When I saw those eyes.
Bitt' ihn, o Mutter,	Tell him, O mother,
Bitte den Knaben,	Tell Cupid
Nicht mehr zu zielen,	Not to aim at me any more,
Weil er mich tödtet.[2]	For he's killing me.

Translated by Heyse

17 Liebe mir im Busen zündet[3]   Love in my breast

Liebe mir im Busen	Love in my breast
Zündet' einen Brand.	Has kindled a fire.
Wasser, liebe Mutter,	Water, dear mother,
Eh das Herz verbrannt!	Before my heart's consumed!
Nicht das blinde Kind[4]	Do not punish the blind child
Straft für meine Fehle;	For my faults;
Hat zuerst die Seele	He cooled my soul
Mir gekühlt so lind.	So gently at first.
Dann entflammt's geschwind	Then swiftly, alas,
Ach, mein Unverstand;	My folly is inflamed.
Wasser, liebe Mutter,	Water, dear mother,
Eh das Herz verbrannt!	Before my heart's consumed!
Ach, wo ist die Flut,	Ah, where is the flood
Die dem Feuer wehre?	That might quench this fire?
Für so große Glut	For so great a flame
Sind zu arm die Meere.	The seas are too small.
Weil es wohl mir tut	Since it does me good,
Wein' ich unverwandt;	I weep without restraint;
Wasser, liebe Mutter,	Water, dear mother,
Eh das Herz verbrannt!	Before my heart's consumed!

---

1 The mythical basilisk was allegedly able to cause death with a single glance.
2 Heyse does not translate the third verse (not included here).
3 There is no Spanish source. The poem is by Heyse.   4 Cupid.

18 Schmerzliche Wonnen und wonnige Schmerzen[1]

Schmerzliche Wonnen und wonnige Schmerzen,
Wasser im Auge und Feuer im Herzen,
Stolz auf den Lippen und Seufzer im Sinne,
Honig und Galle zugleich ist die Minne.

Oft, wenn ein Seelchen vom Leib sich geschieden,
Möcht' es Sankt Michael tragen zum Frieden;
Aber der Dämon auch möcht' es verschlingen;
Keiner will weichen, da geht es ans Ringen.

Seelchen, gequältes, in ängstlichem Wogen
Fühlst du dich hierhin und dorthin gezogen,
Aufwärts und abwärts. In solches Getriebe
Stürzt zwischen Himmel und Höll' uns die Liebe.

Mütterchen, ach, und mit siebenzehn Jahren
Hab' ich dies Hangen und Bangen erfahren,
Hab's dann verschworen mit Thränen der Reue;
Ach, und schon lieb' ich, schon lieb' ich aufs neue!

Painful bliss and blissful pain

Painful bliss and blissful pain,
Tears in the eyes, and fire in the heart,
Pride on the lips and sighs in the mind,
Love is a mixture of honey and gall.

Often, when a soul has departed the body,
St Michael seeks to bear it to rest;
But the devil too tries to devour it;
Neither will yield, so a tussle ensues.

Tormented soul, you feel yourself
Tugged back and forth, up and down
In anguished distress. Such is the turmoil
Love hurls us into between heaven and hell.

Ah, mother, I at seventeen
Have already felt this great anxiety,
And then forswore it with tears of remorse;
And ah, already I'm in love, in love again!

En los tus amores [19]

En los tus amores
carillo no fies
cata que no llores
lo que agora ries.

No ves tu la luna
carillo menguarse
y amor y fortuna
que suele mudarse:
y suele pagarse
de amores no fies
cata que no llores
lo que agora ries.

Guardate carillo
no estes tan vfano
porque en el verano
canta bien el grillo:
no seas agudillo
de amores no fies,
cata que no llores
lo que agora ries.

Donde te desuias
escucha me vn cacho
que amor es mochacho
y haze niñerias:

---

1 Geibel's letter to Heyse of 23 February 1852 suggests that much of the 'translation' is in fact his own poem. There is no original Spanish poem.

ni yguales son dias
de amores no fies
cata que no llores
lo que agora ries.

Ni siempre es de dia
ni siempre haze escuro
ni el bien y alegria
es siempre seguro:
que amor es periuro
de amores no fies
cata que no llores
lo que agora ries.

Anon.
(Not in Böhl)

19 Trau nicht der Liebe

Trau nicht der Liebe,
Mein Liebster, gieb Acht!
Sie macht dich noch weinen,
Wo heut du gelacht.

Und siehst du nicht schwinden
Des Mondes Gestalt?
Das Glück hat nicht minder
Nur wankenden Halt.
Dann rächt es sich bald;
Und Liebe, gieb Acht!
Sie macht dich noch weinen,
Wo heut du gelacht.

Drum hüte dich fein
Vor thörigem Stolze!
Wohl singen im Mai'n
Die Grillchen im Holze;
Dann schlafen sie ein,
Und Liebe, gieb Acht!
Sie macht dich noch weinen,
Wo heut du gelacht.

Wo schweifst du nur hin?
Laß Rath dir ertheilen:
Das Kind mit den Pfeilen
Hat Possen im Sinn.
Die Tage, die eilen,
Und Liebe, gieb Acht!
Sie macht dich noch weinen,
Wo heut du gelacht.

Nicht immer ist's helle,
Nicht immer ist's dunkel;
Der Freude Gefunkel
Erbleichet so schnelle.
Ein falscher Geselle
Ist Amor, gieb Acht!

Put no trust in love

Put no trust in love,
My beloved, take care!
It will make you weep,
Though you laughed today.

Do you not see the moon
Waning?
Happiness is no less
Inconstant.
It soon avenges itself;
And love, beware!
It will make you weep,
Though you laughed today.

So be on your guard
Against foolish pride!
Though crickets in May
Chirp in the trees,
They then fall asleep,
And love, beware!
It will make you weep,
Though you laughed today.

Where are you roaming?
Be well advised,
Cupid with his arrows
Has tricks up his sleeve.
The days hasten by,
And love, beware!
It will make you weep,
Though you laughed today.

It is not always light,
It is not always dark;
The spark of joy
Quickly fades.
A false companion
Is Love, beware!

NO STANZA BREAK

Er macht dich noch weinen, / It will make you weep,
Wo heut du gelacht. / Though you laughed today.

Translated by Heyse

Que por mayo era por mayo [20]

Que por mayo era por mayo
cuando los blandos calores,
cuando los enamorados
van servir á sus amores
sino yo, triste mezquino,
que yago en estas prisiones,
que ni sé cuando de dia,
ni menos cuando es de noche,
sino por una avecilla
que me cantaba al albor:
matómela un ballestero,
déle Dios mal galardon.

Anon.
(Böhl, vol. I, p. 247)

20 Ach, im Maien war's, im Maien[1] / Ah, in May it was, in Maytime

Ach, im Maien war's, im Maien, / Ah, in May it was, in Maytime,
Wo die warmen Lüfte wehen, / When the warm breezes blow,
Wo verliebte Leute pflegen / When those in love are wont
Ihren Liebchen nachzugehn.[2] / To seek their sweethearts.

Ich allein, ich armer Trauriger, / I alone, sad wretch,
Lieg' im Kerker so verschmachtet, / Lie languishing in gaol,
Und ich seh nicht, wann es taget, / And cannot tell when day dawns,
Und ich weiß nicht, wann es nachtet. / And cannot tell when night falls.

Nur an einem Vöglein merkt' ich's, / But I used to know by a little bird
Das dadrauß im Baume sang; / That sang out there in May;
Das hat mir ein Schütz getödtet – / A marksman then killed it –
Geb' ihm Gott den schlimmsten Dank! / May God give him the worst of rewards!

Translated by Heyse

Todos duermen corazon [21]

Todos duermen corazon,
todos duermen y vos non!

El dolor que habeis cobrado
siempre os terná desvelado,
que el corazon lastimado
recuérdalo la pasion.

Anon.
(Böhl, vol. I, p. 303)

---

1 Heyse gave his translation the title 'Romance del Prisionero'. Almost no other song by Wolf has so many examples of poor accentuation. Perhaps the melody was already formed in his mind before he read the poem in detail; or perhaps, as Eric Sams suggests, Wolf's melody was inspired by the happy opening line. Whatever – the blithe melody scarcely expresses a prisoner's grief from a dark dungeon.
2 Heyse: nachzugehen. Wolf, by reducing the verb to three syllables, destroys the rhyme scheme.

21 Alle gingen, Herz, zur Ruh

Alle gingen, Herz, zur Ruh,
Alle schlafen, nur nicht du.¹

Denn der hoffnungslose Kummer
Scheucht von deinem Bett den Schlummer,
Und dein Sinnen schweift in stummer
Sorge seiner Liebe zu.*²

Translated by Geibel
Also set by Schumann
* Wolf repeats 'seiner Liebe zu'.

All have gone to rest, O heart

All have gone to rest, O heart,
All are sleeping, all but you.

For hopeless grief
Banishes slumber from your bed,
And your thoughts drift in speechless
Sorrow to your love.*

Alguna vez [22]

Alguna vez
o pensamiento,
serás contento.

Si amor cruel
me hace guerra,
seis pies de tierra
podrán mas que él:
allí sin él
y sin tormento
serás contento.

Lo no alcanzado
en esta vida,
ella perdida
será hallado,
y sin cuidado
de mal que siento,
serás contento.

Cristóbal de Castillejo (?1492–1550)
(Böhl, vol. I, p. 295)

22 Dereinst, dereinst, Gedanke mein

Dereinst, dereinst,
Gedanke mein
Wirst ruhig sein.

Läßt Liebesglut
Dich still nicht werden:
In kühler Erden
Da schläfst du gut;
Dort ohne Liebe
Und ohne Pein
Wirst ruhig sein.

Was du im Leben
Nicht hast gefunden,
Wenn es entschwunden
Wird dir's gegeben.

One day, one day

One day, one day,
My thoughts,
You shall be at rest.

Though love's ardour
Gives you no peace,
You shall sleep well
In cool earth;
There without love
And without pain
You shall be at rest.

What you did not
Find in life
Will be granted you
When life is ended.

1 Wolf told Oskar Grohe that when composing this couplet he had been thinking of his own sleepless nights.
2 Only the second example thus far of repetition in the *Spanisches Liederbuch*.

NO STANZA BREAK

Dann ohne Wunden
Und ohne Pein
Wirst ruhig sein.

Then, free from torment
And free from pain,
You shall be at rest.

Translated by Geibel
Also set by Leopold Damrosch, Edvard Grieg,
Jensen and Schumann

De dentro tengo mi mal [23]

De dentro tengo mi mal
que de fuera no hay señal.

Mi nueva y dulce querella
es invisible á la gente:
el alma sola la siente
que el cuerpo no es digno de ella:

como la viva centella
se encubre en el pedernal,
de dentro tengo mi mal.

Luis de Camões[1] (?1525–1580)
(Böhl, vol. I, p. 291)

23 Tief im Herzen trag' ich Pein

Tief im Herzen trag' ich Pein,
Muß nach außen stille sein.

Den geliebten Schmerz verhehle
Tief ich vor der Welt Gesicht;
Und es fühlt ihn nur die Seele,
Denn der Leib verdient ihn nicht.
Wie der Funke frei und licht
Sich verbirgt im Kieselstein,
Trag' ich innen tief die Pein.

Deep in my heart I bear my grief

Deep in my heart I bear my grief,
Outwardly I must be calm.

I conceal this sweet agony
Far from the world's gaze;
It is felt only by my soul,
For the body does not deserve it.
As a spark, free and bright,
Lies hidden in the flint,
So I bear my grief deep within.

Translated by Geibel
Also set by Schumann

Ven muerte tan escondida [24]

Ven muerte tan escondida
que no te sienta comigo,
porque el gozo de contigo
no me torne á dar la vida.

Ven como rayo que hiere
que hasta que ha herido
no se siente su ruido,

por mejor herir do quiere:
asi sea tu venida,
sino desde aqui te digo,
que el gozo que habré contigo
me dará de nuevo vida.

Comendador Escrivá (c. 1450–c. 1520))
(Böhl, vol. I, p. 268)

---

[1] A Portuguese poet who also wrote in Castilian. His masterpiece, *Os Lusiadas*, was published in 1572.

24 Komm, o Tod, von Nacht umgeben

Komm, o Tod, von Nacht umgeben,
Leise komm zu mir gegangen,
Daß die Lust, dich zu umfangen,
Nicht zurück mich ruf' ins Leben.[1]

Komm, so wie der Blitz uns rühret,
Den der Donner nicht verkündet,
Bis er plötzlich sich entzündet
Und den Schlag gedoppelt führet.
Also seist du mir gegeben,
Plötzlich stillend mein Verlangen,
Daß die Lust, dich zu umfangen,
Nicht zurück mich ruf' ins Leben.

Translated by Geibel

Come, O Death, night-enshrouded

Come, O Death, night-enshrouded,
Come, steal up to me,
So that my joy in embracing you
Does not recall me to life.

Come, as the lightning strikes
Unheralded by thunder,
Until it suddenly flashes,
And deals a double blow.
Thus may you be granted me,
Suddenly stilling my longing,
So that my joy in embracing you
Does not recall me to life.

Aunque con semblante airado [25]

Aunque con semblante airado
me mirais, ojos serenos,
no me negareis al menos
que me habeis mirado.

Por mas que querais mostraros
airados para ofenderme,
que ofensa podeis hacerme
que iguale al bien de miraros?

Que aunque de mortal cuidado
dejeis mis sentidos llenos,
no me negareis al menos
ojos, que me habeis mirado.

Anon.
(Böhl, vol. I, p. 274)

25 Ob auch finstre Blicke glitten

Ob auch finstre Blicke glitten,
Schöner Augenstern,[2] aus dir,
Wird mir doch nicht abgestritten,
Daß du hast geblickt nach mir.

Wie sich auch der Strahl bemühte,
Zu verwunden meine Brust,
Gibt's ein Leiden, das die Lust,
Dich zu schaun, nicht reich vergüte?

Even though black looks

Even though black looks
Flashed from your beautiful eyes,
It cannot be denied
That you looked at me.

Even though their rays
Sought to wound my breast,
Is there any suffering not recompensed
By the joy of seeing you?

1 The first four lines of the poem are quoted in Chapter 38 of the *Segunda parte del ingenioso caval-lero Don Quixote de la Mancha* by Cervantes (1615). They are sung by Don Clavigo in an attempt to woo the Infanta Antonomasia. The seduction is narrated by La Trifaldi who tells us that such verses 'cast a spell over you when they are sung and hold you fascinated as you read them'. She also tells us that Don Clavigo was a poet and a great dancer who 'played the guitar in such a way as to make it talk' (trans. Samuel Putnam). Edgar Allan Poe quotes the same stanza in his burlesque 'How to Write a Blackwood Article'.
2 'Augenstern' denotes both 'pupil of the eye' and 'sweetheart'.

NO STANZA BREAK

EMANUEL GEIBEL

Und so tödtlich mein Gemüte
Unter deinem Zorn gelitten,
Wird mir doch nicht abgestritten,
Daß du hast geblickt nach mir.¹

However mortally my feelings
Have suffered from your anger,
It cannot be denied
That you looked at me.

Translated by Heyse
Also set by Jensen

Cubridme de flores [26]

Cubridme de flores
que muero de amores!

Porque de su aliento el aire
no lleve el olor sublime,
   cubridme!

Sea porque todo es uno,
alientos de amor y olores
   de flores.

De azuzenas y jazmines
aqui la mortaja espero,
   que muero!

Si me preguntais de qué
respondo: en dulces rigores
   de amores.

 ?Maria Doceo
 (Böhl, vol. 1, p. 35)

26 Bedeckt mich mit Blumen²

Bedeckt mich mit Blumen,
Ich sterbe vor Liebe.

Daß die Luft mit leisem Wehen
Nicht den süßen Duft mir³ entführe,
   Bedeckt mich!

Ist ja alles doch dasselbe,
Liebesodem oder Düfte
   Von Blumen.

Von Jasmin und weißen Liljen
Sollt ihr hier mein Grab bereiten,
   Ich sterbe.

Und befragt ihr mich: Woran?
Sag' ich: Unter süßen Qualen
   Vor Liebe.*

Cover me with flowers

Cover me with flowers,
I am dying of love.

Lest the soft breezes
Rob me of their sweet scent,
   Cover me!

For the breath of love
And the scent of flowers
   Is all one.

Of jasmine and white lilies
You shall here prepare my grave,
   I am dying.

And if you ask me: Of what?
I'll say: In sweet torment
   Of love.*

Translated by Geibel
Also set by Damrosch, Hiller, Rubinstein and Schumann
* Wolf repeats 'vor Liebe'.

---

1 Heyse omits the third stanza (not included here).
2 See HW to Heinrich Potpeschnigg, 6 December 1897, p. 64. 3 Wolf adds „mir".

Si dormis doncella [27]

Si dormis doncella
despertad y abrid,
que venida es la hora
si quereis partir.

Si estais descalza
no cureis de os calzar,
que muchas las agoas
teneis de pasar.

Las agoas tan hondas
de Guadalquivir,
que venida es la hora
si quereis partir.

Gil Vicente[1] (?1465–c. 1537)
(Böhl, vol. I, p. 302)

27 Und schläfst du, mein Mädchen

Und schläfst du, mein Mädchen,
Auf, öffne du mir;
Denn die Stund' ist gekommen,
Da wir wandern von hier.

Und bist ohne Sohlen,
Leg' keine dir an;
Durch reißende Wasser
Geht unsere Bahn.

Durch die tief tiefen Wasser
Des Guadalquivir;[2]
Denn die Stund' ist gekommen,
Da wir wandern von hier.*

And if you're sleeping, my girl

And if you're sleeping, my girl,
Arise, and let me in;
For the time has come
To go forth from here.

And if you're not wearing shoes,
Put none on;
For our way lies
Through raging waters.

Through the deep deep waters
Of the Guadalquivir;
For the time has come
To go forth from here.*

Translated by Geibel
Also set by Hiller, Jensen and Schumann
* Wolf repeats the final line.

En campaña, madre [28]

En campaña, madre
tocan á leva,
vanse mis amores
sola me dejan.

Apenas del dia
se muestra el alva,
cuando hace salva
la infantaría,
y la gloria mia
cuando el son siente
parte incontinente,
porque es á leva:
vanse mis amores
sola me dejan.

---

1 A Portuguese poet who wrote some of his plays and poetry in Castilian, including several that were set by Schumann in his *Spanisches Liederspiel* and *Spanische Liebeslieder*: 'Sanossa está la ninna' ('Weh, wie zornig ist das Mädchen'), 'Si dormis, doncell' ('Und schläfst du, mein Mädchen'), 'Del rosal vengo, mi madre' ('Von dem Rosenbusch, o Mutter'), 'Muy graciosa es la doncella' ('O wie lieblich ist das Mädchen').
2 Spanish river, some 350 miles long, that rises in the Sierra del Pozo Morena, flows through Andalusia and enters the Atlantic about 20 miles north of Cadiz.

EMANUEL GEIBEL

Quedo cual el dia
faltando el sol queda,
sin que aliviar pueda
la tristeza mia:
no quiero alegría
si ausente le tengo,
y no me entretengo

sino con pena:
vanse mis amores
sola me dejan.

Anon.
(Böhl, vol. 1, p. 300)

28 Sie blasen zum Abmarsch   Bugles are sounding the march off

Sie blasen zum Abmarsch,
Lieb Mütterlein.
Mein Liebster muß scheiden
Und läßt mich allein!

The bugles are sounding the march off,
Dear mother.
My beloved must part
And leaves me alone!

Am Himmel die Sterne
Sind kaum noch geflohn,
Da feuert von ferne
Das Fußvolk schon.
Kaum hört er den Ton,
Sein Ränzelein schnürt er,
Von hinnen marschiert er,
Mein Herz hinterdrein.
Mein Liebster muß scheiden
Und läßt mich allein!

The stars in the sky
Have hardly yet faded,
And the infantry already
Fires from afar.
On hearing the sound
He fastens his pack,
And marches away,
Taking my heart with him.
My beloved must part
And leaves me alone!

Mir ist wie dem Tag,
Dem die Sonne geschwunden.
Mein Trauern nicht mag
So balde gesunden.
Nach nichts ich frag',
Keine Lust mehr heg' ich,
Nur Zwiesprach pfleg' ich
Mit meiner Pein –
Mein Liebster muß scheiden
Und läßt mich allein!

I'm like a day
Without sun.
My sorrow cannot
Be so quickly healed.
I ask for nothing,
I have no more joy,
I commune only
With my agony –
My beloved must part
And leaves me alone!

Translated by Heyse
Also set by Jensen

No lloreis ojuelos[1] [29]

No lloreis ojuelos,
porque no es razon
que llore de zelos
quien mata de amor.

Quien puede matar
no intente morir,
si hace con reir
mas que con llorar.

---

1   Heyse left the first 44 lines of this poem untranslated.

No lloreis ojuelos,
porque no es razon
que llore de zelos
quien mata de amor.

Lope de Vega
There are 44 additional lines
in Böhl de Faber's *Floresta*.
(Böhl, vol. III, p. 209)

29 Weint nicht, ihr Äuglein[1]

Weint nicht, ihr Äuglein!
Wie kann so trübe
Weinen vor Eifersucht,
Wer tödtet durch Liebe?

Wer selbst Tod bringt
Der sollt' ihn ersehnen?
Sein Lächeln bezwingt
Was trotzt seinen Thränen.
Weint nicht, ihr Äuglein!
Wie kann so trübe
Weinen vor Eifersucht,
Wer tötet durch Liebe?

Translated by Heyse

Weep not, dear eyes

Weep not, dear eyes!
How can one who kills through love
Weep so bitterly
From jealousy?

Should he who brings death
Crave it?
Whoever resists his tears
Will be won over by his smiles.
Weep not, dear eyes!
How can one who kills through love
Weep so bitterly
From jealousy?

Qui tal fet lo mal del peu [30]

Qui tal fet lo mal del peu
la marioneta
quien te hizo el del talon
la marion.

Contaros quiero mi mal
que nos quiero negar cosa
questa noche en vn rosal
yendo a coger vna rosa:
me ficat vna spineta
la marioneta
que mallega al coraçon
la marion.

Cantaros quiero mi pena
amigas por buen niuel
que entrando en vn vergel
por coger vn açucena:
me ficat vna squerdeta
la marioneta
de dulce conuersacion
la marion.

Cantaros quiero de cierto
que me acontescio mezquina
y es que cogiendo en vn huerto
vna hermosa clauellina:
me ficat vna busqueta
la marioneta
que no hay cura a su lision
la marion.

Señora si vos queredes
yo soy muy buen cirurgiano
que la sacare en la mano
que nada no sentiredes:
y restareu guarideta
la marioneta
no sentireys mas passion
la marion.

Anon.
(Not in Böhl)

1 Heyse: Aeuglein.

30 „Wer tat deinem Füßlein weh?"
Limusinisch[1]

„Wer tat deinem Füßlein weh?
La Marioneta,
Deiner Ferse weiß wie Schnee?
La Marion."

Sag' Euch an, was krank mich macht,
Will kein Wörtlein Euch verschweigen:
Ging zum Rosenbusch zur Nacht,
Brach ein Röslein von den Zweigen;
Trat auf einen Dorn im Gang,
La Marioneta,
Der mir bis ins Herze drang,
La Marion.

Sag' Euch alle meine Pein,
Freund, und will Euch nicht berücken:
Ging in einen Wald allein,
Eine Lilie mir zu pflücken;
Traf ein Stachel scharf mich dort
La Marioneta,
War ein süßes Liebeswort,
La Marion.

Sag' Euch mit Aufrichtigkeit
Meine Krankheit, meine Wunde:
In den Garten ging ich heut,
Wo die schönste Nelke stunde;
Hat ein Span mich dort verletzt,
La Marioneta,
Blutet fort und fort bis jetzt,
La Marion.

„Schöne Dame, wenn Ihr wollt,
Bin ein Wundarzt guter Weise,
Will die Wund' Euch stillen leise,
Daß Ihr's kaum gewahren sollt.
Bald sollt Ihr genesen sein,
La Marioneta,
Bald geheilt von aller Pein,
La Marion."*

'Who hurt your little foot?'

'Who hurt your little foot?
La Marioneta,
Your heel as white as snow?
La Marion.'

I'll tell you what afflicts me,
I'll not withhold a single word:
Last night I went to the rosebush,
And plucked a rose;
I trod on a thorn as I went,
La Marioneta,
Which pierced me to the heart,
La Marion.

I'll tell you all my woes,
My friend, and not deceive you:
I went into a wood alone
To pick myself a lily;
A sharp thorn pricked me there,
La Marioneta,
It was a sweet word of love,
La Marion.

I'll tell you frankly
Of my sickness, my wounds:
I went into the garden today,
Where the loveliest carnation grew;
A splinter hurt me there,
La Marioneta,
The wound bled and bleeds still,
La Marion.

'Beauteous lady, if you will,
I'm a surgeon of good repute,
I'll heal your wound so tenderly
That you'll scarcely notice it.
You'll soon be well again,
La Marioneta,
Soon be free of all your pain,
La Marion.'*

Translated by Geibel
* Wolf twice repeats the last line.

---

[1] From Limousin, the département of Corrèze and Haute-Vienne; the original language is a form of Provençal.

31 Deine Mutter, süßes Kind

Deine Mutter, süßes Kind,
Da sie in den Weh'n gelegen,
Brausen hörte sie den Wind.

Und so hat sie dich geboren
Mit dem falschen wind'gen Sinn.
Hast du heut ein Herz erkoren,
Wirfst es morgen treulos hin.
Doch den zähl' ich zu den Toren,
Der dich schmäht der Untreu wegen:
Dein Geschick war dir entgegen;
Denn die Mutter, süßes Kind,
Da sie in den Weh'n gelegen,
Brausen hörte sie den Wind.

Don Luis el Chico[1]

Your mother, sweet child

Your mother, sweet child,
When she lay in labour,
Could hear the roaring wind.

And so you were born
As false and fickle as the wind.
If you choose a lover today,
You'll discard him faithlessly tomorrow.
Yet I count him a fool
Who chides you for your infidelity:
Your destiny was against you;
For your mother, sweet child,
When she lay in labour,
Could hear the roaring wind.

Pues que no me sabeis dar [32]

Pues que no me sabeis dar
sino tormento y pasion,
yo vendo mi corazon:
hay quien le quiera comprar?

Quiérole poner en precio:
tres blancas me dan por él,
no es fugitivo y es fiel
antes se vende por recio:
vendo por ejecucion
á quien mas quisiera dar:
que vendo mi corazon,
hay quien le quiera comprar?

Sabe darme mil enojos
y nunca placer jamas:
hay quien puje? hay quien dé mas?
allá va con sus antojos:
testigo hago la ocasion
pues que mas no puedo hallar
que vendo mi corazon:
quien me le quiere comprar?

Sin él quedaré sin pena,
téngala quien la quisiere!
quien le compra? quien le quiere?
ea! que buena! que buena!
este es el postrer pregon,
ya se habrá de rematar:
que vendo mi corazon,
hay quien le quiera comprar?

Á la una, y á las dos:
á la tercera es la paga:
ea! que buena pro le haga.
Señora, tomalde vos!
con el clavo y eslabon
le podeis luego herrar,
pues os doy mi corazon
si no le quereis comprar.

Anon.
(Böhl, vol. 1, pp. 358 and 359)

---

1 Sleeman and Davies argue convincingly that the 'author' Don Luis el Chico is none other than Heyse. There is no Spanish source.

32 Da nur Leid und Leidenschaft

Da nur Leid und Leidenschaft
Mich bestürmt in deiner Haft,
Biet' ich jetzt mein Herz zu Kauf.
Sagt, hat einer Lust darauf?

Soll ich sagen, wie ich's schätze,
Sind drei Batzen nicht zuviel.
Nimmer war's des Windes Spiel,
Eigensinnig blieb's im Netze.
Aber weil mich drängt die Not
Biet' ich jetzt mein Herz zu Kauf,
Schlag' es los zum Meistgebot –
Sagt, hat einer Lust darauf?

Täglich kränkt es mich im Stillen
Und erfreut mich nimmermehr.
Nun wer bietet? – wer giebt mehr?
Fort mit ihm und seinen Grillen!
Daß sie schlimm sind, leuchtet ein,
Biet' ich doch mein Herz zu Kauf.
Wär' es froh, behielt' ich's fein –
Sagt, hat einer Lust darauf?

Kauft ihr's, leb' ich ohne Grämen.
Mag es haben, wem's beliebt!
Nun wer kauft? wer will es nehmen?
Sag' ein Jeder, was er giebt.
Noch einmal vorm Hammerschlag
Biet' ich jetzt mein Herz zu Kauf,
Daß man sich entscheiden mag –
Sagt, hat einer Lust darauf?

Nun zum ersten – und zum zweiten –
Und beim dritten schlag ich's zu!
Gut denn! Mag dir's Glück bereiten;
Nimm es, meine Liebste du!
Brenn' ihm mit dem glüh'nden Erz
Gleich das Sklavenzeichen auf;
Denn ich s c h e n k e dir mein Herz,
Hast du auch nicht Lust zum Kauf.

Translated by Heyse

Since only pain and passion

Since only pain and passion
Have assailed me in your custody,
I now offer my heart for sale.
Speak, does no one want it?

If I'm to value it,
Then threepence isn't too much.
It was never the wind's plaything,
It stayed obstinately in your toils.
But because I'm hard pressed,
I now offer my heart for sale,
Shall knock it down to the highest bidder –
Speak, does no one want it?

Each day it silently grieves me
And delights me no more.
So, who'll bid? – who'll give more?
Away with it and all its whims!
It's obvious they are bad,
That's why I offer my heart for sale.
If it were happy, I'd gladly keep it –
Speak, does no one want it?

Buy it, and I'll live free of grief.
Let it go to him who wants it!
So, who'll buy? Who'll take it?
Let everyone say what they'll give.
Once again, under the hammer,
I offer my heart for sale,
So make up your minds.
Speak, does no one want it?

Going for the first time – and the second –
Going, going, gone!
Well done! May you have joy of it;
Take it, my sweetheart!
Brand the slave mark into it at once
With a red-hot iron;
For I'll make you a *gift* of my heart,
Though you do not wish to buy it.

Mal haya quien los envuelve [33]

Mal haya quien los envuelve
los mis amores,
mal haya quien los envuelve!

Los mis amores primeros
en Sevilla quedan presos:
los mis amores,
mal haya quien los envuelve!

En Sevilla quedan presos
con cordon de mis cabellos:
los mis amores,
mal haya quien los envuelve!

Gil Vicente
(Böhl, vol. I, p. 302)

33 Wehe der, die mir verstrickte

Wehe der, die mir verstrickte
Meinen Geliebten!
Wehe der, die ihn verstrickte!

Ach, der Erste, den ich liebte,
Ward gefangen in Sevilla.
Mein Vielgeliebter,
Wehe der, die ihn verstrickte!

Ward gefangen in Sevilla
Mit der Fessel meiner Locken.
Mein Vielgeliebter,
Wehe der, die ihn verstrickte!*

Woe to the woman

Woe to the woman
Who ensnared my beloved!
Woe to the woman who ensnared him!

Ah, the first man I loved
Was captured in Seville.
My best beloved,
Woe to the woman who ensnared him!

He was captured in Seville
By the fetters of my tresses.
My best beloved,
Woe to the woman who ensnared him!*

Translated by Heyse
* Wolf adds an extra 'Wehe!'

Vete amor, y vete [34]

Vete amor, y vete,
mira que amanece.

Gente passa por la calle,
y pues passa tanta gente,
sin duda que la mañana
ya sus alas blancas tiende.
Y pues de la vezindad
tanto me temo, y te temes,
porque al vulgo no declares
lo que te quiero, y me quieres.

Vete amor, y vete,
mira que amanece.

Si el Sol en saliendo barre
la aljofar que el campo tiene,
tambien de mi lado quita
la perla que me enriqueze.
Lo que a otros parece dia,
a mi noche me parece,
pues luego que sale el Alua,
la noche de ausencia viene.

Vete amor, y vete,
mira que amanece.

Dexa los dulces abraços,
que si entre ellos te entretienes,

EMANUEL GEIBEL

vn mal nos podra dar largo
aqueste contento breue.
Vn dia de purgatorio
no haze mucho quien le tiene,
pues la esperança de gloria
sus graues penas descrece.

Vete amor, y vete,
mira que amanece.

Anon.
(Not in Böhl)

34 Geh, Geliebter, geh jetzt![1]   Go beloved, go now!

    Geh, Geliebter, geh jetzt!
    Sieh, der Morgen dämmert.

Leute gehn schon durch die Gasse,
Und der Markt wird so belebt,
Daß der Morgen wohl, der blasse,
Schon die weißen Flügel hebt.
Und vor unsern Nachbarn bin ich
Bange, daß du Anstoß giebst;
Denn sie wissen nicht, wie innig
Ich dich lieb' und du mich liebst.

    Drum, Geliebter, geh jetzt!
    Sieh, der Morgen dämmert.

Wenn die Sonn' am Himmel scheinend
Scheucht vom Feld die Perlen klar,
Muß auch ich die Perle weinend
Lassen, die mein Reichtum war.
Was als Tag den Andern funkelt,
Meinen Augen dünkt es Nacht,
Da die Trennung bang mir dunkelt,
Wenn das Morgenroth erwacht.

    Geh, Geliebter, geh jetzt!
    Sieh, der Morgen dämmert.

Fliehe denn aus meinen Armen!
Denn versäumest du die Zeit,
Möchten für ein kurz Erwarmen
Wir ertauschen langes Leid.

    Go, beloved, go now!
    Look, the day is dawning.

Already people pass in the street,
And the market's so busy
That pale morning
Must be spreading its white wings.
And I'm fearful of our neighbours,
That you'll scandalise them;
For they do not know how fervently
I love you and you love me.

    Therefore, beloved, go now!
    Look, the day is dawning.

When the sun, shining in the sky,
Chases the dewy pearls from the field,
I must also, weeping, leave the pearl
That was my treasure.
What to others shines as day,
My eyes see as night,
For parting darkens my mind,
When the red of morning dawns.

    Go, beloved, go now!
    Look, the day is dawning.

Fly then from my arms!
For if you let time slip by,
We shall pay with long sorrow
For our brief embrace.

1 The theme of illicit and secret love was one with which Wolf and his mistress Melanie Köchert were familiar – which explains, perhaps, the passionate nature of the music. One of Melanie Köchert's children, shaken by the way in which Frieda Zerny was threatening her mother's relationship with Wolf (see pp. 520–21), recalls secretly listening to Wolf and Zerny rehearse a particularly difficult passage in 'Geh, Geliebter, geh jetzt!', and saying to herself: „Sie kann ihn nicht wirklich lieben, wenn sie so etwas nicht singen kann!" ('She can't really love him if she can't sing something like that!' (Estate of Walter Legge). Wolf omits the third verse of Geibel's translation, not printed here.

NO STANZA BREAK

Ist in Fegefeuersqualen
Doch ein Tag schon auszustehn,
Wenn die Hoffnung fern in Strahlen
Läßt des Himmels Glorie sehn.

    Drum, Geliebter, geh jetzt!
    Sieh, der Morgen dämmert.

Translated by Geibel
Also set by Damrosch

One day in Purgatory
Can after all be borne,
When Hope, radiant from afar,
Reveals the glory of heaven.

    Therefore, beloved, go now!
    Look, the day is dawning.

Johann Wolfgang von Goethe
(1749–1832)

			page
Sehnsucht	by August 1875		123
Der Fischer	by August 1875		124
Wanderlied	by August 1875	fragment	
Auf dem See	by August 1875		124
Erster Verlust	30 January 1876		125
Geistesgruß	28 February –3 April 1876	TTBB	126
Mailied	28 February –3 April 1876	TTBB	126
Mai	25 April –1 May 1876	fragment	
Gretchen vor dem Andachtsbild der Mater Dolorosa	22 August –9 September 1878		127
Wanderers Nachtlied	30 January 1887		129
Beherzigung	1 March 1887		128
Die Spröde	13–14 February 1889	fragment	
Gedichte von J. W. v. Goethe für eine Singstimme und Klavier			
Harfenspieler I	27 October 1888, orchestrated 2 December 1890		130
Harfenspieler II	29 October 1888, orchestrated 4 December 1890		131
Harfenspieler III	30 October 1888, orchestrated 4 December 1890		131
Philine	30 October 1888		136
Spottlied aus *Wilhelm Meister*	2 November 1888		132
Der Schäfer	4 November 1888		151
Anakreons Grab	4 November 1888, orchestrated by mid-April 1890 lost and 13 November 1893		156
Der Rattenfänger	6 November 1888, orchestrated 5 February 1890		141
Gleich und gleich	6 November 1888		153
Dank des Paria	9 November 1888		157
Frech und froh I	14 November 1888		147
St. Nepomuks Vorabend	15 November 1888		150

Gutmann und Gutweib	28 November 1888	143
Ritter Kurts Brautfahrt	9 December 1888	142
Der Sänger	14 December 1888	139
Mignon	17 December 1888, orchestrated 31 October 1893, to replace a lost version of 1890	137
Mignon II	18 December 1888	133
Mignon I	19 December 1888	133
Frühling übers Jahr	21 December 1888	155
Mignon III	22 December 1888	134
Epiphanias	27 December 1888, fragment orchestrated 25 April 1894	149
Cophtisches Lied I	28 December 1888	145
Cophtisches Lied II	28 December 1888	146
Beherzigung	30 December 1888	148
Blumengruß	31 December 1888	153
Prometheus	2 January 1889, orchestrated 12 March –c. April 1890	169
Königlich Gebet	7 January 1889	158
Grenzen der Menschheit	9 January 1889	172
Ganymed	11 January 1889, lost orchestrated by mid-April 1890	171
Was in der Schenke waren heute	16 January 1889, afternoon	162
So lang man nüchtern ist	16 January 1889, evening	161
Ob der Koran von Ewigkeit sei?	17 January 1889	160
Sie haben wegen der Trunkenheit	18 January 1889, afternoon	162
Trunken müssen wir alle sein!	18 January 1889, evening	161
Phänomen	19 January 1889	158
Erschaffen und Beleben	21 January 1889, afternoon	159
Nicht Gelegenheit macht Diebe	21 January 1889, evening	163
Hochbeglückt in deiner Liebe	23 January 1889, afternoon	164
Wie sollt' ich heiter bleiben	23 January 1889, evening	167
Als ich auf dem Euphrat schiffte	24 January 1889, afternoon	164
Dies zu deuten, bin erbötig!	24 January 1889, evening	165
Wenn ich dein gedenke	25 January 1889, afternoon	168
Komm, Liebchen, komm!	25 January 1889, evening	166
Hätt ich irgend wohl Bedenken	26 January 1889	165
Locken, haltet mich gefangen	29 January 1889	168
Nimmer will ich dich verlieren!	30 January 1889	169
Frech und froh II	2 February 1889	148

Der neue Amadis	5 February 1889	152
Genialisch Treiben	10 February 1889	151
Die Bekehrte	12 February 1889	154
Die Spröde	21 October 1889	154

POET

It has become fashionable to label Goethe unmusical. In April 1816 he failed to acknowledge Schubert's gift of sixteen settings of his poems, including such masterpieces as 'Gretchen am Spinnrade', 'Meeres Stille', 'Der Fischer' and 'Erlkönig'; he did not warm to Beethoven when they met in 1812; he preferred Carl Friedrich Zelter and Johann Friedrich Reichardt to composers deemed greater by posterity. And he wrote in his autobiography, *Dichtung und Wahrheit*: „Das Auge war vor allen anderen das Organ, womit ich die Welt erfasste" ('It was through the visual, above all other senses, that I comprehended the world') – a statement that seems to be confirmed by his indefatigable study of natural phenomena and his delight in art and architecture, in *seeing*. Lynceus's line at the end of *Faust*, „Zum Sehen geboren, zum Schauen bestellt" ('I was born for seeing, employed to watch') has an unmistakably autobiographical ring. Goethe was, above all, a visual being, an Augenmensch.

Yet he was also, from his earliest days in Frankfurt, intensely musical. His father bought a Giraffe, an upright Hammerklavier, for 60 florins in 1769, played the lute and flute and occasionally made music with friends – there is an amusing passage in *Dichtung und Wahrheit* that describes his father playing the lute, „die er länger stimmte, als er darauf spielte" ('which he spent longer tuning than playing'). His mother, who was more artistic, played the piano and sang German and Italian arias with great enthusiasm. Goethe and his sister Cornelia started piano lessons in 1763, and although the pieces he learned were probably simple dances, marches and songs, he would have been able to supply his own thorough-bass, since the scores of the period rarely contained written-out harmonies. It was during this early Frankfurt period that his interest in opera was kindled. He attended many performances of French and Italian operas, and in his early teens wrote a libretto, *La sposa rapita*, which he later burned. But the overwhelming musical experience of his youth was the visit to Frankfurt in 1763 of the six-year-old Mozart. The fourteen-year-old Goethe was smitten, and his adoration lasted until he died some sixty years later.

While studying in Strasbourg he began to learn the cello: „Ich kann das Violoncello spielen, aber nicht stimmen" ('I can play the cello but not tune it'), he wrote with unaccustomed modesty. In Alsace he gathered folk songs, roaming the countryside like a forerunner of Kodály or Bartók. A new world of music was opening before him: folksong, with its „alte Melodien, wie sie Gott erschaffen" ('ancient melodies, as created by God'), as he wrote to Herder, who had first aroused his interest in the Volkslied. And it was to Herder that he sent 12 *Lieder des Volkes* – a pioneering effort by Goethe in a field that blossomed during the Romantic period. His concept, incidentally, of what a song ought to be – strophic with a simple melody – was almost certainly influenced by his interest in folksong and the Lieder of the young Bernhard Theodor Breitkopf.

Back in Frankfurt and working as a lawyer, he became increasingly interested in the relationship between music and poetry. He greatly admired Gluck and asked him to set his poetry – Gluck declined. Goethe was also keen to find composers to set the Singspiele that he was now beginning to write. He persuaded Johann André to write the music for *Erwin und Elmire*, and though André's music has long been forgotten, two poems from the play have become known the world over through the music of Mozart ('Das Veilchen') and Grieg ('Zur Rosenzeit'). It is the same with his other Singspiele, composed by the likes of André, Philipp Christoph Kayser and Reichardt: their settings have been largely forgotten, but individual songs from the works have been rescued from oblivion by Schubert ('Erlkönig' from *Die Fischerin*, 'Liebe schwärmt auf allen Wegen' from *Claudine von Villa Bella*), Wolf ('Der Schäfer' from *Jery und Bätely*) and many other celebrated composers. His ambitions as a librettist came to nothing, partly because he failed to find a composer of genius. These works, however, are delightful pieces. As Hugo von Hofmannsthal wrote in an essay to accompany *Goethes Opern und Singspiele*: „Der Geist der Poesie weht auch hier unmittelbar uns an." ('Here too the spirit of poetry breathes on us.') And one is left with the feeling that had Goethe collaborated with composers of the calibre of Mozart and Richard Strauss, these Singspiele might now be part of the operatic repertoire.

Goethe's contribution to the musical life of Weimar, where he was summoned in 1775 by Duke Karl August, cannot be overestimated. He himself was impresario, author, director, business manager and actor. 'Auf Miedings Tod', a poem written in 1782 on the death of his stage manager, Johann Martin Mieding, speaks volumes about the poet's love of the theatre and his affection for all those connected with it. Goethe was director of the Hoftheater from 1791 to 1817, and mounted productions by an astonishing variety of composers, including Mozart, Gluck, Beethoven, Dittersdorf, Paisiello, Cimarosa, Cherubini, Boïeldieu, Paër, Spontini and others. In particular he championed the operas of Mozart, when it was not entirely fashionable to do so. During his directorship, *Le nozze di Figaro* was performed 20 times; *Die Entführung aus dem Serail*, 49; *Don Giovanni*, 68; and *Die Zauberflöte*, 82. So fascinated was he by *The Magic Flute* that he wrote a continuation of it, with most of Emanuel Schikaneder's characters reappearing. Tamino and Pamina are married, but their child has been confined to a coffin by the Queen of the Night's magic. The coffin must be carried by bearers without ever being set down, in accordance with the prophecy: „Solang ihr wandelt, lebt das Kind" ('The child shall live, as long as you wander'). The bearers' loyalty is finally rewarded, the child recovers and the libretto ends in celebration. Redemption through striving seems to be the idea.

Goethe's attitude to the relationship between words and music in opera differed radically from the one he adopted vis-à-vis the Lied. In opera, he insisted that the libretto should always serve the music – something that is abundantly clear in his letters to those composers, such as Kayser and Reichardt, who were setting the Singspiele he wrote for the court at Weimar. For example, in 1790 he wrote to Reichardt, „Zur Oper bereite ich mich. Um so etwas zu machen, muß man alles poetische Gewissen, alle poetische Scham nach dem edlen Beispiele der Italiener ablegen." ('I'm preparing for the opera. To do that one must follow the noble example of the Italians and put aside all poetic conscience and poetic modesty.') In matters of song, however, he was adamant that music should merely serve the poetry. In the *Annals* of 1801 he makes it clear that through-composed songs lose their lyrical character by what he calls a „falsche Teilnahme am Einzelnen" ('a misplaced concern with detail'). Nor are these isolated examples – throughout his writings on music, and especially in the voluminous Zelter correspondence, he stresses that in Lieder the accompaniment should be subservient to the poem.

Goethe's poetry has attracted a huge array of composers from across the globe. Early Goethe, middle Goethe, late Goethe; lyric, philosophical, epic, epigrammatic, pornographic, occasional verse; plays, novels, Singspiele – everything he wrote had a musical quality about it. In *Dichtung und Wahrheit* (Part 4, Book 16) he describes how he would wake up in the middle of the night and rush to his desk in order to write down poems such as 'Der Musensohn' that were already fully formed in his brain; and how he preferred to use a pencil, since the scratching of the quill would disturb his 'somnambulistic writing'. Much of his lyric poetry was inspired by the women he loved – and Goethe's amorous escapades were extraordinary. Four years before his death in 1832 at the age of eighty-two, he confided to Johann Peter Eckermann that men of genius (among whom he numbered himself) experienced „eine wiederholte Pubertät" (a repeated puberty) that allowed them to live a life of undiminished intensity.

Among the many women of his youth were Friederike Brion (Beethoven's 'Mailied', Schubert's 'Willkommen und Abschied') and Lili Schönemann (Beethoven's 'Neue Liebe, neues Leben'). In Weimar he became infatuated – perhaps platonically – with the older Charlotte von Stein (Schubert's 'Wandrers Nachtlieder', 'An den Mond'). After his return from Italy in 1788 he started a relationship with the sixteen years younger Christiane Vulpius (Strauss's 'Gefunden'), a young woman working at an artificial-flower factory in Weimar; to the moral outrage of Weimar society he took her into his house, where she lived with him as his mistress and bore him five children, only one of whom survived infancy. Goethe eventually married her in 1806; she died a decade later – see note 1, p. 156. In 1807 he developed a passion for the eighteen-year-old Wilhelmine Herzlieb (Mendelssohn's 'Die Liebende schreibt'). Approaching his sixty-fifth birthday, he fell in love with the thirty-year-old Marianne Jung (Schubert's 'Suleika 1 and 2'), shortly before her marriage to his friend and benefactor Geheimrat von Willemer. Nine years later, aged seventy-four, he was swept off his feet by the beautiful Ulrike von Levetzow, then aged seventeen. Goethe's love poetry was almost always joyous and lifeaffirming – it was only within the framework of fiction (*Faust*, *Wilhelm Meister*, *Egmont* . . .) that he seemed capable of writing tortured and unrequited poems. Exceptions such as the *Trilogie der Leidenschaft* and 'Wonne der Wehmut' (Beethoven and Schubert) merely prove the rule.

Music was to Goethe an essential part of life, and above all, perhaps, it brought solace. It is music that saves Faust from suicide, music that soothes Werther in his bleakest moments, music that restores both Tasso and Wilhelm Meister. The vast majority of vocal music in Goethe's time was sacred, and he was convinced that religion could not dispense with music, since it awoke in man higher feelings, what he called a „Vorgeschmack der Seligkeit" ('a foretaste of heavenly rapture'). Among his favourite sacred works were Bach's chorales, Mozart and Haydn masses and Handel's *Messiah*. Goethe's own musical soirées usually began with sacred music, and his only attempt at composition was, significantly, a setting of a religious text. He was himself no more than a competent player, but he was convinced that music-making could have only a beneficial effect on humanity. As he put it in a letter to Joseph Pleyer, dated August 1822, „Wer Musik nicht liebt, verdient nicht, ein Mensch genannt zu werden; wer sie nur liebt, ist erst ein halber Mensch; wer sie aber treibt, ist ein ganzer Mensch." ('He who does not love music does not deserve to be called a human being; he who merely loves it is only half a human being; but he who makes music is a whole human being.')

Seventeen of the 51 songs that comprise Wolf's *Goethe-Lieder* are taken from the poet's *West-östlicher Divan*. First published in 1819, it owes its inspiration to the Persian poet Hafiz (1320–1389), whose verse Goethe had read in a translation by Joseph, Freiherr von Hammer-Purgstall, that he had come across in 1814. The word 'Divan' is of Persian origin and referred originally to a kind of register or record, and in many European languages it is related to the words for border or customs controls (cf. 'douane' in French and 'dogana' in Italian); only later did the word come to designate the collected works of a poet. In the winter of 1815, Goethe gathered the poems he had so far completed and arranged them in chronological order under the provisional title '*Versammlung* deutscher Gedichte, mit stetem Bezug auf den *Divan* des persischen Sängers Mahomed Schemseddin *Hafis*'. He now prepared the poems for publication in a cycle of twelve books, accentuating the close collaboration of two kindred spirits and the mingling of two cultures („west-östlich") by giving each book a transliterated title and its German equivalent. The German titles are *Buch des Sängers, Buch Hafis, Buch der Liebe, Buch der Betrachtungen, Buch des Unmuts, Buch der Sprüche, Buch des Timur, Buch Suleika, Das Schenkenbuch, Buch der Parabeln, Buch des Parsen, Buch des Paradieses*. Goethe did not attempt to imitate the metrical form of the originals, which were usually ghazals, but wrote instead rhyming verse, mostly arranged in four-line stanzas, that is characterised by a sort of mellifluous wiriness.

It was on 4 August 1814 in Wiesbaden that Goethe met Marianne Jung (1784–1860) for the first time. She had come to Frankfurt in 1798 at the age of fourteen with a theatrical troupe, and two years later, the twice-widowed Frankfurt banker Geheimrat Johann Jakob Willemer (1760–1838), whom Goethe had known since 1778, had taken her into his home to have her educated with his own children. He married her on 27 September 1814, and when Goethe spent the summer of 1815 at the 'Gerbermühle', Willemer's summer residence outside Frankfurt, the sixty-six-year-old poet fell in love with the thirty-year-old wife of his own benefactor. She returned his love, and although after September 1815 they did not see each other again, they continued to correspond at irregular intervals. In a letter dated 10 February 1832, some six weeks before his death, Goethe informed her that he wished to return all her letters, with the request that they should be left unopened „bis zu unbestimmter Stunde" ('until an unspecified time'). He actually posted them on 29 February, enclosing this poem, written on 3 March 1831, whose tone suggests – whatever some scholars might say to the contrary – that their relationship was more than merely platonic:

Vor die Augen meiner Lieben,	To the eyes of my beloved,
Zu den Fingern, die's geschrieben –	To the fingers that wrote them,
Einst mit heißestem Verlangen	To the breast from which they poured –
So erwartet, wie empfangen –	These letters – once awaited and received
Zu der Brust, der sie entquollen,	With such ardour and passion –
Diese Blätter wandern sollen;	Shall now return;
Immer liebevoll bereit,	Ever ready, full of love,
Zeugen allerschonster Zeit.	To bear witness to that most beautiful time.

The *Buch Suleika* poems from the *West-östlicher Divan*, which ostensibly celebrated the love of Hatem and Suleika, enabled Goethe to give clandestine expression to his own passion for Marianne, although it should be remembered that a number of them had been written before they met. Some, however, she did inspire (see note 2 to 'Locken, haltet mich gefangen', p. 168), and some she wrote herself, including 'Hochbeglückt in deiner Liebe'. Their mutual love and the part she played in the composition of the *West-östlicher Divan* was revealed only decades later by Herman Grimm in his article 'Goethe und Suleika', published in the *Preussische Jahrbücher* of 1869.

Of the seventeen poems that Wolf set from the *West-östlicher Divan*, ten came from the 'Book of Suleika'. The texts of a further ten Wolf songs were taken from the novel *Wilhelm Meisters Lehrjahre*, which had first been published in 1795–6 and immediately found favour with the new generation of Romantics. Thomas Carlyle translated the novel into English in 1824 and it was for a while one of the most popular of all Goethe's works. Although it is rarely read today, the lyrics that punctuate the novel have become known to millions of music-lovers, thanks principally to the settings by Schubert, Schumann and Wolf. Some knowledge of the context of these songs within the novel is needed for a proper understanding of the poems. The texts of Wolf's three *Harfenspieler* songs are all masterpieces of introspection and melancholy. Augustin the Harper, of noble Italian birth, enters a monastery in defiance of his father's wishes, and experiences spiritual highs and lows. On his father's death, he resolves to leave the monastery because of his love for Sperata, a young woman who lives in the neighbourhood; to this end, his older brother approaches the priest and requests him to release Augustin from his vows. The priest then reveals that Sperata is none other than Augustin's sister, making any union between the two impossible. Sperata had been conceived when Augustin's parents were elderly and 'in order not to expose himself to ridicule' the father decided to conceal the birth from the outside world. After the clandestine birth, the child Sperata was brought up in the countryside by a friend of the family as his own daughter. When these facts are revealed to Augustin, he furiously refuses to believe them and declares that Sperata is already his wife and is carrying his child. He secretly leaves his family and sets sail on a ship that will, he believes, bring him across the lake to Sperata; but the sailors, apprised of the situation by Augustin's brothers, take him back to the monastery. Augustin finally renounces the relationship and seeks solace in music, singing and playing the harp incessantly in the cloisters of the monastery. Sperata meanwhile gives birth to their child, who is given the name Mignon. Persuaded by the priests that Mignon should never have existed, being the fruit of an incestuous relationship, Sperata gradually rejects her child, who is then taken in by foster-parents.

Mignon, as she grows up, often wanders off and goes missing. One day, she fails to return and Sperata, assuming that she has died, thanks God for having taken the poor creature. Sperata now has visions and is regarded by the community as a sort of saint. When she dies, her body is placed in a chapel, where it shows no signs of decay but instead turns whiter. People make pilgrimages to her chapel from far and wide. Augustin also visits his dead beloved and says cryptically, „Ich kann jetzt nicht bei ihr bleiben, ich habe noch einen sehr weiten Weg zu machen." ('I cannot stay with her now, I still have a very long way to go.') He soon disappears, and makes his way across the mountains to Germany. Mignon, of course, has not died, and we learn in the novel that, having been kidnapped in Italy, she joins a circus troupe in Germany. It is not until the end of the novel, in

Book 8, Chapter 9, that the reader learns about the Harper's story and Mignon's early history.

The Harper's three songs occur in Books 2 and 5 of the novel. Chapter 13 of Book 2 begins:

> In der verdrießlichen Unruhe, in der er [Wilhelm] sich befand, fiel ihm ein, den Alten aufzusuchen, durch dessen Harfe er die bösen Geister zu verscheuchen hoffte. Man wies ihn, als er nach dem Manne fragte, an ein schlechtes Wirtshaus in einem entfernten Winkel des Städtchens, und in demselben die Treppe hinauf bis auf den Boden, wo ihm der süße Harfenklang aus einer Kammer entgegen schallte. Es waren herzrührende, klagende Töne, von einem traurigen, ängstlichen Gesange begleitet. Wilhelm schlich an die Türe, und da der gute Alte eine Art von Phantasie vortrug, und wenige Strophen teils singend, teils rezitierend immer wiederholte, konnte der Horcher nach einer kurzen Aufmerksamkeit ungefähr folgendes verstehen:

> In the morose restlessness of his present mood he [Wilhelm] decided to visit the old man whose harp, he hoped, would banish the evil spirits. On enquiring about the man, he was directed to a squalid inn in a remote corner of the little town, and then up the stairs to the garret, where the harp's sweet tones reached his ear from a small room. They were moving, plaintive tones accompanied by sad, timid singing. Wilhelm crept up to the door, and as the good old man was performing a sort of improvisation and kept on repeating the few stanzas partly as chant and partly as recitative, the listener, after paying attention for a little while, could make out something like this:

Having listened to this song ('Wer nie sein Brot mit Tränen aß'), Wilhelm enters. They talk of solitude, whereupon the Harper improvises 'Wer sich der Einsamkeit ergibt'. 'An die Türen will ich schleichen' occurs much later in the novel: in Chapter 14 of Book 5, Wilhelm overhears the Harper singing the final verse, and the narrative runs:

> Das Lied, das er [Wilhelm] sehr wohl verstehen konnte, enthielt den Trost eines Unglücklichen, der sich dem Wahnsinne ganz nahe fühlt.

> The song, which he [Wilhelm] could understand very clearly, expressed the consolation of a wretch who feels that madness is nigh.

For information on Mignon's life, see notes to songs 5, 6, 7 and 9 of the *Goethe-Lieder*, pp. 133–9.

COMPOSER

HW to Alexander Pöch, August 1875, p. 117, reveals Wolf's ardent desire to become a composer, and it was a cunning move to dedicate the Piano Sonata to his father. In a letter to his parents, dated 29 July 1875, he had already written: „Mir ist die Musik wie Essen u. Trinken" ('Music is like meat & drink to me') and he was clearly thrilled with the first Lieder he wrote to poems by Heinrich Zschokke, Goethe and Nikolaus Lenau. These early songs were probably composed while he was still at school in Marburg, and the choice of Goethe as poet for four of the songs ('Sehnsucht', 'Der Fischer', 'Wanderlied' and 'Auf dem See') was partially determined by Wolf's wish to show his father that he was capable of setting Germany's greatest poet. HW to his parents, 15 March 1876, p. 118, which mentions with pride that he had set three Goethe choruses, illustrates how, even at this early stage, Wolf was gathering together in one opus several settings of a single poet – Wolf was unaware that the poem of one of the choruses, 'Im Sommer', was actually by Johann Georg Jacobi and not by Goethe.

When Wolf embarked on his *Gedichte von J. W. v. Goethe*, he was well aware of the gargantuan task confronting him. How could he do justice to the depth and range of Germany's greatest poet? And how dare he invite comparisons with the greatest Goethe Lieder by Reichardt, Zelter, Beethoven, Schubert, Schumann, Loewe and others? Although he did not shirk this challenge (he composed twenty poems that Schubert had set, including ten *Wilhelm Meister* settings), he cleverly cast his net wide for poems that had not previously attracted composers. Thus it was that he was drawn to seventeen poems from the *West-östlicher Divan*: two from the 'Book of the Minstrel', five from the 'Book of the Cup-bearer' and ten from the 'Book of Suleika', none of which according to Ernst Challier's *Großer Lieder-Katalog* (1885) had *ever* been set to music before, apart from 'Phänomen' (Brahms), 'Erschaffen und Beleben' (Zelter) and long-forgotten settings of 'Als ich auf dem Euphrat schiffte' by Konrad Heubner and Johanna Kinkel. Wolf rather pointedly ended his *Gedichte von J. W. v. Goethe* with 'Prometheus', 'Ganymed' and 'Grenzen der Menschheit' – a scarcely veiled challenge to Schubert who had set these poems with such genius (see HW to Emil Kauffmann, 22 December 1890, p. 121).

Wolf frequently quotes snippets of Goethe in his correspondence, nowhere more memorably than when he expressed his devotion to Margarethe Klinckerfuß. As a seventy-year-old, she wrote a book of reminiscences, *Aufklänge aus versunkener Zeit*, in which she recalls how she (aged nineteen in 1896) and Wolf had played a Bruckner symphony together as a piano duet. After the *adagio* he had kissed her gently on the brow and said: „Wie einig wir sind, als hätten wir uns lebenslang aufeinander eingespielt!" ('How together we are, as though we had practised together all our lives!') He then allegedly recited a passage from

Goethe's great poem to Charlotte von Stein ('Warum gabst du uns die tiefen Blicke'):

Sag', was will das Schicksal uns bereiten?	Tell me, what does fate have in store for us?
Sag', wie band es uns so rein genau?	Tell me, how did it fashion so pure a bond?
Ach, du warst in abgelebten Zeiten	Ah, you were in bygone times
Meine Schwester oder meine Frau ...	My sister or my wife ...

See also HW to his parents, Easter Sunday 1878 and 29 April 1878; to his father, 16 October 1878; to Oskar Grohe, 8 July 1893, and to Karl Mayr, 15 March 1897, pp. 118, 119, 191, 122 and 436, for further examples of Wolf's affection for other works by Goethe.

LETTERS

HW to Alexander Pöch, Windischgraz, August 1875

Ich gebe dir aber die Nachricht dass ich auf's Jahr nach Wien gehe u. z. ins – – Conservatorium. Das Studium wird aufgegeben, da sowol Dr. Hauseker,[1] der Rezensent der Concerte u. des Theaters ist u. was Musik anbelangt allen musikalischen Größen in Gratz obenan steht als auch Loninger, der früher Professor am Conservatorium zu Leipzig war, den Vater beredeten u. ihm mein entschiedenes Talent zur Musik vorstellten, das er mich in's Conservatorium geben soll; und zwar bilde ich mich hauptsächlich in der Compositionslehre aus um mich zum Compositeur heranzubilden. Zu diesem Behufe habe ich, wie du vielleicht schon weist, die Sonate,[2] dann 10 Variationen über ein Original Thema, dann die Lieder „Nacht u. Grab von Heinrich Tschokke, Sehnsucht, der Fischer, Wanderlied (für Männer Quartet)[3] u. Meeresstille von Goethe[4] [...] componirt.

I write to tell you that I shall move next year to Vienna and study at the Conservatoire. I shall give up school, since Dr Hauseker, the theatre & music critic who knows more about music than all the other bigwigs in Gratz, and Loninger, who used to be professor at the Leipzig Conservatoire, have convinced my father of my considerable musical talent & persuaded him that I should attend the Conservatoire – where I shall concentrate on composition and learn all that is necessary to become a composer. To this end I have

---

1 Dr Friedrich von Hausegger (1837–1899).
2 Wolf proudly dedicated the Piano Sonata to his father: *Sonate, gewidmet dem Herrn Philipp Wolf von Hugo Wolf.*
3 No version for male quartet has been found.
4 Wolf mistakes the poet: 'Meeresstille' is by Lenau not Goethe.

composed, as you perhaps know, the Sonata, then 10 Variations on an Original Theme, then these songs: Heinrich Tschokke's 'Nacht & Grab', and Goethe's 'Sehnsucht', 'Der Fischer', 'Wanderlied' (for male quartet) & 'Meeresstille'.

HW to his parents, Vienna, 15 March 1876

Zu Hause angekommen machte ich mich gleich an die Arbeit eines neuen Chores „Im Sommer" von Goethe,[1] dem 3 andere Chöre folgten;[2] diese 4 Chöre sind ohne Klavierbegleitung und im Tenorschlüssel geschrieben, was mir anfangs etwas schwer ging. Sie sind sehr schön gearbeitet, und hoffe, daß dieselben Richter[3] gut gefallen werden.

No sooner had I arrived home than I began to work on a new chorus, Goethe's 'Im Sommer', and then 3 others. These 4 choruses are without piano accompaniment and written in the tenor clef – which I initially found rather difficult. They are very beautifully crafted, and I hope that they will please Richter.

HW to his parents, Vienna, Easter Sunday 1878

Früh morgens um ¼ auf 8 Uhr machte ich den ersten Sprung aus dem Bett, aber nicht um mich anzuziehen, sondern um das bekannte Gegenmittel für den Krampf, der mir in den Fuß fuhr, zu gebrauchen. Nach einer Viertelstunde jedoch mußte ich ernst mit dem Aufstehen anfangen, da mir die Vögel und die Sonne gar zudringlich zu verstehen gegeben, daß es Zeit sei. Das erste, was ich tat, war, die Osterszene aus dem Goetheschen „Faust" zu lesen, die mich in einen Taumel des Entzückens versetzte – ich glaubte mit den Bürgern und Studenten mitzuspazieren, so vertiefte ich mich in diese goldenen Zeiten – ein wahres Labsal.

At 7.45 in the morning I jumped out of bed, not to get dressed but to take the usual remedy for cramp, from which I've been suffering in my foot. After a quarter of an hour, however, I had to think seriously about getting up, because the birds and sun made it abundantly clear that it was time. The first thing I

---

1 The poet of 'Im Sommer' is in fact Jacobi not Goethe.
2 The three other choruses are 'Geistesgruß' (Goethe), 'Mailied' (Goethe) and perhaps the missing 'Die schöne Nacht' (Goethe). These choruses for male voices were composed for performance in the Ritterbund, an amateur music society in Windischgraz.
3 Hans Richter (1843–1916). Wolf first met Richter in February 1876 when he showed him his recent compositions. The conductor not only encouraged the young Wolf but arranged complimentary tickets for him at the Bayreuth Festival. Richter was impressed by Wolf's *Penthesilea* but when he conducted it at a trial performance in 1886 without, according to Wolf, any understanding of the work, Wolf's fury knew no bounds. Whether Richter deliberately sabotaged the success of *Penthesilea* by conducting it without conviction because of Wolf's derogatory comments about Brahms cannot be proved.

did was to read the Easter scene from Goethe's *Faust* that transported me into paroxysms of delight – I immersed myself so deeply in this golden era that I actually imagined I was walking among the citizens and students. A veritable restorative.

HW to his parents, Vienna, 29 April 1878

Zu schwach, die erhebendsten Worte zur Feier dieser zwei schönen Tage[1] zu finden und mein innigstes Empfinden nicht mit einem Bombast von Redensarten zu verunstalten, greife ich zum Grössten deutschen Dichter zu Goethe und rufe Ihnen die schönen Worte des Alten an Doctor Faust in's Gedächtniß zurück:

> So nehmet auch den schönsten Krug,
> Den wir mit frischem Trunk gefüllt!
> Ich bring' ihn zu und wünsche laut,
> Daß er nicht nur den Durst Euch stillt;
> Die Zahl der Tropfen, die er hegt,
> Sei Euren Tagen zugelegt![2]

Too weak to find the most sublime words for these two lovely days of celebration, and also not to spoil my most fervent feelings with bombast, I have recourse to the greatest German poet, to Goethe, and remind you both of the beautiful words of the old man to Doctor Faust:

> So take the choicest jug
> That we have filled with fresh wine!
> I drink a toast and say aloud:
> May it quench more than your thirst;
> May the sum of drops that it contains
> Be added to your days of life!

HW to his father, Waidhofen a. d. Ybbs, 27 August 1878

Jetzt bin ich mit der Komposition „Gretchen vor dem Andachtsbild der mater dolorosa" aus Goethes I. Teil „Faust" beschäftigt. Es wird dies die beste von meinen bis jetzt geschriebenen Kompositionen sein, die dann im November zur Aufführung gelangen.[3]

I'm now busy composing 'Gretchen vor dem Andachtsbild der Mater Dolorosa' from Goethe's *Faust*, Part I. This will be the best of all my compositions to date and will be premiered in November.

---

1 A letter-card to celebrate the birthday of his parents: 30 April (mother), 1 May (father).
2 *Faust*, Part I, 'Vor dem Tor', lines 985–90.
3 The first verifiable performance took place in Vienna on 5 October 1936.

HW to Rudolf von Larisch, Döbling, 19 December 1888

Heute bin ich rasend eilig. Ich beabsichtige, in diesem Jahr noch eine Anzahl Goethe'scher Lieder zu komponieren und fühle mich auch sehr aufgelegt hiezu. So komponierte ich gestern „Mignon" („Nur wer die Sehnsucht kennt"), vorgestern „Mignon" („Kennst du das Land") und heute und morgen hoffe ich noch mit den zwei anderen Mignon's fertig zu werden. Sie sehen, daß es mir an Arbeit nicht gebricht.

Today I'm in a mad hurry. I intend before this year is out to compose a number of Goethe songs, and feel very much in the mood for this. Yesterday I composed 'Mignon' ('Nur wer die Sehnsucht kennt'), the day before yesterday 'Mignon' ('Kennst du das Land') and today and tomorrow I hope to finish Mignon's two other songs. I've no lack of work, you see.

HW to Melanie Köchert, Munich, 12 October 1890

Die Produktion hat stattgefunden u. sind alle bis auf Merz[1] erschienen. Ich habe fast nur Goethe vorgetragen, doch wurde vieles gar nicht verstanden so z. B. „Phänomen" u. „dieß zu deuten". Auch die heiligen 3 Könige thaten nicht ihre gewohnte Wirkung; kurz, es ging ziemlich spießig.

    Gura,[2] der am längsten bei mir aushielt, sang mir, da nur noch Liliencron anwesend war, meine Harfnerlieder vom Blatt weg vor u. z. in geradezu vollendeter Weise. Er war ganz begeistert davon u. stellt dieselben weit über die Schumann'schen u. Schubert'schen. Ganz entzückt war er von „auf einer Wanderung", die er wie sie im Original niedergeschrieben, singen will.

    Lewy[3] gefielen am besten die beiden cophtischen „als ich auf dem Euphrat schiffte" u. seltsamerweise „wenn ich dein gedenke" u. „wie sollt ich heiter bleiben". Der Rattenfänger wollte nicht verfangen, hingegen waren alle in Extase über „trunken müssen wir alle sein" u. „komm, Liebchen, komm". Im Ganzen gewann ich den Eindruck, daß ich <u>nicht</u> verstanden wurde, daß man zu sehr mit dem musikalischen sich beschäftigte u. darüber das Neue u. eigenartige meiner musikalisch-dichterischen Auffassung vergaß.

The recital has taken place & everyone turned up apart from Merz. I performed Goethe almost exclusively, but much of it was not understood at all – for instance 'Phänomen' & 'Dies zu deuten, bin erbötig'. The Three Holy Kings also failed to make their usual impression; in fact, the song fell rather flat.

---

1   Oskar Merz (1851–1908), opera critic of the Münchner *Neueste Nachrichten*.
2   Eugen Gura (1843–1906) first met Wolf on 11 October 1890 in Munich. This bass-baritone did much to promote the Lieder of Wolf, who in a letter to Melanie Köchert described his voice as divine („göttlich") and his singing as heavenly („himmlisch").
3   Hermann Levi (1839–1900), who conducted the first performance of *Parsifal* at Bayreuth.

[Eugen] Gura, who held out longest, sang for me, while only [Detlev von] Liliencron was still present, my *Harfnerlieder* at sight and in consummate fashion. He was utterly enraptured & thought them far superior to the settings by Schumann and Schubert. He was wholly delighted with 'Auf einer Wanderung', which he wants to sing just as it is in the original.

Levi liked the two Coptic songs best, 'Als ich auf dem Euphrat schiffte' &, oddly enough, 'Wenn ich dein gedenke' & 'Wie sollt' ich heiter bleiben'. 'Der Rattenfänger' made little impression, but everyone was ecstatic about 'Trunken müssen wir alle sein!' & 'Komm, Liebchen, komm!' On the whole I got the impression that I was not understood, that they occupied themselves too much with musical matters, & in doing so forgot about what is new & original in my musico-poetical conception.

HW to Emil Kauffmann, Ober-Döbling, 22 December 1890

Was Sie mir über Prometheus u. Ganymed schreiben hat mich auf das innigste erfreut. Auch ich bin der Ansicht, daß Schubert die Composition dieser beiden Gedichte nicht gelungen ist u. daß es einer nach-Wagner'schen Zeit erst vorbehalten war, diese großartigen Gedichte im Goethe'schen Geiste zu vertonen. Es ist geradezu unglaublich, wie Leute von so feinem Verständniß als z. B mein Freund Schalk[1] gegen meinen Prometheus zu Gunsten des Schubert'schen opponiren konnten. Auch Levi u. Porges[2] in München wollte mein Prometheus nicht einleuchten, wohingegen mir von anderer Seite (z. B. Weingartner) gerade diesem Stück gegenüber die begeisterste Anerkennung ausgesprochen wurde. Gegen einmal gefaßte Vorurtheile anzukämpfen ist wahrlich eine harte Arbeit u. für den davon betroffenen Künstler äußerst betrübend. Mich wundert wahrlich, daß man meine Harfner u. Mignon-Lieder noch so passiren läßt und dieß Alles nur, weil ein großes Genie (Schubert) sich einmal auch schwach gezeigt hat.[3]

What you write to me about 'Prometheus' & 'Ganymed' delighted me. I too am of the opinion that Schubert's settings of these two poems were not successful, & that it has been left to a post Wagner era to compose these magnificent poems in a way that is true to Goethe. It's simply unbelievable that people of such fine discernment as my friend Schalk can prefer Schubert's 'Prometheus' to mine. Neither did Levi & Porges in Munich understand my 'Prometheus', whereas for others ([Felix] Weingartner, for example) it was precisely this song that was praised to the skies. Once a prejudice has been formed, it is genuinely difficult & deeply depressing for an artist to fight against it. I find it truly

---

1 Franz Schalk (1863–1931), violinist, conductor, close friend and champion of Wolf's songs.
2 Heinrich Porges (1837–1900), choral conductor and one of Munich's most respected critics.
3 Wolf's unjustified criticism of Schubert shows how even in 1890 Schubert could be underestimated when he aimed for the profound.

surprising that my Harper & Mignon songs should pass muster, just because a great genius (Schubert) had, for once, a bad day.

HW to Oskar Grohe, Traunkirchen, 8 July 1893

Ich wollte Sie wären gerade zur Zeit hier jetzt, wo ein Tag um den Andern wetteifert sein freundlichstes Gesicht uns zu zeigen. Schon fühle ich die Wirkung des Goethe'schen Wortes, daß nichts schwerer zu ertragen sei, als eine Reihe von schönen Tagen.[1] Das mag übrigens auch seinen Grund in der schauderhaften Langeweile haben, die mich nun lange genug schon plagt u. die sich als eine allzu getreue Gefährtin mir erweist.

I wish you could be here now, when days compete with each other in showing me their most friendly countenance. I feel the force of Goethe's words that nothing is more difficult to bear than a sequence of beautiful days. The reason I feel this is the atrocious boredom that has assailed me now for long enough & proves to be an all too faithful companion.

HW to Paul Müller, Vienna, 24 February 1896

Daß das Lied „so lang man nüchtern ist" einen so großen Eindruck auf Sie gemacht freut mich höchlichst. Ich habe seinerzeit, als ich dasselbe Lied Capellmeister Nikisch[2] gelegentlich einer Zusammenkunft in Ischl vorspielte, ihn damit geradezu in Ekstase versetzt. Gravirender aber für Ihre geistreiche Auslegung der Goethe'schen Beobachtung ist das Lied Phänomen, das schon manchem feinfühligen Kenner zu tiefsinnigen Bemerkungen Anlaß gegeben.

I'm delighted that 'So lang man nüchtern ist' made such a huge impression on you. When I played the same song to Kapellmeister Nikisch at a gathering in Ischl, it sent him into ecstasies. Of far greater significance for your clever interpretation of Goethe's powers of observation is my song 'Phänomen' that has occasioned profound comments from many a sensitive connoisseur.

---

[1] Alles in der Welt läßt sich ertragen,   Everything in the world can be borne,
Nur nicht eine Reihe von schönen Tagen.   Except a sequence of beautiful days.

[2] Arthur Nikisch (1855–1922), Hungarian-German conductor who made his first appearance in Vienna in 1874. He reneged on his promise to perform Wolf's *Penthesilea* in Boston. Nikisch accompanied his mistress, the mezzo-soprano Elena Gerhardt, in numerous recitals that featured Wolf's songs.

LIEDER

Sehnsucht[1]

Was zieht mir das Herz so?
Was zieht mich hinaus?
Und windet und schraubt mich
Aus Zimmer und Haus?
Wie dort sich die Wolken
Um Felsen verziehn!
Da möcht ich hinüber,
Da möcht ich wohl hin!*

Nun wiegt sich der Raben
Geselliger Flug;
Ich mische mich drunter
Und folge dem Zug.
Und Berg und Gemäuer
Umfittigen wir;
Sie weilet da drunten;
Ich spähe nach ihr.*

Da kommt sie und wandelt!
Ich eile sobald,
Ein singender Vogel,
Zum buschigten[2] Wald.
Sie weilet und horchet
Und lächelt mit sich:
„Er singt es so lieblich[3]
Und singt es an mich."*

Die scheidende Sonne
Vergüldet die Höhn;
Die sinnende Schöne,
Sie läßt es geschehn.
Sie wandelt am Bache
Die Wiesen entlang,
Und finst'rer und finst'rer[4]
Umschlingt sich der Gang.*

Longing

What pulls at my heart so?
What draws me outside?
And wrenches and wrests me
From room and from house?
How the clouds disperse
About those cliffs!
That is where I'd like to be,
That is where I'd like to go.*

Now the ravens flock together
In undulating flight;
I mingle with them
And follow their path.
We circle around
Mountains and ruins:
Her home's in the valley,
I look out for her there.*

There she comes strolling along!
I hasten at once,
Like a singing bird,
To the bushy wood.
She lingers and listens
And smiles to herself:
'He sings so sweetly
And he sings for me.'*

The setting sun
Gilds the mountains;
My musing fair one
Gives it no thought.
She walks through the meadows
That border the brook,
And the winding path
Grows ever darker.*

Poem written before 18 December 1802
Also set by Ludwig van Beethoven, Fanny Mendelssohn Hensel, Johann Friedrich Reichardt, Wolfgang Rihm and Franz Schubert
* Wolf repeats the final two lines of each verse.

1 Wolf sets only verses 1–4 of Goethe's poem. 2 Goethe: buschigen.
3 Goethe: Er singet so lieblich. 4 Goethe: Und finster und finst'rer.

Der Fischer[1, 2]

Das Wasser rauscht', das Wasser schwoll,
Ein Fischer saß daran,*
Sah nach der Angel[3] ruhevoll,*
Kühl bis ins Herz hinan.*[4]
Und wie er sitzt und wie er lauscht,
Teilt sich die Flut empor;
Aus dem bewegten Wasser rauscht
Ein feuchtes Weib hervor.*

The angler

The water rushed, the water rose,
An angler on the bank*
Sat gazing calmly at his line,*
Cool to his very heart.*
And as he sits and as he harks,
The waters surge and part;
And from the water's churning swell
A water-nymph arose.*

Poem written 1778
Also set by Hensel, Reichardt, Schubert, Robert Schumann, Siegmund von Seckendorff, Richard Strauss, Václav Tomášek, Johann Vesque von Püttlingen and Carl Friedrich Zelter
* Wolf repeats these lines.

Auf dem See[5]

Und frische Nahrung, neues Blut
[Saug' ich aus freier Welt;][6]

On the lake

And fresh nourishment, new blood
[I suck from these open spaces;]

1 Herder opens his *Stimmen der Völker in Liedern* (1779) with Goethe's 'Der Fischer', changing the title to 'Das Lied vom Fischer' and writing in the introduction that Goethe's poem should inspire other German poets to write such folk poetry: „Die deutsche Poesie muß, wenn sie wirklich Volksdichtung werden will, den Weg gehen, den dieses Gedicht zeigt." ('If German poetry seeks to be true folk poetry, it must follow the path shown by this poem.')
2 Wolf sets only the first verse of Goethe's poem.
3 Goethe: nach dem Angel. From Martin Luther and Hans Sachs on, 'Angel' was a masculine noun, although Goethe was later to use the feminine form.
4 Goethe: Kühl bis ans Herz hinan.
5 In 1775 Goethe was summoned by Carl August, the eighteen-year-old ruler of the small Duchy of Saxe-Weimar-Eisenach, to join the cultured circle of the court. Three months before he received the invitation, he wrote an impromptu poem in his notebook under the heading '15. Junius 1775 Donnerstags morgen aufm Zürchersee' and later revised it for publication in 1789, giving it the title 'Auf dem See'. The poem, on the surface, is about rowing on Lake Zurich, but there is a deeper symbolism at work that reflects Goethe's uncertainty of mind, regarding his relationship with the sixteen-year-old Anna Elisabeth Schönemann (the Lili and Belinde of his poetry) to whom he became engaged in April 1775. Although Goethe confided to Eckermann half a century later that Lili was the only woman he had ever truly loved, he broke off the relationship later in the year when he had returned from his Swiss journey. Goethe talks about Lili in Part 4, Chapter 17, of *Dichtung und Wahrheit* and quotes the whole poem in Part 4, Chapter 18. The initial iambic rhythm conveys the pull of the oars, and the harmony he feels with nature is expressed in the opening two lines. The peaceful mood does not last; the iambics cease, he rests on his oars and, to a new trochaic metre, reflects on his life. The 'golden dreams' refer to his love for Lili, whom he now wished to shun; he resolves to forget the dream, and instead embrace the present. To a quicker rhythm he rows ashore and glimpses the ripening fruit in the morning light. 'Ripening fruit' ('Reifende Frucht') – given the abundance of imagery in the first stanza connected with nurture ('saug'/'suckle', 'Busen'/'breast', 'wiegen'/'cradle' and, in the original version, the umbilical cord: „Ich saug an meiner Nabelschnur/Nun Nahrung aus der Welt" ('I now suck from my umbilical cord nourishment from the world around') – implies a new maturity as he faces the future and subsequently the fresh challenge of Weimar.
6 Wolf omits this line.

Wie ist Natur so hold und gut,	How sweet and kindly Nature is,
Die mich am Busen hält!	Who holds me to her breast!
Die Welle wieget unsern Kahn	The waves cradle our boat
Im Rudertakt hinauf,*	To the rhythm of the oars,*
Und Berge, wolkig himmelan,	And soaring cloud-capped mountains
Begegnen unserm Lauf.*	Meet us in our course.*
Aug', mein Aug', was sinkst du nieder?	Why, my eyes, do you look down?
Goldne Träume, kommt ihr wieder?	Golden dreams, will you return?
Weg, du Traum!§ so hold¹ du bist;	Away, O dream,§ however wondrous;
Hier auch Lieb' und Leben ist.*	Here too is love and life.*
Auf der Welle blinken	Stars in their thousands drift
Tausend schwebende Sterne,	And glitter on the waves,
Weiche Nebel trinken	Gentle mists drink in
Rings die türmende Ferne;*	The looming skyline;*
Morgenwind umflügelt	Morning breezes flutter
Die beschattete Bucht,	Round the shaded bay,
Und im See bespiegelt*	And the ripening fruit*
Sich die reifende Frucht.*	Is reflected in the lake.*

Poem written June 1775 and later revised
Also set by Hensel, Carl Loewe, Nikolai Medtner, Felix Mendelssohn, Reichardt, Schubert, Schumann, Strauss and Tomášek
* Wolf repeats these lines.
§ 'Weg, du Traum!' is twice repeated.

Erster Verlust[2]

First loss

Ach! wer bringt die schönen Tage,	Ah! who will bring the fair days back,
Jene Tage der ersten Liebe,	Those days of first love,
Ach! wer bringt nur eine Stunde*	Ah! who will bring but one hour back*
Jener holden Zeit zurück!*	Of that radiant time!*

1 Goethe: gold.
2 Having completed the Singspiel *Scherz, List und Rache*, Goethe immediately set about writing another operetta text, in order to increase the meagre store of good German libretti. On 7 November 1785, he wrote to Charlotte von Stein: „Ich habe auch eine a l t e Operette wieder vorgenommen und sie reicher ausgeführt." ('I have turned my attention once more to an *old* operetta, and have expanded the material.') The work in question was *Die ungleichen Hausgenossen*, for which he had already produced sketches. He worked on the piece, on and off, for another six months, but it remained nothing more than a fragment, possibly because his energies were now directed towards his imminent journey to Italy. Three poems, including 'Erster Verlust', were fortunately salvaged by Goethe and printed in the *Schriften* of 1789. The text to 'Erster Verlust' is a conflation of two arias from Mozart's *Le nozze di Figaro* ('Porgi amor' and 'Dove sono'), which Goethe's brother-in-law Christian Vulpius was translating at the very time Goethe was writing *Die ungleichen Hausgenossen* – a work that, like *Le nozze di Figaro*, presents us with a pair of ill-assorted lovers. Almost all of Goethe's poems of unrequited love were written within the framework of fiction (novels, plays or Singspiele), and personal utterances of unhappiness, such as 'An die Entfernte', 'Wonne der Wehmut' and the *Trilogie der Leidenschaft* are remarkably rare.

Einsam nähr' ich meine Wunde,
Und mit stets erneuter Klage
Traur' ich um's verlorne Glück.*

Ach! wer bringt die schönen Tage,*
Jene holde Zeit zurück!*

In my loneliness I feed my wound,
And with ever renewed lament
Mourn the happiness I lost.*

Ah! who will bring the fair days back,*
That radiant time!*

Poem written in 1785
Also set by Alban Berg, Hensel, Nikolai Medtner, Mendelssohn, Reichardt, Schubert, Tomášek and Zelter
* Wolf repeats these lines.

Geistesgruß[1]

Hoch auf dem alten Turme steht
Des Helden edler Geist,
Der, wie das Schiff vorüber geht,
Es wohl zu fahren heißt.

„Sieh, diese Sehne[2] war so stark,
Dies Herz so fest und wild,
Die Knochen voll von Rittermark,
Die[3] Becher angefüllt;

Mein halbes Leben stürmt' ich fort,
Verdehnt' die Hälft' in Ruh,
Und du, du Menschen-Schifflein dort,
Fahr' immer, immer zu!"[4]

Ghostly greeting

High on the ancient tower
Stands the hero's noble shade,
And bids the passing ship
A prosperous voyage.

'See, these sinews were so strong,
This heart so wild and steadfast,
These limbs full of knightly valour,
These goblets filled with wine;

'For half my life I ventured forth,
Half I spent in repose,
And you, little ship of mankind,
Sail onward, ever on!'

Poem written 18 July 1774
Also set by Medtner, Reichardt, Schubert, Tomášek and Zelter

Mailied[5]

Zwischen Weizen und Korn,
Zwischen Hecken und Dorn,

May song

Amid corn and rye,
Amid hedges and thorn,

---

[1] The poem was written during Goethe's journey along the Lahn and the Rhine from Ems to Neuried in the company of Johann Kaspar Lavater, the celebrated Swiss theologian, and Johann Bernhard Basedow, an eminent scholar. Goethe mentions the occasion in *Dichtung und Wahrheit*, Part 3, Chapter 14. The poem was actually dictated to Maler Schmoll who wrote it into Lavater's diary, where the entry for 18 July 1774 reads: „Herrlich altes Schloß Lahnegg, herab auf die Lahn blickend. Goethe diktierte." ('Splendid old Lahnegg Castle, looking down on the River Lahn. Goethe dictated.') In another poem, 'Zwischen Lavater und Basedow', Goethe describes himself sitting between the two celebrities, „Das Weltkind in der Mitten" ("The worldling in the middle').
[2] Goethe: Senne.   [3] Goethe: Der Becher.
[4] Wolf's a cappella setting for TTBB features multiple repetitions. See also HW to his parents, 15 March 1876, p. 118.
[5] Gojmir Krek points out ('Hugo Wolf in Slovenci', *Novi Akordi*, IX, 1910) that Wolf's opening melody is almost identical with the folk song 'Se davno mrači, moj'ga pobča še ni'.

Zwischen Bäumen und Gras,
Wo gehts Liebchen?
Sag mir das!

    Fand mein Holdchen
    Nicht daheim;
    Muß das Goldchen
    Draußen sein.
    Grünt und blüht
    Der schöne Mai,[1]
    Liebchen ziehet
    Froh und frei.

An dem Felsen beim Fluß,
Wo sie reichte den Kuß,
Jenen ersten im Gras,
Seh ich etwas!
Ist sie das?

Amid trees and grass,
Where's my love walking?
Tell me!

    I did not find my sweetling
    At home;
    The precious creature
    Must be out there.
    May's growing green
    And blossoming fair,
    My sweetheart wanders
    Happy and free.

Under the cliff by the river,
Where she once kissed me –
That first kiss in the grass –
I can see something!
Is it she?

Poem written *c.* 1810
Also set by Robert Franz, Medtner, Arnold Schoenberg, Zelter and Alexander von Zemlinsky

Gretchen vor dem Andachtsbild der Mater Dolorosa[2]

Ach neige,
Du Schmerzenreiche,
Dein Antlitz gnädig meiner Not!

Das Schwert im Herzen,[3]
Mit tausend Schmerzen
Blickst auf zu deines Sohnes Tod.

Gretchen before an image of the Mater Dolorosa

Ah, incline thy countenance,
Thou who art full of sorrow,
To my distress!

With the sword in thy heart,
And a thousand griefs,
Thou dost look up at thy dying Son.

---

1   Goethe: Schön der Mai. See HW to his parents, 15 March 1876, p. 118.
2   Gretchen at the end of 'Meine Ruh' ist hin' (Schubert's 'Gretchen am Spinnrade') subliminally longs for a consummated relationship with Faust („Ach dürft' ich fassen/Und halten ihn,/Und küssen ihn,/So wie ich wollt',/An seinen Küssen/Vergehen sollt'!"). At their next meeting she innocently asks him if he believes in God, and he replies with his famous pantheistic creed that is quite beyond her naive comprehension of the world. He urges her to sleep with him. She replies that her mother would wake and discover them; but when he suggests that she give her a sleeping draught, she consents. By the time of her next song in *Faust* („Ach, neige,/Du Schmerzenreiche") Gretchen is pregnant, abandoned by Faust, and her mother has died from an overdose of the sleeping draught. As Gretchen decorates the shrine of the Mater Dolorosa (Our Lady of Sorrows) in the ramparts of the city wall ('Zwinger') outside the cathedral, she chants the opening of her song, whose incantatory refrain gives way to a more personal and *staccato* utterance („Wer fühlet,/Wie wühlet") describing the pain of the foetus and the shame within her. Wolf, who had recently contracted syphilis, must have been drawn to the theme of the poem – sin and a prayer for forgiveness. See also HW to his father, 27 August 1878, p. 119.
3   Some medieval paintings of the Mater Dolorosa depict the Holy Virgin with a sword piercing her heart.

Zum Vater blickst du,	Thou dost raise thine eyes to the Father
Und Seufzer schickst du	And utter sighs
Hinauf um sein' und deine Not.	For His affliction and thine own.
Wer fühlet,	Who can feel
Wie wühlet	How the pain
Der Schmerz mir im Gebein?	Churns in my very bones?
Was mein armes Herz hier banget,	What my poor heart dreads,
Was es zittert, was verlanget,	Why it quakes, what it craves,
Weißt nur du, nur du allein!	Only thou, thou canst know!
Wohin ich immer gehe,	Wherever I go,
Wie weh, wie weh, wie wehe	How it throbs, throbs, throbs
Wird mir im Busen hier!	Here in my breast!
Ich bin, ach! kaum alleine,	Alas, no sooner am I alone,
Ich wein', ich wein', ich weine,	I weep, I weep, I weep,
Das Herz zerbricht in mir.[1]	My heart breaks.
Die Scherben vor meinem Fenster[2]	The flower pots outside my window
Betaut ich mit Tränen, ach!	I bedewed, ah! with my tears,
Als ich am frühen Morgen	When early this morning
Dir diese Blumen brach.	I picked for thee these flowers.
Schien hell in meine Kammer	When the bright sun
Die Sonne früh herauf,	Shone early into my room,
Saß ich in allem Jammer	I sat in all my misery
In meinem Bett schon auf.	Bolt upright in my bed.
Hilf! rette mich von Schmach und Tod!*	Help! save me from disgrace and death!*
Ach, neige,	Ah, incline thy countenance,
Du Schmerzenreiche,	Thou who art full of sorrow,
Dein Antlitz gnädig meiner Not!	To my distress!

Poem written 1771–5
Also set by Bernhard Klein, Loewe, Schubert,[2] Giuseppe Verdi and Richard Wagner
* Wolf repeats this line.

Beherzigung[3]   ## Counsel

Feiger Gedanken	Timid uncertainty
Bängliches Schwanken,	Of craven thoughts,
Weibisches Zagen,	Effeminate hesitation,

1   Schubert set the poem as 'Gretchens Bitte' in May 1817 but left it unfinished. He modulated to C major after „Das Herz zerbricht in mir" and indicated that the key signature of the next section was to have been in A flat. Benjamin Britten completed the song in December 1938.
2   At the start of this scene, Gretchen is decorating the shrine of the Holy Virgin with flowers she has picked from the pots outside her window.
3   The publication of *Sechs Gedichte von Scheffel, Mörike, Goethe und Just. Kerner* and *Sechs Lieder für eine Frauenstimme* was due largely to the wisdom and generosity of Friedrich Eckstein, a friend of

Ängstliches Klagen	Anxious lamenting
Wendet kein Elend,	Cannot avert misery,
Macht dich nicht frei.	Cannot make you free.
Allen Gewalten	But defying
Zum Trutz sich erhalten,	All tyranny,
Nimmer sich beugen,	Never submitting,
Kräftig sich zeigen,	Showing oneself forceful
Rufet die Arme	Will call forth
Der Götter herbei.*	The succour of gods.*

Poem written 1777
Also set by Johannes Brahms, Reichardt and Zemlinsky
* Wolf twice repeats the final line.

Wanderers Nachtlied[1]

Wanderer's nightsong

Der du von dem Himmel bist,	Thou who art from heaven,
Alles Leid und Schmerzen stillest,	And dost soothe all grief and pain,
Den, der doppelt elend ist,	Refreshing the doubly wretched
Doppelt mit Erquickung füllest,	Doubly with delight,
Ach! ich bin des Treibens müde!	Ah! I am weary of this restlessness!
Was soll all der Schmerz und Lust?	Why all this pain and all this joy?
Süßer Friede!	Sweet peace!
Komm, ach komm in meine Brust!*	Come, ah come into my breast!*

---

independent means, who was always ready to help the composer in times of emotional and financial need. Wolf's father had died on 9 May 1887, and Wolf now fell prey to one of those bouts of melancholy that affected him throughout his life. Eckstein's offer to facilitate the publication of twelve songs, the choice of which he left to the composer, was nothing less than a lifeline. He contacted the Viennese publishing house of Emil Wetzler, and it was not long before Wolf obliged with the two sets. Apart from 'Beherzigung', the songs are 'Wächterlied auf der Wartburg' (Scheffel), 'Der König bei der Krönung' (Mörike), 'Biterolf' (Scheffel), 'Wanderers Nachtlied' (Goethe) and 'Zur Ruh, zur Ruh!' (Kerner), all of which had been composed between 1883 and 1887. During the preparations for publication Wolf informed Eckstein on 15 February 1888 that he would like to dedicate the *Sechs Lieder für eine Frauenstimme* to his mother, and the *Sechs Gedichte von Scheffel, Mörike, Goethe und Just. Kerner* to his father.

'Beherzigung' is sung by Magus in Act II of Goethe's *Lila*, which he wrote, with music by Baron von Seckendorf, for the birthday of the young Duchess Luise on 30 January 1777. The original play deals with a depressive count who is rescued from melancholy by a Fairy Sunlight. In a revised version of the play, the depression was transferred to the Count's wife Lila, whose sanity has been impaired – first, by a false report of her husband's death, and then by the news that his mind has been inhabited by demons. Doctor Verazio, by suggesting that all her friends and relatives impersonate these monsters in order to demonstrate their harmlessness, hopes to effect Lila's recovery. 'Feiger Gedanken', spoken by Doctor Verazio in disguise at the start of Act II, gives sententious advice to Lila on how best to recover from her melancholy. The play is also a thinly veiled parable on the Duchess Luise's marriage to Duke Carl August.

1   Goethe's original title was 'Um Frieden', and the poem was printed as such in 1780 in J. C. Pfenniger's *Christliches Magazin*, with music by Goethe's friend Ph. Chr. Kayser. Goethe's later title was 'Wandrers Nachtlied' not 'Wanderers Nachtlied'. He was known as 'Der Wanderer' among

Poem written 12 February 1776
Also set by Bettina von Arnim, Hensel, Philipp Christoph Kayser, Franz Liszt, Loewe, Joseph Marx, Medtner, Ernst Pepping, Hans Pfitzner, Reichardt, Schubert, Tomášek, Zelter and Winfried Zillig
* Wolf repeats the final two lines.

Gedichte von J. W. v. Goethe für eine Singstimme und Klavier
Poems by J. W. v. Goethe for voice and piano

1 Harfenspieler I[1]

Wer sich der Einsamkeit[2] ergibt,
Ach! der ist bald allein;

The Harper I

He who surrenders to loneliness,
Ah! he is soon alone;

---

his family and closest friends (see *Dichtung und Wahrheit*, Part 3, Chapter 12) and set out from Frankfurt on many journeys on foot: to the Rhine, to Darmstadt and through Thuringia, for example. He sent a copy of the poem to Charlotte von Stein with the date: „Am Hang des Ettersberg d. 12. Febr. 1776" ('On the slopes of the Ettersberg, 12 Feb. 1776'). Charlotte was a lady-in-waiting at the Weimar court, married to the Master of the Horse, and mother of seven children. Of all the women in Goethe's life, it was she who exercised the greatest influence on him. Some of his greatest lyric poems – including 'Jägers Abendlied', 'Rastlose Liebe' and 'An den Mond' – were addressed to her, and she also inspired the roles of Iphigenia in *Iphigenia auf Tauris* and Leonora von Este in *Torquato Tasso*. Above all she 'Poured the balm of composure into my hot blood' („Tropftest Mäßigung dem heißen Blute"), as Goethe wrote in 'Warum gabst du uns die tiefen Blicke', the autobiographical poem in which he pays tribute to the way in which she calmed his *Sturm und Drang* spirit.

1   Eric Fenby – normally no fan of Wolf, considering him 'a sad and morbid fellow' – describes the opening chords of 'Wer sich der Einsamkeit ergibt' as bringing 'tears to one's eyes'. Fenby mentions a recording in Elgar's possession of Herbert Janssen singing Wolf songs 'beautifully with the deepest feeling, every syllable declaimed perfectly, with just that graveness of voice that gets to the very heart of the words'. Janssen (1892–1965) was a German baritone of Swedish descent who became an American citizen in 1946. Alongside a glittering operatic career (there's a complete recording of *Fidelio* under Toscanini), he was regarded as one of the greatest Lieder interpreters of his generation – evidenced by the 23 songs he recorded for The Hugo Wolf Society, accompanied by Gerald Moore (11 songs), Coenraad van Bos (7) and Michael Raucheisen (5). The selection included *Harfenspieler I–III*, 'Anakreons Grab' and 'Gebet'.

2   Johann Georg Zimmermann (1728–1795) distinguishes in his much read *Über die Einsamkeit* (1784–5) between productive and non-productive or pathological solitude. Goethe, who knew Zimmermann and his works, writes in *Dichtung und Wahrheit* (Part 3, Book 15): „Ich fühlte recht gut, daß sich etwas Bedeutendes nur produzieren lasse, wenn man sich isoliere. Meine Sachen, die so viel Beifall gefunden hatten, waren Kinder der Einsamkeit [. . .]" ('I felt most strongly that something significant could be produced only when the poet isolates himself. My writings, which have been so acclaimed, were children of solitude [. . .])' See also note 2 on pp. 139–41. The Harper's solitude is of a different order. Devoured by guilt because of his incestuous relationship with Sperata, and spurned by society, his own isolation leads to pathological introspection and madness. The *ei* assonance of 'Wer sich der Einsamkeit ergibt', always associated with the word 'Einsamkeit' ('loneliness'), throbs through the poem an astonishing 24 times in 16 lines, as Goethe plays with the words „Einsamkeit" (loneliness), „einsam" (lonely) and „allein" (alone). The final line of the poem, printed as four quatrains in the novel, presents a problem for the translator. To what does „sie" ('it') refer? Although the nearest feminine antecedents are „Pein" (pain) and „Qual" (torment), the personal pronoun surely refers to 'Einsamkeit': 'Loneliness will leave me alone!'

JOHANN WOLFGANG VON GOETHE

Ein jeder lebt, ein jeder liebt,
Und läßt ihn seiner Pein.

Ja! laßt mich meiner Qual!
Und kann ich nur einmal
Recht einsam sein,
Dann bin ich nicht allein.

Es schleicht ein Liebender lauschend sacht,
Ob seine Freundin allein?
So überschleicht bei Tag und Nacht
Mich Einsamen die Pein,

Mich Einsamen die Qual.
Ach werd' ich erst einmal
Einsam im Grabe sein,
Da läßt sie mich allein!

Others live, others love,
And leave him to his pain.

Yes! leave me to my torment!
And if I can but once
Be truly lonely,
Then I'll not be alone.

A lover steals up listening,
To learn if his beloved's alone.
So by day and so by night,
I am lonely and stalked by pain,

I am lonely and stalked by torment.
Ah, when once I lie
Lonely in my grave,
Loneliness will leave me alone!

Poem written before 1783
Also set by Hensel, Reichardt, Schubert, Schumann and Zelter

2 Harfenspieler II[1]

An die Türen will ich schleichen,
Still und sittsam will ich stehn;
Fromme Hand wird Nahrung reichen,
Und ich werde weiter gehn.
Jeder wird sich glücklich scheinen,
Wenn mein Bild vor ihm erscheint;
Eine Träne wird er weinen,
Und ich weiß nicht, was er weint.

The Harper II

I'll steal from door to door,
Quietly and humbly I'll stand;
Pious hands will proffer food,
And I'll wander on my way.
Each will think himself happy,
When my figure comes in view;
He will shed a tear,
And I'll not know why he weeps.

Poem written before 1795
Also set by Norbert Burgmüller, Medtner, Modest Mussorgsky, Reichardt, Schubert, Schumann and Zelter

3 Harfenspieler III

Wer nie sein Brot mit Tränen aß,
Wer nie die kummervollen Nächte
Auf seinem Bette weinend saß,
Der kennt euch nicht, ihr himmlischen
  Mächte!

The Harper III

Who never ate his bread with tears,
Who never through the sorrowful nights
Sat weeping on his bed,
He knows you not, you heavenly powers!

[1] The theme of the poem is the Harper's incipient madness. He has just attempted to murder a child with a knife, and Wilhelm also suspects him of arson. Having sung 'An die Türen will ich schleichen' to the end, the Harper is handed over, for his own safety and that of the community, to a kind pastor. See *Wilhelm Meisters Lehrjahre*, Book 5, Chapter 14. The syphilitic Wolf himself was taken within a decade to Dr Svetlin's mental asylum.

Ihr führt ins Leben uns hinein,
Ihr laßt den Armen schuldig werden,
Dann überlaßt ihr ihn der Pein:
Denn alle Schuld rächt sich auf Erden.[1]

You lead us into life,
You let the poor wretch incur guilt,
Then abandon him to agony:
For all guilt is avenged on earth.

Poem written in 1783
Also set by Burgmüller, Franz Lachner, Liszt, Heinrich Marschner, Reichardt, Schubert, Schumann and Zelter

4 Spottlied aus *Wilhelm Meister*[2]

Satirical song from *Wilhelm Meister*

Ich armer Teufel, Herr Baron,
Beneide Sie um Ihren Stand,
Um Ihren Platz so nah dem Thron
Und um manch schön Stück Ackerland,
Um Ihres Vaters festes Schloß,
Um seine Wildbahn und Geschoß.

I, my lord baron, am just a poor devil,
I envy you because of your rank,
Because of your place so near the throne,
Your many stretches of fertile land,
Your father's stately castle,
His game preserves and shoots.

Mich armen Teufel, Herr Baron,
Beneiden Sie, so wie es scheint,
Weil die Natur vom Knaben schon
Mit mir es mütterlich gemeint.
Ich ward, mit leichtem Mut und Kopf,
Zwar arm, doch nicht ein armer Tropf.

But it seems, my lord baron,
That you envy me, poor devil that I am,
Since nature, from boyhood on,
Has always been a mother to me.
My good heart and mind have made me
Poor, it's true, but not a poor fool.

Nun dächt' ich, lieber Herr Baron,
Wir ließens bleiben, wie wir sind:
Sie blieben des Herrn Vaters Sohn,
Und ich blieb' meiner Mutter Kind.
Wir leben ohne Neid und Haß,
Begehren nicht des andern Titel,
Sie keinen Platz auf dem Parnaß
Und keinen ich in dem Kapitel.

So, my lord baron, I thought
We might leave things as they are:
You remain your esteemed father's son,
And I my mother's child.
We'll live without envy or hate,
Not coveting the other's titles –
No place on Parnassus for you,
And none in the Peerage for me.

Poem written *c.* 1785

---

[1] The Harper refers to his incestuous relationship with Sperata that led to the birth of Mignon, although it is only at the end of the novel, when Mignon is already dead, that we discover the true nature of their relationship. Wolf's highly individual marking for 'Harfenspieler III', *Langsam und mit tief klagendem Ausdruck* (*Slowly and with deep lamentation*) suggests that the syphilitic Wolf felt overwhelming pity for the Harper's plight. It is the most deeply felt of the three settings. The song occurs at the beginning of Book 2, Chapter 13, of *Wilhelm Meister*.

[2] The poem from Book 3, Chapter 9, refers to the Baron, a patron who has artistic pretensions; he is unpopular among the troupe because of his invidious treatment of the actors who, to gain their revenge, circulate anonymously a malicious poem about him – much to Wilhelm's displeasure.

5 Mignon I[1]

Heiß mich nicht reden, heiß mich schweigen,
Denn mein Geheimnis ist mir Pflicht;
Ich möchte dir mein ganzes Innre zeigen,
Allein das Schicksal will es nicht.

Zur rechten Zeit vertreibt der Sonne Lauf
Die finstre Nacht, und sie muß sich erhellen;
Der harte Fels schließt seinen Busen auf,
Mißgönnt der Erde nicht die tiefverborgnen Quellen.

Ein jeder sucht im Arm des Freundes Ruh,

Dort kann die Brust in Klagen sich ergießen;
Allein ein Schwur drückt mir die Lippen zu,
Und nur ein Gott vermag sie aufzuschließen.

Mignon I

Bid me not speak, bid me be silent,
For I am bound to secrecy;
I should love to bare my soul to you,
But Fate has willed it otherwise.

At the appointed time the sun dispels
The dark, and night must turn to day;
The hard rock opens up its bosom,
Without begrudging earth its deeply hidden springs.

All humans seek peace in the arms of a friend,

There the heart can pour forth its lament;
But my lips, alas, are sealed by a vow
And only a god can open them.

Poem written *c.* 1790
Also set by Reichardt, Anton Rubinstein, Schubert, Schumann, Pyotr Ilyich Tchaikovsky, Tomášek, Zelter and Johann Rudolf Zumsteeg

6 Mignon II[2]

Nur wer die Sehnsucht kennt
Weiß, was ich leide!
Allein und abgetrennt
Von aller Freude,

Mignon II

Only those who know longing
Know what I suffer!
Alone and cut off
From every joy,

1 The poem comes from the close of Book 5, Chapter 16, of *Wilhelm Meisters Lehrjahre*, where we are told that it was a song that „Mignon mit großem Ausdruck einigemal rezitiert hatte" ('Mignon had several times recited with great expression'). The words refer obliquely to Mignon's secret and unreciprocated love for Wilhelm. The vow to which Mignon refers in the last verse is made by her after the Mother of God has appeared to her in a vision, as she is being kidnapped and transported to Germany. To ensure Her protection, Mignon vows that she will never trust anyone and never tell her story. The relevant passage in Book 8, Chapter 3, reads:

> Da überfiel das arme Geschöpf eine gräßliche Verzweiflung, in der ihm zuletzt die Mutter Gottes erschien, und ihr versicherte, daß sie sich seiner annehmen wolle. Es schwur darauf bei sich selbst einen heiligen Eid, daß sie künftig niemand mehr vertrauen, niemand ihre Geschichte erzählen und in der Hoffnung einer unmittelbaren göttlichen Hülfe leben und sterben wolle.

> The poor creature was then overcome by a terrible despair in the course of which the Mother of God appeared to her and assured her that she would take care of her. She then swore to herself a sacred vow that she would in future trust nobody, tell nobody her story, and that she would live and die in the hope of divine intervention.

Never once in the course of the novel is Mignon aware of the incestuous nature of her relationship with the Harper.

2 Goethe enclosed a copy of the poem in a letter to Charlotte von Stein on 20 June 1785. It is sung in *Wilhelm Meisters Lehrjahre* (Book 4, Chapter 11) by the Harper and Mignon. Wilhelm, injured while fighting off a band of robbers, has just been rescued by a beautiful lady who by the end of the

Seh ich ans Firmament	I search the sky
Nach jener Seite.	In that direction.
Ach! der mich liebt und kennt	Ah! he who loves and knows me
Ist in der Weite.	Is far away.
Es schwindelt mir, es brennt	My head reels,
Mein Eingeweide.[1]	My womb's ablaze.
Nur wer die Sehnsucht kennt	Only those who know longing
Weiß, was ich leide!	Know what I suffer!

Poem written June 1785
Also set by Beethoven, Hensel, Conradin Kreutzer, Loewe, Medtner, Reichardt, Schubert, Schumann, Tchaikovsky, Tomášek and Zelter

7 Mignon III[2]

Mignon III

So[3] laßt mich scheinen, bis ich werde;	Let me seem an angel till I become one,
Zieht mir das weiße Kleid nicht aus!	Do not take off my white dress!

---

novel will become his wife. As Wilhelm recovers from his fever, he wonders about the identity of the woman who, with her companions, has saved him. The narrative runs:

> Er verfiel in eine träumende Sehnsucht, und wie einstimmend mit seinen Empfindungen war das Lied, das eben in dieser Stunde Mignon und der Harfner als ein unregelmäßiges Duett mit dem herzlichsten Ausdrucke sangen.
>
> He fell into a dreamy state of longing, and the song, which Mignon and the Harper sang at that very moment with the most heartfelt expression as an irregular duet, seemed to chime with his own emotions.

In *Wilhelm Meisters Theatralische Sendung*, however, which was Goethe's original version of the novel, it is sung by Mignon alone to a harp accompaniment as an expression of her visceral desire for Wilhelm. Her longing for him has nothing to do with the generalised 'Sehnsucht' beloved of Novalis and other German Romantics. As the physician, having examined Mignon, explains to Wilhelm (*Wilhelm Meisters Lehrjahre*, Book 8, Chapter 3): Mignon is sick with unrequited desire; she wants a consummated relationship. And when she sees Wilhelm flirting with Philine, she struggles for breath and flees to the Harper's abode where she spends the night „unter entsetzlichen Zuckungen" ('suffering terrible convulsions'). Mignon's obsessional love is conveyed by the insistent 'ei' assonance (10 examples in 12 lines), and the feminine rhymes (all ending in *e*) that limp their way through this expression of thwarted desire. Apart from Reichardt's setting, written especially for inclusion in the novel, Schubert alone set the poem as a duet, while all other composers, including Beethoven, Schumann, Tchaikovsky and Wolf, chose to write a solo song. The poem, as well as mirroring Mignon's deep love, also expresses obliquely Goethe's own longing for Italy – it was written in 1785, a year before he fled Weimar clandestinely at the dead of night to escape the stultifying effect of court life and to renew himself in Italy. Schubert set the poem six times, Beethoven four. See HW to Rudolf von Larisch, 19 December 1888, p. 120, to savour Wolf's excitement at composing these *Mignon-Lieder*. See also p. 130, note 2, and p. 139, note 2.

1   Compare Gretchen in *Urfaust* – her longing for a consummated relationship with Faust is expressed in similar fashion: „Mein Schoß! Gott! drängt/Sich nach ihm hin." ('My womb! God!/ Yearns for him.')

2   'So laßt mich scheinen' is the most cryptic of Mignon's songs, and for a proper understanding of the poem, some knowledge of its context within *Wilhelm Meisters Lehrjahre* is required. In Book 8, Chapter 2, Natalie (the woman Wilhelm Meister will eventually marry) gives Wilhelm this account of a children's party that she has arranged:

Ich eile von der schönen Erde	I hasten from the beautiful earth
Hinab in jenes feste Haus.[1]	Down to that impregnable house.

Es fand sich eben, daß der Geburtstag von Zwillingsschwestern, die sich immer sehr gut betragen hatten, nahe war; ich versprach, daß ihnen diesmal ein Engel die kleinen Geschenke bringen sollte, die sie so wohl verdient hätten. Sie waren äußerst gespannt auf diese Erscheinung. Ich hatte mir Mignon zu dieser Rolle ausgesucht, und sie ward an dem bestimmten Tage in ein langes, leichtes, weißes Gewand anständig gekleidet. Es fehlte nicht an einem große goldenen Gürtel um die Brust, und an einem gleichen Diadem in den Haaren. Anfangs wollte ich die Flügel weglassen, doch bestanden die Frauenzimmer, die sie anputzten, auf ein Paar goldene Schwingen, an denen sie recht ihre Kunst zeigen wollten. So trat, mit einer Lilie in der einen Hand, und mit einem Körbchen in der andern, die wundersame Erscheinung in die Mitte der Mädchen, und überraschte mich selbst. Da kommt der Engel, sagte ich. Die Kinder traten gleichsam alle zurück! Endlich riefen sie aus: es ist Mignon, und getrauten sich doch nicht, dem wundersamen Bilde näher zu treten.

Hier sind eure Gaben, sagte sie, und reichte das Körbchen hin. Man versammelte sich um sie, man betrachtete, man befühlte, man befragte sie.

Bist Du ein Engel? fragte das eine Kind.

Ich wollte ich wär' es, versetzte Mignon.

Warum trägst Du eine Lilie?

So rein und offen sollte mein Herz sein, dann wär' ich glücklich.

Wie ist's mit den Flügeln? laß sie sehen!

Sie stellen schönere vor, die noch nicht entfaltet sind.

Und so antwortete sie bedeutend auf jede unschuldige, leichte Frage. Als die Neugierde der kleinen Gesellschaft befriedigt war, und der Eindruck dieser Erscheinung stumpf zu werden anfing, wollte man sie wieder auskleiden. Sie verwehrte es, nahm ihre Zither, setzte sich hier auf diesen hohen Schreibtisch hinauf, und sang ein Lied mit unglaublicher Anmut.

It so happened that the birthday of twin sisters, who had always been very well behaved, was approaching; I promised that this time an angel would bring them the little presents that they had well deserved. They looked forward to the angel's appearance with great excitement. I had chosen Mignon to play this role, and on the day in question she was appropriately dressed in a long, light and white robe. She even had a girdle of gold about her breast and a diadem of gold in her hair. At first I was minded to omit the wings, but the women who were dressing her insisted on a pair of great golden pinions on which they could demonstrate their skill. And so this wondrous vision appeared, a lily in one hand and a little basket in the other, in the midst of the girls, and took me by surprise as well. 'Here comes the angel,' I said. All the children stepped back a little, but finally exclaimed, 'It's Mignon', but did not venture to come any closer to the wondrous sight.

'Here are your presents,' she said, and handed them the little basket. They gathered around her, gazed at her, touched her and questioned her.

'Are you an angel?' one child asked.

'I wish I were,' Mignon replied.

'Why are you carrying a lily?'

'If my heart were as pure and open, I would be happy.'

'What are the wings for? Let us see!'

'They represent more beautiful ones that have not yet grown.'

And so she answered each innocent, simple question in a significant manner. When the curiosity of the little group had been satisfied and the first impressions of her appearance had begun to wear off, they wanted to undress her. She resisted, took her zither, sat down here on this high writing desk and sang this song with astonishing charm.

3 The meaning of 'So' is in this context 'As an angel'.
1 Schubert, in his B major setting (D877) changes 'feste' to 'dunkle' (dark) – which alters the meaning.

Dort ruh ich eine kleine Stille,	There in brief repose I'll rest,
Dann öffnet sich der frische Blick,	Then new vistas shall I see;
Ich lasse dann die reine Hülle,	My pure raiment then I'll leave,
Den Gürtel und den Kranz zurück.	With girdle and rosary, behind.
Und jene himmlischen Gestalten,	And the heavenly beings there,
Sie fragen nicht nach Mann und Weib,	Do not ask who is man or woman,
Und keine Kleider, keine Falten	And no garments, no folds
Umgeben den verklärten Leib.	Drape the transfigured body.
Zwar lebt ich ohne Sorg und Mühe,[1]	Though I lived without trouble and toil,
Doch fühlt ich tiefen Schmerz genung;	I have felt deep pain enough;
Vor Kummer altert ich zu frühe –	I grew old with grief before my time –
Macht mich auf ewig wieder jung!	O make me forever young again!

Poem written June 1796
Also set by Reichardt, Schubert and Schumann

8 Philine[2]

Singet nicht in Trauertönen	Do not sing in mournful tones
Von der Einsamkeit der Nacht;	Of the solitude of night;
Nein, sie ist, o holde Schönen,	No, fair ladies, night is made
Zur Geselligkeit gemacht.	For shared delight.
Wie das Weib dem Mann gegeben[3]	Woman was given to man
Als die schönste Hälfte war,	As his better half,
Ist die Nacht das halbe Leben,	Night is likewise half of life,
Und die schönste Hälfte zwar.	And the better half by far.
Könnt ihr euch des Tages freuen,	Can you take pleasure in day,
Der nur Freuden unterbricht?	Which only interrupts delight?
Er ist gut, sich zu zerstreuen;	It may serve as a distraction,
Zu was anderm taugt er nicht.	But is good for nothing else.
Aber wenn in nächt'ger Stunde	But when in hours of darkness
Süßer Lampe Dämmrung fließt,	Twilight flows from the sweet lamp,
Und vom Mund zum nahen Munde	And love as well as laughter
Scherz und Liebe sich ergießt;	Streams from almost touching lips,

1   The line refers to the happy life Mignon led in Italy.
2   The poem deals with one of the strolling company of actors Wilhelm Meister meets and joins in *Wilhelm Meisters Lehrjahre*. Philine is a light-hearted soubrette who at the beginning of Book 5, Chapter 10, impatiently interrupts the company's discussion of their production of *Hamlet*. Not for her their restrained and calculated performances; she wants something more extrovert and impulsive. To make her point she sings this ditty 'to a very delicate and pleasing melody' („eine sehr zierliche und gefällige Melodie") – which is precisely what Wolf gives us. Wolf once compared his beloved, Frieda Zerny, with Philine. See p. 522.
3   Schumann omitted this verse from his setting of 'Singet nicht in Trauertönen', either because its tone accorded less well with the opening melody, or because he felt its sexual nature would offend.

JOHANN WOLFGANG VON GOETHE

Wenn der rasche lose Knabe,[1]
Der sonst wild und feurig eilt,
Oft, bei einer kleinen Gabe,
Unter leichten Spielen weilt;

Wenn die Nachtigall Verliebten
Liebevoll ein Liedchen singt,
Das Gefangnen und Betrübten
Nur wie Ach und Wehe klingt:

Mit wie leichtem Herzensregen
Horchet ihr der Glocke nicht,
Die mit zwölf bedächt'gen Schlägen
Ruh und Sicherheit verspricht!

Darum an dem langen Tage
Merke dir es, liebe Brust:
Jeder Tag hat seine Plage,
Und die Nacht hat ihre Lust.[2]

When the impulsive, roguish boy,
Used to wild and fiery haste,
In return for some small token
Often lingers, dallying;

When, full of love, the nightingale
Sings a little song for lovers,
Which to the captive and the wretched
Seems only to tell of grief and pain:

With what lightly pounding heart
Do you then listen to the bell,
That with twelve solemn strokes
Pledges security and rest!

And so remember this, dear heart,
Throughout the livelong day:
Every day has its troubles,
And every night its joys.

Poem written c. 1785
Also set by Reichardt, Rubinstein, Schumann and Tomášek

9 Mignon[3]

Kennst du das Land, wo die Zitronen
    blühn,[4]
Im dunkeln Laub die Goldorangen glühn,[5]

Ein sanfter Wind vom blauen Himmel weht,
Die Myrte still und hoch der Lorbeer steht.
Kennst du es wohl?
        Dahin! Dahin
Möcht ich mit dir, o mein Geliebter, ziehn!

Mignon

Do you know the land where lemons
    blossom,
Where oranges grow golden among dark
    leaves,
A gentle wind drifts across blue skies,
The myrtle stands silent, the laurel tall,
Do you know it?
        It is there, it is there
I long to go with you, my love.

1 Cupid.
2 Wolf ends his song with a reprise of the initial rondo theme, which illustrates to perfection Goethe's text:

> Sie machte eine leichte Verbeugung als sie geendigt hatte, und Serlo rief ihr ein lautes Bravo zu. Sie sprang zur Tür hinaus und eilte mit Gelächter fort. Man hörte sie die Treppe hinunter singen und mit den Absätzen klappern.

> She bowed slightly when she had finished, and Serlo shouted Bravo. She skipped through the door and ran off laughing. You could hear her singing and clattering her heels as she went down the stairs.

3 Mignon's fate was to be captured in Italy by a troupe of circus performers and abducted to Germany, which is where we find her in 'Kennst du das Land', which she sings as an expression of her longing to return to her homeland. Challier records over sixty settings of the poem by 1885, including those by Beethoven, Liszt, Reichardt, Rubinstein, Schubert, Schumann, Spohr, Tchaikovsky

and Zelter. The most ambitious setting is by Wolf, and some commentators claim that his version is impossibly sophisticated for a thirteen-year-old girl to sing – which was basically Goethe's criticism of Beethoven's setting. But the poem is sophisticated too: the progression from general to specific longing, as first she has a vision of Italy, then of her house, then of the Alps that bar her way; the use of Fremdwörter ('Orangen', 'Zitronen') to convey her longing for her 'foreign' homeland; the subtle assonance of 'stehn und sehn'; the impassioned enjambement of the refrain; the insistent sibilants of the final phrase and, most wonderful of all, the sudden open-vowelled pleading of 'Vater' contrasting with the closed vowels of 'Beschützer' and 'Geliebter'. Wolf matches all this. The beautiful, plangent melody gradually grows more exalted until in the final verse G flat shifts to F sharp minor, *tremolandi* thunder out in both hands, and the music, ineffably overwrought, mirrors Mignon's ecstatic, unattainable vision of her homeland beyond the Alps.

Goethe's poem opens Book 3 of *Wilhelm Meisters Lehrjahre*, and the poet's commentary on how Mignon sang the poem almost certainly had some influence on Wolf's setting. It is not always realised by audiences that Mignon sings this song in Italian, and what we read and hear is Wilhelm's 'inadequate' translation:

> Melodie und Ausdruck gefielen unserm Freunde [Wilhelm] besonders, ob er gleich die Worte nicht alle verstehen konnte. Er ließ sich die Strophen wiederholen und erklären, schrieb sie auf und übersetzte sie ins Deutsche. Aber die Originalität der Wendungen konnte er nur von ferne nachahmen. Die kindliche Unschuld des Ausdrucks verschwand, indem die gebrochene Sprache übereinstimmend, und das Unzusammenhängende verbunden ward. Auch konnte der Reiz der Melodie mit nichts verglichen werden.
>
>   Sie fing jeden Vers feierlich und prächtig an, als ob sie auf etwas sonderbares aufmerksam machen, als ob sie etwas wichtiges vortragen wollte. Bei der dritten Zeile ward der Gesang dumpfer und düsterer; das: *kennst du es wohl?* drückte sie geheimnisvoll und bedächtig aus, in dem: *dahin! dahin!* lag eine unwiderstehliche Sehnsucht, und ihr: *Laß uns ziehn!* wußte sie, bei jeder Wiederholung, dergestalt zu modifizieren, daß es bald bittend und dringend, bald treibend und vielversprechend war.
>
>   Nachdem sie das Lied zum zweitenmal geendigt hatte, hielt sie einen Augenblick inne, sah Wilhelmen scharf an und fragte: kennst du das Land? – Es muß wohl Italien gemeint sein, versetzte Wilhelm, woher hast du das Liedchen? – Italien! sagte Mignon bedeutend: gehst du nach Italien, so nimm mich mit, es friert mich hier. – Bist du schon dort gewesen, liebe Kleine? fragte Wilhelm. – Das Kind war still und nichts weiter aus ihm zu bringen.

Our friend [Wilhelm] liked in particular the melody and the expression, although he could not understand all the words. He asked for the verses to be repeated and explained, wrote them down and translated them into German. But he was able to give only a remote approximation of the phrases. The childlike innocence of expression vanished as her *staccato* utterances were smoothed over, and what was disjointed was linked together. And the unique charm of the melody could not be reproduced.

  She began each verse with a certain solemn grandeur, as if she were drawing attention to something unusual and imparting something of importance. When she reached the third line, the voice became more sombre and gloomy; the words *kennst du es wohl?* were given mystery and weight, the *dahin! dahin!* was suffused with irresistible longing, and she knew how to vary *Laß uns ziehn!* each time it was repeated, so that one time it was entreating and urgent, the next time pressing and full of promise.

  After she had finished the song for a second time she paused for a moment, looked sharply at Wilhelm and asked, 'Do you know the land?' 'It must be Italy that is meant,' said Wilhelm. 'Where did you learn the little song?' 'Italy,' said Mignon, significantly. 'If ever you go to Italy, take me with you, I'm freezing here.' 'Have you ever been there, you little treasure?' asked Wilhelm. The child was silent and it was impossible to get any more out of her.

4   Goethe seems to have modelled these lines on this passage from 'Summer' in James Thomson's *The Seasons* (1746):

JOHANN WOLFGANG VON GOETHE

Kennst du das Haus? Auf Säulen ruht sein Dach,[1]	Do you know the house? Columns support its roof,
Es glänzt der Saal, es schimmert das Gemach,	Its hall gleams, its apartments shimmer,
Und Marmorbilder[1] stehn und sehn mich an:	And marble statues stand and stare at me:
Was hat man dir, du armes Kind, getan?	What have they done to you, poor child?
Kennst du es wohl?	Do you know it?
Dahin! Dahin	It is there, it is there
Möcht ich mit dir, o mein Beschützer, ziehn.[2]	I long to go with you, my protector.
Kennst du den Berg und seinen Wolkensteg?	Do you know the mountain and its cloud-girt path?
Das Maultier sucht im Nebel seinen Weg,	The mule seeks its way through the mist,
In Höhlen wohnt der Drachen alte Brut,	In caverns dwell the dragons' ancient brood;
Es stürzt der Fels und über ihn die Flut –	The cliff falls sheer, the torrent over it,
Kennst du ihn wohl?	Do you know it?
Dahin! Dahin	It is there, it is there
Geht unser Weg! o Vater, laß uns ziehn!	Our pathway lies! O father, let us go!

Poem written 1782–3
Also set by Beethoven, Berg, Hensel, Liszt, Stanisław Moniuszko, Reichardt, Schubert, Schumann, Ludwig Spohr, Gasparo Spontini, Tchaikovsky, Tomášek and Zelter

10 Der Sänger[3]

The minstrel

„Was hör' ich draußen vor dem Tor,	'What do I hear outside the gate,
Was auf der Brücke schallen?	What sounds from the bridge?
Laß den Gesang vor unserm Ohr	Let that song resound for us
Im Saale widerhallen!"	Here inside this hall!'
Der König sprach's, der Page lief;	So spake the king, the page ran,
Der Knabe kam, der König rief:	The boy returned, the king exclaimed:
„Laßt mir herein den Alten!"	'Let the old man enter!'

> Bear me, Pomona! to thy citron groves;
> To where the lemon and the piercing lime,
> With the deep orange glowing through the green,
> Their lighter glories blend. Lay me reclined
> Beneath the spreading tamarind, that shakes,
> Fanned by the breeze, its fever-cooling fruit.

5 This line in *Wilhelm Meisters Theatralische Sendung* reads „Im grünen Laub die Gold-Orangen glühn", thus capping Thomson's alliterative cluster in 'With the deep orange glowing through the green'.
1 Mignon remembers the Palladian-like villa that she came across in her wanderings – see Book 8, Chapter 5.
2 Wilhelm had bought Mignon's liberty by paying the showman 30 crowns.
3 Goethe's 'Der Sänger', which is sung by the Harper on his first appearance in *Wilhelm Meisters Lehrjahre* in Book 2, Chapter 11, was written a year after Goethe had accepted the high office of Kammerpräsident from the Duke of Weimar. The poem expresses an inner revolt against the political, social and administrative duties that interfered with his art. He confided to Eckermann (*J. P. Eckermanns Gespräche mit Goethe*) on 27 January 1824:

„Gegrüßet seid mir, edle Herrn,	'Hail to you, O noble lords,
Gegrüßt ihr, schöne Damen!	Hail to you, fair ladies!
Welch reicher Himmel! Stern bei Stern!	How rich a galaxy! Star on star!
Wer kennet ihre Namen?	Who can tell their names?
Im Saal voll Pracht und Herrlichkeit	In this hall of pomp and splendour,
Schließt, Augen, euch: hier ist nicht Zeit,	Close, O eyes: here is no time
Sich staunend zu ergötzen."	For amazement and delight.'
Der Sänger drückt' die Augen ein,	The minstrel shut tight his eyes
Und schlug in vollen Tönen;	And struck up with full tone;
Die Ritter schauten mutig drein,	The knights looked on gallantly,
Und in den Schoß die Schönen.	The ladies lowered their gaze.
Der König, dem das Lied gefiel,	The king, enchanted with the song,
Ließ, ihn zu ehren für sein Spiel,	Sent for a golden chain
Eine goldne Kette reichen.	To reward him for his playing.
„Die goldne Kette gib mir nicht,	'Give not the golden chain to me,
Die Kette gib den Rittern,	Give the chain to your knights,
Vor deren kühnem Angesicht	Before whose bold countenance
Der Feinde Lanzen splittern;	The enemy lances shatter;
Gib sie dem Kanzler, den du hast,	Give it to your chancellor
Und laß ihn noch die goldne Last	And let him add its golden weight
Zu andern Lasten tragen.	To his other burdens.
Ich singe, wie der Vogel singt,	I sing as the bird sings
Der in den Zweigen wohnet;	High up in the branches;
Das Lied, das aus der Kehle dringt,	The song that bursts from the throat
Ist Lohn, der reichlich lohnet.	Is its own abundant reward.
Doch darf ich bitten, bitt' ich eins:	But if I may, I'll beg one boon:
Laß mir den besten Becher Weins	Let the best wine be brought to me
In purem Golde reichen."	In a beaker of pure gold.'
Er setzt' ihn an, er trank ihn aus:	He raised the glass, he drank it dry:
„O Trank voll süßer Labe!	'O draught full of sweet refreshment!
O wohl dem hochbeglückten Haus,	O happy the highly favoured house,
Wo das ist kleine Gabe!	Where that is a trifling gift!
Ergeht's euch wohl, so denkt an mich,	If you should prosper, then think of me,
Und danket Gott so warm, als ich	And thank God as warmly
Für diesen Trunk euch danke."	As I thank you for this draught.'

Poem written 1783
Also set by Loewe, Reichardt, Schubert, Schumann and Zelter

Mein eigentliches Glück war mein poetisches Sinnen und Schaffen. Allein wie sehr war dieses durch meine äußere Stellung gestört, beschränkt und gehindert. Hätte ich mich mehr vom öffentlichen und geschäftlichen Wirken und Treiben zurückhalten und mehr in der Einsamkeit leben können, ich wäre glücklicher gewesen und würde als Dichter weit mehr gemacht haben.

I was truly happy only when thinking about and writing poetry – but how such activity was disturbed, limited and hindered by my position at court! Had I been able to withdraw more from

11 Der Rattenfänger[1]

Ich bin der wohlbekannte Sänger,
Der vielgereiste Rattenfänger,
Den diese altberühmte Stadt
Gewiß besonders nötig hat.
Und wären's Ratten noch so viele,
Und wären Wiesel mit im Spiele;
Von allen säubr' ich diesen Ort,
Sie müssen miteinander fort.

Dann ist der gutgelaunte Sänger
Mitunter auch ein Kinderfänger,
Der selbst die wildesten bezwingt,
Wenn er die goldnen Märchen singt.
Und wären Knaben noch so trutzig,
Und wären Mädchen noch so stutzig,
In meine Saiten greif ich ein,
Sie müssen alle hinterdrein.

Dann ist der vielgewandte Sänger
Gelegentlich ein Mädchenfänger;
In keinem Städtchen langt er an,
Wo er's nicht mancher angetan.
Und wären Mädchen noch so blöde,[2]

The ratcatcher

I am that celebrated minstrel,
The much travelled ratcatcher,
Of whom this famous old city
Assuredly has special need.
And however many rats there are,
And were there weasels too,
I'll rid the place of every one,
One and all, they must away.

Then this good-humoured minstrel
Is a child-catcher too from time to time,
Who can tame even the wildest,
When he sings his golden tales.
And however defiant the boys might be,
And however suspicious the girls,
I only have to pluck my strings,
For them all to follow me.

And then this many-sided minstrel
Is occasionally a maiden-catcher;
He's never arrived in any town
Without bewitching many.
And however bashful the girls might be,

---

public and business concerns, and live more in solitude, I should have been happier and would have achieved much more as a writer.'

'Der Sänger' was highly prized by Goethe, who placed it at the head of his *Balladen und Romanzen* in the 1800 edition of his *Complete Works*, where the text differs in several places from that printed in the novel.

1 Robert Browning's poem popularised for English readers the thirteenth-century legend of the Pied Piper of Hamelin, and Goethe did much the same for the German public. He himself discovered the legend in Johann Ludwig Gottfried's *Chronika* of 1642 and also read the traditional folk poem 'Der Rattenfänger von Hameln' published by Arnim and Brentano in *Des Knaben Wunderhorn*. Reviewing the anthology, Goethe wrote: „Zuckt aufs Bänkelsängerische, aber nicht unfein" ('smacks of the street-ballad, but not unrefined'). Goethe's own version makes no attempt to tell the whole story. Of the eleven settings listed by Challier, only those by Tomášek and Schubert met with any success. Wolf's version of Goethe's ballad is superior to both of these and is set to a breathtaking tarantella rhythm that introduces us to a more demonic, lascivious and swaggering Piper than Browning's hero. The prelude, marked *sehr lebhaft*, is a remarkable piece of bravura writing: beginning *ff*, it is played high above the stave, but by the time the voice enters it has descended in volume and pitch, transformed into a lute-like, lilting accompaniment with arpeggiated chords in the left hand simulating the twanging of lute strings. The same music reappears between the verses and again at the end of the song, as the postlude vanishes into thin air – a Wolfian trademark familiar from 'Begegnung', 'Der Gärtner', 'Er ist's', 'Nixe Binsefuß', 'Nun wandre, Maria' and 'Lied vom Winde'.
2 'blœde' is a Middle High German word meaning 'zaghaft' = 'hesitant' or 'bashful', and seems a more appropriate translation here than 'stupid', the normal translation today of 'blöd'. There is a poem by Mörike, 'Liebesvorzeichen', whose fifth stanza uses 'blöde' in this sense of 'bashful':

Dazwischen dacht' ich wohl im stillen: Meanwhile, I thought to myself:
Was hast du vor? sie ist ein Kind!   What can you be thinking of? She's but a child!

Und wären Weiber noch so spröde: | And however prudish the women,
Doch allen wird so liebebang | All of them grow weak with love
Bei Zaubersaiten und Gesang.[1] | At the sound of magic lute and song.

Poem written before 1803
Also set by Schubert and Tomášek

12 Ritter Kurts Brautfahrt[2] | Sir Kurt's wedding-ride

Mit des Bräutigams Behagen | With a bridegroom's relish
Schwingt sich Ritter Kurt aufs Roß; | Sir Kurt vaults onto his steed
Zu der Trauung soll's ihn tragen: | Which will carry him to his wedding
Auf der edlen Liebsten Schloß, | At his noble beloved's castle,
Als am öden Felsenorte | When, in a rocky desert place,
Drohend sich ein Gegner naht; | A threatening foe appears;
Ohne Zögern, ohne Worte | Without hesitation, without a word
Schreiten sie zu rascher Tat. | They swiftly join battle.

Lange schwankt des Kampfes Welle, | For long the combat ebbs and flows,
Bis sich Kurt im Siege freut; | Until Kurt rejoices in victory;
Er entfernt sich von der Stelle, | He now withdraws from that place,
Überwinder und gebläut. | Bruised but victorious,
Aber was er bald gewahret | But what does he soon descry
In des Busches Zitterschein! | Among the thicket's flickering leaves?
Mit dem Säugling still gepaaret, | With a baby quietly at her breast
Schleicht ein Liebchen durch den Hain. | A young girl glides through the wood.

Und sie winkt ihm auf das Plätzchen: | And she beckons him towards her:
„Lieber Herr, nicht so geschwind! | 'Not so fast, dear sir!
Habt Ihr nichts an Euer Schätzchen, | Have you nothing for your sweetheart,
Habt Ihr nichts für Euer Kind?" | Have you nothing for your child?'
Ihn durchglühet süße Flamme, | A sweet flame pervades his being,
Daß er nicht vorbei begehrt, | So that he has no desire to ride on past,

Die Lippen, die von Reife quillen, | Her lips swell with ripeness –
Wie blöde noch und fromm gesinnt! | How bashful still and innocent!

1 Goethe's poem originally had three verses but at the end of the 1861 edition of the poem the words „Von Anfang" appear, thus justifying Wolf's repeat of the first verse.
2 Goethe's poem was inspired by an incident on pp. 339–40 of the *Mémoires du maréchal de Bassompierre*, published in Cologne in 1666. Moritz von Schwind, the friend of Schubert, based one of his paintings on Goethe's ballad. Ernst Decsey, Wolf's first biographer, identified two musical borrowings: one from Karl Goldmark's *Die Königin von Saba* and one from Adalbert von Goldschmidt's *Die sieben Todsünden*. Richard Sternfeld in 'Zum Gedächtnis eines Meisters des deutschen Liedes' describes Wolf's mischievous expression when he played these passages: „Noch sehe ich seine schelmischen Augen, als er mir zeigte, wie er hier bei den Textworten 'Aber ach! da kommen Juden' sich den Spaß gemacht hatte, in der Begleitung zwei markante Themen seiner Wiener Kollegen anzubringen." ('I can still remember the roguish expression in his eyes when he showed me how at "but alas! here come the Jews" he had enjoyed quoting in the accompaniment two striking themes by his Viennese colleagues.')

Und er findet nun die Amme,	And he finds the wet-nurse
Wie die Jungfrau, liebenswert.	As lovable as the maiden.
Doch er hört die Diener blasen,	But he hears his servants sound their trumpets,
Denket nun der hohen Braut,	And thinks now of his noble bride,
Und nun wird auf seinen Straßen	And as he goes on his way,
Jahresfest und Markt so laut,	The noise of fair and market grows loud,
Und er wählet in den Buden	And he chooses in the booths
Manches Pfand zu Lieb' und Huld.	Many a pledge of love and devotion.
Aber ach! da kommen Juden	But alas! along come the Jews
Mit dem Schein vertagter Schuld.	With an overdue promissory note.
Und nun halten die Gerichte	And now the courts of justice
Den behenden Ritter auf.	Detain the agile knight.
O verteufelte Geschichte!	O fiendish story!
Heldenhafter Lebenslauf!	What a fate for a hero to bear!
Soll ich heute mich gedulden?	How can I remain patient today?
Die Verlegenheit ist groß:	The discomfort is considerable:
Widersacher, Weiber, Schulden,	Adversaries, women, debts –
Ach! kein Ritter wird sie los.*[1]	Ah! no knight is ever free of them.

Poem written c. 1802
Also set by Reichardt and Zelter
* Wolf repeats the final line.

13 Gutmann und Gutweib[2]

Goodman and goodwife

Und morgen fällt Sankt Martins Fest,	It is Saint Martinmas eve,
Gutweib liebt ihren Mann;	Goodwife loves her husband;
Da knetet sie ihm Puddings ein	She's been kneading him puddings
Und bäckt sie in der Pfann'.	And now cooks them in the pan.
Im Bette liegen beide nun,	Both of them now lie in bed,
Da saust ein wilder West;	A furious west wind starts to blow;

1 The only example of repetition thus far in the Goethe-Lieder.
2 This is Goethe's adaptation of a Scottish ballad he found in *Ancient and Modern Scots Songs* (vol. 1), edited by David Herd (Edinburgh, 1769). The poem had been set with great success by Carl Loewe and it is more than likely that Wolf knew this ballad of 1833. Frank Walker tells us that many of Wolf's friends he interviewed for his biography of the composer testified to the intense manner in which Wolf sang Loewe ballads. The original 'Get up and bar the door' is a more racy affair than Goethe's version (the man threatens to shave off Gutmann's beard and kiss his wife) but Goethe was obviously fond of his translation, as Eckermann makes clear in his account of two conversations he had with the poet on 4 February and 6 April 1829. Goethe had shown him an engraving after a picture by Adriaen von Ostade and likened the domestic interior to that of his poem: „Hier, sagte er, haben Sie die Szene zu unserm Good man und good wife." ('This is the scene of our Good man and good wife.') Goethe also enclosed his poem in a letter to his Scottish admirer Thomas Carlyle on 20 July 1827. Throughout much of his life Goethe was interested, like Herder in *Stimmen der Völker in Liedern* (1807), in creating an anthology of world poetry, and 'Gutmann und Gutweib' (or 'Altschottisch', as it was called in *Kunst und Altertum*) was probably written with that in mind.

Und Gutmann spricht zur guten Frau:
„Du, riegle die Türe fest."

„Bin kaum erholt und halb erwarmt,
Wie käm' ich da zu Ruh;
Und klapperte sie einhundert Jahr,
Ich riegelte sie nicht zu."

Drauf eine Wette schlossen sie
Ganz leise sich ins Ohr:
So wer das erste Wörtlein spräch',
Der schöbe den Riegel vor.

Zwei Wanderer kommen um Mitternacht
Und wissen nicht, wo sie stehn,
Die Lampe losch, der Herd verglomm,
Zu hören ist nichts, zu sehn.

„Was ist das für ein Hexen-ort?
Da bricht uns die Geduld!"
Doch hörten sie kein Sterbenswort,
Deß war die Türe schuld.

Den weißen Pudding speisten sie,
Den schwarzen ganz vertraut;
Und Gutweib sagte sich selber viel,
Doch keine Silbe laut.

Zu diesem sprach der jene dann:[1]
„Wie trocken ist mir der Hals!
Der Schrank, der klafft, und geistig riecht's,
Da findet sich's allenfalls.

„Ein Fläschchen Schnaps ergreif' ich da,
Das trifft sich doch geschickt!
Ich bring' es dir, du bringst es mir,
Und bald sind wir erquickt."

Doch Gutmann sprang so heftig auf
Und fuhr sie drohend an:
„Bezahlen soll mit teurem Geld,
Wer mir den Schnaps vertan!"

Und Gutweib sprang auch froh heran,
Drei Sprünge, als wär' sie reich:
„Du, Gutmann, sprachst das erste Wort,
Nun riegle die Thüre gleich."

And Goodman says to his wife:
'Get up and bar the door.'

'I've hardly had time to warm myself,
How would I ever get to sleep;
And though it banged for a hundred years,
I would never bar that door.'

Whereupon they whispered a bet
Into each other's ear:
Let him who speaks the first word
Get up and bar the door.

Two travellers arrive as midnight strikes,
Without knowing where they were,
The lamp went out, the coals burned low,
There was neither light nor sound.

'What kind of haunted place is this?
Our patience is at an end!'
But there was not a word in reply,
For that the door was to blame.

And first they ate the white pudding,
And then calmly ate the black;
And Goodwife said much to herself,
But not a word out loud.

One traveller now said to the other:
'My throat's so parched and dry!
The cupboard's wide open, it smells of spirits,
That'll be where they keep it.

I'll grab that bottle of Schnapps,
Just what the doctor ordered!
I'll serve you and you'll serve me,
And soon we'll be refreshed.'

But Goodman bounded out of bed,
And bellowed in their face:
'Whoever's taken my own Schnapps
Shall pay for it in hard cash!'

At which our Goodwife gave three skips
And danced about with glee:
'Goodman, you have spoken first,
Get up and bar the door!'

Poem written 1827
Also set by Loewe

[1] Goethe: Zum andern sprach der eine dann.

Goethe's source, as it appears in *Ancient and Modern Scots Songs*:

Get up and bar the door [13]

It fell about the Martinmas time,
    And a gay time it was then,
When our goodwife got puddings to make,
    And she's boild them in the pan.

The wind sae cauld blew south and north,
    And blew into the floor;
Quoth our goodman to our goodwife,
    'Gae out and bar the door.'

'My hand is in my hussyfskap,[1]
    Goodman, as ye may see;
An it shoud nae be barrd this hundred year,
    It's no be barrd for me.'

They made a paction tween them twa,
    They made it firm and sure,
That the first word whaeer shoud speak,
    Shoud rise and bar the door.

Then by there came two gentlemen,
    At twelve o clock at night,
And they could neither see house nor hall,
    Nor coal nor candle-light.

'Now whether is this a rich man's house,
    Or whether is it a poor?'
But neer a word wad ane o them speak,
    For barring of the door.

And first they ate the white puddings,
    And then they ate the black;
Tho muckle thought the goodwife to hersel,
    Yet neer a word she spake.

Then said the one unto the other,
    'Here, man, tak ye my knife;
Do ye tak aff the auld man's beard,
    And I'll kiss the goodwife.'

'But there's nae water in the house,
    And what shall we do than?'
'What ails ye at the pudding-broo,
    That boils into the pan?'

O up then started our goodman,
    An angry man was he:
'Will ye kiss my wife before my een,
    And scad me wi pudding-bree?'[2]

Then up and started our goodwife,
    Gied three skips on the floor:
'Goodman, you've spoken the foremost word,
    Get up and bar the door.'

14 Cophtisches Lied I[3]

Lasset Gelehrte sich zanken und streiten,
Streng und bedächtig die Lehrer auch sein!
Alle die Weisesten aller der Zeiten
Lächeln und winken und stimmen mit ein:

Coptic song I

Let scholars quarrel and squabble,
And teachers deliberate with rigour!
All the wisest men throughout the ages
Nod and smile in agreement with me:

---

1 Housewife's bag that held darning or mending materials.
2 Pudding bree or pudding broo = 'the water in which puddings have been boiled' (*OED*).
3 When Goethe returned from his Italian journey, the Duke and Dowager Duchess at the Weimar court invited him to oversee the building of a new theatre and take charge of the management. Goethe reluctantly agreed, but volunteered to write some new plays. One of these was *Der Groß-Cophta* (1791), a comedy in five acts that is in fact a rather pedestrian affair about, among other things, the Queen of France's necklace. While in Italy, Goethe had collected information about the

NO STANZA BREAK

Töricht, auf Beßrung der Toren zu harren!	Foolish to wait for fools to learn better!
Kinder der Klugheit, o habet die Narren	Children of wisdom, o simply make fools
Eben zum Narren auch, wie sich's gehört!	Of the fools, as is fit!

Merlin der Alte, im leuchtenden Grabe,	Old Merlin from his gleaming grave,
Wo ich als Jüngling gesprochen ihn habe,	Where I consulted him in my youth,
Hat mich mit ähnlicher Antwort belehrt:	Gave me a similar answer too:
Töricht, auf Beßrung der Toren zu harren!	Foolish to wait for fools to learn better!
Kinder der Klugheit, o habet die Narren	Children of wisdom, o simply make fools
Eben zum Narren auch, wie sich's gehört!	Of the fools, as is fit!

Und auf den Höhen der indischen Lüfte	And on India's windswept heights,
Und in den Tiefen ägyptischer Grüfte	And in the depths of Egyptian tombs,
Hab ich das heilige Wort nur gehört:	This alone was the gospel I heard:
Töricht, auf Beßrung der Toren zu harren!	Foolish to wait for fools to learn better!
Kinder der Klugheit, o habet die Narren	Children of wisdom, o simply make fools
Eben zum Narren auch, wie sich's gehört!	Of the fools, as is fit!

Poem written c. 1788
Also set by Max Bruch and Reichardt

15 Cophtisches Lied II[1]

Coptic song II

Geh! gehorche meinen Winken,	Go! do what I suggest,
Nutze deine jungen Tage,	Make use of your young days,
Lerne zeitig klüger sein:	Learn in good time to be wiser:

---

life of Giuseppe Balsamo who, under the false name of Count Cagliostro, had played a major role in the infamous Necklace Affair at the French court, scheming with a disgraced cardinal to acquire the valuable necklace for a certain Countess Jeanne de la Motte. He was rumbled and imprisoned in the Bastille for his pains. Both songs in the Singspiel are sung by the charlatan Count Rostro – a hardly disguised pseudonym for Cagliostro – who regards himself as one of the 'wise' and all scholars as mere pedants. Goethe's original intention had been to write a comic opera libretto called *Die Mystifizierten*, but the project was never finished. However, this 'Cophtisches Lied' („Lasset Gelehrte sich zanken und streiten") and 'Ein anderes' („Geh, gehorche meinen Winken") were salvaged. Unable to incorporate them into *Der Groß-Cophta*, Goethe revised them and they were first published in Schiller's *Musenalmanach* of 1796. In 'Lasset Gelehrte sich zanken und streiten', Wolf repeats the refrain (on how to deal with fools) each time at a lower pitch – a comically ironic touch, especially apt in verse 3, when Goethe tells us that the oracle speaks from 'the depths of Egyptian tombs'. Coptic is the language of the Christian descendants of the ancient Egyptians. For a fuller account of the song, see Susan Youens, *Hugo Wolf: The Vocal Music*, pp. 104–9.

Friedrich Schiller's story 'Der Geisterseher' is also based on the impostor figure of Cagliostro. Goethe became obsessed with Cagliostro and wrote about him on four occasions: as an opera buffa libretto, a play, a lecture for the Freitagsgesellschaft (Friday Club) in Weimar on 23 March 1792 and as an episode in his *Italienische Reise*. Cagliostro was notorious as clairvoyant, faith-healer, alchemist, magician and forger. He and his wife, Lorenza Feliciana, alias Countess Serafina di Cagliostro, who as a courtesan contributed to their living costs, plied their trade in countless cities throughout Europe, including Malta, Naples, Paris, London, Barcelona, Madrid, Lisbon, Aix-en-Provence, Strasbourg, Rome and St Petersburg.

1 *Carpe diem* is the theme of the second Coptic song, in which Goethe also advises us to be philosophical about our fate: we must either be successes or failures, a notion that Wolf, with his pictorial

Auf des Glückes großer Waage	On the mighty scales of Fortune
Steht die Zunge selten ein;	The pointer seldom remains at rest;
Du mußt steigen oder sinken,	You must rise or you must fall,
Du mußt herrschen und gewinnen,	You must either win and rule,
Oder dienen und verlieren,	Or must lose and be a slave,
Leiden oder triumphieren,	You must suffer or triumph,
Amboß oder Hammer sein.	Be anvil or hammer.

Poem written c. 1788
Also set by Bruch and Reichardt

16 Frech und froh I[1] — Cheerful impudence I

Mit Mädchen sich vertragen,	Getting on well with girls,
Mit Männern 'rumgeschlagen,	Knocking about with men,
Und mehr Kredit als Geld;	And with more credit than cash;
So kommt man durch die Welt.	That's how to get through life.
Mit vielem läßt sich schmausen,	With a lot you can feast like a lord,
Mit wenig läßt sich hausen;	With a little you can make ends meet;
Daß wenig vieles sei,	But only pleasure can succeed
Schafft nur die Lust herbei.	In making a lot out of little.
Will sie sich nicht bequemen,	If they won't consent,
So müßt ihr's eben nehmen.	Simply take what you want.
Will einer nicht vom Ort,	If someone won't leave,
So jagt ihn grade fort.	Then chase him away.
Laßt alle nur mißgönnen,	Let them all begrudge
Was sie nicht nehmen können,	What they're unable to have,
Und seid von Herzen froh;	And be truly free of care;
Das ist das A und O.	That's the beginning and end of it.
So fahret fort zu dichten,	Continue to write verses,
Euch nach der Welt zu richten.	Continue to conform.
Bedenkt in Wohl und Weh	In weal and woe bear in mind
Dies goldne ABC.*	This golden ABC.*

Poem written c. 1774
Also set by Beethoven, Reichardt and Schubert
* Wolf repeats the final line.

---

sense, conveys in the piano accompaniment, which suggests the slow tipping of the scales in the piano interlude before „Du mußt steigen oder sinken" ('You must climb or fall').

1 Ernst Challier in his *Großer Lieder-Katalog* of 1885 lists a single setting of 'Mit Mädeln sich vertragen', by M. Hirschfeld. The first 'Frech und froh' poem occurs in Goethe's Singspiel *Claudine von Villa Bella*, where it is sung in Act I by the robber Rugantino to a zither accompaniment. He sings verses 1, 3 and 5, while his cronies intone verses 2 and 4. The poem advocates a happy-go-lucky approach to life: consort with girls, live off credit rather than cash, let no one stand in your way. This is the golden rule – and Wolf wittily sets „Dies goldne ABC" to the equivalent musical notes (B in German = B flat), accompanied by piano octaves in both hands.

17 Frech und froh II[1]

Liebesqual verschmäht mein Herz,
Sanften Jammer, süßen Schmerz;
Nur vom Tücht'gen will ich wissen,
Heißem Äugeln,[2] derben Küssen.
Sei ein armer Hund erfrischt
Von der Lust, mit Pein gemischt!
Mädchen, gib der frischen Brust
Nichts von Pein, und alle Lust.

Poem written *c.* 1788

Cheerful impudence II

My heart scorns pangs of love,
The gentle moan, the sweet distress;
Tell me about none but the vigorous,
Passionate ogling, rough kisses.
Let poor wretches find refreshment
In pleasure mingled with pain!
Give this fresh heart, my girl,
No pain and nothing but pleasure.

18 Beherzigung[3]

Ach, was soll der Mensch verlangen?
Ist es besser, ruhig bleiben?
Klammernd fest sich anzuhangen?
Ist es besser, sich zu treiben?
Soll er sich ein Häuschen bauen?
Soll er unter Zelten leben?
Soll er auf die Felsen trauen?
Selbst die festen Felsen beben.

Eines schickt sich nicht für alle!
Sehe jeder wie er's treibe,
Sehe jeder wo er bleibe,
Und wer steht, daß er nicht falle![4]

Poem written ?1777
Also set by Zelter and Zillig

Take this to heart

Ah, what should a man desire?
Is it better to live quietly?
Hanging on, holding tight?
Is it better to press on?
Should he build himself a house?
Should he live in tents?
Should he rely on rocks?
Even solid rocks can quake.

There is no answer fit for all!
Let each man look to himself,
Let each man decide where to dwell,
And he who stands, let him take heed
    lest he fall!

---

1 The second poem, unlike the first (which has no title in the Singspiel), was called 'Frech und froh' by Goethe: it enjoins the girl to give the poet nothing but pleasure, and nothing of pain. The song begins with sighs and groans (descending dotted crotchets and a telling *sforzando*), but by the end all has turned to pleasure, with an extended melisma on 'alle' (lasting three bars) in the final phrase 'alle Lust' – all is pleasure.
2 Goethe: Äuglen.
3 Doubt surrounds the date of Goethe's poem. Heinrich Viehoff and others believe it was written in the early Weimar period as a rebuke to friends who offered advice or criticised his lifestyle; for Heinrich Düntzer, who dates it to about 1788, it is no longer an occasional poem ('Gelegenheitsgedicht') but an epigram that applies to all men. Goethe eventually removed it from the *Vermischte Gedichte* section of the 1789 edition of his works and placed it among the *Epigramme*. Wolf's music is aptly didactic, set to somewhat dry and discordant music that suits Goethe's punchy sermon.
4 Cf. 1 Corinthians 10:12: 'Wherefore let him that thinketh he standeth take heed lest he fall.'

19 Epiphanias[1]

Die heiligen[2] drei König' mit ihrem Stern,
Sie essen, sie trinken, und bezahlen nicht gern;
Sie essen gern, sie trinken gern,
Sie essen, trinken, und bezahlen nicht gern.

Die heil'gen drei König' sind kommen allhier,
Es sind ihrer drei und sind nicht ihrer vier;
Und wenn zu dreien der vierte wär',
So wär' ein heil'ger drei König mehr.

Ich erster bin der weiß' und auch der schön',[3]
Bei Tage solltet ihr erst mich sehn!
Doch ach, mit allen Spezerein
Werd ich sein Tag kein Mädchen mehr erfrein.

Ich aber bin der braun' und bin der lang',[4]
Bekannt bei Weibern wohl und bei Gesang.
Ich bringe Gold statt Spezerein,
Da werd ich überall willkommen sein.

Ich endlich bin der schwarz' und bin der klein'[5]
Und mag auch wohl einmal recht lustig sein.
Ich esse gern, ich trinke gern,
Ich esse, trinke und bedanke mich gern.

Die heil'gen[6] drei König' sind wohlgesinnt,
Sie suchen die Mutter und das Kind;

Epiphany

The holy three kings with their star,
They eat, they drink, and are loath to pay;
They like to eat, they like to drink,
They eat, drink and are loath to pay.

The holy three kings have come to this place,
They are three in number and not four;
And if to the three a fourth were added,
There'd be one holy three king more.

I, the first, am the handsome white one,
Just wait till you see me by day!
But ah! despite all my spices,
I'll never win a girl again.

But I'm the brown one, I'm the tall one,
Well known to women and to song.
I bring gold instead of spices,
So I'll be welcome everywhere.

I, lastly, am the little black one,
And would like a good time too for once.
I like to eat, I like to drink,
I like to eat, drink and say thank you too.

The holy three kings are well disposed,
They seek the Mother and the Child;

---

1 Goethe's 'Epiphanias' (a title he later changed to 'Epiphaniasfest') was written originally for performance at the Weimar court in 1781. The actress Corona Schröter, who composed the first version of 'Erlkönig', played the part of 'Der erste', disguised as a man. The performance was a light-hearted protest against the police ban on such processions at Epiphany, and also against those members of the court who were over-reverential in religious matters. Wolf wrote the song as a birthday present for his married mistress, Melanie Köchert, and it was performed by her three children, Hilde, Ilse and Irmina, on 6 January 1889 at the Köchert home (Neuer Markt 15) to celebrate Melanie's thirty-first birthday. They dressed up as the Three Kings, with Wolf providing the accompaniment from behind a screen. In the extensive postlude each king in turn, to his own characteristic accompaniment, takes his bow. Wolf intended to orchestrate the song, as we learn from a letter to Frieda Zerny of 24 April 1894: „Ochs schrieb mir, daß es nun zu spät an der Zeit sei die heilg. 3 Könige in's Programm aufzunehmen. Mir auch recht. So kann ich denn mit Musse an die Instrumentation des Stückes gehen." ('Ochs has written to say that it's now too late to include the Three Kings in the programme [for a concert on 28 April]. Which is fine by me. I shall now be able to tackle the orchestration at leisure.') The orchestrated version remained a fragment, however: a mere introduction and 21 bars.
2 Goethe: heil'gen, although the 1861 edition reads 'heiligen'.   3 Casper.
4 Melchior.   5 Balthasar.   6 See note 2, above.

Der Joseph fromm sitzt auch dabei,
Der Ochs und Esel liegen auf der Streu.

Wir bringen Myrrhen, wir bringen Gold,
Dem Weihrauch sind die Damen hold;
Und haben wir Wein von gutem Gewächs,
So trinken wir drei so gut als ihrer sechs.

Da wir nun hier schöne Herrn und Fraun,
Aber keine Ochsen und Esel[1] schaun,
So sind wir nicht am rechten Ort
Und ziehen unseres Weges weiter fort.

Pious Joseph is sitting there too,
The ox and ass lie on the straw.

We bring myrrh, we bring gold,
And frankincense that the ladies love;
And if we've wine from a fine year,
We drink enough, we three, for six.

But since we see fine squires and ladies,
But no oxen or asses here,
We cannot be in the right place,
And so must proceed on our way.

Poem written c. 1781
Also set by Pepping, Bernard van Dieren and Zelter

20 St. Nepomuks Vorabend[2]

St Nepomuk's Eve

Lichtlein schwimmen auf dem Strome,
Kinder singen auf der Brücken,
Glocke, Glöckchen fügt vom Dome
Sich der Andacht, dem Entzücken.

Lichtlein schwinden, Sterne schwinden;
Also löste sich die Seele
Unsres Heil'gen; nicht verkünden
Durft' er anvertraute Fehle.

Lichtlein, schwimmet! Spielt, ihr Kinder!
Kinderchor, o singe, singe!
Und verkündiget nicht minder,
Was den Stern zu Sternen bringe.

Little lights are floating on the river,
Children are singing on the bridge,
Bells great and small from the cathedral
Join in the devotions, the delight.

Little lights vanish, stars vanish;
Thus did the soul of our saint
Pass away; he could not divulge
A confessed misdeed.

Little lights, float! Play, you children!
Children's choir, sing, oh sing!
And proclaim no less what it is
That brings a star to other stars.

Poem written 15 May 1820
Also set by Hermann Zilcher and Zelter

---

1 'Ochsen' and 'Esel' can also be used as derogatory words for 'fools' – a scarcely veiled reference, perhaps, to the instigators of the police ban. Wolf would frequently turn and look accusingly at the audience at the mention of 'Ochsen' and 'Esel'.

2 'St. Nepomuks Vorabend' tells of St John of Nepomuk (c. 1348–1393), condemned to death by drowning by King Wenceslas IV of Bohemia for refusing to divulge the sins that Queen Johanna had allegedly revealed to him during confession (stanza 2). According to tradition, stars shone round his corpse as it floated down the Moldau. Goethe's poem was written while he was taking the waters in Karlsbad (now Karlovy Vary); nine days later he sent the poem to Zelter, who replied on 2 June 1820 that he had already set it as a solo song and a duet. The poem describes the celebration of the saint's death arranged each year on the eve of his name day, when candles, placed on wooden planks and protected by a transparent screen to simulate the stars, are floated downstream. The high-lying accompaniment of Wolf's song, above the stave throughout, evokes the sound of bells, and if the instruction to singer and pianist to perform 'slowly and with the utmost delicacy throughout' is heeded, an impression of ethereal beauty can be achieved. Nepomuk was canonised in 1863, and a bronze statue of the saint now stands on the Charles Bridge in Prague at the spot where he was

21 Genialisch Treiben[1]

So wälz' ich ohne Unterlaß,
Wie Sankt Diogenes, mein Faß.
Bald ist es Ernst, bald ist es Spaß;
Bald ist es Lieb', bald ist es Haß;
Bald ist es dies, bald ist es das;
Es ist ein Nichts und ist ein Was.
So wälz' ich ohne Unterlaß,
Wie Sankt Diogenes, mein Faß.

Poem written ?1775, first published 1811
Also set by Zelter

Genius at work

So I trundle my tub incessantly,
Like Saint Diogenes.
Sometimes it's serious, sometimes a joke;
Sometimes it's love, sometimes it's hate;
Sometimes it's this, sometimes it's that;
It's nothing and it's something.
So I trundle my tub incessantly,
Like Saint Diogenes.

22 Der Schäfer[2]

Es war ein fauler Schäfer,
Ein rechter Siebenschläfer,
Ihn kümmerte kein Schaf.
Ein Mädchen konnt' ihn fassen,
Da war der Tropf verlassen,
Fort Appetit und Schlaf!

The shepherd

There was once a lazy shepherd,
A veritable sleepy-head,
Who cared nothing for his sheep.
A girl took his fancy,
The fool was then forlorn,
Gone all appetite and sleep!

---

allegedly thrown into the river. St Nepomuk was considered the protector of bridges, and statues of him were erected on many other bridges throughout Bohemia, as Goethe wittily implies in the opening sestet of a longer poem, 'Celebrität', written in 1806, fourteen years before 'St. Nepomuks Vorabend':

Auf großen und auf kleinen Brucken
Stehn vielgestaltete Nepomucken
Von Erz, von Holz, gemahlt, von Stein,
Colossisch hoch, und puppisch klein.
Jeder hat seine Andacht davor,
Weil Nepomuck auf der Brucken das Leben
    verlor.

On large and on small bridges
Stand Nepomuks in many a guise
In bronze, in wood, painted, in stone,
As tall as a colossus, as small as a doll.
Folk say their prayers before them,
Because Nepomuk lost his life on a bridge.

1 Diogenes, the Cynic philosopher, was said to have lived in a tub. Goethe's poem had already been set by Zelter as a three-voice six-part canon that manages successfully to convey the image of a barrel trundling along. Goethe wrote to Zelter on 18 November 1810 to thank him for the song, which had become „Der Liebling unsres kleinen Publikums" ('the favourite of our little circle'). Wolf's setting is also a wonderfully witty song about the irresponsibility of genius and the chaotic lives artists lead. Goethe's iterative and silly rhyme scheme – each line ends in words that rhyme with 'Faß' ('barrel') – inspired Wolf to compose a boisterous and humorous scherzo. Goethe was clearly fond of the poem and several times referred to it in his correspondence, for example in a letter to Friedrich von Stein, dated 14 August 1794: „Für meine Person finde ich nichts Rätlicheres, als die Rolle des Diogenes zu spielen und mein Faß zu wälzen." ('As for me, the best advice I can take is to play the role of Diogenes and trundle my tub.')
2 Goethe's poem forms part of *Jery und Bätely*, a Singspiel he wrote in 1779 and revised as late as 1828. He lavished much care on this trifle, which also contains the ravishing duet 'Es rauschet das Wasser', set by Brahms as his Op. 28/3. 'Der Schäfer' is sung by Thomas, who ridicules Jery for his

Es trieb ihn in die Ferne,	He was driven to distant parts,
Des Nachts zählt' er die Sterne,	Counting the stars at night,
Er klagt' und härmt' sich brav:	Moaning and complaining mightily.
Nun, da sie ihn genommen,	Now that she's taken him,
Ist alles wiederkommen,	It's all come back again,
Durst, Appetit und Schlaf.	Thirst, appetite and sleep.

Poem written *c.* 1779
Also set by Arnim Knab, Reichardt and Erich Zeisl

23 Der neue Amadis[1,2]   A latter-day Amadis

Als ich noch ein Knabe war,	When I was still a little boy,
Sperrte man mich ein;	They used to lock me in;
Und so saß ich manches Jahr	So for many a year I had
Über mir allein,	To sit there all alone,
Wie im[3] Mutterleib.	As in my mother's womb.
Doch du warst mein Zeitvertreib,	But you passed the time for me,
Goldne Phantasie,	Golden Fantasy,
Und ich ward ein warmer Held,	And I became an ardent hero,
Wie der Prinz Pipi,[4]	Like young Prince Pipi,
Und durchzog die Welt.	And I roamed the world.
Baute manch kristallen Schloß	I built and shattered
Und zerstört' es auch,	Many a castle of glass,
Warf mein blinkendes Geschoß	I hurled my shining spear

---

unrequited love for Bätely. Wolf's song begins with a yawn in the accompaniment (slow trills in both hands). The marking is 'slothfully and sluggishly', an effect that Wolf conveys by the trilling of the prelude and the drooping phrases of the piano and voice in unison. After a more animated central section to depict the lover's heartburn, the song ends as it had begun – in a sleepy yawn. With Haydn's 'Lob der Faulheit', this must be one of the laziest songs in the Lieder repertoire. The title, 'Der Schäfer', was a late addition by the poet when he was preparing his *Gedichte* for publication. The poem is printed as two sestets in the Singspiel and four three-line verses in the *Nachlaß*.

1 The title of 'Der neue Amadis' refers to Amadis de Gaul, a hero of fourteenth-century Portuguese and subsequently Spanish romance. Goethe recalls the early days in his childhood when he first became aware of the stirrings of his poetic imagination. The poem formed part of the set of poems he prepared for Charlotte von Stein in 1777. In a letter to Charlotte dated 9 December 1777, Goethe wrote: „Wenn ich so allein bin, erkenn ich mich recht wieder wie ich in meiner ersten Jugend war, da ich so ganz allein unter der Welt umhertrieb." ('When I am so alone, I recognise myself as I was in the early days of my adolescence, when I drifted along so utterly alone and remote from the world.') An 1815 edition of Goethe's verse opened with this poem.

2 In December 1917, the imprisoned Rosa Luxemburg asked Sonja Liebknecht to copy out for her 'Der neue Amadis', saying, „Ich liebe das Gedicht so sehr – natürlich dank Hugo Wolfs Lied." ('I love the song so much – thanks of course to Hugo Wolf's song.') (See *Die Fackel*, July 1920.)

3 Goethe: in.

4 In 'The Dolphin', a fairy tale by Marie Catherine d'Aulnoy that was all the rage in the eighteenth century, there is a hero called 'Byby'. The tales were probably read to the child Goethe, who in this poem changes 'Byby' to 'Pipi'. The same fairy tale also mentions a 'castle of glass'.

Drachen durch den Bauch,	Through dragons' bellies,
Ja, ich war ein Mann!	Yes, I was a man!
Ritterlich befreit' ich dann	Chivalrously I then rescued
Die Prinzessin Fisch;	Princess Fish;
Sie war gar zu obligeant,	She was most obliging,
Führte mich zu Tisch,	Conducted me to table,
Und ich war gelant.	And I was gallant.
Und ihr Kuß war Götterbrot,	And her kiss was ambrosia,
Glühend wie der Wein.	Glowing like wine.
Ach! ich liebte fast mich tot!	Ah! I almost died of love!
Rings mit Sonnenschein	She glittered, enamel-like,
War sie emailliert.	In sunshine.
Ach! wer hat sie mir entführt?	Ah, who has abducted her?
Hielt kein Zauberband	Did no magic bond
Sie zurück vom schnellen Fliehn?	Detain her from hasty flight?
Sagt, wo ist ihr Land?	Say, where is her country?
Wo der Weg dahin?	Where the way to it?

Poem written c. 1774
Also set by Knab, Ernst Krenek, Reichardt and Corona Schröter

24 Blumengruß[1] — Flower greeting

Der Strauß, den ich gepflücket,	May this garland I have gathered
Grüße dich vieltausendmal!	Greet you many thousand times!
Ich habe mich oft gebücket,	I have often stooped down,
Ach, wohl eintausendmal,	Ah, surely a thousand times,
Und ihn ans Herz gedrücket	And pressed it to my heart
Wie hunderttausendmal!*	Something like a hundred thousand!*

Poem written c. 1810
Also set by Rued Immanuel Langgaard, Paul Graener, Knab, Reichardt, Anton Webern and Zelter
* Wolf repeats the final line.

25 Gleich und gleich[2] — Like to like

Ein Blumenglöckchen	A little flower-bell
Vom Boden hervor	Had sprung up early
War früh gesprosset	From the ground

---

1 Challier lists 27 settings of 'Blumengruß' before Wolf created his page-long gem on 31 December 1888. The drooping piano figuration is all tenderness and wistfulness, and suggests the stooping of the lover, as he picks the flower – but it speaks too perhaps of his forlorn hope. Goethe's poem was given by the poet to Zelter, who set it to music in September 1810 with the title 'Willkommen dem 28. August 1749' – a touching gesture on Goethe's sixty-first birthday.
2 Goethe sent this poem to Zelter on 22 April 1814 shortly after he had finished it, and Zelter responded by setting it as a seventieth birthday present for the poet in August 1819.

In lieblichem Flor;	In lovely blossom;
Da kam ein Bienchen	Along came a little bee
Und naschte fein: –	And sipped daintily: –
Die müssen wohl beide	They must have been
Für einander sein.	Made for each other.

Poem written 1814
Also set by Franz, Medtner, Webern, Zelter

26 Die Spröde[1] / The coy shepherdess

An dem reinsten Frühlingsmorgen	On the clearest of spring mornings
Ging die Schäferin und sang,	The shepherdess went out and sang,
Jung und schön und ohne Sorgen,	Carefree, young and beautiful,
Daß es durch die Felder klang,	Till it echoed through the fields:
So la la! le ralla![2]	So la la! le ralla!

Thyrsis bot ihr für ein Mäulchen	Thyrsis offered her, for a kiss,
Zwei, drei Schäfchen gleich am Ort,	Two, three lambs there and then,
Schalkhaft blickte sie ein Weilchen;	She looked on roguishly awhile,
Doch sie sang und lachte fort,	But went laughing and singing on her way,
So la la! le ralla!	So la la! le ralla!

Und ein andrer bot ihr Bänder,	And another offered her ribbons,
Und der dritte bot sein Herz;	And a third offered his heart;
Doch sie trieb mit Herz und Bändern	But she made fun of heart and ribbons,
So wie mit den Lämmern Scherz,	As she had done with the lambs,
Nur la la! le ralla!	All she sang was la la, le ralla!

Poem written c. 1796
Also set by Domenico Cimarosa, Knab, Medtner, Wilhelm Petersen, Tomášek and Zelter

27 Die Bekehrte[3] / The repentant shepherdess

Bei dem Glanz der Abendröte	In the red glow of sunset
Ging ich still den Wald entlang,	I wandered quietly through the wood,
Damon saß und blies die Flöte,	Damon sat and played his flute,

---

1 'Die Bekehrte' and 'Die Spröde' were the last of the *Goethe-Lieder* to be composed (12–14 February 1889) – but only 'Die Bekehrte' was finished. Wolf abandoned 'Die Spröde' after ten bars, and it was not until October that he completed the song – and the *Goethe-Lieder*.
2 Wolf extends the shepherdess's humming in each verse.
3 Goethe's two poems were sung originally by Rosalba in *Der Directeur in der Klemme* (1797), a German version of Cimarosa's *L'impresario in angustie* (1786), which Goethe's brother-in-law Christian Vulpius had prepared for the Weimar stage; the poems were later always printed together in his *Gedichte* under the present titles. The carefree shepherdess in 'Die Spröde' rejects the advances of three lovers; but in 'Die Bekehrte' she describes how, having surrendered herself to Damon, she longs for him when he then deserts her – see Wolf's settings of Mörike's 'Der Knabe und das

Daß es von den Felsen klang,	Making the cliffs resound,
So la la!¹	So la la!
Und er zog mich zu sich nieder,	And he drew me down to him,
Küßte mich so hold, so süß.	Kissed me so gently, so sweetly,
Und ich sagte: „Blase wieder!"	And I said: 'Play once more!'
Und der gute Junge blies,	And the good lad played,
So la la!	So la la!
Meine Ruh' ist nun verloren,	Now my peace of mind is lost,
Meine Freude floh davon,	My joy has flown away,
Und ich hör' vor meinen Ohren	And ringing in my ears I hear
Immer nur den alten Ton,	Nothing but the old refrain,
So la la! le ralla!	So la la, le ralla!

Poem written c. 1796
Also set by Ferruccio Busoni, Cimarosa, Knab, Medtner, Tomášek and Zelter

28 Frühling übers Jahr²   Perennial spring

Das Beet, schon lockert	Flowers break free from the earth
Sich's in die Höh,	And shoot up from their beds,
Da wanken Glöckchen	Little bells sway
So weiß wie Schnee;	White as snow;
Safran entfaltet	Crocuses blaze
Gewalt'ge Glut,	With intense colour,
Smaragden keimt es	Budding emerald
Und keimt wie Blut.	And budding blood red.
Primeln stolzieren	Primroses strut
So naseweis,	So saucily,
Schalkhafte Veilchen,	Roguish violets
Versteckt mit Fleiß;	Are carefully hidden;
Was auch noch alles	And a great deal else
Da regt und webt –	Stirs and grows,
Genug, der Frühling,	Enough – it's spring,
Er wirkt und lebt.	Active and alive.

Immlein' and 'Ein Stündlein wohl vor Tag' for a similar treatment of the theme. The accompaniment at the end of the second verse of 'Die Bekehrte' falters in a manner reminiscent of the piano part in Schubert's 'Gretchen am Spinnrade', after Gretchen recalls Faust's kiss; to clinch the connection, one needs only to read the opening of the third verse: „Meine Ruh ist nun verloren . . . ". 'Die Spröde' takes place at break of day, 'Die Bekehrte' in the evening.
1   As in 'Die Spröde', Wolf extends the refrain at the end of each verse. The right hand of the accompaniment simulates Damon's flute.
2   'Frühling übers Jahr', like Schumann's 'Frühlingsnacht', manages to be both spring song and love song; Wolf's ubiquitous bell-like accompaniment (43 bars of treble clef chiming before the bass appears) must surely have been suggested by the third and fourth lines of Goethe's poem: „Da wanken Glöckchen/So weiß wie Schnee" ('Little bells sway/White as snow').

Doch was im Garten	But in all the garden
Am reichsten blüht,	The most gorgeous flower
Das ist des Liebchens[1]	Is my sweetheart's
Lieblich Gemüt.	Lovely soul.
Da glühen Blicke	Her ever-loving
Mir immerfort,	Glowing glances
Erregend Liedchen,	Inspire my songs,
Erheiternd Wort;	Enliven our talk;
Ein immer offen,	An ever-open
Ein Blütenherz,	Blossoming heart,
Im Ernste freundlich	Friendly in grave matters,
Und rein im Scherz.	And pure in jest.
Wenn Ros' und Lilie	Summer may bring
Der Sommer bringt,	The rose and lily,
Er doch vergebens	But it vies in vain
Mit Liebchen ringt.	With my darling.

Poem written 15 March 1816
Also set by Loewe

29 Anakreons Grab[2]

Wo die Rose hier blüht, wo Reben um Lorbeer sich schlingen,
    Wo das Turtelchen lockt, wo sich das Grillchen ergötzt,
Welch ein Grab ist hier, das alle Götter mit Leben
    Schön bepflanzt und geziert? Es ist Anakreons Ruh.
Frühling, Sommer und Herbst genoß der glückliche Dichter;
    Vor dem Winter hat ihn endlich der Hügel geschützt.

Poem written c. 1785

1   'Liebchen' refers to Goethe's wife Christiane who three years previously in 1813 had been the recipient of another flower poem, 'Gefunden', written by Goethe to celebrate the twenty-fifth anniversary of their first meeting (see Strauss's lovely setting, Op. 56/1). Her health had deteriorated in the three years that separate the two poems and she died of what was probably stomach cancer on 6 June 1816, a few months after Goethe had written 'Frühling übers Jahr', which depicts her in their Weimar garden enjoying a brief period of better health. The garden in question was probably the one attached to Goethe's Gartenhaus, which had been bought for him by Carl August in 1776. This was Goethe's permanent residence until 1782, after which he moved into the more spacious house on the Frauenplan. However, he continued to use the Gartenhaus for recreational purposes, gradually extending and beautifying the garden. Situated in the Park an der Ilm, this is the most suggestive of all the Goethe sites in Weimar, and it was here that poems such as 'An den Mond', 'Wandrers Nachtlied', 'Rastlose Liebe' and 'Jägers Abendlied' were written, and where he also worked at *Torquato Tasso*, *Faust* and the prose version of *Iphigenia auf Tauris*. On 1 May 1827 Goethe wrote a little poem, 'Goethes Gartenhaus am untern Park bei Weimar', beginning „Übermüthig sieht's nicht aus", describing the modest house and garden he so cherished.
2   Anacreon was a Greek poet from Teos who, according to Valerius Maximus, choked to death on a grape stone at the age of eighty-five. Pausanias in his *Descriptions of Greece* reports that the Athenians erected a statue of him as a drunk man singing and that he was, after Sappho of Lesbos, the first poet to write erotic love poetry. Only fragments of his work survive. His poems, in praise of

Anacreon's grave

Here, where the rose blooms, where vine and laurel intertwine,
   Where the turtle-dove calls, where the cricket rejoices,
Whose grave is this that all the gods have adorned
   With beautiful life? It is Anacreon's resting-place.
Spring, summer and autumn the happy poet enjoyed;
   This mound has at the last sheltered him from winter.

30 Dank des Paria[1]

Großer Brahma! nun erkenn' ich,
Daß du Schöpfer bist der Welten!
Dich als meinen Herrscher nenn' ich;
Denn du lässest alle gelten.

Und verschließest auch dem Letzten
Keines von den tausend Ohren;
Uns, die tief Herabgesetzten,*
Alle hast du neu geboren.

Wendet euch zu dieser Frauen,
Die der Schmerz zur Göttin wandelt;[2]
Nun beharr' ich anzuschauen
Den, der einzig wirkt und handelt.

Poem written c. 1822
Also set by Loewe
* Wolf repeats the line.

The pariah's thanks

Great Brahma! now I recognise
That you created all worlds!
Master I call you,
For all creatures have value in your eyes.

And even to the lowliest you close
None of your thousand ears;
Us, the deeply despised,*
And all men, you have born anew.

Direct your prayers towards this woman,
Whom pain has transformed into a goddess!
Steadfastly now I persist in beholding
Him who alone can cause and act.

---

wine, women (and boys) and song, are written in a metre that derives from his name: Anacreontic. German poets such as Johann Wilhelm Ludwig Gleim, Friedrich von Hagedorn, Gotthold Ephraim Lessing and Johann Peter Uz exemplified this style in the eighteenth century. 'Anakreons Grab' became one of Wolf's most popular songs, and in a letter to Melanie Köchert of 10 June 1896 he describes it as 'unvermeidlich' ('unavoidable', 'ubiquitous'). The accompaniment seems to suggest the gentle bending of trees above his grave, and although the tonality darkens at 'Grab' ('grave'), the whole song breathes serenity and peace, particularly at the wonderful pause between 'Es ist' and the pianissimo 'Anakreons Ruh'.

Eduard Mörike's *Anakreon und die sogenannten Anakreontischen Lieder*, published in 1864, contains over a hundred translations of Anacreon's fragments, epigrams and lyrics, including 'Die Leier' – a poem more familiar in Franz von Bruchmann's translation that Schubert composed in the winter of 1822 as 'An die Leier'. Moritz von Schwind, when asked to illustrate Mörike's 'Erinna an Sappho', wrote a letter to the poet expressing his surprise that Mörike had found the time to pen these translations, adding that if such work 'cost us a single one of your poems, it would be too high a price to pay for the whole of Anacreon'.

1   Goethe's poem is the last of a trilogy, *Paria*, written during 1821 and 1822: 'Des Paria Gebet', 'Legende' and 'Dank des Paria', all three of which were set by Carl Loewe. The idea of 'Dank des Paria' is central to Goethe's humanistic philosophy, familiar to us from Schubert's 'Der Gott und die Bayadere': pariahs of society are human beings too and should not be despised.

2   Verse 3 refers to the events of 'Legende'. A brahminee is beheaded by her brahmin husband for harbouring mildly erotic thoughts for a beautiful youth glimpsed by the shores of the Ganges. On discovering the atrocity, her son hurries back to the place of execution with a magic sword, sees two

31 Königlich Gebet[1]

Ha, ich bin der Herr der Welt! mich lieben
Die Edlen, die mir dienen.
Ha, ich bin der Herr der Welt! ich liebe
Die Edlen, denen ich gebiete.
O gib mir, Gott im Himmel! daß ich mich
Der Höh' und Liebe nicht überhebe.

Poem written 1775/6

A royal prayer

Ha, I am master of the world, loved
By the nobles in my service!
Ha, I am master of the world, I love
The nobles, whom I command!
O Lord in Heaven, grant that I do not abuse
This eminence and this love.

from the *Buch des Sängers des West-östlichen Divans*
Book of the Minstrel in the West-Eastern Divan

On 11 May 1820 Goethe wrote a letter to Zelter that expresses the pleasure that he, as an old man, derived from the Mohammedan religion:

> Diese Mohamedanische Religion, Mythologie, Sitte geben Raum einer Poesie wie sie meinen Jahren ziemt. Unbedingtes Ergeben in den unergründlichen Willen Gottes, heiterer Überblick des beweglichen, immer kreis- und spiralartig wiederkehrenden Erde-Treibens, Liebe, Neigung zwischen zwei Welten schwebend, alles Reale geläutert, sich symbolisch auflösend. Was will der Großpapa weiter?

> The Mohammedan religion, mythology and customs invite a poetry that befits a man of my age. Absolute surrender to the inscrutable will of God, the serene survey of earthly striving, always in motion, circling, spiralling back to where it began, love and affection swaying between two worlds, everything that is real purified, dissolving into the symbolic. What else could a grandfather desire?

32 Phänomen[2]

Wenn zu der Regenwand
Phöbus sich gattet,
Gleich steht ein Bogenrand
Farbig beschattet.

Phenomenon

When Phoebus couples
With a curtain of rain,
Up springs a curved rim,
Shaded in colour.

---

bodies and two heads, and joins his mother's head onto one of the female bodies, that of a common criminal. The resultant hybrid – a brahminee head and a pariah's body – terrifies the mother, but she is now able, because of this divine intervention (the whole scenario had been planned by the gods) to act as an intermediary between immortals and mortals.

1 The poem, copied out in Goethe's own hand for Charlotte von Stein, was first published in the *Werke* of 1815. In Wolf's *Gedichte von J. W. v. Goethe*, it contrasts neatly with 'Dank des Paria'. For a similar theme, see the early Mörike song 'Der König bei der Krönung', p. 367.

2 'Phänomen' was written by the sixty-four-year-old Goethe on his way to Wiesbaden, where he would meet Marianne von Willemer, as yet unknown to him. The poem describes the formation of a rainbow. In mist or cloud, we are told, the rainbow can seem white – a fact that inspires the poet to

Im Nebel gleichen Kreis	I see the same arc
Seh ich gezogen,	Described in mist,
Zwar ist der Bogen weiß,	Though the bow be white,
Doch Himmelsbogen.	It is a bow of heaven.
So sollst du, muntrer Greis,	So, spry old man,
Dich nicht betrüben;	Do not lose heart;
Sind gleich die Haare weiß,	Your hair may be white,
Doch wirst du lieben.	Yet you will love.

Poem written 25 July 1814
Also set by Brahms and Rihm

33 Erschaffen und Beleben[1] — Creation and animation

Hans Adam war ein Erdenkloß,	Hans Adam was a lump of clay
Den Gott zum Menschen machte,	That God made into man,
Doch bracht er aus der Mutter Schoß	But from his mother's womb
Noch vieles Ungeschlachte.	He brought much that was uncouth.
Die Elohim[2] zur Nas' hinein	The gods, via his nose,
Den besten Geist ihm bliesen,	Blew the best spirit in,
Nun schien er schon was mehr zu sein,	Now he seemed to make progress,
Denn er fing an zu niesen.	For he began to sneeze.
Doch mit Gebein und Glied und Kopf	Yet with his head and bones and limbs,
Blieb er ein halber Klumpen,	He still remained half a lump,
Bis endlich Noah[3] für den Tropf	Till Noah for the oaf at last
Das Wahre fand, den Humpen.	Found the very thing – a tankard.
Der Klumpe fühlt sogleich den Schwung,	That brings life into the lump
Sobald er sich benetzet,	As soon as he wets his whistle,
So wie der Teig durch Säuerung	Just as dough, through leavening,
Sich in Bewegung setzet.	Is quickened into life.

---

end his terse, epigrammatic poem with an objective correlative, fraught with autobiographical significance: old men should take heart, for even if their hair is white, they shall still find love – a remarkable prophecy of the passionate relationship he was to enjoy with the then thirty-year-old Marianne. The white rainbow is not a product of his imagination; on 25 July 1814, at the start of his travels in the Rhine and Main areas, he witnessed this rare phenomenon, a colourless rainbow, which he took as a happy omen. The poem was penned on the same day. While Brahms (Op. 61/3) achieves his effect through multicoloured arpeggios, Wolf depicts the chromatic rainbow by managing to touch, in a mere 16 bars, almost every known key – a technical *tour de force* that never once seems contrived. See HW to Melanie Köchert, 12 October 1890, p. 120, and to Paul Müller, 24 February 1896, p. 122.

1 'Erschaffen und Beleben', entitled originally 'Der Urvater', traces with typical Goethean irreverence the course of Adam's life from birth to death. The poem ends in crapulous merriment, and in Wolf's postlude we hear the exuberant clinking of glasses, as we are led off into the Promised Land. Written at Berka on the Ilm, this was the first of the *West-östlicher Divan* poems to be penned.

2 Goethe has fun treating the Hebrew name of the divinity as a plural – as it is in Hebrew.

3 See Genesis 9:20–21: 'Noah was the first tiller of the soil. He planted a vineyard; and he drank of the wine, and became drunk, and lay uncovered in his tent.'

So, Hafis,[1] mag dein holder Sang,	So, Hafiz, may your sweet song
Dein heiliges Exempel,	And your sacred example
Uns führen, bei der Gläser Klang,	Conduct us, as the glasses clink,
Zu unsres Schöpfers Tempel.	To our Creator's temple.

Poem written 21 June 1814
Also set by Max von Schillings, Strauss and Zelter

from the *Schenkenbuch des West-östlichen Divans*
The Book of the Cup-Bearer in the West-Eastern Divan

The ninth book of the *West-östlicher Divan* is devoted to wine-drinking and the figure of the cup-bearer – favourite themes in the poetry of Hafiz. The cup-bearer ('sāqī' in Arabic and Persian), a stock figure in Persian poetry, is far more than a mere servant. A devoted disciple, keen to learn, he can also scold his master when he drinks too much, and he is sexually alluring. Certain Sufis maintained that to gaze on the 'beardless boy' was to glimpse the beauty of God, a notion that was roundly condemned by critics of the Sufis. None of these poems has a title in the *Divan*.

34 Ob der Koran von Ewigkeit sei?[2]
Has the Koran existed since time began?

Ob der Koran von Ewigkeit sei?	Has the Koran existed since time began?
Darnach frag ich nicht!	I do not enquire!
Ob der Koran geschaffen sei?	Was the Koran created?
Das weiß ich nicht!	I do not know!
Daß er das Buch der Bücher sei,	That it is the Book of Books,
Glaub ich aus Mosleminenpflicht.	I, as a dutiful Muslim, believe.
Daß aber der Wein von Ewigkeit sei,	That wine has existed since time began,
Daran zweifl' ich nicht;	I do not doubt;
Oder daß er vor den Engeln geschaffen sei,	And that it was created before the angels,
Ist vielleicht auch kein Gedicht.	May also be no myth.
Der Trinkende, wie es auch immer sei,	Be that as it may, he who imbibes
Blickt Gott frischer ins Angesicht.	Sees God's countenance more clearly.

Poem written 20 May 1815

---

1   Hafiz is described as a 'sacred example': a Muslim, he was forbidden to drink by his religion, but he nevertheless wrote many poems on the delights of wine.
2   Muslim theologians had debated for many centuries whether the Koran was created by God or had always existed (as God's speech). 'Ob der Koran von Ewigkeit sei?' begins grandly (rising octaves) as Goethe ponders the question, but this solemnity soon degenerates into drunken mirth (hilarious syncopated chords) as he turns his attention to the origin of wine.

JOHANN WOLFGANG VON GOETHE

35 Trunken müssen wir alle sein![1]

Trunken müssen wir alle sein!*
Jugend ist Trunkenheit ohne Wein;
Trinkt sich das Alter wieder zu Jugend,
So ist es wundervolle Tugend.
Für Sorgen sorgt das liebe Leben,
Und Sorgenbrecher sind die Reben.

Da wird nicht mehr nachgefragt!
Wein ist ernstlich untersagt.
Soll denn doch getrunken sein,
Trinke nur vom besten Wein:
Doppelt wärest du ein Ketzer
In Verdammnis um den Krätzer.[2]

We must all be drunk!

We must all be drunk!*
Youth is drunkenness without wine;
If old age can drink itself young again,
That's a marvellous virtue.
Dear life takes care to burden us with cares,
And the grape it is that cures care.

No more questions, then!
Wine is strictly forbidden.
But if you are to drink,
Drink only the best wine:
You'd be an infidel twice over,
If damned for drinking gut-rot.

Poem written before 30 May 1815
* Wolf repeats the line at the end of the song, after which 'trunken' is sung twice more by the inebriated singer.

36 So lang man nüchtern ist[3]

So lang man nüchtern ist,
Gefällt das Schlechte;
Wie man getrunken hat,
Weiß man das Rechte;
Nur ist das Übermaß
Auch gleich zuhanden;
Hafis, o lehre mich,
Wie du's verstanden!

Denn meine Meinung ist
Nicht übertrieben:
Wenn man nicht trinken kann,
Soll man nicht lieben;
Doch sollt ihr Trinker euch
Nicht besser dünken,
Wenn man nicht lieben kann,
Soll man nicht trinken.

As long as one is sober

As long as one is sober,
The bad things please;
When one has drunk,
One knows what is right.
But then excess
Is ever at hand:
Oh, teach me, Hafiz,
How you see it!

For my view is,
With no exaggeration,
That if one cannot drink,
One should not love;
But you topers
Should not think yourselves superior:
If one cannot love,
One should not drink.

1 Cf. Baudelaire's prose-poem 'Enivrez-vous', from *Le Spleen de Paris*. Wolf marks his song *Bacchantisch*, and when he performed it at Alfred Schmied's, he wrote to Melanie Köchert (12 October 1890, p. 120) that he sent everyone into ecstasies.
2 'Krätzer' is still used today to denote a pale wine from the Alto Adige; in Goethe's time, however, it simply meant inferior wine. The verb 'kratzen' means to 'scratch', the implication perhaps being that the wine scratched the throat on its way down.
3 Goethe in mock-philosophical mood: topers make the best lovers, unless too much alcohol reduces their libido. A minor is also Wolf's key in 'Zur Warnung', his most comic song about the effects of alcohol. See HW to Paul Müller, 24 February 1896, p. 122.

Poem written 26 July 1814
Also set by Felix Mendelssohn and Zelter

37 Sie haben wegen der Trunkenheit[1]

Sie haben wegen der Trunkenheit
Vielfältig uns verklagt,
Und haben von unsrer Trunkenheit
Lange nicht genug gesagt.
Gewöhnlich der Betrunkenheit
Erliegt man, bis es tagt;
Doch hat mich meine Betrunkenheit
In der Nacht umhergejagt.
Es ist die Liebestrunkenheit,
Die mich erbärmlich plagt,
Von Tag zu Nacht, von Nacht zu Tag
In meinem Herzen zagt.
Dem Herzen, das in Trunkenheit
Der Lieder schwillt und ragt,
Daß keine nüchterne Trunkenheit
Sich gleich zu heben wagt.
Lieb-, Lied- und Weinestrunkenheit,
Ob's nachtet oder tagt,
Die göttlichste Betrunkenheit,
Die mich entzückt und plagt.

They have accused us of drunkenness

They have accused us of drunkenness
In many different ways,
And have nowhere nearly found all
There's to say about our drunkenness.
It's normal to lie drunk
Until the break of day,
But my drunkenness
Chases me around all night.
It's being drunk with love
That torments me so terribly.
Night and day, day and night,
It wavers in my heart –
My heart, which so swells and rises
With the drunkenness of song,
That sober drunkenness
Dares not raise its head.
The drunkenness of love, song and wine,
Whether it be night or day,
This most divine drunkenness
Enraptures and torments me.

Poem written 24 September 1815

38 Was in der Schenke waren heute[2]

Was in der Schenke waren heute
Am frühsten Morgen für Tumulte!
Der Wirt und Mädchen! Fackeln, Leute!

Was gab's für Händel, für Insulte!

What an uproar there was

What an uproar there was in the tavern
At the crack of dawn!
Innkeeper and serving-girls! Torches, crowds!

Such haggling and such insults!

1 The poet complains that he is continually being accused of drunkenness, but he challenges the accusation by saying that his real problem is being drunk with love. At the mention of 'Liebestrunkenheit' the uncertain harmonies and slurred vocal line are replaced by more coherent music, until on the final page the pianist's left hand reintroduces the swaying rhythm associated with alcoholic inebriation. Contrary to received opinion, Wolf rarely drank immoderately. Edmund Hellmer reports in *Hugo Wolf. Erlebtes und Erlauschtes* (p. 114) that he never saw Wolf drink more than one glass.
2 The poem, which is closely based on a ghazal by Hafiz, was first published in vol. VI of 'Über Kunst und Altertum' in 1827, and was then added to the *Divan* in the same year. The poem depicts a frenzied scene of debauchery at the tavern: girls, torches, crowds, haggling, insults and shrill music – all of which is marked *Äußerst rasch und wirbelnd* (exceedingly fast and whirling). The final stanza introduces a moral note, which Wolf signals by a succession of weighty octaves in both hands – but the serious mood is soon over, and the song whirls to a drunken conclusion.

Die Flöte klang, die Trommel scholl!	Flutes were played, drums were banged!
Es war ein wüstes Wesen –	What wild debauchery!
Doch bin ich, Lust und Liebe voll,	But I too was there myself,
Auch selbst dabei gewesen.	Full of pleasure and love.
Daß ich von Sitte nichts gelernt,	That I've learned nothing of decorum
Darüber tadelt mich ein jeder;	Is what they all reproach me with;
Doch bleib' ich weislich weit entfernt	But I wisely stay aloof
Vom Streit der Schulen und Katheder.	From disputing professors and scholars.

Poem not included in the *Divan* until 1827

from the *Buch Suleika des West-östlichen Divans*
The Book of Suleika in the West-Eastern Divan (Nos. 39–48)

The eighth book of the *West-östlicher Divan* was inspired largely by Goethe's admiration for the poems of Hafiz and his love for Marianne von Willemer who contributed five poems of her own to the collection, as she confided in a letter to Herman Grimm of 5 April 1856: 'Hochbeglückt in deiner Liebe', 'Als ich auf dem Euphrat schiffte', 'Was bedeutet die Bewegung?', 'Ach, um deine feuchten Schwingen' and 'Wie mit innigstem Behagen'. Goethe referred to Marianne as Suleika, a variant on the Arabic or Persian name Zulaykhā, meaning 'brilliant' or 'beautiful'. The poetic pen-name that Goethe gave himself was Hatem, a reference to the pre-Islamic poet Ḥātim al-Ṭa'ī who was praised for his legendary generosity – see note 2 to 'Locken, haltet mich gefangen' (No. 47, p. 168). None of these ten poems has a title in the *Divan*.

39 Nicht Gelegenheit macht Diebe[1]
Hatem

Opportunity does not make thieves
Hatem

Nicht Gelegenheit macht Diebe,	Opportunity does not make thieves,
Sie ist selbst der größte Dieb;	It is itself the greatest thief;
Denn sie stahl den Rest der Liebe,	For it stole what was left of the love
Die mir noch im Herzen blieb.	That still remained in my heart.
Dir hat sie ihn übergeben,	It handed over to you
Meines Lebens Vollgewinn,	All I had gained in life,
Daß ich nun, verarmt, mein Leben	So that now, impoverished,
Nur von dir gewärtig bin.	I am wholly dependent on you.

1 'Nicht Gelegenheit macht Diebe' and 'Hochbeglückt in deiner Liebe' appear together in the *West-östlicher Divan*, the first spoken by Hatem (Goethe), the second by Suleika (Marianne). Wolf also places them together and uses a falling chromatic scale in the piano writing of both. 'Nicht Gelegenheit macht Diebe' is the earliest of the *Divan* poems to be addressed to Marianne.

Doch ich fühle schon Erbarmen	But I sense compassion
Im Karfunkel deines Blicks	In your garnet glances,
Und erfreu in deinen Armen	And in your embrace
Mich erneuerten Geschicks.	Rejoice in my reborn destiny.

Poem written 12 or 15 September 1815

40 Hochbeglückt in deiner Liebe[1]
Suleika

Sublimely happy in your love
Suleika

Hochbeglückt in deiner Liebe	Sublimely happy in your love,
Schelt ich nicht Gelegenheit;	I do not chide opportunity;
Ward sie auch an dir zum Diebe,	Though it played the thief on you,
Wie mich solch ein Raub erfreut!	How such a theft delights me!
Und wozu denn auch berauben?	But why speak of stealing?
Gib dich mir aus freier Wahl;	Surrender to me of your own free will;
Gar zu gerne möcht ich glauben –	I would gladly believe
Ja, ich bin's, die dich bestahl.	That it was I indeed who robbed you.
Was so willig du gegeben,	What you gave so willingly
Bringt dir herrlichen Gewinn,	Brings you glorious gain,
Meine Ruh, mein reiches Leben	My peace, my rich life
Geb ich freudig, nimm es hin!	I gladly give, take it from me!
Scherze nicht! Nichts von Verarmen!	No jesting! No mention of impoverishment!
Macht uns nicht die Liebe reich?	Does not love make us rich?
Halt ich dich in meinen Armen,	When I hold you in my arms,
Jedem Glück ist meines gleich.	My joy's as great as anyone's.

Poem written 16 September 1815

41 Als ich auf dem Euphrat schiffte[2]
Suleika

As I sailed on the Euphrates
Suleika

Als ich auf dem Euphrat schiffte,	As I sailed on the Euphrates,
Streifte sich der goldne Ring	The golden ring you lately gave me
Fingerab in Wasserklüfte,	Slipped from my finger
Den ich jüngst von dir empfing.	Down into the watery abyss.

---

1 Marianne von Willemer told Herman Grimm in a letter of 5 April 1856 that she wrote her poem as a reply to Goethe's 'Nicht Gelegenheit macht Diebe'. As the manuscript has not been preserved, the extent of Goethe's subsequent collaboration is unclear, although he did change Marianne's 'ganzes Leben' to 'reiches Leben' in verse 3.

2 The roles are now reversed in these next two songs, which are related musically and thematically. Suleika, in 'Als ich auf dem Euphrat schiffte', narrates the riddle that Hatem, in 'Dies zu deuten, bin erbötig!', then interprets. And the meaning of the riddle? Just as the Doge of Venice symbolically weds La Serenissima by sailing out to sea on Ascension Day in the golden ship of state known as the *Bucintoro* and sinking a precious ring into the depths, so does the apparent loss of Suleika's ring symbolise her spiritual betrothal to Hatem. Wolf sets the poem as a bewitching barcarolle.

Also träumt ich. Morgenröte	So I dreamed. Red dawn
Blitzt ins Auge durch den Baum,	Flashed into my eyes through the tree,
Sag, Poete, sag, Prophete!	Tell me, poet, tell me, prophet!
Was bedeutet dieser Traum?[1]	What is the meaning of this dream?

Poem written 17 September 1815
Also set by Johanna Kinkel

42 Dies zu deuten, bin erbötig!   I am disposed to interpret this dream!
Hatem   *Hatem*

Dies zu deuten, bin erbötig!	I am disposed to interpret this dream!
Hab ich dir nicht oft erzählt,	Have I not often told you
Wie der Doge von Venedig	How the Doge of Venice
Mit dem Meere sich vermählt?	Wedded himself to the sea?
So von deinen Fingergliedern	Thus from your fingers
Fiel der Ring dem Euphrat zu.	The ring fell into the Euphrates.
Ach, zu tausend Himmelsliedern,	Ah, sweet dream, you inspire me
Süßer Traum, begeisterst du!	To a thousand heavenly songs!
Mich, der von den Indostanen	I, who wandered
Streifte bis Damaskus hin,	From Hindustan to Damascus
Um mit neuen Karawanen	To journey with new caravans
Bis ans Rote Meer zu ziehn,	As far as the Red Sea –
Mich vermählst du deinem Flusse,	You wed me to your river,
Der Terrasse, diesem Hain,	To the terraces, to this grove:
Hier soll bis zum letzten Kusse	Here, until our final kiss,
Dir mein Geist gewidmet sein.	I dedicate my soul to you.

Poem written 17 September 1815

43 Hätt ich irgend wohl Bedenken[2]   Could I ever hesitate
Hatem   *Hatem*

Hätt ich irgend wohl Bedenken,	Could I ever hesitate to offer you
Balch,[3] Bochâra, Samarkand,	Balkh, Bokhara, Samarkand,

---

1   The last two lines are quoted by Wolf in a letter to Frieda Zerny of 3 March 1894: he has been day-dreaming about his mistress and wonders what the dream might signify.
2   'Hätt ich irgend wohl Bedenken' quivers with quaver triplet chords in the right hand, while the left hand and voice express the rapture of being in love. In both this poem and 'Komm, Liebchen, komm!', the poet compares himself with the Emperor and sees himself as an equal in the latter („ich bin so groß als Er") and superior in 'Hätt ich irgend wohl Bedenken'. 'Bettler' in the final verse is meant ironically. The Emperor, who owns all these wonderful towns, could give them away but does not do so, for he has no loving soul. The poet cannot give them away either, for he, as a beggar, does not own them; but he could give them away if he owned them: for in his soul he is a true Emperor. 'Bettler' ('beggar') is meant as something positive.
3   Balkh is a town in the Balkh province of Afghanistan, south of the Oxus.

Süßes Liebchen, dir zu schenken,	O my sweetest love,
Dieser Städte Rausch und Tand?	With all their gaudy delights?
Aber frag einmal den Kaiser,	But try asking the Emperor
Ob er dir die Städte gibt?	Whether he would give you these cities?
Er ist herrlicher und weiser;	He may be grander and wiser;
Doch er weiß nicht, wie man liebt.	But does not know how one should love.
Herrscher, zu dergleichen Gaben	Sovereign, you will never resolve
Nimmermehr bestimmst du dich!	To bestow such gifts!
Solch ein Mädchen muß man haben	Better by far to have such a girl
Und ein Bettler sein wie ich.	And be a beggar like me.

Poem written 17 February 1815

44 Komm, Liebchen, komm![1] / Come, my love, come!

Hatem / *Hatem*

Komm, Liebchen, komm! umwinde mir die Mütze!	Come, my love, come! Wind my head-dress on!
Aus deiner Hand nur ist der Tulbend schön.	Only when wound by you is the turban beautiful.
Hat Abbas[2] doch, auf Irans höchstem Sitze,	Even Abbas, on Iran's loftiest throne,
Sein Haupt nicht zierlicher umwinden sehn!	Did not see his head more gracefully enwreathed!
Ein Tulbend war das Band, das Alexandern[3]	It was a turban that cascaded
In Schleifen schön vom Haupte fiel	In fine folds from Alexander's head,
Und allen Folgeherrschern, jenen Andern,	And with all rulers that succeeded him
Als Königszierde wohlgefiel.	Found favour as a royal embellishment.

---

1 See HW to Melanie Köchert, 12 October 1890, p. 120. 'Komm, Liebchen, komm!' is steeped in melodic beauty, the tune appearing first in the piano, then the voice, and finally in the exultant and tender postlude. Goethe's birthday was celebrated in style at the Willemer home on 28 August 1815 and Sulpiz Boisserée gives the following description:

> Auf den Körben lag ein Turban vom feinsten indischen Mußlin, mit einer Lorbeerkrone umkränzt ... Frau Städel hatte dazu die Aussicht aus Goethes Fenster auf die Stadt Frankfurt recht hübsch gezeichnet und Frau Willemer einen kleinen Kranz von Feldblumen aufgeklebt, worein sie einen passenden Spruch aus dem „Divan" [des Hafis] geschrieben hatte ...
>
> A turban of finest Indian muslin lay on top of the baskets, wreathed with a crown of laurel ... Frau Städel had made a very pretty drawing of the view from Goethe's window onto the town of Frankfurt, and Frau Willemer had fastened onto it a little garland of wild flowers with a suitable quote from the *Divan* [of Hafis] ...

2 Shah Abbas, the founder of the Safavid dynasty in Iran, who reigned from 1586 to 1628. He promoted the prosperity of his people and tolerated the Christians.
3 Alexander of Macedon, commonly known as Alexander the Great (356BC–323BC).

Ein Tulbend ist's, der unsern Kaiser schmücket,	It is a turban that adorns our Emperor,
Sie nennen's Krone. Name geht wohl hin!	A crown they call it. What's in a name?
Juwel und Perle! sei das Aug entzücket!	Jewels and pearls may delight the eyes!
Der schönste Schmuck ist stets der Musselin.	But the most beautiful adornment is muslin.
Und diesen hier, ganz rein und silberstreifig,	So wind this muslin here, so pure and silver-threaded,
Umwinde, Liebchen, um die Stirn umher.	Wind it, my love, about my brow.
Was ist denn Hoheit? Mir ist sie geläufig!	What, then, is majesty? It's well known to me:
Du schaust mich an, ich bin so groß als Er.	You gaze at me, I am as great as He.

Poem written 17 February 1815

45 Wie sollt' ich heiter bleiben[1]
Hatem

How could I remain cheerful
Hatem

Wie sollt' ich heiter bleiben,	How could I remain cheerful,
Entfernt von Tag und Licht?	When sundered from day and light?
Nun aber will ich schreiben,	But now I shall write,
Und trinken mag ich nicht.	And do not wish to drink.
Wenn sie mich an sich lockte,	When she enticed me to her,
War Rede nicht im Brauch,	There was no need of words;
Und wie die Zunge stockte,	And as my tongue faltered,
So stockt die Feder auch.	So does my quill now.
Nur zu! geliebter Schenke,	But come, beloved cup-bearer,
Den Becher fülle still!	Fill my cup in silence!
Ich sage nur: Gedenke!	I've only to say, 'Remember!'
Schon weiß man, was ich will.*	And he knows at once my wish.*

Poem written 1 October 1815
* Wolf repeats the final line.

---

[1] 'Wie sollt' ich heiter bleiben' and 'Wenn ich dein gedenke' form another pair, both sung this time by Hatem, as he meditates in a reverie on his loved one. The poem was sent by Goethe, who signed himself Hatem, to Marianne on 16 December 1815. The first verse ran originally:

Mir will es finster bleiben	I find it dark
Im vollsten Mondenlicht,	In full moonlight,
Ich mag nicht singen, schreiben,	I do not wish to sing or write,
Und trinken mag ich nicht.	And nor do I wish to drink.

See HW to Melanie Köchert, 12 October 1890, p. 120.

46 Wenn ich dein gedenke
Hatem

Wenn ich dein gedenke,
Fragt mich gleich der Schenke:
„Herr, warum so still?
Da von deinen Lehren
Immer weiter hören
Saki[1] gerne will."

Wenn ich mich vergesse
Unter der Zypresse,
Hält er nichts davon,
Und im stillen Kreise
Bin ich doch so weise,
Klug wie Salomon.

Poem written late September or early October 1815

47 Locken, haltet mich gefangen[2]
Hatem

Locken, haltet mich gefangen
In dem Kreise des Gesichts!
Euch geliebten braunen Schlangen
Zu erwidern hab ich nichts.

Nur dies Herz, es ist von Dauer,
Schwillt in jugendlichstem Flor;
Unter Schnee und Nebelschauer
Rast ein Ätna dir hervor.

Du beschämst wie Morgenröthe
Jener Gipfel ernste Wand,
Und noch einmal fühlet Hatem
Frühlingshauch und Sommerbrand.

Schenke, her! Noch eine Flasche!
Diesen Becher bring ich Ihr!
Findet sie ein Häufchen Asche,
Sagt sie: der verbrannte mir.

Poem written 30 September 1815

When I think of you
Hatem

When I think of you,
My cup-bearer at once enquires:
'Master, why so silent?
For Saki would gladly
Listen forever
To your teaching.'

When I lose myself in thought
Beneath the cypress tree,
He's not impressed at all;
Yet in that silent sphere
I am as shrewd
And wise as Solomon.

O curls, hold me captive
Hatem

O curls, hold me captive
In the circle of her face!
I have nothing to match
You much loved tawny serpents.

This heart alone is constant,
Swelling in most youthful blossom;
Beneath snow and drops of mist
An Etna gushes out towards you.

Like red dawn, you bring a blush
To the earnest brow of those peaks,
And once again Hatem feels
The breath of spring and summer's fire.

Cup-bearer, fill! Another flagon!
I raise this glass to her!
If she finds a heap of ashes,
She'll say: 'He burned away for me.'

---

1   Persian for 'publican', here used as a proper noun. See HW to Melanie Köchert, 12 October 1890, p. 120.
2   Hatem casts all tranquillity aside in 'Locken, haltet mich gefangen', the first of the final pair that completes Wolf's *Divan* settings. The piano accompaniment strains the medium to the utmost as it strives to express the tumultuous feelings that Suleika arouses in him. That Hatem is none other than Goethe himself is made clear in the rhyme scheme of stanza 3, where 'Morgenröte' instead of rhyming with 'Goethe' clashes with 'Hatem'. The first line of the poem in the *West-östlicher Divan* read: 'Locken! haltet mich gefangen'.

48 Nimmer will ich dich verlieren![1]
Suleika

Nimmer will ich dich verlieren!
Liebe gibt der Liebe Kraft.
Magst du meine Jugend zieren
Mit gewalt'ger Leidenschaft.
Ach! wie schmeichelt's meinem Triebe,
Wenn man meinen Dichter preist.
Denn das Leben ist die Liebe,
Und des Lebens Leben Geist.

Poem first published 1819

May I never lose you!
Suleika

May I never lose you!
Love gives strength to love.
May you adorn my youth
With your mighty passion.
Ah! how flattered my ardour feels
When my poet is praised.
For love is life,
And spirit the life of life itself.

49 Prometheus[2]

Bedecke deinen Himmel, Zeus,
Mit Wolkendunst,
Und übe, dem Knaben gleich,
Der Disteln köpft,
An Eichen dich und Bergeshöhn;
Mußt mir meine Erde
Doch lassen stehn,
Und meine Hütte, die du nicht gebaut,
Und meinen Herd,

Prometheus

Cover your heaven, Zeus,
With cloudy vapour,
And test your strength, like a boy
Beheading thistles,
On oaks and mountain peaks;
Yet you must leave
My earth alone,
And my hut you did not build,
And my hearth,

1   Suleika/Marianne replies to her lover's ardour in 'Nimmer will ich dich verlieren!' with an equally tempestuous outpouring of passion. „Denn das Leben ist die Liebe" ('For love is life') she exclaims in a phrase that culminates in a top A sung *ff*, as the *tremolandi* ring out in both hands. The Weimarer Ausgabe and the Jubiläums Ausgabe of Goethe's works attribute the poem to Marianne von Willemer. Since Goethe's sketches for the poem were discovered among Sulpiz Boisserée's papers, it is now thought that the poem is Goethe's with contributions from Marianne. This is the last of the *West-östlichen Divan* songs.
2   Some myths claim that mankind was created by Prometheus who, to bring his creation to life, stole fire from heaven. As a punishment, he was chained to a mountain in the Caucasus where an eagle would each day devour his liver, which, however, grew again each night, thus ensuring eternal torture. He was eventually freed by Hercules who, en route to his eleventh labour, killed the eagle. In several of his *Sturm und Drang* poems Goethe changes myth to accord with his own *Weltanschauung*. Prometheus, for example, is freed from his grisly fate not by Hercules, but by his own strength. Goethe, especially in his early works, saw himself as a sort of god: „Bin ich ein Gott? Mir wird so licht!" Faust/Goethe exclaims (line 439). Poems such as 'An Schwager Kronos' and 'Prometheus' must have appealed mightily to anyone, like Schubert, living in the repressed atmosphere of Metternich's Vienna: these poems, written in the early 1770s, express a reaction against rationalism, a reliance on individuality and an exaltation of freedom. The poem was intended as a monologue for the unfinished *Prometheus* drama that Goethe had begun in 1773. 'Prometheus' was one of the nine Goethe songs that Wolf later decided to orchestrate, but this version does not, paradoxically, convey the titanic might of the piano-accompanied song, in which the 22-bar prelude, containing almost all of the song's subsequent material, screams defiance at the gods. Like Beethoven's *Grosse Fuge* for string quartet, the piano version of 'Prometheus' appears inadequate to convey the might of the composer's thought, and for that very reason can seem wonderfully vulnerable and violent in performance. Those great massed octaves in both hands express rebellion, fury and disdain in a way that is denied to a full orchestra.

Um dessen Glut	Whose warmth
Du mich beneidest.	You envy me.
Ich kenne nichts Ärmeres	I know nothing more paltry
Unter der Sonn' als euch, Götter!	Beneath the sun than you, gods!
Ihr nährt kümmerlich	Meagrely you nourish
Vom Opfersteuern	Your majesty
Und Gebetshauch	On levied offerings
Eure Majestät,	And breath of prayer,
Und darbtet, wären	And would starve, were
Nicht Kinder und Bettler	Not children and beggars
Hoffnungsvolle Toren.	Ever-hopeful fools.
Da ich ein Kind war,	When I was a child,
Nicht wußte wo aus noch ein,	Not knowing which way to turn,
Kehrt' ich mein verirrtes Auge	I raised my misguided eyes
Zur Sonne, als wenn drüber wär'	To the sun, as if above there were
Ein Ohr, zu hören meine Klage,	An ear to hear my lament,
Ein Herz, wie mein's,	A heart like mine,
Sich des Bedrängten zu erbarmen.	To pity me in my anguish.
Wer half mir	Who helped me
Wider der Titanen Übermut?	Withstand the Titans' insolence?
Wer rettete vom Tode mich,	Who saved me from death
Von Sklaverei?	And slavery?
Hast du nicht Alles selbst vollendet,	Did you not accomplish all this yourself,
Heilig glühend Herz?	Sacred glowing heart?
Und glühtest jung und gut,	And did you not – young, innocent,
Betrogen, Rettungsdank	Deceived – glow with gratitude for your deliverance
Dem Schlafenden da droben?	To that slumberer in the skies?
Ich dich ehren! Wofür?	I honour you? Why?
Hast du die Schmerzen gelindert	Did you ever soothe the anguish
Je des Beladenen?	That weighed me down?
Hast du die Tränen gestillet	Did you ever dry my tears
Je des Geängsteten?	When I was terrified?
Hat mich nicht zum Manne geschmiedet	Was I not forged into manhood
Die allmächtige Zeit	By all-powerful Time
Und das ewige Schicksal,	And everlasting Fate,
Meine Herrn und deine?	My masters and yours?
Wähntest du etwa,	Did you suppose
Ich sollte das Leben hassen,	I should hate life,
In Wüsten fliehen,	Flee into the wilderness,
Weil nicht alle	Because not all
Blütenträume reiften?[1]	My blossoming dreams bore fruit?

---

[1] In its earliest form there is a fascinating variant that reveals much about Goethe's linguistic excesses in the *Sturm und Drang* period: the penultimate stanza originally ended: „Weil nicht

JOHANN WOLFGANG VON GOETHE   171

Hier sitz' ich, forme Menschen	Here I sit, making men
Nach meinem Bilde,	In my own image,
Ein Geschlecht, das mir gleich sei,[1]	A race to resemble me,
Zu leiden, zu weinen,	To suffer, weep,
Zu genießen und zu freuen sich,	Know joy and delight,
Und dein nicht zu achten,	And ignore you,
Wie ich!	As I do!

Poem written late autumn 1773, revised 1774
Also set by Reichardt and Schubert

50 **Ganymed**[2]   **Ganymede**

Wie im Morgenglanze	How in the morning radiance
Du rings mich anglühst,	You glow at me from all sides,
Frühling, Geliebter!	Spring, beloved!
Mit tausendfacher Liebeswonne	With thousandfold delights of love,
Sich an mein Herze drängt	The holy sense
Deiner ewigen Wärme	Of your eternal worth
Heilig Gefühl,	Presses against my heart,
Unendliche Schöne!	Beauty without end!

Daß ich dich fassen möcht'	To clasp you
In diesen Arm!*[3]	In these arms!*

Ach an deinem Busen	Ah, on your breast
Lieg' ich und schmachte,	I lie and languish,
Und deine Blumen, dein Gras	And your flowers, your grass
Drängen sich an mein Herz.	Press against my heart.

---

alle Knabenmorgen-/Blütenträume reiften" – a quadruple neologism that was finally trimmed to 'Blütenträume' in the *Schriften* of 1789.

1   Wolf, understanding that the poem is about the sacred nature of individuality, sets 'mir' to a *marcato* minim, whereas Schubert illogically stresses 'gleich', so that the phrase runs '*resemble* me' instead of 'resemble *me*'. See HW to Emil Kauffmann, 22 December 1890, p. 121, for Wolf's view of Schubert's setting.

2   Wolf's song, especially in the rise and fall of the piano's quavers above the stave, conveys a sensuality that is less apparent in Schubert's more melodious setting – see HW to Emil Kauffmann, 22 December 1890, p. 121, for Wolf's view of Schubert's song. Ganymede in myth was a beautiful young Phrygian shepherd raised up to Olympus by Zeus (see Rembrandt's wittily grotesque painting in Dresden), who had fallen in love with the boy and wished him to replace Hebe as his cup-bearer. In typical *Sturm und Drang* fashion, Goethe changes the myth (as he did in 'Prometheus') and has Ganymede borne aloft by the intensity of his own feelings. The poem is drenched in amorous language: 'Frühling, *Geliebter*', '*Liebes*wonne', '*lieblicher* Morgenwind', '*liebend* nach mir aus dem Nebeltal', 'neigen sich der sehnenden *Liebe*', 'All*liebender* Vater!' The many variations on the word 'Liebe' reflect not just Ganymede's adoration of the natural world, but also the ubiquitous presence of lascivious Jove, who appears in multiple guises throughout the poem.

3   Wolf quotes the music and words of this two-lined verse in a letter of 3 March 1894 to Frieda Zerny to assure her of his love, following Melanie Köchert's discovery of their affair – see p. 520.

NO STANZA BREAK

Du kühlst den brennenden	You cool the burning
Durst meines Busens,	Thirst of my breast,
Lieblicher Morgenwind!	Sweet morning breeze!
Ruft drein die Nachtigall	The nightingale calls out to me
Liebend nach mir aus dem Nebeltal.	Longingly from the misty valley.
Ich komm', ich komme!	I come, I come!
Ach wohin, wohin?	Where? Ah, where?
Hinauf strebt's, hinauf!	Upwards! Upwards I'm driven.
Es schweben die Wolken	The clouds drift
Abwärts, die Wolken	Down, the clouds
Neigen sich der sehnenden Liebe,	Yield to yearning love.
Mir! Mir!	To me! To me!
In eurem Schoße	Enveloped by you
Aufwärts!	Aloft!
Umfangend umfangen!	Embraced and embracing!
Aufwärts an deinen Busen,	Upwards to your bosom,
Allliebender Vater!	All-loving Father!

Poem written early 1774
Also set by Loewe, Reichardt and Schubert
* Wolf repeats the line.

51 Grenzen der Menschheit[1]   Limitations of mankind

Wenn der uralte,	When the Ancient of Days,
Heilige Vater	The holy father
Mit gelassener Hand	With a serene hand
Aus rollenden Wolken	From rolling clouds
Segnende Blitze	Scatters beneficent thunderbolts

1   Although there are a few pre-Weimar poems in free verse ('Ganymed' and 'Prometheus', for example), it was during the Weimar period that Goethe produced a series of such poems. Between 1779 and 1783 he wrote four great philosophical pieces, 'Gesang der Geister über den Wassern', 'Meine Göttin', 'Das Göttliche' and 'Grenzen der Menschheit'; and although all are written in free verse, a regular rhythm gradually becomes perceptible during the course of each poem, as we see in 'Grenzen der Menschheit', where a pattern imposes itself. The poem deals with man's insignificance before the power of the gods, a theme similar to Lear's 'As flies to wanton boys, are we to the gods;/They kill us for their sport'. There is a magisterial solemnity about 'Grenzen der Menschheit', a contemplative tone that would have been impossible in the pre-Weimar period.

    By opening his *Gedichte von J. W. v. Goethe* with three Harper songs and three Mignon songs from *Wilhelm Meisters Lehrjahre* and concluding it with 'Prometheus', 'Ganymed' and 'Grenzen der Menschheit' – nine of Schubert's greatest Goethe settings – Wolf might be accused of arrogance; some friends certainly thought that this was a provocative gesture. Gustav Schur, however, in *Erinnerungen an Hugo Wolf*, reports that Wolf once defended himself from such accusations: „Man bedroht mich ja förmlich mit Schubert, ich kann mir doch nicht das Maul verbinden, weil ein Genie vor mir gelebt und herrliche Lieder geschrieben hat." ('People positively threaten me with the name of Schubert, but I cannot shut my mouth simply because a genius lived before me and wrote wonderful songs.')

Über die Erde sä't,
Küss' ich den letzten
Saum seines Kleides,
Kindliche Schauer
Treu in der Brust.[1]

Denn mit Göttern
Soll sich nicht messen
Irgend ein Mensch.
Hebt er sich aufwärts,
Und berührt
Mit dem Scheitel die Sterne,
Nirgends haften dann
Die unsichern Sohlen,
Und mit ihm spielen
Wolken und Winde.

Steht er mit festen,
Markigen Knochen
Auf der wohlgegründeten
Dauernden Erde;
Reicht er nicht auf,
Nur mit der Eiche
Oder der Rebe
Sich zu vergleichen.

Was unterscheidet
Götter von Menschen?
Daß viele Wellen
Vor jenen wandeln,
Ein ewiger Strom:
Uns hebt die Welle,
Verschlingt die Welle,
Und wir versinken.

Ein kleiner Ring
Begrenzt unser Leben,
Und viele Geschlechter
Reihen sich dauernd
An ihres Daseins
Unendliche Kette.

Poem written autumn ?1781
Also set by Berg and Schubert

Over the earth,
I kiss the extreme
Hem of his garment,
Childlike awe
In my loyal breast.

For no man
Should measure himself
Against the gods.
If he reaches up
And touches
The stars with his head,
His uncertain feet
Lose their hold,
And clouds and winds
Make sport of him.

If he stands with firm,
Sturdy limbs
On the solid
Enduring earth,
He cannot even reach up
To compare himself
With the oak
Or vine.

What distinguishes
Gods from men?
Before them
Many waves roll onwards,
An eternal river;
We are lifted by the wave,
Engulfed by the wave,
And we founder.

A little ring
Bounds our life,
And many generations
Constantly succeed each other
Like links in the endless chain
Of existence.

---

1   Schubert: Tief in der Brust.

Friedrich Hebbel
(1813–1863)

		page
Das Kind am Brunnen	16–27 April 1878	178
Das Vöglein	2–23 May 1878	179
Knabentod	3–6 May 1878	180
Schön Hedwig	?1878	lost

POET

After the death of his father, a bricklayer, who had wished his son to follow the same trade, the fourteen-year-old Friedrich Hebbel worked as a secretary to the parish bailiff in Wesselburen near Heide and, inspired by the latter's extensive library, resolved to become a writer. Lacking funds, he wrote to the poet Ludwig Uhland and others without success. Eventually, he was helped financially by Amalia Schoppe, who published some of his poems in her journal, the *Neue Pariser Modeblätter*. When they fell out, he began a relationship with a seamstress, Elise Lensing, and although he was unfaithful she continued to support him from her meagre earnings. They never married but she bore his child – *Mutter und Kind*, a long poem in seven cantos, dates from 1857. At the age of twenty-two Hebbel went to Munich on foot in the hope of creating a stir in the literary world, leaving Elise behind. He stayed in Munich from 1836 to 1839, returned on foot to Elise, wrote one of his most successful plays, *Judith*, which was premiered in 1840 and published the following year. He was granted a two-year stipend from King Christian VIII of Denmark, but when his time in Copenhagen brought no tangible rewards, he tried his luck in Rome and Naples, leaving Elise again, despite the death of his first child and the birth of his second.

Success finally came in 1845. He became engaged to a wealthy actress, Christine Enghaus, who introduced him to leading figures in Vienna's theatrical world and created the roles of the eponymous heroine in *Judith*, Klara in *Maria Magdalene* (1844), Mariamne in *Herodes und Mariamne* (1849) and Brunhild in *Die Nibelungen* (1862). Several of his plays were successfully staged at Vienna's Burgtheater and he was soon to become a celebrated playwright. Wealthy enough to travel, he now spent much time in Weimar, where he met Liszt and Hans and Cosima von Bülow. His *Genoveva* (1843) fascinated Robert Schumann, and Hebbel travelled to Dresden to discuss the possibility of writing a libretto, a task that Schumann finally took on himself, much to the disappointment of Robert

Reinick (see p. 432). Schumann dedicated his 'Nachtlied', Op. 108, to Hebbel, who returned the compliment by dedicating his play *Michel Angelo* (1850) to the composer. At the end of his life Hebbel worked hard to complete Schiller's *Demetrius* in time for the centenary of Schiller's birth, and wrote two of his best plays: *Agnes Bernauer* (1852) and *Gyges und sein Ring* (1856). He was a prolific poet: *Gedichte* (1842) and *Neue Gedichte* (1848) were followed by *Gedichte von Friedrich Hebbel* (1857), which he dedicated to Uhland. This last collection included a cycle of eleven poems, entitled 'Dem Schmerz sein Recht', which expresses Hebbel's vulnerability to isolation and despair, and his longing for escape; Alban Berg set the celebrated fourth poem of the cycle, 'Schlafen, Schlafen, nichts, als Schlafen!', as the opening song of his Op. 2.

Hebbel's poetry, even though it now seems to lack the lyrical flair of Eichendorff, Goethe, Heine and Mörike, has fared better than his plays, which have not stood the test of time. His prose works include a novel and seven dense Novellen, now little read. Most readable of all his writings are the *Tagebücher*, begun in 1835 and continued until his death. Carl Hanser Verlag has recently published an entertaining anthology of aphorisms and longer entries from the *Diaries*, chosen and introduced by Alfred Brendel: *Weltgericht mit Pausen*. Mörike, whom Hebbel visited in 1856, neatly summed up Hebbel's personality: „Dieser Hebbel ist ein Glutmensch durch und durch, zugleich von einem schneidenden Verstand." ('This Hebbel is a man of passion through and through, but he also has an incisive intellect.') His poems have been set by a select group of composers, including Brahms, Cornelius, Liszt, Pfitzner, Reger, Schoeck, Schumann, Rudi Stephan and Wolf. His collected verse, published in 1857, included the four poems set by Wolf: 'Das Kind am Brunnen', 'Das Vöglein', 'Knabentod' and 'Schön Hedwig', the manuscript of which is lost.

COMPOSER

The description in the biography by Emil Kuh (the poet of Liszt's 'Die Glocken von Marling') of Hebbel's poverty and his struggle to become an accepted writer must have resonated deeply with the young composer, who was always short of funds. As a young man, Wolf read widely, looking for suitable texts to set, and he immersed himself in Hebbel's works, both poetry and plays: *Judith* (1841), *Julia* (1851) and *Gyges und sein Ring* (1856). As a young man, he often overestimated the quality of the Lieder he had written (HW to his parents, 20 April 1878, and to Oskar Grohe, 16 March 1894, pp. 176 and 177), although 'Das Kind am Brunnen' and 'Knabentod' give us a tantalising foretaste of Wolf's genius for setting such eerie ballads as 'Nixe Binsefuß' and 'Die Geister am Mummelsee' from the *Mörike-Lieder*. Hebbel's 'Das Vöglein' was set as a duet by Schumann in his *Liederalbum für die Jugend*, Op. 79, where it is still called 'Das Glück', a title that Hebbel was to change to 'Das Vöglein' in later editions. The happy mood of the poem would have appealed to Wolf, who had just met Vally Franck, his first sweetheart. 'Das Vöglein' is the second song of Wolf's *Sechs Lieder für eine Frauenstimme* – see p. 4, for details relating to the publication.

LETTERS

HW to his parents, Vienna, 10 April 1878

Ich lese jetzt Friedrich Hebbel, dessen ausführliche Biographie, ein wahres Meisterwerk von E. Kuh,[1] ich heute ausgelesen. Wie schlecht es Hebbel ging, welche Schwierigkeiten er zu überwinden hatte, davon kann man sich keine Vorstellung machen, und trotzdem es mir nicht am besten geht (ich habe nämlich eine Lektion wieder verloren, weil die Kinder Dr. B.s[2] für 5 Wochen nach Meran fuhren, und esse, da es nicht anders geht, nur einmal im Tag), so preise ich mich glücklich, daß es nicht ärger ist.

I am now reading Friedrich Hebbel, the detailed biography of whom by E. Kuh – a veritable masterpiece – I finished today. One simply cannot imagine how Hebbel suffered and what difficulties he had to overcome; and though things for me are not going as well as they might (I've lost another teaching job, because Dr. B's children are spending 5 weeks in Meran, and am of necessity eating only once a day), I consider myself fortunate that it is not worse.

HW to his parents, Vienna, 20 April 1878

Heute mache ich die letzten Federstriche am Liede „Das Kind am Brunnen" von Hebbel, und ich glaube, daß es der „Spinnerin" nicht nachstehen wird. [. . .] Ich lese noch etwas Hebbel, wahrscheinlich das Trauerspiel „Julia", und begebe mich dann zur Ruhe.

Today I'm putting the final touches to the song 'Das Kind am Brunnen' by Hebbel, and I think that it will turn out every bit as good as 'Die Spinnerin'. [. . .] I shall now read some more Hebbel, probably the tragedy 'Julia', and then go to bed.

---

1 Emil Kuh, *Friedrich Hebbel* (1877).
2 Dr Josef Breuer (1842–1925), who collaborated with Sigmund Freud on *Studien über Hysterie* (Vienna, 1895). The children were the eight-year-old Robert and his seven-year-old sister Bertha. Wolf became a close friend of the whole family, and spent the summer of 1878 with them in Waidhofen, where 'Gretchen vor dem Andachtsbild der Mater Dolorosa' was composed. Breuer also contributed financially to Wolf's visit to Bayreuth in 1882.

FRIEDRICH HEBBEL

HW to his parents, Vienna, 12 May 1878

Ich habe jetzt wieder 5 Lieder beisammen, von denen eines besser als das andere sein sollte. Ich jedoch bin nicht zufrieden, rastlos treibt es mich, mein schwaches Talent zu überbieten, meinen Gesichtskreis zu erweitern, meinem Denken, Handeln und Empfinden einen womöglich gereiften Ausdruck zu verleihen. Hie und da sehe ich auch mein Streben durch einigen Erfolg belohnt. Doch befriedigt er mich nicht, sondern reizt mich nur an, noch größere Anforderungen an mich zu stellen. Die Leute versprechen sich viel von mir, ich fühle auch die Kraft, mich über das gewöhnliche Niveau emporzuarbeiten. Doch verlassen mich auch oft die Kräfte [. . .] aber auf einmal entsteht ganz unbewußt eine Arbeit unter meinen Händen, die mich wieder überzeugt, daß das Talent in mir nicht eingeschlafen, sondern nur geschlummert habe. Die Probe davon lieferte ich an dem am 6. Mai komponierten Gedichte „Knabentod" von Hebbel, welches in der Erfindung sowohl als musikalischen Ausführung einen bedeutenden Fortschritt zeigt.

Once again I now have 5 songs together, each, I'm told, better than the last. And yet I'm not satisfied, I feel a compulsive urge to outdo my meagre talent, to widen my horizons, to develop my thoughts, my actions and my sensitivity to their full maturity. Here and there I see my striving rewarded with some success. But success, instead of satisfying me, spurs me on to make even greater demands on myself. People have great hopes of me, and I feel I have the strength to rise above mere mediocrity. But my powers often abandon me [. . .] yet suddenly, quite unconsciously, I create something that convinces me that my talent has not died away but was only slumbering – as I proved with 'Knabentod', which I set to a poem by Hebbel on 6 May. It shows significant progress in both invention and musical execution.

HW to Oskar Grohe, Vienna, 16 March 1894

Zu meinem kürzlich eingetretenen 34. Geburtstag wurden mir Hebbels sämmtliche Werke in Prachteinband beschert. Obwohl ziemlich vertraut mit seinen Dichtungen, macht mir die neuerliche Bekanntschaft mit denselben viel Vergnügen. Die Judith verräth bei all ihren Extravaganzen u. fürchterlichen Übertreibungen doch ein eminent dramatisches Talent. Es ist Rasse darin. Ganz einzig u. hochpoetisch in seiner Art aber ist der Ring des Gyges. Das wäre sogar was für Musik. Kennen Sie die Dichtung? Wenn nicht, verschaffen Sie sich's doch. Das Stück wird Sie entzücken.

For my recent 34th birthday I was given the complete works of Hebbel in a luxury edition. Although I know his writings fairly well, this renewed acquaintance with his works has given me much pleasure. *Judith*, for all its extravagancies & terrible exaggerations, reveals an important dramatic talent. Real breed. Utterly unique &, in its own way, highly poetic is *Der Ring des Gyges* [*Gyges und sein Ring*]. That could even be put to music. Do you know it? If not, acquire it. The play will enchant you.

LIEDER

Das Kind am Brunnen

Frau Amme, Frau Amme, das Kind ist erwacht!
    Doch die liegt ruhig im Schlafe.
Die Vöglein zwitschern, die Sonne lacht,
    Am Hügel weiden die Schafe.

Frau Amme, Frau Amme, das Kind steht auf,
    Es wagt sich weiter und weiter!
Hinab zum Brunnen nimmt es den Lauf,
    Da stehen Blumen und Kräuter.

Frau Amme, Frau Amme, der Brunnen ist tief!
    Sie schläft, als läge sie drinnen!
Das Kind läuft schnell, wie es nie noch lief,
    Die Blumen locken's von hinnen.

Nun steht es am Brunnen, nun ist es am Ziel,
    Nun pflückt es die Blumen sich munter,
Doch bald ermüdet das reizende Spiel,
    Da schaut's in die Tiefe hinunter.

Und unten erblickt es ein holdes Gesicht,
    Mit Augen so hell und so süße,
Es ist sein eignes, das weiß es noch nicht,
    Viel stumme, freundliche Grüße!

Das Kindlein winkt, der Schatten geschwind
    Winkt aus der Tiefe ihm wieder.
Herauf! Herauf! So meint es das Kind;[1]
    Der Schatten: Hernieder! Hernieder!

Schon beugt es sich über den Brunnenrand,
    Frau Amme, du schläfst noch immer!
Da fallen die Blumen ihm aus der Hand
    Und trüben den lockenden Schimmer.

1 Hebbel: so meint's.

The child at the well

Wet-nurse, wet-nurse, the child has awoken!
    But she is still fast asleep.
The birds twitter, the sun is laughing,
    The sheep on the hillside are grazing.

Wet-nurse, wet-nurse, the child's getting up,
    Further and further he ventures!
Down to the well he now goes running,
    Where flowers and herbs are growing.

Wet-nurse, wet-nurse, the well is deep!
    She sleeps, as though she were in it!
The child runs faster than ever before,
    The flowers entice him away.

He's now by the well, he has reached his goal,
    And is happily picking the flowers,
But the enchanting game begins to pall,
    And he looks down into the depths.

And there he discovers a lovely face,
    With eyes so bright and so sweet,
It is his own, he is not yet aware –
    Such friendly and silent greetings!

The little child waves, the shadow at once
    Returns the wave from the depths.
Come up! Come up! the child would say;
    The shadow: Come down! Come down!

Already he's leaning over the well,
    Wet-nurse, still you are sleeping!
The flowers then fall from his hand
    And cloud the alluring glitter.

Verschwunden ist sie, die süße Gestalt,
    Verschluckt von der hüpfenden Welle,
Das Kind durchschauert's fremd und kalt,
    Und schnell enteilt es der Stelle.

The sweet figure has vanished from view,
    Swallowed up by the rippling wave,
A strange cold shiver runs through the child,
    And swiftly he hastes from the scene.

Das Vöglein[1]

Vöglein vom Zweig
    Gaukelt hernieder;
Lustig sogleich
    Schwingt es sich wieder.

Jetzt dir so nah,
    Jetzt sich versteckend;
Abermals da,
    Scherzend und neckend.

Tastest du zu,
    Bist du betrogen,
Spottend im Nu
    Ist es entflogen.

Still! Bis zur Hand
    Wird's dir noch hüpfen,
Bist du gewandt,
    Kann's nicht entschlüpfen.

Ist's denn so schwer,
    Das zu erwarten?
Schau' um dich her:
    Blühender Garten!

Ei, du verzagst?
    Laß es gewähren,
Bis du's erjagst,
    Kannst du's entbehren.

Wird es auch dann[2]
    Wenig nur bringen;
Aber es kann
    Süßestes singen.

Also set by Robert Schumann

The little bird

The little bird flutters
    Down from its branch;
And in a trice
    Happily flies back again.

Now it is near you,
    Now it is hiding,
There it comes again,
    Playing and teasing.

If you try to touch it,
    You'll be foiled,
Off it flies in a flash,
    Mockingly away.

Hush! Right up to your hand
    It will come hopping,
If you are quick,
    It won't escape.

Is it really so hard
    To wait for that moment?
Look about you
    At the garden in bloom!

What? You despair?
    Let it have its own way –
Until you catch it,
    You can manage without.

Even then it will
    Bring you little;
But it can
    Sing most sweetly.

---

1 Hebbel's original title was 'Das Glück'.   2 Hebbel: Wird's doch auch dann.

Knabentod[1]

Vom Berg der Knab',
Der zieht hinab
    In heißen Sommertagen;
Im Tannenwald,
Da macht er Halt,
    Er kann sich kaum noch tragen.

Den wilden Bach,
Er sieht ihn jach
    Ins Tal herunter schäumen;
Ihn dürstet sehr,
Nun noch viel mehr:
    Nur hin! Wer würde säumen!

Da ist die Flut!
O, in die Glut,[2]
    Was kann so köstlich blinken!
Er schöpft und trinkt,
Er stürzt und sinkt
    Und trinkt noch im Versinken![3]

A boy's death

From the mountain
The boy comes down,
    During the scorching days of summer;
In the pinewood
He stops to rest,
    Scarcely able to drag himself further.

He catches sight
Of the wild brook in spate,
    Foaming into the valley,
His burning thirst
Grows ever greater:
    Keep moving! Who would delay?

There is the water!
Oh, in that heat
    What else could glitter so wonderfully!
He scoops and drinks water,
He falls and sinks,
    And drinks still as he drowns.

---

[1] See HW to his parents, 12 May 1878, p. 177.
[2] Hebbel: in der Glut.
[3] Wolf omits Hebbel's final stanza, not printed here.

HEINRICH HEINE
(1797–1856)

			page
Die Flucht	late 1875–early January 1876	duet; fragment	
Mädchen mit dem roten Mündchen	17 December 1876		195
Du bist wie eine Blume	18 December 1876		196
Wenn ich in deine Augen seh	21 December 1876		196
Sie haben heut' abend Gesellschaft	18–25 May 1878		197
Ich stand in dunkeln Träumen	26–29 May 1878		197
Das ist ein Brausen und Heulen	31 May 1878		198
Wo ich bin, mich rings umdunkelt	3–4 June 1878		200
Aus meinen großen Schmerzen	5 June 1878		198
Mir träumte von einem Königskind	16 June 1878, rev. 20 January 1881		199
Mein Liebchen, wir saßen beisammen	June 1878		199
Es blasen die blauen Husaren	22 June 1878		200
Manch Bild vergessener Zeiten	24 June 1878	fragment	
Es war ein alter König	4 October 1878		201
Mit schwarzen Segeln	6 October 1878		201
Spätherbstnebel, kalte Träume	7 October 1878		201
Ernst ist der Frühling	13–17 October 1878		202
Wie des Mondes Abbild zittert	13 February 1880		202
Sterne mit den goldnen Füßchen	26 November 1880		203
Das gelbe Laub erzittert	7 December 1880	fragment	
Wo wird einst	24 January 1888		203

POET

Born and raised in Düsseldorf, capital of the tiny Duchy of Berg, Heine was the eldest of four children of Jewish parentage. Crucial to a full understanding of this great poet is a statement he made in *Geständnisse* (*Confessions*), written in 1854, two years before his death: „Trotz meiner exterminatorischen Feldzüge gegen die Romantik, blieb ich doch selbst immer ein Romantiker, und ich war es in einem höheren Grade, als ich es selbst ahnte." ('Despite my exterminatory campaigns against romanticism, I always remained a romantic, and to a greater extent than

I ever thought.') Schumann's *Dichterliebe*, the Op. 24 *Liederkreis* and the 18 songs that Wolf completed are shot through with this ambivalent approach to romanticism: Heine's poems are both romantic and anti-romantic, sentimental and cynical – only rarely did he write a truly happy and requited love poem.

C. W. Orr once said (see Stephen Cary's 'A. E. Housman and the Renaissance of English Song'[1]), 'Housman wrote verse that was (a) beautiful, (b) scanned, (c) rhymed, and (d) made sense [. . .] He is, I think, to English songwriters very much what Heine was to German and Verlaine to French composers.' And it is, at least partially, this syntactical simplicity that has drawn so many composers to his poetry. Heinrich Heine, whose name, alongside Goethe's, is almost synonymous with German art song, has been prodigiously set by Lieder composers. Vesque von Püttlingen leads with 119 mostly ironical settings, followed by Robert Franz with 67; Schumann, 41; Wolf, 18; Liszt and Mendelssohn, 7; Schubert, Brahms and Pfitzner, 6; and Richard Strauss, 5. He has also attracted composers from an astonishing array of non-German-speaking countries, such as Norway (Grieg), Russia (Balakirev, Borodin, Mussorgsky, Tchaikovsky), France (Meyerbeer), America (Ives, Edward MacDowell, Charles Griffes) and England (Maude Valérie White) among many others. Most of these songs were based on poems taken from the *Buch der Lieder* (1827), a collection that in a variety of guises expresses the tortured feelings of a jilted lover.

Several of these unrequited love poems were probably inspired, directly and indirectly, by unreciprocated passion for his cousin Amalie (Molly), whose rejection of Heine is clearly chronicled in the letters he wrote to his school friend Christian Sethe. On 6 July 1816, shortly before arriving in Hamburg, where he was to begin a business career under the sponsorship of wealthy Uncle Salomon, Heine wrote to Sethe that he was looking forward to seeing Molly again for the first time in two years:

> Freu Dich, Freu Dich: in 4 Wochen sehe ich Molly. Mit ihr kehrt auch meine Muse zurück. Seit 2 Jahr habe ich sie nicht gesehen; Altes Herz, was freust du dich und schlägst so laut!

> Rejoice, rejoice: in 4 weeks I shall see Molly. And with her my muse shall return. I have not seen her for 2 years; dear old heart, how you rejoice and beat so loud!

Their meeting took place a month later. Heine was eighteen and a half, Amalie two years younger. Less than four months after this letter, Heine wrote again to Sethe on 27 October 1816. Something shattering must have occurred, for the letter, which had taken almost a month to write, scorns all preliminary niceties and plunges straight into his grief:

---

[1] *NATS Journal*, vol. 49 no. 1 (September–October 1992).

> Sie liebt mich *nicht*! – Mußt, lieber Christian, dieses *letzte* Wörtchen ganz leise, leise aussprechen. In dem ersten Wörtchen liegt der ewig lebendige Himmel, aber auch in dem letzten liegt die ewig lebende Hölle.
>
> She loves me *not*! – Dear Christian, you must utter this *last* little word quietly, very quietly. Eternal Heaven dwells in the first word, just as an eternal living Hell dwells in the last.

The letter, which goes on to describe how Molly had scoffed at the 'schöne Lieder' he had written especially for her, also criticises the philistine atmosphere of Hamburg, and states bitterly that the poems of a Jew would not be received kindly by the Christian community. Yet Heine tells Sethe that he is determined to keep writing poetry, despite his rejection by Molly, and then quotes that wonderful passage from Goethe's *Torquato Tasso* in which the Italian poet in his final speech praises God for having given him the ability to poeticise his suffering:

> Und wenn der Mensch in seiner Qual verstummt,
> Gab mir ein Gott, zu sagen, was ich leide.
>
> Though in their torment men are dumb,
> A god granted me the gift to express my grief.

Amalie's spectre was still haunting him when he visited Hamburg again in 1823 – see note 1 to 'Sie haben heut' abend Gesellschaft', p. 197, for his tormented letter to Moses Moser of 11 July 1823. Several biographers have maintained that Heine, when rejected by Amalie, transferred his affections to her sister Therese – see note 1 to 'Sie haben heut' abend Gesellschaft' and note 1 to 'Du bist wie eine Blume', pp. 197, 196. Marriage between cousins was not at all uncommon in the nineteenth century, and it is certainly possible that Heine, on the rebound, started to woo Therese. There was clearly a bond between them. He mentions her name more than a dozen times in his letters and wrote her a note on 3 December 1843 in which he used the 'Du' form of address (whereas Amalie had always been addressed as 'Sie'). Therese visited him on his sickbed in Paris during the summer of 1853 and on her return wrote him a tender and loving letter, dated 10 August:

> Seit meinem Besuch, welchen ich Dir bei unserem kurzen Aufenthalt in Paris gemacht habe, steht dein Bild fortwährend vor mir [. . .] Hoffentlich, lieber Harry, wirst Du diese Zeilen mit früherer freundlicher Anhänglichkeit annehmen und sie so auffassen, wie sie aus einem warmen, mitfühlenden Herzen an Dich gerichtet werden.
>
> Since I visited you during our short sojourn in Paris, I have had you constantly on my mind [. . .] I hope, dear Harry, that you will accept these lines

with the affection and devotion of former times, and interpret them as coming to you from a warm and sympathetic heart.

Any attempt to identify which sister inspired which poems seems doomed to failure in the absence of any concrete evidence.

Heine felt increasingly isolated in Hamburg and suffered keenly from the prevalent anti-Semitism. In December 1820 he was expelled from the Göttingen Burschenschaft (student fraternity): at a secret meeting on 28 September 1820 in Dresden, the Burschenschaft had decided not to accept any more Jews, since they had „kein Vaterland und für unseres kein Interesse haben können" ('no fatherland, and could therefore be of no interest to our own'). That the rampant anti-Semitism was threatening not only his confidence but his very sense of identity is clear from an extraordinary letter to Sethe, dated 14 April 1822:

> Alles was deutsch ist, ist mir zuwider; und Du bist leider ein Deutscher. Alles Deutsche wirkt auf mich wie ein Brechpulver. Die deutsche Sprache zerreißt meine Ohre [sic]. Die eignen Gedichte ekeln mich zuweilen an, wenn ich sehe, daß sie auf deutsch geschrieben sind. [. . .] Des Tags verfolgt mich ein ewiges Mißtrauen, überall hör ich meinen Namen und hinterdrein ein höhnisches Gelächter.
>
> All that is German repulses me; and you, unfortunately, are German. Everything German acts on me like an emetic. The German language shrills in my ears. There are times when my own poems disgust me, when I see that they are written in German. [. . .] An eternal mistrust pursues me each day, I hear my name uttered everywhere, followed by mocking laughter.

The theme of unrequited love that runs through the early poetry is also a metaphor for Heine's rejection by society and his increasing fear of isolation. He recovered from his 'Amalie' trauma, and in 1831, attracted by Louis-Philippe, the new citizen-king, emigrated to Paris where he frequented the salon world, meeting such celebrities as George Sand, Liszt, Ferdinand Hiller, Meyerbeer and Berlioz. In August 1841 he married his lover of many years, Crescencia Eugénie Mirat – the Mathilde of his poetry. He fell ill at the end of 1844 and sought a cure at a spa in the Pyrenees during 1846 but by the spring of 1848 was confined to what he wrily called his 'Matratzengruft' ('Mattress-grave'), suffering, according to recent research, not from syphilis or opium abuse, but from lead poisoning. Half blind, half deaf, unable to walk, racked with pain from spinal spasms that he sought to alleviate through opium, he continued to dictate letters and poems to his secretary. „Meine Phantasie spielt mir in schlaflosen Nächten die schönsten Comödien und Possen vor," ('During sleepless nights, my imagination conjures up the most beautiful drolleries and farces,') he wrote to his publisher

Julius Campe in October 1854. *Romanzero*, the most successful of his later poetry collections, was published in 1851 and reprinted four times between October and December of that year, selling 21,000 copies.

The poems selected by Wolf for his 18 *Heine-Lieder* come from three different collections. *Lyrisches Intermezzo* was Heine's title for the 65 poems that did indeed form an intermezzo between two tragedies, *Almansor* and *William Ratcliff*, in the volume that he published in April 1823: *Tragödien nebst einem Lyrischen Intermezzo*. The two tragedies are now rarely read but many of the 65 poems have been immortalised by Lieder composers. It is in the *Lyrisches Intermezzo* poems that Heine found his true manner, which he described in a letter to Moses Moser of 14 December 1825 as his „lyrisch-maliziöse zweystrophige Manier" ('lyrically malicious two-stanza manner'). Whereas several of the poems in *Junge Leiden*, Heine's previous book of poems, written between 1817 and 1821, bore individual titles, *Lyrisches Intermezzo* abandons that practice. Heine does not wish the poems to be read separately but only in their context. As he put it to Campe in a letter dated 12 August 1852, „Sie wissen, ich bin ein großer Meister in der Anordnung" ('You know that I am a great master of arrangement'). Successive poems are linked either verbally or thematically. No. 18, for example, begins, „Ich grolle nicht" and ends, „Ich sah, mein Lieb, wie sehr du elend bist", while No. 19 begins, „Ja, du bist elend und ich grolle nicht". The theme of almost all the poems is his love for a woman who rejects him, and throughout the collection we see the ebb and flow of a relationship: past rapture is often followed by present misery. With the possible exception of No. 3 ('Die Rose, die Lilie, die Taube, die Sonne'), none of the poems are purely happy, and many flame with bitterness and self-mockery.

Heine's typical *Lyrisches Intermezzo* metre owes much to Wilhelm Müller, whose *Die schöne Müllerin* had been published in 1821 as part of *Sieben und siebzig Gedichte aus den hinterlassenen Papieren eines reisenden Waldhornisten*. It was to Müller that Heine sent this letter of appreciation on 7 June 1826:

> Ich bin groß genug, Ihnen offen zu bekennen, daß mein kleines „Intermezzo"-Metrum nicht bloß zufällige Ähnlichkeit mit Ihrem gewöhnlichen Metrum hat, sondern daß es wahrscheinlich seinen geheimsten Tonfall Ihren Liedern verdankt, indem es die lieben Müllerschen Lieder waren, die ich zu eben der Zeit kennen lernte, als ich das „Intermezzo" schrieb. Ich habe sehr früh schon das deutsche Volkslied auf mich einwirken lassen; späterhin, als ich in Bonn studirte, hat mir August Schlegel viel metrische Geheimnisse aufgeschlossen, aber ich glaube erst in Ihren Liedern den reinen Klang und die wahre Einfachheit, wonach ich immer strebte, gefunden zu haben. Wie rein, wie klar sind Ihre Lieder, und sämmtlich sind es Volkslieder.

> I am generous enough to admit to you openly that my modest *Intermezzo* metre does not possess a merely coincidental similarity to your usual metre; I admit too that my *Lyrisches Intermezzo* almost certainly owes its most intimate and characteristic sound to your songs: I actually got to know your *Schöne Müllerin* poems at the very time that I was writing my *Lyrisches Intermezzo*. German folksong influenced me very early in my career; and later, when I was studying in Bonn, August Schlegel revealed to me many metrical secrets; but I think that it was in your songs that I first discovered the pure tone and the true simplicity for which I was always striving. How pure and clear your songs are – folk songs every one of them.

The frequent self-mockery, evident in many of the *Lyrisches Intermezzo* poems, is intensified still further in the 88 poems of *Die Heimkehr* (1823–4) that originally opened the *Reisebilder*. These poems too have proved extremely popular with Lieder composers – Schubert selected six for his *Heine-Lieder* from *Schwanengesang* and Vesque von Püttlingen set all 88. The volume, like *Lyrisches Intermezzo*, continues the theme of disillusionment in love – Heine, it seems, was still trying to exorcise the trauma he had described in the letters to Christian Sethe. When in 1827 Heine published the *Buch der Lieder*, which included all the verse he had previously written apart from several immature poems that he now jettisoned, Campe acquired the exclusive copyright and by the time Heine died almost thirty years later the work had gone into no fewer than 13 editions – printing circa 23,000 copies. While preparing the *Buch der Lieder* for publication, Heine wrote a letter to Friedrich Merckel on 16 November 1826 revealing the highly personal nature of these poems:

> Einige Freunde dringen darauf, daß ich eine auserlesene Gedichtesammlung, chronologisch geordnet und streng gewählt, herausgeben soll, und glauben, daß sie ebenso populär wie die Bürgersche, Göthesche und Uhlandsche u.s.w. werden wird. [. . .] Es wär meine Freude [. . .] zu zeigen, daß ich mir doch zu helfen weiß, und dieses Buch würde mein Hauptbuch seyn und ein psychologisches Bild von mir geben.

> Some friends are urging me to publish a carefully selected and chronologically ordered collection of poems, and they believe it will become just as popular as such volumes by Bürger, Goethe, Uhland, etc. [. . .] It would give me pleasure [. . .] to show that I am capable of this, and to show that this would become my magnum opus, providing a psychological picture of myself.

Despite Heine's pride in the *Buch der Lieder*, he was acutely aware of the formulaic nature of many of these love poems, as this squib from *Die Heimkehr* (verse 1 from poem 42) makes clear:

„Teurer Freund! Was soll es nützen,	'What's the use, dear friend, of strumming
Stets das alte Lied zu leiern?	The same old song in this fashion?
Willst du ewig brütend sitzen	Will you sit forever clucking
Auf den alten Liebes-Eiern?"	On the same old eggs of passion?'

When Heine emigrated to Paris in 1831, he continued to write poems, and *Neue Gedichte*, from which Wolf selected six, were published in 1844. The title is partly ironic; the theme of many of the 'new' poems remained exactly the same. And yet this volume also contained, as a supplement, *Deutschland: Ein Wintermärchen*, which shows Heine in a different light. This political poem is among the finest in the entire history of German polemical literature: witty, acerbic and moving, it is considered by many commentators to be his finest contribution to German letters. Heine himself was all too aware of being labelled a love poet who could churn out exquisitely crafted gems according to a certain successful formula. In the letter to Moser mentioned above, he refers to *Die Nordsee* poems, and writes:

> Du siehst, jeden Sommer entpuppe ich mich, und ein neuer Schmetterling flattert hervor. Ich bin also doch nicht auf eine bloß lyrisch-maliziöse zwey-strophige Manier beschränkt.

> Each summer, you see, I burst from the cocoon and a new butterfly flutters forth. I am therefore not confined to a merely lyrically malicious two-stanza manner.

Die Nordsee: Erste Abtheilung was published in Volume 1 of the *Reisebilder*, *Die Nordsee: Zweite Abtheilung* in Volume 2. These remarkable poems, which were written mostly in free verse and intermingle the themes of seascape and love, have been sadly ignored by most Lieder composers, with the exception of Robert Franz.

In a letter to Vesque von Püttlingen, dated 22 June 1851, Heine mentions an opera libretto he had written for the composer Joseph Klein and a ballet pantomime for a London theatre. Heine also tells Vesque that he had heard only a very few of the multitudinous settings of his verse by Schubert, Schumann and others:

> Ich liebe die Musik sehr, aber ich habe selten das Glück, gute Musik zu hören oder gar meine poetischen Schöpfungen durch Musik unterstützt zu sehen. Von den außerordentlich vielen Composizionen meiner Lieder sind mir während den zwanzig Jahren, die ich in Frankreich lebe, nur sehr wenige, vielleicht kaum ein halbes Duzend, zu Ohren gekommen.

> I love music very much, but I seldom have the fortune to hear good music or even to see my own poetic creations reinforced through music. During the twenty years that I have lived in France, I have heard very few, perhaps half a dozen, of the extraordinary number of settings of my poems.

COMPOSER

Wolf was sixteen when he first turned to Heine, in December 1876, setting three poems from *Das Buch der Lieder*: 'Mädchen mit dem roten Mündchen', 'Du bist wie eine Blume' and 'Wenn ich in deine Augen seh'. A year and a half later, during May and June 1878, he set another nine poems (one unfinished) also from the *Buch der Lieder*, seven of which he now fashioned into a *Liederstrauß*: 'Sie haben heut' abend Gesellschaft', 'Ich stand in dunkeln Träumen', 'Das ist ein Brausen und Heulen', 'Aus meinen großen Schmerzen', 'Mir träumte von einem Königskind', 'Mein Liebchen, wir saßen beisammen' and 'Es blasen die blauen Husaren'. He called his work *Liederstrauß: Sieben Gedichte aus dem Buch der Lieder von Heinrich Heine, componirt von Hugo Wolf, 1 Heft, Sommer 1878*. Still a decade from the Mörike songs, in this early *Liederstrauß* there are signs of the mature composer, and the songs are of genuine interest; indeed, they need no special pleading. „Mein Lodi im Lied ist bekanntlich das Jahr 1878 gewesen; damals komponierte ich fast jeden Tag e i n gutes Lied, mitunter auch z w e i." ('My Lodi in song is known to have been the year 1878; in those days I composed almost every day *one* good song, sometimes *two*.') So wrote Wolf to his friend Edmund Lang in February 1888. 'My Lodi in song' is a reference to Napoleon's victory at Lodi (1796) in northern Italy, which brought him recognition and a boost in self-confidence. Although Wolf could occasionally be self-deprecating about his pre-1888 Lieder, he was already following the example of Schumann in *Dichterliebe, Frauenliebe und -leben*, the Heine and Eichendorff *Liederkreise* and the *Kerner-Lieder* by composing settings of one particular poet en masse in the heightened state of creativity that was to be characteristic of him for the rest of his artistic life.

The bouquet of songs, which unlike *Dichterliebe* is not bound together either musically or thematically, opens with 'Sie haben heut' abend Gesellschaft', an astonishing achievement for an eighteen-year-old, every bit as good as Pfitzner's fine setting of 1888. The waltz tune of the dance, at which the tormented and jilted poet looks on, is heard in the prelude. The dotted rhythmic figures and the horn-call motif lend it a jaunty character, and at the outset the singer seems to sing in harmony with it. But during the course of the song Wolf changes the rhythm, melody and harmony to convey the singer's bleak inner world – unloved and unnoticed by the woman. The postlude takes up a quarter of the entire song, and clearly represents an attempt on Wolf's part to emulate those Schumann postludes, such as in 'Ein Jüngling liebt ein Mädchen', that rewrite the poem. Here, he repeats the first four bars of the waltz in its original guise, before allowing the 'merry' tune to disintegrate into a statement of enormous emotional upheaval and fury, abounding in *sforzandi*; and eight bars from the end he instructs the pianist to play 'wildly'.

'Ich stand in dunkeln Träumen' had been immortalised by Schubert in his posthumously published *Schwanengesang* and by Clara Schumann in her Op. 13. Wolf's setting, marked *Innig, ziemlich langsam*, betrays his debt to Schumann, and the way in which he develops the chromatic motif reminds us of songs such as 'Zwielicht' from the Eichendorff *Liederkreis*. 'Das ist ein Brausen und Heulen' begins and ends with wild octaves and violent syncopations to depict the storm in nature and the despair in the heart of the lover. Wolf's setting of 'Aus meinen großen Schmerzen', though little known, is more than a match for Franz's celebrated version of the same poem – a delicious miniature for piano solo, a sort of *moto perpetuo*, to which the singer contributes his neutral vocal line of limited range. Wolf always had the ability to create a song with two distinct voices – here, the small songs that warble their way sweetly and ineffectually from start to finish, and the poet's tortured utterances. Dream sequences, as we know from *Dichterliebe*, are a commonplace in the *Buch der Lieder*, and the beginning of Wolf's setting of 'Mir träumte von einem Königskind' bears a striking resemblance to Schumann's 'Ich hab' im Traum geweinet': both dispense with a piano introduction, both share the same 6/8 metre, and both declaim the first four notes on a single repeated pitch. Wolf intended originally to place 'Wo ich bin, mich rings umdunkelt' as the fifth song of his *Liederstrauß*, but eventually replaced it with 'Mir träumte von einem Königskind'. Wolf's loathing of Brahms is well known (see APPENDIX 1), and it's interesting to compare their versions of 'Mein Liebchen, wir saßen beisammen'. Brahms called his song 'Meerfahrt', and perhaps its most striking feature is the succession of anguished *forte* dissonances that depict the lovers' failure to reach the beautiful island. In Wolf there is no such anguish: the exquisite accompaniment suggests the murmuring sea and plashing oars, recalling a prelude by Chopin, a composer he greatly admired.

The final song of the *Liederstrauß*, 'Es blasen die blauen Husaren', needs some explanation. The poem is the second of a pair from Heine's *Die Heimkehr*. „An deine schneeweiße Schulter" is the opening line of the first poem (not set by Wolf), and against that snowy shoulder the poet rests his head. But his happiness is short-lived, for as he hears the bugles ring out, he realises that her feelings lie elsewhere. The two of them nonetheless spend the night together, before she goes off to join her soldier lover. The second song begins with a military march (a forerunner of 'Sie blasen zum Abmarsch' from the *Spanisches Liederbuch* and 'Ihr jungen Leute' from the *Italienisches Liederbuch*), which announces the return of the soldiers. Despite his sweetheart's infidelity, the poet goes out to meet her, but in the second stanza his disgust gets the better of him, as he realises – Heine's phrase is typically lubricious – that many soldiers have enjoyed her.

The seven songs of the *Liederstrauß* were composed in just over a month – from 18 May ('Sie haben heut' abend Gesellschaft') to 22 June ('Es blasen die blauen Husaren') – and were not published in Wolf's lifetime, although he tried his luck with Breitkopf & Härtel and André; he also hoped that Kistner would acquire them – see HW to Henriette Lang, 26 January 1881 (p. 192). He spent much of the summer of 1878 with Dr Breuer and his family in Waidhofen on the Ybbs – much against the wishes of his parents who wanted him to spend the summer with them in Windischgraz. Soon after returning to Vienna in the autumn, he set about composing a second *Liederstrauß* but did not complete it. The facsimile of the first page lists seven Lieder but indicates only five titles. All the poems are taken from Heine's *Neue Gedichte*, treating the same old theme of unhappy love. 'Es war ein alter König' (No. VIII) dates from 4 October and provides an interesting alternative to Grieg's celebrated setting of the same poem. 'Mit schwarzen Segeln' (No. IX) followed on 6 October, 'Spätherbstnebel, kalte Träume' (numbered VIII, like 'Es war ein alter König') the next day, while 'Ernst ist der Frühling' (No. X), a delightful song of gentle melancholy, was composed between 13 and 17 October. 'Manch Bild vergessener Zeiten' (No. XI) remains a sketch of 30 bars, and was not included in the new *Liederstrauß*, perhaps because the poem was taken from the *Buch der Lieder* and not the *Neue Gedichte*. The same number, XI, is given to 'Sterne mit den goldnen Füßchen' (26 November 1880), a fine song with a gossamer accompaniment that anticipates 'O wär dein Haus durchsichtig wie Glas' from the *Italienisches Liederbuch*. No. XII was to have been 'Wie des Mondes Abbild zittert', composed on 13 February 1880. No. XIII is given no title and merely has a key signature of five sharps. The fourteenth song is listed as 'Das gelbe Laub erzittert', a sketch of eight bars in E flat minor.

Almost all of Wolf's Heine songs deal with unhappy or unfaithful love, and it seems probable that he chose them to exorcise his feelings vis-à-vis Vally Franck's suspected infidelities. See note 2, p. 198, to 'Aus meinen großen Schmerzen'.

After the break with Vally, Wolf spent the spring of 1882 in Maierling and while there read Heine's *Die Harzreise*. He was fascinated by the character of Prinzessin Ilse and harboured ambitions to write an opera on the subject, possibly to his own libretto, but nothing came of the project. The *Vier Gedichte nach H. Heine, Shakespeare und Lord Byron* were published in 1897 by Heckel in Mannheim. 'Wo wird einst' is Wolf's eighteenth and final setting of Heine.

Though none of these *Heine-Lieder* appeared in print during the composer's lifetime, Lauterbach & Kuhn published six of them in the autumn of 1903. The editor was Ferdinand Foll, a close friend of Wolf and an admirer of his music. Foll did much to propagate Wolf's Lieder before and after the composer's death. He called the twelve songs *Lieder aus der Jugendzeit* and they comprise: 'An*' (Lenau, p. 313), 'Wanderlied' (Anon., p. 6), 'Traurige Wege', 'Nächtliche Wanderung' (both Lenau, pp. 310 and 311), 'Das Kind am Brunnen' (Hebbel, p. 178), 'Über Nacht' (Sturm, p. 470), 'Ich stand in dunkeln Träumen', 'Das ist ein Brausen und Heulen', 'Wo ich bin, mich rings umdunkelt', 'Aus meinen großen

Schmerzen', 'Es war ein alter König' and 'Ernst ist der Frühling' (all Heine, pp. 197–202). The edition was taken over by Bote & Bock in 1908.

LETTERS

HW to his father, Vienna, 16 October 1878

Außer zwei Heineschen Gedichten,[1] die recht gut gefallen, habe ich nichts komponiert, woran wohl viel die Wohnung und vielleicht auch die unbehagliche Witterung schuld sein mag. Überm Winter jedoch gedenke ich manches noch zustande zu bringen. Soeben bin ich im Begriffe, ein Heinesches Lied aufzuschreiben,[2] und da Dr. Schoenaich[3] schon sehr danach verlangt, es zu hören, kann ich mich nicht mehr allzulange mit dem Briefe beschäftigen. Vier Tage trage ich das Lied schon im Kopfe herum und war bis jetzt noch nicht gestimmt, es auszuarbeiten.

Apart from two Heine poems that have gone down very well, I have composed nothing – largely due to my apartment and perhaps also the unpleasant weather. During the winter, nevertheless, I hope to achieve considerably more. I am at the moment in the process of composing a Heine song, and as Dr Schoenaich is longing to hear it, I cannot spend too long on this letter. For four days I've carried the song around in my head, but wasn't till now in the mood to finish it.

HW to his father, Maierling, 5 September 1880

Nebst den Schuhen[4] für mich eine unterhaltende Lektüre für Sie. H. Heines Reisebilder[5] werden Ihnen die Zeit hinweggaukeln. Sie werden sich amüsieren und alle Jeremiaden dabei vergessen. Anbei „Der Prinz von Homburg"[6] und

---

1   After his return to Vienna, Wolf in fact composed not two but three Heine songs: 'Es war ein alter König' (4 October), 'Mit schwarzen Segeln' (6 October) and 'Spätherbstnebel, kalte Träume' (7 October).
2   'Ernst ist der Frühling' (13–17 October).
3   Gustav Schönaich (1841–1906) exercised a huge influence on Wolf in the late 1870s. A keen admirer of Wagner and highly cultured, he lent Wolf money on several occasions, though not wealthy himself, and took great interest in Wolf's development as a composer. In a letter to his father of 18 December 1877, Wolf compares Schönaich to Faust and himself to his amanuensis Wagner, and then quotes lines 596–601 and 941–2 from *Faust*, ending with: „Mit Euch, Herr Doktor, zu spazieren/ Ist ehrenvoll und ist Gewinn." ('To walk with you, my master,/Brings me honour and much gain.')
4   Wolf asks his father later in the letter to post him the shoes as soon as they have been mended.
5   Heine's *Reisebilder*, a four-volume collection of prose and verse, appeared between 1826 and 1831. Volume 1 (1826) contains *Die Harzreise*, a partly lyrical and partly satirical account of a walking tour through the Harz mountains that Heine had made in 1824.
6   *Der Prinz von Homburg*, a five-act drama in blank verse by Heinrich von Kleist (1777–1811), completed in 1810 and published in 1821 – his greatest play.

unser Liebling „Der zerbrochene Krug".¹ Der Band Heine gehört Frl. F.,² ich bitte deshalb, für das Buch Sorge zu tragen, daß es am Ende nicht in eine Schüssel Milchbrein hineinplumpst. Lesen Sie nur gleich die Harzreise. Die „Ideen" sind köstlich über alle Maßen. O, Sie werden entzückt sein. Die andern 2 Bändchen können Sie behalten, Heine aber bei Gelegenheit, wenn Sie ihn ausgelesen, zurückschicken. Wenn es Ihnen gefällt, <u>schicke ich den 2. Band nach</u>.³

For me the shoes, for you an entertaining book. H. Heine's *Reisebilder* will while away the time for you. You will be amused and forget all your woes. I also enclose *Der Prinz von Homburg* and our favourite *Der zerbrochene Krug*. The Heine volume belongs to Fräulein F. – so please make sure it doesn't fall into a bowl of semolina. Read the *Harzreise* straightaway. Heine's *Ideen* [*Ideen: Das Buch Le Grand*] are absolutely exquisite. Ah, you will be enraptured. You can keep the other 2 little volumes, but send back the Heine some time when you have read it. If you like it, <u>I'll send you the second volume</u>.

HW to Henriette Lang, Vienna, Rennweg 3, 26 January 1881

Vielleicht interessiert es Sie, daß meine Lieder (7 von Heine)⁴ bei Kistner in Leipzig demnächst erscheinen werden.

It might interest you that my songs (7 by Heine) will soon be published by Kistner in Leipzig.

HW to Oskar Grohe, Döbling, 13 May 1893

Um jedoch die Wirkung dieser Danaergabe einigermassen abzuschwächen bin ich so „anmaßend" ein noch nicht publicirtes Lied von mir beizulegen,⁵ das ich eigens für Sie abschreibe. Mit demselben hat es die merkwürdige Bewandtniß, daß es aus einer Zeit stammt, in der mir nach jahrelangem Irren, Suchen u. Verzweifeln zum erstenmale der Knopf – wie man bei uns zu sagen pflegt –

---

1   *Der zerbrochene Krug*, a one-act comedy in blank verse by Kleist, written between 1803 and 1807, and published in 1811.
2   Valentine (Vally) Franck (1856–?), Wolf's beloved. The relationship ended in March or April 1881. See pp. 480–83.
3   Wolf's mother later returned the book to her son, writing somewhat ungrammatically: „Das Buch von Freulein Vali schließe ich bei und danke herzlich. Heine hat mich köstlich unterhalten sein Humor ist vol Satir und sehr treffend, ich staune nur dass es ausgegeben wurde, es nicht gleich konfeszirten." ('I enclose Fräulein Vally's book with many thanks. Heine has thoroughly entertained me. His humour is full of well-aimed satire, but I'm astonished that it was published and not confiscated on the spot.')
4   Presumably the Heine *Liederstrauß* (18 May–22 June 1878). The songs were not published in Wolf's lifetime.
5   'Wo wird einst'.

aufging. Es war sozusagen das Vorspiel zu meinen Mörike-Liedern, denn wenige Wochen darnach war die Liedersintfluth bei mir ausgebrochen.

In order to diminish a little the effect of this Greek gift, permit me in my arrogance to enclose an unpublished song of mine that I've copied out especially for you. Curiously enough, it was composed at a time when – after years of false starts, searching & despairing, the penny – as we say – finally dropped. It was, as it were, the prelude to my *Mörike-Lieder*, for a few weeks later the flood of Lieder burst forth.

HW to Oskar Grohe, Traunkirchen, 8 June 1893

Ich führe hier die Existenz einer Auster, denn das bißchen Lektüre, das ich treibe, ist kaum nennenswert. Nur das mechanische Üben auf dem Flügel macht mir noch Spaß, zumal abends in die Nacht hinein, wenn die Finger immer geläufiger werden; da entfalte ich mitunter eine mechanische Fertigkeit, daß ich selber davor erschrecke. Gestern z.B. spielte ich in später Nachtstunde bei offenem Klavier den Walkürenritt nach der Klindworthschen[1] Bearbeitung in einem rasenden Tempo, ohne jemals daneben gegriffen zu haben. Die Finger flogen nur so blitzartig über die Tasten, daß mir ganz schaurig dabei zumute ward. Hätte ich zur gestrigen Geisterstunde Publikum um mich gehabt, die Leute hätten gedacht, der Teufel musiziere ihnen was vor, so grausig war die Sache zum Anhören. Leider aber spiele ich gerade vor Leuten immer zaghaft und befangen, und so werd' ich als Klavierspieler auch nie was aufstecken.
    Daß Ihnen mein Heinesches Lied so gefällt, höre ich gern.[2]

I'm living the life of an oyster here, for the little that I read is hardly worth mentioning. Mechanical piano practice alone gives me any pleasure, especially as night draws on and the fingers move with ever greater fluency. I then occasionally develop a mechanical skill that frightens me. Yesterday, for example, at a late hour and with the piano on full stick, I performed the Ride of the Valkyries in Klindworth's arrangement at breakneck speed without ever playing a wrong note. My fingers moved like lightning so swiftly over the keys that I was terrified. Had I had an audience yesterday at that witching hour

---

[1] Karl Klindworth (1830–1916), a friend of Liszt and Wagner, was a composer, conductor, virtuoso pianist, violinist and publisher. Eric Sams writes perceptively of Klindworth:

> Before Schubert could write his first great songs, it was first necessary for the piano to evolve so that it could render orchestral sound-effects, and thus enable Lied composers to compress the intensity of large-scale musical expression within the more personal and intimate frame of voice and keyboard, household and drawing-room, friends and lovers. That task of compression was dramatically eased for Wolf by the techniques of piano reduction used by Karl Klindworth and other fine pianists, including Liszt, in their vocal scores of Wagner operas.

[2] 'Wo wird einst'.

they would have thought it was the devil playing to them – it was so terrifying. Unfortunately, when I play in public, I am always hesitant and embarrassed, and so I'll never make it as a pianist.

Delighted that you so like my Heine song.

HW to Frieda Zerny, Vienna, 24 April 1894

„Ich sitze u. sinne u. sinne u. träume – und denk an die Liebste mein."

Diese Worte Heine's, die Schumann in einer herrlichen Composition verewigte,[1] wollen mir zur Stunde gar nicht aus dem Sinne gehen. Es ist gerade Mittagszeit. Ich sitze im Garten unter dem Schatten einer prächtigen Kastanie, vor mir auf dem Gartentischchen Deine lieben Zeilen, die mir soeben der Briefbote überbrachte. Was wird das heute ein melancholisches Mittagessen geben! o diese Oede, wenn ich vergebens Dein Bild beschwöre, das noch vor kurzem in hellster Wirklichkeit diese sommerlichen Räume so reizend belebte! Ach Frieda, Du mußt wiederum zu mir kommen od. ich komm zu Dir. Dieses Getrenntsein ist gar zu öd u. traurig.

'I sit & muse & muse & dream – and think of my dearest love.'

I cannot get these words of Heine, immortalised by Schumann in a splendid composition, out of my head. It has just turned noon. I'm sitting in the garden beneath the shade of a splendid chestnut tree, the postman has just brought your dear letter which lies open in front of me on the little garden table. Today's lunch will be a melancholy occasion! How desolate! I conjure up in vain your image that, just a little while ago, brightened this summery place in such a charming way! Ah Frieda! You must come to me again, or I to you. Being apart is far too desolate & sad.

HW to Oskar Grohe, Vienna, 28 December 1896

Demnächst werde ich an Heckel wiederum drei Lieder senden, darunter das von Heine, wovon Du eine Abschrift besitzest, ferner das Lied des transferirten Zettel aus dem Sommernachtstraum u. ein soeben zu Weihnachten componirtes neues Lied nach einem herrlichen Gedicht von Lord Byron.[2]

I shall soon send Heckel another three songs, including the Heine setting, of which you have a copy, Bottom's Song from *A Midsummer Night's Dream*,

---

1 'Mein Wagen rollet langsam' by Robert Schumann, Op. 142/4, also set by Richard Strauss as 'Waldesfahrt', Op. 69/4.
2 Wolf intended to publish 'Wo wird einst', the 'Lied des transferierten Zettel' and 'Keine gleicht von allen Schönen' – but between 29 and 31 December he composed 'Sonne der Schlummerlosen', thus adding another song to the opus number. Wolf had sent Grohe a copy of 'Wo wird einst' shortly after the death of Grohe's wife Jeanne, on 13 May 1893.

& a new song that I've just composed at Christmas to a splendid poem by Lord Byron.

HW to Hugo Faisst, Vienna, 14 April 1897

Es freut mich ganz besonders, daß Dir No. 1 von Heine so gut gefällt. Ich habe dieses Stück vor nun 9 Jahren am selben Abend in Perchtoldsdorf componirt, an dem auch das Gesellenlied entstanden ist. Das sind freilich große Contraste. Dennoch wundert es mich, daß Du gerade auf das 1. verfallen bist,[1] da es sich doch zuweilen in der Tenorlage bewegt, während die Gedichte nach Byron auch den, leider von mir vernachlässigten Baritönen zugänglich sind.[2]

I'm delighted that No. 1 (by Heine) pleases you so much. I composed this song 9 years ago in Perchtoldsdorf on the same evening as 'Gesellenlied'. What contrasts! Yet I'm surprised that you go for the first one, for some of the music is in the tenor register, while the Byron songs are suitable also for the baritone voice that I have unfortunately neglected.

LIEDER

Mädchen mit dem roten Mündchen[3]

Maiden with the red lips

Mädchen mit dem roten Mündchen,
Mit den Äuglein süß und klar,
Du mein süßes,[4] kleines Mädchen,
Deiner denk' ich immerdar.

Lang ist heut der Winterabend,
Und ich möchte bei dir sein,
Bei dir sitzen, bei[5] dir schwatzen
Im vertrauten Kämmerlein.

An die Lippen wollt' ich pressen
Deine kleine, weiße Hand,
Und mit Tränen sie benetzen,
Deine kleine, weiße Hand.

Maiden with the red lips,
With the sweet and limpid eyes,
You, my dearest little maiden,
I think of you all the time.

The winter evening's long tonight,
And I'd love to be by your side,
Sit with you and talk with you
In your cosy little room.

I long to press to my lips
Your little white hand,
And moisten it with tears,
Your little white hand.

Die Heimkehr 50; poem written spring 1824
Also set by Carl Bohm, Leopold Damrosch, Robert Franz, Franz Lachner and Johann Vesque von Püttlingen

1 'Wo wird einst'.
2 Faisst was an amateur singer, a baritone.
3 Cf. Wilhelm Müller's 'Fastnachtslied von den goldenen Zöpfen': „Mägdlein mit den goldnen Zöpfen,/Mägdlein mit dem goldnen Haar!"
4 Heine: liebes.   5 Heine: mit.

Du bist wie eine Blume[1]

Du bist wie eine Blume,
So hold und schön und rein;
Ich schau' dich an, und Wehmut
Schleicht mir ins Herz hinein.

Mir ist, als ob die Hände
Auf's Haupt dir legen sollt',
Betend, daß Gott dich erhalte
So rein, so schön und hold.[2]

You are like a flower

You are like a flower,
So sweet and fair and pure;
I gaze at you, and sadness
Steals into my heart.

I feel as if I should lay
My hands upon your head,
Praying that God preserve you
So pure, so fair, so sweet.

Die Heimkehr 47; poem first published 1825
Also set by Lord Berners, Norbert Burgmüller, Ferruccio Busoni, Georg Henschel, Charles Ives, Franz Lachner, Franz Liszt, Sergei Rachmaninov, Anton Rubinstein, Robert Schumann and Vesque von Püttlingen[3]

Wenn ich in deine Augen seh

Wenn ich in deine Augen seh,
So schwindet all mein Leid und Weh;
Doch wenn ich küsse deinen Mund,
So werd ich ganz und gar gesund.

Wenn ich mich lehn' an deine Brust,
Kommt's über mich wie Himmelslust;
Doch wenn du sprichst: Ich liebe dich!
Dann[4] muß ich weinen bitterlich.[5]

When I look into your eyes

When I look into your eyes,
All my pain and sorrow vanish;
But when I kiss your lips,
Then I am wholly healed.

When I lay my head against your breast,
Heavenly bliss steals over me;
But when you say: I love you!
I must weep bitter tears.

1 According to Heine's niece, Maria Embden-Heine (*Erinnerungen an H. Heine*), the poem was addressed to a destitute Jewish girl from Gnesen in Poland, whose name was Mirjam. Heine, having encountered her on the street, asked his friend Rahel Varnhagen von Ense to look after her. Embden-Heine then asserts that Heine fell in love with Mirjam who did not reciprocate his affection and returned soon after to Poland. Whatever the truth of such an assertion (and we should be wary of taking her account as gospel as she was writing more than half a century after the alleged encounter), the mood of Heine's poem conveys some painful experience. Far from being the romantic outpouring we hear in Schumann's lovely song from *Myrthen*, it is full of bitterness. The first verse, unless the opening line be construed as a cliché, is devoid of irony, but the mood is one of melancholy, not happiness: the enjambement conjures up graphically the moment that sadness steals into his heart. This mood of genuine sadness, however, is short-lived. Verse 2 shows us the lover praying that God might *preserve* his sweetheart (be it Mirjam or whoever) pure and unsullied. If the stress falls not on 'Gott' but 'erhalte', the whole mood of the poem changes: it is too late – the poet has already been rebuffed and the girl belongs to another. Heine's bitterness at being rejected is then expressed in the final line of the poem, a jingly reversal of the original refrain, which deflates the mood of the opening. It is scarcely surprising that Wolf's song, written at the age of sixteen, does not address the irony.
  Lewis Browne (*That Man Heine*) suggests that Heine is addressing Therese, while Ernst Elster states categorically that the poem was inspired by Therese – see *Heines Werke*, vol. I, pp. 9 and 459.
2 Heine: So rein und schön und hold.
3 Ernst Challier lists no fewer than 160 settings by 1885, and concludes that no other German poem was set more often in the nineteenth century.
4 Heine: So muß ich weinen bitterlich.
5 The last line is a fine example of Heine's trademark 'Stimmungsbrechung' (a word or line that deflates or punctures the previous mood). The first seven lines of 'Wenn ich in deine Augen seh' are

Lyrisches Intermezzo 4; poem written during the winter of 1821–2
Also set by Frank Bridge, Franz, Alexander Glazunov, Fanny Mendelssohn Hensel, Joseph Klein, Lachner, Nikolai Rimsky-Korsakov and Schumann

Liederstrauß
A Bouquet of Songs

1 Sie haben heut' abend Gesellschaft[1]   They are partying tonight

Sie haben heut' abend Gesellschaft,	They are partying tonight
Und das Haus ist lichterfüllt.	And the house is filled with light.
Dort oben am hellen Fenster	Up there at the bright-lit window
Bewegt sich ein Schattenbild.	A shadowy figure moves.
Du schaust mich nicht, im Dunkeln	You do not see me, in the dark
Steh' ich hier unten allein;	I stand down here below,
Noch wen'ger kannst du schauen	Even less can you see
In mein dunkles Herz hinein.	Into my dark heart.
Mein dunkles Herze liebt dich,	My dark heart loves you,
Es liebt dich und es bricht,	It loves you and it breaks,
Und bricht und zuckt und verblutet,	It breaks and quivers and bleeds to death,
Du aber siehst es nicht.*[2]	But this you do not see.*

Die Heimkehr 60; poem written autumn 1823
Also set by Lachner, Hans Pfitzner and Vesque von Püttlingen
* Wolf repeats the last line.

2 Ich stand in dunkeln Träumen   I stood in dark dreams

Ich stand in dunkeln Träumen,	I stood in dark dreams,
Und starrte ihr Bildnis an,	And gazed at her likeness,
Und das geliebte Antlitz	And that beloved face
Heimlich zu leben begann.	Sprang mysteriously to life.

---

a crescendo of ecstasy, but the final line, instead of providing the expected climax, points bathetically to the poet's bitterness: her confession of love was a lie. Other common deflating devices used by Heine are half-rhymes, Ogden Nash-like rhymes, archaisms, hyperbole, jingly assonance and diminutives.

1   In July 1823 Heine visited Hamburg for the first time after the break with his cousin Amalie. Although he did not see her again during his stay with Uncle Salomon, the pain he felt at their separation still persisted, as can be seen from the letter he wrote Moses Moser on 11 July 1823: „Die alte Leidenschaft bricht nochmals mit Gewalt hervor. Ich hätte nicht nach Hamburg gehn sollen; wenigstens muß ich machen, daß ich so bald als möglich fortkomme." ('The old passion erupts again with fury. I should not have come to Hamburg again; I must see to it that I escape as soon as possible.') 'Sie haben heut' abend Gesellschaft' was written a few months later. In another letter to Moser of 23 August 1823, Heine tells his friend that he had *'grafted a new folly on to the old one'* („w i e d i e n e u e T h o r h e i t a u f d e r a l t e n g e p r o p f t i s t"). It seems that he had transferred his affections to Therese, Amalie's sister.
2   Heine: Aber du siehst es nicht.

Um ihre Lippen zog sich	A smile played wondrously
Ein Lächeln wunderbar,	About her lips,
Und wie von Wehmutstränen	And her eyes glistened,
Erglänzte ihr Augenpaar.	As though with sad tears.
Auch meine Tränen flossen	And my tears too
Mir von den Wangen herab –	Streamed down my cheeks –
Und ach, ich kann's[1] nicht glauben,	And ah, I cannot believe
Daß ich dich verloren hab'!*	That I have lost you!*

Die Heimkehr 23; poem first published 1826
Also set by Edvard Grieg, Lachner, Franz Schubert, Clara Schumann and Vesque von Püttlingen
* Wolf repeats the final two lines.

3 Das ist ein Brausen und Heulen   How the weather roars and howls

Das ist ein Brausen und Heulen,	How the weather roars and howls:
Herbstnacht und Regen und Wind;	Autumn night and rain and wind;
Wo mag wohl jetzo weilen	Where can she now be, I wonder,
Mein armes, banges Kind?	My poor dear frightened child?
Ich seh' sie am Fenster lehnen	I see her leaning by the window
Im einsamen Kämmerlein;	In her lonely little room;
Das Auge gefüllt mit Tränen,	With tear-filled eyes
Starrt sie in die Nacht hinein.*	She stares out into night.*

Lyrisches Intermezzo 57; poem written autumn 1822
Also set by Franz and Charles Griffes
* Wolf repeats the last line.

4 Aus meinen großen Schmerzen[2]   From my great sorrows

Aus meinen großen Schmerzen	From my great sorrows
Mach' ich die kleinen Lieder;[3]	I make little songs;

---

[1] Heine: Und ach, ich kann es nicht glauben.
[2] See p. 482. Wolf used to sing 'Aus meinen großen Schmerzen' in a 'toneless, veiled voice' whenever he suspected Vally Franck of being disloyal. Helene Bettelheim-Gabillon, Vally's close friend, writes in her memoirs:

> Über den Wert der Komposition hatte ich damals kein Urteil und ich kann mich auch nicht entsinnen, ob mir das Lied als solches gefiel oder nicht – aber ich wußte, wem seine „großen Schmerzen" galten, und der Ausdruck seiner Leidenschaft und seines tiefgequälten Gemütes, der sich in seinen Zügen spiegelte, und in seiner klanglosen, verschleierten Stimme zitterte, hatte etwas so Ergreifendes, daß mir der Eindruck unvergessen blieb.
>
> About the worth of the composition I could at that time form no opinion, and I cannot recall whether the song as such pleased me or not – but I knew to whom his 'große Schmerzen' referred, and the expression of his passion and his deeply wounded feelings that was reflected in his features and quivered in his toneless, veiled voice had something so gripping about it that I have never forgotten it.

Die heben ihr klingend Gefieder
Und flattern nach ihrem Herzen.

Sie fanden den Weg zur Trauten,
Doch kommen sie wieder und klagen,
Und klagen, und wollen nicht sagen,
Was sie im Herzen schauten.*¹

They raise their resonant plumage
And flutter to her heart.

They found their way to my dear one,
But they come back and complain,
Complain, and will not tell me
What they saw in her heart.*

Lyrisches Intermezzo 36; poem first published 1823
Also set by Franz and Lachner
* Wolf repeats the final two lines.

5 Mir träumte von einem Königskind

I dreamt of a princess

Mir träumte von einem Königskind,
Mit nassen, blassen Wangen;
Wir saßen unter der grünen Lind',
Und hielten uns liebeumfangen.²

I dreamt of a princess
With pale and humid cheeks;
We sat beneath the green linden tree,
Clasped in a loving embrace.

„Ich will nicht deines Vaters Thron,
Ich will nicht sein Szepter aus Golde,³
Ich will nicht seine demantene Kron',
Ich will dich selber, du Holde!"

'I do not want your father's throne,
I do not want his sceptre of gold,
I do not want his diamond crown,
It is you I want, my love!'

Das kann nicht sein, sprach sie zu mir,
Ich liege ja im Grabe,
Und nur des Nachts komm' ich zu dir,
Weil ich so lieb dich habe.

That cannot be, she said to me,
For I lie in the grave below,
And only at night do I come to you,
Because I love you so.

Lyrisches Intermezzo 41; poem written between winter 1821 and December 1822
Also set by Franz Abt, Lachner, Carl Orff and Vesque von Püttlingen

6 Mein Liebchen, wir saßen beisammen

My sweetest, we sat in our skiff

Mein Liebchen, wir saßen beisammen
Traulich im leichten Kahn.
Die Nacht war still und wir schwammen
Auf weiter Wasserbahn.

My sweetest, we sat in our skiff,
Closely next to each other.
The night was still, and we drifted
Along a wide waterway.

Die Geisterinsel, die schöne,
Lag dämmrig im Mondenglanz;
Dort klangen liebe Töne
Und wogte der Nebeltanz.

The beautiful haunted island
Glimmered in the moon's dim light;
Sweet music resounded,
And dancing mists swirled.

---

3 Heine also parodied his poem – see 'Ich mache die kleinen Lieder', the fifth song of 'Zum Polterabend'.
1 The accompaniment bears a striking resemblance to Schubert's 'Auf dem Wasser zu singen'.
2 Heine: liebumfangen.   3 Heine: Und nicht sein Zepter von Golde.

Dort klang es lieb und lieber	The sounds grew ever sweeter,
Und wogt' es hin und her;	The mists swirled this way and that;
Wir aber schwammen vorüber,	But we drifted past,
Trostlos auf weitem Meer.	Desolate on the wide sea.

Lyrisches Intermezzo 42; poem written between winter 1821 and December 1822
Also set by Johannes Brahms, Franz, Eduard Lassen, Edward MacDowell, Felix Mendelssohn and Joseph Ropartz

7 Es blasen die blauen Husaren[1]   The Blue Hussars blow their bugles

Es blasen die blauen Husaren,	The Blue Hussars blow their bugles,
Und reiten zum Tor hinaus;	And ride out through the gate;
Da komm ich, Geliebte, und bringe	I come to you, love, and bring you
Dir einen Rosenstrauß.	A bouquet of roses.
Das war eine wilde Wirtschaft!	What wild company you kept!
Kriegsvolk und Landesplag'!	Soldiers at war and a real scourge!
Sogar in deinem Herzen[2]	And many soldiers
Viel Einquartierung lag.*	Billeted in your breast.

Die Heimkehr 74; poem first published 1826
Also set by César Cui and Vesque von Püttlingen
* Wolf repeats the final line, and then the opening two lines of the poem.

Wo ich bin, mich rings umdunkelt[3]   Darkness gathers about me

Wo ich bin, mich rings umdunkelt	Darkness gathers about me,
Finsternis, so dumpf und dicht,	So heavily and close,
Seit mir nicht mehr leuchtend funkelt,	Now that your sparkling eyes,
Liebste, deiner Augen Licht.	Beloved, no longer shine on me.
Mir erloschen ist der süßen	The golden splendour of love's sweet firmament
Liebessterne goldne Pracht,	Is now extinguished for me,
Abgrund gähnt zu meinen Füßen –	The abyss gapes beneath my feet –
Nimm mich auf, uralte Nacht!*	Receive me, O primeval night!*

Lyrisches Intermezzo 63; poem written during the winter of 1821–2
Also set by Griffes, Ropartz, Richard Strauss and Vesque von Püttlingen
* Wolf repeats the final line.

---

1 See p. 189 for an explanation of this poem. The Prussian uhlans wore blue uniforms. Düsseldorf was the garrison town of the regiment.
2 Heine: Herzchen.
3 'Wo ich bin, mich rings umdunkelt' was to have been the fifth song of the Heine *Liederstrauß*, but Wolf decided to substitute it with 'Mir träumte von einem Königskind'.

Es war ein alter König[1]

Es war ein alter König,
Sein Herz war schwer, sein Haupt war grau;
Der arme alte König,
Er nahm eine junge Frau.

Es war ein schöner Page,
Blond war sein Haupt, leicht war sein Sinn;
Er trug die seidne Schleppe
Der jungen Königin.

Kennst du das alte Liedchen?
Es klingt so süß, es klingt so trüb!
Sie mußten beide sterben,
Sie hatten sich viel zu lieb.

There was an old king

There was an old king,
His heart was heavy, his hair was grey;
The poor old king,
He took a young wife.

There was a beautiful page,
His hair was blond, his heart was light;
He held the silken train
Of the young queen.

Do you know the old song?
It sounds so sweet, it sounds so sad!
They both had to die,
They loved each other too much.

Neue Gedichte, 'Neuer Frühling' 29; poem published in 1844 as part of *Neue Gedichte*
Also set by Peter Cornelius, Grieg, Henschel, Ferdinand Hiller, Heinrich Marschner, Rubinstein, Vesque von Püttlingen and Alexander von Zemlinsky

Mit schwarzen Segeln

Mit schwarzen Segeln segelt mein Schiff
Wohl über das wilde Meer;
Du weißt, wie sehr ich traurig bin,
Und kränkst mich noch so schwer.

Dein Herz ist treulos wie der Wind
Und flattert hin und her;
Mit schwarzen Segeln segelt mein Schiff
Wohl über das wilde Meer.

With black sails

With black sails my ship sets forth
Out over the stormy sea;
Though you know how sad I am,
Still you wound me so cruelly.

Your heart is fickle like the wind
And flutters to and fro;
With black sails my ship sets forth
Out over the stormy sea.

Neue Gedichte; poem first published in 1833, the eleventh poem of 'Seraphine' from *Verschiedene*.[2]
Also set by Franz and Griffes

Spätherbstnebel, kalte Träume[3]

Spätherbstnebel, kalte Träume,
Überfloren Berg und Tal,
Sturm entblättert schon die Bäume,
Und sie schaun gespenstig[4] kahl.

Late autumn mists, cold dreams

Late autumn mists, cold dreams
Drape mountain and valley,
Storms already denude the trees,
And they appear spectrally bare.

---

1 See HW to his father, 16 October 1878, p. 191.
2 The title is a pun. 'Verschiedene' means 'deceased', 'departed' and also 'sundry', 'diverse'.
3 See HW to his father, 16 October 1878, p. 191. The diminished sevenths of the accompaniment must surely have been inspired by Schubert's setting of 'Die Stadt' in *Schwanengesang*.
4 Heine: gespenstisch.

Nur ein einz'ger, traurig schweigsam
Einz'ger Baum steht unentlaubt,
Feucht von Wehmutstränen gleichsam,
Schüttelt er sein grünes Haupt.

Ach, mein Herz gleicht dieser Wildnis,
Und der Baum, den ich dort schau'
Sommergrün, das ist dein Bildnis,
Vielgeliebte* schöne Frau!

Only one, standing in sad silence,
One lone tree still shows its leaves,
Wet, as with the tears of sadness,
It shakes its verdant crown.

Ah, my heart is like this wilderness,
And the tree that I see there,
Summer-green, is the image of you,
Fair lady much loved.*

Neue Gedichte, 'Neuer Frühling' 43; poem published 1844 as part of *Neue Gedichte*
Also set by Alban Berg
* Wolf repeats 'Vielgeliebte'.

Ernst ist der Frühling[1]

Ernst ist der Frühling, seine Träume
Sind traurig, jede Blume schaut
Von Schmerz bewegt, es bebt geheime

Wehmut im Nachtigallenlaut.

O lächle nicht, geliebte Schöne,
So freundlich heiter, lächle nicht!
O weine lieber, eine Träne*
Küss' ich so gern dir vom Gesicht.

Solemn is the spring

Solemn is the spring, its dreams
Are sad, every flower seems
To tremble with pain, the song of the
    nightingale
Quivers with sadness.

O do not smile, my fair beloved,
Do not smile so cheerfully!
O rather weep, I would love so dearly
To kiss from your face a tear.*

Neue Gedichte, 'Neuer Frühling' 38; poem published in 1844 as part of *Neue Gedichte*
Also set by Berg, Hans von Bülow and Charles Villiers Stanford
* Wolf repeats 'eine Träne'.

Wie des Mondes Abbild zittert

Wie des Mondes Abbild zittert
In den wilden Meereswogen,
Und er selber still und sicher
Wandelt an dem Himmelsbogen:

Also wandelst du, Geliebte,
Still und sicher, und es zittert

How the moon's reflection trembles

How the moon's reflection trembles
In the sea's wild heaving waves,
While the moon, calmly and surely,
Moves through the vault of heaven:

Thus you move, beloved,
Calmly and surely, and only

---

1 Susan Youens writes in *Hugo Wolf: The Vocal Music* (p. 60) that the song

> ... seems in retrospect a study for the Mörike lied 'Im Frühling' ten years before the fact. One wonders if Wolf remarked the resemblance when he came to compose the later masterpiece. The two songs share the same 6/4 meter, the similar interplay of triple and duple divisions of the measure, and, most notably, the interwoven motion of the individual melodic lines in the piano and vocal part, the instrumental melodies and the singer's part of equal importance over a bass foundation in even dotted half-notes.

Nur dein Abbild mir im Herzen,	Your reflection trembles in my heart,
Weil mein eignes Herz* erschüttert.	For my own heart* is shattered.

Neue Gedichte, 'Neuer Frühling' 23; poem published in 1844 as part of *Neue Gedichte*
Also set by Franz and Stanford
* Wolf repeats 'eignes Herz'.

Sterne mit den goldnen Füßchen[1] — Stars with tiny golden feet

Sterne mit den goldnen Füßchen	Stars with tiny golden feet
Wandeln droben bang und sacht,	Move anxiously and gently across the skies,
Daß sie nicht die Erde wecken,	So as not to wake the earth,
Die da schläft im Schoß der Nacht.	Sleeping in the lap of night.
Horchend stehn die stummen Wälder,	The silent forests hearken –
Jedes Blatt ein grünes Ohr!	Each leaf a verdant ear!
Und der Berg, wie träumend streckt er	And the mountain, as though dreaming,
Seinen Schattenarm hervor.	Stretches out his shady arm.
Doch was rief dort? In mein Herze	But what cried there? My heart
Dringt der Töne Widerhall.	Is pierced by the echo of a sound.
War es der Geliebten Stimme,	Was it my beloved's voice,
Oder nur die Nachtigall?	Or just the nightingale?

Neue Gedichte, 'Neuer Frühling', 37; poem published in 1844 as part of *Neue Gedichte*
Also set by Franz and Stanford

Wo wird einst[2] — Where shall the weary traveller

Wo wird einst des Wandermüden	Where shall the weary traveller
Letzte Ruhestätte sein?	Find his final resting-place?
Unter Palmen in dem Süden?[3]	Under palm trees in the south?
Unter Linden an dem Rhein?	Under lime trees by the Rhine?

---

1 This is the first of Wolf's songs whose accompaniment is written almost entirely in the treble clef, a device that became one of his most characteristic trademarks. See also 'Blumengruß', 'St. Nepomuks Vorabend', 'Die Spröde', 'Mausfallen-Sprüchlein', 'O wär dein Haus' and 'Zum neuen Jahr'.
2 See HW to Oskar Grohe, 13 May 1893, and to Hugo Faisst, 14 April 1897, pp. 192 and 195. The poem was published for the first time in 1869 as part of *Letzte Gedichte und Gedanken von Heinrich Heine*, edited by Adolf Strodtmann, Heine's first biographer, who provided the title 'Wo?' The poem, written in Heine's own hand, can be seen in the Pierpont Morgan Library in New York. Scholars disagree about the date: Elster's second edition of the poems suggests merely that it was written „wahrscheinlich vor 1840"– probably before 1840. 'Wo' adorns Heine's gravestone in Paris in the Montmartre Cemetery. His tombstone is topped by a magnificent bust of the poet, carved by Louis Hasselriis (1844–1912), a well-known Danish sculptor famed for his public statuary.
3 A letter written by Heine from Norderney to Christian Sethe, dated 1 September 1825, anticipates the mood of 'Wo?':

Werd' ich wo in einer Wüste	Will I, somewhere in a desert,
Eingescharrt von fremder Hand?	Be buried by a stranger's hand?
Oder ruh' ich an der Küste	Or shall I find rest on the shore
Eines Meeres in dem Sand?	Of some ocean in the sand?
Immerhin! Mich wird umgeben	No matter, I shall be surrounded
Gottes Himmel,[1] dort wie hier,	By God's Heaven, there as here,
Und als Totenlampen schweben	And, as funeral lamps, the stars
Nachts die Sterne über mir.	Shall float each night above me.

Romanzen und vermischte Gedichte 1; poem written ?1839
Also set by Wolfgang Rihm and Othmar Schoeck

> Es ist ein mißmüthiges Wetter, ich höre nichts als das Brausen der See – O läg ich doch begraben unter den weißen Dünen. – Ich bin in meinen Wünschen sehr mäßig geworden. Einst wünschte ich begraben zu seyn unter einer Palme des Jordans.
>
> The weather is miserable, all I hear is the roaring of the sea – Ah, if only I were lying beneath the white dunes. – My wishes have become extremely modest. One day I would like to be buried beneath a palm by the River Jordan.

Similar images are conjured up in Chapter 4 of *Ideen. Das Buch Le Grand* (1826):

> Ein Baum wird meinen Grabstein beschatten. Ich hätte gern eine Palme, aber diese gedeiht nicht im Norden. Es wird wohl eine Linde sein, und sommerabends werden dort die Liebenden sitzen und kosen.
>
> A tree will shade my tombstone. I'd like it to be a palm-tree, but palms don't flourish in northern climes. It will probably be a lime tree, and on summer evenings lovers will sit there and talk amorously.

1 Heine: Gotteshimmel.

Karl Herloßsohn
(1804–1849)

		page
Der Schwalben Heimkehr	August 1877–29 December 1877	205

POET

Karl Herloßsohn, christened Herloß, was born in Prague, where he began his law studies, which he continued in Vienna. He worked as a private tutor before moving to Leipzig in 1825 to study medicine. While there he founded *Der Komet*, a literary journal that he himself ran. By 1831 he had received his D.Phil. in Jena and was gradually beginning to publish. 'Der Schwalben Heimkehr' appeared originally in 1842 under the title 'Agathe' in *Buch der Liebe. Nebst einem Anhange. Von C. Herloßsohn*. The poem was then printed again, with minor changes, in 1848 in *Das Buch der Lieder von C. Herloßsohn*, where it is titled 'Abschied'. The poem's extraordinary popularity was partly due to Franz Abt's 1842 setting of 'Agathe', which was published in Volume 1 of Ludwig Erk's *Deutscher Liederschatz*. Thanks to this celebrity, the poem then appeared in a number of anthologies, including *Dichtergrüße. Neuere deutsche Lyrik ausgewählt von Elise Polko*, under the title 'Scheiden'. This anthology was possibly Wolf's source for the song, since it also includes seven other poems that he was to set: 'Perlenfischer' (Roquette), 'Das taube Mütterlein' (Halm), which exists only as a sketch, 'Mädchen mit dem roten Mündchen' (Heine), 'Du bist wie eine Blume' (Heine), 'Die Spinnerin' (Rückert), 'Die Stimme des Kindes' (Lenau), 'Im stillen Friedhof' (Pfau). Wolf set only the first of Herloßsohn's three verses.

LIED

Der Schwalben Heimkehr[1]

Wenn die Schwalben heimwärts zieh'n,
    Wenn die Rosen nicht mehr blüh'n,
    Wenn der Nachtigall Gesang
    Mit der Nachtigall verklang,

The swallows' homecoming

When the swallows fly homeward,
    When the roses no longer bloom,
    When the song of the nightingale
    Faded with the nightingale,

---

[1] In several later editions of Herloßsohn's poem the title was changed to 'Scheiden'.

Fragt das Herz in bangem Schmerz:	My heart enquires with anxious pain:
Ob ich euch wieder seh'?[1]	Shall I ever see you again?
Scheiden, ach Scheiden, Scheiden thut weh!	Parting, parting, ah parting causes grief.

Also set by Franz Abt and Osnat Netzer

1 Herloßsohn: Ob ich dich auch wieder seh'?

Paul Heyse
(1830–1914)

Italienisches Liederbuch
nach Paul Heyse für eine Singstimme und Klavier

Italian Songbook
after Paul Heyse for voice and piano

The titles below consist of the first line of each poem. Wolf criticised B. Schott's Söhne for the way the song titles were abbreviated in the Index of Book I of the *Italienisches Liederbuch* when it was published in Mainz in 1892 – see HW to B. Schott's Söhne, 20 December 1892, p. 226.

According to Ernst Challier, only two of the 46 poems had ever been set to music before Wolf: 'Wie lange schon' (by Hermann Goetz and Hans Huber) and 'Ein Ständchen Euch zu bringen' (by Richard Heuberger).

page

Book I

Mir ward gesagt, du reisest in die Ferne	25 September 1890	232
Ihr seid die Allerschönste weit und breit	2 October 1890	233
Gesegnet sei, durch den die Welt entstund	3 October 1890	233
Selig ihr Blinden	4 October 1890	234
Wer rief dich denn? Wer hat dich herbestellt?	13 November 1890, noon	234
Der Mond hat eine schwere Klag' erhoben	13 November 1890, afternoon	235
Nun laß uns Frieden schließen, liebstes Leben	14 November 1890	235
Daß doch gemalt all deine Reize wären	29 November 1891	236
Du denkst mit einem Fädchen mich zu fangen	2 December 1891	237
Mein Liebster ist so klein	3 December 1891	240
Und willst du deinen Liebsten sterben sehen	4 December 1891, afternoon	241
Wie lange schon war immer mein Verlangen	4 December 1891, evening	237

Geselle, woll'n wir uns in Kutten hüllen	5 December 1891	239
Nein, junger Herr, so treibt man's nicht, fürwahr	7 December 1891	238
Hoffärtig seid Ihr, schönes Kind	7/8 December 1891	238
Auch kleine Dinge können uns entzücken	9 December 1891	232
Ein Ständchen Euch zu bringen kam ich her	10 December 1891	244
Ihr jungen Leute, die ihr zieht ins Feld	11 December 1891	241
Heb' auf dein blondes Haupt und schlafe nicht	12 December 1891	242
Mein Liebster singt am Haus im Mondenscheine	12 December 1891	243
Wir haben beide lange Zeit geschwiegen	16 December 1891	242
Man sagt mir, deine Mutter woll' es nicht	23 December 1891	243

Book II

Ich esse nun mein Brot nicht trocken mehr	25 March 1896	245
Mein Liebster hat zu Tische mich geladen	26 March 1896	246
Ich ließ mir sagen und mir ward erzählt	28 March 1896	246
Schon streckt' ich aus im Bett die müden Glieder	29 March 1896	247
Du sagst mir, daß ich keine Fürstin sei	30 March 1896	247
Laß sie nur gehn, die so die Stolze spielt	30–31 March 1896	248
Wie viele Zeit verlor ich, dich zu lieben!	2 April 1896	253
Und steht Ihr früh am Morgen auf vom Bette	3–4 April 1896	251
Wohl kenn' ich Euren Stand, der nicht gering	9 April 1896	248
Wie soll ich fröhlich sein und lachen gar	12 April 1896, a.m.	249

O wär' dein Haus durchsichtig wie ein Glas	12 April 1896, p.m.	254
Sterb' ich, so hüllt in Blumen meine Glieder	13 April 1896, a.m.	250
Gesegnet sei das Grün und wer es trägt!	13 April 1896, p.m.	254
Wenn du mich mit den Augen streifst und lachst	19 April 1896	253
Was soll der Zorn, mein Schatz, der dich erhitzt?	20 April 1896	249
Benedeit die sel'ge Mutter	21 April 1896	252
Schweig' einmal still, du garst'ger Schwätzer dort!	23 April 1896, a.m.	256
Nicht länger kann ich singen	23 April 1896, p.m.	256
Wenn du, mein Liebster, steigst zum Himmel auf	24 April 1896	252
Ich hab' in Penna einen Liebsten wohnen	25 April 1896, a.m.	258
Heut Nacht erhob ich mich um Mitternacht	25 April 1896, p.m.	255
O wüßtest du, wie viel ich deinetwegen	26 April 1896	257
Verschling' der Abgrund meines Liebsten Hütte	29 April 1896	257
Was für ein Lied soll dir gesungen werden	30 April 1896	244

POET

Paul Heyse was surrounded in childhood by literature and music. His mother, Julie Solomon, was a cousin of Felix Mendelssohn's mother, and the young Paul not only frequented the homes of the Mendelssohn and Levy families but also attended the Sunday salons in Fanny Mendelssohn's *Gartensaal*, where he encountered a number of composers, including Liszt. A devotee of Brahms's music, he met the composer during his stay in Munich, and Max Kalbeck records Brahms's opinion of the poet:

> Heyse war früher – jetzt habe ich ihn lange nicht gesehen – einer der
> reizendsten Männer. Ich kann mir wohl denken, daß er von Frauen,
> die ihn näher kannten, sehr geliebt wurde. Er war schön und dazu dies

überaus liebenswürdige Talent! Ich kenne kaum einen Menschen, der eine Gesellschaft, in die er eintrat, so erleuchtete, wie er . . .[1]

Heyse used to be – it's been a long time since I saw him – one of the most charming of men. I can imagine that he was greatly loved by the women who knew him well. He was handsome and had, in addition, this exceedingly delightful talent! Almost nobody lit up a room in the way he did on making an entry . . .

This is also the impression we get from Adolph von Menzel's imposing portrait of the poet. Heyse was on friendly terms for a while with Peter Cornelius – until they disagreed about Wagner and went their separate ways. Cornelius was a passionate admirer of Wagner, whose music Heyse detested to such an extent that he had the words „Kein Bayreuth-Anhänger darf herein" ('No Bayreuth aficionado may enter here') positioned in a prominent place at his home.

As a young man of seventeen, Heyse studied classical philology at Berlin University, and it was during his stay in Berlin that he met his future wife Margarethe at a literary society in the house of her father Franz Kugler, whose poetry inspired a number of Lieder composers, especially Brahms and Loewe. Heyse took Margarethe to Italy for their honeymoon during 1852–3, and their marriage lasted until her death in 1862 following the birth of their fourth child. Five years later Heyse married the seventeen-year-old Anna Schubart. Their daughter Marianne died, aged one, in 1869, and in 1871 Heyse lost his eleven-year-old son, Ernst, on the very night that his sixth child Wilfried was born. Wilfried too died young, aged six, in 1877. Just as Eichendorff and Rückert had tried to exorcise their grief at the deaths of their own children (see pp. 21 and 450), so too Heyse wrote *Meinen Todten* (*To my dead children*) in memory of his children – a sequence of fine poems that seems to have been ignored by Lieder composers.

In 1847 Heyse joined a literary society, the Tunnel über der Spree, where he rubbed shoulders with Eichendorff and Theodor Fontane. Four years later he embarked on his first Italian journey, which inspired what was to become his most famous Novelle, *La Rabbiata*. While in Rome, he researched Romance manuscripts in the Vatican Library, was caught copying material and expelled. During his stay in Sorrento he jotted down the songs that his landlady sang at mealtimes – some of which were later to find their way into the *Italienisches Liederbuch*. On his return to Berlin he drifted for a while, until he was summoned to Munich by King Maximilian II, who granted him a generous pension. Heyse became a leading light in the Münchner Dichterkreis, a group of poets that included Friedrich von Bodenstedt, Felix Dahn, Emanuel Geibel, Martin Greif, Heinrich Leuthold, Hermann Lingg and Adolf Friedrich, Graf von Schack,

---

1 Max Kalbeck, *Johannes Brahms*, 4 vols (Hans Schneider, 1976), vol. III, p. 85.

all of whom were to inspire Lieder composers. They specialised in epic and lyric poetry, and their work was characterised by a rather conservative formal beauty and themes that were somewhat removed from the ugliness of everyday reality – not dissimilar to the poetry of the Georgian movement in England. Heyse lived in Munich for more than fifty years, contributed many articles to local newspapers and wrote more than 150 Novellen, 8 novels and more than 50 plays. Wolf did not have a high opinion of the Novellen, writing to Melanie Köchert on 6 October 1893:

> Nur an die moralischen Novellen von Heyse konnte ich meinen aparten Geschmack noch nicht gewöhnen, was auch meine Schwester Kathi dagegen einzuwenden hatte. Da ist mir der „Rothe" doch lieber, als diese fade, schale, heysische Limonade.

> My idiosyncratic taste still can't get used to Heyse's moralistic Novellen, however much my sister Kathi objects to this. I prefer red wine to Heyse's insipid, stale lemonade.

Heyse lived in the Luisenstraße in a house that became a celebrated centre of Munich's cultural life, and he was made an honorary citizen of Munich on his eightieth birthday. His voluminous correspondence includes a fascinating exchange of letters with Eduard Mörike, published by Peter Lang Verlag as *Ein Gefühl der Verwandtschaft* – see Mörike to Paul Heyse, 5 November 1861, p. 215. Mörike dedicated 'Besuch in der Kartause' to Heyse and sent the great poem to his friend on 12 December 1861 with the comment: „Epistel in Jamben aparte für Dich *pour passer le temps*, ein halb elegischer Scherz, der Hauptsache nach nicht gefabelt." ('An epistle written in iambics especially for you *pour passer le temps*, playful and elegiac, for the most part not invented.')

Although Heyse was a respected poet (*Gedichte*, 1872; *Skizzenbuch*, 1877), it was as a translator that he became best known. Rightly so. The *Italienisches Liederbuch*, published in 1860, contains his translations of over 300 anonymous Italian poems, of which 135 are *rispetti*. In the Foreword, addressed to his friend Jacob Burckhardt, Heyse reminisces about the evenings they spent together at the home of Franz Kugler in the latter's house in Berlin's Friedrichstraße, where they would sing and play folk songs, as Heyse describes in his poem 'An Emanuel Geibel'. Kugler was not the only influence on the young Heyse. Almost as important, he goes on to say, were the folk songs he read in Wilhelm Müller's *Egeria* (1829) and August Kopisch's *Agrumi* (1838) and, of course, the anthologies of Italian folk songs that had appeared earlier in the nineteenth century – Heyse's source for his *Italienisches Liederbuch*: Niccolò Tommaseo's *Canti popolari Toscani Corsi Illirici Greci* (1841), Angelo Dalmedico's *Canti del popolo Veneziano* (1848), Oreste Marcoaldi's *Canti popolari inediti umbri liguri piceni piemontesi latini* (1855) and Giuseppe Tigri's *Canti popolari Toscani* (1856). The 46 poems that inspired Wolf's *Italienisches Liederbuch* and the 27 that Heyse contributed to the *Spanisches Liederbuch* are more than merely elegant translations of the mostly anonymous originals; they tend to be richer in hyperbole and alliteration, and many manage to be witty and moving in equal measure. Translations such as 'Gesegnet sei, durch den die Welt entstund' deserve a place in any anthology of German poetry. Heyse was raised to the nobility in 1910, the year in which he was awarded the Nobel Prize for Literature. His own poetry has been set by, among others, Brahms, Bruch, Cornelius, Jensen, Marx, Schoenberg, Schreker, Schumann and Zemlinsky.

Heyse's *Zwölf Dichterprofile* contains short poems on many of the poets who feature in *The Complete Songs of Hugo Wolf*: 'Friedrich Hölderlin', 'Joseph v. Eichendorff', 'Friedrich Rückert', 'Nicolaus Lenau', 'Adalbert v. Chamisso', 'Eduard Mörike', 'Emanuel Geibel', 'Gottfried Keller', 'Theodor Storm' and 'Hermann Lingg'. He also wrote poems on Hermann Allmers, Franz Kugler and Joseph Victor von Scheffel.

COMPOSER

As was the case with all Wolf's mature songbooks, the *Italienisches Liederbuch* was composed in feverish bouts. „Ich spüre verdächtige Anzeichen zur Composition in mir und erwarte ich jeden Moment eine Explosion," ('Suspicious signs of creativity are stirring within me, and I expect an imminent explosion,') we read in a letter to Gustav Schur, dated 24 September 1890 (p. 215). He was right. Two days later the first of the songs was penned – 'Mir ward gesagt, du reisest in die Ferne' (HW to Gustav Schur, 27 September 1890, p. 216). Three more followed in early October and then three in November. A year of creative paralysis ensued, and the letters of this period, like this one to Emil Kauffmann of 1 June 1891, speak of gloom and self-disgust: „Ich bin am Ende. Möge es bald ein vollständiges sein – ich wünschte nichts sehnlicher." ('I've reached the end – may it come soon and completely. That is my most fervent wish.') Despite a visit to Bayreuth and the support of friends, despair and melancholy were beginning to crush him. „Mit dem Komponieren ist es rein aus. Ich glaube, daß ich wohl nie mehr eine Note aufschreiben werde," ('I have finished composing. I think I shall probably never write another note,') he wrote to Grohe on 12 June. This time he was wrong. Inspiration suddenly returned with the composition on 29 November 1891 of 'Daß doch gemalt all deine Reize wären'; in the course of the next month, fourteen further songs were composed. All of them (the 22 songs of what is now known as Book I) were sold for a fee of 1000 marks to Schott's, who published them in 1892. Wolf suffered at this time from fevers, headaches and sore throats (common symptoms of secondary syphilis), and from 1892 to 1894 he composed hardly a note of original music. There was a recovery, however, in 1895 when he worked feverishly at his new opera, *Der Corregidor*, which was premiered the following year. And on 25 March 1896 he resumed the *Italienisches Liederbuch*, composing the remaining 24 songs in a spate of inspiration in little more than a month.

Wolf ignored the ballads, ritornelle and death laments of Heyse's collection, and concentrated almost exclusively on the *rispetti* – short love poems, usually of eight or ten lines, that depict a wide variety of emotions. Giuseppe Tigri, in the Introduction to his *Canti popolari Toscani*, defines *rispetti* as 'rispettosi saluti che si facciono fra di loro gli innamorati' – 'respectful greetings that lovers exchange with one another'. These greetings, however, are not always 'respectful': the love poems set by Wolf chart, against a Tuscan landscape of Orvieto, Siena and the Arno, the everyday squabbles, tiffs, jealousies, flirtations, machinations, frivolities, joys and despairs of men and women in love. Like much demotic verse (*Des Knaben Wunderhorn*, for example), the language is simple and the lines frequently end-stopped. If Heyse's translations often intensify the simple, unemotional Italian of the original poems, Wolf's settings, particularly of the more serious poems, represent a further heightening of emotion. Miniatures they may be, but many of these songs strike unforgettably at the heart. The punchline of several *rispetti* are transformed by Wolf into moments of unforgettable poignancy – like the final line of 'Gesegnet sei, durch den die Welt entstund'. We expect the *crescendo* enumeration of God's creations to climax in the final line; instead, there is hushed adoration at 'Schönheit und dein Angesicht', as the singer is struck almost dumb with awe at the image of his beloved's face. Similar magic is wrought in 'Der Mond hat eine schwere Klag' erhoben' at 'die beiden Augen dort': through a shift in tonality, the pithy point of the poem receives an emotional charge quite absent from the original poem and its translation. Time and again Wolf deepens the translations. The downward leap of a sixth at the close of 'Wer rief dich denn?' betrays an underlying commotion that is foreign to the angry tone of the poem. And there is new tenderness in many other of Wolf's settings, such as 'Wir haben beide lange Zeit geschwiegen' and 'Nun laß uns Frieden schließen'.

This last song, when the *Italienisches Liederbuch* is given complete, usually occasions a wrangle between the singers as acrimonious as the quarrelling in the songs. Sopranos usually lay claim to it, since most of the serious songs in the collection are given to men – not because of Wolf's own bias, but because it is in the nature of *rispetti* to let men speak of adoration; the women's songs flame more with mockery, scorn, rage and jealousy. The soprano, however, has the best comic songs, which are among the finest in the entire Lieder repertoire. We are introduced to an unforgettable array of oddities in songs that are alternately irrepressibly abandoned ('Ich hab' in Penna'), teasing ('Mein Liebster ist so klein') or affectionate ('Mein Liebster hat zu Tische'). 'Not without humour' is Wolf's indication to his interpreters in 'Wie lange schon' – and there can hardly be a more comic postlude, which ends with the wretched violinist's laborious trill.

The *Italienisches Liederbuch* is unlike any of Wolf's other collections. The opening song – the sixteenth in order of composition – states that 'even small things can delight us', and Wolf presumably opened his final songbook with 'Auch kleine Dinge' to indicate the miniature form of these songs. Of 46, only six are three pages long, the majority occupying a mere two pages, while two songs ('Heut' Nacht erhob ich mich' and 'Nicht länger kann ich singen') fill a single page. The volume contains no grand-scale songs like Goethe's 'Prometheus' or Mörike's 'Der Feuerreiter'; there are no passionate songs like 'Mignon' ('Kennst du das Land'), no religious fervour, as in the *Spanisches Liederbuch*, no introspection to match the Harper's songs. Yet there is an *Innigkeit*, an emotional immediacy, about them and an understanding of the human heart that is in no way diminished by the miniature form. Or as Wolf put it in a letter to Kauffmann of 23 December 1892:

> Und ein warmes Herz, deß kann ich mich verbürgen, pocht in diesen kleinen Leibern meiner jüngsten Kinder des Südens, die trotz allem ihre deutsche Herkunft nicht verleugnen können. Ja, das Herz schlägt ihnen deutsch, wenn auch die Sonne auf „italienisch" [. . .] dazu scheint.

> And a warm heart, I can assure, beats in the little bodies of my youngest children from the South, who, in spite of everything, cannot deny their German origin. Yes, their heart beats in German, even if the sun shines in 'Italian'.

Because Wolf never heard a complete performance of his *Italienisches Liederbuch*, no established performing tradition developed during his lifetime. In the years since his death, there have been several ways of presenting this great work. Paul Müller, writing in 1926, criticises complete performances of the *Italienisches Liederbuch*:

> Man hat sogar mehrfach den Versuch gemacht, das ganze „Italienische Liederbuch" in Form von Wechselgesängen an einem Abend vorzutragen. Diesen Versuch halte ich für durchaus verfehlt.

> Several attempts have even been made to perform the whole of the *Italienisches Liederbuch* on one evening, with two singers alternating with one another. I regard this to be most ill-considered.

Complete performances of the work are, however, now the norm. Singers and pianists often concoct an entertaining order of their own, shuffling the songs in a dramatic way, so that lover replies to sweetheart and vice versa – often semi-staged. Or the songs are grouped according to literary provenance: the poems from Tommaseo's *Canti popolari*, Tigri's *Canti popolari Toscani*, Marcoaldi's *Canti popolari inediti* and Dalmedico's *Canti del popolo Veneziano* being performed separately. Another possibility is to perform the songs in their order of composition – which means starting not with 'Auch kleine Dinge' (9 December 1891) but with 'Mir ward gesagt, du reisest in die Ferne' (25 September 1890). But perhaps the best way is to perform the songs in the order that Wolf himself chose in the two volumes published during his lifetime: Book I in 1892 and Book II in 1896. The advantages are twofold: it creates a natural interval (crucial in a recital of 46 songs); and it allows us to see the stylistic differences, particularly in the piano writing, between the two books. Wolf told a friend, Edwin Mayser, that the second part of the *Italienisches Liederbuch* contained far more 'absolute music' than the first part, and that the accompaniments to many of the songs in Book II could be just as well played by a string quartet. The implication is that the accompaniments in Book I strive to depict the character of each poem through musical detail, whereas those in Book II are more concerned with providing the songs with a complex polyphonic texture.

Another composer drawn to Heyse's *Italienisches Liederbuch* was Joseph Marx (1882–1964) who in 1912 selected 17 poems that had not been set by Wolf. Ermanno Wolf-Ferrari (1876–1948) also composed two sets of *4 Rispetti* (Opp. 11 and 12) and an *Italienisches Liederbuch*, Op. 17, a collection of 44 songs, composed to the original Italian texts and provided with a German translation by Franz Rau. And one of the finest of all settings is 'Am Sonntag Morgen' by Johannes Brahms. For all Wolf's detestation of that composer (see APPENDIX 1), it is possible that he knew and admired 'Am Sonntag Morgen', and for that reason declined to set it himself.

LETTERS

Eduard Mörike to Paul Heyse, 5 November 1861

Ich habe kürzlich Deine, mit wunderbarer Kunst reprodicirten, ital. Volkslieder kennen gelernt.

I have recently got to know your most artistically fashioned Italian folk songs.

HW to Gustav Schur, Unterach, 24 September 1890

Ich spüre verdächtige Anzeichen zur Composition in mir und erwarte ich jeden Moment eine Explosion. Die wundervolle Ruhe u. gänzliche Abgeschlossenheit hier berauschen mich förmlich.

Suspicious signs of creativity are stirring within me, and I expect an imminent explosion. The wonderful stillness here & the utter seclusion are absolutely enchanting.

HW to Gustav Schur, Unterach, 27 September 1890

Inzwischen habe ich aus dem italienischen Liederbuch eines u. den Schluß eines andern componirt. Du wirst über das eine entzückt sein u., so weit ich mir über das andere klar bin, ebenfalls grunzen. Das erste beginnt mit den anzüglichen Worten: „Mir ward gesagt, Du reisest in die Ferne."

Meanwhile I've finished *one* of the *Italian Songbook* songs and composed the end of another. You will be delighted at the former & chuckle likewise at the latter if my judgement can be trusted. The first begins with these suggestive words: 'Mir ward gesagt, Du reisest in die Ferne.'

HW to Gustav Schur, Rinnbach, 5 October 1890

Das Wetter hat sich wieder aufgeklärt u. da ich jetzt im Zuge bin (4 italienische, darunter ein „Schlager" sind vorhanden)[1] gedenke ich auf ein paar Tage nach Unterach zurückzugehen.

The weather has cleared up & now that things are going well (4 Italians including a real 'corker' have been completed), I plan to return to Unterach for a few days.

HW to Melanie Köchert, Döbling, 13 November 1890

Heute in den Mittags u. Nachmittagsstunden kam ich auf die gute Idee mir zwei „italienische" einfallen zu lassen „wer rief dich denn?" u. „der Mond hat eine schwere Klag' erhoben". Wenn's so weiter geht kann ich bis zum Samstag vielleicht mit einem halben Dutzend aufwarten. Die Einsamkeit u. der Mangel an menschlicher Gesellschaft frischt mich wieder auf. Ich bin voller Freuden u. äußerst guter Dinge.

Today I had the bright idea around lunchtime & in the afternoon of composing two Italians: 'Wer rief dich denn?' & 'Der Mond hat eine schwere Klag' erhoben'. If I continue at this pace, I might be capable of serving up half a dozen by Saturday. The solitude & lack of human company has refreshed me. I'm full of joy & in excellent spirits.

[1] 'Mir ward gesagt, du reisest in die Ferne', 'Ihr seid die Allerschönste', 'Gesegnet sei, durch den die Welt entstund', 'Selig ihr Blinden'. The 'corker' probably refers to the wonderful 'Gesegnet sei, durch den die Welt entstund'. Wolf was a guest of the Köchert family in Rinnbach.

HW to Oskar Grohe, Döbling, 14 November 1890

Seit drei Tagen wohne ich wieder in Döbling, Hirschengasse 68,[1] wo ich wahrscheinlich auch überwintern dürfte. Des beschränkten Raumes wegen muß ich mich mit einem Pianino, einem der elendsten Möbel, die je ein Geräusch von sich gegeben, behelfen. Trotz alledem und obschon mich dieses verfluchte Instrument keineswegs anlockt, mich in eine musikalische Stimmung zu versetzen, komponierte ich gestern[2] zwei italienische und heute[3] eines. Ich bin sehr gespannt, wie lange diese Laune anhalten wird. Es wäre mir sehr angenehm, könnt ich jetzt so fort werkeln, da ich den Zyklus der italienischen gern vor Weihnachten noch beendet sähe.

For three days now I've been living in Döbling, Hirschengasse 68, where I shall probably also spend the winter. Because of the confined space, I'm having to make do with a small upright piano, one of the most wretched items of furniture from which sound ever issued. Despite all this and although I find this damned instrument utterly unalluring and incapable of putting me into a musical frame of mind, I composed two Italians yesterday and one today. I'm curious to see how long this mood lasts. It would be wonderful if I could keep going like this, because I'd like to see the Italian cycle finished before Christmas.

HW to Oskar Grohe, Döbling, 30 December 1890

Überhaupt ist meine Stimmung seit einiger Zeit ein sehr verdüstertes Moll. Die verfluchte Ballade will mir nun einmal nicht einfallen und die Ouvertüre kann infolgedessen nicht geschrieben werden. Ich fürchte, dieses Werk[4] wird ein Torso bleiben. Aber auch mit den „Italienischen" will's nicht gehen. Es will überhaupt gar nichts gehen. 's ist eine Hundeexistenz, wenn man nicht arbeiten kann. Wenn ich auf gute Manier abkratzen könnte, wär's mir eben recht. Möge sich die Hölle meiner erbarmen. – Wie recht hat Kleist, wenn er sagt: „Der Himmel gibt einem ein ganzes oder gar kein Talent; die Hölle hat mir meine halben gegeben."[5] Und ich fühl's, ich bin auch so ein Höllensohn, und also gehöre ich dorthin, von woher ich kam.

My mood has for some time now been very minor key and dark. I'm getting no inspiration for the wretched ballad and the overture can therefore not be

---

1 Now Billrothstraße, one of the many homes of Heinrich Köchert where Wolf was a frequent guest.
2 'Wer rief dich denn?' and 'Der Mond hat eine schwere Klag' erhoben'.
3 'Nun laß uns Frieden schließen'.
4 *Das Fest auf Solhaug*.
5 Wolf misquotes. On 5 October 1803 Kleist wrote from Geneva to his sister Ulrike: „Die Hölle gab mir meine halben Talente, der Himmel schenkt dem Menschen ein ganzes oder gar keins." ('Hell has given me half a talent, Heaven gives us either true talent or none at all.')

written. I fear that this work will remain a torso. And it's the same with the 'Italians'. I'm making no progress with anything. It's a dog's life when you can't work. If I could now politely snuff it, I'd be happy. May Hell take pity on me. How right Kleist was when he said, 'Heaven gives you either great talent or none at all; Hell has given me half a talent.' I'm well aware that I'm a son of Hell – that's where I belong and where I came from.

HW to Detlev von Liliencron, Ebensee, 1 August 1891

Mein lebhaftester Wunsch ist es noch in dieser Saison einen Cyklus italienischer Lieder, übersetzt von P. Heyse, zu veröffentlichen. Wenn es dennoch nicht dazu kommen sollte läge die Schuld einzig u. allein nur an mir, der ich leider seit langem schon nicht mehr die Musse finde diesen Cyklus zu beenden, wie ich denn überhaupt seit begonnenem Frühjahr keine Note mehr geschrieben.

My most fervent wish is to publish during this season a cycle of Italian songs, translated by P. Heyse. If it proves impossible the fault will be entirely mine, for it's been an age since I've found the leisure to finish this cycle, just as I've been unable to write a single note since early spring.

HW to Emil Kauffmann, Traunkirchen, 12 October 1891

Ich fange nachgerade an überzeugt zu werden, daß ich zu jenem unglückseligen Schlag von Menschen gehöre, die viel versprechen u. wenig halten, u. ich müßte es sehr um Ihretwillen herzlichst bedauern, wenn sich diese meine innerste Überzeugung über lang od. kurz bewahrheiten sollte. Die Oper u. immer wieder die Oper! Wahrlich, mir graut schon vor meinen Liedern. Die schmeichelhafte Anerkennung als „Liederkomponist" betrübt mich in die innerste Seele.[1] Was anders will es denn bedeuten, als eben einen Vorwurf, daß ich immer nur Lieder componire, daß ich doch nur ein kleines genre beherrsche u. dieses nicht einmal vollkommen, da sich in ihm ja nur Ansätze zum dramatischen Schaffen vorfänden. Also wäre ich nicht einmal ein ordentlicher Lyriker!

I'm beginning to be convinced that I am one of those wretched types who promise much & achieve little, & I would sincerely regret it, for your sake, if this my innermost conviction should sooner or later prove true. Opera & always opera! Truly, I have come to dread my songs. The flattering recognition I've gained as a 'song composer' makes me sick at heart. What else does it mean, other than a reproach that I only ever write songs, that I am only master of a

---

[1] See note 1 to HW to B. Schott's Söhne, 7 June 1892, p. 222.

small genre, & do not even have complete mastery of that, since my songs only reveal the <u>rudiments</u> of a dramatic talent. So I am not even a decent songwriter!

HW to Melanie Köchert, Döbling, 2 December 1891

Ich glaube, verehrteste gnädige Frau, dieses schöne Briefpapier in keiner bessern Art einweihen zu können, als durch die wunderbare Mittheilung, daß mir zwei italienische Lieder gelungen sind.[1] „Ein süßer Schrecken geht durch mein Gebein".[2] Ich bin wie im Elysium. – 33 ist die Zahl! Will's Gott, schreib' ich heute noch ein drittes. Wer hätte so was gedacht!

I can think of no better way, dearest lady, of consecrating this beautiful writing paper than by giving you the wonderful news that I have successfully completed two Italian songs. 'A sweet tremor pervades my frame!' It's as though I'm in Elysium. – 33 of them! God willing, I shall compose a third one today. Who would have thought it!

HW to Emil Kauffmann, Döbling, 15 December 1891

Seit den ersten Tagen des Dezembers fing mein geistiges Uhrwerk plötzlich an lustig zu ticken, u. Sie können sich nun, bei dieser Wahrnehmung, meinen freudigen Schrecken vorstellen. In dieser kurzen Zeit hatte ich bis vor zwei Tagen 13 Lieder aus dem italienischen Liederbuch geschrieben u. mir freventlich vorgenommen bei dem 33. erst anzuhalten. Nun folgt schon die Strafe für meine gottlose Vermessenheit, indem ich seit zwei Tagen vergeblich auf Einfälle warte. Gott, und ich wäre so glücklich, könnte ich noch im Dezember den Band zu Ende führen. Aber mit Gewalt läßt sich dabei nun einmal nichts erreichen u. ich bin – wie immer – aufs Abwarten angewiesen. Wenns nur nicht zu lange dauert! Die Lieder aber sind, eines wie das andere, auf's beste gelungen. Es ist wieder eine ganz andere Welt u. Sie werden nicht wenig erstaunen über meine Proteusnatur, die sich nun einmal in jede Haut hineinfinden kann. Ich halte die Italienischen für das originellste u. künstlerisch vollendetste unter allen meinen Sachen. Sie werden sicherlich Ihre helle Freude daran haben.

From the first days of December my brain suddenly began to tick away merrily, & you can well imagine the joy and shock this has caused me. In this short period of time up until two days ago, I composed 13 songs from the *Italian Songbook*, & I have outrageously resolved not to stop until there are 33. I am now punished for my wicked audacity, since for two days now I've been waiting in vain for inspiration. God! And I would be so happy if I could finish the

---

1 'Du denkst mit einem Fädchen mich zu fangen' and 'Mein Liebster ist so klein'.
2 Wolf quotes from Mörike's 'Neue Liebe'.

volume in December. But nothing can be achieved by forcing matters, & I shall as usual just have to wait. If only it's not too long! The songs, each one of them, are wonderful. They inhabit a completely different world & you will not be a little astonished at my Protean nature that can respond to every new stimulus. I consider my Italians to be the most original and artistically consummate of all my compositions. You will certainly be delighted.

HW to his mother, Döbling, 17 December 1891

Bis vor 4 Tagen ging Alles herrlich. In den ersten zwei Wochen dieses Monates habe ich 14 Lieder componirt u. hoffte bis zum Ende des Dezember noch einmal so viele zu schreiben. Ich fühlte mich jedoch schon seit einigen Tagen sehr unpass u. gestern ist nun eine recht tüchtige Influenza zum Ausbruch gekommen. Trotz der schrecklichsten Halsschmerzen trotz Fieber u. Kopfweh u. eines wüthenden Schnupfens kann ich es nicht über mich bringen, das Bett zu hüten. Hoffentlich werden bis morgen die Fiebererscheinungen verschwunden sein. Das Schlimmste aber ist, daß ich nun wenig Hoffnung habe noch in diesem Monat das italienische Liederbuch zu beendigen. Mein elender Zustand raubt mir alle Lust zum arbeiten u. doch finde ich einzig und allein nur in meinem Arbeiten die richtige Erholung für mein geistiges wie physisches Dasein. Gott schenke mir bald wieder volle Gesundheit, auf daß ich wieder meinen Pflichten obliegen kann.

Until 4 days ago all was going wonderfully well. In the first two weeks of this month I wrote 14 songs & hoped by the end of December to have composed as many again. But for some days now I have been feeling very unwell, & yesterday I developed a terrible influenza. Despite the most terrible sore throats, despite fever & headaches & a raging cold, I cannot bring myself to stay in bed. I hope that by tomorrow all signs of fever will have disappeared. The worst thing is that I now have little hope of finishing the *Italian Songbook* this month. My wretched condition deprives me of all desire to work, & yet it is only through work that I can restore myself mentally and physically. May God soon give me back my full health so that I can once again fulfil my duties.

HW to his mother, Döbling, 29 December 1891

Das Christkindl hat mich mit mancherlei bedacht. Aus nah u. fern sind Überraschungen eingetroffen. Das schönste Christkindl hab' ich mir aber durch meine neuen Lieder gemacht, die ich für das allerbeste ansehe, was ich bisher geschrieben.

Father Christmas has showered me with gifts: surprises from far & near! But I've given myself the loveliest Christmas present in the shape of my new songs which I consider to be the finest I have ever composed.

HW to Emil Kauffmann, Döbling, 2 April 1892

Mein italienisches Liederbuch ist leider noch nicht abgeschlossen. Es fehlen noch 11, da ich mirs in den Kopf gesetzt 33 Italienische zu veröffentlichen. Tagtäglich harre ich der günstigen Stimmung, aber immer vergeblich. Ich bin schon ganz wild u. verzweifelt darüber.

My *Italian Songbook* is unfortunately still not completed. There are still 11 to be composed, as I got it into my head to publish 33. Every day I wait for inspiration, but always in vain. It makes me utterly wild & desperate.

HW to B. Schott's Söhne, Döbling, 20 April 1892

Vor längerer Zeit schon hatte ich Ihnen einen Band italienischer Lieder offerirt, welche Offerte bislang mit Stillschweigen beantwortet wurde.[1] Es liegt mir daran, daß diese Sammlung Lieder (33 an der Zahl)[2] zu Weihnachten im Handel erscheine u. frage ich mich deshalb noch einmal an, ob Sie darauf reflectiren wollen, in welchem Falle mit dem Stich der Platten nicht allzu lange gezögert werden möge.

Quite some time ago I offered you a volume of Italian songs – and have since heard nothing. It is important to me that this collection of songs (33 in all) should be on sale at Christmas, & therefore I would ask you again to consider the matter, so that the engraving of the plates might not be delayed too long.

HW to B. Schott's Söhne, Döbling, 10 May 1892

Geehrtester Herr Doctor!
    Mit heutigem geht sogleich die Sendung des allerdings noch nicht completen italienischen Liederbuches an Ihre werthe Adresse ab. Die noch fehlenden (ungefähr ein Dutzend) sollen baldigst nachfolgen. [. . .]

1   Dr Strecker of B. Schott's Söhne replied on 27 April:

> Wegen der italienischen Lieder haben Sie mich fälschlich in Verdacht, dass ich bislang darüber geschwiegen hätte. Sie schrieben vor einiger Zeit, dass Sie im Begriffe stünden diese Lieder zu vollenden. Sonst Nichts. Da sie nun fertig sind, bitte ich Sie dieselben nach Mainz zu schicken.

> You accuse me wrongly of not having replied to you about the Italian songs. Some time ago you wrote that you were in the process of finishing these songs. That was all. Now that they are finished, please send them to me in Mainz.

2   Only 22 had at this point been composed.

Wie Sie nach flüchtiger Durchsicht schon bemerken werden, ist die Begleitung fast durchweg höchst einfach gehalten, wie denn auch an die Singstimme so viel wie gar keine Anforderungen gestellt werden. Zudem sind die Gedichte dießmal durchgehend erotischen Inhaltes, mithin allgemein verständlich u. zugänglich. Übersetzt hat dieselben Paul Heyse.

Most respected Herr Doktor!

I am posting you today the songs of my *Italian Songbook*, even though the collection is still not finished. The still outstanding songs (about a dozen) will follow as soon as possible. [. . .]

A fleeting glance at the music will tell you that the accompaniments have been kept extremely simple, just as very few demands have been made of the voice. In addition, the poems this time are in general of an erotic nature, and therefore intelligible & accessible. They were translated by Paul Heyse.

Dr Strecker of B. Schott's Söhne to HW, 18 May 1892

Mit diesen Zeilen bezwecke ich hauptsächlich Ihnen den Empfang Ihres Briefes v. 10. & der italienischen Lieder anzuzeigen. Ich habe sie mir sogleich spielen lassen & kann Ihnen sagen, dass sie mir viel besser gefallen wie die Mehrzahl der spanischen.

The purpose of this letter is to confirm receipt of your letter of the 10th & the Italian songs. I had them performed immediately, & I can say to you that I like them much better than most of the Spanish songs.

HW to B. Schott's Söhne, Döbling, 7 June 1892

Ihre Vorschläge in punkto der Reihenfolge der Italienischen sollen nach Möglichkeit berücksichtigt werden.[1] Das praktische derselben liegt zu sehr auf der Hand, um nur irgend einen Grund dagegen geltend zu machen. Dennoch kann ich mich zu einer definitiven Angabe der Reihenfolge in Ihrem Sinne zur Stunde noch nicht entschließen, da die Einreihung der noch folgenden Lieder auch zu berücksichtigen sein wird.

Your suggestions concerning the order of the Italian songs should, where possible, be adhered to. It's quite clearly the most practical solution, and there is no reason to argue against it. And yet I cannot at this point decide on a definitive order, as we have to bear in mind where the next songs will be fitted in.

1   Dr Strecker had suggested in a letter of 4 June that all the songs of three pages should be grouped at the end of the volume. At the end of the same letter he advised Wolf to take a break from Lieder and concentrate instead on more substantial compositions: „Ueberhaupt möchte ich rathen, dass Sie jetzt eine Pause im Lied-Componiren eintreten lassen & etwas Grösseres produciren." ('And anyway, I would advise you to stop writing songs for a while and concentrate instead on larger forms.')

HW to Jeanette Grohe, Traunkirchen, 20 July 1892

Dieser Tage wurden mir auch schon Correcturen von den Italienischen zugeschickt. Leider bin ich noch immer nicht so weit, die Sammlung als abgeschloßen betrachten zu können, obschon es mein sehnlichster Wunsch ist, alles Italienische (wozu auch die unvollendete Serenade gehört) mir für immer vom Halse zu schaffen, um ganz nur meinen spanischen Operngelüsten zu fröhnen.

I've recently also been sent the proofs of the Italian songs. Unfortunately I'm not yet in a position to consider the volume finished – although it's my most fervent wish to dispose of everything Italian (including the unfinished *Serenade*) so that I can indulge my Spanish opera cravings.

HW to Oskar Grohe, Traunkirchen, 10 August 1892

Die Herausgabe der Italienischen muß auf unbestimmte Zeit verschoben werden, da ich noch immer mit einem bedeutenden Rest im Rückstande bin. Bei dem herrlichen sonnigen Wetter u. der köstlichen Ruhe, die mich hier umgiebt, hätte ich Musse genug die Sammlung zu beschließen, wenn es bei dem allein sein Bewenden haben könnte. Damit ist aber noch wenig gethan. Um nur einigermassen in irgend einem Contact zur Musik zu bleiben mache ich zeitweilig Fingerübungen auf dem Piano, wobei ich dann die erstaunliche Entdeckung mache, daß meine Sinne auf Klang u. Ton noch reagiren u. sogar eine Dissonanz von einer Consonanz unterscheiden mögen. Somit ist nicht alle Hoffnung verloren meine Componistenlaufbahn als ein zweiter Diabelli od. Czerny dereinst zu beschließen. Gratuliren Sie mir doch dazu.

Publication of the Italian songs must be postponed for an indefinite period, as I'm still behind with finishing all the rest. Given the sunny weather & the delicious peace that surrounds me, I have leisure enough to be able to finish the collection – if only it were as simple as that. But I have yet to accomplish much. In order to stay to some degree in touch with music, I occasionally practise finger exercises on the piano, and in so doing have made the astonishing discovery that I am still able to react to sounds & timbre & can even distinguish a dissonance from a consonance. There is still some hope therefore that I shall finish my composer's career as a latterday Diabelli or Czerny. You should congratulate me.

HW to Siegfried Ochs, Döbling, 16 October 1892

Wenn es mir gelingen sollte Schott zum Ankauf meiner neuesten Liedersammlung, der Italienischen, zu bewegen, beabsichtige ich ganz nach Berlin zu übersiedeln u. z. noch in diesem Winter. Glauben Sie, daß es mir dort an Klavierlectionen od. Accompagnements mangeln könnte? Wenn, dann wär' es allerdings schlimm, da ich zu meinem Lebensunterhalte darauf angewiesen wäre. Würden Sie wohl auch darüber ein Wort an mich fallen lassen?

If I manage to persuade Schott's to purchase my latest collection of songs, the Italians, I intend to move once and for all to Berlin, as early as this winter. Do you think that there might be a lack of opportunity for me to give piano lessons or to accompany? It would be serious if that were so, because I still depend on giving lessons for my livelihood. Could you drop me a line about it?

HW to B. Schott's Söhne, Döbling, 18 October 1892

Ich glaube diese Zeilen am schicklichsten einzuleiten mit den Versen meines letzten der italienischen Lieder: „Wir haben Beide lange Zeit geschwiegen. Auf einmal kam uns nun die Sprache wieder." Eine künstlerische Nöthigung ist es nun freilich nicht, die mir für dießmal die Zunge löst, vielmehr beabsichtige ich ganz gemeine, prosaische, aber, wie ich hoffe, nützliche Dinge, sowohl für Sie als auch für mich, in Vorschlag zu bringen. Wir werden mithin vom Geschäfte reden. [. . .][1]

Nun denn, ich bin entschloßen, so weit es in meinen Kräften steht, für meine Sache, die ja auch die Ihre ist, in Berlin zu wirken, vorausgesetzt, daß Sie mir, geehrtester Doctor, dabei behülflich sein wollen. Zu diesem Behufe biete ich Ihnen das italienische Liederbuch zum Kaufe an, da ich sonst keine Möglichkeit ersehe, mir die zu meinem Unternehmen nöthigen Geldmittel zu verschaffen. Wenn Sie, wie ich zuversichtlich hoffe, dieses mein Ansinnen freundlich acceptiren, erwarte ich dießbezüglich Ihre weiteren Vorschläge. Noch habe ich zu bemerken, daß die Sammlung der Italienischen doch um weitere zehn Lieder bereichert werden dürfte, falls sich noch rechtzeitig die günstige Stimmung dafür einstellt. Wie viel Zeit bleibt mir überlassen, wenn die complete Sammlung 14 Tage vor Weihnacht erscheinen soll?

I think it would be most appropriate to begin this letter with a quote from the most recent of my Italian songs: 'For a long time we have both been silent. Now all at once speech has returned.' It is not for any artistic need that I break the silence; instead, I intend to broach several quite ordinary, prosaic but, also I hope, useful matters – both for you and me. We shall therefore talk business. [. . .]

---

1 Dr Strecker replied from Paris on 21 October, advising Wolf – if he wished the *Italienisches Liederbuch* to appear before Christmas – to refrain from adding any further songs. He ended the letter by suggesting Goethe's *Hermann und Dorothea* as a possible subject for an opera. Dr Strecker wrote again on 12 November, offering Wolf 1000 marks with exclusive rights for Book I of the *Italienisches Liederbuch*.

Well then – I am resolved, as far as it is in my power to do so, to transfer my activities to Berlin, providing you, respected sir, will help me. For this purpose, I am giving you the opportunity of purchasing the *Italian Songbook*, as I see no other way of raising the necessary money for my undertaking. If you will be kind enough – as I confidently hope you shall be – to accept my request, I await your further proposals. I should tell you that the collection will be increased by another ten songs, if inspiration should return in time. How long could you give me to do this, for the complete songbook to appear 14 days before Christmas?

HW to Emil Kauffmann, Döbling, 22 November 1892

Die Italienischen, die so weit sie fertig wurden, als I. Band eines ital. Liederbuches demnächst erscheinen werden, sollen dießmal Ihren Weihnachtsbaum schmücken. Ich habe die Sammlung an Schott um 1000 Mk. verkauft, um auf solche Weise sein Interesse an dem Vertrieb meiner Sachen zu erhöhen. Hoffentlich wird sich dieses Opfer seinerzeit in anderweitiger Weise verzinsen u. es wird ermöglichen höhere Preise zu stellen.

The Italian songs which will appear, as they stand, as Book I of an *Italian Songbook*, shall this year decorate your Christmas tree. I have sold the collection to Schott's for 1000 marks in order to encourage him to sell my works. I hope this sacrifice will one day pay dividends in other ways & enable me to set higher prices.

HW to Käthe Wolf, Ober-Döbling, 7 December 1892

Van Dyck[1] ist heutzutage der berühmteste Tenor u. wenn der einmal meine Sachen singen wird, dann solls aus einer andern Tonart gehen. Hoffentlich ist diese Zeit schon vor der Thüre. Ein neuer Band Lieder wird zu Weihnachten erscheinen. Der 1. Band der „Italienischen". Schott hat mir denselben abgekauft u. z. um die Bagatelle von 1000 Mark. Ich bin somit, wie Du Dir denken kannst, für den Moment bei Casse. Da ich von diesem Gelde Schulden in der Höhe von 200 fl. berichtigt bleibt mir noch ein Rest von 660 Mk. od. ungefähr 400 fl.

---

1   Ernest van Dyck (1861–1923), Flemish tenor engaged at the Wiener Hofoper. One of the most celebrated Wagner tenors of his day, he sang the roles of Lohengrin and Parsifal at Bayreuth. He appeared regularly at Covent Garden from 1891 and was more at home in the French repertoire than the German, creating the title role in Massenet's *Werther* (1892). He was also a friend of Emmanuel Chabrier, who dedicated the operatic 'Toutes les fleurs' to the *Heldentenor*. Wolf rehearsed him for the role of Siegmund in *Die Walküre*, for which the Vienna Hofoper paid him 200 florins. Wolf soon realised that his own initial euphoria had been misplaced: in a letter to Kauffmann of 10 March 1893 he states that Van Dyck was interested only in well-paid operatic roles.

Dieses Geld benöthige ich einstweilen gar nicht u. ich beabsichtige sogar es in eine Sparkasse anzulegen. <u>Nun höre!</u> Sollte die gute, arme Mutter irgendwie in Verlegenheit kommen u. nicht mehr als 400 fl. benöthigen, so wird sie jetzt wissen, wo sie das Geld <u>augenblicklich</u> haben kann.

Van Dyck is today's most famous tenor, & should *he* sing my songs, things will be different! I hope this day is imminent. A new volume of songs will appear at Christmas. Schott's have bought Book I of the 'Italians', for a mere pittance: 1000 marks. I'm therefore, as you can well imagine, in funds. Though I have to pay debts of 200 florins from this amount, I still have 660 marks or some 400 florins. I don't at present have any need of this money, & I even intend to put it in a savings bank. <u>Now listen!</u> Should our dear good mother get into financial difficulties & need no more than 400 florins, she will know where she will <u>immediately</u> be able to find the money.

HW to B. Schott's Söhne, Döbling, 20 December 1892

Und nun zu den „Freuden", die mir der neue Band so reichlich beschieden! Dieselben beginnen bereits mit dem Titelblatte. Da heisst es: comp. 1889–90 <u>sollte</u> aber heissen <u>90–91</u> wie ausdrücklichst angegeben wurde. Nun scheint aber das Titelblatt der Spanischen als Modell für das der Italienischen gedient zu haben, wobei die Jahreszahl 89-90 gedankenlos beibehalten wurde. Würde mir nun, wie ich ausdrücklich darum bat, eine Correctur des Titelblattes zugeschickt worden sein wäre dieser lapsus, der meine Lieder um ein Jahr älter macht, leicht zu vermeiden gewesen.

 Die nächste „Freude" erblühte mir schon auf der darauffolgenden Seite, die das Inhaltsverzeichniss schmückt. Da giebt es lustige Dinge zu lesen wie: gesegnet sei . . . pag. 8 oder: wir haben Beide . . . pag. 40 od. „und willst du" . . . pag. 36 u. s. f. Dießmal rächt sich Ihre Vorliebe für die großen unförmigen Typen, die es allerdings nicht gestatten konnten den <u>ganzen</u> Vers abzudrucken, wie dieß z. B. in der Buchausgabe der Fall ist u. wie dieß als etwas selbstverständliches überhaupt nicht anders sein kann.

And now to the 'joys' that the new volume vouchsafes me in such generous measure! They begin already on the title page, where we read: composed 1889–90, which <u>should</u> be <u>90–91</u> as was most clearly indicated. The title page of the Spanish songs seems to have served as your model, and so you retained 89–90 without thinking. Had I been sent the proofs of the title page, as I expressly requested, this lapse, which makes my songs a year older, would never have happened.

 The next 'joys' revealed themselves to me in all their glory on the very next page which is adorned by the table of contents. What curious titles can be found there! 'Gesegnet sei' . . . page 8; or 'Wir haben beide' . . . page 40; or 'Und willst du' . . . page 36, etc., etc. You are paying here for your predilection for large, unwieldy type, which prevents you from printing the whole line, as is done in the book edition & should always be done as a matter of course.

HW to Emil Kauffmann, Döbling, 23 December 1892

Soeben bringt mir der Bote einen Brief aus Tübingen. Welche Freude! Ich ersehe daraus, daß Sie über die neueste Wendung der Dinge noch nicht unterrichtet sind. Davon sollen Sie nun gleich das Nöthige erfahren. Zuvördest benachrichtige ich Sie, daß ich meine Pläne auf Berlin fallen gelassen u. daß ich in Wien bleiben werde. Die Veranlaßung hierzu bot mir der Sänger van Dyck, mit dem ich seit einigen Wochen correpetire. Sie müssen nämlich wissen, daß van Dyck heutzutage als eine Berühmtheit allerersten Ranges gilt, daß es mir mithin nicht gleichgültig sein konnte, zu diesem Künstler in Beziehungen zu treten. Obschon sich sonderbarer Weise bis zur Stunde noch keine passende Gelegenheit gefunden mit ihm über meine Angelegenheiten zu conferiren, gebe ich mich doch zuversichtlich der Hoffnung hin, dereinst Capital (im künstlerischen Sinne natürlich) aus ihm zu schlagen. Wenn es mir gelingen sollte van Dyck für meine Sachen ernstlich zu interessiren, dann bin ich sozusagen ein gemachter Mann. Ich muß aber dabei äußerst vorsichtig zu Werke gehen, um jeden Verdacht zu vermeiden, der auf mein egoistisches Vorhaben fallen könnte, denn diese verfluchten Herrn Tenoristen sind unberechenbar in ihrer wahnsinnigen Eitelkeit u. dabei rachsüchtig wie ein Corsicaner.

The postman has just delivered a letter from Tübingen. What joy! I see from it that you have not yet been informed about the recent turn of events. I shall now tell you at once all you need to know. Before that, I must tell you that my plans for Berlin have been dropped & that I shall remain in Vienna. The reason for this is the singer van Dyck whom I've been rehearsing for some weeks. You must know that van Dyck is regarded today as a celebrity of the very first rank, and that it cannot be a matter of indifference to me to be associated with this artist. Though I have not yet, strangely enough, found a suitable opportunity to discuss my affairs with him, I confidently harbour the hope of making capital (in the artistic sense, of course) out of him in the future. If I were to succeed in seriously interesting van Dyck in my things, I would, so to speak, be made for life. But I must proceed with great caution, in order to avoid all suspicion of my egotistical purpose, for these confounded tenors are incalculable in their insane vanity &, in addition, as revengeful as Corsicans.

HW to Heinrich Potpeschnigg, Vienna, 16 December 1894

Deine jüngsten Zeilen haben mir eine wahre Herzensfreude bereitet. Was Du mir über Fräulein Spurny berichtest klingt ja überaus verheissungsvoll. [...] Die Mitwirkung der Violine im Musikanten[1] muß sich reizend gemacht haben – u. gar hinter dem Vorhang! Was für raffinierte Leute ihr doch seid!

Your recent letter warmed the cockles of my heart. What you tell me about Miss Spurny sounds so promising. [...] The participation of a violinist in the 'Musikant' song must have been delightful – & from behind the curtain! What refined folk you are!

HW to Paul Müller, Perchtoldsdorf, 31 March 1896

Ich wohne hier in derselben Villa, in der die Mörike-Lieder, das spanische Liederbuch u. der 1. Akt u. die Hälfte des 2. Aktes vom Corregidor entstanden. Vom 2. Band des italienischen Liederbuches liegen bereits fünf vor. Drei davon sind humoristischen Inhaltes u. höchst ergötzlich.

I'm living here in the same house in which the *Mörike-Lieder*, the *Spanisches Liederbuch*, and Act 1 and half of Act 2 of *Der Corregidor* were composed. Five of the songs from Book II of the *Italienisches Liederbuch* are already finished. Three of them are humorous & quite delightful.

HW to Melanie Köchert, Perchtoldsdorf, 3 April 1896

Dieses Gedicht[2] ist ganz einfach in der Begleitung behandelt u. sehr naiv im Ton gehalten.

My setting of this poem is treated very simply in the accompaniment & kept very naive in tone.

HW to Emil Kauffmann, Perchtoldsdorf, 8 April 1896

Mir geht es seit den Feiertagen recht elend; ich werde von einem schrecklichen Schnupfen in Verbindung mit Rachenkatarrh geplagt. Nun sind es schon fünf Tage her, daß ich keine Note geschrieben u. ich war schon so schön im

---

1 Wolf is presumably referring to 'Wie lange schon war immer mein Verlangen' that Spurny and Potpeschnigg performed at a Liederabend in Graz on 10 December 1894 (see Jestremski, p. 536). Although he uses the word „Musikanten" in his letter, suggesting that the song in question is 'Der Musikant' from the *Eichendorff-Lieder*, there is no mention of a violin in that poem. It is more likely that he was referring to 'Wie lange schon war immer mein Verlangen', and simply confused 'Musikanten' with 'Musikus'.
2 'Wie viele Zeit verlor ich, dich zu lieben!'

Zug. Am 3. April hatte ich das 8. der italienischen Lieder zum 2. Bande aufgeschrieben. Wäre nicht dieser tückische Schnupfen über mich gekommen, läge sicherlich schon ein Dutzend vor.

My health has been wretched since the holidays; I am plagued by a terrible cold and inflammation of the throat. For five days now I have not written a single note – & it was all going so well. On 3 April I had composed the 8th song of Book II of the *Italian Songbook*. If it weren't for this spiteful cold, I'd have certainly finished a dozen by now.

HW to Hugo Faisst, Perchtoldsdorf, 13 April 1896

Heute habe ich das 12.[1] der neuen italienischen Lieder geschrieben. Die meisten davon sind tief gehalten, also daß sie Dir sehr bequem liegen werden.[2]

Today I finished the 12th of the new Italian songs. They are mostly for low voice, so that they should suit you very well.

HW to Heinrich Potpeschnigg, Perchtoldsdorf, 15 April 1896

Vorgestern habe ich das 12. der neuen Italienischen geschrieben. Leider hat gestern u. heute meine gute Stimmung etwas nachgelassen, so daß ich mich veranlaßt sah, zwei weitere Lieder stante pede in den Ofen zu prakticiren, weil sie mir zu schwächlich schienen.

The day before yesterday I finished the 12th of the new Italians. Unfortunately, my inspiration has yesterday & today abated somewhat, so that I was immediately obliged to throw two further songs into the fire, because they seemed too feeble.

HW to Melanie Köchert, Perchtoldsdorf, 23 April 1896

Ich habe zwei Cabinetstücke[3] geschrieben, die über alle bisher componirten gehen. [...] Diese zwei Stücke sind im Buch getrennt. Sie passen aber unverkennbar zusammen.

I have written two songs that are superior to all else I have composed – veritable jewels. Although these two poems do not follow one another in the volume, they belong unmistakably together.

---

[1] 'Sterb' ich, so hüllt in Blumen meine Glieder'.
[2] Faisst was an amateur singer, a baritone.
[3] 'Nicht länger kann ich singen' and 'Schweig' einmal still!'

HW to Frida von Lipperheide, Perchtoldsdorf, 27 April 1896

Trotz des mörderisch kalten u. hässlichen Aprilwetters habe ich gestern den 2. Band des italienischen Liederbuches mit dem 22. Lied – also gerade so viele, als der 1. Band umfaßt – beendigt.[1] Meine Freude über dieses prächtige Gelingen ist ganz unbeschreiblich, denn diese neuen Italienischen übertreffen an plastischer Anschaulichkeit Alles bisher von mir produzirte. Für die braven Conservativen sind diese Sachen allerdings nicht geschrieben, bei denen wird es wohl nur ein bedenkliches Schütteln des „Kopfes" hervorrufen. Ich brauche eben, um mit unserm Gewährsmann Nietzsche zu reden, neue Ohren für neue Musik, u. das ist doch gewiß nicht mehr als billig.[2]

Despite the murderously cold & horrid April weather I yesterday finished Book II of the *Italian Songbook*, bringing the number to 22 – exactly the same number, therefore, as in Book I. My joy at this splendid achievement is utterly indescribable, for these new Italians are more vivid and sculpted than anything I have composed previously. These songs have of course not been written for worthy conservatives, who would merely criticise them with a shake of the 'head'. To quote Nietzsche, an authority on such matters, I need new ears for new music, & that is only just.

HW to his mother, Perchtoldsdorf, 28 April 1896

Liebe Mutter, ich habe jetzt in der kurzen Zeit vom 25. März bis 26. April 22 neue Lieder geschrieben, die wohl zu den besten gehören, was überhaupt auf dem Gebiet der Liederkomposition geleistet wurde.

Dear Mother, I have in the short period between 25 March and 26 April composed 22 new songs, which are, I think, among the finest in the history of Lieder composition.

HW to Melanie Köchert, Stuttgart, 14 May 1896

Ich habe soeben ein opulentes Frühstück bei Faischtling absolvirt u. ihm darauf das Lied „Ich hab in Penna einen Liebsten wohnen" auswendig vorgespielt, worüber er in eine ganz kanibalische Extase gerathen. Er wollte es immer u. immer wieder hören.

1 Wolf composed another two Lieder on 29 and 30 April ('Verschling' der Abgrund' and 'Was für ein Lied soll dir gesungen werden', bringing the final number of songs in Book II to 24.
2 A reference to Nietzsche's Foreword to *Der Antichrist*, where he writes: „Neue Ohren für neue Musik. Neue Augen für das Fernste. Ein neues Gewissen für bisher stumm gebliebene Wahrheiten". ('New ears for new music. New eyes for what is most distant. A new conscience for truths that have hitherto remained unheard.')

I've just consumed an opulent breakfast at Faischtling's & then played for him by heart 'Ich hab' in Penna einen Liebsten wohnen', which sent him into a cannibalistic ecstasy. He wanted to hear it over & over again.

HW to Hugo Faisst, Vienna, 25 July 1896

Soeben sind die Correcturbogen von den neuen Italienischen eingetroffen. So viel ich bis jetzt ersehen wimmelt es nur so von Fehlern darin.

The proofs of the new Italians have just arrived. Teeming with errors, as far as I can see.

LIEDER

Italienisches Liederbuch
nach Paul Heyse für eine Singstimme und Klavier.

Italian Songbook
after Paul Heyse, for voice and piano

These anonymous poems from the sixteenth to the nineteenth centuries were collected by Dalmedico, Marcoaldi, Tigri and Tommaseo at a time of heightened Italian patriotism during the Austrian Occupation. This example of folk culture – similar to *Des Knaben Wunderhorn* in Germany – was an expression of the popular spirit in which all Italians could take pride.

The punctuation and orthography of these anonymous poems do not always conform to modern practice. Tommaseo and Tigri, for example, print 'chè', 'nè' and 'perchè', which in modern Italian would be rendered 'ché', 'né' and 'perché'; while 'siete' often appears as 'sete'. The German texts reproduce the orthography of Heyse's first edition.

I. BAND   **BOOK I**

Le cose piccoline son pur belle! [1]

Le cose piccoline son pur belle!   L'è piccolina, e di buon frutto mena.
Le cose piccoline son pur care!   Ponete mente come l'è la rosa:
Ponete mente come son le perle: L'è piccolina, e l'è tanto odorosa.
Son piccoline e si fanno pagare.   *rispetto* (Tommaseo, *Canti popolari*,
Ponete mente come l'è l'uliva: vol. I, p. 244)

1 Auch kleine Dinge können uns entzücken[1]

Auch kleine Dinge[2] können uns entzücken,	Even small things can delight us,
Auch kleine Dinge können theuer sein.	Even small things can be precious.
Bedenkt, wie gern wir uns mit Perlen schmücken	Think how gladly we deck ourselves with pearls –
Sie werden schwer bezahlt und sind nur klein.	They fetch a great price and are only small.
Bedenkt, wie klein ist die Olivenfrucht,	Think how small the olive is,
Und wird um ihre Güte doch gesucht.	And yet is prized for its goodness.
Denkt an die Rose nur, wie klein sie ist	Think only of the rose, how small it is,
Und duftet doch so lieblich, wie ihr wisst.	And yet smells so sweet, as you know.

M' è stato detto che voli partire [2]

M' è stato detto che voli partire:	Ricordati di me, speranza mia:
Specchio degli occhi miei do' vuoi andare?	Di lacrime ti bagnerò lo loco,
E se tu parti mandamelo a dire,	Ricordati di me, pensaci un poco.
Di lacrime ti voglio accompagnare:	
Di lacrime ti bagnerò la via,	*rispetto* (Marcoaldi, *Canti popolari inediti*, p. 44)

2 Mir ward gesagt, du reisest in die Ferne[3]

Mir ward gesagt, du reisest in die Ferne.	They told me you were going far away.
Ach, wohin gehst du, mein geliebtes Leben?	Ah, whither are you bound, love of my life?
Den Tag, an dem du scheidest, wüßt' ich gerne;	The day you leave, I would gladly know;
Mit Thränen will ich das Geleit dir geben.	I shall accompany you with tears.
Mit Thränen will ich deinen Weg befeuchten –	I shall bedew your path with tears;
Gedenk' an mich, und Hoffnung wird mir leuchten!	Think of me, and hope will give me light!
Mit Thränen bin ich bei dir allerwärts –	With tears I'm with you, wherever you be –
Gedenk' an mich, vergiß es nicht, mein Herz!	Think of me, do not forget, my heart!

---

1   In one anthology of popular poetry, 'Le cose piccoline son pur belle!' was printed under the heading of 'Amore ineguale', suggesting that the theme of the poem, like that of 'Wohl kenn ich Euren Stand', is disparity in social class.

2   The prosody is not perfect (Wolf stresses 'Dinge' instead of 'kleine') – but this is one of his most magical songs, and sensitive performers can easily diminish the heaviness of the dotted crotchet on 'Dinge'.

3   This was the first of the songs in the *Italienisches Liederbuch* to be composed. Wolf places the song second, just as Heyse had placed the poem second in his collection.

E sete la più bella mentovata [3]

E sete la più bella mentovata;
Più che non è di maggio rosa e fiore,
Più che non è d'Orvieto la facciata,
E di Viterbo la fonte maggiore.
Di grazia e di beltà sei tanto piena:
Lo porti il vanto del duomo di Siena.
Di grazia e di beltà sei piena tanto:
E del duomo di Siena porti il vanto.

rispetto (Tigri, *Canti popolari Toscani*, 2nd edn (1860), p. 20)

3 Ihr seid die Allerschönste weit und breit

You are the fairest far and wide

Ihr seid die Allerschönste weit und breit,
Viel schöner als im Mai der Blumenflor.
Orvieto's Dom steigt so voll Herrlichkeit,
Viterbo's größter Brunnen nicht empor.
So hoher Reiz und Zauber ist dein[1] eigen,
Der Dom von Siena muß sich vor dir neigen.
Ach, du bist so an Reiz und Anmuth reich,
Der Dom von Siena selbst ist dir nicht gleich.

You are the fairest far and wide,
Fairer by far than flowers in May.
Not Orvieto Cathedral or Viterbo's
Grandest fountain rises with such majesty.
Your charms and magic are such
That Siena Cathedral must bow before you.
Ah, you are so rich in charm and grace,
Even Siena Cathedral cannot compare.

Sia benedetto chi fece lo mondo [4]

Sia benedetto chi fece lo mondo:
Lo seppe tanto bene accomodare.
Fece lo mare, e non vi fece fondo,
Fece le navi per poter passare.
Fece le navi e fece il paradiso:
E fece le bellezze al vostro viso.

rispetto (Tigri, 2nd edn (1860), p. 28)
Also set in Italian by Ermanno Wolf-Ferrari

4 Gesegnet sei, durch den die Welt entstund

Blessed be he, through whom the world began

Gesegnet sei, durch den die Welt entstund;

Wie trefflich schuf er sie nach allen Seiten!
Er schuf das Meer mit endlos tiefem Grund,
Er schuf die Schiffe, die hinübergleiten,
Er schuf das Paradies mit ew'gem Licht,
Er schuf die Schönheit und dein Angesicht.

Blessed be he, through whom the world began;
How excellent on every side he made it!
He made the sea of unfathomable depths,
He made the ships that glide across,
He made Paradise with perpetual light,
He made beauty and your countenance.

---

[1] Note the switch to the intimate 'Du' form of address that dominates the last four lines of the poem.

Beati ciechi voi che non vedete [5]

Beati ciechi voi che non vedete
E che di donne non v'innamorate:
Beati sordi voi che no' intendete,
E i lagni degli amanti disprezzate:
Beati muti voi che non potete
Palesare la vostra volontate:
Beati morti voi che in terra siete,
L'amor non vi tormenta e riposate.

rispetto (Marcoaldi, p. 139)

5 Selig ihr Blinden

Blessed are the blind

Selig ihr Blinden, die ihr nicht zu schauen
Vermögt die Reize, die uns Glut entfachen;
Selig ihr Tauben, die ihr ohne Grauen
Die Klagen der Verliebten könnt verlachen;
Selig ihr Stummen, die ihr nicht den Frauen
Könnt eure Herzensnoth verständlich machen;
Selig ihr Todten, die man hat begraben!
I h r sollt vor Liebesqualen Ruhe haben.

Blessed are the blind, who cannot see
The charms that kindle desire in us;
Blessed are the deaf, who without fear
Can laugh at lovers' laments;
Blessed are the dumb, who cannot tell
Women of their heart's anguish;
Blessed are the dead in their graves!
You shall be safe from the pangs of love.

Chi ti ci fa venir, chi ti ci chiama? [6]

Chi ti ci fa venir, chi ti ci chiama?
Chi ti ci fa venir mal volontieri?
Vanne pure dov'hai fissa la dama,
Vanne pure dov'hai fissi i pensieri,
Vanne pure dov'hai 'l pensier sicuro:
Che tu venga da me non me ne curo.
Vanne pure dov'hai fissa la dama.
Chi ti ci fa venir? Chi ti ci chiama?

rispetto (Tommaseo, vol. I, p. 293)

6 Wer rief dich denn? Wer hat dich herbestellt?[1]

Who called you, then? Who sent for you?

Wer rief dich denn? Wer hat dich herbestellt?
Wer hieß dich kommen, wenn es dir zur Last?
Geh zu dem Liebchen, das dir mehr gefällt,
Geh dahin, wo du die Gedanken hast.

Who called you, then? Who sent for you?
Who asked you to come, if it's a burden?
Go to the sweetheart you like better,
Go there – where your thoughts are, and desires.

Geh nur, wohin dein Sinnen steht und Denken!
Daß du zu mir kommst, will ich gern dir schenken.
Geh zu dem Liebchen, das dir mehr gefällt!
Wer rief dich denn? Wer hat dich herbestellt?

Just go to her you dream and think of!
Do not come here for my sake.
Go to the sweetheart you like better!
Who called you, then? Who sent for you?

---

1 The song is a wonderful example of Wolf's ability to deepen the emotion of the original. The Italian poem and Heyse's translation maintain the woman's bluster to the end; in Wolf's setting, the downward leap of a sixth on 'herbestellt' betrays an underlying commotion that is foreign to the angry tone of the original poem: it was she who summoned him.

La luna s'è venuta a lamentare [7]

La luna s'è venuta a lamentare
Inde la faccia del divino Amore;
Dice che in cielo non ci vuol più stare;
Chè tolto gliel'avete lo splendore.
E si lamenta, e si lamenta forte;
L'ha conto le sue stelle, non son tutte.
E gliene manca due, e voi l'avete:
Son que' du' occhi che in fronte tenete.

rispetto (Tigri, 2nd edn (1860), p. 22)

7 Der Mond hat eine schwere Klag' erhoben[1] / The moon has raised a grave complaint

Der Mond hat eine schwere Klag' erhoben
Und vor dem Herrn die Sache kund gemacht:
Er wolle nicht mehr stehn am Himmel droben,
Du habest ihn um seinen Glanz gebracht.
Als er zuletzt das Sternenheer gezählt,
Da hab' es an der vollen Zahl gefehlt;
Zwei von den schönsten habest du entwendet,
Die beiden Augen dort, die mich verblendet.

The moon has raised a grave complaint
And made the matter known unto the Lord:
No longer does it wish to dwell in the sky above,
For you have robbed it of its radiance.
When last it counted all the stars,
The full number was not complete;
You have purloined two of the loveliest:
Those two eyes that have dazzled me.

Facciam la pace, caro bene mio [8]

Facciam la pace, caro bene mio,
Che questa guerra non può più durare.
Se non la vuoi far tu, la farò io:
Fra me e te non ci è guerra mortale.
Fanno la pace principi e signori:
Così la posson far due amatori.
Fanno la pace principi e soldati:
Così la posson far due innamorati.
Fanno la pace principi e tenenti:
Tanto lo posson far du' cor contenti.

rispetto (Tommaseo, vol. I, p. 261)
Also set in Italian by Wolf-Ferrari

8 Nun laß uns Frieden schließen, liebstes Leben[2] / Let us now make peace, my dearest love

Nun laß uns Frieden schließen, liebstes Leben,
Zu lang ist's schon, daß wir in Fehde liegen.

Let us now make peace, my dearest love,
We have been feuding far too long.

---

1 The song appears in a very different guise in the Korngold–Marischka version of Johann Strauss's *Eine Nacht in Venedig* where it is sung by the Duke at the end of Act I as he looks up to Delacqua's balcony. This version, starring Richard Tauber, was first performed at the Theater an der Wien in 1923.
2 The song is almost always sung too slowly. The *Italienisches Liederbuch* is Wolf's only songbook for which he provided metronome markings, and his metronome speed for 'Nun laß uns Frieden schließen, liebstes Leben' is crotchet = 72 – a reminder that there is an urgency about the poem and music, and that peace has not yet been made.

NO STANZA BREAK

Wenn d u¹ nicht willst, will ich mich dir ergeben;	If *you're* not willing, I'll yield to you;
Wie könnten wir uns auf den Tod bekriegen?	How could we wage war unto death?
Es schließen Frieden Könige und Fürsten,	Peace is made by kings and princes,
Und sollten Liebende nicht darnach² dürsten?	Why should not lovers crave the same?
Es schließen Frieden Fürsten und Soldaten,	Peace is made by soldiers and princes,
Und sollt' es zwei Verliebten wohl mißrathen?	So why should two lovers not succeed?
Meinst du, daß, was so großen Herrn gelingt,	Do you think what such great lords can manage
Ein Paar zufriedner Herzen nicht vollbringt?	Cannot be done by two contented hearts?

Le tue bellezze fossero dipinte [9]

Le tue bellezze fossero dipinte,	Ogni pagano tornasse alla fede,
Fussan portate innanzi al re Pagano!	Si facesse cristiano e amasse tene.
Chè lui te ne farebbe un gran presente,	Ogni pagano alla fede tornasse,
La sua corona ti darebbe in mano.	Si facesse cristiano e poi t'amasse.
E manderebbe in bando alla sua gente,	
Che tornasse alla fede ogni pagano.	*rispetto* (Tommaseo, vol. I, p. 42)

9 Daß doch gemalt all deine Reize wären³

If only all your charms had been painted

Daß doch gemalt all deine Reize wären,	If only all your charms had been painted,
Und dann der Heidenfürst das Bildniß fände.	And the heathen chief then found the picture!
Er würde dir ein groß Geschenk verehren,	He would honour you with a great gift
Und legte seine Kron' in deine Hände.	And lay his crown into your hands.
Zum rechten Glauben müßt'⁴ sich bekehren	His entire kingdom, to its farthest corner,
Sein ganzes Reich bis an sein fernstes Ende.	Would be converted to the true faith.
Im ganzen Lande würd' es ausgeschrieben,	It would be proclaimed throughout the land
Christ soll' ein Jeder werden und dich lieben.	That all must turn Christian and love you.
Ein jeder Heide flugs bekehrte sich	All the heathen would be converted at once
Und würd' ein guter Christ und liebte dich.	And become good Christians and love you.

---

1   Wolf responds memorably to the italicised 'd u' by setting the word to a dotted crotchet tied to a crotchet over the barline.
2   Heyse: danach.
3   This was the song with which Wolf continued the *Italienisches Liederbuch* after his inspiration had dried up shortly after composing 'Nun laß uns Frieden schließen' on 14 November 1890. More than a year separates the two songs.
4   Heyse: müßte.

Ti pensi di legarmi con un filo [10]

Ti pensi di legarmi con un filo,
Con uno sguardo farmi innamorare.
Non ti fidar di me quando che rido:
Che più in alto l'ho fatti calare.

E l'ho fatti calar; credilo a mene.
So' innamorata, ma non già di tene.

rispetto (Tommaseo, vol. I, p. 273)

10 Du denkst mit einem Fädchen mich zu fangen

You think you can catch me with a thread

Du denkst mit einem Fädchen mich zu fangen,
Mit einem Blick schon mich verliebt zu machen?
Ich fing schon Andre, die sich höher schwangen;
Du darfst mir ja nicht trau'n, siehst du mich lachen.
Schon Andre fing ich, glaub' es sicherlich.
Ich bin verliebt, doch eben nicht in dich.*[1]

You think you can catch me with a thread,

Make me fall in love with a mere glance?

I've caught others who flew higher,

You shouldn't trust me if you see me laugh.

I've caught others, believe you me.
I am in love – but not with you.'

* Wolf repeats the final line.

Oh quanto tempo l'ho desiderato [11]

Oh quanto tempo l'ho desiderato
Un damo aver che fosse sonatore!
Eccolo qua che Dio me l'ha mandato
Tutto coperto di rose e viole:

Eccolo qua che vien pianin pianino
A capo basso, e suona il violino.

rispetto (Tigri, 1st edn (1856), p. 72;
2nd edn (1860), p. 82)

11 Wie lange schon war immer mein Verlangen[2]

How long have I yearned

Wie lange schon war immer mein Verlangen:
Ach, wäre doch ein Musikus mir gut!
Nun ließ der Herr mich meinen Wunsch erlangen
Und schickt mir einen, ganz wie Milch und Blut.
Da kommt er eben her mit sanfter Miene,
Und senkt den Kopf und spielt die Violine.

How long have I yearned
To have a musician as lover!
Now the Lord has granted me my wish

And sent me one, all pink and white.

And here he comes with gentle mien,
And bows his head and plays the violin.

Also set by Hermann Goetz and Hans Huber

---

1 Wolf indicates that 'doch eben nicht in dich' should be sung with laughter in the voice. This is the first of only two repetitions in the *Italienisches Liederbuch*. See also 'Benedeit die sel'ge Mutter'.
2 See HW to Heinrich Potpeschnigg, 16 December 1894, p. 228.

Giovinottino, non si fa così [12]

Giovinottino, non si fa così:
Si fa le cose lecite ed oneste.
Ma mi tieni la dama d'ogni dì,
Le altre le tieni nel dì delle feste.

Giovanottino, se così farai,
La dama d'ogni dì la perderai.

rispetto (Tommaseo, vol. I, p. 283)

12 Nein, junger Herr, so treibt man's nicht, fürwahr

Nein, junger Herr, so treibt man's nicht, fürwahr;
Man sorgt dafür, sich schicklich zu betragen.
Für Alltags bin ich gut genug, nicht wahr?
Doch Beßre suchst du dir an Feiertagen.
Nein, junger Herr, wirst du so weiter sünd'gen,
Wird dir den Dienst dein Alltagsliebchen künd'gen.

No, young man, that's no way to carry on

No, young man, that's no way to carry on;
People should try to behave properly.
I'm good enough for weekdays, am I?
But on holidays you look for better.
No, young man, if you keep transgressing so,
Your weekday love will give you notice.

Bella che troppo in alto vi tenete [13]

Bella che troppo in alto vi tenete,
Con molta fantasia vi fate amare.
A chi vi parla, alquanto rispondete,
Che vi rincresce il troppo salutare.
Figlia non sei d'un Alessandro Magno,

Nemmen padrona di qualunque regno;
E se l'oro non vuo', prendilo stagno;
Se tu non vuo' l'amor, prendi lo sdegno.

rispetto (Tommaseo, vol. I, p. 239)

13 Hoffärtig[1] seid Ihr, schönes Kind

Hoffährtig seid Ihr, schönes Kind, und geht
Mit Euren Freiern um auf stolzem Fuß.
Spricht man Euch an, kaum daß Ihr Rede steht,
Als kostet' Euch zuviel ein holder Gruß.
Bist keines Alexanders Töchterlein,
Kein Königreich wird deine Mitgift sein,
Und willst du nicht das Gold, so nimm das Zinn;
Willst du nicht Liebe, nimm Verachtung hin.

You are haughty, beautiful child

You are haughty, beautiful child,
Act high and mighty with your suitors.
If you're spoken to, you hardly deign reply,
As if a friendly greeting cost too much.
Yet you are no Alexander's daughter,
No kingdom shall be your dowry,
So if you don't want gold, take tin,
If you don't want love, take contempt.

---

1 Heyse: Hoffährtig.

Compagno mio, vustu che andèmo frate [14]

Compagno mio, vustu che andèmo frate,
Lassar el mondo a chi lo vol godere?
Porta per porta nu anderèmo a bate:
'Fate la carità al povero frate?'
O caro Padre, un poco di ritorno,
Gnancóra el pan no xe vegnùo dal forno.
O caro Padre fe' una ritornata,
Chè go una puta in leto amalata.
Se l'è amalata fèmela vedere,
Che no la fusse in ponto de morire.
Se l'è amalata lassela vardare,
Che no la se volesse confessare.
Serè ste porte, serè sti balconi,
Che nissun senta la so confessione.

vilota (Dalmedico, *Canti del popolo Veneziano*, p. 41)

14 Geselle, woll'n wir uns in Kutten hüllen[1]

Comrade, shall we disguise ourselves in cowls

Geselle, woll'n wir uns in Kutten hüllen,
Die Welt dem lassen, den sie mag ergötzen?
Dann pochen wir an Thür um Thür im Stillen:
„Gebt einem armen Mönch[2] um Jesu willen."
– O lieber Pater, du mußt später kommen,
Wenn aus dem Ofen wir das Brod genommen.
O lieber Pater, komm nur später wieder,
Ein Töchterlein von mir liegt krank danieder.
– Und ist sie krank, so lass't mich zu ihr gehen,
Daß sie nicht etwa sterbe unversehen.
Und ist sie krank, so lass't mich nach ihr schauen,
Daß sie mir ihre Beichte mag vertrauen.
Schließt Thür und Fenster, daß uns Keiner störe,
Wenn ich des armen Kindes Beichte höre!

Comrade, shall we disguise ourselves in cowls
And leave the world to those that enjoy it?
Quietly we'll go knocking at door after door:
'Give to a poor monk, for Jesus' sake!'
'O dear Father, you must come later,
When we've taken the bread from the oven.
O dear Father, come back later,
One of my daughters lies ill in bed.'
'If she is, let me go to her,
So she might not die unshriven.
If she's ill, then let me see her,
That she may confess her sins to me.
Close door and window, let no one disturb us,
When I hear the poor child's confession!'

---

1 The first thirteen songs of the *Italienisches Liederbuch* are settings of *rispetti*, lapidary expressions of love. Here, for the first time, Wolf composes a Venetian *vilota* which has a much more narrative feel.

2 Wolf, in a letter to his mother (29 April 1892), called himself an „Ungläubiger", an 'atheist', but he also had a pronounced spiritual side. And in a letter to his parents of 17 July 1880 he described his feelings as he stood in the Cistercian monastery of Heiligenkreuz near Maierling: „ich war so entzückt und ergriffen, daß ich keinen anderen Wunsch mehr übrig hatte als den: Mönch zu sein!" ('I was so enchanted and moved that I only had one wish: to become a monk!') See also p. 344.

E lo mio damo è tanto piccolino [15]

E lo mio damo è tanto piccolino,
Chè co' capelli mi spazza la casa.
Andò nell'orto a côrre un gelsomino,
Ebbe paura d'una gran lumaca.
E venne in casa, e si messe a sedere,
Passò una mosca e lo fece cadere.
E lu' si rizza, e andò alla finestra,
Passò un tafano e gli rompè la testa:
E maledisco le mosche e i tafani,
E chi s'innamorò de maremmani;
E maledisco le mosche e i cugini,
E chi s'innamorò de' piccolini.

rispetto (Tigri, 2nd edn (1860), p. 280)

15 Mein Liebster ist so klein / My sweetheart's so small

Mein Liebster ist so klein, daß ohne Bücken	My sweetheart's so small that without bending down
Er mir das Zimmer fegt mit seinen Locken.	He can sweep my room with his curls.
Als er ins Gärtlein ging, Jasmin zu pflücken,	When he went to the garden to pick jasmine
Ist er vor einer Schnecke sehr erschrocken.	He was terrified by a snail.
Dann setzt' er sich ins Haus um zu verschnaufen	Then when he came indoors to recover,
Da warf ihn eine Fliege übern Haufen;	A fly knocked him head over heels;
Und als er hintrat an mein Fensterlein,	And when he stepped over to my window,
Stieß eine Bremse ihm den Schädel ein.	A horse-fly caved his head in.
Verwünscht sei'n alle Fliegen, Schnaken, Bremsen	A curse on all flies (crane- and horse-)
Und wer ein Schätzchen hat aus den Maremmen!	And anyone with a sweetheart from the Maremma!
Verwünscht sei'n alle Fliegen, Schnaken, Mücken	A curse on all flies, craneflies and midges
Und wer sich, wenn er küßt, so tief muß bücken![1]	And on all who have to stoop so low to kiss!

Giovanettini che andate alla guerra [16]

Giovanettini che andate alla guerra,
Tenete conto del mio innamorato.
Diteli che non metta l'arme in terra,
Perch'alla guerra lui non c'è mai stato.
Diteli che non dorma a ciel sereno,
Le chiavi del suo cor le porto in seno.
Ditegli che non dorma nel profondo,
Mi ricordo di lui 'n tempo del mondo.

rispetto (Tommaseo, vol. i, p. 183)

---

[1] The idea of stooping for a kiss is absent from the original Italian poem. 'Mein Liebster ist so klein' is one of the most endearing songs of the collection, despite the somewhat mocking text. Wolf too was physically small – not much over five feet – and he obviously had a soft spot for this diminutive lover from the Maremma. The opening is marked *sehr zart* (very delicately and tenderly), and the idea of smallness is conveyed throughout the song by tiny intervals. Particularly tender is the little postlude, where the ascending and then descending figure suggests the lover straining up on tiptoe to reach the girl's lips, before settling back on his heels again.

16 Ihr jungen Leute, die ihr zieht ins Feld — You young men going off to war

Ihr jungen Leute, die ihr zieht ins Feld,	You young men going off to war,
Auf meinen Liebsten sollt ihr Achtung geben.	You must take care of my sweetheart.
Sorgt, daß er tapfer sich im Feuer hält;	Make sure that he's brave under fire,
Er war noch nie im Kriege all sein Leben.	He's never been to war in all his life.
Laßt nie ihn unter freiem Himmel schlafen;	Never let him sleep in the open;
Er ist so zart, es möchte sich bestrafen.	He's so delicate, it might harm him.
Lasst mir ihn ja nicht schlafen unterm Mond;	Don't let him sleep out under the moon;
Er ginge drauf, er ist's ja nicht gewohnt.	He'd die – he's not used to it, you see.

Se vuoi vedere il tuo servo morire [17]

Se vuoi vedere il tuo servo morire,
Testi capelli non te li arricciare,
Giù per le spalle lasciateli ire
Che paion fila d'oro naturale.
Paiono fila d'oro, oro infilato,
Son belli li capelli, e chi l'ha in capo.
Paiono fila d'ora e seta fina:
Son belli li capelli, e chi li striga.

rispetto (Tommaseo, vol. I, p. 78)

17 Und willst du deinen Liebsten sterben sehen[1] — And if you would see your lover die

Und willst du deinen Liebsten sterben sehen,	And if you would see your lover die,
So trage nicht dein Haar gelockt, du Holde.	Do not curl your hair, my love!
Laß von den Schultern frei sie niederwehen;	Let it cascade from your shoulders;
Wie Fäden sehn sie aus von purem Golde.	It looks like threads of pure gold.
Wie goldne Fäden, die der Wind bewegt –	Like golden threads blown by the wind,
Schön sind die Haare, schön ist, die sie trägt!	How lovely your hair, how lovely she that wears it!
Goldfäden, Seidenfäden ungezählt –	Golden threads, silken threads without number –
Schön sind die Haare, schön ist, die sie strählt!	How lovely your hair, how lovely she who combs it!

Alza la bionda testa, e non dormire [18]

Alza la bionda testa, e non dormire,
Non ti lasciar superar dallo sonno.
Quattro parole, amore, io son per dire
Che tutte e quattro son di gran bisogno:
La prima ell'è che mi fate morire,
E la seconda, che un gran ben vi voglio:
La terza, che vi sia raccomandata;
L'ultima, che di voi so' innamorata.[2]

rispetto (Tigri, 2nd edn (1860), p. 72)
Also set in Italian by Wolf-Ferrari

---

1 The 55 arpeggiated chords of the accompaniment are a wonderfully graphic way of depicting a young woman combing her locks.
2 The singer in the Italian original is a woman but Heyse's version is gender unspecific.

18 Heb' auf dein blondes Haupt und schlafe nicht

Heb' auf dein blondes Haupt und schlafe nicht,
Und laß dich ja vom Schlummer nicht bethören.
Ich sage dir vier Worte von Gewicht,
Von denen darfst du keines überhören.
Das erste: daß um dich mein Herze bricht,
Das zweite: dir nur will ich angehören,
Das dritte: daß ich dir mein Heil befehle,
Das letzte: dich allein liebt meine Seele.

Raise your blonde head and do not sleep

Raise your blonde head and do not sleep,
And let not slumber beguile you.

Four things of moment I have to tell you,
None of which you must ignore.
The first: my heart is breaking for you,
The second: I wish to be yours alone,
The third: you are my one salvation,
The last: my soul loves you alone.

Ha tanto tempo ch'eravamo muti! [19]

Ha tanto tempo ch'eravamo muti!
Eccoci ritornati alla favella:
E gli angioli dal ciel sono venuti,
L'hanno posta la pace in tanta guerra:
E son venuti gli angioli di Dio,
L'hanno posta la pace nel cor mio.
E son venuti gli angioli d'amore,
L'hanno posta la pace nel mio cuore.

rispetto (Tommaseo, vol. I, p. 264)

19 Wir haben beide lange Zeit geschwiegen[1]

Wir haben beide lange Zeit geschwiegen,
Auf einmal kam uns nun die Sprache wieder.
Die Engel, die herab vom Himmel fliegen,
Sie brachten nach dem Krieg den Frieden wieder.
Die Engel Gottes sind herabgeflogen,
Mit ihnen ist der Frieden eingezogen.
Die Liebesengel kamen über Nacht
Und haben Frieden meiner Brust gebracht.

For a long time we have both been silent

For a long time we have both been silent,
Now all at once speech has returned.
The angels of God have descended,
They have brought back peace after war.
The angels of God have descended
And with them peace has returned.
The angels of love came in the night
And have brought peace to my breast.

Amor, che passi la notte cantando [20]

Amor, che passi la notte cantando,
Ed io meschina son nel letto e sento!
Vôlto le spalle alla mia mamma, e piango;
Di sangue son le lacrime che getto;
Di là dal letto ho fatto un grosso fiume,
Da tanto lacrimar non vedo lume;
Di là dal letto un grosso fiume ho fatto,
Da tanto tacrimar son cieca affatto.

rispetto (Tigri, 2nd edn (1860), p. 2)

---

1 See HW to B. Schott's Söhne, 18 October 1892, p. 224.

20 Mein Liebster singt am Haus im Mondenscheine[1]

Mein Liebster singt am Haus im Mondenscheine,
Und ich muß lauschend hier im Bette liegen.
Weg von der Mutter wend' ich mich und weine,
Blut sind die Thränen, die mir nicht versiegen.
Den breiten Strom am Bett hab' ich geweint,
Weiß nicht vor Thränen, ob der Morgen scheint.
Den breiten Strom am Bett weint' ich vor Sehnen;
Blind haben mich gemacht die blut'gen Thränen.

My sweetheart sings outside in the moonlight

My sweetheart sings outside in the moonlight,
And I must lie in bed and listen.
I turn away from my mother and weep,
My tears are blood, which will not dry.
I have wept that broad stream by the bed,
I do not know, for tears, if day has dawned.
I've wept that broad stream with longing;
The tears of blood have blinded me.

M'è stato detto che tua madre 'n vuole [21]

M'è stato detto che tua madre 'n vuole:
Contentala, bellin, non ci venire;
Giovanettino, qui non abbadare;
Faglie dispetto, amor, vienmi a trovare.
Giovanettin, non abbadare a questo:
Faglie dispetto, amor, vienci più spesso.

Giovanettin, non abbadar costì,
Faglie dispetto, amor, vienci ogni dì.

rispetto (Tigri, 2nd edn (1860), p. 263)
Also set in Italian by Wolf-Ferrari

21 Man sagt mir, deine Mutter woll' es nicht

Man sagt mir, deine Mutter woll' es nicht;
So bleibe weg, mein Schatz, thu' ihr den Willen.
Ach Liebster, nein! thu' ihr den Willen nicht,
Besuch' mich doch, thu's ihr zum Trotz, im Stillen!
Nein, mein Geliebter, folg' ihr nimmermehr,
Thu's ihr zum Trotz, komm öfter als bisher!
Nein, höre nicht auf sie, was sie auch sage;
Thu's ihr zum Trotz, mein Lieb, komm alle Tage!

They tell me your mother disapproves

They tell me your mother disapproves;
Then stay away, beloved, do her bidding.
Ah no, my love, do not do her bidding,
Defy her, visit me in secret!
No, my love, do not ever obey her,
Defy her, come more often than before!
No, don't listen to her, whatever she says;
Defy her, my love, come every day!

1   The accompaniment resembles a Chopin mazurka, reminding us of Wolf's admiration for the Polish composer. Writing to Henrietta Lang on 19 October 1882 after the death of her uncle Anton, Wolf tells her that three days previously he had played some of her uncle's favourite songs with Paula von Goldschmidt, including Chopin's 'Zwei Leichen' and 'Polens Grabgesang' ('Two corpses', Op. 74/11, and 'Poland's Funeral Hymn' in E flat minor, Op. 74/17). Other Chopin echoes can be found in 'Mein Liebchen, wir saßen beisammen', 'Tief im Herzen trag' ich Pein' and 'Karwoche'. See also pp. 477–8.

Io son venuto a farvi serenata [22]

Io son venuto a farvi serenata,
Padron di casa, se contento siete.
So che ci avete una giovin garbata:
Dentro le vostre mura la tenete.
E se per sorte fosse addormentata,
Questo da parte mia voi le direte:

Che ci è passato un suo caro servente,
Che giorno e notte la tiene in la mente.
Tra giorno e notte son ventiquattr' ore;
E venticinque la tengo nel core.

rispetto (Tommaseo, vol. I, p. 120)

22 Ein Ständchen Euch zu bringen kam ich her

I have come here to serenade you

Ein Ständchen Euch zu bringen kam ich her
Wenn es dem Herrn vom Haus nicht ungelegen.
Iht habt ein schönes Töchterlein. Es wär
Wohl gut, sie nicht zu streng im Haus zu hegen.
Und liegt sie schon im Bett, so bitt' ich sehr,
Thut es zu wissen ihr von meinetwegen,
Daß ihr Getreuer hier vorbeigekommen,
Der Tag und Nacht sie in den Sinn genommen,
Und daß am Tag, der vierundzwanzig zählt,
Sie fünfundzwanzig Stunden lang mir fehlt.

I have come here to serenade you,
If the master of the house does not mind.

You have a beautiful daughter. It were
Better not to keep her too strictly indoors.

And should she have gone to bed,
Then kindly tell her on my behalf
That her true love passed this way,
Who thinks of her by day and night,

And that in a day of four and twenty hours
I miss her twenty-five.

Also set by Richard Heuberger

II. BAND

BOOK II

Non so quale canzona mi cantare [23]

Non so quale canzona mi cantare,
Che s'affacesse alla vostra persona:
Di sottoterra la vorrei cavare,
Che detta non l'avesse creatura.

Che detta non l'avesse nè sentita
Uomo nè donna nè persona antica.

rispetto (Tommaseo, vol. I, p. 11)

23 Was für ein Lied soll dir gesungen werden[1]

What kind of song shall be sung to you

Was für ein Lied soll dir gesungen werden,
Das deiner würdig sei? Wo find' ich's nur?

What kind of song shall be sung to you
That does you justice? Wherever can I find it?

---

[1] No song of Wolf's better illustrates his contention that 'the main focus in my songs is the piano part' (see HW to Karl Mayr, 22 April 1897, p. 285). The melody in the piano binds the whole song

NO STANZA BREAK

Am liebsten grüb' ich es tief aus der Erden,	I'd like best to delve it deep from the earth,
Gesungen noch von keiner Creatur.	As yet unsung by any creature.
Ein Lied, das weder Mann noch Weib bis heute	A song that till now no man nor woman
Hört' oder sang, selbst nicht die ältesten Leute.	Has ever heard or sung, however old they be.

Non posso più mangiarlo il pane asciutto [24]

Non posso più mangiarlo il pane asciutto
Che m'è 'ntrato una spina in chesto piede,
Rimiro in qua, in là; miro per tutto:
Non c'è nessuno che mi voglia bene.
Ci fosse almeno un po' di vecchierello
Che mi volesse un po' bene chello!

Ti dico e tu m'intendi per diletto
Un vecchierello fusse del mi' tempo,
Ti dico: e tu m'intendi per affanni,
Un vecchierello di quattordici anni.

rispetto (Tommaseo, vol. I, p. 234)

24 Ich esse nun mein Brot nicht trocken mehr

I no longer eat my bread dry

Ich esse nun mein Brot nicht trocken mehr,[1]	I no longer eat my bread dry,
Ein Dorn ist mir im Fuße stecken blieben.	I have a thorn stuck in my foot.
Umsonst nach rechts und links blick' ich umher,	In vain I look around to left and right
Und Keinen find' ich, der mich möchte lieben.	And find no one who will love me.
Wenn's doch auch nur ein altes Männlein wäre,	If there were only a little old man
Das mir erzeigt' ein wenig Lieb' und Ehre.	Who loved and honoured me a little.
Ich meine nämlich, so ein wohlgestalter,	I mean, in other words, a well-proportioned,
Ehrbarer Greis, etwa von meinem Alter.	Honourable old man of about my age.
Ich meine, um mich ganz zu offenbaren,	I mean, to be entirely frank,
Ein altes Männlein so von vierzehn Jahren.	A little old man of about fourteen.

El mio moroso m'a invidato a cena [25]

El mio moroso m'a invidato a cena,
E nol gaveva casa da menarme.
Ghe manca 'l fogo e ghe manca la legna,
Ghe manca la pignata da tacare.
Ghe manca 'l caratèlo del vin bon,

E non gavea bocal da travasarlo.
Curta la tola e streta la tovagia,
El pan xe duro e 'l cortelo no tagia.

vilota (Dalmedico, p. 141)

---

together, while the singer weaves his way in and out of the accompaniment, stressing now this word now that, in a sort of heightened recitative. This was the last of the 46 songs to be composed, and Wolf proudly placed it at the beginning of Book II, as a scarcely veiled homage to Melanie Köchert.

1 Because he wets the bread with his tears [Heyse's footnote].

25 Mein Liebster hat zu Tische mich geladen   My sweetheart invited me to dinner

Mein Liebster hat zu Tische mich geladen	My sweetheart invited me to dinner,
Und hatte doch kein Haus mich zu empfangen,	Yet had no house to receive me,
Nicht Holz noch Herd zum Kochen und zum Braten,	No wood nor stove for boiling or roasting,
Der Hafen auch war längst entzwei gegangen.	And the cooking pot had long since split in two.
An einem Fäßchen Wein gebrach es auch,	There was not even a small cask of wine,
Und Gläser hatt' er gar nicht im Gebrauch;	And he simply never used glasses;
Der Tisch war schmal, das Tafeltuch nicht besser,	The table was tiny, the tablecloth no better,
Das Brod steinhart und völlig stumpf das Messer.[1]	The bread rock hard and the knife quite blunt.

Me xe stà dito, e me xe stà contà [26]

Me xe stà dito, e me xe stà contà,
Che Toni belo no pol magnar gnente.
L'è tanto co una tosa incapricià,
Che sète pani no ghe toca un dente.
E dopo cena l'à magnà un salà,
Con altri vinticinque pani arente.
E se Tonina bela no ghe cria,
Vegniva l'ano de la carestìa.

vilota (Dalmedico, p. 139)

26 Ich ließ mir sagen und mir ward erzählt[2]   I enquired and have been informed

Ich ließ mir sagen und mir ward erzählt,	I enquired and have been informed
Der schöne Toni hungre sich zu Tode;	That handsome Toni's starving to death;
Seit ihn so überaus die Liebe quält,	Ever since love's tormented him so cruelly,
Nimmt er auf einen Backzahn sieben Brode.[3]	He eats only seven loaves per molar.
Nach Tisch, damit er die Verdauung stählt,	After meals, to steel his digestion,
Verspeis't er eine Wurst und sieben Brode,	He devours a sausage and seven loaves,
Und lindert nicht Tonina seine Pein,	And if Tonina doesn't ease his pain,
Bricht nächstens Hungersnoth und Theurung ein.	We'll soon be faced with famine and starvation.

1 The poem is an expression of frustration. I picture the young woman (as in Mozart's 'Der Zauberer') talking to her girlfriends. Only at the end of the poem does she refer to her most serious complaint: her lover's sexual inadequacy.
2 In a letter to Melanie Köchert of 28 March 1896 Wolf writes: „Ich habe heute den schönen, hungrigen Toni componirt – wie? Das läßt sich unmöglich beschreiben. Ich weiß nur das Eine, daß der Humor in der Musik erst mit diesem Lied in die Welt getreten ist!" ('Today I set handsome, starving Toni to music – how, I cannot describe. But one thing I do know – this song introduces humour into music for the first time!') An extraordinary example of Wolf's hyperbole!
3 The pianist plays seven *fortissimo*, mostly dotted chords to illustrate 'sieben Brote', and the ensuing hemidemisemiquavers vividly conjure up the guzzling of the loaves.

E m'ero spolto per andare a letto [27]

E m'ero spolto per andare a letto:
Bella, tu mi venisti in fantasia.
Presto mi rizzo, mi calzo e mi vesto;
Piglio il mi' ribechino, e vado via.
E per tutta la vïa e canto e suono:
Fo innamorar le citte, e le abbandono.
E per tutta la vïa e suono e canto:
Fo innamorar le citte, e poi le lasso.

rispetto (Tigri, 2nd edn (1860), p. 101)

27 Schon streckt' ich aus im Bett die müden Glieder

I'd already stretched my tired limbs out in bed

Schon streckt' ich aus im Bett die müden Glieder,
Da tritt dein Bildniß vor mich hin, du Traute.

Gleich spring' ich auf, fahr' in die Schuhe wieder
Und wandre durch die Stadt mit meiner Laute.
Ich sing' und spiele, daß die Straße schallt;

So Manche lauscht – vorüber bin ich bald.

So manches Mädchen hat mein Lied gerührt,
Indeß der Wind schon Sang und Klang entführt.

I'd already stretched my tired limbs out in bed,
When you appeared to me in a vision, my love.

I jump straight up, put my shoes back on
And wander through the town with my lute.
The streets resound with my singing and playing;

Many a girl listens, but I have soon passed by.

Many a girl is moved by my song,
While already my singing's wafted away on the wind.

Tu vai dicendo ch'io non son regina [28]

Tu vai dicendo ch'io non son regina;
Nè anche tu se' figluol del re di Spagna.
Bello, quando ti levi la mattina,
Le tue carrozze non vanno in campagna.
Tu vieni a minchionar la mia bassezza.
La povertà non guasta gentilezza.
Tu vieni a minchionare l'esser mio:
Poi va' per terra te, come vo' io.

rispetto (Tommaseo, vol. I, p. 238)

28 Du sagst mir, daß ich keine Fürstin sei

You tell me I'm no princess

Du sagst mir, daß ich keine Fürstin sei;
Auch du bist nicht auf Spaniens Thron entsprossen.
Nein, Bester, stehst du auf bei Hahnenschrei,
Fährst du aufs Feld und nicht in Staatskarossen.
Du spottest mein um meine Niedrigkeit,
Doch Armuth thut dem Adel nichts zu Leid.
Du spottest, daß mir Krone fehlt und Wappen,
Und fährst doch selber nur mit Schusters Rappen.

You tell me I'm no princess;
But you're not Spanish royalty either.

No, my dear, when you rise at cock crow,
You go to the fields, and not by state coach.

You mock my lowly station,
But poverty doesn't harm the noble soul.
You mock me for having no crown or crest,
But Shanks's pony is all you ride yourself.

Conosco il vostro stato, fior gentile [29]

Conosco il vostro stato, fior gentile:
Non è dover che v'abbassiate tanto
D'amarmi me che son povera e vile,
Chè voi de' belli ne portate il vanto:
E voi de' belli il vanto ne portate,
Conosco ben che voi mi canzonate;
Voi mi burlate, me lo dice ognuno,
Ma siete bello, e perciò vi perdono.

rispetto (Tigri, 2nd edn (1860), p. 137)

29 Wohl kenn' ich Euren Stand, der nicht gering

Your station, I'm aware, is no mean one

Wohl kenn' ich Euren Stand, der nicht gering.
Ihr brauchtet nicht so tief herabzusteigen,
Zu lieben solch ein arm und niedrig Ding,
Da sich vor Euch die Allerschönsten neigen.
Die schönsten Männer leicht besiegtet Ihr,[1]
Drum weiß ich wohl, Ihr treibt nur Spiel mit mir.
Ihr spottet mein, man hat mich warnen wollen,
Doch ach, Ihr seid so schön! wer kann Euch grollen?

Your station, I'm aware, is no mean one.
You had no need to descend so low
To love such a poor humble wretch as me,
When even the fairest bow before you.
You far surpass the handsomest of men,
So I know full well you're just trifling with me.
You're mocking me, they tried to warn me,
But ah! you're so handsome. Who could chide you?

Lassatela passar che fa la brava [30]

Lassatela passar che fa la brava,
La bizzarrina del campo de' fiori.
Se vede bene all'occhi quanto è vaga;
Ogni tre dì li muta li amatori.
E fa come lo fiume di Toscana,
Raccoglie tutta l'acqua de' valloni.
E fa come lo fiume di Firenza,
Quando l'ha tanti amanti, e quando è senza.

rispetto (Tommaseo, vol. 1, p. 345)

30 Laß sie nur gehn, die so die Stolze spielt

Let her go, then, who acts so haughtily

Laß sie nur gehn, die so die Stolze spielt,
Das Wunderkräutlein aus dem Blumenfeld.
Man sieht, wohin ihr blankes Auge zielt,
Da Tag um Tag ein Andrer ihr gefällt.
Sie treibt es grade wie Toscana's Fluß,
Dem jedes Berggewässer folgen muß.
Sie treibt es wie der Arno, will mir scheinen:
Bald hat sie viel Bewerber, bald nicht einen.[2]

Let her go, then, who acts so haughtily,
Like the magic herb in a field of flowers.
You can see what her bright eyes are after,
For every day she fancies a different man.
She carries on just like Tuscany's river
That every mountain stream must follow.
She carries on just like the Arno, it seems to me,
Now wooed by many, now by none.

---

1 This line is often misconstrued to imply that it is the woman – not the man – who conquers the most handsome of men. But it is the woman who speaks, as the original Italian makes clear.
2 The Arno in the hot summer months is abandoned by her tributaries [Heyse's footnote].

E come vuoi ch'io faccia a stare allegra [31]

E come vuoi ch'io faccia a stare allegra,
Che meco tu fai sempre il corrucciato?
Ogni cent'anni ci vieni una sera,
E par che tu ci sia stato mandato.
Chè vieni, se non son contenti i tuoi?
Rendimi il core, e va dove tu vuoi.
Co' tuoi di casa non ci stare in guerra.
Che ciò ch'è scritto in ciel, sarà anche in terra.
Co' tuoi di casa in guerra non ci stare.
Che ciò ch'è scritto in ciel, non può mancare.

rispetto (Tommaseo, vol. I, p. 225)

31 Wie soll ich fröhlich sein und lachen gar

Wie soll ich fröhlich sein und lachen gar,
Da du mir immer zürnest unverhohlen?
Du kommst nur Einmal alle hundert Jahr,
Und dann, als hätte man dir's anbefohlen.
Was kommst du, wenn's die Deinen ungern sehn?
Gieb frei mein Herz, dann magst du weitergehn.
Daheim mit deinen Leuten leb' in Frieden,
Denn was der Himmel will, geschieht hienieden.
Halt Frieden mit den Deinigen zu Haus,
Denn was der Himmel will, das bleibt nicht aus.

How can I be happy and laugh indeed

How can I be happy and laugh indeed,
When you always rage at me so openly?
You only visit me *once* in a hundred years,
And then as if you'd been ordered to.
Why come if your family's against it?
Set my heart free and go on your way.
Live in peace with your family at home,
Since what heaven ordains, happens here on earth.
Keep the peace with your family at home,
Since what heaven ordains shall come to pass.

Caro amor mio, non mi far l'adirato [32]

Caro amor mio, non mi far l'adirato.
Averla contro me non hai ragione.
Piglia un coltel che sia bene appuntato,
Vieni alla volta mia, passami il core.
Se non serve un coltel, prendi una spada,
E del mio sangue fanne una fontana.
Se non serve un coltel, prendi un pugnale,
E lava nel mio sangue ogni mio male.

rispetto (Tommaseo, vol. I, p. 345)

32 Was soll der Zorn, mein Schatz, der dich erhitzt?

Was soll der Zorn, mein Schatz, der dich erhitzt?
Ich bin mir keiner Sünde ja bewußt.
Ach, lieber nimm ein Messer wohlgespitzt

Und tritt zu mir, durchbohre mir die Brust.
Und taugt ein Messer nicht, so nimm ein Schwert,

Why this anger, my love, that inflames you so?

Why this anger, my love, that inflames you so?
I am not conscious of any sin.
Ah, I'd rather you take a well-sharpened knife

And come to me and pierce my breast.
And if a knife won't do, then take a sword

Daß meines Blutes Quell gen Himmel fährt.
Und taugt ein Schwert nicht, nimm
   des Dolches Stahl
Und wasch' in meinem Blut all meine Qual.

That my blood might spurt up to the sky.
And if a sword won't do, take a dagger
   of steel
And wash away my torment in
   my own blood.

Se moro, ricopritemi di fiori [33]

Se moro, ricopritemi di fiori,
E sottoterra non mi ci mettete:
Mettetemi de là de chelle mura
Dove più volte vista mi ci avete.
Mettetemi de là, all'acqua, al vento:
Che se moro per voi, moro contento.
Mettetemi de là, all'acqua, al sole:
Che se moro per voi, moro d'amore.

rispetto (Tommaseo, vol. I, p. 348)

33 Sterb' ich, so hüllt in Blumen meine Glieder

If I should die, shroud my limbs in flowers

Sterb' ich, so hüllt in Blumen meine Glieder;
Ich wünsche nicht, daß ihr ein Grab
   mir grabt.
Genüber jenen Mauern legt mich nieder,
Wo ihr so manchmal mich gesehen habt.
Dort legt mich hin, in Regen oder Wind;
Gern sterb' ich, ist's um dich, geliebtes Kind.
Dort legt mich hin in Sonnenschein
   und Regen;
Ich sterbe lieblich, sterb' ich deinetwegen.

If I should die, shroud my limbs in flowers;
I will not have you dig a grave for me.

Lay me down to face those walls
Where you have so often seen me.
There lay me down in rain or wind;
I die gladly, if it's for you, dear child.
There lay me down in sunshine
   and rain;
I die happily if I die for you.

E la mattina quando vi levate [34]

E la mattina quando vi levate,
Le nuvile dal ciel fate sparire.
Il sole a' monti lo fate apparire,
E quando vi vestite e vi calzate
Ill'angioli vi viengono a servire.
Quando che suona a messa,
   voi ci andate,
Tutta la gente la fate venire.
Quando l'uscio di chiesa voi entrate,
Le lampane coll'occhi l'accendete:
Pigliate l'acqua santa e vi segnate,
In testa bianca fronte la spargete.
Fate l'inchino, e poi v'inginocchiate:
Tutta la bella grazia che vo' avete!
La grazia e la beltà che il ciel vi dona:
Bella che di beltà porti corona.
La grazia e la beltà che il ciel vi manda;
Bella che di beltà porti la palma.

rispetto (Tommaseo, vol. I, p. 53)

34 Und steht Ihr früh am Morgen auf vom Bette[1]

Und steht Ihr früh am Morgen ·
   auf vom Bette,
Scheucht Ihr vom Himmel alle Wolken fort,
Die Sonne lockt Ihr auf die Berge dort,
Und Engelein erscheinen um die Wette
Und bringen Schuh und Kleider Euch sofort.
Dann, wenn Ihr ausgeht in die heil'ge Mette,
So zieht Ihr alle Menschen mit Euch fort,
Und wenn Ihr naht der benedeiten Stätte,
So zündet Euer Blick die Lampen an.
Weihwasser nehmt Ihr, macht des Kreuzes
   Zeichen
Und netzet Eure weiße Stirn sodann
Und neiget Euch und beugt die Knie
   ingleichen –
O wie holdselig steht Euch Alles an!
Wie hold und selig hat Euch Gott begabt,

Die Ihr der Schönheit Kron' empfangen habt!
Wie hold und selig wandelt Ihr im Leben;

Der Schönheit Palme ward an Euch gegeben.

And when you rise from your bed at dawn

And when you rise from your bed
   at dawn,
You chase all clouds from the sky,
You lure the sun onto those hills
And cherubs vie with each other
To bring at once your shoes and clothes.
Then, when you go to holy Mass,
You draw everyone along with you,
And when you near the sanctuary
Your glance lights up the lamps.
You take holy water, make the sign
   of the cross,
Then moisten your white brow,
And bow and fall to your knees –

Ah, how beautifully it all becomes you!
What blessed grace has God bestowed
   on you,
Who have received the crown of beauty!
How graciously, how blessedly you walk
   through life;
The palm of beauty was bestowed on you.

Benedetta sia la madre [35]

Benedetta sia la madre
Che ti fece così bella.
Più di te gentil donzella
Più di te non so bramar.
Tu sei la più graziosa,
Tu sei la più vezzosa,
Tu sei la gioja mia,
Benedetta sei tu.

Ammirando la vaghezza
Di bellezza così rara,
Ti confesso, mia cara,
Mi facesti sospirar;
E nel petto mi sentii
Una fiamma sì vivace,
Che disturba la mia pace
Mi fa sempre delirar.

venezian., MS
(Heyse, *Italienisches Liederbuch*, p. 272)

---

1 In a letter to Melanie Köchert of 3 April 1896 Wolf wrote of this song: „Ich bin mit der Musik ungefähr bei der Hälfte dieses herrlichen Gedichtes angelangt. Ob es aber heute noch fertig gebracht wird ist zweifelhaft." ('I've composed about half of this wonderful poem – but whether I shall finish it today is doubtful.') He didn't; it was completed the following morning.

35 Benedeit die sel'ge Mutter[1]

Blessed be your mother in heaven

Benedeit die sel'ge Mutter
Die so lieblich dich geboren,
So an Schönheit auserkoren,
Meine Sehnsucht fliegt dir zu!
Du so lieblich von Gebärden,
Du die Holdeste der Erden,
Du mein Kleinod, meine Wonne,
Süße, benedeit bist du!

Wenn ich aus der Ferne schmachte
Und betrachte deine Schöne,
Siehe wie ich beb und stöhne,
Daß ich kaum es bergen kann!
Und in meiner Brust gewaltsam
Fühl ich Flammen sich empören,
Die den Frieden mir zerstören,
Ach, der Wahnsinn faßt mich an!*[2]

Blessed be your mother in heaven,
Who bore you to be so sweet,
So elect in beauty –
My yearning wings its way to you!
You, so gracious of gesture,
You, the fairest on earth,
You, my jewel, my rapture,
A blessing on you, my sweet!

When I languish from afar
And behold your beauty,
See how I so tremble and groan,
Till I can hardly conceal it!
And in my breast I feel the force
Of violent flames
That destroy my peace,
Ah, madness seizes hold of me!*

* Wolf repeats the opening verse at the end of the song.

Quando bellino, al cielo salirai [36]

Quando bellino, al cielo salirai,
Ti verrò incontro con il cuore in mano:
Tu pien d'amore al sen mi abbraccerai,
Ed io ti menerò dal gran Soprano.
Il Soprano, veduto il nostro amore,
Farà dei cuori innamorati un cuore.

Ed un cuore farà de' nostri cuori,
In paradiso, in mezzo alli splendori.

rispetto (Tigri, 1st edn (1856), p. 192; 2nd edn (1860), p. 237)

36 Wenn du, mein Liebster, steigst zum Himmel auf

When you, my love, ascend to heaven

Wenn du, mein Liebster, steigst zum Himmel auf,
Trag' ich mein Herz dir in der Hand entgegen.
So liebevoll umarmst du mich darauf,
Dann woll'n wir uns dem Herrn zu Füßen legen.
Und sieht der Herrgott unsre Liebesschmerzen,
Macht er Ein Herz aus zwei verliebten Herzen,
Zu Einem Herzen fügt er zwei zusammen,
Im Paradies, umglänzt von Himmelsflammen.

When you, my love, ascend to heaven,
I'll come to you with heart in hand.
Then you will embrace me so lovingly
And we shall fall at the Lord's feet.

And when the Lord sees our love's anguish,
He'll make *one* heart of two loving hearts,
He'll fashion two hearts into *one*,
In Paradise, ringed by heavenly radiance.

1 This is the only poem not to be found in Dalmedico, Marcoaldi, Tigri or Tommaseo. Heyse called it a Venetian popular song.
2 In less than eighteen months, Wolf was taken to Dr Svetlin's mental asylum.

E quanto tempo ho perso per amarte! [37]

E quanto tempo ho perso per amarte!
Egli era meglio avessi amato Iddio.
Del paradiso n'avere' una parte,
Qualche Santo averei dal lato mio.
E per amarvi voi, fresco bel viso,
Io mi ritrovo fuor del paradiso:
E per amarvi voi, fresca viola,
Del paradiso mi ritrovo fuora.

rispetto (Tigri, vol. I, p. 145, and Tommaseo, vol. I, p. 226)

37 Wie viele Zeit verlor ich, dich zu lieben![1]

How much time I've lost in loving you!

Wie viele Zeit verlor ich, dich zu lieben!
Hätt' ich doch Gott geliebt in all der Zeit,
Ein Platz im Paradies wär' mir verschrieben,
Ein Heil'ger säße dann an meiner Seit'.
Und weil ich dich geliebt, schön frisch Gesicht,
Verscherzt' ich mir des Paradieses Licht,
Und weil ich dich geliebt, schön Veigelein,
Komm' ich nun nicht ins Paradies hinein.

How much time I've lost in loving you!
Had I but loved God in all that time,
A place in Paradise would now be mine,
And a saint would be seated at my side.
And because I've loved you, fair and fresh of face,
I have forfeited the light of Paradise,
And because I've loved you, fair violet,
I shall never now gain Paradise.

Quando incontri i miei occhi, e fai un riso [38]

Quando incontri i miei occhi, e fai un riso,
E poi li abbassi, e pieghi il mento al seno,
Ti prego prima a darmene un avviso,
Perchè in quel mentre io tenga il cuore a freno.
Perchè in quel mentre io tenga a freno il cuore,
Che mi vorrebbe uscir dal grande amore.
Perchè in quel mentre io tenga il core in petto,
Che mi vorrebbe uscir dal gran diletto.

rispetto (Tommaseo, vol. I, p. 70)

38 Wenn du mich mit den Augen streifst und lachst

When you caress me with your eyes and laugh

Wenn du mich mit den Augen streifst und lachst,
Sie senkst und neigst das Kinn zum Busen dann,
Bitt' ich, daß du mir erst ein Zeichen machst,
Damit ich doch mein Herz auch länd'gen kann,

When you caress me with your eyes and laugh,
Then lower them and bow your head to your breast,
I beg you to give me first a sign,
That I might keep my heart in check.

---

1 The poem appears in both Tigri and Tommaseo, where it is headed respectively 'Unhappy love' and 'Bitter reproaches'. Does the poem express delight or despair? Either interpretation is possible, but Wolf's music seems to speak of both grief and deep love. See HW to Melanie Köchert, 3 April 1896, p. 228.

Daß ich mein Herz mag bänd'gen,   That I might tame and keep my heart
    zahm und still,   in check,
Wenn es vor großer Liebe springen will,   When it would leap up for great love,
    Daß ich mein Herz mag halten   That I might keep my heart
    in der Brust,   in my breast,
Wenn es ausbrechen will vor großer Lust.   When it would break out in its great joy.

Sia benedeto 'l verde e chi lo porta [39]

Sia benedeto 'l verde e chi lo porta,   De verde va vestido lo mio amore.
Che mi de verde vôi farme una vesta.   Verde co verde se confà con tuto:
De verde va vestida la campagna,   Fora del verde nasse ogni bel fruto.
De verde va vestido chi me ama.
De verde va vestido 'l caciatore,   *vilota* (Dalmedico,[1] p. 19)

39 Gesegnet sei das Grün und wer es trägt!

Blessed be green and those who wear it!

Gesegnet sei das Grün und wer es trägt!   Blessed be green and those who wear it!
Ein grünes Kleid will ich mir machen lassen.   I shall have a green dress made.
Ein grünes Kleid trägt auch die Frühlingsaue.   The meadows too wear green in spring,
Grün kleidet sich der Liebling meiner Augen.   And the darling of my eyes wears green.
    In Grün sich kleiden ist der Jäger Brauch,   Huntsmen are wont to dress in green,
Ein grünes Kleid trägt mein Geliebter auch;   My sweetheart too is clad in green;
    Das Grün steht allen Dingen lieblich an,   All things look well in green,
Aus Grün wächs't jede schöne Frucht heran.   Every lovely fruit grows from green.

Vorria che la tua casa tralucesse [40]

Vorria che la tua casa tralucesse,   Quanti risguardi ti daria il mio cuore,
Bellin, quando ci passo per la via: Non son gocciole d'acqua quando piove.
Tu fossi dentro ed io lì ti vedesse,
Quanti risguardi il mio cuor ti daria!
Quanti risguardi ti daria il cuor mio,   *rispetto* (Tigri, 1st edn (1856), p. 196;
Non son gocciole d'acqua giù pel rio;   2nd edn (1860), p. 126)

40 O wär' dein Haus durchsichtig wie ein Glas

Ah, were your house transparent like a glass

O wär' dein Haus durchsichtig wie ein Glas,   Ah, were your house transparent
        like a glass,
Mein Holder, wenn ich mich vorüberstehle!   When I steal past, my darling!

---

1   Dalmedico, writing in 1857, states in his 'Cenni sulle Vilote' that until fifty years ago these songs used to be sung by lovers beneath the windows of their sweethearts to the accompaniment of a fiddle, mandolin or guitar – or all these instruments together.

NO STANZA BREAK

Dann säh' ich drinnen dich ohn' Unterlaß,
Wie blickt' ich dann nach dir mit ganzer
    Seele!
Wie viele Blicke schickte dir mein Herz,
Mehr als da Tropfen hat der Fluß im März!
Wie viele Blicke schickt' ich dir entgegen,
Mehr als da Tropfen niedersprühn im Regen!

Then I should always see you within,
How I should gaze at you with all my soul!

My heart would send you more glances
Than the river has drops in March!
How many glances would I send you,
More than drops cascading down in rain!

Stanotte a mezzanotte mi levai [41]

Stanotte a mezzanotte mi levai,
Trovai 'l mio cuore che del petto usciva;
E io gli dissi: cor, dove ne vai?
Mi disse: a veder voi che ne veniva.

Mira, il mi' core se non ti vuol bene!
Esce dal petto e ti viene a vedere.

rispetto (Tommaseo, vol. I, p. 118)

41 Heut Nacht erhob ich mich um Mitternacht[1]

Last night I rose at midnight

Heut Nacht erhob ich mich um Mitternacht,
Da war mein Herz mir heimlich
    fortgeschlichen.
Ich frug: Herz, wohin stürmst du so
    mit Macht?
Es sprach: Nur Euch zu sehn, sei es entwichen.
Nun sieh, wie muß es um mein Lieben stehn:
Mein Herz entweicht der Brust, um dich[2]
    zu sehn!

Last night I rose at midnight,
And found my heart had secretly
    slipped away.
I asked: 'Heart, where are you storming to
    with such force?'
It said it had only stolen away to see you.
Now you can see how much I must love you:
My heart steals from my breast
    to behold you!

Non posso più cantar [42]

Non posso più cantar, che tira vento
E m'entra in bocca, e non mi lassa dire:
L'ho ben paura di perdarlo il tempo.
Fossi sicur, non andere' a dormire,

Fossi sicuro, a dormir 'n andarei:
Chesto bel tempo non lo perdarei.

rispetto (Tommaseo, vol. I, p. 127)

---

1 This was one of Melanie Köchert's favourite poems, as we see from the letter Wolf wrote her on 25 April 1896: „Ich weiß, daß Ihnen dieses Gedicht ganz besonders gefallen, umso mehr freut es mich, daß dasselbe in der Sammlung nicht fehlt." ('I know that this poem has given you particular pleasure, and so it makes me all the happier that it's included in the collection.')
2 The switch from 'Euch' to intimate 'dich' is signalled by a melting modulation to D major.

42 Nicht länger kann ich singen[1]

Nicht länger kann ich singen, denn der Wind
Weht stark und macht dem Athem was zu schaffen.
Auch fürcht' ich, daß die Zeit umsonst verrinnt.
Ja wär' ich sicher, ging' ich jetzt nicht schlafen.
Ja wüßt' ich was, würd' ich nicht heimspazieren
Und einsam diese schöne Zeit verlieren.

I can sing no more

I can sing no more, for the wind
Blows fiercely and takes my breath away.
I fear too that I am wasting my time.
If I were sure of you, I should not now go to bed.
If I really knew, I should not walk home
And waste this lovely time in solitude.

Stattene zitta, brutta cicalina [43]

Stattene zitta, brutta cicalina:
I tuoi rispetti m'hanno stomacato.
Se tu durassi fino a domattina,
Non canteresti un rispetto garbato.
Stattene zitta, e vattene alla paglia:
Canta meglio di te un asin che raglia.

rispetto (Tigri, 1st edn (1856), p. 41;
2nd edn (1860), p. 3)

43 Schweig' einmal still, du garst'ger Schwätzer dort!

Schweig' einmal still, du garst'ger Schwätzer dort!
Zum Ekel ist mir dein verwünschtes Singen.
Und triebst du es bis morgen früh so fort,
Doch würde dir kein schmuckes Lied gelingen.
Schweig' einmal still und lege dich aufs Ohr!
Das Ständchen eines Esels zög' ich vor.

Shut up for once, you odious ranter!

Shut up for once, you odious ranter!
Your cursed singing makes me sick.
And were you to keep it up till morning,
You'd still not manage a decent song.
Shut up for once and go to bed!
I'd sooner hear a donkey's serenade.

---

1   Wolf's marking requires the song to be performed *recht kläglich*. 'Kläglich' can mean either plaintively or pathetically/wretchedly/lamentably, and in view of the many *staccati*, *marcati* and trills, Wolf possibly intended the singer to perform as unmusically as the violinist in the postlude to 'Wie lange schon war immer mein Verlangen'. But Eric Sams considers the song to be 'far from comic' and writes that the 'aloofly classical texture of the music' suggests 'an other-worldly passion wholly wasted on a mundane recipient whose instant reaction in the second song is to double the speed of the music, as if to say 'for heaven's sake get on with it'. Wolf links 42 and 43, even though they are printed separately in Heyse's *Italienisches Liederbuch*. Falling intervals in both songs, suggesting a donkey's bray, become explicit in Wolf's setting of 'Esel' in 'Schweig einmal still', and in the ensuing postlude. See also HW to Melanie Köchert, 23 April 1896, p. 229.

Se ti savessi, o falsa renegada [44]

Se ti savessi, o falsa renegada,
Le pene che ò patìo per el to amore,
Quando ti gèri in camera serada,
E mi, meschin, de fora a le verdure.
La piova me pareva aqua rosada,
E i lampi me parea segni d'amore,
E la tempesta me pareva dài,

Quando che gèra soto i to tolài,
E soto i to tolài gera 'l mio leto,
El ciel sereno gèra 'l mio coverto.
El scalin de la porta, el mio cussin:
Che vita che faceva, o poverin!

vilota (Dalmedico, p. 116)

44 O wüßtest du, wie viel ich deinetwegen

O wüßtest du, wie viel ich deinetwegen,
Du falsche Renegatin, litt zur Nacht,
Indeß du im verschlossnen Haus gelegen
Und ich die Zeit im Freien zugebracht.
Als Rosenwasser diente mir der Regen,
Der Blitz hat Liebesbotschaft mir gebracht;
Ich habe Würfel mit dem Sturm gespielt,
Als unter deinem Dach ich Wache hielt.
    Mein Bett war unter deinem Dach bereitet,
Der Himmel lag als Decke drauf gebreitet,
    Die Schwelle deiner Thür, das war
        mein Kissen –
Ich Aermster, ach, was hab' ich ausstehn
    müssen!

Ah, if only you knew how much for you

Ah, if only you knew how much for you,
False traitress, I have suffered at night,
While you lay in your locked house
And I spent the time outside.
Rain served me for rose-water,
Lightning brought me tidings of love;
I played dice with the storm,
While keeping watch beneath your eaves.
    My bed was laid beneath your eaves,
With the sky spread out as my blanket,
    Your threshold was my pillow –

Poor me, how I've had to suffer!

La casa del mi' amor vada in profondo [45]

La casa del mi' amor vada in profondo,
Un lago d'acqua possa diventare
Dentro ci piova coccole di piombo,
Dentro ci vada un serpente a alloggiare,
E ci vada un serpente avvelenato,
Avveleni il mio amor che m'ha lasciato.

E ci vada un serpente avvelenito,
Avveleni il mio amor che m'ha tradito.

rispetto (Tommaseo, vol. I, p. 338)
Also set in Italian by Wolf-Ferrari

45 Verschling' der Abgrund meines Liebsten Hütte

Verschling' der Abgrund meines Liebsten
    Hütte,
An ihrer Stelle schäum' ein See zur Stunde.

Bleikugeln soll der Himmel drüber schütten,
Und eine Schlange hause dort im Grunde.

May a chasm engulf my lover's cottage

May a chasm engulf my lover's cottage,

May a foaming lake appear promptly
    in its place,

May heaven rain lead bullets on it,
And a serpent make its lair there.

Drin hause eine Schlange gift'ger Art,
    Die ihn vergifte, der mir untreu ward.

Drin hause eine Schlange, giftgeschwollen,
    Und bring' ihm Tod, der mich verrathen wollen!

May a poisonous snake dwell there
    And poison him who was unfaithful to me.

May a snake dwell there swollen with venom
    And bring death to him who sought to betray me!

Ce l'ho un amante alla Città di Penna [46]

Ce l'ho un amante alla Città di Penna,
E l'altro l'ho al bel porto d'Ancona:
N'ho uno sul gran pian della Maremma,
L'altro a Viterbo ch'è terra di Roma:
Ne ho uno giù pel pian del Casentino.

Quello del mio paese è più vicino:
Ne ho uno verso il pian della Magione,
Quattro alla Fratta, e diece a Castiglione.

rispetto (Tigri, 2nd edn (1860), p. 179)

46 Ich hab' in Penna einen Liebsten wohnen[1]

I have one lover living in Penna

Ich hab' in Penna einen Liebsten wohnen,
In der Maremmenebne einen andern,
Einen im schönen Hafen von Ancona,
Zum Vierten muß ich nach Viterbo wandern;
Ein Andrer wohnt in Casentino dort,
Der Nächste lebt mit mir am selben Ort,
Und wieder einen hab' ich in Magione,
Vier in La Fratta, zehn in Castiglione.

I have one lover living in Penna,
Another in the plain of Maremma,
One in the beautiful port of Ancona,
For the fourth I must go to Viterbo;

Another lives over in Casentino,
The next with me in my own town,
And I've yet another in Magione,
Four in La Fratta, ten in Castiglione.

---

[1] 'Ich hab in Penna' concerns a nymphomaniac, a sort of female counterpart to Mozart's Don Giovanni – and the comparison is apt, even though Wolf's heroine, with 21 conquests, is no match for the Don's 2,064. Wolf must have known Leporello's 'Madamina, il catalogo è questo', for there are unmistakable echoes of the Catalogue Aria, such as the rapid quaver movement and the whiplash scale passage at 'Maggione' which scuttles down the stave just like Mozart's accompaniment. And the final phrase of the song, 'zehn in Castiglione' is breathtakingly similar in rhythm to Leporello's 'Ma in Espagna' – the cadence in Wolf's song is marked *frei*, as though it were the conclusion of a cabaletta (the preceding quaver rests, however, must be kept in strict rhythm: ten of them, implying that all the lovers in Castiglione are being mentally adumbrated). The song is usually sung flirtatiously but there is another way. In the semi-staged performances of the cycle by Werner Güra, Anke Vondung and Christoph Berner, Vondung sang it with all the fury that she could muster – not to the audience but into Güra's face. It is the culmination of all the quarrelling that has flared throughout the cycle: *you* might not think me attractive, she screams, but other men *do*. See HW to Melanie Köchert, 14 May 1896, p. 230.

Edmund Hoefer
(1819–1882)

			page
Fröhliche Fahrt	6–7 May 1876, revised 6 September 1876	SATB unaccompanied	259

POET

Hoefer was a popular novelist in the second half of the nineteenth century: *Aus alter und neuer Zeit* (1854), *Wie das Volk spricht* (1855), *Bewegtes Leben* (1856), *Vergangene Tage* (1859), *Norien. Erinnerungen einer alten Frau* (1859), *Deutsche Herzen* (1860), *Der große Baron* (1861), *Unter der Fremdherrschaft* (1863), *Tolleneck* (1864) and *Altermann* (1864) are just some of his books that were once widely read. His poems were published in 1853 by M. Simions Verlag, Leipzig, as *Gedichte von Edmund Hoefer*.

COMPOSER

Wolf tells us on the score of 'Fröhliche Fahrt' that it was 'begun at 4.15 on the Saturday afternoon of 6 May' and 'finished on Sunday, 7 May at 10.15 in the morning, in the Prater'. He also tells us that it was extremely cold. He revised the work in September, and then used the back of the score to write down his SATB setting of August Mahlmann's 'Gottvertrauen'. See p. 315.

LIED

Fröhliche Fahrt[1]

Glücklich[2] wer zum Liebchen zieht
In die blaue Fern' hinein,[3]
Da tanzt der Schritt, da klingt das Lied,
Da blitzt der Sonnenschein.

Joyous journey

Happy is he who sets out to his love
Far into the distant blue,
His step dances, his song resounds,
The sunshine glitters brightly.

[1] Wolf sets the first two of Hoefer's four stanzas, with several repetitions of text.
[2] Hoefer: O glücklich.   [3] Hoefer: In blaue Fern' hinein!

Es sagt kein Wort, es singt kein Lied
Das Glück so hold[1] und rein:
O glücklich, wer zum Liebchen zieht
In die blaue Fern' hinein![2]

Hinaus, hinaus mit Sing und Sang',
Hinein ins Blau, ins Blau!
Der Tag mit klarem Fittig sank
Auf Wald und Busch und Au.
Was zaghaft dir das Herz umschlingt,
Wirf's ab, du altes Haus,
Und zieh noch einmal lustbeschwingt
Zur Ferne froh hinaus.

No word can describe, no song express
Such pure and gracious happiness:
Oh, happy is he who goes to his love
Far into the distant blue!

Away we go with songs and singing,
Out into the blue, the blue!
Dusk has descended with limpid wings
On forest, bush and meadow.
Whatever constricts your timid heart,
Cast it aside, old fellow,
And set out once more, winged with joy,
Happily into the distance.

1   Hoefer: frisch.   2   See note 3, p. 259.

August Heinrich Hoffmann von Fallersleben
(1798–1874)

		page
Liebesfrühling	9 August 1878	263
Auf der Wanderung	10 August 1878	264
Ja, die Schönst'! ich sagt' es offen	11 August 1878	265
Nach dem Abschiede	31 August–1 September 1878	265
Die Nachtigallen schweigen	10 September 1878	fragment

POET

Christened August Heinrich Hoffmann, the poet added 'von Fallersleben' (his birthplace and where he first went to school) to lend distinction to his name. He attended the celebrated Katharineum School in Braunschweig, where he came across the political and patriotic poetry of Theodor Körner in *Leyer und Schwert*. In the spring of 1816 he entered Göttingen University to study theology, but his fondness for poetry – he had already written much verse – caused him to switch to language and literature. During his travels in the autumn of 1818 he formed a friendship with the Grimm brothers, and on his return in 1819 transferred to the University of Bonn, where he became the librarian's secretary and earned a partial living by giving tuition and writing anonymously a large number of student songs. Five years later he was appointed official curator at the central library in Breslau, and in 1830 professor of German language and literature. By this time he was a passionate collector and editor of medieval texts.

After Hoffmann's extensive travels through Austria, Switzerland and France, his poetry turned political. He expressed his support for German unity in *Unpolitische Lieder* (1840), which led to dismissal from his post at Breslau University, and Campe, his publishers, were no longer allowed to operate in Prussia. Several years of political activity in the north and west of Germany followed, before he settled in Schwerin. Although he took little part in the March Revolution of 1848, his 'Deutschland, Deutschland über alles', written in 1841, was often sung as a patriotic hymn before it became the official national anthem. Although the Prussian authorities agreed to an amnesty, he was not allowed to resume his professorship and was ordered to leave Berlin. He considered renouncing his Prussian nationality and seriously entertained the idea of emigrating to America, but on returning to Braunschweig in the summer of 1848 he met his sister's daughter, the eighteen-year-old Ida zum Berge. They married the following year when Hoffmann was fifty-one. In 1860 he moved to Corvey in Westphalia as librarian to the Duke of Ratibor, whose library of some 36,000 books he catalogued and expanded into one of the most celebrated in Germany.

Hoffmann was also a renowned collector and publisher of folk songs and one of Germany's most gifted writers of children's verse: poems such as 'Wer hat die schönsten Schäfchen', 'Kuckuck, Kuckuck ruft aus dem Wald', 'Winter, ade!' and 'Alle Vögel sind schon da' used to be known to hundreds of thousands of children in German-speaking lands. *Fünfzig Kinderlieder* (1843), *Fünfzig neue Kinderlieder* (1845) and *Hundert Schullieder* (1847) made him a household name throughout Germany. His huge reputation was to some extent due to the numerous musical settings of his verse, and throughout his career he courted song composers. He met the twenty-year-old Brahms in Göttingen in July 1853, and Liszt in Weimar during 1854; Mendelssohn, Schumann, Nicolai, Reissiger and Spohr all agreed to supply melodies for his *Fünfzig neue Kinderlieder*; and Ludwig Erk for the *Deutsches Volksgesangbuch* (1848). Like many a poet before and after him, he was not averse to writing to composers, asking them to set his poems – see the letter to Schumann of late December 1843, p. 263. He also tried to interest Schumann in an opera libretto, *In beiden Welten*, which he had written in less than a fortnight. Schumann didn't bite. Hoffmann's prolific output exceeded two hundred publications. There are four editions of his *Gedichte*, published in 1834, 1837, 1843 and 1853 – a nightmare for scholars, since the textual variations in each volume are legion.

COMPOSER

Wolf's four Hoffmann von Fallersleben songs were composed in 1878, 'My Lodi in song', as Wolf later called it (see p. 188). He was already in the habit of composing settings of one particular poet en masse in a heightened state of creativity – characteristic of him for the rest of his artistic life. He now turned to Hoffmann von Fallersleben, whose works he had recently bought. Wolf planned two cycles: *Des fahrenden Schülers Lieben und Leiden* and *Dichterleben*, consisting respectively of three and fourteen songs – see HW to his father, 27 August 1878, p. 263. 'Auf der Wanderung' and 'Ja, die Schönst'! ich sagt' es offen' from *Des fahrenden Schülers Lieben und Leiden* were composed on 10 and 11 August; 'Liebesfrühling' and 'Nach dem Abschiede' from *Dichterleben* on 9 August and at the end of the same month. It seems that Wolf intended to compose two cycles simultaneously.

AUGUST HEINRICH HOFFMANN VON FALLERSLEBEN

LETTERS

Hoffmann von Fallersleben and Richter Ende to Robert Schumann, late December 1843

Wir beabsichtigen jetzt eine neue Sammlung von Kinderliedern mit Original- und Volksmelodien nebst Pianofortebegleitung herauszugeben. Um dieser Sammlung einen eigenthümlichen Werth zu verleihen vor allen andern, bitten wir Sie, dieselbe mit einer Composition des beifolgenden Gedichtes[1] zu bereichern.

We now intend to bring out a new collection of children's songs with both original and folk melodies, complete with pianoforte accompaniment. In order to give this collection a special quality and make it superior to all other anthologies, we request you to enrich it with a musical setting of the enclosed poem.

HW to his father, Waidhofen a. d. Ybbs, 27 August 1878

Die Produktivität im Komponieren hat sich zeitweise wieder eingestellt. Ich schrieb 3 Lieder „des fahrenden Schülers". Einige für den aus 14 Liedern bestehenden Zyklus „Dichterleben", sämtliche Texte von Hoffmann v. Fallersleben, dessen Gedichte ich mir gekauft.

My rate of composition has picked up once again. I've written 3 songs on poems from *Des fahrenden Schülers Lieben und Leiden*; and several from the cycle of 14 poems called *Dichterleben*, all by Hoffmann v. Fallersleben whose poems I have bought.

LIEDER

Liebesfrühling[2]

Wie oft schon ward es Frühling wieder
Für die erstorbne öde Welt!
Wie oft schon schollen frohe Lieder
Ihm überall durch Wald und Feld!

Love's springtime

How often has spring returned
For the dead and desolate world!
How often was spring greeted everywhere
By happy songs in forest and field!

---

1 The poem in question is 'Soldatenlied', to which Schumann gave no opus number.
2 The original title in *Dichterleben* read: 'Wie oft schon!'

Wie oft schon ward es Frühling wieder!	How often has spring returned!
Doch Frühling ward es nicht für mich:	But no spring burgeoned for me:
Es schweigen meines Herzens Lieder,	The songs of my heart are silent,
Denn Frühling* wird es nur durch dich.	For spring* can be brought only by you.

* Wolf repeats 'Frühling' to a *fortissimo* dynamic.

Auf der Wanderung[1]   On a walk

Über die Hügel und über die Berge hin	Over the hills and over the mountains
Sing' ich und ruf' ich, wie glücklich ich bin.	I sing and cry out how happy I am.
Sonniges Wetter,	Sunny weather,
Rauschende Blätter,	Rustling leaves,
Vogelgeschmetter,[2]	Carolling birds,
Wonnige Lust!	Rapturous delight!
Dörfer und Mühlen, Wälder und grüne Au'n,	Villages and mills, woods and green meadows,
Schlößer und Burgen, lieblich zu schau'n,	Castles and palaces, fair to the eye,
Freundliche Städtchen,	Friendly small towns,
Niedliche Mädchen:	Pretty girls:
Gretchen und Käthchen,	Gretel and Katy,
Kennst du mich noch?	Do you remember me?
Warum nicht kennen? Willkommen in unsrem[3] Land!	Why do you not? Welcome to our land!
Bist[4] mir willkommen, und reich mir die Hand!	You are welcome, so give me your hand!
Laßt uns dann singen,	Then let us sing,
Tanzen und springen,	Dance and leap,
Lustig uns schwingen –	Let us make merry,
Kirmes ist heut!	Today's church fair!
Lustig das Leben zu Fuß mit dem Wanderstab	Life is fun, to hike with a staff
Über die Berge, hinauf und herab!	Over mountains, up hill and down dale!
Sonniges Wetter,	Sunny weather,
Rauschende Blätter,	Rustling leaves,
Vogelgeschmetter,[5]	Carolling birds,
Wonnige Lust!	Rapturous delight!

1 This is the eighth poem of Hoffmann von Fallersleben's *Des fahrenden Schülers Liebe und Leiden*. Wolf omits Hoffmann's fourth verse.
2 Hoffmann: Vögelgeschmetter.   3 Hoffmann: unserm.   4 Hoffmann: bis.
5 See note 2.

Ja, die Schönst'! ich sagt' es offen

Ja, die Schönst'! ich sagt' es offen,
Und ich war's mir frisch[1] bewußt.
Kühnes Wagen, süßes Hoffen,
Frischer Muth und Wanderlust!*

Und nun möcht' ich schier verzagen
Und im[2] Herzeleid vergehn,
Denn nach diesen kurzen Tagen
Ist's um alles schon geschehn.

Laß sie sinken, laß sie fallen,
Laß sie alle stürzen ein,
All die Zinnen, Thürm' und Hallen!
Ist die Schönste darum mein?

Sind nicht Riegel, Schlößer, Thore,
Ist nicht Alles aufgetan?
Nur dein Herz, o Leonore,
Bleibt verschlossen mir fortan.*

Yes, the fairest!

Yes, the fairest! I've said it openly,
And have always been aware of it.
Dauntless adventure, sweet hope,
A fresh spirit and thirst for travel!*

And now I am near to despair
And overwhelmed with sorrow,
For after these short-lived days
Everything has come to naught.

Let them crumble, let them fall,
Let them all come tumbling down:
Pinnacles, towers and halls!
Would the fairest thereby be mine?

Have not bolts, locks, gates
All been opened up?
Only your heart, Leonora,
Continues to be closed to me.*

* Wolf repeats the final two lines of the first and last verse.

Nach dem Abschiede

Dunkel sind nun alle Gassen,
Und die Stadt ist öd' und leer;
Denn mein Lieb hat mich verlassen.
Meine Sonne scheint nicht mehr.*

Büsch' und Wälder, Flüss' und Hügel
Liegen zwischen ihr und mir –
Liebe, Liebe, gieb mir Flügel,
Daß ich fliegen kann zu ihr!

Liebe, laß ihr Bild erscheinen!
O so blick' ich sie doch an,
Daß, wenn meine Augen weinen,
Sich mein Herz erfreuen kann.

After parting

The streets are now all dark,
And the town is desolate and empty;
For my love has left me.
My sun no longer shines.*

Bushes and forests, rivers and hills
Intervene between us:
Love, Love, give me wings,
That I might fly to her!

Love, let her image appear!
For me to gaze on her,
So that, when I weep,
My heart may delight.

* Wolf repeats the line to a *piano* and then to a *pianissimo* dynamic.

1 Hoffmann: froh.   2 Hoffmann: in.

HENRIK IBSEN
(1828–1906)

		page
Drei Gesänge aus H. Ibsens 'Das Fest auf Solhaug'		
Ballade. Gesang Margits	7–23 January 1891	272
Gudmunds erster Gesang	30 October 1891, rev. 12 November 1896	272
Gudmunds zweiter Gesang	7 March 1891	273

POET

Norwegian playwright, often considered to be the founder of modern prose drama. Ibsen wrote some 25 plays between 1850 and 1899, several of which have been adapted as operas. *The Vikings at Helgeland* was set by Karel Moor as *Hjördis* (1905), and the American Robert Ward turned *Hedda Gabler* (1890) into an opera, which was premiered as *Claudia Legare* in 1978 at the Minnesota Opera. *The Master Builder* (1892) became Anton Ruppert's *Baumeister Solness* (1996) and Martin Halpern's *The Scaffolding* (2005). *Peer Gynt* (1867) was set as an opera by Werner Egk (1938), but no composer can rival Edvard Grieg's Ibsen compositions: *Peer Gynt* (1902) and the *Seks Digte af Henrik Ibsen*, Op. 25: 'Spillemænd', 'En Svane', 'Stambogsrim', 'Med en Vandlilje', 'Borte!' and 'En Fuglevise' (1876). *The Feast at Solhaug* was set by Wilhelm Stenhammar in 1893, and both Hans Pfitzner and Harald Sæverud composed incidental music to the play.

Ibsen's *Gildet paa Solhoug* was written in Bergen in 1855 and premiered on 2 January 1856 to mark the anniversary of the Norwegian National Theatre. Its mixture of poetic form (much of it is written in rhyming verse) and folklore contributed to its initial success. Ibsen was actually serenaded after the premiere in Bergen, and it was the first of his plays to be performed outside Norway: staged in Stockholm during the autumn of 1857, and in Copenhagen four years later. The critics were not so impressed and unfairly accused Ibsen of plagiarism. Georg Brandes, for example, declared that it was 'nothing more or less than a colourless imitation of *Svend Dyrings Huus* [a play by Henrik Hertz, written in 1837]'. Brandes later became a friend of the playwright and revised his opinion. Discussing Ibsen's Preface to the revised edition of the play (1883), Brandes implied that there was something strongly personal about the theme. 'Where this personal nucleus lies', he writes, 'must be left unsaid by a critic who has received no confidential communication from the author.' What Brandes was unable to explain, because of loyalty to his friend Ibsen, James Walter McFarlane and Graham Orton reveal in the first volume of *The Oxford Ibsen*. After the first night of *Gildet paa Solhoug*, Magdalene Thoresen persuaded her husband, the Reverend Johan Thoresen, to invite the young playwright to their home. Ibsen accepted the invitation and the dinner took place five days later. During the evening Ibsen met and fell in love with one of the daughters of the house, the nineteen-year-old Suzannah. A few weeks later he was formally engaged and the marriage took place two years later. It seems that Magdalene, who was thirty-six at the time, was also attracted to Ibsen; when it is understood that she had married Johan, a much older widower, not out of passion but for companionship and security, the similarity to the Margit–Bengt–Gudmund–Signe configuration in the play becomes clear – see notes to the songs below.

COMPOSER

Although Wolf hoped that he would eventually be able to earn a living as a composer, he was perpetually short of money. His delight at being offered 300–400 florins by the Burgtheater to write incidental music to Ibsen's *Das Fest auf Solhaug* in a translation by Emma Klingenfeld, when he had recently contributed 500 marks in cash towards the cost of publishing the *Spanisches Liederbuch*, can be imagined (HW to his mother, 8 November 1890, p. 268). In the event he received only 200 florins. Delight soon turned to despair (a typical Wolfian characteristic) when he realised that the material was uninspired (HW to Oskar Grohe, 14 November 1890, p. 269). He even felt tempted to plagiarise Brahms (HW to Engelbert Humperdinck, 11 November 1890, p. 269)! However, he persevered, was pleased by what he had achieved, convinced that he was destined to become a celebrated opera composer (HW to Oskar Grohe, 18 December 1890, p. 269). He finally completed five choruses, two instrumental preludes and three solo songs. The premiere took place on 21 November 1891: the play was not a success, enjoyed only a short run, and Wolf's contributions were drastically reduced in number by the director (HW to his mother, 27 November 1891, p. 270) and were hardly mentioned in the press. And yet, with typical inconsistency, Wolf harboured hopes at the time of composing *Manuel Venegas* in 1897 that he could develop *Das Fest auf Solhaug* into a full-scale opera – the reason why he resisted the idea of reusing the chorus from *Das Fest* in his second opera (HW to Melanie Köchert, 31 July 1897, p. 270). In the year that Wolf died, the Vienna Hugo-Wolf-Verein arranged for Heckel to publish Wolf's *Solhaug* music in its entirety and in March 1904 there was a complete performance of the play with all Wolf's incidental music – uncut and untampered with – at the Stadttheater in Graz in a new translation by Christian Morgenstern, who was later to make his name as the poet of *Galgenlieder* (1905) and *Palmström* (1910), which include some of the wittiest poems in German literature. *Das Fest auf Solhaug* is the only music that Wolf wrote to commission.

LETTERS

HW to Wilhelm Schmid, Vienna, 8 November 1890

Auch bin ich jetzt contraktlich gebunden die Wege Ibsen'scher Romantik zu wandeln, da ich mich dem Director unseres k. k. Hofburgtheaters verpflichtet habe die Musik zu dem romantischen Schauspiele „das Fest auf Solhaug" zu schreiben, eine Aufgabe, die, obschon gegen meine künstlerischen Principien, doch den Reiz für sich hat: dem dramatischen einen Schritt näher gerückt zu sein.

I am now bound by contract to wander the paths of Ibsen romanticism, for I have promised the director of our Hofburgtheater to compose the incidental music to the romantic drama *Das Fest auf Solhaug*, a task that, though not in line with my artistic principles, is attractive in that it will bring me a step nearer to my operatic ambitions.

HW to his mother, Vienna, 8 November 1890

Meine Aktien sind jetzt furchtbar im Steigen begriffen, da Schott in Mainz alles von mir verlegt. Ich hoffe vom nächsten Jahr an in geordneten Verhältnissen leben zu können, da ich mir von dem Ertrag meiner Kompositionen wohl etwas verhoffen darf. Wenn ich nur dieses Jahr noch überdaure! Gleichzeitig denke ich vom Direktor des Hofburgtheaters, in dessen Auftrag ich eine Musik zu einem neuen Schauspiel von Ibsen, „das Fest auf Solhaug", zu schreiben habe, 3–400 fl. zu bekommen, als Honorar für meine Arbeit.

My reputation is improving radically, as Schott's in Mainz are to publish all my music. From next year I hope to be living a settled existence, and I also harbour some hope that I shall be able to live off the proceeds of my compositions. If only I can survive this year! At the same time I shall receive 3–400 florins from the director of the Hofburgtheater who has commissioned me to write incidental music to Ibsen's *Das Fest auf Solhaug*.

HW to Engelbert Humperdinck, Döbling, 11 November 1890

Zudem fühle ich mich momentan zum Arbeiten gar nicht aufgelegt u. doch soll ich demnächst dem Director unseres k. k. Hofburgtheaters eine Arbeit liefern: eine Musik zu Ibsen's „das Fest auf Solhaug". Der Teufel soll das musiciren! Wenn Gelegenheit Diebe macht, so möge man mich's nicht verübeln, wenn ich die Musik zu diesem Gelegenheitsstück irgendwo stehle. Ich wäre fast im Stande bei Brahms eine Anleihe zu machen [. . .]

And anyway I am simply not in the mood for work at the moment, although I must in the near future finish a work for the director of the Hofburgtheater: incidental music to Ibsen's *Das Fest auf Solhaug*. The devil's work! If opportunity makes the thief, no one will take it amiss if I steal the music from somewhere for this occasional piece. I would almost be capable of borrowing from Brahms [. . .]

HW to Oskar Grohe, Döbling, 14 November 1890

Das Ibsensche Stück gefällt mir alle Tage weniger. Es ist recht brav gestümpert und dabei verdammt wenig Poesie.
　　Ich weiß wahrlich nicht, wo ich den Mörtel hernehmen soll, diese hausbackene Zimmermannsarbeit musikalisch zu verkleistern. Das ganze Zeug widersteht mir, und doch soll ich dran.

I like the Ibsen play less every day – it's cobbled together in an extremely amateurish way and with damned little poetry.
　　I really don't know where I shall get the mortar from to glue together musically this home-made piece of carpentry. The whole thing is repugnant to me and yet I must get on with it.

HW to Oskar Grohe, Döbling, 18 December 1890

Meine Musik zum Fest auf Solhaug ist, bis auf die Ballade u. die Ouvertüre beendet u. gefiel Alles, was ich meinen Freunden daraus vorgespielt. Sie werden sich höchlichst verwundern über das theatralische dieser Musik der sich der routinirteste Operncomponist nicht zu schämen brauchte. Ich glaube nun mehr denn je, daß ich zum Operncomponisten berufen bin.

My incidental music to *Das Fest auf Solhaug* is finished apart from the ballad & the overture, & my friends have enjoyed all that I've played them. You will be astonished at the theatrical nature of this music, which even the most experienced opera composer need not be ashamed of. I now believe more than ever that I am destined to be an opera composer.

HW to his mother, Döbling, 27 November 1891

Die Aufführung des „Festes auf Solhaug" hat nun allerdings stattgefunden, doch spielte der musikalische Teil dabei eine so nebensächliche Rolle, daß es sich kaum verlohnt, desselben zu erwähnen. Anfänglich schien's, als wollte man den musikalischen Partien einige Bedeutung beilegen, aber gar bald fing man an, mit dem Rotstift in meiner Partitur zu streichen, daß schließlich fast gar nichts mehr zu spielen übrigblieb und das wenige Beibehaltene in so unerhörter Weise zum Vortrag gelangte, daß kein Mensch, ich selbst nicht, wußte, was im Orchester vorging. Genug, die ganze Affaire ist ziemlich jämmerlich verlaufen, und ich bin nur froh, daß ich die 200 fl. für meine Arbeit bereits eingesteckt hatte, ehe noch die Proben angesetzt waren.

The premiere of *Das Fest auf Solhaug* has taken place, but my music played such an unimportant part that it's scarcely worth mentioning. To start with, it seemed as though they were going to attach some importance to the music, but it was not long before they began taking a red pencil to so many passages in the score that almost nothing remained to be played, and the little that did remain was performed in such an excruciating manner that no one, not even I, knew what the orchestra was playing. Enough! The whole thing went off very badly, and I'm only happy that I pocketed the 200 florins for my work before the rehearsals began.

HW to Melanie Köchert, Vienna, 31 July 1897

Von meiner Idee: den Chor aus dem Fest auf Solhaug in's Textbuch einzuschmuggeln bin ich nun gänzlich abgekommen u. z. deswegen, weil ich aus dem Ibsen'schen Stück mit Gottes u. Freund Hoernes' Hilfe eine Oper machen will. Als ich letzthin die Partitur der Solhaugmusik zur Hand nahm, that es mir furchtbar leid, daß diese frischen Klänge nie ertönen sollen. Und es weht doch so echt dramatische Luft Einen daraus an.

I have now decided once and for all not to go through with my idea of smuggling the chorus from *Das Fest auf Solhaug* into the libretto [to *Manuel Venegas*], because with the help of God and our friend Hoernes I shall turn Ibsen's play into an opera. When I recently picked up the score of the Solhaug music, I was terribly dismayed that this fresh music might never be performed – and yet one is assailed by such a genuinely dramatic atmosphere.

---

1   Moriz Hoernes (1852–1917), the librettist of *Manuel Venegas*.

LIEDER

When Ibsen wrote *Gildet paa Solhoug* in 1855, the Norwegian language was still in a state of flux and was to remain so throughout the nineteenth century. Danish had been the official language of Norway under Danish rule since 1537, and even when Norway became an independent country in 1814, the Danish language still contaminated the work of government, church, theatre and most of the professions. Gradually this changed. Norwegian orthography was introduced into the Danish language, which gave rise to Dano-Norwegian Riksmål (State language), now referred to as Bokmål (Book or literary language). Ibsen's language in *Gildet paa Solhoug* might best be described as slightly Norwegianised Danish, an early form of today's Bokmål.

Drei Gesänge aus H. Ibsens 'Das Fest auf Solhaug'
Three Songs from Ibsen's *The Feast at Solhaug*

Margit:
(Act I scene 3)

Bjergkongen red sig syd under Ø,
(Saa klageligt rinde mine Dage.)
Vilde han fæste den væne Mø.
(Ret aldrig Du kommer tilbage.)

Bjergkongen red til Herr Haakens Gaard,
(Saa klageligt rinde mine Dage.)
Liden Kirsten stod ude, slog ud sit Haar.
(Ret aldrig Du kommer tilbage.)

Bjergkongen fæsted' den væne Viv,
(Saa klageligt rinde mine Dage.)
Han spændte en Sølvgjord omkring
    hendes Liv.
(Ret aldrig Du kommer tilbage.)

Bjergkongen fæsted' den Lillievaand,
(Saa klageligt rinde mine Dage.)
Med femten Guldringe til hver
    hendes Haand.
(Ret aldrig Du kommer tilbage.)

Tre Sommere gik og der gik vel fem;
(Saa klageligt rinde mine Dage.)
Kirsten sad i Bjerget i alle dem.
(Ret aldrig Du kommer tilbage.)

Fem Sommere gik, og der gik vel ni;
(Saa klageligt rinde mine Dage.)
Liden Kirsten saae ikke Solen i Li.
(Ret aldrig Du kommer tilbage.)

Dalen har Blomster og Fuglesang,
(Saa klageligt rinde mine Dage.)
I Bjerget er der Guld og en Nat saa lang.
(Ret aldrig Du kommer tilbage.)

Ballade. Gesang Margits[1]

Bergkönig ritt in[2] die Lande weit –
　So traurig vergehn mir die Tage.
Er wollte sich frei'n[3] die schönste Maid –
　Ach, enden wird nie meine Klage!

Bergkönig ritt vor Herrn Hakons Thor –

Klein Kirsten strählte ihr Haar davor.

Bergkönig freite das schlanke Weib –
Umfing ihr mit silbernem Gürtel den Leib.

Bergkönig führte sie heim alsdann –
Zehn güldene Ringe steckt er ihr an.

Es kam und schwand wohl Jahr um Jahr –
Im Berge saß Kirsten auf immerdar.

Das Thal hat Vögel und Blumenpracht –
　So traurig vergehn mir die Tage.
Im Berg ist Gold und ewige Nacht –
　Ach, enden wird nie meine Klage!

Gudmund:
(Act I scene 11)

　Jeg vandred' i Lien saa tung og saa ene,
　De Smaafugle kviddred' fra Busker
　　og Grene;
　Saa listeligt kviddred' de Sangere smaa:
　Hør til, hvordan Kjærlighed monne
　　opstaa!

Gudmunds erster Gesang[4]

Ich wandelte sinnend allein auf der Halde,
Da zwitscherten ringsum die Vöglein
　im Walde.
So hell erscholl ihr listiges Lied:

Margit's song

Mountain-king rode through all his lands,
　How sadly my days pass by,
He wished to woo the fairest maid,
　Ah! my lamenting will never end!

Mountain-king rode up to Lord Hakon's
　gate,
There stood little Kirsten, combing her hair.

Mountain-king courted the slender girl,
Encircled her waist with a golden belt.

Mountain-king then led her home,
With ten gold rings he adorned her hands.

Many a year came and went,
Kirsten stayed in the mountain all that time.

The valley glitters with birds and flowers,
　How sadly my days pass by,
In the mountains lie gold and endless night –
　Ah! my lamenting will never end!

Den voxer som Egen i Aarene lange,
Den næres ved Tanker og Sorger og Sange.
Den spirer saa let; i den flygtigste Stund
Fæster den Rødder i Hjertets Grund!

Gudmund's first song

Pensively I wandered alone on the hills,
The birds all around chirped in the wood,

So clearly their sly song resounded:

1　Margit, trapped in a loveless marriage to Bengt Gauteson, a wealthy squire on Solhaug, sings this ballad about a doomed relationship, in which she sees herself as 'Klein Kirsten' and her husband as 'Bergkönig' – Wolf aptly begins the song with a funeral march. Her misery is compounded when she realises, immediately after she has finished the ballad, that it was taught her by her cousin Gudmund, whom she secretly loves.
2　Klingenfeld: durch die Lande weit.　　3　Klingenfeld: freien.
4　Gudmund sings this song shortly after his return to Solhaug following an absence of twelve years. After a touching scene with Margit, he talks to her sister Signe, now a grown woman, and

Hör' an,* wie die Liebe im Herzen erblüht!
Sie wächst wie die Eiche wohl Jahre lang,
Sie nährt sich von Sorge, von Traum und Gesang. –
Sie keimet geschwind: in der flüchtigsten Stund'
Fasset sie Wurzel im Herzensgrund.

* Wolf repeats 'Hör' an'.

Listen* how love blossoms in the heart!
It grows like the oak for many a year,
It feeds off sorrow and dreams and song,

It flowers swiftly: in the most fleeting hour,
It takes root deep within the heart.

Gudmund:
(Act II scene 7)

Jeg red mig udi Lunde,
Jeg seiled' over Sø;
Det var sig i mit væne Hjem,
Der fæsted' jeg min Mø.

Det var den Alfekvinde,
Hun er saa led og gram:

Ret aldrig skal den Jomfru skjær
Til Kirken følge ham.

Hør mig, Du Alfekvinde,
Lad fare den Besvær;
To Hjerter kan ei skilles ad,
Der har hinanden kjær.

Gudmunds zweiter Gesang[1]

Ich fuhr wohl über[2] Wasser
Und in die Ferne weit –
Als ich zurück zur Heimat kam,
Freit' ich die schönste Maid.

Da war die Elfenfraue,
Die thät's mit Zürnen sehn;
Und nimmer soll sein feines Lieb
Mit ihm zur Kirche gehn.

Hör' an, du Elfenfraue:
Laß fahren die Beschwer!
Zwei Herzen, die sich lieben,
Die trennst du nimmermehr!*

* Wolf repeats the final line.

Gudmund's second song

I sailed across the water
And far away –
When I returned to my homeland,
I wooed the loveliest maid.

But the elf-woman
Looked angrily on –
Never, she said, would his dear love
Go to church with him.

Listen, you elf-woman:
Complain no more!
If two hearts are in love,
You will never part them!*

---

accompanies himself on the harp – Wolf's original music is scored for harp and strings. When he has finished the song, Signe repeats the line about love blossoming swiftly after years of steady growth. Margit senses to her dismay that her sister and Gudmund have fallen in love.

1 Realising that Gudmund loves her sister Signe, the jealous Margit threatens him. His response, which depicts Margit as the 'Elfenfraue', expresses arcanely his own love for Signe.
2 Klingenfeld: über's Wasser.

Johann Georg Jacobi
(1740–1814)

			page
Im Sommer	28 February –3 April 1876	TTBB	275

POET

Best known to lovers of Lieder through Mozart's 'An Chloe' and Schubert's seven settings, especially 'Am Tage aller Seelen', Jacobi was Professor of Philosophy at Halle and, later, Freiburg University. A great admirer of Anacreon, he published his own poems, which have an anacreontic feel to them, in 1816. He also founded the periodical *Iris* in which Goethe published a number of his poems for the first time. The poet of Wolf's 'Im Sommer' was named originally as Goethe, due to an unauthorised edition of Goethe poems, edited by Christian Friedrich Himburg in 1779. Jacobi's authorship had already been made clear, however, when he published the poem under his own name in *Iris* (vol. 7, 1776). Alfred Nicolovius, Goethe's great-nephew, on discovering in 1826 the true authorship of the poem, informed his great-uncle of the matter, and described many years later the old man's reaction to the news in a letter to the editor of a selection of Goethe's verse: „Als ich Goethe persönlich diesen Beleg vorlegte, schlug er das Gedicht in seinen Werken auf, ergriff ein Lineal und eine Feder, und strich es mit einem beinahe feierlichen Suum cuique! aus." ('When I personally furnished Goethe with the proof, he located the poem in his collected works, seized a ruler and pen and struck it out with an almost ceremonial Suum cuique!')

LETTER

See HW to his parents, 15 March 1876, p. 118.

JOHANN GEORG JACOBI

LIED

Im Sommer[1]

Wie Feld und Au
So blinkend im Thau!
Wie Perlen schwer
Die Pflanzen umher!
Wie durch's Gebüsch
Die Winde so frisch![2]
Wie laut, im hellen Sonnenstrahl
Die süßen Vöglein allzumal!

   Ach! aber da,
Wo Liebchen ich sah,
Im Kämmerlein,
So nieder und klein,
So rings bedeckt,
Der Sonne versteckt –
Wo bleibt[3] die Erde weit und breit,
Mit aller ihrer Herrlichkeit?

In summer

How field and meadow
Glisten in the dew!
How laden with pearls
The plants all around!
How fresh the winds
Through the undergrowth!
How loud in bright sunshine
The sweet birds sing!

   Alas, but there,
Where I saw my love,
In her little room,
So small and low,
Sheltered on all sides,
Hidden from the sun –
Where now is the widespread earth
With all its splendour?

Also set by Felix Mendelssohn

---

1 Jacobi: 'Der Sommer-Tag'. See HW to his parents, 15 March 1876, p. 118.
2 Jacobi: Wie durch den Hain/ Die Lüfte so rein!
3 Jacobi: blieb.

GOTTFRIED KELLER
(1819–1890)

                                                                                page

Alte Weisen

Tretet ein, hoher Krieger	25 May 1890	286
Singt mein Schatz wie ein Fink	2 June 1890	287
Wie glänzt der helle Mond	5–23 June 1890	289
Das Köhlerweib ist trunken	7–23 June 1890	288
Wandl' ich in dem Morgentau	8–23 June 1890	288
Du milchjunger Knabe	16 June 1890	287

POET

After the death of his father when Keller was five, his mother maintained the family by letting apartments in her house. Keller was expelled from school in 1834 – an injustice to which he gave expression in his great novel *Der grüne Heinrich* (1854–5 and 1879–80). The novel is heavily autobiographical: the hero, Heinrich Lee, the only son of a devoted mother, leaves home to study painting – as did Keller, who established himself in Munich, the artistic capital of Germany, but eventually gave up his ambitions for lack of funds and talent. When Keller turned to literature, he was active as poet, short-story writer and art critic. His early poetry was influenced by the political verse of Heine and Hoffmann von Fallersleben, but he soon found his own voice. Although his poetry lacks the musicality of Eichendorff, Goethe, Heine, Hölderlin and Mörike, there is a pictorial quality about his poems that has endeared him to a number of Lieder composers, chief among them Brahms, Pfitzner, Wolf and above all Othmar Schoeck, whose *Gaselen* (1923), *Lebendig begraben* (1927) and *Unter Sternen* (1943) comprise respectively 10, 14 and 25 Keller settings.

During his studies at Heidelberg University from 1848 to 1850, Keller lost his Christian faith, but his resolve to become a successful writer was strengthened. He intended to become a dramatist but lacked the flair – see HW to Melanie Köchert, 26 June 1894, p. 283. Fiction, on the other hand, became increasingly important: not just the novel but short stories, many of which were gathered in *Die Leute von Seldwyla*, a collection of Novellen dealing with the eccentric inhabitants of a fictitious Swiss town, that remains his most popular work. It was published in two volumes in 1856, then revised and enlarged in 1873–4. Volumes of his poetry were published in 1846 and 1851. The *Gesammelte Briefe* (see HW to Melanie Köchert, 26 June 1894, p. 283) were published in four volumes from 1950 to 1954, edited by C. Helbing.

Keller, who was of even smaller stature than Wolf (1.5 metres to Wolf's 1.54), never married, though there were many women in his life. He became engaged in 1866 to a young woman of twenty-two who committed suicide when Keller's character was slandered in several newspapers politically hostile to him. Prodigiously shy, he proposed by letter to Luise Rieter in 1847 and Johanna Kapp in 1849, both of whom declined. Although attracted to Betty Tendering, the sister of his publisher's wife, he felt unable to declare his love for her – she is almost certainly the model for Dortchen Schönfund in *Der grüne Heinrich*. In 1861 he was appointed Erster Staatsschreiber, and for fifteen years he discharged the duties of clerk to the Canton of Zurich. Keller lived with his mother in Zurich, and when she died, with his sister, who kept house for him.

Keller described the poems of *Von Weibern* (Wolf's *Alte Weisen*) in a letter of July 1852 to his composer friend Wilhelm Baumgartner (1820–1867), who set a number of Keller poems that were a great success in Switzerland – see *Gottfried Kellers Leben. Seine Briefe und Tagebücher* edited by Jakob Baechtold for a full list of Baumgartner's Keller settings:

> Meine Gedichte sind sehr dünn und pauvre und ein verunglücktes Ding ... Jedoch bin ich gerade mit dem fremden Tadel nicht ganz einverstanden. 'Von Weibern' halte ich für ganz erträglich; es sollen gerade keine Schilderungen der Leidenschaft, sondern bloß weibliche Marotten und Schicksale sein, und auch dies nicht ausdrücklich, sondern leichte, wunderliche Klänge, von denen ich selbst nicht recht weiß, wie sie entstanden.

> My poems are very slender and meagre and rather wretched ... And yet I don't exactly agree with the censure they have received from critics. The *Von Weibern* poems are perfectly passable: they are not supposed to depict passions but rather female fads and fates – not explicitly but through light and strange colours. I don't really know how this came about.

And Max Friedlaender, having visited Keller in the summer of 1884, left this account of their conversation in *Brahms' Lieder*:

> Als ich im Sommer 1884 zwei Nachmittage in der Wohnung des Dichters in Zürich verlebte, sagte er mir: „Ich wollte in dieser Liederreihe ursprünglich die auf- und absteigende Liebe eines jungen Mannes zu einer voll erblühten verwöhnten Schönheit schildern. Anfangs weist sie den grünen Anbeter schnöde ab, später aber, als sie einen Zahn verliert und auch sonst älter zu werden merkt, will sie ihn mit allen Mitteln wieder erobern. Doch es ist schon zu spät."

When I spent two afternoons in the summer of 1884 at the poet's house in Zurich, he said to me: 'My original intention was to portray in this series of poems the waxing and waning of the love of a young man for a mature pampered beauty. At the outset, she contemptuously dismisses the young and inexperienced lover. But later, when she loses a tooth and realises that she is growing older, she tries to win him back by every means at her disposal, but it is too late.'

COMPOSER

Keller's *Der grüne Heinrich* was Wolf's favourite novel; he read, re-read and read it aloud to his friends throughout his life – see HW to his mother, 24 March 1894, p. 283. Wolf's six *Alte Weisen* were composed in May and June 1890 as a tribute to Keller on his seventieth birthday, but by the time the songs were finished, the poet had died. Whereas Brahms for his 'Therese' and 'Salome' had used the 1851 edition of Keller's poems (the *Neuere Gedichte* written in 1846 in which the cycle is called *Von Weibern. Alte Lieder*), Wolf, like Pfitzner, used the later version of the poems, now called simply *Alte Weisen*, that were included in Keller's *Collected Works*, published in 1883, where these lyrics no longer had girls' names as titles. Wolf chose six of Keller's twelve poems, most of which are about dominant and ageing women. The first he composed was 'Tretet ein, hoher Krieger', a poem in which the woman conquers a soldier with her charms, and uses all the appurtenances of war as domestic implements. Unlike Pfitzner's setting, which maintains the march-like momentum throughout (suggesting that the woman is as military as the man), Wolf's march collapses and develops into a dance. It is instructive to compare the second song of Wolf's collection, 'Singt mein Schatz wie ein Fink' with Brahms's version, composed in 1877. Keller's original subtitle, 'Salome', implies that this country girl is a potential monster, a man-eater. But such an interpretation hardly suited Brahms in the *Mädchenlieder* of Op. 69, composed with Elisabet von Herzogenburg in mind. He therefore substituted 'stolzen' ('proud') with 'teuren' ('dear') in the final verse, and turns the poem into a genuine love song. Wolf detested Brahms's interpretation, especially at „O ihr Jungfrauen im Land,/Von dem Berg und über See!", for which he branded Brahms „ein Meister des Dudelsackes u. der Ziehharmonika" ('a master of the bagpipe & concertina', see HW to Melanie Köchert, 20 August 1890, p. 281). Instead of Brahms's simple melodic approach, Wolf gives us a song that develops from a light-hearted beginning to a vicious conclusion, with a postlude that breathes *fortissimo* fire.

In 'Du milchjunger Knabe', Wolf depicts the woman as a harmonically adventurous and teasing flirt, similar to Barbara in her treatment of Heinrich Lee in *Der grüne Heinrich*. His A major setting of 'Wandl' ich in dem Morgentau' is the most lyrical of the set: the woman, seeing all nature in love, laments her own loneliness. Compared with Pfitzner's melancholy setting, Wolf makes her sound merely gently resigned. 'Das Köhlerweib ist trunken' is in violent contrast, with the piano providing a vivid description of shrill, demonic laughter, as the once rich and beautiful charcoal-burner's wife lurches drunkenly through the forest, reminiscent of the gypsies in *Romeo und Julia auf dem Dorfe*, the Novelle that inspired Delius's *A Village Romeo and Juliet* (1899–1901). 'Wie glänzt der volle Mond' concludes the set: an old woman, feeling death approach, imagines the scene that will await her in Paradise. Keller, the atheist, eschews all sentimentality and depicts her with affectionate humour. Wolf seems to misinterpret (or re-interpret?) the text, and writes one of his most beautiful songs, with *pianissimo* repeated chords high above the stave, suggesting the night sky, and a sweet and harmonious close.

LETTERS

HW to Gustav Schur, Unterach, 28 May 1890

Wenn Sie nun erfahren, daß ich am Pfingstsonntag eines meiner schönsten Lieder (u. wie ich hoffe dereinst populärsten) geschrieben, wird Sie das sehr kalt lassen, denn Sie werden mit Recht erwarten, daß ich am Pfingstmontag 2 am Dienstag wieder zwei u. heute noch mindestens 3 componirte. Ach, ach wie ganz anders ist alles geworden. Ich habe seit dem Einen („Tretet ein, hoher Krieger" von Gottfried Keller) gar keines mehr geschrieben u. ich müßte untröstlich darüber sein, wenn mir dies Malheur bei gesundem Leibe passirt wäre. Ich bin aber noch immer Patient, Dank meiner Unvorsichtigkeit gleich nach meiner Landung ein Seebad genommen zu haben. Die Folge ist eine schreckliche Halsentzündung.

The information that on Whit Sunday I composed one of my most beautiful songs (& in the future one of the most popular, I hope) will certainly not impress you, because you will justifiably expect me to have written 2 on Whit Monday, another two on the Tuesday & at least 3 more today. But alas, it all turned out quite differently. Since that first one ('Tretet ein, hoher Krieger' by Gottfried Keller) I have written no more, & I would be inconsolable if this misfortune had occurred when I was well. But I am still a patient. Thanks to my having swum in the sea immediately after I arrived here, I now have a terrible sore throat.

HW to Ilse Köchert, Unterach, 3 June 1890

Der Mutter magst Du sagen, daß ich gestern Abend noch ein schönes Lied von Gottfr. Keller „singt mein Schatz wie ein Fink" componirt [. . .]

Tell your mother that yesterday evening I composed another beautiful Gottfr. Keller song: 'Singt mein Schatz wie ein Fink' [. . .]

HW to Rudolf von Larisch, Unterach, 5 June 1890

Mit meiner Produktivität sieht's etwas mager aus. Zwei Lieder von Gottfried Keller, sind die ganze Ausbeute. Freilich es sind zwei „Löwen", aber ich bin nun einmal gewohnt, meine Jungen dutzendweise zur Welt zu bringen und so bringen diese zwei Racker zu wenig Abwechslung in mein musikalisches Leben.

I have composed rather little of late. Two Gottfried Keller songs – that's all. Both are corkers, but I'm now used to bringing my children into the world by the dozen – so these two rascals change too little in my musical life.

HW to Melanie Köchert, Unterach, 24 June 1890

Hurrah! der Bann ist gebrochen!
    Gestern die verwünschte Apfelblüth' wundervoll componirt.[1] St. Petrus[2] flickt, was nur das Zeug hält. Das trunkene Köhlerweib[3] nach einer Skizze vom 7. d. M. ebenfalls vollendet. Heult schauderhaft. Habe endlich, endlich die 6 beinander. Nun komme, was will; mein Tagewerk ist vollbracht.

Hooray! The spell is broken!
    Yesterday I composed the confounded apple-blossom – wonderfully. St Peter cobbles with might and main. The drunken charcoal-burner's wife is likewise finished, from a sketch I started on the 7th of this month. She's making dreadful screeching noises. Finally, finally, I've got all 6 together. No matter what happens now: my day's labour is done.

HW to Gustav Schur, Unterach, 24 June 1890

Ich habe nun sechs neue Lieder nach Gottfr. Keller beisammen. Wollen wir die nicht auch losschlagen? Falls Sie an Breitkopf und Härtel noch nicht geschrieben haben, erwähnen Sie auch die Kellerschen Lieder. Ich wäre allenfalls einverstanden, dieselben mir abkaufen zu lassen um den Preis von 600 Mark.[4]

---

1 'Wandl' ich in dem Morgentau'.   2 'Wie glänzt der helle Mond'.
3 'Das Köhlerweib ist trunken'.
4 A huge amount compared to the 1000 marks he received from Schott for the 46 songs of the *Italienisches Liederbuch*.

I've now got six new Gottfr. Keller songs together. Why don't we flog them too? If you haven't yet written to Breitkopf & Härtel, do mention the Keller songs. I would be prepared to let them go for 600 marks.

HW to Melanie Köchert, Ober-Döbling, 20 August 1890

Larisch besuchte mich heute, u. da ihm meine Keller'schen noch unbekannt waren spielte ich ihm als Ersatz zwei Keller'sche von Brahms vor, die ich soeben dem ausgesuchten Sortiment Lacoms[1] entnommen. O Sie hätten ihre [sic] Freude daran erlebt! Welch' ein Meister des Dudelsackes u. der Ziehharmonika ist doch Brahms! [...]

Eine wegen ihrer ganz besonderes originellen Deklamation bemerkenswerthe Stelle kann ich mir nicht versagen hier anzuführen [he quotes the music to 'O ihr Jungfrau im Land,/Von dem Berg und über See!'] u. so in der bekannten edlen Volksthümlichkeit jodelt es bis zum Schluß. –

B. hat glücklicherweise nur 2 Keller'sche in die Unsterblichkeit hinübergerettet, u. z. unter den Überschriften „Therese" (du milchjunger Knabe) u. „Salome" (Singt mein Schatz). Bei ersterem ist sogar die Schlußstrophe variirt. Es heißt dort:

> eine Meermuschel liegt
> auf dem Schrank meiner Bas':
> da halte dein Ohr d'ran,
> dann hörst du etwas![2]

B. scheint eine ältere Ausgabe der K. Gedichte für seine verbrecherischen Bedürfnisse benützt zu haben.

Larisch visited me today, & since my Keller songs were still unknown to him, I played him instead two Keller songs by Brahms which I'd just selected from Lacom's[1] assorted collection. Oh, you would have loved it! What a master of the bagpipe & concertina Brahms is! [...]

I can't resist quoting one passage remarkable for its quite outstandingly original declamation [he quotes the music to 'O ihr Jungfrau im Land,/Von dem Berg und über See!'] – & so it yodels on to the end in the celebrated, noble folksong manner.

Fortunately, B. conferred immortality on only two Keller poems, with the titles 'Therese' ('Du milchjunger Knabe') & 'Salome' ('Singt mein Schatz'). The final verse of the former has a variant, and reads:

---

1   C. Lacom was a small Viennese firm that published the *Eichendorff-Lieder* and the *Goethe-Lieder*. It was via Lacom that Wolf corresponded secretly with Melanie Köchert – see p. 491.
2   See note 4 to 'Du milchjunger Knabe', p. 287.

> a sea-shell lies
> on my aunt's cabinet;
> just put it to your ear
> and you'll hear something!

B. seems to have used an older edition of Keller's poems for his criminal purposes.

HW to Melanie Köchert, Mainz, 22 October 1890

Schott u. ich sind nun mehr eins. Er hat mich wie einen alten Freund empfangen, mich gleich zum Abendbrot geladen, wo wir, ganz unter uns, champagnisirten. Ich hab' ihm eine Menge schon vorgespielt u. er geht mit Eifer auf die Sachen ein, ob er schon ziemlich conservativ in manchen Punkten denkt. Über Keller haben wir heute bis in die Nacht gestritten – natürlich in aller Freundschaft – ohne Resultat. Er ist <u>gegen</u> die Gedichte. Aber seine Frau, ein sehr nettes Weibchen, hab' ich auf meiner Seite. Dr. Strecker[1] (so heisst Schott) ist noch ein junger u. feingebildeter Mensch von den aller aller aller allerangenehmsten Manieren.

Ich bin ein für allemal bei ihm zum Essen eingeladen u. seine Tafel ist eine fürstliche. Er möchte nun vor allem die Christnacht[2] verlegen. Ich habe den Eindruck empfangen, daß er auf alle meine Forderungen eingehen wird. Ein wahrer Prachtkerl durch u. durch! Kann auch Brahms nicht ausstehen. Kurz ein Kapitalkerl!

Schott's & I are now of the same mind. He [Ludwig Strecker] received me like an old friend, immediately invited me to dinner – at which we drank champagne – just the two of us. I played him many of my things & he is most enthusiastic, although rather conservative in many areas. We argued about Keller till late into the night – amicably, of course – without agreeing. He is <u>against</u> the poems. But his wife, a very nice little woman, is on my side. Dr Strecker (that is Schott's name) is still young & a very educated man with the most most most most exquisite manners.

I have a standing invitation to dine there, and his table is lavish. He would now like above all to publish my 'Christnacht'. I have the impression that he will agree to all my demands. A splendid fellow through & through! And he can't abide Brahms! In short, a capital fellow!

---

1 For another view of Dr Strecker, see 'Unser Feind ist, großer Gott', the seventh song of Richard Strauss's *Krämerspiegel* (1918), a work in which the poet Alfred Kerr pillories many music publishers of the time.
2 See p. 427.

HW to Detlev von Liliencron, Ebensee, 1 August 1891

Ihre Klagen über den niederträchtigen Vertrieb meiner Compositionen wären im vergangenen Jahre wohl noch berechtigt gewesen, als derlei Fälle, wie Sie einen anführen, an der Tagesordnung waren. Seitdem dürfte diese üble Wirthschaft wohl ein Ende genommen haben, da Schott in Mainz den Verlag aller meiner Compositionen übernommen hat. Als erstes erschienen bei ihm das spanische Liederbuch (44 Gedichte) u. „alte Weisen" von Gottfried Keller (6 Gedichte) – Sollten Sie ein Verlangen danach haben so bitte ich Sie es mir nur kund zu thun u. Sie sollen augenblicklich damit bedient sein, da es mir nur ein Vergnügen sein kann für die freundliche Zusendung Ihrer Werke mich revanchiren zu können.

Your complaints about the despicable marketing of my compositions would last year still have been justified, when such cases as the one you describe were the order of the day. Since that time, this shambles should now be a thing of the past, since Schott's in Mainz have taken over the publishing of all my compositions. First to appear was the *Spanisches Liederbuch* (44 poems) & Gottfried Keller's *Alte Weisen* (6 poems). Please let me know if you would like copies & you will receive them immediately – it will give me great pleasure to repay your kindness in sending me your works.

HW to his mother, Vienna, 24 March 1894

Zu meinem Geburtstag wurden mir sämmtliche Werke von Gottfr. Keller im Prachteinband verehrt. Ich lese jetzt schon zum xtenmale den grünen Heinrich u. erfreue mich immer wieder an der herrlichen Dichtung. Erinnern Sie sich noch an meine Vorlesung?[1]

For my birthday I received the *Complete Works* of Gottfr. Keller in a de luxe edition. I'm now reading *Der grüne Heinrich* for the umpteenth time & am enjoying once more the splendid work. Do you remember me reading it to you?

HW to Melanie Köchert, Vienna, 26 June 1894

Die Briefe Gottfr. Kellers sind jetzt meine einzige Unterhaltung. Ich verlange mir aber auch keine bessere. Bereits bin ich schon über die Hälfte des Buches hinaus, trotzdem eine Anzahl der Briefe mit Bedacht gelesen sein wollen. Hochinteressant sind seine Ansichten u. Abhandlungen über das

---

[1] Wolf enjoyed recitation, and would often insist that a singer recite a poem before performing it.

moderne Drama, für das er einen ebenso richtigen Instinkt als eine schwache Begabung zeigt.

Gottfr. Keller's letters are now my sole source of entertainment. And I can ask for no better. I am already over halfway through, even though a number of the letters have to be read slowly and with care. Highly interesting are his views & writings on modern drama, for which he has absolutely the right instinct but little talent.

HW to Melanie Köchert, Vienna, 3 July 1894

Ich lese jetzt nichts wie Keller u. immer wieder nur Keller. Gestern vor'm Einschlafen nahm ich einen Band Wagner zur Hand, klappte aber das Buch bald wieder zu, so widerlich berührte mich diese weitausgeholte bandwurmartige Schreibart. Da ist der knorrige Gottfried, in punkto Stil wenigstens, doch ein ganz anderer Herr. Mich heimelt seine Prosa mehr noch an als selbst die Goethe'sche, mit der sie übrigens eine große Verwandschaft aufweist. Aber Kellers Sprache ist plastischer, farbiger u. bei aller Künstlichkeit kräftiger und naiver, als die seines großen Vorbildes.

I'm now reading nothing but Keller, and again more Keller. Before going to sleep last night, I took down a volume of Wagner but soon put it aside, because I was offended by his repellent long-winded, tapeworm style of writing. Gnarled old Gottfried, as far as style is concerned, is a different kettle of fish. His prose beguiles me even more than Goethe's, to which it bears a strong resemblance, by the way. But Keller's language is more pliable, colourful &, in its deftness, stronger and more objective than that of his great model.

HW to Heinrich Potpeschnigg, Vienna, 17 December 1896

Wenn Du Dir ein besonderes bene anthun willst verschaffe Dir sofort den 3. Band von Keller's Leben u. Briefen. Herausgeber Baechtold verlegt bei Wilh. Hertz in Berlin. Der Band enthält etliche hundert Briefe von Keller, von denen einer lustiger u. bummelwitziger als der andere ist. Ich kugle mich nur so bei der Lectüre.[1]

---

[1] Wolf was a voracious reader of catholic taste. Byron, Goethe, Kleist, Nietzsche, Schopenhauer, Shakespeare and Stifter were among his favourite authors, but he also had a penchant for books that made him laugh. He was especially fond of Claude Tillier's *Mon Oncle Benjamin*, Mark Twain's *The Adventures of Huckleberry Finn*, Charles Dickens's *Pickwick Papers*, Laurence Sterne's *Tristram Shandy*, Jonathan Swift's *Gulliver's Travels* – books that he would read over and over again. With the exception of Mark Twain (1835–1910), Wolf's favourite books were almost all written by authors who were no longer alive.

If you want to give yourself a special treat, acquire <u>at once</u> Volume 3 of Keller's *Life & Letters*. Edited by Baechtold and published by Wilh. Hertz in Berlin. It contains several hundred of Keller's letters, each one funnier & wittier than the other. I double up with laughter as I read them.

HW to Karl Mayr, Vienna, 15 March 1897

Bezüglich des Programmes Ihrer verehrten Braut für den Münchener-Liederabend würde ich vorschlagen anstatt der abgedroschenen Verborgenheit das 1. der Keller'schen Lieder („tretet ein") u. an Stelle des nicht minder abgeleierten Elfenliedes das Keller'sche „wandl' ich in dem Morgenthau" zu wählen.

Concerning your fiancée's programme for the Liederabend in Munich, I would suggest she choose the first Keller song ('Tretet ein, hoher Krieger') instead of the trite 'Verborgenheit', & Keller's 'Wandl' ich in dem Morgentau' instead of the no less hackneyed 'Elfenlied'.

HW to Karl Mayr, Vienna, 22 April 1897

Auf den Liederabend, den Frl. Clementine in Gemeinschaft mit Faisst in München abzuhalten gedenken, bin ich sehr gespannt.[1] Sehen Sie sich im besagten Falle doch ja um einen tüchtigen Begleiter um, denn, wie Sie ja selber wissen, ruht der Schwerpunkt meiner Lieder im Klavierpart, der unter allen Umständen nur den Händen eines wahrhaft gebildeten Musikers anzuvertrauen sein wird. Sehr lieb wäre mir's, wenn Frl. Clementine die beiden Keller'schen Weisen „tretet ein hohe [sic] Krieger" u. „du milchjunger Knabe" in ihr Programm aufnehmen wollte. Man kann doch nicht immer „den hellen Mond" glänzen lassen.[2] Überhaupt Abwechslung. Neues u. immer Neues! Wozu habe ich denn gegen 250 Lieder geschrieben, wenn immer nur die alten Bekannten den Leuten aufgetischt werden? Man kann ja Altes mit Neuem untermischen – variatio delectat.

I am very excited about the Liederabend that Miss Clementine plans to give in Munich with Faisst. Make sure you have a decent accompanist, because, as you well know, the main focus in my songs is the piano part, which should in all circumstances be entrusted only to a truly educated musician. It would gratify me greatly if Miss Clementine would include in her programme the two Keller songs: 'Tretet ein, hoher Krieger' & 'Du milchjunger Knabe'. One can't, after all, allow the 'bright moon' to shine all the time. Ring the changes! Explore new

---

1 The recital never took place.
2 The reference is to the last (and most popular) song of the set. See note 1 to 'Wie glänzt der helle Mond'.

songs, then more new songs! What is the point of me having composed some 250 songs, if it's always the old familiar ones which are served up to audiences? One can blend the old with the new – variatio delectat.

LIEDER

Alte Weisen
Old Saws

1 Tretet ein, hoher Krieger[1]

Tretet ein, hoher Krieger,
Der sein Herz mir ergab!
Legt den purpurnen Mantel
Und die Goldsporen ab.

Spannt das Roß in den Pflug,
Meinem Vater zum Gruß!
Die Schabrack' mit dem Wappen
Gibt 'nen Teppich meinem Fuß!

Euer Schwertgriff muß lassen
Für mich Gold und Stein,
Und die blitzende Klinge
Wird ein Schüreisen sein.

Und die schneeweiße Feder
Auf dem blutroten Hut
Ist zu 'nem kühlenden Wedel
In der Sommerszeit gut.

Und der Marschalk muß lernen
Wie man Weizenbrot backt,
Wie man Wurst und Gefüllsel
Um die Weihnachtszeit hackt!

Nun befehlt Eure Seele
Dem heiligen Christ!
Euer Leib ist verkauft,
Wo kein Erlösen mehr ist!

Also set by Hans Pfitzner

Enter, lofty warrior

Enter, lofty warrior,
You who gave your heart to me!
Lay that crimson cloak aside
And those golden spurs.

Yoke your charger to the plough,
As a greeting for my father!
Give me the crested saddle-cloth
As a carpet for my feet.

Your sword-hilt must yield to me
Its jewels and its gold,
And its flashing blade
Shall serve as a poker.

And the snow-white feather
On your blood-red hat
Shall make a cooling fan
In summertime.

And the marshall must learn
How to bake wheaten bread,
How sausages and stuffing
Are minced at Christmastide.

Commend now your soul
To Christ our Lord!
For your body is sold
Where it cannot be redeemed!

---

1 The poem was called 'Helene' in the 1846 version of *Von Weibern. Alte Lieder*, published in *Neuere Gedichte* (1851). See also HW to Gustav Schur, 28 May 1890, p. 279.

2 Singt mein Schatz wie ein Fink[1]

Singt mein Schatz wie ein Fink,
Sing' ich Nachtigallensang;
Ist mein Liebster ein Luchs,
O so bin ich eine Schlang'!

O ihr Jungfraun im Land,
Vom Gebirg und über See,
Überlaßt mir den Schönsten,
Sonst tut ihr mir weh!

Er soll sich unterwerfen
Zum Ruhm uns und Preis!
Und er soll sich nicht rühren,
Nicht laut und nicht leis!

O ihr teuern Gespielen,
Überlaßt mir den stolzen Mann,
Er soll sehn wie die Liebe
Ein feurig' Schwert werden kann!

Also set by Johannes Brahms and Pfitzner

If my love sings like a finch

If my love sings like a finch,
I'll sing like a nightingale;
If my sweetheart is a lynx,
Then I shall be a snake!

O you maidens on land,
From the mountains and across the sea,
Leave the most handsome one to me,
Or else you'll do me harm!

He shall surrender
To our glory and our praise!
And he shall not stir
Either loudly or softly!

O you dear playmates,
Leave the proud fellow to me,
He shall see how Love
Can become a fiery sword!

3 Du milchjunger Knabe[2]

Du milchjunger Knabe,
Wie siehst du mich an?
Was haben deine Augen
Für eine Frage getan!

Alle Ratsherrn in der Stadt[3]
Und alle Weisen der Welt
Bleiben stumm auf die Frage,
Die deine Augen gestellt!

Ein leeres Schneckhäusel,[4]
Schau, liegt dort im Gras;
Da halte dein Ohr dran,
Drin brümmelt dir was!

Also set by Brahms and Pfitzner

You beardless boy

You beardless boy,
Why do you look at me so?
What kind of question
Have your eyes been asking!

All the town councillors
And all the world's wise men
Are dumbfounded by the question
Your eyes have asked!

Look, there's an empty snail-shell,
Lying there in the grass;
Just put it to your ear,
And you'll hear something whispering!

---

1   The poem was called 'Salome' in the 1846 version of *Von Weibern. Alte Lieder*, published in *Neuere Gedichte* (1851).
2   The poem was called 'Therese' in the 1846 version of *Von Weibern. Alte Lieder*, published in *Neuere Gedichte* (1851). See also HW to Melanie Köchert, 20 August 1890, p. 281.
3   Wolf here uses the 1846 version which has 'in der Stadt' instead of 'der Stadt'.
4   The 1846 version has „Meermuschel/auf dem Schrank meiner Bas'" ('sea-shell on my aunt's cabinet'). Whether 'Schneckhäusel' ('snail-shell') or 'Meermuschel' ('sea-shell'), the meaning seems

4 Wandl' ich in dem Morgentau[1]

Wandl' ich in dem Morgentau
Durch die dufterfüllte Au',
Muß ich schämen mich so sehr
Vor den Blümlein ringsumher!

Täublein auf dem Kirchendach,
Fischlein in dem Mühlenbach,
Und das Schlänglein still im Kraut,
Alles fühlt und nennt sich Braut.

Apfelblüt' im lichten Schein
Dünkt sich stolz ein Mütterlein;
Freudig stirbt so früh im Jahr
Schon das Papilionenpaar.

Gott, was hab' ich denn getan,
Daß ich ohne Lenzgespan,
Ohne einen süßen Kuß
Ungeliebt sterben muß?

Also set by Pfitzner

When I walk in the morning dew

When I walk in the morning dew
Through the scent-filled meadow,
I'm forced to feel so ashamed
By the flowers all around!

The dove on the church roof,
The fish in the millstream,
And the silent snake in the grass,
All feel and call themselves a bride.

Apple blossom in the sunlight
Proudly deems itself a mother;
The butterfly pair is glad
To die so early in the year.

God, what then have I done
That, with no springtime mate,
And not a single sweet kiss,
I must die unloved.

5 Das Köhlerweib ist trunken[2]

Das Köhlerweib ist trunken
Und singt im Wald,
Hört, wie die Stimme gellend
Im Grünen hallt!

Sie war die schönste Blume,
Berühmt im Land;
Es warben Reich' und Arme
Um ihre Hand.

Sie trat in Gürtelketten[3]
So stolz einher;

The charcoal-burner's wife is drunk

The charcoal-burner's wife is drunk
And singing in the wood,
Listen how her screeching voice
Echoes through the countryside!

She was once the fairest flower,
Celebrated far and wide,
Rich and poor came wooing
To win her hand.

She wore a chatelaine
And walked with haughty pride;

---

to be this: the young man is a milksop ('milchjung'), inexperienced in love and the ways of the world. Therese (the woman's name in the earlier Keller version) is an older woman and she dismisses the young man as being too uninitiated in sexual matters. She advises him to put the sea-shell to his ear – because, if he does so, he will hear the booming of the ocean – elemental, powerful, mysterious. And that will teach him a thing or two about sensuality. 'Snail-shell' is surely weaker, and less effective.

1 The poem was called 'Das rote Bärbchen' in the 1846 version of *Von Weibern. Alte Lieder*, published in *Neuere Gedichte* (1851).
2 The poem was called 'Kunigunde' in the 1846 version of *Von Weibern. Alte Lieder*, published in *Neuere Gedichte* (1851). It is the only one of these six poems that is not a Rollengedicht: it is the poet who speaks.
3 A set of short chains on a belt worn for carrying keys.

Den Bräutigam zu wählen	To choose a bridegroom
Fiel ihr zu schwer.	Proved too hard a task.
Da hat sie überlistet	Then red wine
Der rote Wein –	Outwitted her –
Wie müssen alle Dinge	How transitory
Vergänglich sein!	Everything must be!
Das Köhlerweib ist trunken	The charcoal-burner's wife is drunk
Und singt im Wald;	And singing in the wood;
Wie durch die Dämmerung gellend	How her screeching song resounds
Ihr Lied erschallt!	In the gathering dusk!

6 Wie glänzt der helle Mond[1]

How cold and distant the bright moon shines

Wie glänzt der helle Mond so kalt und fern,	How cold and distant the bright moon shines,
Doch ferner schimmert meiner Schönheit Stern!	But my beauty's star gleams more distant still!
Wohl rauschet weit von mir des Meeres Strand,	The sea pounds the shore far away from me,
Doch weiterhin liegt meiner Jugend Land!	But farther still lies the land of my youth!
Ohn' Rad und Deichsel gibt's ein Wägelein,	There is a wagon without wheels or shafts,
Drin fahr' ich bald zum Paradies hinein.	I'll soon drive in it to Paradise.
Dort sitzt die Mutter Gottes auf dem Thron,	The Mother of God sits there on her throne,
Auf ihren Knieen schläft ihr sel'ger Sohn.	With her blessed Son asleep on her lap.
Dort sitzt Gott Vater, der den heil'gen Geist	There sits God the Father, with the Holy Ghost
Aus seiner Hand mit Himmelskörnern speist.	Whom He feeds from His hand with manna.
In einem Silberschleier sitz' ich dann	Then I'll sit in a silver veil
Und schaue meine weißen Finger an.	And gaze at my white fingers.
Sankt Petrus aber gönnt sich keine Ruh,	Only Saint Peter will grant himself no rest,
Hockt vor der Tür und flickt die alten Schuh.[2]	He squats at the Gate and cobbles old shoes.

---

1   The poem was called 'Creszens' in the 1846 version of *Von Weibern*. *Alte Lieder*, published in *Neuere Gedichte* (1851). See also HW to Karl Mayr, 22 April 1897, p. 285. In a letter to Hugo Faisst of 18 March 1897 Wolf upbraids the soprano Clementine Schönfield for choosing ad nauseam such songs as 'Verborgenheit', 'Elfenlied' and 'Wie glänzt der helle Mond' in her programmes.
2   St Peter was traditionally a cobbler by profession. He also appears in 'Das himmlische Leben' from *Des Knaben Wunderhorn* that Mahler was to set a decade later as the final movement of his Fourth Symphony. Both the Wolf and the Mahler are characterised by a charming blend of naivety and gravitas.

JUSTINUS KERNER
(1786–1862)

		page
Zur Ruh, zur Ruh!	16 June 1883	294

POET

Justinus Andreas Christian Kerner lost his father at the age of thirteen and was apprenticed in 1801 to a cabinet-maker, Professor Karl Philipp Conz, a minor poet and friend of Friedrich von Schiller. Recognising Kerner's literary talent, Conz took on responsibility for his apprentice's further education, and in 1804 Kerner matriculated at Tübingen University, where he studied medicine. Part of his training was to observe the deranged poet Friedrich Hölderlin, who had been removed to a Tübingen clinic in 1806. Having qualified in 1808, Kerner travelled widely in Germany and Austria, and became acquainted with many other distinguished literary figures, including Ludwig Uhland, Gustav Schwab, Friedrich de la Motte Fouqué, Rahel Varnhagen, Adelbert von Chamisso and Friedrich Schlegel. Kerner's eccentric personality is mirrored in the manner in which he met his wife. Observing on one of his excursions a sad young woman, Friederike Ehmann, he addressed her with the first stanza of Goethe's poem 'Trost in Tränen':

Wie kommt's, daß du so traurig bist,	How is it that you're so sad,
Da alles froh erscheint?	When everyone is happy?
Man sieht dir's an den Augen an,	I can see clearly from your eyes
Gewiß du hast geweint.	That you've been weeping.

She replied with the second stanza, and their engagement was the eventual consequence. They married in 1813, by which time Kerner was practising medicine in Wildbach and Welzheim. He eventually settled in Weinsberg as a district physician and remained there for the rest of his life, devoting himself to his patients and indulging his interests in the occult. In Weinsberg he was a much loved host to countless visitors, including Ferdinand von Freiligrath, Emanuel Geibel, Nikolaus Lenau, Eduard Mörike, who lived two hours away in Cleversulzbach, Julius Mosen (the poet of Schumann's 'Der Nußbaum'), Wilhelm Müller and Ludwig Uhland. Theobald Kerner has left us an intimate description of these poets and his father's life in Weinsberg, published as *Das Kernerhaus und seine Gäste* (1894). Kerner's interest in psychic abnormalities led him to publish *Die*

Seherin von Prevorst (1829) – the results of his treatment of a patient, one Friederike Hauffe, a somnambulist and clairvoyant. One of his most original books was *Kleksographien. Mit Illustrationen nach den Vorlagen des Verfassers*, published posthumously in 1890 – a collection of poems and grotesque drawings created by folding sheets of paper containing blots of ink. *Reiseschatten* (1811) includes the play *Nachspiel der zweiten Schattenreihe oder Der Totengräber von Feldberg*, and *Bilderbuch aus meiner Kindheit* (1849) gives an account of his childhood. His poetry was published in several volumes: *Gedichte* (1826) which contains the 'An Anna' poems set by Schumann in 1828; *Dichtungen* (1834), which includes all the poems set by Schumann as Op. 35; *Lyrische Gedichte* (1847 and 1854); *Der letzte Blumenstrauß* (1852) and *Winterblüthen von Justinus Kerner* (1859). His friendship with the Swabian poet Ludwig Uhland proved especially stimulating, and for five years from 1807 they corresponded and commented on each other's poems. Much of Kerner's poetry shows the influence of folksong, and one poem from *Reiseschatten*, 'Der schwere Traum', was included by Arnim and Brentano in *Des Knaben Wunderhorn* under the title 'Icarus' – both editors believing it to be an anonymous folk song. Kerner's lyrical poems have not, strangely, attracted many Lieder composers, with the exception of Robert Schumann, whose *Zwölf Gedichte von Justinus Kerner* (1840) remains one of the finest *Liederreihen* in the repertoire. Other composers drawn to his poetry include Friedrich Silcher, Louis Spohr, Johannes Brahms and Clara Schumann.

COMPOSER

In the autumn of 1887 Friedrich Eckstein, at Wolf's request, approached the Viennese publishing house of Emil Wetzler with a proposal to publish Wolf's Lieder. Wolf then prepared two sets of songs for publication: *Sechs Lieder für eine Frauenstimme* and *Sechs Gedichte von Scheffel, Mörike, Goethe und Just. Kerner*. In a letter to Edmund Lang (15 February 1888, p. 292), Wolf declared his intention to dedicate the first set to his mother, and the second to his father. 'Zur Ruh, zur Ruh!' – the final poem of *Winterblüthen von Justinus Kerner* – was set by Wolf as part of his *Sechs Gedichte von Scheffel, Mörike, Goethe und Just. Kerner*. It and 'Morgentau' were the first Wolf songs to be performed in public at a recital given by Rosa Papier (mezzo) and Elise von Révfy (piano) on 2 March 1888 before a packed audience in the Saal Bösendorfer. 'Zur Ruh, zur Ruh!', which at Wolf's request had been transposed down to suit Papier's voice, was encored. Theodor Helm, reviewing the concert at Wolf's behest on 9 March 1888 (see HW to Theodor Helm, March 1888, p. 292), wrote in the *Deutsche Zeitung*: „In der That sind uns in den beiden Wolf'schen Liedern Proben eines echten lyrischen Talentes begegnet." ('Both songs indeed suggest that Wolf possesses a true lyrical talent.') Wolf described the review as 'tasteless journalistic drivel' (HW to Modesta and Josef Strasser, 31 March 1888, p. 293).

At Wolf's funeral on 24 February 1903 (see APPENDIX 2), the first verse of 'Zur Ruh, zur Ruh!' was recited by Michael Haberlandt (see p. 484) at the end of his oration in the Zentralfriedhof by the side of Wolf's open grave. Whereas the dying man of the poem addresses himself, bidding farewell first to his body and then to his eyes, Haberlandt speaks to the deceased composer, adapting Kerner's words with touching devotion:

Zur Ruh, zur Ruh,	To rest, to rest,
Ihr müden Glieder!	You weary limbs!
Schließt fest euch zu,	Close tight,
Ihr Augenlider!	You eyelids!
Du bist allein,	You are alone,
Fort ist die Erde;	The world is left behind;
Nacht muß es sein,	Night must come
Daß Licht dir werde.	That you may find light.

LETTERS

HW to Edmund Lang, Perchtoldsdorf, 15 February 1888

Bitte, gehen Sie gelegentlich [sic] zu Wetzler u. sagen ihm, daß mit der Herstellung der Titelblätter nicht geeilt werden möge, da ich jetzt die Absicht habe beiden Heften eine Widmung voranzusetzen, u. z. möchte ich die Lieder für eine Frauenstimme meiner Mutter, das andere Heft aber dem Andenken meines Vaters weihen.

Please go to Wetzler & tell him that there is no hurry with the title-pages, as it is now my intention to place a dedication at the head of both volumes; I would like to dedicate the songs for a woman's voice to my mother, and the other volume to the memory of my father.

HW to Theodor Helm, Perchtoldsdorf, March 1888

Wenn Sie durch ein paar Worte über die Lieder selbst und nicht nur über den günstigen Eindruck derselben auf das Publikum schreiben wollten, steht Ihnen auch das zweite Lied im Manuscripte zu Gebote. Ich denke, Sie machen – wenn Sie damit einverstanden sind – einstweilen das Publikum auf das Erscheinen zweier Liederhefte (12 Lieder) aufmerksam und betonen, daß Sie sich eine Würdigung derselben gelegentlich vorbehalten. Daß ich großen Werth daruf lege, mit Zois und Herzfeld[1] nicht in einen Topf geworfen zu werden, ist selbstverständlich. Wenn Sie einstweilen dem Publikum gewissermaßen eine Perspektive auf meine letzten Lieder, auf die originelle Art derselben, auf die neuen Bahnen, die ich mit Sicherheit betrete, kurz eine Perspektive auf etwas Ursprüngliches, Neues und deshalb nicht gleich Vertrautes eröffnen wollten, würden Sie mich meiner Ansicht nach, ohne mich gerade zu lobhudeln, in das rechte Licht setzen.

If you wanted to say a few words about the songs themselves and not merely about the favourable impression they made on the audience, I have the second song in manuscript form for you. I think you should for the time being – if you are in agreement – inform the public that two song collections will be published, and that you will, when you find the time, review them. It goes without saying that it is very important for me not to be mentioned in the same breath as Zois and Herzfeld. If you draw the public's attention to the originality of my latest songs and how they most certainly break new ground – in short, show them how new, original and, therefore, not immediately familiar they are, you will in my opinion be showing me in the correct light, without being fulsome.

HW to Modesta and Josef Strasser, Perchtoldsdorf, 31 March 1888

Eure Fassungslosigkeit über die dumme Recension in der Deutschen Zeitung setzt mich in erstaunen. Denkt doch, daß dieß dummes Geschwefel ist und obenein von einem Menschen herrührt, der absolut einen D . . . versteht. Abgeschmacktes Zeitungsgewäsche!

Your disbelief at the stupid review in the *Deutsche Zeitung* astonishes me. Just think – this is stupid waffle, written moreover by someone who knows absolutely b . . . all. Tasteless journalistic drivel.

---

[1] Hans Freiherr Zois von Edelstein (1861–1924), Austrian composer; Victor von Herzfeld (1856–1920), Austrian composer and violinist.

LIED

Zur Ruh, zur Ruh![1]

Zur Ruh, zur Ruh,
Ihr müden Glieder!
Schließt fest euch zu,
Ihr Augenlider!
Ich bin allein,
Fort ist die Erde;
Nacht muß es sein,
Daß Licht mir werde.[2]

O führt mich ganz,
Ihr innern Mächte!
Hin zu dem Glanz
Der tiefsten Nächte.
Fort aus dem Raum
Der Erdenschmerzen
Durch Nacht und Traum
Zum Mutterherzen!

To rest, to rest!

To rest, to rest,
You weary limbs!
Close tight,
You eyelids!
I am alone,
The world is left behind;
Night must come
That I may find light.

O lead me on,
You inner powers,
To the radiance
Of the darkest nights!
Far away from earth
And its anguish
Through night and dream
To a mother's heart!

---

1 Frank Walker writes perceptively that this song, in its application of 'Wagnerian technique and principles', was 'a milestone in Wolf's own progress towards mastery and in the history of song'. Composed perhaps as Wolf's threnody on the death of Wagner a few months earlier.
2 The bold ascending melody at „Nacht muß es sein, daß Licht mir werde" conveys symbolically the journey from 'night' to 'light'.

THEODOR KÖRNER
(1791–1813)

		page
Ständchen	25 March–12 April 1877	297

POET

Körner, who came from a literary family (his parents were close friends of Friedrich von Schiller), first attracted attention with *Knospen* (1810), but it was his patriotic poetry, published posthumously under the title *Leyer und Schwert* ('Lyre and Sword') that made a great impression on the young Schubert, whom he met and encouraged in Vienna in 1813, and his contemporaries. His bellicose nature led him to fight a duel while at Leipzig University, and he was forced to flee the city to avoid arrest. He arrived in Vienna on 26 August 1811 and wrote plays with such success that he was appointed resident dramatist at the Burgtheater in January 1813. Two months later he, like Joseph von Eichendorff, enlisted in Adolf von Lützow's Freikorps (Free Corps), to fight against Napoleon. There is a wonderful painting in Berlin's Nationalgalerie, *Auf Vorposten* (*At the Sentry Post*) by Georg Friedrich Kersting, a friend of Caspar David Friedrich, depicting Körner with his comrades Karl Friedrich Friesen and Heinrich Hartmann leaning against oak trees, that symbol of German identity, waiting for the French to attack. All three were killed in the Wars of Liberation and all three were friends of the artist, who painted this picture and *Die Kranzwinderin* in memory of his fallen comrades. Körner, who demanded in his poetry that men should prize the freedom of the fatherland more highly than their own lives, was a recruiting officer for the Freikorps, and died at the battle of Gadebusch. Several composers have been drawn to his verse, most notably Schubert (14 settings), Weber (12), Loewe (2), and Franz and Richard Strauss (one each). Schubert also composed *Der vierjährige Posten* to one of his libretti. Körner, who lived in the Wipplingerstraße in the very apartment that Schubert was later to share with Mayrhofer, left behind five tragedies, five comedies, a number of short stories and several volumes of poetry. His father, who wrote an Introduction to the second enlarged edition of *Leyer und Schwert* (1814), refers to Körner's „Vertrauen zu Gott, sein fester Glaube an den Sieg des Rechts, der Freiheit, der Brüdereintracht, des Mutes, der Todesverachtung [. . .]" ('firm belief in the victory of justice, freedom, brotherly love, courage and defiance of death'). 'Ständchen', which was published posthumously in *Vermischte Gedichte*, shows a more romantic side of Körner.

COMPOSER

Wolf included 'Ständchen' in a volume of songs with the title LIEDER *und* GESÆNGE. *1tes Heft. In Musik gesetzt von* HUGO WOLF that he sent in the summer of 1877 to the Ministry of Culture and Education, hoping to be granted a bursary (see p. 4). The first verifiable performance of 'Ständchen' took place in Vienna on 5 October 1936. Wolf also considered writing two operas on plays by Körner: *Alfred der Große. Oper in zwei Aufzügen* and *Rosamunde. Ein Trauerspiel in fünf Aufzügen* (1812) – see HW to Anna Vinzenzberg, 28 July 1876, below.

LETTER

HW to Anna Vinzenzberg, Windischgraz, 28 July 1876

Ich bin ganz glücklich bei meinem kleinen Zimmer, wo ich nun ungestört größere Werke schaffen kann. Schade, daß ich mit so einem elenden Kasten mich abbalgen muß; den ersten Tag fielen schon 4 Hämmer u. z bei der Tannhäuser-Ouvertüre.[1]

Alfred den Großen werde ich nicht bearbeiten, wol aber Alboin u. Rosamunde, wo zu Körner schon in seinen Briefen Anweisungen zur Behandlung giebt. Jetzt werde ich eine Ouvertüre componiren, wozu ich aber noch keinen Stoff habe.

I am extremely happy in my little room, where I can now compose larger works without being disturbed. A pity that I have to slave away on such a wretched honkytonk of a piano; four hammers fell off in my first few days here while I was playing the *Tannhäuser* overture.

I shall not adapt *Alfred the Great*, but will probably compose *Alboin & Rosamunde*, regarding which Körner gives some performance hints in his letters. I am now going to compose an overture, for which, however, I as yet have no material.

---

1 A touching example of the sixteen-year-old Wolf's obsession with Wagner.

LIED

Ständchen

Alles wiegt die stille Nacht
    Tief in süßen Schlummer;
Nur der Liebe Sehnsucht wacht
    Und der Liebe Kummer.[1]
Mich umschleichen bandenfrei
    Nächtliche Gespenster;
Doch ich harre still und treu
    Unter deinem Fenster.

Holdes Mädchen, hörst du mich?
    Willst du länger säumen?
Oder wiegt der Schlummer dich
    Schon in süßen Träumen?
Nein, du bist gewiß noch wach;
    Hinter Fensters Gittern
Seh' ich ja im Schlafgemach
    Noch das Lämpchen zittern.

Ach, so blicke, süßes Kind,
    Aus dem Fenster nieder!
Leise wie der Abendwind
    Flüstern meine Lieder;
Doch verständlich sollen sie
    Meine Sehnsucht klagen
Und mit sanfter Harmonie
    Dir: „Ich liebe!" sagen.

Was die treue Liebe spricht,
    Wird die Liebe hören.
Aber länger darf ich nicht
    Deine Ruhe stören.
Schlummre, bis der Tag erwacht,
    In dem warmen Stübchen;
Drum, feins Liebchen, gute Nacht,
    Gute Nacht, feins Liebchen![2]

Serenade

The silent night lulls everything
    Into deep, sweet slumber;
Only Love's longing lies awake,
    And Love's sorrow too.
Nocturnal spectres prowl
    Untrammelled around me;
But I wait, silent and faithful,
    Underneath your window.

Lovely girl, can you not hear me?
    How much longer will you delay?
Or does sleep cradle you
    Already in sweet dreams?
No, you are surely still awake;
    For behind your lattice window
I can see the little lamp
    Flickering in your bedroom.

Ah, then look down, sweet girl,
    From your window!
Softly as the evening breeze
    My songs murmur;
Yet they shall clearly
    Lament my longing
And in gentle harmony
    Say 'I love you!'

What true love utters,
    Love will hear.
But I must no longer
    Disturb your rest.
Sleep on in your warm little room
    Till morning dawns;
So, my dearest love, good night,
    Good night, my dearest love!

---

1 Körner: der liebe Kummer.
2 Wolf adds „Gute Nacht, gute Nacht!" at the end of the song.

Nikolaus Lenau
(1802–1850)

			page
Der Raubschütz	1875–24 June 1876	fragment	
Frühlingsgrüße	3 January 1876		306
Meeresstille	begun January 1876		306
Liebesfrühling	29 January 1876		307
Die Stimme des Kindes	February 1876	Chorus for 4–6 mixed voices with piano	307
Stille Sicherheit	autumn 1876		308
Scheideblick	c. December 1876,		308
Abendbilder	4 January–24 February 1877		309
An*	27 April–8 May 1877		313
Wunsch	26 November 1877	fragment	
Traurige Wege	22–25 January 1878 revised 3 February 1878		310
Nächtliche Wanderung	19–21 February 1878		311
Der schwere Abend	?1879	lost	
Herbstentschluß	8 July 1879		311
Frage nicht	21 July 1879		312
Herbst	24 July 1879		313
Herbstklage	11 September 1879	fragment	
Der kriegslustige Waffenschmied	28 May 1880	fragment	
An die Wolke	7 January 1881	fragment	

POET

Perhaps the most melancholy of all German-speaking poets, Nikolaus Franz Niembsch, Edler von Strehlenau (the pseudonym Lenau is derived from the final two syllables) was the son of a dissolute Austrian cavalry officer and a middle-class Hungarian girl from a good family. He lost his father when he was five and suffered in his youth from deep depressions. He studied numerous subjects, including philosophy, law, agriculture and medicine, at several different universities, and qualified in none. On receiving a substantial inheritance in 1830, he moved to Stuttgart, where he was in regular contact with Ludwig Uhland, Gustav Schwab and, above all, Justinus Kerner. Lenau's love for Schwab's niece, Lotte Gmelin, inspired the five *Schilflieder*, two of which were later memorably set by Mendelssohn ('Auf dem Teich, dem regungslosen') and Berg ('Auf geheimem Waldespfade'). Lenau met the nineteen-year-old Lotte in Stuttgart on 22 August 1831 and was entranced by her youth and her singing of Beethoven's 'Adelaide'. But he could not commit himself to the relationship, broke it off in May 1832 and poured out his heart in a letter to Kerner:

> O Kerner! Kerner! ich bin kein Aszet; aber ich möchte gerne im Grabe liegen. Helfen Sie mir von dieser Schwermut, die sich nicht wegscherzen, nicht wegpredigen, nicht wegfluchen läßt!

> O Kerner! Kerner! I am no ascetic; but I wish I were lying in my grave. Help me to conquer this melancholy which cannot be joked, preached or cursed away!

Disappointed by the social and political conditions in Austria, he emigrated in 1832 to America where he tried unsuccessfully to become a farmer. On his return to Stuttgart six months later, he fell in love with the twenty-four-year-old Sophie von Löwenthal. His relationship with her was never easy. They met in the autumn of 1834; she was unhappily married to Max von Löwenthal, a high official in the Austrian Civil Service, and they had three children. What began as a light-hearted flirtation developed, on Lenau's side, into a crazed passion. They corresponded for many years, and as with Wolf's letters and notes to Melanie Köchert (see p. 491), Lenau used both the 'Sie' form of address for communications that might also be read by her husband, and the intimate 'Du' form in the *Tagebuchblätter* – what Lenau called the *Zettel* or love notes – to express his passion. Let one example from many suffice, written from Stuttgart on 7 May 1841:

> Du schreibst, daß Du Deine Garderobe für Ischl zurichtest; ach, hätt' ich nur irgend ein Kleidungsstück, ein nahes, von Dir da! weißt Du, eines, das Du nah am Leibe getragen! Das noch warm wäre von Deinem süßen Leibe! Ach, Sopherl, ich liebe ja Deinen Leib selbst so sehr, nur weil er herumliegt um die schönste, beste, allersüßeste Seele auf Erden.

> You write that you are preparing your wardrobe for Ischl; ah, if only I had an article of your clothing, something that you wear next to your body! Something still warm from your sweet body! Ah, Soph! I love your body so much only because it encloses the most beautiful, the best, the sweetest soul in the world.

Sophie inspired some of Lenau's finest poems, including 'Meine Rose' (posted with a letter in August 1836, and later immortalised by Schumann as Op. 90/2) and 'An*', which Wolf was to set in May 1877. „O, spiele nicht mit meinem Herzen!" ('Oh do not trifle with my heart!') runs a line from that poem, and there is a sense in which Sophie, although she loved him, never had any intention of sacrificing her well-ordered domestic life and her social standing in Viennese society. Despite his subsequent behaviour, she remained fond of him and when in May 1847 he languished in the asylum at Ober-Döbling, she visited him once a fortnight and gazed at him through the door of his cell.

It is hardly surprising that Lenau began to look elsewhere. Like Wolf, he next fell for a singer, but whereas Wolf sought to conceal from Melanie his attachment to Frieda Zerny (see pp. 491–2 and 520–22), Lenau actually wrote to Sophie from Vienna on 25 June 1839, informing her of his infatuation with the celebrated mezzo:

> Ich speiste mit Fräulein Unger und Graf Heißenstamm, dem dramatischen Dichter. Unger sang vor Tisch, unter Heißenstamms Begleitung, den Wanderer und das Gretchen von Schubert, hinreißend schön. [. . .] Wir setzten uns zu Tisch. Die Unger war sehr freundlich und gesprächig. „Ich bitte mir meinen Lenau zum Nachbarn aus", sagte sie, und so ward ich ihr Nachbar.

> I dined with Fräulein Unger and Count Heißenstamm, the playwright. Before we sat down, Unger, accompanied by Heißenstamm, sang Schubert's 'Der Wanderer' and 'Gretchen am Spinnrade', most beautifully. [. . .] We then took our places at table. Unger was most friendly and communicative. 'I would like my Lenau to sit beside me,' she said, and I obliged.

Karoline Unger (1803–1877), one of the most celebrated mezzo-sopranos of her day, had been taught by Johann Michael Vogl and was the first mezzo to sing in Beethoven's 'Choral' Symphony. Her relationship with Lenau blossomed, but Sophie's attempts to thwart the liaison were finally successful – not before Lenau had written her this sentence in a letter of 11 July 1839:

> Karoline liebt mich und will mein werden. Sie sieht es als ihre Sendung an, mein Leben zu versöhnen und zu beglücken.

> Karoline loves me and wishes to be mine. She sees it as her mission to alleviate and gladden my life.

Sophie also opposed his subsequent engagement to Marie Behrends. Lenau suffered a nervous breakdown and, on 29 September 1844 (the year in which his *Gedichte* went into a seventh edition), a mild heart attack. On 19 October he was declared insane, the result of a syphilitic infection contracted in his youth, and on the 22nd he was taken to the asylum at Winnenthal. Three years later he was transferred to the asylum at Ober-Döbling outside Vienna, a stone's throw from the Köchert villa where Wolf would often stay. He died on 22 August 1850.

Lenau was intensely musical, played the violin to a high standard (he owned a Guarneri), adored *Fidelio* and was among the first to appreciate late Beethoven, in particular the Ninth Symphony and the Late Quartets. He appears as the central character, Dr Moorfeld, in Ferdinand Kürnberger's *Der Amerika-Müde* (1855). Although Lenau published several epics, such as *Faust. Ein Gedicht* (1836), *Savonarola* (1837), *Die Albingenser* (1842) and *Don Juan*, which was published posthumously in 1851, he is best remembered for his lyric poetry, which has attracted numerous composers, most notably Berg, Franz, Liszt, Mendelssohn, Pfitzner, Schoeck, Schumann (who dedicated his Op. 90 songs to the memory of the poet), Strauss and Wolf.

COMPOSER

Wolf, like Lenau, suffered from syphilis and died in an asylum. Thirteen complete Lenau settings survive, but none of these early songs – they were composed between 1876 and 1879 – has found a regular place in the repertoire. There is, however, much to admire, and Wolf clearly thought they were good enough for publication. 'Liebesfrühling' is an *allegro scherzando* description of springtime love that he started on 29 January 1876 at five o'clock in the evening and finished at a quarter to one in the morning, as he noted meticulously on the manuscript. In February 1878 he sent four Lenau Lieder, including 'An*' and 'Traurige Wege', to the publishing house of Johann André in Offenbach/Main, expressing the hope that they would be published 'in four or eight weeks'. When they were rejected, he sent them to Friedrich von Hausegger in Graz, who described them, to Wolf's disgust, as 'reminiscent of Mendelssohn' – see HW to his parents, 10 April 1878, p. 305. He then offered them, with the addition of 'Nächtliche Wanderung', to Breitkopf & Härtel in the spring of 1878, and once more they were rejected. There is a strong influence of Schumann in these songs, especially 'Traurige Wege' and 'An*'. Wolf wrote a dedication in the autograph manuscript of 'An*' that was subsequently partially erased: „Fräulein Valentine Franck . . ." It is clear that Wolf regarded several of his Lenau settings as a sort of personal confession, reflecting his ultimately hopeless love for Vally. They were not published in his lifetime, but that did not prevent him from planning three separate collections, as these manuscript titles show: *Herbstgesänge von N. Lenau componirt von Hugo Wolf*; *Gedichte von N. Lenau componirt von Hugo Wolf* and *Gedichte von N. Lenau. Frage nicht. Traurige Wege. Nächtliche Wanderung. Herbstentschluß. An* componirt von Hugo Wolf*.

Wolf included 'An*' in a volume of songs with the title LIEDER und GESÆNGE. *1tes Heft. In Musik gesetzt von* HUGO WOLF that he sent in the summer of 1877 to the Ministry of Culture and Education, hoping it would earn him a bursary (see p. 4).

One way for the impecunious Wolf to earn money was by giving piano lessons, and in 1879 he had the good fortune to have Vally Franck as a pupil. She was the first big love of his life, and it can be seen from one of Vally's letters, dated 25 August 1879, to her friend Helene Gabillon, that Wolf's love was for a while requited – see Valentine Franck to Helene Gabillon, 25 August 1879, p. 305. 'The dear creature has remained true to me and himself. I receive many loving letters and now and then compositions.' The compositions probably refer to three Lenau songs, 'Herbstentschluß', 'Frage nicht' and 'Herbst', the first two of which had been intended to form part of a group of Lieder dedicated to Vally: *Lieder und Gesänge von N. Lenau und J. Eichendorff. Fräulein V .... F .... geweiht, von Hugo Wolf*. 'Herbstentschluß', with its tumultuous piano accompaniment of *tremolando* semiquavers, is the most ambitious of these passionate songs, 'Frage nicht' the most autobiographical, an intimate avowal of his love for Vally, in which he instructs the pianist to begin the song 'convulsively, like a passionate outburst'. Given their intensely private nature, it is easy to see why Wolf did not include these Lieder in his first song collections, which appeared in 1888; less easy to understand is why they are still not better known, when they have for many years been available in the *Nachgelassene Lieder*, and were given such committed performances on disc by Dietrich Fischer-Dieskau and Daniel Barenboim in the mid-1970s.

LETTERS

HW to his parents, Vienna, 15 March 1876

Ich komponiere jetzt sehr fleißig; hab' gleich darauf, als Sie mir von dem sog. Ritterbund[1] die Anzeige machten, einen Chor, „Die Stimme des Kindes" von Lenau, komponiert, u. z. für 4 Männerstimmen und Klavierbegleitung. Mit der fertigen Arbeit ging ich am 28. Febr., gerade als die Oper „Rienzi" von Richard Wagner gegeben wurde, zum Kapellmeister der Oper, Hans Richter. Ich fand ihn beim Speisen, ließ ihn herausrufen und erklärte ihm mein Erscheinen. Hierauf führte er mich hinein, wo ich beiläufig eine gute ½ Stunde warten mußte, bis er vom Speisen fertig war. Hierauf spielten wir den Chor auf einem Bösendorfer-Flügel, er die Partitur, ich die Klavierstimme, so gut es bei mir gehen mochte, denn Richter spielte die Partitur viel besser als ich die

---

1 The Ritterbund succeeded the Kasinoverein ('cinema club'), an institution in Windischgraz that organised social occasions and concerts.

Klavierstimme. Der Chor gefiel ihm sehr gut, aber wie ich immer das Pech mit der Stimmenführung habe, die Bässe gingen im Verhältnis zum Tenor viel höher als der Tenor selbst; damit wird die Melodie selbstverständlich verschwommen. Er zeigte mir hierauf die verschiedenen Lagen, schrieb mir alles auf und gab mir die Erlaubnis, ihm andere Chöre, aber im Tenorschlüssel, zu bringen. Zu Hause angekommen machte ich mich gleich an die Arbeit eines neuen Chores „Im Sommer" von Goethe, dem 3 andere Chöre folgten;[2] diese 4 Chöre sind ohne Klavierbegleitung und im Tenorschlüssel geschrieben, was mir anfangs etwas schwer ging. Sie sind sehr schön gearbeitet, und hoffe, daß dieselben Richter gut gefallen werden. Hauptsächlich ging ich zum Richter, um Karten für die Oper zu erhalten und Protektion bei Richard Wagner zu erlangen. Das zweite schlug nun fehl, da Richter sagte, daß ich mit meinem ersten Chor „Die Stimme des Kindes" vor dem Meister nicht erscheinen solle, weil eben die Bässe erst umgearbeitet werden müßten.

I am now composing very industriously; when you mentioned the so-called Ritterbund to me, I immediately composed a chorus, 'Die Stimme des Kindes', to words by Lenau, for four male voices with piano accompaniment. On 28 Feb. I went with the completed work to Hans Richter, the Kapellmeister of the Opera, just as Richard Wagner's opera *Rienzi* was being given. I found him at table, had him called out and explained to him why I had come. He then led me inside, where incidentally I had to wait for a good half-hour until he had finished dining. Whereupon we played the chorus on a Bösendorfer grand, he the voice parts, I the piano accompaniment, as well as I was able, for Richter played the score much better than I the piano part. He liked the chorus very much, but as I always have bad luck with part-writing, the bass line went much higher than the tenor line – thus, of course, blurring the melody. He then showed me the various registers, wrote it all out for me and gave me permission to bring him some more choruses, but written in the tenor clef. On arriving home, I got straight to work on a new chorus, 'Im Sommer', by Goethe, and this was followed by three other choruses. These 4 choruses are without piano accompaniment and written in the tenor clef, which I found rather difficult at first. They are very finely crafted, and I hope that Richter will be pleased with them. The main reason for going to Richter was to acquire tickets for the Opera and to obtain Wagner's patronage. The second goal was unsuccessful, since Richter said that I ought not to appear before the Master with my first chorus, 'Die Stimme des Kindes', because the basses would first need to be revised.

---

2 'Im Sommer' is actually by Johann Georg Jacobi; the other choruses are 'Geistesgruß' (Goethe), 'Mailied' (Goethe) and, perhaps, 'Die schöne Nacht' (Goethe), which, though mentioned on the cover of the Goethe choruses, has not survived.

HW to his parents, Vienna, 18 December 1877

Am 1. Jänner wird entschieden, wer den Preis erhaltet; ich habe große Hoffnungen. Das Scherzo aus der Symphonie gefällt allgemein, ein Lied „An***" von Lenau, das ich bei Goldschmidt vorgespielt, entzückte die Zuhörer, und so glaube ich, mit Recht große Hoffnungen auf den Preis setzen zu dürfen.

The winner of the prize will be announced on 1 January; I have high hopes. The *scherzo* from my Symphony has pleased everyone here, and a song, 'An***' (Lenau) that I played at Goldschmidt's, entranced the audience – and so I am right to harbour great hopes of winning the prize.

HW to his parents, Vienna, 17 February 1878

Das Neueste auf meiner Künstlerlaufbahn ist ein Ereigniss, das Sie sehr angenehm berühren wird, nähmlich in 4 od. 8 Wochen erscheinen von mir 4 Lieder bei Joh. André in Offenbach am Main in Druck. Die Lieder habe ich bereits eingesandt u. z. geschah dies auf Verwendung Kastners,[1] der mit André auf gutem Fuße steht. Hauseggers[2] Schreiben folgt bei, bitte es mir jedoch zu retourniren. Die Lieder habe ich Hauseg. noch nicht eingesendet, weil ich nur eine Abschrift davon besitze – werde jedoch sobald selbe copirt sind ihm schicken. Es sind die 3 Lieder aus Windischgraz nähmlich „An*", „Wanderlied" u. „Morgenthau" u. eines das beste, was ich erst vor Kurzem in Wien geschrieben „Traurige Wege" von Lenau. Für den Druck zahle ich selbstverständlich nichts, werde aber auch nicht bezahlt, nur bei der 2. Verlegung wenn die Lieder gut abgehen, bekomme ich Honorar.[3]

The latest bulletin in my career as an artist will please you most agreeably: 4 of my songs will be published by Joh. André in Offenbach am Main within 4 to 8 weeks. I've already delivered the songs, thanks to the influence of Kastner who is on good terms with André. I enclose Hausegger's letter, but please return it to me. I haven't yet sent the songs to Hauseg., because I only have one copy – but as soon as they are copied, I shall send him them. These are the 3 songs I composed in Windischgraz: 'An*', 'Wanderlied' & 'Morgentau' & best of all Lenau's 'Traurige Wege' that I composed recently in Vienna. Of course, I shall not pay for them to be published, but I shall get no fee until the second edition – if the songs sell well.

---

1   Emerich Kastner (1847–1916), Austrian writer on music.
2   Dr Friedrich von Hausegger (1837–1899), lawyer, critic and musicologist, taught at the University of Graz from 1872.
3   The songs were not published in Wolf's lifetime.

HW to his parents, Vienna, 10 April 1878

Die Lieder samt einem Brief Dr. Hauseggers habe ich vor einigen Tagen erhalten, ohne jedoch nur das geringste Resultat erzielt zu haben. In seinem Schreiben heißt es, daß er vor Überbürdung zu wenig Zeit habe, die Lieder eingehender zu analysieren, ja, daß er kaum so viel Zeit erübrigen kann, um dieselben nur flüchtig durchzusehen. Was er über die Lieder ausspricht, will ich hier anführen: „Im allgemeinen haben mir die einen Mendelssohnschen Charakter tragenden Lieder bei der Durchsicht einen nicht ungünstigen Eindruck gemacht [. . .]" Dies seine eigenen Worte, die ich ihm aber sehr verarge, denn eine größere Beleidigung könnte mir wohl niemals ins Gesicht geworfen werden, als mich der Nachahmung Mendelssohns zu zeihen und obendrein noch im Lied! Wahrscheinlich hat er sie vorm Schlafengehen, nachdem nicht allein schon seine physischen, sondern auch psychischen Kräfte sehr erschlafft waren, durchgesehen, denn sonst könnte er niemals zu diesem Fazit gelangen. Sogar ein starker Schumannscher Zug geht durch die Lieder, am meisten in den „Traurigen Wegen", aber Mendelssohn nimmermehr.

A few days ago I received back the songs, together with a letter from Dr Hausegger, without having in the slightest achieved my goal. He writes that, because of excessive work pressures, he has had too little time to analyse the songs in greater detail – indeed, he can hardly spare the time even to give them a fleeting glance. This is what he has to say about the songs: 'Perusing these songs, those resembling Mendelssohn have on the whole left me with a not unfavourable impression [. . .]' I violently object to these words of his, for no greater insult could be thrown in my face than to accuse me of imitating Mendelssohn – and in the Lied of all things! He probably looked through them just before going to bed, when not only his physical but also his mental powers were seriously flagging – otherwise, he could never have arrived at this conclusion. A strong Schumannian trait runs through the songs, especially in 'Traurige Wege', but absolutely not Mendelssohn.

Valentine Franck to Helene Gabillon, 25 August 1879

Das liebe Geschöpf ist mir und sich treu geblieben, ich erhalte viele und liebe Briefe, ab und zu auch Compositionen. Nicht verhehlen kann ich Dir, daß ich die Briefe beantworte, die Compositionen spiele und die mir geschickten Bücher lese. Wie das enden soll, wissen die Götter, einstweilen geht die Selbstständigkeit und Originalität meines Styles verloren, denn ich schreibe schon ganz wie Hugo.

The dear creature has remained true to me and himself. I receive many loving letters and now and then compositions. I cannot deny that I answer the letters, play the compositions, and read the books sent to me. How that will end only the gods can tell; meanwhile the independence and originality of my style are lost, for I write now exactly like Hugo.

LIEDER

Frühlingsgrüße[1]

Nach langem Frost, wie weht die Luft
   so lind!
Da bringt Frühveilchen mir ein bettelnd
   Kind.*

Es ist betrübt, daß so den ersten Gruß
Des Frühlings mir das Elend bringen muß.

Und doch der schönen Tage Liebespfand[2]
Ist mir noch werter aus des Unglücks Hand.

So bringt dem Nachgeschlechte unser Leid
Die Frühlingsstimmen einer bessern Zeit.*

* Wolf repeats these verses.

Spring greetings

How gently, after long frosts, the breezes
   blow!
A beggar child then brings me early
   violets.*

It is sad that spring's first greeting
Must be brought to me by misery.

And yet the love-token of happy days
Is more precious when given by misfortune.

And so our pain hands to those who follow
The spring voices of happier times.*

Meeresstille

Sturm mit seinen Donnerschlägen
Kann mir nicht wie du
So das tiefste Herz bewegen,
Tiefe Meeresruh'!

Du allein nur konntest lehren
Uns den schönen Wahn
Seliger Musik der Sphären,
Stiller Ozean du!*

Nächtlich Meer, nun ist dein Schweigen
So tief ungestört,
Daß die Seele wohl ihr eigen
Träumen§ klingen hört;

Sea calm

The tempest with its peals of thunder
Cannot move the heart
As profoundly as you,
Profound sea calm!

Only you were able to teach
Us the fair illusion
Of the spheres' blissful music,
Calm ocean!*

Nocturnal sea, your silence is now
So profoundly peaceful,
That the soul can perhaps hear
The sound of its own dreaming;§

1 The sixteen-year-old Wolf's immature style is shown in his melismatic setting of the final line of Lenau's poem: 'Frühlingsstimmen' consists of four semiquavers on 'Frühlings' and sixteen on 'stimmen'!
2 Lenau: liebes Pfand.

Daß, im Schutz geschloßnen Mundes,	So peaceful – that, safeguarded by silence,
Doch mein Herz[§] erschrickt,	My heart[§] grows afraid,
Das Geheimnis heil'gen Bundes	And presses more tightly[§] to itself
Fester[§] an sich drückt.	The secret of this sacred bond.

* Wolf repeats 'stiller' and adds 'du' for metrical reasons, thereby destroying Lenau's rhyme scheme.
[§] Wolf repeats the words 'Träumen', 'Herz' and 'Fester'.

Liebesfrühling / Love's spring

Ich sah den Lenz einmal,	I once saw spring,
Erwacht im schönsten Tal;	Awakened in the loveliest valley;
Ich sah der Liebe Licht[1]	I saw the light of love
Im schönsten Angesicht.	In the loveliest face.
Und wandl' ich nun allein	And when I now walk alone
Im Frühling durch den Hain,	In spring through the wood,
Erscheint aus jedem Strauch	Her face also appears to me
Ihr Angesicht mir auch.	From every bush.
Und seh' ich sie am Ort,	And if I see her at the spot,
Wo längst der Frühling fort,	That spring has long since left,
So sprießt ein Lenz und schallt	A spring shoots up and resounds
Um ihre süße Gestalt.*[2]	About her sweet figure.*

Also set by Robert Franz and Othmar Schoeck
* The whole of the final verse is repeated. Wolf also adds an extra 'süße' in the penultimate bar of the vocal line.

Die Stimme des Kindes[3] / The voice of the child

Ein schlafend Kind! o still! in diesen Zügen*	A sleeping child! O silence! With these features*
Könnt ihr das Paradies zurückbeschwören;	You could conjure up paradise again;
Es lächelt süß, als lauscht' es Engelschören,	It smiles sweetly, as though listening to angelic choirs,
Den Mund umsäuselt himmlisches Vergnügen.	Its mouth fanned by heavenly joy.
O schweige, Welt,[§] mit deinen lauten Lügen,	Cease, O world,[§] your noisy lies,
Die Wahrheit dieses Traumes nicht zu stören!	So as not to disturb the truth of this dream!

1 Wolf's manuscript has 'liebes Glück', but Dr Hans Jancik has restored 'Licht' (and also the rhyme) in his edition of the song in the *Gesamtausgabe*.
2 This is the first example of the repetition of a complete verse in Wolf's Lieder.
3 The poem is the last in a sequence of four poems by Lenau called *Stimmen*, the others being 'Stimme des Windes', 'Stimme des Regens' and 'Stimme der Glocken'. Although Wolf indicated that the chorus was 'for men's voices' (see HW to his parents, 15 March 1876, p. 302), the score is for mixed choir. Wolf added the definite article to Lenau's title.

NO STANZA BREAK

Laß mich das Kind im Traume sprechen hören	Let me hear the child sweetly tell its dream
Und mich, vergessend, in die Unschuld fügen!†	And bear me, oblivious, to the realm of innocence.†
Das Kind, nicht ahnend mein bewegtes Lauschen,	The child, unaware of my tremulous listening,
Mit dunklen Lauten hat mein Herz gesegnet,	Has blessed my heart with mysterious sounds,
Mehr als im stillen Wald des Baumes Rauschen.‡	More than a murmuring tree in the silent wood.‡
Ein tiefres Heimweh hat mich überfallen,	A deeper nostalgia has assailed me,
Als wenn es auf die stille Heide regnet,	As when rain falls on the silent heath,
Wenn im Gebirg die fernen Glocken hallen.⁵	When distant bells echo on the mountains.⁵

* Wolf repeats 'o still' and 'in diesen Zügen' many times. § Wolf repeats 'o schweige, Welt'.
† Wolf repeats this line. ‡ Wolf repeats this line several times.
⁵ The last verse is repeated many times.

Stille Sicherheit

Quiet certainty

Horch, wie still es wird im dunkeln Hain,
Mädchen, wir sind sicher und allein.

Hark how quiet it grows in the dark wood,
My girl, we are safe and alone.

Still umsäuselt hier den Wiesenhang[1]
Schon der Abendglocke müder Klang.

Quietly the weary sound of evening bells
Murmur around the meadow's slope.

Auf den Blumen, die sich dir verneigt,
Schlief das letzte Lüftchen ein und schweigt.

On the flowers, that incline toward you,
The last breeze has died and now is silent.

Sagen darf ich dir – wir sind allein –:
Daß mein Herz ist ewig, ewig dein!*

I can tell you – we are alone –
My heart is ever, ever yours!*

Also set by Franz and Schoeck
* Wolf repeats the final line.

Scheideblick

A parting glance

Als ein unergründlich Wonnemeer
Strahlte mir dein tiefer Seelenblick;
Scheiden mußt' ich ohne Wiederkehr,
Und ich habe scheidend all mein Glück
Still versenkt in dieses tiefe Meer.

Like an unfathomable sea of rapture
Your soul's deep gaze shone on me;
I had to part, never to return,
And parting, I sank all my happiness
Silently into this deep sea.

1 Lenau: Still versäuselt hier am Wiesenhang.

Abendbilder

3 Oden von N. Lenau

1. Friedlicher Abend senkt sich aufs Gefilde;
Sanft entschlummert Natur, um ihre Züge

    Schwebt der Dämmrung zarte Verhüllung, und sie

    Lächelt, die holde;

    Lächelt, ein schlummernd Kind in Vaters Armen,
    Der voll Liebe zu ihr sich neigt; sein göttlich
    Auge weilt auf ihr, und es weht sein Odem
    Über ihr Antlitz.

2. Schon zerfließt das ferne Gebirg mit Wolken
    In ein Meer; den Wogen entsteigt der Mond, er
    Grüßt die Flur, entgegen ihm grüßt das schönste
    Lied Philomelens

    Aus dem Blütenstrauche, der um das Plätzchen
    Zarter Liebe heimlichend sich verschlinget:
    Mirzi horcht am Busen des Jünglings ihrem Zaubergeflöte.

    Dort am Hügel weiden die Schafe beider
    Traulichen Gemenges in e i n e r Herde,
    Ihre Glöcklein stimmen so lieblich ein zu
    Frohen Akkorden.

3. Stille wird's im Walde; die lieben kleinen
    Sänger prüfen schaukelnd den Ast, der durch die
    Nacht dem neuen Fluge sie trägt, den neuen

    Liedern entgegen.

    Bald versinkt die Sonne; des Waldes Riesen
    Heben höher sich in die Lüfte, um noch
    Mit des Abends flüchtigen Rosen sich ihr
    Haupt zu bekränzen.

Images of evening

3 Odes by N. Lenau

1. A peaceful evening descends on the fields;
Nature gently falls asleep, around her features

    Floats the soft veil of twilight, and she,

    The gracious one, smiles;

    Smiles, a slumbering child in the arms of her father,
    Who bends lovingly over her; his divine
    Eye dwells on her, and his breath passes
    Over her countenance.

2. Now the distant mountains dissolve with the clouds
    Into a sea; the moon emerges from the waves, and
    Greets the meadow, and Philomel's most beautiful song returns
    Its greeting

    From the flowering shrub that secretly garlands
    This place of tender love:
    Mirzi, in her lover's arms, listens to the Magical fluting.

    There on the hillside both their herds graze
    Close together in one *single* pasture,
    Their little bells ringing in charming Harmony.

3. Silence falls on the forest; the dear little
    Singers, shaking the branch that
    Bore them during the night, test it for their new flights,
    And new songs.

    Soon the sun sinks, the forest giants
    Reach higher into the air, to garland
    Their heads awhile yet with evening's
    Fleeting roses.

Schon verstummt die Matte; den satten Rindern	The meadow now falls silent; the sated bullocks
Selten nur enthallt das Geglock am Halse,	Only rarely tinkle the bells round their necks,
Und es pflückt der wählende Zahn nur läßig Dunklere Gräser.	And only casually do they munch Darker grasses.
Und dort blickt der schuldlose Hirt der Sonne	And there the innocent shepherd looks pensively
Sinnend nach; dem Sinnenden jetzt entfallen	At the sun; meditatively he lets fall
Flöt' und Stab, es falten die Hände sich zum Stillen Gebete.	His flute and staff and folds his hands In silent prayer.

Also set by Fanny Mendelssohn Hensel

Traurige Wege[1]   Sad pathways

Bin mit dir im Wald gegangen;	I walked with you in the forest;
Ach, wie war der Wald so froh!	Ah, how beautiful the forest was!
Alles grün, die Vögel sangen,	All was green, the birds were singing,
Und das scheue Wild entfloh.	And the startled wild beasts fled.
Wo die Liebe frei und offen	Where Love, freely and openly,
Rings von allen Zweigen schallt,	Echoed all around the branches,
Ging die Liebe ohne Hoffen	Our love, devoid of hope,
Traurig durch den grünen Wald. –	Moved sadly through the green forest.
Bin mit dir am Fluß gefahren;	I went with you to the river;
Ach, wie war die Nacht so mild!	Ah, how soft the night was!
Auf der Flut, der sanften, klaren,	On the clear and tranquil waters
Wiegte sich des Mondes Bild.	The moon's reflection swayed.
Lustig scherzten die Gesellen;	Our companions laughed out loud;
Unsre Liebe schwieg und sann,	Our love was silent and sensed
Wie mit jedem Schlag der Wellen	How with every plashing wave
Zeit und Glück vorüberrann.	Time and happiness slipped away.
Graue Wolken niederhingen,	Grey clouds hung down from heaven,
Durch die Kreuze strich der West,	The West Wind blew among the crosses,
Als wir einst am Kirchhof gingen;	When we passed by the graveyard once;
Ach, wie schliefen sie so fest!	Ah, how deeply they were sleeping!
An den Kreuzen, an den Steinen	By the crosses, by the stones
Fand die Liebe keinen Halt;	Love could find no anchor;
Sahen uns die Toten weinen,	Did the dead see us weeping,
Als wir dort vorbeigewallt?	As we passed them by?

Also set by Hensel

1   See HW to his parents, 17 February and 10 April 1878, pp. 304 and 305.

Nächtliche Wanderung

Die Nacht ist finster, schwül und bang,
Der Wind im Walde tost;
Ich wandre fort die Nacht entlang
Und finde keinen Trost.

Und mir zur Seite, engelmild
Und, ach! so schmerzlich traut,
Zieht mein Geleite hin, das Bild
Von meiner toten Braut.

Ihr bleiches Antlitz bittet mich,
Was mich ihr süßer Mund
So zärtlich bat und feierlich
In ihrer Sterbestund':

„Bezwinge fromm die Todeslust,
Die dir im Auge starrt,
Wenn man mich bald von deiner Brust
Fortreißet und verscharrt!"

Da unten braust der wilde Bach,
Führt reichen, frischen Tod,
Die Wogen rufen laut mir nach:
„Komm, komm und trinke Tod!"

Das klingt so lieblich wie Musik,
Wird wo ein Paar getraut:
Doch zieht vom Sprunge mich zurück
Das Wort der toten Braut.

Stets finstrer wird der Wolkendrang,
Der Sturm im Walde brüllt,
Und ferne hebt sich Donnerklang,
Der immer stärker schwillt.

O, schlängle dich, du Wetterstrahl,
Herab, ein Faden mir,
Der aus dem Labyrinth der Qual
Hinaus mich führt zu ihr!

Herbstentschluß

Trübe Wolken, Herbstesluft,
Einsam wandl' ich meine Straßen,
Welkes Laub, kein Vogel ruft –
Ach, wie stille! wie verlassen!

A walk at night

The night is dark, sultry and uneasy,
The wind rages in the forest;
I keep walking into the night
And can find no solace.

And at my side, like a gentle angel,
And ah! so painfully close,
The image of my dead bride
Accompanies me.

Her pale face begs me
What her sweet lips
So tenderly and solemnly
Begged as she lay dying:

'Overcome this wish for death,
In your glassy eyes,
When I am soon torn from your arms
And buried in a grave!'

Down there the wild stream roars,
Bringing an ample fresh death,
The waves are calling loud to me:
'Come, come, and savour death!'

That sounds as lovely as music
Played on a wedding day:
But I am prevented from leaping in
By the words of my dead bride.

Darker and darker the clouds pile up,
The storm rages in the forest,
And a clap of thunder far away
Grows louder and louder.

Uncoil for me, O teeming rain,
A rope down here to earth,
That from this labyrinth of pain
I might be drawn up to her!

Autumn resolution

Dismal clouds, autumn breezes,
Solitary I go my way,
Withered leaves, no birds sing –
Ah! how silent! how forsaken!

Todeskühl der Winter naht;
Wo sind, Wälder, eure Wonnen?
Fluren, eurer vollen Saat
Goldne Wellen sind verronnen!

Es ist worden kühl und spät,
Nebel auf der Wiese weidet,
Durch die öden Haine weht
Heimweh; – alles flieht und scheidet.

Herz, vernimmst du diesen Klang
Von den felsentstürzten Bächen?
Zeit gewesen wär' es lang,
Daß wir ernsthaft uns besprächen!

Herz, du hast dir selber oft
Weh getan und hast es andern,
Weil du hast geliebt, gehofft;
Nun ist's aus, wir müssen wandern!*

Auf die Reise will ich fest
Ein dich schließen und verwahren,
Draußen mag ein linder West
Oder Sturm vorüberfahren;

Daß wir unsern letzten Gang
Schweigsam wandeln und alleine,
Daß auf unsern Grabeshang
Niemand* als der Regen weine!

Also set by Schoeck
* Wolf repeats 'müssen wandern' and 'niemand'.

Winter draws near, deathly cold,
Where, O woods, are your delights?
Meadows, the golden ripples
Of your ripe corn have vanished!

It has grown chilly and late,
Mists graze upon the meadow,
Winds of nostalgia blow
Through the woods; – all things flee and part.

Heart, can you hear this sound
Of torrents gushing down the rocks?
It is high time that we
Talked seriously together!

Heart, you have often wounded yourself,
And others too,
Because you have loved, have hoped;
All is now over, we must depart!*

On the journey I shall guard you,
Clasp you firmly to my breast;
Even though a mild west wind
Or a storm break loose;

Let us take our final steps
Silently and alone,
And upon our gravestone
Let no one* but the rain lament!

Frage nicht[1]

Wie sehr ich dein, soll ich dir sagen?
Ich weiß es nicht und will nicht fragen;
Mein Herz behalte seine Kunde,
Wie tief es dein im Grunde.

O still! ich möchte sonst erschrecken,
Könnt' ich die Stelle nicht entdecken,

Do not ask

I should tell you how much I love you?
I do not know and shall not ask;
Let my heart keep for itself
The depth of its love for you.

O be silent! or else I might take fright,
Were I unable to find the place in my heart,

---

1 The song was composed on 21 July 1879, a few months before Vally Franck wrote that devastating letter to Helene Gabillon (see p. 481) describing how her relationship with Wolf had suffered a setback. The passionate nature of the prelude and the emotive markings – *Sehr langsam und mit der innigsten Empfindung* and *krampfhaft, wie in leidenschaftlicher Aufwallung* (*Very slow and with the most fervent feeling* and *convulsively, like a passionate outburst*) – convey the intense nature of Wolf's relationship with Vally.

Die unzerstört für Gott verbliebe,
Beim Tode deiner Liebe.

That would always live for God alone,
If your own love were to die.

Also set by Franz and Schoeck

Herbst

Nun ist es Herbst, die Blätter fallen,
Den Wald durchbraust des Scheidens Weh,
Den Lenz und seine Nachtigallen
Verträumt' ich auf der wüsten See.

Der Himmel schien so mild, so helle,
Verloren ging sein warmes Licht;
Es blühte nicht die Meereswelle,
Die rohen Winde sangen nicht.

Und mir verging die Jugend traurig,
Des Frühlings Wonne blieb versäumt;
Der Herbst durchweht mich trennungsschaurig,
Mein Herz dem Tod entgegenträumt.

Autumn

Autumn is come, the leaves are falling,
The ache of parting soughs through the wood,
Spring and its nightingales I dreamt away,
As I sailed on the desolate sea.

The heavens seemed so mellow, so clear,
Their warm light has vanished;
The ocean waves did not blossom,
The biting winds did not sing.

And my youth passed sadly by,
The joys of spring were not tasted;
Autumn pierces me with a parting shudder,
My heart dreams on towards death.

An*[1]

O, wag' es nicht, mit mir zu scherzen,
Zum Scherze schloß ich keinen Bund;
O, spiele nicht mit meinem Herzen![2]
Weißt du noch nicht, wie sehr es wund?

Weil ich so tief für dich entbrannte,
Weil ich mich dir gezeigt so weich,
Dein Herz die süße Heimat nannte
Und deinen Blick mein Himmelreich:

O, rüttle nicht den Stolz vom Schlummer,
Der süßer Heimat sich entreißt,
Dem Himmel mit verschwiegnem Kummer
Auf immerdar den Rücken weist.

To*

Oh, do not dare to jest with me,
It was not to jest that I vowed to wed you;
Oh, do not trifle with my heart!
Do you still not know how wounded it is?

Because I burned for you with such passion,
Because I showed myself so tender,
Because I called your heart my homeland
And a glance from you my heaven:

Oh, do not shake pride awake from slumber,
He who abandons his sweet homeland,
Turns his back in silent sorrow
For ever more on that heaven.

---

1 For publication details see pp. 3–4.
2 Lenau here has Sophie von Löwenthal in mind – see p. 300. Although 'An*' was composed before Wolf met Vally Franck, he later revised the song and included it in a group of Lieder he called *Gedichte von N. Lenau*, which he dedicated to his beloved. A few words of the dedication have been erased but some of the text is still decipherable: *Fräulein Valentine Franck* [. . .] *Antwort auf den* [. . .] *unterthänigst* [. . .]. Vally's letter to Helene Gabillon of 25 August 1879 (quoted above, see p. 305) mentions the fact that Wolf sent her many of his compositions in the summer of 1879.

Lenz Lorenzi

(dates unknown)

			page
Grablied	by early September 1876	SATB, for unaccompanied choir	314

POET

Frank Walker in *Hugo Wolf: A Biography* writes that Lorenzi was a friend of the Wolf family.

COMPOSER

The autograph manuscript states that 'Grablied' was written in the Lechner Wald, a wood near Windischgraz. It seems likely that the song, along with other a cappella choral pieces, was written for performance by family friends and acquaintances.

LIED

Grablied

Wach' auf, erwache wieder,
Lächle uns noch einmal an –
Doch nein, schlumm're sanft, du Müder,
Kaum entfloh'n der Erde Wahn.

Schlumm're süß im ew'gen Frieden,
Engel halten dir die Wacht,
Finde, den das Glück gemieden,
Stille Ruh'* in Grabes Nacht.

* Wolf repeats 'stille Ruh''.

Dirge

Wake up, awaken once more,
Smile at us again –
But no, slumber gently on, you weary one,
Scarcely yet escaped from earth's folly.

Slumber sweetly in eternal peace,
Angels will watch over you,
You, whom happiness shunned –
Find silent peace* in the night of the grave.

August Mahlmann
(1771–1826)

			page
Gottvertrauen	September 1876	SATB unaccompanied	315

POET

Mahlmann's father was a well-to-do merchant who sent his son to a private school in Leipzig; August later transferred to the Fürstenschule in Grimma and then studied law at Leipzig University. Having worked for a while as a private tutor, he embarked in 1797 on a journey through Denmark, Sweden and Russia. After his return to Leipzig he bought the Junius bookshop, which he sold a few years later following substantial financial losses. He was appointed chief editor of the *Zeitung für die elegante Welt* (1805–16) and then of the *Leipziger Zeitung*. Although he had scientific interests, he became best known for a series of stage plays, including *Der Hausbau* (1801) and *Herodes vor Bethlehem, oder der triumphirende Viertelsmeister* (1803). The complete edition of his works appeared in 1839. Several Lieder composers have been drawn to his poetry, most notably Hindemith, Loewe, Schumann, Spohr, Wolf and Zumsteeg.

LIED

Gottvertrauen

An Himmels Höh'n
Die Sterne gehn
In fester, stiller Bahn;
Der Mensch, das schwache Kind der Zeit,
Blickt zu der ew'gen Herrlichkeit
Mit glaubensvollem Trost hinan.

Durch Wolken bricht
Der Hoffnung Licht
Zur Erdenwelt herab;
Wer's aufnahm in sein frommes Herz,
Der wandelt ohne Furcht und Schmerz
Mit Gottvertrau'n zum stillen Grab!

Trust in God

High up in Heaven
The stars pursue
Their fixed, silent course,
Man, that weak child of the present time,
Gazes up to the eternal splendour
With the comfort born of belief.

The light of hope
Breaks through the clouds
To the world here below;
Whoever absorbed it into a devout heart
Will journey without fear and pain
And trusting God to his grave!

Friedrich von Matthisson
(1761–1831)

		page
Andenken	23–25 April 1877	318

POET

Matthisson's father, a clergyman, died before his son was born, and Friedrich was educated by his grandfather before entering the seminary at Klosterbergen in Magdeburg. Having studied theology and philology, he began his nomadic existence as a tutor to the great and good. Throughout his life he moved in aristocratic and literary circles, witnessed by a remarkable document, *Das Stammbuch Friedrich von Matthissons*, a sort of glorified autograph album that contains contributions from a number of figures who loom large in the history of the Lied: Claudius, Herder, Klopstock, Müller, Salis-Seewis, Schiller, Schubart and Stolberg. He married in 1793; a son, Ludwig, was born two years later but died in 1799. Many years after his divorce from his first wife, Matthisson married a woman some thirty years his junior. She predeceased him, and their child also died at an early age. Child mortality was a commonplace in the nineteenth century, and many poets who feature in this volume wrote poems on the death of their children, among them Eichendorff, Heyse and Rückert. Matthisson's 'Todtenkranz für ein Kind', set by both Schubert and Mendelssohn, is a touching poem of two short stanzas that shows a depth of feeling not always evident in his poetry. His poems might have been praised by Schiller for their melancholy sweetness and bucolic descriptions, but they rarely move the reader.

Matthisson's essentially musical verse was admired by Schubert, over half of whose 29 settings were composed between 1812 and 1814. Many other composers have been drawn to his poetry, including Giuliani, Josefine Lang, Loewe, Mendelssohn, Reichardt, Ries, von Krufft, Weber, Zelter and Zumsteeg. His best-known poem has an intriguing history. While in the service of Princess Luise, Matthisson allegedly fell in love with a maid of honour, Annette von Glafey, who inspired 'Adelaide'. Because Matthisson was seventeen years her senior and yet to be ennobled, Annette's father ruled out any possibility of marriage. Another version of their relationship maintains that Annette's love for Matthisson was unrequited and resulted in her entering a religious order. Whatever the truth of these assertions, Matthisson deliberately chose a woman's name that included the word 'Adel' ('noble'), and Beethoven's song has become known to thousands of Lieder enthusiasts across the globe. Robert Louis Stevenson, writing from Edinburgh to Mrs Sitwell on 16 September 1873, praised the poem and Beethoven's music:

> I have tried to write some verses; but I find I have nothing to say that has not been already perfectly said and perfectly sung in *Adelaïde*. I have so perfect an idea out of that song! The great Alps, a wonder in the starlight – the river, strong from the hills, and turbulent, and loudly audible at night – the country, a scented *Frühlingsgarten* of orchards and deep wood where the nightingales harbour – a sort of German flavour over all – and this love-drunken man, wandering on by sleeping village and silent town, pours out of his full heart, *Einst, O Wunder, einst* etc. I wonder if I am wrong about this being the most beautiful and perfect thing in the world – the only marriage of really accordant words and music – both drunk with the same poignant, unutterable sentiment.

When the song was mentioned to Beethoven many years later, he contented himself with the lapidary reply, „Das Gedicht ist sehr schön." ('The poem is very beautiful.')

Second only in popularity to 'Adelaide' is 'Andenken' which has been set by more composers than any other Matthisson poem, although Ernst Challier, who lists 25 songs in his *Großer Lieder-Katalog* of 1885, was not aware of the settings by Mendelssohn, Salieri, Schubert and Wolf. Matthisson's 'Andenken', written in 1792, was not published until 1802, when it was included in the almanac *Flora, Teutschlands Töchtern geweiht* (*Flora, dedicated to the daughters of Germany*). One of these daughters, Matthisson's close friend Friederike Brun, was inspired by 'Andenken' to write a poem of her own beginning „Ich denke dein,/Wenn sich im Blütenregen/Der Frühling malt" ('I think of you, when the spring is reflected in showers of blossom'). In 1796, a year before Schubert's birth, Goethe attended a party at which this poem by Friederike Brun was sung to music by Zelter; after hearing the song, Goethe wrote that Zelter's melody 'appealed to me enormously, and I could not refrain from writing a poem ['Nähe des Geliebten'] to fit it [. . .].' He retained the idea and same metrical pattern of Brun's poem, but whereas she had started each verse, apart from the fourth, with „Ich denke dein" ('I think of you'), Goethe varied each opening line, thus adding great movement and life to the poem, especially in the final verse, where the woman, having worked herself up into a frenzy of expectation, has convinced herself (through thought, sight and hearing) that she is actually by her lover's side – a hope that is dashed by the final line's despairing conditional tense.

Having worked as a private tutor for Princess Luise von Anhalt-Dessau and the Duke of Württemberg, Matthisson was ennobled, and the author of the 1811 edition of his poems is announced as Friedrich von Matthisson. He was a prolific writer and his *Schriften* appeared in eight volumes between 1825 and 1829, the first of which contains his poems and the remainder his *Erinnerungen* (*Memoirs*); a ninth volume was added in 1833 containing a biography by Heinrich Döring. A *Literarischer Nachlaß* was published in four volumes by F. R. Schoch in 1832.

COMPOSER

Wolf included 'Andenken' in the volume of songs with the title LIEDER *und* GESÆNGE. *1tes Heft. In Musik gesetzt von* HUGO WOLF he sent in the summer of 1877 to the Ministry of Culture and Education (see p. 4).

LETTER

HW to Bertha von Lackhner,[1] Vienna, 13 March 1883

Ich denke Dein	I no longer think of thee
Nicht mehr beim Brein,	As I eat semolina,
Bei Kochsalat,	Salad,
Oder Spinat. –	Or spinach. –
Ich friß mich satt	I stuff my mouth
Von früh bis spat	From morn to dusk
Und denke Dein	And think of thee
Bei Ochs u. Schwein!	As I eat ox and pork!

LIED

Andenken

Ich denke dein,
Wenn durch den Hain
Der Nachtigallen
Akkorde schallen!
Wann denkst du mein?

Remembrance

I think of you
When through the grove
The nightingales'
Songs resound!
When do you think of me?

[1] Wolf had turned vegetarian during the summer of 1881 in honour of Wagner, who, in *Religion und Kunst*, had denounced the eating of meat. Wolf's parody of Matthisson's poem, however, enclosed in this letter to Bertha von Lackhner, reveals that by March 1883 he was once again eating meat with relish. Bertha treated Wolf as an adopted son whenever he stayed in Maierling in 1880 and 1882. In an attempt to make him feel as comfortable as possible, she cooked for him with motherly devotion. Wolf, like Mozart, had a scatological side, and he signed his name at the end of this letter as „Ihr unverbeßerlicher Piss" ('Your incorrigible Piss').

FRIEDRICH VON MATTHISSON

Ich denke dein	I think of you
Im Dämmerschein	In the twilight
Der Abendhelle	Of evening
Am Schattenquelle!	By the shadowed spring!
Wo denkst du mein?	Where do you think of me?
Ich denke dein	I think of you
Mit süßer Pein,	With sweet agony,
Mit bangem Sehnen	With fearful longing
Und heißen Thränen!	And passionate tears!
Wie denkst du mein?	How do you think of me?
O denke mein,	O think of me
Bis zum Verein	Until we are united
Auf besserm Sterne!	On a better star!
In jeder Ferne	However far away,
Denk' ich nur dein!*	I think only of you!*

Also set by Ludwig van Beethoven, Mendelssohn, Antonio Salieri, Franz Schubert, Carl Maria von Weber and Johann Rudolf Zumsteeg
* The final two words are twice repeated by Wolf.

Michelangelo Buonarroti
(1475–1564)

		page
Drei Gedichte von Michelangelo		
Wohl denk' ich oft an mein vergang'nes Leben	18 March 1897	327
Alles endet, was entstehet	20 March 1897	328
Fühlt meine Seele	22–28 March 1897	329

POET

Giorgio Vasari, in his celebrated *Lives*, heads the chapter on Michelangelo 'MICHELANGELO BONARROTI FIORENTINO, Pittore Scultore et Architetto'. These three nouns are inscribed on Michelangelo's tomb designed by Vasari in Florence's Santa Croce; there is no mention of poetry. Though Michelangelo wrote verse from an early age, though some of his poems circulated during his lifetime in often unauthorised publications, though Vasari in *Le Vite* tells us that 'he delighted in composing serious madrigals, upon which commentaries have since been made', and though he himself started to prepare a large anthology for publication – it was only many years after his death, in 1623, that his great-nephew Buonarroti the Younger published some hundred of his poems. The originals have a roughness about them, comparable to his unfinished sculptures. Unfortunately, his great-nephew saw fit to smooth out their rough edges in the name of elegant Petrarchism. He also drastically revised them: by changing the gender of the addressees in many of the poems from male to female (as an early editor of Shakespeare's sonnets was also to do) he hoped to conceal Michelangelo's homosexuality – a travesty that was put right by John Addington Symonds, who translated the original sonnets into English and wrote a two-volume biography, published in 1893. It was not until 1863 that a more reliable Italian version of the poems, edited by Cesare Guasti, appeared, but this edition, by grouping Michelangelo's poems according to genre, obscured the chronology – a drawback of Carl Frey's scholarly edition of 1897. Enzo Noè Girardi's fine edition of 1960 restores the chronological order and supplies a paraphrase of each poem and extensive notes.

Michelangelo wrote some 300 poems, many of which are either incomplete or little more than sketches. There are around 180 completed poems of sonnet length, and it is on these that his reputation as a poet rests. Only a few of them comment on his work as painter and sculptor, the best being 'I' ho già fatto un gozzo in questo stento', which self-mockingly enumerates the physical agonies he suffered while painting the ceiling of the Sistine Chapel. His themes are almost always profound: beauty, love, moral rectitude, the struggle between flesh and spirit, and the transience of life. A turning point in his development as a poet was his meeting with Tommaso Cavalieri in late 1532. This young nobleman, twenty-three at the time of their first encounter, exceptionally handsome and gifted, was described by the poet as the 'light of our century, the paragon of all the world'. Michelangelo addressed thirty or so poems to his lover – probably the first sequence of poems in any modern tongue written by one man to another, predating Shakespeare's by some fifty years. Considered by a few critics to be platonic, there's an undeniable – even disturbing – sensuality about many of the poems, as in the sonnet 'D'altrui pietoso e sol di sé spietato', which describes his wish to clothe Cavalieri's living body with his own dead skin. The other great muse in his poetry was Vittoria Colonna. They met in Rome in 1536 when she was forty-six and Michelangelo sixty-one. She, the widowed granddaughter of Federigo da Montefeltro, appealed to a very different side of his nature. They would often meet on Sundays in the cloisters of San Silvestro on the Quirinal, and their imagined conversations were recorded in dialogue form by Francisco de Hollanda, a young Portuguese painter. It was through Vittoria Colonna that Michelangelo came to reject worldly fame and instead seek God. In one poem, 'Un uomo in una donna', he compares Vittoria to a god speaking inside a woman. It was she who introduced him to the reforming elements of the Church and the writings of Savonarola – see note 1 to 'Alles endet, was entstehet', p. 328. He drew a *Pietà* for her, and also a crucified Christ that, according to his biographer Ascanio Condivi, was made 'per amor di Lei'. Kenneth Clark puts it well, when he writes that for Michelangelo she 'symbolised a release from the tyranny of the senses. His long struggle with physical passion was almost over, and as with many other great sensualists, its place had been taken by an obsession with death.'

Walter Robert-tornow (1852–1895), the German translator of Michelangelo's poetry, remained stunted in growth after an accident sustained at the age of three and was educated privately, until he matriculated at Berlin University to study philology and art history. After the death in 1884 of Georg Büchmann, he edited the next five editions of the latter's *Geflügelte Worte* (Dictionary of Quotations) adding more than 700 new entries. From April 1888 he acted as chief librarian to Kaiser Friedrich III, and died at the age of forty-three on Helgoland. He wrote poetry but knew his limitations and eventually found his métier as a translator or, rather, 'Nachdichter' – a translator who creates versions of the original instead of exact translations. His translator's motto ran:

| Wenn möglich, treu, | If possible, faithful, |
| Wenn nötig, frei. | If necessary, free. |

It took him six years to finish his Michelangelo translations, which were published posthumously in 1896, edited by Georg Thouret.

COMPOSER

Wolf's Michelangelo songs were the last he composed before he was taken to Dr Svetlin's mental asylum. 'Wohl denk' ich oft' translates an eight-line stanza by Michelangelo, 'I' vo pensando al mio viver di prima', which forms part of one of his longest mock love poems, beginning 'Io crederrei, se tu fussi di sasso'; 'Alles endet, was entstehet' comes from one of the *Canti de' Morti* ('Chiunche nascie a morte arriva'); and 'Fühlt meine Seele' is a translation of 'Non so se s'è la desiata luce', addressed probably to Tommaso Cavalieri. Wolf had received a copy of the original Italian poems in Thouret's edition with German translations by Walter Robert-tornow from Paul Müller during Christmas 1896 (HW to Paul Müller, 25 December 1896, below) and intended to set at least six of them (HW to Karl Heckel, 19 March 1897, p. 323). Four were eventually composed, but he was dissatisfied with 'Irdische und himmlische Liebe' (HW to Oskar Grohe, 13 May 1897, p. 326) and later destroyed it. He actually wrote out the texts of songs 5 and 6, his customary practice before composing a song: 'Durch Liebestreue glaubt' ich Dich zu zwingen' and 'Du giebst mir Licht!' When asked by Edmund Hellmer why he had composed the songs for bass, Wolf replied: „Selbstverständlich muß ein Bildhauer Baß singen." ('Of course a sculptor has to sing bass.') Hellmer reviewed the songs in the *Deutsche Zeitung* on 8 December 1898 and predicted that they would be successful because the poems mirrored Wolf's own life. Wolf was convinced that these 'deeply serious' songs would make him famous and intended to orchestrate them (HW to Heinrich Potpeschnigg, 9 September 1898, p. 326) – something he never achieved.

LETTERS

HW to Paul Müller, Vienna, 25 December 1896

Ich benutze die frühe Morgenstunde des Christtages, um Ihnen für Ihr pompöses Geschenk zu danken. Nein, war das eine herrliche Überraschung! Mit den Gedichten Michel-Angelos haben Sie mir eine nicht zu beschreibende Freude gemacht. Ich sehe schon einen stattlichen Liederband nach

Michel-Angelo vor mir. Sind das herrliche, urkräftige Sachen! Dem Manne glaubt man doch jedes Wort, das seiner Feder entflossen. Zu meiner Schande muß ich gestehn, daß mir der Dichter Michelangelo bisher eine terra incognita war. Um so größer nun ist mein Entzücken über diese neue Entdeckung. Haben Sie tausend Dank dafür.

I'm using the early hours of Christmas Day to thank you for your magnificent present. What a splendid surprise! You have given me indescribable joy with these poems of Michelangelo. I already have visions of an imposing volume of Michelangelo Lieder. These wonderful poems have such primeval force! One believes every single word that flows from his pen. To my shame, I have to admit that Michelangelo the poet was terra incognita for me – which makes my new discovery all the more delightful. A thousand thanks.

HW to Paul Müller, Vienna, 18 March 1897

Heute 18. März das erste Gedicht aus dem Bande Michelangelo componirt ['Wohl denk' ich oft']. Das Stück beginnt mit einer schwermüthig sinnenden Figur in den Bässen, die in langsamer Bewegung aufwärts steigen, u. schließt in Dur (Tonart g moll) mit triumphalen Fanfaren. Grandios!

Today, 18 March, I composed the first song from the Michelangelo volume ['Wohl denk' ich oft']. The piece begins with a soulful, pensive motif in the bass, which slowly ascends the scale & closes in D major (the song's key is G minor) with triumphant fanfares. Magnificent!

HW to Karl Heckel, Vienna, 19 March 1897

Inzwischen habe ich 3 Gedichte von Michelangelo componirt u. denke es auf ein halb Dutzend noch zu bringen.

Meanwhile I've composed 3 of Michelangelo's poems & intend to bring the number to half a dozen. [Wolf tells Heckel in the postscript that he mislaid the letter; it was not posted until after 28 March, by which time he had composed three Michelangelo songs.]

HW to Oskar Grohe, Vienna, 24 March 1897

Vor kurzem entstanden einige Gesangsstücke nach Gedichten von Michelangelo, zu denen mir ein paar wahrhaft sublime Einfälle verhalfen. Leider bin ich in den letzten Tagen durch meine lärmende Nachbarschaft in meiner Thätigkeit etwas aufgehalten worden, doch hoffe ich den Faden bei nächster Gelegenheit wieder aufnehmen zu können, denn ich habe jetzt, um mit Gottfr. Keller zu reden, Werg auf meiner Kunkel.[1] Um Dir einen Begriff davon zu geben, was für ein verfluchter Kerl der Michelangelo als Poet auch war theile ich Dir das zuerst von mir componirte Lied mit; dasselbige ist an einen Freund gerichtet [. . .]. Die Musik dazu, welche mit einer schwermüthigen Einleitung beginnt u. diesen Ton bis zu den vorletzten Versen festhält, nimmt unversehens einen strammen Charakter an (entwickelt aus dem vorangegangnen Motiv) u. schließt mit triumphalen Fanfaren, gleichsam einem Tusch, den ihm die huldigenden Zeitgenossen brachten, festlich ab. – Du wirst Deine helle Freude daran haben. Bedeutender aber scheint mir noch das 2. Gedicht zu sein, das ich für das Beste halte, was ich bis dato gestümpert habe –

> „Alles endet was entstehet
> Alles endet, was vergehet"[2]

Wenn Du vor Ergriffenheit dabei nicht Deinen Verstand verlierst, so hast Du nie einen besessen. Es ist wahrlich, um dabei verrückt zu werden, dabei von einer verblüffenden, wahrhaft antiken Einfachheit. Na, Du wirst Augen machen! Ich fürchte mich förmlich vor dieser Composition, weil mir dabei um meinen Verstand bange wird.

A few truly sublime flashes of inspiration enabled me recently to compose some songs to poems by Michelangelo. In the past few days my progress has been somewhat held up by noisy neighbours, but I hope to be able to resume as soon as possible, because I have, to quote Gottfr. Keller, tow on my distaff. To give you some idea of what a damned fine poet Michelangelo was, here is the text of the first song I composed, which is addressed to a friend [. . .]. The music, which begins with a mournful introduction and maintains the same mood up to the penultimate line, unexpectedly takes on a robust character (developed from the previous motif) & concludes solemnly with triumphant fanfares like a flourish of trumpets sounded for him [Michelangelo] in homage by his contemporaries. You will be delighted with it. But the second poem strikes me as more significant, and I believe it's the best of all my botchings to date.

> 'All must end that has beginning,
> All things round us perish.'

If the emotion doesn't cause you to lose your mind, then you've never had one. It really is something to drive you crazy, and it has at the same time an

---

1   Wolf was clearly fond of the phrase that appears, in slightly different form, in Keller's novel *Der grüne Heinrich*, which Wolf so admired. Keller's original wording in the novel (Volume 1, Chapter 15) is „Werg an die Kunkel".

2   Wolf misremembers the second line, which should run: 'Alles, Alles rings vergehet'. I have translated the correct text.

astonishing and truly antique simplicity. You'll be amazed. I'm genuinely afraid of this composition, because it makes me fear for my own sanity.[1]

HW to Hugo Faisst, Vienna, 29 March 1897

Ich benütze eine kleine Erholungspause in meinem Schaffensdrange (4[2] herrliche Gedichte nach Michelangelo sind mir in den letzten Märztagen auf's beste gelungen) um Deinen letzten Brief zu beantworten.

I'm taking a little break from my heightened state of creativity (in the last days of March I composed most successfully 4 splendid Michelangelo songs) to thank you for your last letter.

HW to Paul Müller, Vienna, 6 April 1897

Von morgen ab werde ich mein altes Quartier in Perchtoldsdorf für 14 Tage beziehen, um in Muße der Beschäftigung mit den Gedichten Michelangelos zu obliegen. Adressiren Sie einfach Perchtoldsdorf an d. Südbahn. Man kennt mich dort wie's schlechte Geld. Das 1. Lied kommt unter dem Collectivum „Riechbüchsen"[3] vor. Da ich den Gedichteband nicht bei mir habe, führe ich die ersten Verse an. „Wohl denk' ich oft an mein vergangnes Leben". Das 2. Lied befindet sich auf pag. 19 Gesang der Todten.[4] Ich habe dasselbe vanitas vanitatum betitelt. Das 3. heisst: „Deiner Augen Macht." Das 4. Irdische u. himmlische Liebe, der Anfangsvers: Zur Schönheit meine Blicke suchend gleiten.

From tomorrow I shall spend a fortnight in my old quarters in Perchtoldsdorf in order to attend at leisure to Michelangelo's poems. Address all letters to Perchtoldsdorf on the southern railway. They know me there like a bad penny. The first song appears under the section called 'Smelling salts'. As I don't have the volume of poems with me, here is the first line: 'Wohl denk' ich oft an mein vergang'nes Leben'. The second song is on page 19 of the Song of the Dead section. I have called it 'Vanitas vanitatum'. The third is called: 'Deiner Augen Macht'. The fourth 'Irdische u. himmlische Liebe', which begins: 'Zur Schönheit meine Blicke suchend gleiten'.

---

1 Prophetic words: less than six months later, on 20 September, Wolf was taken to Dr Svetlin's mental asylum.
2 See HW to Oskar Grohe, 13 May 1897, p. 326.
3, 4 These are Robert-tornow's headings, not Michelangelo's.

HW to Emil Kauffmann, Vienna, 10 April 1897

In jüngster Zeit beschäftigten mich lebhaftest die Gedichte Michelangelos; drei dieser herrlichen, urkräftigen u. förmlich gemeisselten Gedichte sind von mir auch schon vertont worden.

Michelangelo's poems have occupied me most intensively in recent days; three of these splendid, primeval & downright sculpted poems have already been set by me.

HW to Oskar Grohe, Vienna, 13 May 1897

Von den Gedichten Michelangelos sind erst drei componirt. Das vierte ist mir mißlungen. Ich will noch zwei Gedichte hinzucomponiren u. dann erhältst Du alle mitsammen.

Only three of the Michelangelo poems have been composed. The fourth did not work out. I shall compose another two & you will then receive them all.

HW to Heinrich Potpeschnigg, Traunkirchen, 9 September 1898

Deine Vorliebe für die Michelangelogesänge wird merkwürdiger Weise von allen meinen Freunden getheilt. Es scheint fast, als sollten diese drei tiefernsten Gesänge berufen sein mich populär zu machen. Wunderliche Welt! Ich beabsichtige übrigens die Michelangelolieder zu instrumentiren;[1] Dr. Obrist würde dieselben in einem der Abonnementkonzerte in Stuttgart mit Hinzuziehung des Sängers Frausche,[2] der die 3 Gesänge bereits mehrmals mit großem Erfolge dort vorgetragen, aufführen. Mit Orchester müßte die Wirkung dieser 3 Stücke allerdings eine ungleich größere sein, als mit Klavierbegleitung. Ich habe nicht übel Lust mich gleich an die Arbeit zu machen.

All my friends share strangely enough your predilection for the Michelangelo songs. It almost seems as if these three deeply serious songs were destined to make me popular. Strange world! I intend by the way to orchestrate the Michelangelo Lieder; Dr Obrist would then perform them in one of the subscription concerts in Stuttgart with the singer Frauscher, who has already performed the 3 songs several times there with great success. The effect of these 3 pieces with orchestra would be immeasurably greater than with piano accompaniment. I've a good mind to start work immediately.

1 Wolf never orchestrated the songs: on 4 October 1898, following a suicide attempt, he was taken to the Niederösterreichische Landesirrenanstalt, where he spent the rest of his life. The songs were later orchestrated by Kim Borg and performed by Walter Berry at Perchtoldsdorf on 29 June 1978.
2 Moritz Frauscher (1859–1916) was a bass who gave the first performance of the *Michelangelo-Lieder* before they were published. Heinrich Werner, in a letter to Potpeschnigg of 17 November 1898, described Frauscher as „einer der herrlichsten Wolfsänger" ('one of the most splendid singers of Wolf').

LIEDER

Drei Gedichte von Michelangelo
Three Michelangelo poems
(Translated by Walter Robert-tornow)

The Italian texts printed here are taken from Robert-tornow's *Die Gedichte des Michelangelo Buonarroti*, and differ slightly from other versions of the same poems. Michelangelo did not give titles to the poems.

[1]
I' vo pensando al mio viver di prima,
   Inanzi ch' i' t'amassi, come gli era.
   Di me non fu ma' chi facesse stima;
   Perdendo ogni dì il tempo insino
     a sera.
Forse pensavo di cantare in rima,
   O di ritrarmi da ogni altra stiera?
   Or si sa 'l nome, o per tristo o per
     buono;
   E sassi pure ch' al mondo i' ci sono!

1 Wohl denk' ich oft an mein vergang'nes Leben[1]   I often recall my past life

Wohl denk' ich oft an mein vergang'nes Leben,
   Wie es, vor meiner Liebe für Dich, war;
   Kein Mensch hat damals Acht auf mich gegeben,
   Ein jeder Tag verloren für mich war.
   Ich dachte wohl, ganz dem Gesang zu leben,
   Auch mich zu flüchten aus der Menschen Schaar ...
   Genannt in Lob und Tadel bin ich heute,
   Und, daß ich da bin, wissen alle Leute![2]

I often recall my past life,
   As it was before I loved you;
   No one then paid heed to me,
   Each day for me was a loss.
   I thought to live for song alone,
   And flee the thronging crowd ...
   Today my name is praised and censured,
   And the entire world knows that I exist!

[2]
Chiunche nascie a morte arriva
   Nel fuggir del tempo; e 'l sole
   Niuna cosa lascia viva.
   Manca il dolcie e quel che dole,
   E gl' ingiegni e le parole;
   E le nostre antiche prole
Al sole ombre, al vento un fumo.
Come voi uomini fumo,
Lieti e tristi, come siete;
E or siàn, come vedete,
Terra al sol di vita priva.
   Ogni cosa, ec.

---

1 Robert-tornow headed the second section of his book 'Freunde', and Wolf, taking his cue from this, called the poem 'An einen Freund' when he wrote to Heinrich Potpeschnigg on 20 March 1897. See HW to Paul Müller, 18 March 1897, p. 323, for Wolf's description of the song.
2 How the proud Wolf must have relished this line!

2 Alles endet, was entstehet[1]

Alles endet, was entstehet,
   Alles, Alles rings vergehet,[2]
   Denn die Zeit flieht, und die Sonne
   Sieht, daß Alles rings vergehet,
   Denken, Reden, Schmerz und Wonne;
   Und die wir zu Enkeln hatten,
   Schwanden wie bei Tag die Schatten,
   Wie ein Dunst im Windeshauch.
   Menschen waren wir ja auch,[3]
   Froh und traurig, so wie ihr;
   Und nun sind wir leblos hier,
   Sind nur Erde, wie ihr sehet;
   Alles endet, was entstehet,
   Alles, Alles rings vergehet![4]

All must end that has beginning

All must end that has beginning,
   All things round us perish,
   For time is fleeting, and the sun
   Sees that all things round us perish,
   Thought, speech, pain and rapture;
   And our children's children
   Vanished as shadows by day,
   As mists in a breeze.
   We were also human beings,
   With joys and sorrows like your own;
   And now there is no life in us,
   We are but earth, as you can see;
   All must end that has beginning,
   All things round us perish!

[3]
Non so se s'è la desiata luce
   Del suo primo fattor, che l'alma sente;
   O se dalla memoria della gente
   Alcun'altra beltà nel cor traluce;
O se fama o se sognio alcun prodduce
   Agli occhi manifesto, al cor presente;
   Di sè lasciando un non so che cocente,
   Ch'è forse or quel ch' a pianger
      mi conduce;

Quel ch' i' sento e ch' i' cerco: e chi mi guidi
   Meco non è; nè so ben veder dove
   Trovar mel possa, e par c' altri mel
      mostri.
Questo, signior, m'avvien, po' ch' i' vi vidi;
   C'un dolce amaro, un sì e no mi muove:
   Certo saranno stati gli occhi vostri.

---

1 Robert-tornow's original title for this translation was 'Gesang der Todten'; Wolf, in a letter to Hugo Faisst of 21 April 1898, calls it 'Vanitas vanitatum'. The influence of the apocalyptic Dominican friar Savonarola is unmistakable. Michelangelo's biographer Condivi, who had lengthy conversations with the sculptor, wrote, 'Michelangelo has similarly with great diligence and attention read the holy scriptures [...] as well as the writings of those who have busied themselves with their study, such as Savonarola, for whom he has always had a strong affection, and the memory of whose living voice he still carries in his mind.'
2 This line does not appear in Robert-tornow's translation.
3 The line is spoken by the dead from their tombs.
4 The final two lines of Robert-tornow's translation run:

    Sind nur Erde, wie ihr sehet;
    Alles, (Alles rings vergehet!)

3 Fühlt meine Seele[1]

Fühlt meine Seele das ersehnte Licht
    Von Gott, der sie erschuf? Ist es der Strahl
    Von and'rer Schönheit aus dem
        Jammerthal,
    Der in mein Herz Erinn'rungweckend[2]
        bricht?
Ist es ein Klang, ein Traumgesicht,[3]
    Das Aug' und Herz mir füllt mit
        einem Mal
    In unbegreiflich glüh'der Qual,[4]
    Die mich zu Thränen bringt? Ich weiß
        es nicht.
Was ich ersehne, fühle, was mich lenkt,
    Ist nicht in mir: Sag' mir, wie ich's
        erwerbe?[5]
    Mir zeigt es wohl nur eines And'ren Huld.
Darein bin ich, seit ich Dich sah, versenkt;
    Mich treibt ein Ja und Nein, ein Süß
        und Herbe ...
    Daran sind, Herrin,[6] Deine Augen[7] Schuld!

Does my soul feel

Does my soul feel the longed-for light
    Of God who created it? Is it the ray
    Of some other beauty from this vale
        of tears
    That storms my heart, awakening
        memories?
Is it a sound, a vision in a dream
    That suddenly fills my eyes and heart

    With inconceivable, searing pain,
    Reducing me to tears? I do not know.

What I long for, what I feel, what guides me
    Is not in me: tell me how to achieve it!

    Only another's favour is likely to reveal it.
This has absorbed me, since seeing you;
    I am torn between yes and no, bitterness
        and sweetness ...
    Your eyes, my lady, are the cause!

---

1 The title of Robert-tornow's translation is 'Deiner Augen Macht'. He calls the section in which this sonnet appears 'Minnelieder vor der Vittoriazeit' ('Love songs before the Vittoria era'), and the poem in its final version was probably written for Tommaso Cavalieri.
2 Robert-tornow: erinn'rungsweckend.
3 Robert-tornow: Ist es ein Klang, ist es ein Traumgesicht?
4 Robert-tornow: Mit einer unbegreiflich glüh'nden Qual.
5 Robert-tornow: Sag' mir, wo ich's erwerbe?
6 Robert-tornow changes Michelangelo's 'signior' to 'Herrin', thus altering the gender of the addressee, presumably to make the poem more respectable, as Buonarroti the Younger had done.
7 Franz Grasberger reproduces a facsimile of Wolf's setting of this line at the beginning of his edition of *Briefe an Melanie Köchert*, and it is more than likely that Wolf was thinking of Melanie and her brown eyes when composing the final bars of this song. The text in Wolf's source-book is headed „Deiner Augen Macht" – the power of your eyes.

EDUARD MÖRIKE
(1804–1875)

		page
Suschens Vogel	24 December 1880	364
Mausfallen-Sprüchlein	18 June 1882	365
Die Tochter der Heide	11 July 1884	366
Der König bei der Krönung	13 March 1886	367
Gedichte von Eduard Mörike für eine Singstimme und Klavier		
Der Tambour	16 February 1888	371
Der Knabe und das Immlein	22 February 1888	368
Jägerlied	22 February 1888	370
Ein Stündlein wohl vor Tag	22 February 1888	370
Der Jäger	23 February 1888	403
Nimmersatte Liebe	24 February 1888	374
Auftrag	25 February 1888	415
Zur Warnung	25 February 1888	414
Lied vom Winde	29 February 1888	401
Bei einer Trauung	1 March 1888	416
Der Genesene an die Hoffnung	6 March 1888	368
Zitronenfalter im April	6 March 1888	385
Der Gärtner	7 March 1888	383
Elfenlied	7 March 1888	382
Abschied	8 March 1888	417
Denk' es, o Seele!	10 March 1888, orchestrated 4 May 1891	402
Auf einer Wanderung	11–25 March	381
Gebet	13 March 1888, orchestrated 4 September 1890	393
Verborgenheit	13 March 1888	378
Lied eines Verliebten	14 March 1888	406
Selbstgeständnis	17 March 1888	416
Erstes Liebeslied eines Mädchens	20 March 1888	405
Fußreise	21 March 1888	375
Rat einer Alten	22 March 1888, a.m.	404
Begegnung	22 March 1888, p.m.	374
Das verlassene Mägdlein	24 March 1888	373
Storchenbotschaft	27 March 1888	413

Frage und Antwort	29 March 1888	399
Lebe wohl	31 March 1888	399
Heimweh	1 April 1888	400
Seufzer	12 April 1888, orchestrated 28 May 1889	388
Auf ein altes Bild	14 April 1888, orchestrated for woodwind, ?May 1889	389
An eine Äolsharfe	15 April 1888	376
Um Mitternacht	20 April 1888	385
Auf eine Christblume II	21 April 1888	388
Peregrina I	28 April 1888	397
Peregrina II	30 April 1888	398
Agnes	3 May 1888	380
In der Frühe	5 May 1888, orchestrated 6 May 1890	390
Er ist's	5 May 1888, orchestrated 20 February 1890	372
Im Frühling	8 May 1888	379
Nixe Binsefuß	13 May 1888	409
Die Geister am Mummelsee	18 May 1888	411
An den Schlaf	4 October 1888, a.m., orchestrated 4 September 1890	393
Neue Liebe	4 October 1888, evening, orchestrated 5 September 1890	394
Zum neuen Jahr	5 October 1888	392
Schlafendes Jesuskind	6 October 1888, a.m., orchestrated ?May 1889	390
Wo find' ich Trost?	6 October 1888, p.m., orchestrated 6 September 1890	395
Karwoche	8 October 1888, orchestrated 29 May 1889	391
Gesang Weylas	9 October 1888, orchestrated 21 February 1890	410
Der Feuerreiter	10 October 1888, arranged for chorus and orchestra, October–November 1892	407
An die Geliebte	11 October 1888	396
Auf eine Christblume I	26 November 1888, orchestrated 25 September 1890	386

POET

Eduard Mörike, the fourth child of Dr Karl Friedrich Mörike and his wife Charlotte, was born in 1804 in Ludwigsburg. He was one of thirteen children, seven of whom survived infancy. His childhood seems to have been happy. He was passionately fond of his mother, who had good looks (which Mörike didn't inherit), a gift for story-telling and drawing (which he did), and humour and intelligence in abundance. Eduard was blue-eyed and fair-haired and seems to have been the most spoilt and vulnerable of all the brothers and sisters. Throughout his life he would return to Ludwigsburg at regular intervals, and delight in renewing acquaintance with the scenes of his childhood: the picturesque villages and gentle slopes of the landscape, in particular the Emichsburg with the sad wailing of its Aeolian harps, which always fascinated him – see 'An eine Äolsharfe'. When Dr Mörike died in 1817, the childhood idyll came to an abrupt end and the family moved to Stuttgart, where Eduard was taken into the house of his uncle, Obertribunalpräsident Eberhard von Georgii, an embodiment of fine taste and eighteenth-century Enlightenment. Eduard attended the Gymnasium, specialising in Greek and Latin. German schoolboy classicists of that era had to translate Greek and Latin verse into German, using the original verse forms – a practice that almost certainly stimulated his interest in versification.

Eduard failed his Landexamen at the age of fourteen and his school reports, though describing his character as 'gutartig' (good-natured), also complain that he was 'nachlässig' (apathetic) and not 'zweckmäßig genug' (sufficiently practical). Because of his somewhat dreamy and thoughtful temperament, it was decided that he should take Holy Orders. In 1818, despite very poor marks in mathematics, he gained a place in the Klosterschule at Urach, one of the many famous Protestant seminaries to produce men of great distinction, including Hegel, Schelling, Hölderlin and Wilhelm Hauff. His experience there was quite different from that of Hans Giebenrath at his Klosterschule in Maulbronn, described by Hermann Hesse in *Unterm Rad*, and Eduard seemed to experience none of Giebenrath's misery. Although he did not excel as a scholar and found Hebrew impossible, he was happy and attained more than average marks in theology and literature. He made many friends, including the loyal Wilhelm Hartlaub, a fine pianist who fostered his love of music and was always available to help him in times of emotional need. It was to Hartlaub that Mörike dedicated the first edition of his *Gedichte*: „Seinem Freunde WILHELM HARTLAUB zum Zeichen unveränderlicher Liebe gewidmet" ('Dedicated to his friend WILHELM HARTLAUB as a sign of his unswerving love').

Like several poets mentioned in this book (Johann Wolfgang von Goethe, Gottfried Keller, Franz Kugler, Robert Reinick and Joseph Victor von Scheffel), Mörike was a gifted amateur artist, whose drawings and caricatures delighted and amused his friends. Although he possessed only a rudimentary knowledge of art history – Moritz von Schwind was shocked that he had never seen a painting by Raphael, referring to his friend's ignorance as „ein Skandal, ein Aergernis, eine Sünde wider den heiligen Geist" (a scandal, an outrage, a sin against the Holy Spirit) – Mörike's fantastical doodlings, his caricatures and sketches of buildings and landscapes reveal a Carl Spitzweg-like elegance and humour. The hero of his first published work, *Maler Nolten*, was a painter, and one of his last poems, 'An Moriz von Schwind' (1868) contains these revealing lines that are an eloquent testimony to his artistic ambitions:

> Ich knüpfte seufzend endlich meine Mappe zu,
> Saß da und hing den Kopf. – Warum? Gesteh' ich dir
> Die große Torheit? Jene alte Grille war's,
> Die lebenslang mir mit der Klage liegt im Ohr,
> Daß ich nicht Maler werden durfte. Maler, ja!
> Und freilich keinen gar viel schlechteren als dich,
> Dacht' ich dabei.

> I finally closed my portfolio with a sigh,
> Sat there and bowed my head. – Why? Shall I confess
> My great folly? It was that old fantasy of mine,
> That life-long lament I kept hearing,
> That I could not become a painter. A painter, yes!
> And one not so inferior to you,
> I mused.

Music too was an important part of Mörike's childhood, and he was extremely susceptible to its beauty: when Pauline Viardot visited him with Turgenev on 31 January 1865 to perform her own settings of his poems, he is reported to have hidden behind a screen to hide his tears. All members of the Mörike family were musical, and his brother Karl not only played the piano well but was later to compose the first settings of Mörike's poetry. Eduard, typically, refused to have piano lessons, for fear of being asked to perform in public, but he did play the Jew's harp and was passionate about Mozart: in a letter to Johannes Mährlen of 5 June 1832, Mörike described how a violent thunderstorm conjured up in his mind the overture to *La clemenza di Tito*. He also loved the voice of Marie Mörike, the wife of his cousin Karl, whose voice he described in his poetry – see note 1 to 'Auf einer Wanderung', p. 381. He admired Gluck, Mozart, Haydn (he wrote a charming distich, 'Joseph Haydn', about the composer's humour) and Beethoven – „Dagegen eine Symphonie Beethovens aus C moll! Hinreißend!" ('But a Symphony in C minor by Beethoven! Ravishing!') he writes to his mother and sister in November 1838 – but utterly rejected Liszt and Wagner, Wolf's greatest idol. His composer friend Ernst Friedrich Kauffmann had already dubbed Wagnerians as 'false prophets' and Mörike in *Mozart auf der Reise nach Prag* has Mozart exclaim: „Je nun, im Lauf der nächsten sechzig, siebzig Jahre, nachdem ich lang fort bin, wird mancher falsche Prophet aufstehen." ('Indeed, in the course of the next sixty, seventy years, after I have long been gone, many a false prophet will arise.') The Novelle was published in 1855, by which time Wagner had composed *Der fliegende Holländer* (1843 premiere), *Tannhäuser* (1845) and *Lohengrin* (1850). Mörike seems to have had little time for contemporary composers, though he told Hartlaub in May 1838 that he liked several of Mendelssohn's *Lieder ohne Worte*. Whether Mörike would have appreciated Wolf's Lieder is doubtful: in a letter to Hartlaub of 19–20 August 1865, he expresses a preference for Ludwig Hetsch, considering him superior to Robert Franz, Louis Köhler and Franz Schubert. Mörike's delight in Hetsch's songs is clear from his correspondence – and it is to Hetsch and Kauffmann that he dedicated his most famous prose work, *Mozart auf der Reise nach Prag*.

His first unhappiness in love – almost as devastating in its effect as the more celebrated Maria Meyer affair a couple of years later – was experienced when he was seventeen, in 1821. His feelings for his cousin Klärchen Neuffer, who had been a constant childhood companion, deepened, and when she rejected his advances, he was devastated. After such a rebuff, he avoided her anxiously for years on end, but managed to exorcise the pain by writing the charming 'Erinnerung', encapsulating in 62 short lines the whole Eduard–Klärchen relationship. When Klärchen died in 1837, Mörike expressed his grief in 'Vicia faba minor', a four-line poem in which he describes her as a 'Verführerin' ('seductress') who had ensnared him.

In 1822, Mörike entered the theological college at Tübingen, where he met Ludwig Bauer, with whom he created the mythical land of Orplid – probably to escape the boredom of academic routine. Although he excelled in German and philosophy, he was not a good student, and in homiletics he was given a shattering report: 'The plan of his sermon was mediocre; it was inadequately worked out and unattractively delivered.' A year later, he fell in love with Maria Meyer – an experience that inspired some of his greatest poetry, and also scarred him for life – see HW to Melanie Köchert, 15 October 1890, p. 355. In the summer of 1824, still reeling from the Maria Meyer episode, he attended a performance of *Don Giovanni* in Stuttgart's Hoftheater, with his younger brother August, sister Luise and several friends. A few days later the brother he loved passionately was dead, possibly by suicide, although the local doctor certified the death as a stroke, to soften the blow for his family. Mörike was thunderstruck – see note 2 to 'An eine Äolsharfe', p. 376. After August's death, he grew closer to his sister Luise, to whom he always turned for comfort in affairs of his heart. He sought her help in avoiding a meeting with Klärchen; and the poem 'Nachklang' acknowledges the part she played in helping him to come to terms with his grief over Maria Meyer. Three years later, in 1827, Luise fell gravely ill. Mörike, who by now had left university, was with her during the final weeks of her illness. After her death he began work as a curate, the routine possibly providing a steadying structure for him as he grieved.

Not that routine was welcome. „Alles, nur kein Geistlicher" ('Anything but a priest') he had written to his friend Johannes Mährlen in mid-February 1828, the year in which he applied for jobs as librarian, private tutor, editor, proofreader and common-or-garden secretary. Having decided, *faute de mieux*, to become a priest, he was required to practise for some years as a supply preacher (Vikar), and he wandered from one poorly paid post to another – the very names redolent of provincial backwaters: Möhringen, Köngen, Pflummern, Plattenhardt, Owen, Eltingen, Ochsenwang, Weilheim and Otlingen. He carried out his duties unenthusiastically and with no sense of vocation, and even resigned his curacy for more than a year to see whether he could earn his living as a free-lance writer. Realising that he needed financial security if he was to live the life of a poet, he returned to the pastoral fold, and it was not until 1834, when he was the oldest curate in Württemberg, that he was given his own parish at Cleversulzbach, where he held office until 1843. He disliked all forms of work that required regular application and was notorious for his laziness and hypochondria. He hated writing sermons and had no ambition to make a career in the Church – a contributory cause, incidentally, for the failure in 1833 of his relationship with Luise Rau, a clergyman's daughter, to whom he had become engaged in 1829. She inspired some of the most beautiful love letters in the German language, and also some of the finest love poems, some of which – 'An die Geliebte', 'Karwoche' and 'Lebe wohl', for example – were enclosed in letters to her, in the same way that Goethe had sent Charlotte von Stein such gems as 'Der du von dem Himmel bist', 'Warum gabst du uns die tiefen Blicke' and 'An den Mond'. Some sixty of Mörike's letters to Luise survive. When Wilhelm Hartlaub urged his friend to show him them, Mörike observed, „Sie sind ihrer Natur nach ziemlich eintönig. Nur wirst Du daraus sehen, daß ich das Mädchen unsäglich liebte. [. . .] Es schwindelt mir, wenn ich hineinblicke und denke, wir sind auseinander." ('They are by their very nature rather monotonous. But you will see from them that I loved the girl more than words can express. [. . .] My head reels when I look at them and think that it is all over.')

After the break with Luise Rau, Mörike lived with his mother and sister Klara in the parsonage at Cleversulzbach. Nine years he spent there, attending unwillingly to his duties and travelling little. He suffered increasingly from hypochondria, and while on sick leave from his parish would languish in bed with a cup of tea, a book and a pipe – not too dissimilar from the figure in Carl Spitzweg's contemporary painting, *The Poor Poet* (1839). He also tended the plants and vegetables in the parsonage garden and lavished enormous affection on animals and birds – rather like an English poet-priest before him: Robert Herrick. After the death of his sister Luise, he had gained solace from the company of small animals, and gave up an entire room in the house to starlings, quails and finches. Now, in Cleversulzbach, he provided the birds with branches to perch on, and allowed them to fly freely about the room. There was also a Pomeranian, called Joli, and a succession of cats who would often receive missives from Mörike. He tells in one letter how a kitten, on killing her first mouse, had been stroked approvingly by all the family. 'Mausfallen-Sprüchlein' springs to mind, probably the most famous of his animal poems.

From 1837 to 1841 Mörike enjoyed a period of lively correspondence with Hermann Kurz, who assisted him in arranging the poems in the first edition, published by Cotta in 1838. Then there was his friendship with Justinus Kerner (see p. 290), known to us now through Schumann's twelve *Kerner-Lieder* – a skilful physician who would often advise the family on Mörike's hypochondria. They shared a belief in the occult, and Mörike was a frequent contributor to Kerner's spiritualist periodical *Magikon*. Mörike rarely left Cleversulzbach, but in 1838 he spent some months in Stuttgart, supervising the production of *Die Regenbrüder*, an opera by Ignaz Lachner, for which he had written the libretto. Like many lyric poets, including for example Eichendorff, Hebbel and Heyse, Mörike believed himself to be a potential dramatist and gave up writing for the stage only after repeated failures. He won greater success as the editor of an anthology of classical verse, *Klassische Blumenlese*, a collation of the best existing translations, for which he supplied notes on the various authors. For Mörike's own translations, see note to 'Anakreons Grab', p. 157. Mörike confided to Kurz that he found translation easier when his own muse had dried up but it is probably true to say that the publication of *Klassische Blumenlese* was partially undertaken to lighten the chronic load of debt that Mörike was forced to bear. This was due in some degree to his eldest brother Karl, who, having been imprisoned for revolutionary activities, drained Mörike's resources by spending long periods with him at Cleversulzbach.

After their mother's death in 1841 he relied increasingly on his sister Klara, who kept house for him. When his parishioners at Cleversulzbach expressed dissatisfaction with their priest, he was forced to retire, and found employment as a teacher at a girls' school in Stuttgart and lived on a meagre pension with his sister, first at Schwäbisch Hall and then at Bad Mergentheim, where he met his future wife, Margarethe von Speeth. They married in 1851 and moved to Stuttgart the same year. Margarethe was a Catholic, and some of Mörike's Protestant friends disapproved of the marriage, causing him great pain. While living in Stuttgart, he lectured on German literature to the girl pupils of the *Katharinenstift*, and continued to write poems and stories, including his masterpiece *Mozart auf der Reise nach Prag*, which ends with the poem 'Denk es, o Seele!' Margarethe bore him two daughters, but his domestic situation was never really happy. Klara lived with the married couple, and was unwilling to relinquish her domestic duties, which explains Mörike's frequent remark in his diary: *perturbatio domestica*. Mörike never succeeded in freeing himself from financial difficulties, and died almost as poor as Mozart, leaving behind a total fortune of 800 florins – about £90. His final years were largely unproductive and hardly fulfilled the promise of his youth; like Wolf, he suffered periods of writer's block, as he explains in his poem 'Muse und Dichter' ('Muse and Poet'). After the third edition of 1856, only twenty-one new poems found their way into the *Ausgabe letzter Hand*. True, he could still write the occasional poem of great beauty – 'Besuch in der Kartause' from 1861, 'Schlafendes Jesuskind' (1862) and 'Erinna an Sappho' (1863) – but with increasing age he tended to dwell more on the past than the present, and spent a disproportionate amount of time (sixteen years from 1859 till his death) revising the novel of his youth, *Maler Nolten*. He finally left his wife and lived a nomadic existence before being reunited with Margarethe shortly before his death, aged seventy, in 1875.

What are we to make of him? Gottfried Keller, the great Swiss poet, novelist and short-story writer, described his passing: „Wie wenn ein schöner Junitag dahin wäre" ('as if a fine June day had passed away with him') and Mörike was once regarded as a naive romantic, untouched by the events of his time, the epitome of Biedermeier, the author of poetic idylls and delightful fairy tales, a charmingly inadequate, ineffectual clergyman at one with his surroundings in Cleversulzbach, a nature poet par excellence with an engaging sense of humour. And perhaps that is the impression given by the many portraits we have of his bespectacled face, as in the sketch by Kurtz, in the Schiller National Museum in Marbach am Neckar. We now know, however, that the naivety, the idylls and the humour of many Mörike poems are, in fact, a bastion erected by the poet against the extreme emotions that threatened to overwhelm him throughout his life.

The most destructive of these experiences shaping much of his verse was his short-lived acquaintance with Maria Meyer. She was born in Schaffhausen on 27 February 1802, the illegitimate child of a certain Helena Meyer, a prostitute, and an apprentice tawer. Mörike met her when he was nineteen in 1823. We actually know little about her and even less about the details of her relationship with Mörike. She was a Swiss girl of obscure origin, wildly beautiful, extremely well read, a member of the wandering sect of Julia von Krüdener, and affected at times by a sort of religious fervour. Emil Kauffmann's brief account of the short-lived affair can be found in HW to Melanie Köchert, 15 October 1890, p. 355. The first Mörike heard of her was when Herr Mergenthaler, the owner of a Ludwigsburg brewery, found her unconscious on the Stuttgart–Ludwigsburg road. It later turned out that she was prone to epileptic fits and bouts of sleepwalking. She was taken in by the mother of one of Mörike's seminary friends, Rudolf Lohbauer. Overnight, Maria Meyer had become something of a celebrity in the little town, and Mörike, living in Tübingen, exchanged passionate letters with her, all of which he later destroyed. Rumours soon reached him, however, that led him to call her moral integrity into question. Mörike was thrown into utter confusion, all the more so when he heard that she had suddenly left Ludwigsburg. Soon afterwards, she was found in Heidelberg in exactly the same circumstances as she had first appeared on the Ludwigsburg road. This time she was arrested, but subsequently bailed by influential friends and admirers and left to go on her way. In the early summer of 1824 she turned up in Tübingen and wrote Mörike a letter, requesting him to meet her and write her a short dedicatory poem. He refused both requests and fled in turmoil to his mother in Stuttgart. Maria left Tübingen in August 1824 and returned to Switzerland. In April 1826 she came once more to Ludwigsburg, and asked Mörike to meet her. He refused, and for the rest of his life was loath to mention her. She eventually married a carpenter called Andreas Kohler in 1836 and lived with him in Winterthur and the surrounding villages. She died on 2 September 1865, had no children and is buried in the cemetery at Sirnach. For a fuller account of Maria Meyer's life, see Chapter 2 of Susan Youens's *Hugo Wolf and his Mörike Songs*.

The wound that Maria Meyer inflicted on Mörike never healed, as we see from the third Peregrina poem (set by Schoeck but not Wolf):

Krank seitdem,	My heart since then
Wund ist und wehe mein Herz.	Is sick, wounded and sore.
Nimmer wird es genesen!	Never will it heal!

Mörike started to fictionalise the affair, possibly as a cathartic attempt to exorcise the experience. What began as a Novelle in 1827 about a young artist's attraction to an exotic and dangerous woman gradually grew into the novel *Maler Nolten*, which exists in two versions: *MN1* was published in 1832, and the revised version (*MN2*), unfinished at his death, posthumously in 1877. In Part II of *MN2*, Nolten the painter leaves the town with his fiancée Agnes and during the journey hears of the suicide of his actor/poet friend Larkens. Nolten and Agnes are offered accommodation by the chairman of the local town council, one of Larkens's most fervent admirers, and while staying on his estate Nolten finds among Larkens's papers five poems (four in *MN1*) that chronicle Nolten's relationship with the half-gypsy Elisabeth – the fictitious Maria Meyer. The first poem ('Der Spiegel dieser treuen, braunen Augen') recalls their first meeting, and in *MN1* is presciently headed 'Warnung' ('Warning'); the second poem describes their surreal wedding ('Aufgeschmückt ist der Freudensaal') and is titled 'Die Hochzeit' ('The wedding') in *MN1*; the third poem, beginning 'Ein Irrsal kam in die Mondscheingärten', depicts their painful parting and is actually titled 'Scheiden von Ihr' ('Departing from her') in *MN1*; the fourth poem, not included in *MN1*, recalls their first meeting ('Warum, Geliebte, denk' ich dein'); and in the fifth ('Die Liebe, sagt man, steht am Pfahl gebunden'), titled 'Und wieder' ('Re-encounter') in *MN1*, Nolten blames himself for Peregrina's downfall. These five Peregrina poems throw Nolten into emotional turmoil, and with no thought for Agnes's vulnerability, he confesses to her his passionate fling with Elisabeth and also with the Countess Constanze. Appalled at Nolten's story, Agnes suffers a breakdown, loses her mind and eventually commits suicide.

It is possible that the five Peregrina poems (written as far as we can tell between 1824 and 1830), which Mörike distilled from the shattering Maria Meyer episode, also include echoes of the Klärchen Neuffer experience (both women seem to merge in a supernatural poem, 'Nächtliche Fahrt', that Mörike wrote in 1823), but whatever their emotional provenance, there are no love poems in the German language that lurch more violently between ecstatic sensuality and tortured anguish – Heine's *Buch der Lieder* poems seem mostly like pale posturings in comparison.

There is also another relationship that left its mark on Mörike and might have fed into some of the 'Peregrina' poems. In late February 1828 he visited his brother Karl in Scheer, a little town on the Danube. It was there that he seems to have had an affair with Josephine, the daughter of the local Catholic schoolmaster. The poem 'Josephine' describes this young woman and depicts the poet attending a Catholic Mass, consumed with desire for her. Like Peregrina, she had brown eyes and, to judge from another, much shorter 'Josephine' poem ('Dünkt euch die Schöne'), their relationship was consummated. It was during his stay at Scheer that Mörike, probably inspired by Josephine, wrote 'Im Frühling' (see the notes to that poem, p. 379), 'Erstes Liebeslied eines Mädchens', 'Frage und Antwort', 'Lied vom Winde', 'Nimmersatte Liebe', 'Liebesvorzeichen' and 'Mein Fluß', an extraordinary poem (set by Othmar Schoeck), which can be read as a highly charged and fanciful description of love-making and, ultimately, rejection.

In much of his poetry – for example, 'Gebet' and 'Verborgenheit' – Mörike seeks to avoid overwhelming emotions. Despite such a resolve, suggestions of unrequited love and infidelity surface intermittently throughout his verse: 'Suschens Vogel', 'Die Tochter der Heide', 'Der Knabe und das Immlein', 'Ein Stündlein wohl vor Tag', 'Das verlassene Mägdlein', 'Im Frühling', 'Agnes', 'Der Gärtner', 'Zitronenfalter im April', 'Frage und Antwort', 'Lebe wohl', 'Lied vom Winde' and 'Lied eines Verliebten' all have unhappy love as a theme, often veiled, it's true, with a protective layer of whimsy. And there is often an erotic undertow present in his love poetry ('Nimmersatte Liebe', 'Begegnung', 'Erstes Liebeslied eines Mädchens', 'Der Gärtner'); even when he indulges his predilection for idylls ('Gesang Weylas') and humour ('Storchenbotschaft', 'Der Jäger'), an implied sensuality is never far from the surface.

The most effective way of banishing the spectre of Maria Meyer was to immerse himself in mythology and abandon himself to his own imagination – a faculty he possessed in extraordinary measure. From his earliest childhood, he had sought refuge in dream worlds. On hot summer days he spent hours in the attic of his parents' house, where he would light candles. He loved to explore caves, ravines, wells, forests; he sought out the half-light of remote gardens and woods and delighted in the incense-filled interiors of old churches. It's almost as if, burdened by the rigours of the common round, psychosomatic ill-health and an inability to solve everyday problems, he was drawn into a world of dreams and visions and imagination. *Maler Nolten* includes the dramatic phantasy ('Ein phantasmagorisches Zwischenspiel') called *Der letzte König von Orplid* – Orplid being the fantastical island that Mörike had created with his friend Ludwig Bauer while at theological college in Tübingen.

This tendency of Mörike's to dream has led some commentators to depict him as a romantic visionary and little more. The truth is rather different. Many of his schoolfriends in Urach testified to his sense of humour and gift for mimicry. He was, apparently, an enormously gifted raconteur and would often gather around him a crowd of admiring listeners. Wilhelm Hartlaub, who was to remain Mörike's closest friend throughout his life, tells us how he could let his hair down and play the fool. His delight in mimicry stayed with him into adulthood, and he would often reduce his closest friends to helpless laughter as he imitated fictional characters such as Wispel (see Hermann Hesse's delightful short story 'Im Presselschen Gartenhaus'), the Barber, Professor Sichéré, Pourquoi and Monsieur Ognolet. And in his poetry, there is a strain of humorous Lewis Carroll-like infantilism, familiar to Lieder audiences from songs such as 'Mausfallen-Sprüchlein', 'Selbstgeständnis', 'Abschied', 'Storchenbotschaft', 'Auftrag' and 'Zur Warnung'. Mörike on his deathbed begged his sister Klara to pass him a copy of his poems, and asked touchingly, „Nicht wahr, es steht nichts Frivoles drin?" ('There's nothing frivolous about them, is there?')

Whereas his brother Karl was imprisoned for his political activities, Mörike's innate indolence and his capacity for reverie meant that he was somewhat out of touch with the mainstream of contemporary literature, although he wrote, aged fifteen, a long, passionately patriotic poem, 'Die Liebe zum Vaterlande', that expressed his enthusiasm for the Wars of Liberation. In general, however, Mörike, unlike Freiligrath, Heine and Herwegh, tended not to engage with the social and political issues of the day. But he did have views on some weighty questions, such as the greatness of Napoleon, whom he admired, Greek independence and the union of Germany. And he was in touch with several interesting figures of the time. In 1863 he had met Moritz von Schwind, who asked him to illustrate some of his poems, and they remained friends till Mörike's death in 1875. He enjoyed a close friendship with Theodor Storm, to whom he read the proofs of *Mozart auf der Reise nach Prag*. He knew Emanuel Geibel, Paul Heyse and Justinus Kerner, and as a student had accompanied the insane

Friedrich Hölderlin on regular walks with his friends Ferdinand Christian Bauer and Wilhelm Waiblinger – scenes that Hesse vividly reconstructs in 'Im Presselschen Gartenhaus' (1913).

Mörike's fame spread slowly. The first edition of his *Gedichte* was published by Cotta in 1838 – he was paid 330 florins and a thousand copies were printed. Five years later he enquired of Cotta how many copies had been sold, and was informed the total was 405. When he approached the publishers again in 1846, there were still 393 remaining unsold. These were pulped when Cotta published a new edition of a thousand copies in 1848, for which Mörike was paid 400 florins. Several of the poems underwent significant revisions for this new edition, especially 'Der Feuerreiter' and 'Die Elemente'. Further editions followed in 1856 and 1867. The third edition of 1856 still had 300 copies unsold when Cotta decided to publish a fourth edition in 1867. Another thousand copies were now printed, but this time Mörike received 800 florins, twice the fee he had received for the second edition, and Cotta now included a portrait of the poet. When Mörike died in poverty in 1875, he was still scarcely known beyond a small literary circle in southern Germany; and he was mocked by both Nietzsche (see HW to Oskar Grohe, 21 July 1896, p. 362) and Heinrich Heine who, in *Der Schwabenspiegel*, written just before the publication of the first edition of Mörike's *Gedichte* in 1838, has this to say about Mörike's poetry:

> Man sagt mir, er besinge nicht bloß Maikäfer, sondern sogar Lerchen und Wachteln, was gewiß sehr löblich ist. Lerchen und Wachteln sind wahrhaftig wert, daß man sie singe, nämlich wenn sie gebraten sind.

> I am told that he sings not only of May-bugs but also of larks and quails, which is certainly most laudable. Larks and quails are truly worthy of being praised, especially when they are roasted.

Whether Heine would have changed his view having read all the poems (he confesses that he had not done so) is debatable. Mörike still lags far behind Geibel, Heine, Goethe, Hoffmann von Fallersleben and Rückert in the list of the most-set Lieder poets. Although there were contemporary composers who were drawn to his verse, they were mostly from Swabia and almost unknown: his brother Karl, fellow students such as Ernst Friedrich Kauffmann (whose son Emil was to become one of Wolf's most important champions) and Ludwig Hetsch, who set nine of the poems published here; these were soon followed by Friedrich Silcher and such ephemeral talents as Immanuel Faißt, Otto Scherzer, Gustav Pressel and others. Of the specialist Lieder composers, Schoeck set 44 poems, 40 of which appear in his *Das holde Bescheiden*, a collection that duplicates only one song ('Gebet') from Wolf's *Mörike-Lieder*, Franz 12, Schumann 7 and Brahms 3.

Although Wolf's source for his *Mörike-Lieder* was the sixth edition of the *Gedichte* and not *Maler Nolten* (but see note 1 to 'Er ist's', p. 372), it can be extremely useful for singer and pianist to know the context of these poems within the novel – indeed, in some cases ('Lied vom Winde', for example), it will profoundly influence their interpretation. The same, of course, can be said for those songs that composers set from Goethe's *Wilhelm Meisters Lehrjahre* and Eichendorff's *Ahnung und Gegenwart*. The following poems that Wolf set also appear, shorn of their titles, in *Maler Nolten*: part of 'Der Feuerreiter', 'Die Geister am Mummelsee', 'Elfenlied', 'Das verlassene Mägdlein', 'Er ist's', 'Im Frühling', 'Der Jäger', 'Agnes', 'An die Geliebte', 'Karwoche', 'Lied vom Winde', 'Wo find' ich Trost?', 'Seufzer', 'Neue Liebe', two 'Peregrina' poems and a stanza of 'Gebet'.

Required reading for anyone interested in Mörike is *Hugo Wolf and his Mörike Songs* by Susan Youens.

COMPOSER

Wolf owned a volume of Mörike's poetry (*Gedichte von Eduard Mörike. Sechste Auflage.* Stuttgart, G. J. Göschen'sche Verlagshandlung, 1876) from 1878 – probably a present from Adalbert von Goldschmidt. His first Mörike setting, 'Suschens Vogel', dates from 24 December 1880, a song that owes much to Schumann. 'Mausfallen-Sprüchlein', written for the light soprano voice of Mitzi Werner, followed on 18 June 1882, a genuine masterpiece (see HW to Bertha von Lackhner, 21 October 1882, p. 345); 'Die Tochter der Heide', a rambling and not entirely successful setting of Mörike's ballad, dates from 11 July 1884, and 'Der König bei der Krönung' from 13 March 1886 on his twenty-sixth birthday – a declamatory prayer that fails wholly to convince. Two barren Lieder years followed, and then came the explosion, ushered in by 'Der Tambour', composed on 16 February 1888 in Perchtoldsdorf. The remaining fifty-two songs now poured out of him.

Many of the letters are suffused with a self-ironic hyperbole in keeping with Wolf's heightened mood. From the composition of 'Der Tambour' on, he regularly communicates his excitement to friends. He keeps insisting that his most recent song is his greatest, only to renounce such claims the very next day. There was no stopping him. In his trance-like state, he felt capable of setting Mörike's entire poetic output, as he wittily implied in a letter about the composition of 'Nimmersatte Liebe' – see HW to Edmund Lang, 24 February 1888, p. 345. It should not, however, be thought that Wolf's Lieder were somehow miraculously committed to manuscript with no effort – see HW to Melanie Köchert, 24 June 1890, p. 280. Many sketches exist in the Österreichische Nationalbibliothek Musiksammlung. Some are simply jottings without the words ('Kennst du das

Land'), others are fair copies with music and words ('Fühlt meine Seele'). And perfectionist as he was, he would often make further corrections in the engraver's copy and also at the proof sheet stage. See APPENDIX 5 for further information about Wolf's sketches.

Wolf's correspondence with his friends and their own testimonies also provide us with a fairly detailed description of his method of work. For weeks on end he would carry about with him his edition of Mörike's poems, reading and rereading them, immersing himself in them until they seemed to be part of himself. Most days began with a walk to the Hochberg above the 'Häuslein Windebang', the summer-house mentioned in 'Der Knabe und das Immlein' that belonged to the Werner family and where many of his songs were conceived. He would then work at the song in hand, either in his bedroom or study, making sketches and sometimes, with longer songs, a fair copy. He would usually recite the poem aloud, working out the rhythm, harmony and melody on the piano. He would also recite a poem before performing the song, and often insist that the singer recite it. Richard Batka (1868–1922), musicologist, critic and great champion of Wolf's music, describes a Liederabend at which he was present:

> Zunächst las er die Gedichte im schönsten steirischen Dialekt, aber so von innen heraus empfunden, daß nur einem ganz törichten Menschen die Sache hätte komisch erscheinen können. Nach dem Mörikeschen „In ein freundliches Städtchen tret' ich ein" wandte er sich zu uns: „Ist das Gedicht nicht zum Heulen schön?" Und nun fing er an zu singen.

> To begin with he recited the poems with the most beautiful Styrian accent, but in such an intense, internalised way that only an utter fool could have found it funny. Having recited Mörike's 'In ein freundliches Städtchen tret' ich ein', he turned to us and said, 'Isn't the poem screamingly beautiful?' And then he began to sing.

Lunch was usually taken in the Gasthaus 'Zum schwarzen Adler', followed by black coffee and a cigarette and another session of work. Evenings were normally devoted to reading and correspondence. The house at Brunnergasse 26 was, especially in the winter months, extremely cold (see HW to Melanie Köchert, 16 November 1894, p. 361). There was no running water and the only warmth was provided by an old, inadequate tiled stove. Wolf referred to his room as a „schrecklicher Verbannungsort" ('a terrible place of exile'), but it provided him with the absolute silence that he required to compose. When once the silence was broken by children playing outside, he screamed at the miscreants and confiscated their spinning tops and whips. During these months of sustained inspiration, Wolf produced Lieder of a literary pedigree that are matched only by Schubert's seventy or so Goethe settings and Schumann's forty or so songs to texts by Heine.

He was, of course, aware of his debt to Mörike, as Detlev von Liliencron, who was present at the first performance the composer gave of the Mörike songs, tells us in his poem 'An Hugo Wolf', the full text of which can be found in APPENDIX 1:

Vorn im Mörike-Heft,	In the Mörike volume,
Auf erster Seite,	On the first page,
Hattest Du, Bescheidener,	You, modest man,
Des Dichters Bild verehrend aufgestellt.	Had set the poet's portrait in admiration.
Welcher Tonsetzer that je so?	What composer ever did that?

Although Wolf was touched by Liliencron's poem (HW to his mother, 23 December 1890, p. 357), he despised much of his verse, as he explains in a withering letter to Emil Kauffmann written the previous day.

Wolf was brought up in the Catholic tradition by his devout mother, and 9 of the 53 *Mörike-Lieder* are religious in tone: 'Auf ein altes Bild', 'Auf eine Christblume I', 'Auf eine Christblume II', 'Karwoche', 'Neue Liebe', 'Schlafendes Jesuskind', 'Seufzer', 'Wo find' ich Trost?' and 'Zum neuen Jahr'. Although Wolf in a letter to his mother of 29 April 1892 describes himself as an „Ungläubiger" ('unbeliever'), he also had a pronounced spiritual side, as becomes clear in this passage from the same letter in which he pours scorn on prayer:

Worte, Worte, nichts als Worte, die nach der Überlieferung gewerkelt werden, wie das Abc auf den untersten Schulbänken. Solche Worte gleichen der Saat in der Wüste, die der Wind verweht, gleich wie die Worte selber in den Wind gesprochen sind, die aus dem Munde wüster Menschen kommen. Wie der Baum seine Wurzeln tief in die Erde gräbt, um kraftvoll in die Höhe zu streben, so muß auch das <u>lebendige</u> Wort, die Ahnung des Göttlichen im innersten Kerne des menschlichen Wesens Wurzel fassen, damit sich der Spruch bewähre: an ihren Früchten sollt ihr sie erkennen.

Words, words, nothing but words, which are gabbled in the time-honoured way in which the smallest children recite their ABC on the school bench. Such words are like the seeds in the desert blown by the wind, like the words spoken by the dissolute to the winds. Just as a tree sinks its roots deep into the earth to soar up more vigorously, so too must the <u>living</u> word, the presentiment of godliness at the innermost core of every human being, take root, in order for the proverb to be proved true: By their fruits ye shall know them.

Such a view would have been shared by Mörike, the unorthodox Protestant priest. Some two years later, however, Wolf writes to Melanie Köchert (17 May 1895, p. 361) that he and Mörike would not have understood each other. Wolf calls himself a 'modernist' and Mörike was anything but. Musically too, their tastes were different: Mörike disliked Wagner, Wolf worshipped him. Mörike's poetry, however, struck a chord in the composer's heart, and that Mörike today is regarded throughout the world as one of the great German poets has much to do with the beauty of Wolf's wonderful songs. Although Mörike was admired in his own lifetime by a select few such as Fontane, Jakob Grimm, Hebbel, Heyse, Keller, Kerner, Storm and Uhland; although artists such as Ludwig Richter and Moritz von Schwind illustrated his works; although Franz, Schumann and Brahms set his poems – it was only after the publication of Wolf's *Mörike-Lieder* that this Swabian poet became known across the globe.

LETTERS

HW to Bertha von Lackhner, Vienna, 21 October 1882

Unter Anderm singt sie [Frau Paula v. Goldschmidt] auch das (von mir für die Mitz [Mitzi Werner]) componirte „Mausfallen-Sprüchlein" das aber Mitz nicht des Ansehens werth gehalten u. mit dem Frau Paula v. Goldschmidt in Gesellschaften Triumphe feiert. Sie singt nichts anderes mehr, als mein „Mausfallensprüchlein"; ich hab es ihr auch gewidmet.

Among other things she [Frau Paula v. Goldschmidt] sings 'Mausfallen-Sprüchlein' that I composed for Mitz [Mitzi Werner], who does not deem it worthy of consideration, but which Frau Paula v. Goldschmidt sings with great success at soirées. She sings nothing but my 'Mausfallensprüchlein', and I have dedicated it to her.

HW to Edmund Lang, Perchtoldsdorf, 22 February 1888

Soeben habe ich ein neues Lied aufgeschrieben ['Der Knabe und das Immlein']. Ein Götterlied sag' ich Ihnen! ganz göttlich, wunderbar! Bei Gott! mit mir wird's bald zu Ende gehen, da meine Gscheidtheit von Tag zu Tag zu nimmt. Wie weit soll ich's noch bringen? mir grauts daran zu denken. Ich habe nicht den Muth eine Oper zu schreiben, weil ich mich vor den nothwendigen vielen Einfällen fürchte. Einfälle, lieber Freund, sind schrecklich. Ich fühl's. Meine Wangen glühen vor Aufregung wie geschmolzenes Eisen u. dieser Zustand der Inspiration ist mir eine entzückende Marter, kein reines Glück.

Ich habe heute förmlich eine ganze komische Oper auf dem Klaviere zusammen phantasirt. Ich glaube ich brächte wirklich etwas Gutes in dieser Art zu Stande. Aber ich fürchte die Strapazen; ich bin zu feige für einen ordentlichen

Componisten. Was mag mir wohl die Zukunft noch vorbehalten? Diese Frage quält mich u. ängstigt und beschäftigt mich im Wachen u. im Traume. Bin ich ein Berufener? bin ich am Ende gar ein Auserwählter? Gott verhüte das letztere. Das wär' mir eine schöne Bescheerung.

I have just written a new song ['Der Knabe und das Immlein']. A divine song, I tell you! Utterly divine, wonderful! By God! it will soon be all over with me, for my cleverness increases from day to day. How far shall I progress? I shudder to think about it. I haven't the courage to write an opera, as I'm afraid of all the ideas it's necessary to have. Ideas, dear friend, are dreadful. I feel my cheeks glow with excitement like molten iron, & this state of inspiration is more like rapturous torture than unadulterated happiness.

Today I practically sketched out an entire comic opera at the piano. I believe I could compose something really good in this vein. But I am afraid of all the toil; I'm too cowardly to be a proper composer. What will the future hold for me? This question tortures & frightens me and preoccupies me waking & dreaming. Have I been called? Am I really one of the elect? God forbid the latter. That would be a fine state of affairs.

HW to Edmund Lang, Perchtoldsdorf, 22 February 1888

Die Tage von Lodi scheinen sich in der Tat erneuern zu wollen. Meine Lodi im Lied ist bekanntlich das Jahr 78 gewesen;[1] damals komponierte ich fast jeden Tag <u>ein</u> gutes Lied, mitunter auch <u>zwei</u>: Nun reißen Sie Ihre Nasenflügel auf.

Kaum, daß mein Brief expediert wurde, schrieb ich auch schon, den Mörike zur Hand nehmend, ein zweites Lied u.z. im 5/4 Takt, und ich darf wohl sagen, daß selten ein 5/4 Takt so richtig am Platze war, als in dieser Komposition ['Jägerlied']. Auch Sie, als Laie, werden aus dem Rythmus des Gedichtes sofort den 5/4 Takt herausfinden und die Notwendigkeit desselben einsehen. Nun beglückwünschen, oder verwünschen Sie mich, ganz nach Belieben.

Sollte mir Polyhymnia aufsässig genug sein, mit einem dritten Liede zu drohen, werde ich diese Schreckensnachricht persönlich morgen in aller Frühe überbringen.

Augenblicklich ereignet sich nichts musikalisches um mich, es wäre denn das tägliche Abendgebet in langgezogenen Schluchzern von Seiten einer ehrbaren Jungfrau – unserer Diana.[2]

PS Verachten Sie mich. Das Bubenstück ist vollbracht. Auch das <u>dritte</u> Lied „ein Stündlein wohl vor Tag" ist mir gelungen und <u>wie</u>! das ist ein ereignisvoller Tag.

---

1 'My Lodi in song' is a reference to Napoleon's 1796 victory at Lodi in northern Italy, which brought him recognition and a boost in self-confidence.
2 The name of the Newfoundland bitch in the Werner household.

The days of Lodi really seem to be renewing themselves. My Lodi in song is well known to have been 1878; in those days I would compose almost every day <u>one</u> good song and sometimes <u>two</u>. Now listen to this and be amazed!

Scarcely was my letter dispatched than, taking up Mörike, I wrote a second song, in 5/4 time, and I can well say that seldom has 5/4 time been so appropriate as in this composition ['Jägerlied']. You too, as a layman, will at once discover the 5/4 measure in the rhythm of the poem and understand the necessity for it. Now congratulate me or curse me, just as you please.

Should Polyhymnia be sufficiently aggressive to threaten me with a third song, I shall convey the dreadful news to you personally tomorrow at the break of day.

At the moment there is nothing musical happening here, except for the regular evening prayer in long-drawn sobs from a respectable maiden – our Diana.

PS Despise me. The hat-trick is complete. I have also successfully composed a <u>third</u> song, 'Ein Stündlein wohl vor Tag', and <u>what</u> a song! An eventful day.

HW to Friedrich Eckstein, Perchtoldsdorf, 24 February 1888

Vielleicht lockt Sie die Mittheilung, daß ich ein Heft neuer Lieder von Mörike componirt u. ich sage Ihnen (aber ganz leise) so schön, wie sich in der ganzen Liederliteratur kaum Besseres vorfindet. Wenn Sie mir nicht glauben wollen, so hören Sie's an. Kommen Sie! Sie haben völlige Freiheit zu spucken, zu schneitzen, zu rülpsen u. zu kotzen, wann's Ihnen beliebt. Aber <u>kommen</u> Sie! Selbstverständlich bleiben wir auch den Abend beisammen. Also: bei Vermeidung noch gefährlicherer Drohungen – – – kommen Sie bei schönem Wetter zu Ihrem herzlich ergebenen Hugo Wolf.

Perhaps the announcement that I have just composed a set of new poems by Mörike will tempt you, & I can tell you (but very gently) that they are so beautiful that there is scarcely anything better to be found in the entire Lieder repertoire. If you don't believe me, listen to them. Come! You are wholly at liberty to spit, blow your nose, belch or puke, just as you wish. But <u>come</u>! And of course we'll spend the evening together. So – to avoid even more dangerous threats – come in fine weather to your truly devoted Hugo Wolf.

HW to Edmund Lang, Perchtoldsdorf, 24 February 1888

Es ist jetzt punkt 7 Abend und ich bin so überglücklich, wie ein überglücklicher König. Wieder ist mir ein neues Lied gelungen. Schatzerl, wenn's das hörst, holt Dich vor Vergnügen der Teufel.

Der Schluß bricht geradezu in einem Studententon aus. Es geht darin zum Erhängen lustig her. Hier die Worte: [Wolf quotes 'Nimmersatte Liebe'].

Dabei fällt mir gerade ein, daß Sie sich das Ankaufen der Mörike'schen Gedichte füglich ersparen können, da ich, bei meinem wunderlichen Produktionsdrang, in der erfreulichen Lage sein dürfte, Sie über kurz oder lang mit sämtlichen Gedichten meines Lieblings in dieser Weise bekannt zu machen.

It is now precisely 7 in the evening and I am as ecstatic as an ecstatic king. Yet another new song has been successfully completed. My dear fellow, when you hear it, the Devil will take you with pleasure.

The end breaks out in a regular student's song – nothing could be more jolly. Here is the poem [Wolf quotes 'Nimmersatte Liebe'].

It just occurs to me that you may justifiably save yourself the purchase of Mörike's poems, as I, in the grip of my strange creative urge, might sooner or later be in the happy position of acquainting you with the entire poetical works of my favourite.

HW to Franz Schalk, Perchtoldsdorf, 24 February 1888

Ich habe funkelnagelneue Lieder am Lager. Vorgestern, denken Sie nur – schrieb ich gleich deren drei;[1] gestern[2] eines u. so Gott will gelingt mir heute auch noch das Eine od. Andere.

Die Gedichte sind durchgehend von Mörike u. die Compositionen sind sicherlich das Beste, was ich bis zur Stunde aufgeschrieben. –

I have brand-new songs ready. The day before yesterday – just think! – I composed three; yesterday one, & if God wills it, there will be another one or two today.

The poems are all by Mörike, & the songs are certainly the best I have ever written.

HW to Marie Lang, Perchtoldsdorf, 25 February 1888

Ich habe rasend zu thun. Heute sind mir zwei neue Lieder (von Ed. Mörike) eingefallen, von denen das Eine[3] so schauerlich seltsam klingt, daß mir ganz bange davor wird. So etwas war noch nie da. Gott stehe den armen Leuten bei, die das einmal hören werden.

---

1 'Der Knabe und das Immlein', 'Ein Stündlein wohl vor Tag' and 'Jägerlied'.
2 'Der Jäger'.   3 'Zur Warnung'. The second song was 'Auftrag'.

Am frantically busy. Today I composed two new songs (by Ed. Mörike), one of which sounds so strangely creepy that it frightens me. There has never been a song like this. God help the poor people who will one day hear it.

HW to Franz Schalk, Perchtoldsdorf, 14 March 1888

Daß ich seit unserem letzten Wiedersehen 4 neue Lieder (von Mörike)[1] componirt, 4 sehr schöne Lieder die ganz gewiß Ihren Beifall finden werden – das – nicht wahr? – erstaunt Sie nicht, u. offen gestanden – mich auch nicht.

That I have composed 4 new songs (by Mörike) since our last meeting – 4 very beautiful songs of which you will most certainly approve – does not surprise you, does it? &, to be frank, me neither.

HW to Bertha von Lackhner, Perchtoldsdorf, 17 March 1888

Seit dem 22. Feb. bin ich in eine wahre Componir-Wuth gerathen. Ich componire fast alle Tage ein Lied, auch 2, ja selbst 3 Lieder. Und alle, alle gelingen mir, so daß den Leuten, die Sie kennen, die Wahl der Entscheidung für dieß od. jenes schwer fällt. Bis jetzt habe ich seit 22. Febr. 20 Lieder geschrieben, und ich verfluche jeden Tag, den ich in Wien[2] verbringen muß, weil er mich vom Componiren abbringt. Ja, selbst diese Zeilen, die ich flüchtig auf's Papier hinwerfe, muß ich meiner wirklich kostbaren Zeit stehlen u. wie ein Dieb verbringe ich dieses angenehme Geschäft in möglichster Eile.

Since 22 Feb. I have been composing like a madman. Almost every day I compose one song, sometimes 2 or even 3. And all of them turn out well, so that it's difficult for the people you are acquainted with to decide on which they prefer. Since 22 Feb. I have written 20 songs, and I curse every day that I have to spend in Vienna, because it interrupts my composing. Even these lines that I scrawl onto paper steal my so precious time – & like a thief I accomplish this pleasant activity in all possible haste.

HW to Edmund Lang, Perchtoldsdorf, 20 March 1888

Heute, gleich nach meiner Ankunft habe ich mein Meisterstück geliefert. „Erstes Liebeslied eines Mädchens" (Ed. Mörike) ist das weitaus beste, was ich bis jetzt zu Stande gebracht. Gegen dieses Lied ist Alles Vorhergegangene Kinderspiel. Die Musik ist von so schlagender Charakteristik, dabei von einer

---

[1] 'Denk' es, o Seele!' (10 March), 'Auf einer Wanderung' (11 March), 'Gebet' (13 March), 'Verborgenheit' (13 March).
[2] The twice-weekly piano lessons he gave to Countess Harrach earned Wolf much needed income.

Intensität, die das Nervensystem eines Marmorblockes zerreissen könnte. Das Gedicht ist wahnsinnig, die Musik nicht minder u. ebenso Ihr
   Fluchu.[1]

Today, immediately after my arrival, I composed my masterpiece. 'Erstes Liebeslied eines Mädchens' (Ed. Mörike) is by far the best thing I've done. In comparison to this, all the earlier songs are mere child's play. The music is of such striking character, and at the same time so intense, that it would lacerate the nervous system of a block of marble. The poem is mad, the music no less so, and likewise your
   Fluchu.

HW to Edmund Lang, Perchtoldsdorf, 21 March 1888

Ich revocire, daß „erstes Liebeslied eines Mädchens" mein Bestes sei, denn was ich heute Vormittag geschrieben: „Fussreise" (Ed. Mörike) ist noch millionenmal besser. Wenn Sie dieses letzte Lied gehört haben, kann Sie nur noch ein Wunsch beseelen: zu sterben.

I take back my claim that 'Erstes Liebeslied eines Mädchens' is my finest song, for what I wrote this morning, 'Fussreise' (Ed. Mörike), is a million times better. When you have heard this song, you will have but one more wish: to die.

HW to Franz Schalk, Perchtoldsdorf, 21 March 1888

Gestern componirte ich ein Lied, „erstes Liebeslied eines Mädchens" (Ed. Mörike) von dem ich überzeugt war, daß es mein Bestes sei. Heute aber componirte ich ein anderes Lied „Fussreise" (Ed. Mörike) das wirklich schon über alle Bäume geht. Liebster Franziskus! wenn das so fort geht, werden Sie wirklich noch Respekt vor mir kriegen. Sie werden nur stöhnen u. schreien, wenn Sie diese zwei neuen Lieder zu hören bekommen. Einstweilen mögen Sie mit den Gedichten vorlieb nehmen.

Yesterday I composed a song, 'Erstes Liebeslied eines Mädchens' (Ed. Mörike), which I was convinced was my best. But today I composed another song, 'Fußreise', that beats everything. Dearest Franziscus! if it goes on like this, you will begin to respect me. When you listen to these two new songs, you will merely groan & scream. In the meantime, you will have to make do with the poems.

---

1 Wolf was much given to swearing – hence his nickname 'Fluchu' ('fluchen' = to swear). To friends and relatives he would often sign himself Wölfing, Wölferl, Wolferl, Wluhu, Fluchu and Lupusculus.

HW to Josef Strasser, Perchtoldsdorf, 23 March 1888

Ich arbeite mit tausend Pferdekräften von früh bis in die Nacht, ununterbrochen. Was ist jetzt aufschreibe, das, lieber Freund, schreibe ich auch schon für die Nachwelt. Es sind Meisterwerke. Einstweilen allerdings nur Lieder, aber wenn ich Dir sage, dass ich bei den vielen Unterbrechungen durch meine Anwesenheit in Wien, die zweimal in der Woche wegen der Harrach[1] unbedingt nötig ist, und wie ich also trotzdem seit 22. Februar bis zum heutigen Tage 25 Lieder komponiert, von denen eins das andere übertrifft, darüber es unter Musikverständigen nur eine Stimme gibt, dass seit Schubert und Schumann nichts ähnliches da war etz. etz. etz. etz., so magst Du Dir vorstellen was das für Lieder sind. [. . .] Den Wagnerverein[2] habe ich an einem Abend, an dem ich meine neuesten Lieder vortrug, geradezu toll gemacht. Die Kerle gehen für mich in die Hölle, wenn's sein muss. Ich werde dort gefeiert wie ein König.

I'm working with a thousand horsepower, from early morning into the night without interruption. What I now write, dear friend, I write for posterity also. They are masterpieces. For the moment they are admittedly only songs, but when I tell you that in spite of the many interruptions due to the necessity of my being in Vienna twice weekly because of Countess Harrach I have nonetheless since 22 February composed 25 songs, each one of which surpasses the others, and about which there is only one opinion among those of musical discernment – namely that there has been nothing like them since Schubert and Schumann, etc. etc. etc. etc. – you may imagine what sort of songs they are. [. . .] When I performed my latest songs one evening at the Wagnerverein, they went mad. They would die for me if they had to. I'm treated there like a king.

HW to Friedrich Eckstein, Perchtoldsdorf, 27 March 1888

Heute vormittags war ich trotz des schönen Wetters ganz verzweifelt, da mir absolut nichts einfallen wollte, und ich den Tag schon als verloren betrachtete.

Ich bin schon wieder beruhigt. Nachmittag schrieb ich ein ganz besonders gelungenes Lied „Storchenbotschaft" (natürlich Mörike) und so habe ich wieder Hoffnung, daß die Mühle weiter klappert.

---

1 See note 2 to HW to Bertha von Lackhner, 17 March 1888, p. 349.
2 The Wiener Akademischer Wagner-Verein, founded in 1873, played an important role in propagating Wolf's Lieder. Wolf first attended the Verein in 1883, and in 1884 offered the Society his String Quartet in D minor – which was performed for the first time two and a half weeks after Wolf's death by the Prill-Quartett. When Joseph Schalk was appointed artistic director in 1887, he worked hard to champion his new friend's Lieder at the 'Donnerstagabend' concerts. And in 1890, at the instigation of Gustav Schur, treasurer of the Wagner-Verein, a group was formed, consisting mainly of his friends, to help Wolf financially. A fund was established that in the following years was used to contribute towards publication costs, and that also provided Wolf with travelling expenses.

Samstag komponierte ich, ohne es beabsichtigt zu haben, „Das verlassene Mägdlein" – von Schumann [Op. 64/2] bereits himmlisch komponiert. Wenn ich dasselbe Gedicht trotzdem komponierte, geschah es fast wider meinen Willen; aber vielleicht gerade dadurch, daß ich mich von dem Zauber dieses Gedichtes plötzlich gefangen nehmen ließ, ist etwas Vortreffliches entstanden, und ich glaube, daß meine Komposition neben der Schumann'schen sich sehen lassen kann.

This morning I was in utter despair despite the beautiful weather, because I felt totally uninspired and had written the day off.

I am now calm again. In the afternoon I composed an especially successful song, 'Storchenbotschaft' (Mörike of course), so I'm hopeful once more that the mill will continue to clatter.

On Saturday I composed, without meaning to, 'Das verlassene Mägdlein', already set to heavenly music by Schumann. If, despite that, I also set the poem, it happened almost against my will; but perhaps it is precisely because I let myself be captured by the magic of this poem that something splendid resulted, and I believe that my song can bear comparison with Schumann's.

HW to Edmund Lang, Perchtoldsdorf, 14 April 1888

Mein letztes Lied, das ich soeben vollendet ['Auf ein altes Bild'], ist ganz gewiß die Krone von Allen. Ich stehe noch ganz unter dem Stimmungszauber dieses Liedes u. es flimmert mir Alles grün vor den Augen. Ja, es ist sicherlich das weitaus beste, stimmungsvollste, formvollendetste, gedankentiefste u. was es noch dergleichen herrliche Ausdrücke giebt. Was für ein ausgefallener Titel! Das giebt eine Perspektive! Das reizt zu einem sinnvollen Nachspiel! Sapperment! Das soll mir einer nachschreiben! Lieber Freund, ich bin heute dergestalt arrogant, daß sich jeder gemüthliche Diskurs aufhört. Ich sage Ihnen daher nur schnell adio adio adio!

The song I have just finished is without a doubt the finest of them all ['Auf ein altes Bild']. The magical atmosphere of this song still surrounds me, & everything glimmers green before my eyes. Yes, it is far and away the best, the most atmospheric, the best crafted, the most profound & all the other splendid superlatives. What an unusual title! It sets up the song wonderfully well! – inspiring a postlude fraught with significance! The devil! No one can emulate that! Dear friend, I am today so arrogant that there can be no genial discourse. And so in haste I bid you addio addio addio!

HW to Friedrich Eckstein, Unterach, 8 October 1888

Ich will nur noch den „Feuerreiter" hier componiren, damit die 50 voll ist.[1] Ja, liebes Ecksteinderl! Ich habe in den letzten Tagen wieder fleißig „gemörikelt", u.z. lauter Gedichte, die Sie besonders adoriren. „An den Schlaf", „Neue Liebe" (beide am 4. Oktb.) „Zum neuen Jahr" (5. Oktb.) „Schlafendes Jesuskind", „Wo find' ich Trost" (beide am 6 Okt.). Jetzt arbeite ich gerade an der „Charwoche", die über die Massen herrlich wird. Alle Lieder sind wahrhaft erschütternd componirt. Mir sind oft genug dabei die Thränen über die Wangen gerollt. Sie überragen an Tiefe der Auffassung alle übrigen von Mörike.

Gott gebe nur, daß mir Der Feuerreiter gelingt, denn dann erst sind die 50 beinander.

Haben Sie Schritte gethan von wegen des Seperatdruckes der Gedichte. Lassen Sie doch dieselben copiren, daß die Geschichte einmal in's Rollen kommt. Ich arbeite <u>Tag u. Nacht</u>, was Ruhe ist kenn ich nicht mehr.

Ich will die Lieder mit einer <u>Vorrede</u> herausgeben.[2] Was sagen Sie dazu? Noch Eines: Schreiben Sie an den Verleger der Mörike'schen Gedichte, ob er Ihnen ein Bild aus den <u>jungen</u> Tagen des Dichters zum bewußten Zwecke verschaffen könne, aber schnell, schnell, schnell. Mörike muß vor Weihnacht erscheinen, sonst bring ich Sie u. mich um.

Once I've composed 'Der Feuerreiter', the 50 will be complete. Yes, dear Ecksteinderl, I have in recent days once again industriously 'Möriked', and what is more, nothing but poems that you especially adore: 'An den Schlaf', 'Neue Liebe' (both on 4 Oct.), 'Zum neuen Jahre' (5 Oct.), 'Schlafendes Jesuskind', 'Wo find' ich Trost?' (both on 6 Oct.). Just now I am working on 'Charwoche', which will be magnificent beyond all imagining. All the songs are truly shatteringly composed. Often enough the tears rolled down my cheeks as I wrote. They surpass in depth of conception all the other settings of Mörike.

With God's help, I'll finish 'Der Feuerreiter' – then there will be 50.

Have you taken steps to ensure that the poems are published separately? Have them copied out to get the ball rolling. I'm working <u>day & night</u>, I no longer know the meaning of rest.

I would like to publish the songs with a <u>Preface</u>. What do you think? And another thing. Write to the publisher of the Mörike poems to see whether he can supply for our purpose a picture of the <u>young</u> poet, but be quick, quick, quick about it. Mörike must appear before Christmas, otherwise I'll kill you & myself.

---

1   To the intended 50 songs Wolf added three more. 'Gesang Weylas' was composed before 'Der Feuerreiter' (9 October), and two others followed: 'An die Geliebte' on 11 October and 'Auf eine Christblume I' on 26 November – making a total of 53.

2   Wolf wrote no such Preface.

HW to his mother, Döbling, 27 December 1888

Anbei ein Programm. Ich schicke auch zwei Zeitungen mit Recensionen über mich. In der einen „Abendpost" schimpft mein Freund Paumgartner.[1] Wozu hat man denn sonst Freunde? Gerne wäre ich zu Weihnachten nach Hause gekommen, doch hat sich das Erscheinen der Mörike'schen Lieder derartig verzögert, daß an eine Publikation derselben vor Ende des nächsten Monates kaum zu denken ist.[2]

I enclose a programme. I also send you two newspapers with reviews about me. Friend Paumgartner slates me in the 'Abendpost'. But what else are friends for? I would have loved to come home for Christmas, but the publication of the Mörike songs has been so delayed that it is almost certain that they will not appear before the end of next month.

HW to his mother, Perchtoldsdorf, 19 April 1890

Den „Jäger" nennt dieses Kalb von Rezensenten ein frisch empfundenes „Liedchen". Da müsste man Tristan und Isolde ein putziges Operettchen heissen. O, diese Schafsköpfe von Rezensenten![3]

---

1 Hans Paumgartner was one of Wolf's closest friends, and when Philipp Wolf, Hugo's father, got into financial difficulties, it was Paumgartner, a lawyer, who gave him advice. He also tried to interest Hans Richter in Wolf's *Penthesilea*. After the concert at the Wiener Akademischer Wagner-Verein, however, on 15 December 1888, which programmed Beethoven and Wolf, Paumgartner, who had little understanding of Wolf's harmonic language, wrote a withering review in the 'Abendpost' of the *Wiener Zeitung* in which he accused Wolf of a lack of invention („einen Mangel an Erfindung"). The review marked the end of their friendship.
2 The songs were not published until March 1889 – by Emil Wetzler under the title *Gedichte von Eduard Mörike für eine Singstimme und Klavier*.
3 Franz Petrich's review had appeared in the *Grazer Tagespost* on 14 April 1890. Not all the critics were of the same opinion, as can be seen from this rapturous review in the *Grazer Wochenblatt* of 20 April 1890:

> Hugo Wolf ist ein Liedercomponist allerersten Ranges. Seit Schubert haben wir nicht vieles seines Gleichen [. . .] Zehn Lieder von einem und demselben Componisten in einer Reihenfolge gehört haben und doch den Wunsch empfunden, noch mehr von demselben zu vernehmen – das ist ein klarer Beweis für die ungewöhnliche Bedeutung, von dem Werthe der Compositionen. [. . .] Potpeschnigg spielte den Klavierpart meisterhaft.

> Hugo Wolf is a Lieder composer of the highest rank. Since Schubert, there have been few to equal him [. . .] To hear ten songs from one and the same composer one after the other and to wish to hear still more – that clearly testifies to the unusual significance and worth of the compositions. [. . .] Potpeschnigg was the masterly accompanist.

In fact, twelve of Wolf's Lieder were performed (settings of Goethe, Mörike and Eichendorff) alongside songs by Wagner.

This ass of a critic calls 'Der Jäger' a freshly felt ditty. In which case, you would have to call *Tristan und Isolde* a cute little operetta. Oh, these asinine critics!

HW to Emil Kauffmann, Unterach, 5 June 1890

Und selbst Mörike, dieser Liebling der Grazien! zu welchen Excessen läßt seine Muse sich hinreissen, wenn sie der dämonischen Seite der Wahrheit ihr Antlitz zukehrt! das „erste Liebeslied eines Mädchens" bietet ein treffendes Beispiel hierfür.

And even Mörike, this darling of the Graces! – to what excesses does his Muse abandon herself, when she turns her gaze towards the demonic side of truth! 'Erstes Liebeslied eines Mädchens' is a striking example of this.

HW to Oskar Grohe, Unterach, 25 September 1890

Mein Prometheus ist schon längst fertig instrumentirt; desgleichen eine Anzahl geistlicher Lieder von Mörike, darunter die Charwoche, wo find' ich Trost? neue Liebe, An den Schlaf, Gebet, etc. etc.

The orchestration of my 'Prometheus' was finished long ago – likewise that of a number of sacred Mörike songs, including 'Karwoche', 'Wo find' ich Trost?', 'Neue Liebe', 'An den Schlaf', 'Gebet', etc., etc.

HW to Melanie Köchert, Stuttgart, 15 October 1890

Zum Frühstück las mir K. Briefe von Mörike an seinen Vater vor.[1] Du lieber Himmel, was sind das Briefe!!! Dieselben sind fast seinen Gedichten vorzuziehen, so viel Herrliches offenbart sich in ihnen. Wir waren alle bis zu Thränen gerührt. [. . .]

Wundervolle Aufschlüße über Mörike's Verhältniss zu Peregrina gab mir Kauffmann heute auf dem Wege nach Reutlingen. Darnach hiess dieselbe Marie Mayer [*sic*] u. wurde von einem Fuhrmann auf dem Wege nach Ludwigsburg in ohnmächtigem Zustand aufgefunden. Wieder zu sich gebracht u. vom Fuhrmann nach Ludwigsburg befördert erregte Marie Mayer, die jegliche Auskunft über ihr Vorleben u. ihre Heimath verweigerte, gewaltiges Aufsehen durch ihre fabelhafte Schönheit, namentlich ihre faszinirenden Augen. Mörike verliebte sich sterblich in sie. Er war dazumal Student in Tübingen. Sie schrieben sich glühende Liebesbriefe, denn seine Angebetete war von hoher Bildung u. zeigte

---

[1] Emil Kauffmann's father, Ernst Friedrich, was a close friend of Mörike and set a number of his poems to music.

ein besonderes Verständniß für Jean Paul.[1] Beide galten schließlich als Verlobte. –

Eines Tages nun verschwand M. M. spurlos aus Ludwigsburg. Wochenlang konnte man über ihren Aufenthaltsort nichts erfahren. Mörike war in Verzweiflung. Da kam mit einem die Nachrichte aus Carlsruhe, daß eine gewisse M. M. wegen unbefugter Bettelei u. gröblicher Unzucht in Haft gehalten werde. Diese Nachricht kam zu Kauffmann's Eltern, die besagte M. M. längere Zeit in ihrem Hause beherbergten. Mörike wurde davon verständigt. Er war außer sich. – Da plötzlich erschien eines Tages früh am morgen auf den Stufen des Hauses lagernd welches Mörike bewohnte, sein verlorenes Lieb, das er, obschon es noch liebend damals von sich stieß. Deshalb also „ein Irrsal kam in die Mondscheingärten einer einst heiligen Liebe".[2] Wie verständlich werden mir jetzt diese Gedichte. Kauffmann zeigte mir nun das Haus, das Mörike dazumal bewohnte u. so sah ich die Stufen, auf denen Peregrina dem unglücklichen Dichter zum letzten male begegnete. Ist das nicht hoch interessant?

Auch soll der wahnsinnige Hölderlin, der in Tübingen gelebt u. gestorben Mörike als Modell zum Feuerreiter gedient haben.

At breakfast K. read out some of Mörike's letters to his father. Good God, what letters!!! Almost preferable to his poems, they contain so many wonderful things. We were all moved to tears. [. . .]

On the way to Reutlingen today, Kauffmann gave me wonderful insights into Mörike's relationship with Peregrina. According to him, she was called Marie Mayer [sic] & was found in an unconscious state by a carter on his way to Ludwigsburg. When she came to, she was brought by the carter to Ludwigsburg, where, refusing to divulge any information about her past & her homeland, she aroused huge interest through her fabulous beauty and especially her fascinating eyes. Mörike fell head over heels in love with her. At that time he was a student in Tübingen. They exchanged passionate love letters, for the woman he worshipped was <u>highly</u> educated and showed a special understanding of Jean Paul. They were considered to be an engaged couple.

One day M. M. disappeared without trace from Ludwigsburg. For weeks on end there was no information as to her whereabouts. Mörike was in despair. Someone then brought news from Carlsruhe that a certain M. M. had been arrested because of unauthorised begging & gross indecency. The news then reached Kauffmann's parents, who for some time had sheltered the said M. M. in their home. Mörike was informed. He was beside himself. Then one

---

[1] Jean Paul (1763–1825), the pseudonym of Johann Paul Friedrich Richter, a writer of eccentric and discursive novels, much admired by Schumann. Wolf initially found *Der Titan* difficult to digest, hurling the book to the ground in a fit of temper, but eventually the novel became one of his favourites. Wolf visited the novelist's grave in Bayreuth which he adorned with ivy and lilac leaves. He set himself the task of reading all the novels.
[2] See 'Peregrina 2', set by Othmar Schoeck.

day Mörike's lost love appeared early in the morning on the steps of the house where he lived, and although he still loved her, he turned her away. Hence 'a madness entered the moonlit gardens of a once sacred love'. How I now begin to understand these poems. Kauffmann then showed me the house where Mörike once lived, & so it was that I saw the steps on which the wretched poet encountered Peregrina for the last time. Is that not of huge interest?

And the demented Hölderlin, who lived & died in Tübingen, was said to have been Mörike's model for the Feuerreiter.

HW to his mother, Döbling, 23 December 1890

Liliencron, ein in Deutschland sehr renommirter Dichter, hat in dem Gedichtband („der Haidegänger") den ich Ihnen zusende auch mich poetisch gefeiert. Das letzte Gedicht „an Hugo Wolf" betitelt ist auf mich gemünzt u. ist es sehr liebenswürdig vom Poeten mich in so schmeichelhafter Weise in die Ewigkeit zu befördern. Vielleicht freut es Sie, daß Ihr Sohn Hugo bereits bei Lebzeiten angeflötet wird, was nach seinem Tode allerdings auch nicht ausbleiben wird. Aber dann würde mir's eben keinen Spaß mehr machen, während mich jetzt die Geschichte amusirt.

Liliencron, a poet very highly regarded in Germany, has celebrated me in verse in a volume of poetry ('Der Haidegänger') that I'm sending you. The last poem, called 'To Hugo Wolf', relates to me, & it is very sweet of the poet to bestow eternity on me in such a flattering way. Perhaps it will give you pleasure to know that your son Hugo is so lionised during his lifetime – something that will also occur after his death. Then, however, it will give me no pleasure, whereas now it amuses me.

HW to Emil Kauffmann, Döbling, 2 April 1892

An Fräulein Hohenschild war ich durch Freund Grohe empfohlen. Ich machte ihr auch einen Besuch, wurde aber nicht empfangen. Einer Einladung zum Thee nach einigen Tagen konnte ich leider nicht folgen – so ging ich dieser Bekanntschaft verlustig, die für mich gewiß sehr interessant gewesen wäre, denn ein Frauenzimmer, das für meine „Seufzer" schwärmt, muß schlechterdings interessant sein.

Fräulein Hohenschild was recommended to me by our friend Grohe. I paid her a visit but was not received. A few days later she invited me to tea but I was unable to go – I was therefore deprived of making her acquaintance, which would certainly have been of great interest to me, for a woman who enthuses for my 'Seufzer' must ipso facto be interesting.

HW to Siegfried Ochs, Döbling, 16 October 1892

Die Aufführung meines Elfenliedes[1] haben Sie mir halb u. halb schon zugesagt u. ich bin Ihnen dafür herzlich verbunden. Da dieses Stückchen jedoch nur von sehr kurzer Dauer ist, auch seines intimen Charakters wegen kaum eine nachhaltigere Wirkung erzielen dürfte, erlaube ich mir Ihnen vorzuschlagen ein Gegenstück zu demselben in's Programm aufzunehmen. Ich habe im Sommer die Mörike'sche Ballade „der Feuerreiter" für Chor u. grosses Orchester bearbeitet u. halte das Stück in seiner jetzigen Gewandung für äußerst effektvoll. Der Chor singt zum größeren Theil unisono, wodurch Ihnen die Arbeit des Einstudirens entschieden erleichtert wird. Auch an das Orchester werden keine übertriebenen Anforderungen gestellt.

You have half agreed to a performance of my 'Elfenlied', & I am extremely grateful. But as this little piece is of very short duration and can hardly be expected, because of its intimate character, to create any lasting impression, may I suggest that you perform a contrasting piece in the same programme. During the summer I arranged Mörike's ballad 'Der Feuerreiter' for chorus & large orchestra & consider the song in its present guise to be extremely effective. The chorus sings for the most part in unison which will make rehearsals easier. And no especial demands are put on the orchestra.

HW to Richard Sternfeld, Döbling, 20 October 1892

Hingegen scheint es mit der Freundschaft der Frau Herzog[2] zu mir nicht sehr weit her zu sein. Zwar höre ich, daß sie ab u. zu in verschiedenen Städten Deutschlands meine Sachen in ihr Programm aufnimmt, jedoch immer nur ganz vereinzelt, wodurch kein Mensch eine nur halbwegs klare Vorstellung von meiner Art gewinnen kann. Es kann mir nichts daran gelegen sein, gerade nur als Componist des „Gärtners" den Leuten zu gefallen. „Ein schönes Lied zu singen mocht manchem wohl gelingen."[3] Wozu habe ich an 200 Lieder veröffentlicht? Bitter beschwerte sich letzthin mein Freund Kauffmann in Tübingen, als Frau Herzog in Stuttgart nur ein Lied von Mörike sang. Gerade

---

1 Shakespeare's; see p. 468.
2 Emilie Herzog (1859–1923) was a celebrated coloratura soprano who specialised in Mozart roles and championed many of Wolf's songs. Wolf's comments are unfair, since contemporary programmes reveal that Herzog gave public performances of as many as 30 Wolf songs in cities such as Berlin, Stuttgart, Nuremberg, Prague and Vienna. In a private concert she sightread Mörike's 'Elfenlied' to perfection – which delighted Wolf. But in a letter of 30 October 1896 to Hugo Faisst Wolf expressed his bitterness that Herzog had never shown her gratitude.
3 A misquotation of Hans Sachs's couplet from *Die Meistersinger von Nürnberg*, Act III, scene 2: 'Ein schönes Lied zu singen/Mocht vielen da gelingen.' ('Many have succeeded in singing/A single beautiful song.')

in Stuttgart, wo der Mörike-Cultus mehr als irgendwo anders gepflegt wird, hätte Frau H. die Gelegenheit wahrnehmen können, eine ganze Serie aus meiner Sammlung vorzutragen.

On the other hand, Frau Herzog does not show any great signs of friendship. Although I hear that she occasionally programmes my pieces in various German cities, it's always just single songs – which can give no one even a partial idea of my style. Giving joy to people through a single song such as 'Der Gärtner' means nothing to me. 'Many have succeeded in singing one single beautiful song.' What is the point in my having published some 200 songs? My friend Kauffmann recently complained bitterly in Tübingen that Frau Herzog had sung only <u>one</u> Mörike song in Stuttgart. In Stuttgart of all places, where the Mörike cult is stronger than elsewhere, she could have grasped the opportunity to perform a whole series from the Mörike volume.

HW to Melanie Köchert, Vienna, 23 July 1894

Heute schickte mir ein Herr Georg Scherer[1] seine Gedichte aus München ein u. berief sich in einem beigelegten Schreiben auf seine innige Freundschaft mit Ed. Mörike. Inliegend das Schreiben des Betreffenden. Die Gedichte, ein allzu stattlicher Band, sind sehr schön ausgestattet, das ist aber auch das einzig Schöne an ihnen. Im Übrigen ein fades Gewinsel von Herz u. Schmerz, Liebe u. Triebe Thränen u. Flennen u. Sehnen u. Brennen u. was sonst noch als Trödel in der lyrischen Rumpelkammer zu holen ist – lauter wohlfeile Waare. Die Ausgabe ist sogar mit dem Bildniß des „Dichters" geschmückt. Nach der Phisage zu schließen dürfte der Herr Poet ein sehr guter Ehemann u. vortrefflicher Familienvater sein. Seine geistigen Kinder aber sind entschieden auf der Schulbank gezeugt. –

Today a certain Herr Georg Scherer sent me his poems from Munich, & referred in an accompanying letter to his close friendship with Ed. Mörike. I enclose his letter. The poems, an extremely handsome volume, have been beautifully printed, but that is the only beautiful thing about them. For the rest: an insipid moaning about heart, pain, love, passion, tears & snivelling & longing & desiring & whatever other junk can be found in the lumber room of poesy – nothing but cheap fare. The edition has even been adorned with a likeness of

---

[1] Georg Scherer (1828–1909) is best known to lovers of Lieder for his contribution to Brahms's 'Wiegenlied', the second verse of which features his adaptation of a folk song. As an anthologist he compiled a number of folksong volumes including *Deutsche Volkslieder* (1851) and *Die schönsten deutschen Volkslieder* (1868). In his accompanying letter Scherer expressed the wish, „daß eines oder das andere Lied Sie zur Vertonung anregen möge" ('that one or another of the poems might inspire you to compose a song'). As with Liliencron, Wolf did not bite.

the 'poet'. His mug suggests that the Poet is a good husband & splendid paterfamilias. His spiritual children, however, were clearly conceived on the school bench.

HW to Melanie Köchert, Matzen, 23 September 1894

Ab u. zu kommt Maler Rickelt[1] zum Vorschein u. bittet mich ihm etwas vorzuspielen. Meine humoristischen Lieder, namentlich die letzten von Mörike haben es ihm bisher am meisten angethan. Er war ganz erstaunt, daß dergleichen Texte in Musik gesetzt werden konnten. Im Übrigen ist er für Sachen leichtern Genres, wie die Fussreise, der Gärtner, u. dgl. zugänglicher, als für die mehr Vollwichtigen, was man ihm schließlich auch nicht verargen kann.

Rickelt the painter turns up occasionally and asks me to play him something. My humorous songs, especially the last ones in the Mörike volume, have till now affected him most. He was astonished that such texts could be set to music. For the rest, he finds lighter fare such as 'Fußreise', 'Der Gärtner' & the like more accessible than the weightier songs – and you cannot really hold that against him.

HW to Melanie Köchert, Matzen, 25 September 1894

Zugleich mit dem Bruckner'schen Schreiben kam auch eine Sendung von Kauffmann, ein Buch, betitelt: Ed. Mörike als Gelegenheitsdichter, mit zahlreichen erstmal gedruckten Gedichten Mörikes u. Zeichnungen von seiner Hand.[2] Ich habe es nur flüchtig durchgesehen u. köstliche Sachen vorgefunden.

There arrived at the same time as Bruckner's letter a parcel from Kauffmann with a book titled 'Ed. Mörike as Occasional Poet, with a large number of Mörike's poems & drawings published here for the first time'. I have skimmed through it & found some delightful things.

HW to Emil Kauffmann, Matzen, 26 September 1894

Faisst schrieb mir auch unter Anderm, daß der Herausgeber des Mörikebuchs ein Studienkollege von ihm gewesen sei u. er ihn recht gut kenne. Da wundert es mich nur, daß unter den „zahllosen" Componisten, die Mörikes Lieder

---

1 Karl Rickelt (1857–1919) was a painter friend of Wolf.
2 The book by Rudolf Krauss (1861–1945) is entitled *Mörike als Gelegenheitsdichter. Aus seinem Leben. Mit zahlreichen erstmals gedruckten Gedichten Mörikes und Zeichnungen von seiner Hand*, and was published in Stuttgart in 1895. Mörike was an accomplished draughtsman who made several skilful drawings of his friends. He was also adept at wood-carving, and chiselled an inscription on a cross for the grave of Schiller's mother in the graveyard of his church.

componirten meiner Wenigkeit so gar nicht gedacht wurde. Ich dächte in einer Biographie Mörikes vom Jahre 1894 dürfte mein Name doch schon Erwähnung finden. So unbekannt sind „wir", zumal im Schwabenlande, ja doch nicht. Faisst möge doch mit Herrn Rudolf Krauss ein Wörtlein darüber sprechen.

Faisst wrote to me among other things that the editor of the book on Mörike was a fellow student & knew him well. I find it strange though that among the 'numerous' composers who have set Mörike poems yours truly is not even mentioned. I should have thought that in a biography of Mörike published in 1894 my name would have at least been mentioned. After all, 'we' are not so unknown, especially in Swabia. Perhaps Faisst could have a little word with Herr Rudolf Krauss.

HW to Melanie Köchert, Perchtoldsdorf, 16 November 1894

Ich halte mich die meiste Zeit im Freien auf, da die Temperatur draußen wärmer ist als in meinem Zimmer.[1] Im windebangen Häuslein[2] sitzt sich's recht angenehm – ist auch ein schöner Aussichtspunkt u. bequem zu erreichen.

I spend most of the time out of doors because the temperature is warmer there than in my room. The Windebang summer-house, where it's most pleasant to sit, is a beautiful vantage point & easy to reach.

HW to Melanie Köchert, Matzen, 17 May 1895

Die Zeit verbrachte ich während der Fahrt zum Theil mit der Lektüre der Mörike'schen Briefe, von denen die erste Hälfte entschieden als schwach u. ziemlich uninteressant gelten darf.[3] Die andere Hälfte hat auch meinen Beifall gefunden, obschon ich mir die Briefe origineller u. geistreicher vorgestellt hatte. Ein gewißer altfränkischer Ton in ihnen drängt sich allzusehr vor. Wir „Modernen" empfinden eben anders. Ich glaube, wir hätten uns (Mörike & ich) doch nicht gut verstanden.

I spent part of the journey reading Mörike's letters, the first half of which must be considered to be decidedly weak & rather uninteresting. But I approved of the second half, although I had imagined them to be more original and entertaining. A certain old-fashioned tone in them is rather too prominent. We 'moderns' feel things differently. I think that we (Mörike & I) would not have understood each other well.

---

1 There was no running water in the Perchtoldsdorf house, and warmth was provided by a scarcely adequate tiled stove. The conditions were spartan.
2 See note 4 to 'Der Knabe und das Immlein', p. 368.
3 But see HW to Melanie Köchert, 15 October 1890, p. 355.

HW to Friedrich Eckstein, Vienna, 17 July 1896

Liebes Fritzchen! Bitte, bestimme einen Tag, an welchem ich die Seßel, das Tischchen u. das Bild von Mörike abholen laßen kann. Ich benöthige <u>dringend</u> die genannten Dinge.¹

Dear Fritzchen! Please name a day on which I can have the chairs, the small table and the portrait of Mörike delivered. I need these things <u>urgently</u>.

HW to Oskar Grohe, Vienna, 21 July 1896

Nietzsches Aussprüche über Mörike stammen wohl aus seiner unreifsten Zeit. Da sieht man wieder so recht, was für ein Unfug angestiftet wird mit dem in unserer Zeit zur Manie gewordenen Herausgeben des Nachlasses, Gott schütze einen vor solchen Leichenschändern.²

Nietzsche's remarks about Mörike probably stem from his most immature period. One can now see what mischief is caused by today's mania for publishing posthumous works. God protect us from such desecrators.

HW to Hugo Faisst, Vienna, 24 July 1896

Beiliegend sende ich Dir eine Expectoration Nietzsches über Mörike. Wie an so manchen Dingen (siehe Wagner) so hat dieser gewaltige Geist sich auch an Mörike vergriffen. Man traut seinen Augen nicht. [. . .]

---

1   A consequence of Wolf's habit of continually changing his address was to ask friends to store his belongings. It has been estimated that he lodged in some 35 different apartments while he lived in Vienna, and between 1875 and the summer of 1885 he changed apartment in the capital about thirty times. He could not abide noise and could work only in silence.
2   See Friedrich Nietzsche, *Werke II*. Abt. Bd. X. S. 410 (Werner). Nietzsche's polemic is published in the *Nachgelassene Fragmente* and was written in the summer of 1875, presumably occasioned by Mörike's death in June of that year. Discussing German lyrical poetry, he writes:

> Da lese ich, daß gar M ö r i k e der größte deutsche Lyriker sein soll! Ist es nicht ein Verbrechen dumm zu sein, wenn man hier also Goethe n i c h t als den größten empfindet oder empfinden will? – Aber was muß da in den Köpfen spuken, welcher Begriff von Lyrik! Ich sah mir darauf diesen Mörike wieder an und fand ihn, mit Ausnahme von 4–5 Sachen in der deutschen Volkslied-Manier, ganz schwach und undichterisch. Vor allem fehlt es an Klarheit der Anschauung. Und was die Leute an ihm musikalisch nennen, ist auch nicht viel: und zeigt w i e   w e n i g die Leute von Musik wissen: die m e h r ist als so ein süßliches-weichliches Schwimm-schwimm und Kling-kling!

> I read that *Mörike* of all people is supposed to be the greatest German poet! How criminally stupid it is *not* to recognise or to claim Goethe as the greatest. – What weird ideas must people have of what constitutes lyric poetry! Having read this article, I looked at Mörike again and found him, with the exception of 4 or 5 things in the German folksong manner, to be very weak and unpoetic. Above all he lacks clarity of vision. And when people call him musical, it also doesn't add up to much, and shows *how little* they understand about music, which is *more* than his wishy-washy, sing-song sort of poetry!

Heute habe ich eine meiner Wände mit einem wohlgelungenen Bildniß Mörikes (leider aus seinen letzten Tagen) geschmückt.

I enclose Nietzsche's tirade on Mörike. As in so many things (viz. his book on Wagner), this great mind has committed an indecent assault on Mörike. Unbelievable. [. . .]

Today I have adorned one of my walls with an excellent portrait of Mörike (unfortunately in his old age).

HW to Hugo Faisst, Vienna, 8 April 1897

Deine „trostlose Lage"[1] wird hoffentlich nicht von allzulanger Dauer sein, sonst tröste Dich mit dem Mörike Lied „wo find' ich Trost?"

I hope your 'desperate plight' will not last too long – if it does, comfort yourself with the Mörike song 'Wo find' ich Trost?'

HW to Edwin Mayser, Vienna, 1 June 1897

Freund Faisst scheint sich meine „Fussreise" sehr zu Herzen genommen zu haben, da er, freilich auch mit gelegentlicher Zuhilfenahme eines Coupés I. Classe-Blitzzug – der Neidenswerthe! – so rüstig in der Welt umherwandert.

Our friend Faisst seems to have taken my 'Fußreise' very much to heart, since he – how I envy him! – travels the world so intrepidly, with the occasional assistance of a first-class compartment in an express train.

LIEDER

The first edition of the *Gedichte* appeared in 1838. On 3 December 1841, Mörike wrote to Hartlaub:

> Ich habe neulich angefangen, meine Gedichte für den Fall einer neuen Ausgabe durchzugehen und [. . .] verschiedene Verbesserungen vorzunehmen. Am meisten schien mir deren die Romanze vom Feuerreiter und das Gedicht „Die Elemente" zu bedürfen. Beide sind noch in Tübingen im Jahre 1824 gemacht (die erstere im Sommer auf einem schönen Rasenplätzchen beim Philosophen-Brunnen, das andere im Winter). Diese Stücke genießen bei Freunden und Bekannten eines gewissen herkömmlichen Ansehens, das ohne Zweifel dazu beitrug, mich gegen ihre Fehler blind [. . .] zu machen.

Byron was similarly dismissive of Keats's poetry when, in a letter to John Murray from Ravenna in October 1820, he referred to 'Johnny Keats's *p-ss a bed* poetry' and his 'drivelling idiotism'.

1 Faisst's housekeeper was ill.

I've recently begun to go through my poems in the event of a new edition and [...] to make several improvements, which the 'Romanze vom Feuerreiter' and 'Die Elemente' seemed especially to need. Both were written in Tübingen during 1824 – the former in summer on a beautiful lawn by the Philosophers' Well, the latter in winter. These poems are held in the customary high regard by friends and acquaintances, which was partly responsible for making me blind to their defects.

It is always fascinating to see how a great poet polishes and refines his poems – for which reason the variants of the first edition have been indicated in the footnotes to each song. The somewhat archaic orthography of the first edition has been modernised. In the following examples, the original version appears in brackets: rot (roth), Tür (Thür), Träne (Thräne), Tal (Thal), Ängste (Aengste), Widerschein (Wiederschein), bar (baar), kopuliert (copulirt), Rezensent (Recensent) etc.

Suschens Vogel

Ich hatt' ein Vöglein, ach wie fein!
Kein schöners mag wohl nimmer sein:

Hätt auf der Brust ein Herzlein rot
Und sung und sung sich schier zu Tod.

Herzvogel mein, du Vogel schön,
Nun sollt du mit zu Markte gehn! –

Und als ich in[1] das Städtlein kam,
Er saß auf meiner Achsel zahm;

Und als ich ging am Haus vorbei
Des Knaben, dem ich brach die Treu',

Der Knab' just aus dem Fenster sah,
Mit seinem Finger schnalzt er da:

Wie horchet gleich mein Vogel auf!
Zum Knaben fliegt er husch! hinauf;

Der koset ihn so lieb und hold;
Ich wußt' nicht, was ich machen sollt,

Und stund, im Herzen so erschreckt,
Mit Händen mein Gesichte deckt',

Und schlich davon und weinet' sehr,
Ich hört' ihn rufen hinterher:[2]

Suzy's bird

I once had a bird, ah so exquisite!
No fairer bird could ever have been:

It had on its breast a little red heart
And sang and sang till it almost died.

O bird of my heart, you lovely bird,
You must now go to market with me! –

And as I entered the little town,
The bird sat tamely on my shoulder.

And when I went past the house
Of the boy, to whom I had been untrue,

That boy was looking from his window,
And suddenly he snaps his fingers:

How my bird pricked up its ears!
In a flash he flew up to the boy;

Who cuddled him with love and kindness;
I did not know what to do,

And stood there with a frightened heart,
And covered with my hands my face,

And crept away and wept and wept,
I heard him calling after me:

---

1   First edition (1838): durch.   2   First edition (1838): Mir war, als rief' es hinterher.

„Du falsche Maid, behüt' dich Gott,
Ich hab doch wieder mein Herzlein rot."

'You faithless girl, may God protect you!
I have once more my little red heart.'

Poem written 1837

Mausfallen-Sprüchlein[1]
Das Kind geht dreimal um die Falle und spricht:

Kleine Gäste, kleines Haus.
Liebe Mäusin oder Maus,[2]
Stell' dich nur kecklich ein
Heut nacht bei Mondenschein!
Mach' aber die Tür fein hinter dir zu,
Hörst du?*
Dabei hüte dein Schwänzchen!
Nach Tische singen wir,
Nach Tische springen wir
Und machen ein Tänzchen:§
Witt witt!†
Meine alte Katze tanzt wahrscheinlich mit.

Mousetrap incantation
The child walks three times round the trap and says:

Little guests, little house,
Dear Mrs or Mr Mouse,
Just drop in cheekily
Tonight by moonlight!
But be sure to close the door behind you,
Do you hear?*
And watch out for your tail!
After supper we'll sing,
After supper we'll prance
And do a little dance:§
Witt, witt!†
My old cat might well dance with us too.

Also set by Hugo Distler[3] and Emil Kauffmann
* Wolf repeats the phrase, and then again twice more after 'dein Schwänzchen!', and twice more at the end of the song.
§ Wolf repeats 'ein Tänzchen'.   † Wolf repeats the phrase.

1   Wolf wrote the song in Maierling for the light soprano voice of Mitzi Werner – he referred to her „Silberglöckchenstimmlein" (little silver bell of a voice) in a letter to Bertha von Lackhner of 15 June 1881. Mitzi was the sister of Heinrich and daughter of Hugo and Marie, who six years later put their house in Perchtoldsdorf at Wolf's disposal. The Werners were staying in Maierling at a house owned by Dr Joseph Reitzes and rented by the Preyss family: the Marienhof (now shamefully neglected). The twenty-two-year-old composer, who had been invited to stay at the Marienhof by Dr Reitzes, rehearsed the song with Mitzi, who, according to Wolf in a letter to Bertha von Lackhner of 21 October 1882, considered it „nicht des Ansehens werth" – not worthy of consideration (see HW to Bertha von Lackhner, 21 October 1882, p. 345). He also rehearsed the song with Paula von Goldschmidt, the wife of Adalbert von Goldschmidt, to whom he gave singing lessons. There is no song that better illustrates the composer's view expressed later in life that the early songs were to some extent already typical Wolf: „Man spürt schon das kleine Wölferl drin!" ('You can already detect the wolf-cub!') For publication details, see p. 4.
2   The first edition omits the first two lines and begins: „Muse=Mäuschen, stell' dich ein".
3   Hugo Distler (1908–1942), Chorus Master at the Musikhochschule in Stuttgart, composed his *Chorliederbuch* in 1937: settings of 48 Mörike poems for combined male and female choirs. They were first performed in Graz in 1939 and met with great success. Mörike, to judge from a letter to Hartlaub of 15 March 1850, would not have approved. He tells Hartlaub that he had recently been asked by Ludwig Roth to act as literary and musical adviser to a male choir, and that Roth would like his choir to sing, among other things, arrangements of Goethe's lyric poetry. Mörike writes to Hartlaub: „Allein die guten und besten Sachen dieser Art sind größtenteils von einem zarten subjektiven Charakter, und dieser würde nach meinem Gefühl durch eine Mehrzahl von Sängern [...] zerstört."

Die Tochter der Heide[1]

    Wasch' dich, mein Schwesterchen,
        wasch' dich!
Zu Robin's Hochzeit gehn wir heut:
Er hat die stolze Ruth gefreit.
Wir kommen ungebeten;
    Wir schmausen nicht, wir tanzen nicht,
Und nicht mit lachendem Gesicht
    Komm' ich vor ihn zu treten.*

    Strähl' dich, mein Schwesterchen,
        strähl' dich!
Wir wollen ihm singen ein Rätsel-Lied,
Wir wollen ihm klingen ein böses Lied;
    Die Ohren sollen ihm gellen.
Ich will ihr schenken einen Kranz
Von Nesseln und von Dornen ganz:
    Damit fährt sie zur Hölle!*

    Schick' dich, mein Schwesterchen,
        schmück dich!
Derweil sie alle sind am Schmaus,
Soll rot in Flammen stehn das Haus,
    Die Gäste schrein[2] und rennen.
Zwei sollen sitzen unverwandt,
Zwei hat ein Sprüchlein festgebannt;
    Zu Kohle müssen sie brennen!*

    Lustig, mein Schwesterchen, lustig!
Das war ein alter Ammensang.
Den falschen Rob vergaß ich lang.
    Er soll mich sehen lachen!

The daughter of the heath

    Wash yourself, my sister,
        wash yourself!
To Robin's wedding we'll go today:
He has wooed and won that proud Ruth.
We shall come uninvited;
    We shall not feast, we shall not dance,
And I shall not be laughing
    When I step before him.*

    Comb your hair, my sister,
        comb your hair!
We shall sing him a riddle,
We shall strike up a wicked song –
    The noise will shrill in his ears.
To her I'll give a wreath
Of nettles and thorns:
    She can wear it on her way to hell!*

    Make haste, my sister,
        adorn yourself!
While they are all at the feast,
The house shall burn red with flames,
    The guests shall scream and flee.
But two shall sit rooted to the spot,
Two shall be transfixed by a spell;
    They must burn to coal!*

    I was joking, my sister, joking!
That was an old wives' tale.
I've long forgotten faithless Rob.
    He shall see me laugh!

('But the best things of this kind are for the most part delicate and personal in character – and this would, I feel, be destroyed when performed by many singers.') He goes on to say that the only types of poem that lend themselves to choral treatment are war songs and songs for social gatherings. Distler set eighteen of the poems printed here.

1 Mörike explains in a letter of 3 September 1861 to Wilhelm Hartlaub that he wrote 'Die Tochter der Heide' to illustrate an English engraving that was to appear in *Freya*, a Stuttgart magazine published by Krais:

> Es ist eine ländliche Szene am Bach, ursprünglich mit der Unterschrift „Morgentoilette" und will sonst weiter nichts besagen. Doch hat das eigentümliche Gesicht des Mädchens etwas, das mich auf diesen Inhalt führte: Eine Art Pendant zu dem König Milesint mit halb scherzhafter Schlußwendung, worin doch noch ein Stachel von heftiger Eifersucht.

> The rustic scene by the brook is called 'The Morning Toilet', and is of little significance. But there was something about the girl's individual face that led me to pen this poem – a sort of pendant to King Milesint [Mörike's poem is called 'Die traurige Krönung'], with a half-playful ending that also bristles with violent jealousy.

2 Mörike: schreien.

NO STANZA BREAK

Hab' ich doch einen andern Schatz,	For I have got another lover,
Der mit mir tanzet auf dem Platz –	Who'll dance with me there –
Sie werden Augen machen!*	They shall be amazed!*

Poem written 1861
Also set by Distler
* Wolf repeats these lines.

Der König bei der Krönung[1]   The king at his coronation

Dir angetrauet am Altare,	Wedded to you at the altar,
O Vaterland, wie bin ich dein!	O Fatherland, I am wholly thine!
Laß für das Rechte mich und Wahre	Let me now be for what is right and true
Nun Priester oder Opfer sein![2]	Either priest or sacrifice!
Geuß auf mein Haupt, Herr! deine Schale,	Anoint my head, O Lord, from thy chalice
Ein köstlich Öl des Friedens, aus,	With precious oils of peace,
Daß ich wie eine Sonne strahle	That I, like a sun, may shine
Dem Vaterland und meinem Haus!	Upon my Fatherland and home!

Poem written before 1838
Also set by Ernst Friedrich Kauffmann and Max Reger

Gedichte von Eduard Mörike für eine Singstimme und Klavier
Poems by Eduard Mörike for voice and piano

The *Mörike-Lieder* were published by Wetzler at the beginning of March 1889 in ten Hefte (books) – much to the displeasure of Wolf, who felt that the songs should be contained in a single volume. During the nineteenth century it had become common practice to publish songs in this manner (*Die schöne Müllerin* had been divided into five books), and Wolf eventually allowed Wetzler to go ahead. He gave much thought to the order in which these songs appear, creating relatively coherent groups on different themes (love, religion, the supernatural, humour, etc.), while allowing for contrasts within each Heft. He bookends the collection with two deeply personal songs: 'Der Genesene an die Hoffnung', which celebrates his victory over creative inertia, and 'Abschied', which expresses his detestation of music critics.

---

1   In the autumn of 1887 Friedrich Eckstein, at Wolf's request, approached the Viennese publishing house of Emil Wetzler to try to interest the firm in the Lieder of his friend. Wolf then prepared two sets for publication: *Sechs Lieder für eine Frauenstimme* and *Sechs Gedichte von Scheffel, Mörike, Goethe und Just. Kerner*, which features 'Der König bei der Krönung' as the second song. See HW to Edmund Lang, 15 February 1888, p. 292. The song was composed on Wolf's twenty-sixth birthday. Goethe wrote a poem on a similar theme, 'Königlich Gebet' that Wolf set as No. 31 of his *Goethe-Lieder*.

2   The King, in 'Der letzte König von Orplid' from *Maler Nolten*, exclaims: „Ein König, ist er nicht ein Priester auch?" ('Is not a king also a priest?')

HEFT I

1 **Der Genesene an die Hoffnung**[1]

Tödlich graute mir der Morgen:
Doch schon lag mein Haupt, wie süß!
Hoffnung, dir im Schoß verborgen,
Bis der Sieg gewonnen hieß.*
Opfer bracht' ich allen Göttern,
Doch vergessen warest du;
Seitwärts von den ew'gen Rettern
Sahest du dem Feste zu.

O vergib, du Vielgetreue!
Tritt aus deinem Dämmerlicht,
Daß ich dir in's ewig neue,
Mondenhelle Angesicht
Einmal schaue recht von Herzen,
Wie ein Kind und sonder Harm;
Ach, nur Einmal[2] ohne Schmerzen
Schließe mich in deinen Arm!

Poem written 1838
* Wolf repeats this line.

2 **Der Knabe und das Immlein**[3]

Im Weinberg auf der Höhe
Ein Häuslein steht so windebang;[4]
Hat weder Tür noch Fenster,
Die Weile wird ihm lang.

BOOK I

He who has recovered addresses hope

Day dawned deathly grey:
Yet my head lay, how sweetly!
O Hope, safely hidden in your lap,
Till victory was reckoned won.*
I had made sacrifices to all the gods,
But you I had forgotten;
Aside from the eternal saviours
You gazed on at the feast.

Oh forgive, most true one!
Step forth from your twilight
That I, just once, might gaze
With all my heart
At your eternally new and moonbright face,
Like a child and without sorrow;
Ah, just *once*, without pain,
Enfold me in your arms!

The boy and the bee

On the hill-top vineyard
There stands a hut so wind-afraid,
It has neither door nor window
And feels time dragging by.

---

1 'Der Genesene an die Hoffnung' was placed by Wolf at the head of the Mörike volume, thus suggesting he had conquered his self-doubt and unlocked the creative block that had paralysed him since the death of his father in the spring of 1887. He could now look triumphantly to the future – the reason why he repeats „Bis der Sieg gewonnen hieß!" to an accompaniment that bristles with *fortissimi* and *sforzandi*. The poem has biographical significance for Mörike too: it was written in 1838, the year that saw the first edition of his poetry. Cf. Klopstock's 'Die Genesung'.
2 The capital letter denotes italics, which Wolf honours with a dotted crotchet.
3 See HW to Edmund Lang, 22 February 1888, p. 345.
4 For a description of the 'Häuslein Windebang', the little summer-house in Perchtoldsdorf where Wolf sketched many of his songs, see Heinrich Werner: *Hugo Wolf in Perchtoldsdorf*. For the sexual connotation of 'Weinberg', 'Häuslein', 'windebang', 'Garten' and 'Honig' – and the erotic nature of the whole poem – see Susan Youens: *Hugo Wolf and his Mörike Songs*. See also HW to Melanie Köchert, 16 November 1894, p. 361. 'Windebang', literally 'wind-anxious', is an appropriate word to describe the summer-house in the garden of Brunnergasse 26 in Perchtoldsdorf, where Wolf composed most of the *Mörike-Lieder*: it is situated, after all, on a little hill, at the mercy of winds.

Und ist der Tag so schwüle,	And when the day's so sultry
Sind all' verstummt die Vögelein,	And every little bird is silent,
Summt an der Sonnenblume	A solitary bee
Ein Immlein ganz allein.	Buzzes round the sunflower.
Mein Lieb hat einen Garten,	My sweetheart has a garden
Da steht ein hübsches Immenhaus:	With a pretty beehive in it:
Kommst du daher geflogen?	Is that where you've flown from?
Schickt sie dich nach mir aus?	Did she send you to me?
„O nein, du feiner Knabe,	'Oh no, you handsome boy,
Es hieß mich niemand Boten gehn;	No one bade me bear messages;
Dies Kind weiß nichts von Lieben,	This child knows nothing of love,
Hat dich noch kaum gesehn.	Has scarcely even noticed you.
Was wüßten auch die Mädchen,	'And what can girls know
Wenn sie kaum aus der Schule sind!	When hardly out of school!
Dein herzallerliebstes Schätzchen	Your beloved sweetheart
Ist noch ein Mutterkind.	Is still her mother's child.
Ich bring' ihm Wachs und Honig;	'I bring her wax and honey;
Ade! – ich hab' ein ganzes Pfund;	Farewell! I've gathered a whole pound.
Wie wird das Schätzchen lachen,	How your beloved will laugh,
Ihm wässert schon der Mund."	Her mouth's already watering.'
Ach, wolltest du ihr sagen,	Ah, if you'd be so kind to tell her,
Ich wüßte, was viel süßer ist:	I know of something much sweeter:
Nichts Lieblichers auf Erden	There's nothing lovelier on earth
Als wenn man herzt und küßt!*¹	Than when one hugs and kisses!*

Poem written 1837
Also set by Distler, Ludwig Hetsch and Robert Kahn
* Wolf repeats the final two lines.

'Windebang' is also a Swabian tautology, as in the phrase „wind und weh"' ('very anxiously'); and Jeremias Gotthelf in Chapter 36 of his novel of Swiss peasant life, *Der Bauernspiegel* (1837), uses a similar phrase, „wind und bange", to express anxiety: „Ihm ward wind und bange, mich fort zu schaffen." ('He became anxious to get rid of me.') The opening stanza is crucial for an understanding of the poem. Huts, even dilapidated ones, are not in real life wholly without doors or windows, nor are they 'bored'. The 'Häuslein', as Susan Youens explains, is an anthropomorphised symbol for the immature girl. The poem is about inexperience in love, about innocence and anxiety, both on the girl's part (who is 'hardly out of school') and the boy's, who longs for a consummated relationship. Typically for Mörike (viz. 'Begegnung', 'Nimmersatte Liebe', 'Der Gärtner', 'Erstes Liebeslied eines Mädchens' and 'Der Fluß'), 'Der Knabe und das Immlein' brims with understated sexual innuendo. 'My love has a garden' and 'honey' need no explanation; and 'Winde' is often in Mörike associated with passion (see 'Lied vom Winde').
1   Wolf often repeats the final phrase of a song as a sort of peroration. „Nichts Lieblichers auf Erden/Als wenn man herzt und küßt!", sung initially to a *pianissimo* dynamic, is marked *forte* and *hingebend* (with abandon) for the repeat.

3 Ein Stündlein wohl vor Tag[1]

Derweil ich schlafend lag,
Ein Stündlein wohl vor Tag,
Sang vor dem Fenster auf dem Baum

Ein Schwälblein mir, ich hört' es kaum,
Ein Stündlein wohl vor Tag:

Hör' an, was ich dir sag',
Dein Schätzlein ich verklag';
Derweil ich dieses singen tu',
Herzt er ein Lieb in guter Ruh',
Ein Stündlein wohl vor Tag.

O weh! nicht weiter sag'!
O still! nichts hören mag!
Flieg' ab! flieg' ab von meinem Baum!
– Ach, Lieb' und Treu' ist wie ein Traum
Ein Stündlein wohl vor Tag.

An hour before day

As I lay sleeping,
An hour before day,
A swallow sang to me – I could hardly
       hear it –
From a tree by my window,
An hour before day.

Listen well to what I say,
It's your lover I accuse:
While I'm singing this,
He's cuddling a girl in sweet repose,
An hour before day.

Alas! Don't say another word!
Be silent! I don't wish to hear!
Fly away! fly away from off my tree!
– Ah, love and fidelity are like a dream
An hour before day.

Poem written 1837
Also set by Eugen d'Albert, Distler, Robert Franz, Kahn, E. F. Kauffmann, Franz Lachner, Ludwig Thuille, Felix Weingartner and Eric(h) Zeisl

4 Jägerlied[2]

Zierlich ist des Vogels Tritt im Schnee,
Wenn er wandelt auf des Berges Höh':
Zierlicher schreibt Liebchens liebe Hand,
Schreibt ein Brieflein mir in ferne Land'.

In die Lüfte hoch ein Reiher steigt,
Dahin weder Pfeil noch Kugel fleugt:[3]

Huntsman's song

Daintily a bird steps in the snow
On the mountain heights,
Daintier still is my sweetheart's hand,
When she writes to me in far-off lands.

A heron soars high into the air,
Beyond the reach of shot or arrow:

---

1   Although 'Der Knabe und das Immlein' and 'Ein Stündlein wohl vor Tag' are not printed as a pair in any edition of Mörike's poems, Wolf clearly links them. The girl's lament in the second song is based on the same musical material as the opening page of 'Der Knabe und das Immlein'. Wolf intends a compressed narrative. The boy's innocent delight in hugging and kissing in the first song takes on a darker significance in the second: he does indeed delight in such dalliance – so much so that he is unfaithful to his sweetheart who in the second poem laments her lot. Compare Wolf's settings of Goethe's 'Die Spröde' and 'Die Bekehrte' (p. 154). Mörike's refrain, 'Ein Stündlein wohl vor Tag', derives from the first verse of 'Der ernsthafte Jäger' in Des Knaben Wunderhorn. The swallow as a harbinger of doom is a commonplace in German literature: see Immermann's 'Tristan und Isolde' and 'Radoslaus' in Herder's *Volkslieder*.
2   See HW to Edmund Lang, 22 February 1888, p. 345.
3   'Fleugt' is an older form of 'fliegt', creating here a good Swabian rhyme with 'steigt'. Cf. Walter's song at the beginning of Act III in Schiller's *Wilhelm Tell*:

>   Ihm gehört das Weite,   The wide-open spaces are his,
>   Was sein Pfeil erreicht,   Whatever his arrow reaches –

Tausendmal so hoch und so geschwind	The thoughts of faithful love
Die Gedanken treuer Liebe sind.¹	Are a thousand times as swift and high.

Poem written 1837
Also set by Distler, Hetsch, Kahn, E. F. Kauffmann, Robert Schumann and Weingartner

5 Der Tambour²   The drummer-boy

Wenn meine Mutter hexen könnt',	If my mother could work magic,
Da müßt' sie mit dem Regiment	She'd have to go with the regiment
Nach Frankreich, überall mit hin,	To France and everywhere,
Und wär' die Marketenderin.	And be the vivandière.
Im Lager, wohl um Mitternacht,	In camp, at midnight,
Wenn niemand auf ist als die Wacht,	When no one's up save the guard,
Und alles schnarchet, Roß und Mann,	And everyone's snoring, horses and men,
Vor meiner Trommel säß' ich dann:	Then I'd sit by my drum:
Die Trommel müßt' eine Schüssel sein,	My drum would be a bowl
Ein warmes Sauerkraut darein,	Of warm sauerkraut,
Die Schlegel Messer und Gabel,	Drumsticks a knife and fork,
Eine lange Wurst mein Sabel;	My sabre – a long sausage;
Mein Tschako wär' ein Humpen gut,	My shako would be a tankard
Den füll' ich mit Burgunderblut.³	Which I'd fill with red Burgundy.
Und weil es mir an Lichte fehlt,	And because I'd lack light,
Da scheint der Mond in mein Gezelt;	The moon would shine into my tent;
Scheint er auch auf Französ'ch herein,	And though it would shine in French,
Mir fällt doch meine Liebste ein:	I'd still think of my love:
Ach weh!* jetzt hat der Spaß ein End'!⁴	Oh dear!* There's an end to my fun!
– Wenn nur meine Mutter hexen könnt'!*	– If only my mother could work magic!*

Das ist seine Beute,	That is his prey,
Was da fleugt und kreucht.	Whether it flies or crawls.

1 In 1838 at a composer's request, Mörike added a third stanza, which he did not include in his Collected Poems. The song was arranged by Max Reger as part of his *12 Mörike-Lieder von Hugo Wolf für Pianoforte solo bearbeitet* (September 1905). Reger was a passionate admirer of Wolf's music. Apart from the *12 Mörike-Lieder* for piano solo, he orchestrated 'Und willst du deinen Liebsten sterben sehen' and 'Sterb' ich, so hullt in Blumen meine Glieder' from the *Italienisches Liederbuch*; 'Der Freund' and 'Das Ständchen' from the *Eichendorff-Lieder*; the ten sacred songs from the *Spanisches Liederbuch*; and four of the *Mörike-Lieder*. He also arranged Eichendorff's *Sechs geistliche Lieder für gemischten Chor* for male chorus, and dedicated to Wolf his own *12 Lieder für eine Singstimme*, Op. 51.
2 'Der Tambour' was the poem that unleashed Wolf's creative imagination after a long period of inactivity. He was amazed at the nature of this outpouring – see HW to Edmund Lang, 22 February 1888, p. 345. Mörike's poem exhibits several folksong characteristics such as dialect rhymes: 'könnt'/'Regiment', 'fehlt'/'Gezelt', 'End''/'könnt', etc.
3 First edition (1838): Gefüllet mit Burgunderblut.
4 Writing to Frieda Zerny on 3 March 1894 a few days after Melanie Köchert had discovered his affair with the singer, Wolf, while expressing his undying love for Frieda, contemplates suicide as the only way out of the impasse, and adapts this line from 'Der Tambour': „Hat doch dann der Spaß ein End'."

Poem written 1837
Also set by Distler
* Wolf repeats these phrases and ends the song with a repetition of the opening line.

HEFT II	**BOOK II**
6 Er ist's[1]	**Spring is here**
Frühling läßt sein blaues Band[2]	Spring lets its blue banner
Wieder flattern durch die Lüfte;	Flutter on the breeze again;
Süße, wohlbekannte Düfte	Sweet, well-remembered scents
Streifen ahnungsvoll das Land.	Drift portentously across the land.
Veilchen träumen schon,	Violets, already dreaming,
Wollen balde kommen.	Will soon begin to bloom.
– Horch, von fern ein leiser Harfenton![3]	– Listen, the soft sound of a distant harp!
Frühling, ja du bist's![4]	Spring, that must be you!
Frühling, ja du bist's!	Spring, that must be you!
Dich hab' ich vernommen!	It's you I've heard!

Poem written March 1829
Also set by d'Albert, Carl Bohm, Distler, Franz, Kahn, E. F. Kauffmann, Lachner, Reger, Othmar Schoeck, Schumann, Pauline Viardot and Weingartner

1   Mörike wrote the poem on 9 March 1829 during a walk at Pflummern and included it, without title, in *Maler Nolten*, where it is sung by Nolten. Convalescing from an illness, he hears the words (introduced as the first verse of a song) sung by the prison warder's daughter. Her rapture at the approach of spring is expressed through sight („blaues Band"), smell and touch („Düfte streifen") and hearing („Harfenton"); Wolf responds with a tremulous song that charges along. The narrative runs: „Die Strophen bezeichneten ganz jene zärtlich aufgeregte Stimmung, womit die neue Jahreszeit den Menschen, und den Genesenden weit inniger als den Gesunden, heimzusuchen pflegt." ('The verses captured perfectly the mood of tender excitement that the new season is wont to visit on people – affecting the convalescent more profoundly than the healthy man.') In 1844 Mörike prepared a manuscript copy of his poems for the King of Prussia (it has become known as the 'Königshandschrift'), in which he changed the title of 'Er ist's' to 'Frühlingsgefühl'.
2   There is an echo here of Siegmund's „Auf lach ich in heiliger Lust" from Act I, scene 3 of *Die Walküre*.
3   A reference to the fact that itinerant musicians in early nineteenth-century Swabia would emerge from the towns at the onset of spring to ply their trade in the countryside. 'The soft sound of a distant harp' has no connection here with the Aeolian harp of 'An eine Äolsharfe'.
4   In the first edition of *Gedichte* and in the first version (but not the second) of *Maler Nolten*, Mörike repeats and indents the line; and Wolf, in keeping with the exultant tone of the poem, ends the song with another euphoric „ja du bist's!"

7 **Das verlassene Mägdlein**[1] **The forsaken servant-girl**

Früh, wann die Hähne krähn,[2]
Eh' die Sternlein schwinden,[3]
Muß ich am Herde stehn,
Muß Feuer zünden.

Schön ist der Flammen Schein,
Es springen die Funken;
Ich schaue so darein,
In Leid versunken.

Plötzlich, da kommt es mir,
Treuloser Knabe,
Daß ich die Nacht von dir
Geträumet habe.

Träne auf Träne dann
Stürzet hernieder;
So kommt der Tag heran –
O ging' er wieder!

Early at cockcrow,
Before the tiny stars fade,
I must be at the hearth,
Must light the fire.

The flames are beautiful,
The sparks fly;
I gaze at them,
Sunk in sorrow.

Suddenly I realise,
Faithless boy,
That in the night
I dreamt of you.

Tear after tear
Now tumbles down;
So the day dawns –
Oh that it were gone again!

Poem written May 1829
Also set by Distler, Franz, Robert Fuchs, Hetsch, Lachner, Eduard Lassen, Hans Pfitzner, Carl Reinicke, Schumann and Viardot

---

1 'Das verlassene Mägdlein' also appears in *Maler Nolten*, where it is sung, like 'Er ist's', by the daughter of the prison warder, whose voice resembles that of Agnes, to whom Nolten has been unfaithful. Hearing the song, he is moved to tears. The bleakness of the poem is especially evident in verse 1, in which the first and third lines and the second and fourth do not rhyme. Wolf's extraordinary setting intensifies the torment of the poem: the bleak opening melody limps along in A minor, and the succession of cold sevenths and cheerless chords of augmented fifths combine to make this one of the saddest of all his Lieder. The theme of infidelity surfaces again and again in Mörike's poems – a consequence of his rejection by Maria Meyer – see HW to Melanie Köchert, 15 October 1890, p. 355. Wolf greatly admired Schumann's setting of the same poem, describing it as 'himmlisch' – see HW to Friedrich Eckstein, 27 March 1888, p. 351.
2 Wolf quotes the opening six bars of the song in a letter to Melanie Köchert of 19 September 1894 to depict his own sombre mood. Note the aptness of the cock as a symbol of betrayal (Matthew 26:34). The harshness (in this context) of the ä assonance ('Hähne'/'krähn') is similar to Rilke's use of the same sound to suggest the despair of the caged panther in 'Der Panther' from *Neue Gedichte*:

Ihm ist, als ob es tausend Stäbe gäbe
Und hinter tausend Stäben keine Welt.

He thought there were a thousand bars
And beyond a thousand bars no world.

3 Wolf's source for this song was probably Schumann's setting of the same words. Like Schumann, Wolf changed Mörike's 'verschwinden' to 'schwinden' and, in the third stanza, 'drein' to 'darein'.

8 Begegnung[1]

Was doch heut Nacht ein Sturm gewesen,
Bis erst der Morgen sich geregt!
Wie hat der ungebetne Besen
Kamin und Gassen ausgefegt!

Da kommt ein Mädchen schon die Straßen,
Das halb verschüchtert um sich sieht;
Wie Rosen, die der Wind zerblasen,
So unstet ihr Gesichtchen glüht.

Ein schöner Bursch tritt ihr entgegen,
Er will ihr voll Entzücken nahn:
Wie sehn sich freudig und verlegen
Die ungewohnten Schelme an!

Er scheint zu fragen, ob das Liebchen
Die Zöpfe schon zurecht gemacht,
Die heute Nacht im offnen Stübchen
Ein Sturm in Unordnung gebracht.

Der Bursche träumt noch von den Küssen,
Die ihm das süße Kind getauscht,
Er steht, von Anmut hingerissen,
Derweil sie um die Ecke rauscht.

Poem written 1829
Also set by E. F. Kauffmann and Reger

Encounter

What a storm there was last night,
It raged until this morning dawned!
How that uninvited broom
Swept the streets and chimneys clean!

Here comes a girl along the street,
Glancing about her, half afraid;
Like roses the wind has scattered,
Her pretty cheeks keep changing colour.

A handsome lad steps up to meet her,
Approaches her full of bliss,
How joyfully and awkwardly
Those novice rascals exchange looks!

He seems to ask if his sweetheart
Has tidied up her plaited locks,
That last night a storm dishevelled
In her open-windowed room.

The lad's still dreaming of the kisses
The sweet child exchanged with him,
He stands enraptured by her charm,
As she whisks round the corner.

9 Nimmersatte Liebe[2]

So ist die Lieb'! So ist die Lieb'!
Mit Küssen nicht zu stillen:
Wer ist der Tor und will ein Sieb
Mit eitel Wasser füllen?

Insatiable love

Such is love! Such is love!
Not to be quieted with kisses:
What fool would fill a sieve
With nothing else but water?

---

1 The poem is drenched in sexual innuendo: „Was doch heut Nacht ein Sturm gewesen" refers obliquely to their lovemaking: 'Besen' in the nineteenth century also meant 'prick', 'cock' („Unter dem Besen getraut sein" = 'to live in sin'); 'fegen', 'to screw'; 'Gasse', 'vagina' (Mörike would have known Goethe's lubricious Venetian Epigram (No. 5b) „In dem engsten der Gäßchen"); „Im offenen Stübchen" corresponds to the old-fashioned English description of the vagina as a chamber. There is nevertheless, as in 'Nimmersatte Liebe', an exquisite delicacy about the poem. Cf. 'Das Wiedersehen am Brunnen' from *Des Knaben Wunderhorn*.

2 As Wolf tells Edmund Lang (see HW to Edmund Lang, 24 February 1888, p. 347), 'the end breaks out into a regular student's song – nothing could be more jolly'. There is nothing romantic about this poem or music. It might seem surprising to us that a twenty-four-year-old curate should write such erotic verse, but Mörike, like another man of God, John Donne, had a highly developed sensual side of which he was sometimes painfully aware – see 'Verborgenheit', 'Gebet' and HW to Emil Kauffmann, 5 June 1890, p. 355. The poem, like 'Frage und Antwort' and 'Erstes Liebeslied eines Mädchens', was probably inspired by Mörike's love for Josephine, a village schoolmaster's daughter.

NO STANZA BREAK

Und schöpfst du an die tausend Jahr',	And if you drew water for some thousand years,
Und küssest ewig, ewig gar,	And if you kissed for ever and ever –
Du tust ihr nie zu Willen.	You could never satisfy love.
Die Lieb', die Lieb' hat alle Stund	Love, love, has every hour
Neu wunderlich Gelüsten;	New and strange desires;
Wir bissen uns die Lippen wund,	We bit our lips sore,
Da wir uns heute küßten.	When we kissed today.
Das Mädchen hielt in guter Ruh',	The girl kept quiet and still,
Wie's Lämmlein unterm Messer;	Like a lamb beneath the knife;
Ihr Auge bat: nur immer zu,	Her eyes kept pleading: Go on, go on!
Je weher, desto besser!	The more it hurts the better!
So ist die Lieb', und war auch so,	Such is love, and has been so
Wie lang es Liebe gibt,	As long as love's existed,
Und anders war Herr Salomo,[1]	And wise old Solomon himself
Der Weise, nicht verliebt.	Was no differently in love.

Poem written 1828
Also set by d'Albert and Distler

10 Fußreise[2] — A journey on foot

Am frischgeschnittnen Wanderstab,	When, with freshly cut staff,
Wenn ich in der Frühe	I set off early like this
So durch Wälder ziehe,	Through the woods
Hügel auf und ab:	And over the hills:
Dann, wie's Vöglein[3] im Laube	Then, as the bird in the branches
Singet und sich rührt,	Sings and stirs,
Oder wie die goldne Traube	Or as the golden cluster of grapes
Wonnegeister spürt	Senses the spirits of delight

---

1   'But King Solomon loved many strange women [. . .] and he had seven hundred wives, princesses, and three hundred concubines' (1 Kings 11:1–3). Wolf repeats the final two lines, but cleverly varies the prosody. They should be sung initially in one breath, but the singer, when repeating the phrase, must heed Wolf's delightfully saucy semiquaver rest before 'verliebt'.
2   'Fußreise', which sings the glories of creation, quickly became one of Wolf's most popular songs, and he was clearly delighted with it: see HW to Edmund Lang and to Franz Schalk, both 21 March 1888, p. 350. To Richard Sternfeld (HW to Richard Sternfeld, 20 October 1892, p. 358), however, he fulminates against those artists who always perform the most popular songs without exploring the rest of his repertoire. Wolf considered 'Fußreise' to be one of his humorous songs (HW to Melanie Köchert, 23 September 1894, p. 360) and objected to those singers and pianists who chose too fast a tempo. He once said that the Styrian dialect verb 'schlenzen' ('to saunter') best described the tempo he had in mind – although his own marking is *ziemlich bewegt* (appropriately fast). It would have been fascinating to hear the tempo chosen during the first performance of the song on 15 December 1888 in Vienna, when Wolf, in his first public appearance as a pianist, accompanied Ferdinand Jäger. The song was arranged by Max Reger as part of his *12 Mörike-Lieder von Hugo Wolf für Pianoforte solo bearbeitet* (September 1905).
3   Mörike: Vögelein.

In der ersten Morgensonne:	In the early morning sun –
So fühlt auch mein alter, lieber	So the old Adam in me
Adam Herbst- und Frühlingsfieber,	Feels autumn and spring fever,
Gottbeherzte,	The God-inspired,
Nie verscherzte	Never forfeited
Erstlings=Paradieseswonne.	Primal bliss of Paradise.
Also bist du nicht so schlimm, o alter	So you are not as bad, old
Adam, wie die strengen Lehrer sagen;	Adam, as strict teachers say;
Liebst und lobst du immer doch,	You still love and extol,
Singst und preisest immer noch,	Always sing and praise
Wie an ewig neuen Schöpfungstagen,	Your dear Maker and Preserver,
Deinen lieben Schöpfer und Erhalter.	As if Creation were ever new each day.
Möcht' es dieser geben,	May He grant it so,
Und mein ganzes Leben	And my whole life
Wär' im leichten Wanderschweiße	Would be, gently perspiring,
Eine solche Morgenreise![1]	Just such a morning journey!

Poem written September 1828

HEFT III

BOOK III

11 An eine Äolsharfe[2]

Tu semper urges flebilibus modis
Mysten ademptum: nec tibi Vespero

Surgente decedunt amores,
Nec rapidum fugiente Solem.

To an Aeolian harp

But thou in tearful strains dwellest ever
On the loss of thy Mystes; nor do thy loving words cease
When Vesper appears
Or when he flees the swiftly coursing Sun.
             Horace (*Odes* II, No. IX ll. 9–12)

---

1 Wolf was a keen hiker and lover of nature. He made regular sorties into the countryside from most of the places where he lived: St Paul, Maierling, Gmunden, Rinnbach am Traunsee, Schloss Gstatt, Murau, Perchtoldsdorf, Matzen, Urach ... While staying at Urach, he went on a pilgrimage with Emil Kauffmann and Wilhelm Schmid, visiting hallowed Mörike sites connected with Mörike's 'Besuch in Urach'. Might they have sung 'Fußreise' en route? Many of the titles Wolf chose for his songs contain the theme of wandering: 'Wanderers Nachtlied', 'Wanderlied', 'Nächtliche Wanderung', 'Auf der Wanderschaft', 'Auf der Wanderung', 'Auf einer Wanderung'.
2 'An eine Äolsharfe' was indirectly inspired by the Horace ode addressed to Valgius Rufus on the death of Mystes, probably a favourite slave, but the actual subject is the loss thirteen years earlier of Mörike's brother who lies beneath the „frisch grünendem Hügel". Mörike prefaced his poem with verse 3 of Horace's Ode (No. IX from Book II), which serves as a sort of reprimand to those who grieve too long – Mörike's grief at August's death was deep and enduring, and he kept referring to it years later in letters and conversations. The setting for the poem is Ludwigsburg. In a letter to

Angelehnt an die Epheuwand	Leaning against the ivy-clad wall
Dieser alten Terrasse,	Of this old terrace,
Du, einer luftgebornen Muse	O mysterious lyre
Geheimnisvolles Saitenspiel,	Of a zephyr-born Muse,
Fang' an,	Begin,
Fange wieder an	Begin again
Deine melodische Klage!	Your melodious lament!
Ihr kommet, Winde, fern herüber	You winds have come hither from far away,
Ach! von des Knaben,	Ah! from the freshly greening mound
Der mir so lieb war,	Of the boy
Frisch grünendem Hügel.	Who was so dear to me.
Und Frühlingsblüten unterweges streifend,	And caressing spring flowers along the way,
Übersättigt mit Wohlgerüchen,	Saturated with fragrance,
Wie süß*¹ bedrängt ihr dies Herz!	How sweetly* you afflict this heart!
Und säuselt her in die Saiten,	And you murmur into these strings,
Angezogen von wohllautender Wehmut,	Drawn by their sweet-sounding sorrow,
Wachsend im Zug meiner Sehnsucht,	Waxing with my heart's desire,
Und hinsterbend wieder.	Then dying away once more.
Aber auf einmal,	But all at once,
Wie der Wind heftiger herstößt,	As the wind gusts more strongly,
Ein holder Schrei der Harfe	The harp's exquisite cry
Wiederholt, mir zu süßem Erschrecken,	Echoes, to my sweet alarm,
Meiner Seele plötzliche Regung;	The sudden commotion of my soul;
Und hier – die volle Rose streut, geschüttelt,	And here – the full-blown rose, shaken,
All' ihre Blätter vor meine Füße!	Strews all its petals at my feet!

Poem written 1837
Also set by Johannes Brahms and E. Kauffmann
* Wolf twice repeats „wie süß".

---

his fiancée Luise Rau, dated 14 May 1831, Mörike describes an Aeolian harp that he had seen at the Emichsburg in the grounds of the Schloss, telling her how 'the sweet tones fused the entire past within me' („die süßen Töne schmolzen alles Vergangene in mir auf"). The harp was placed by the ivy-covered wall; August's grave was in the distant cemetery, and the grounds between the two were covered with fruit trees. Mörike would also have seen the celebrated Aeolian harp owned by Justinus Kerner. Wolf heard an Aeolian harp for the first time when he visited the castle of Hoch-Osterwitz in Carinthia during the summer of 1888 a few months after his song was composed. His setting is fittingly elegiac in mood, with *pianissimo* arpeggios in the accompaniment depicting the wind playing through the Aeolian harp.
1   Was Wolf's double repetition of „wie süß" inspired by the Brahms setting (Op. 19/5), which repeats the phrase only once?

12 Verborgenheit[1]

Laß, o[2] Welt, o laß mich sein!
Locket nicht mit Liebesgaben,
Laßt dies Herz alleine haben
Seine Wonne, seine Pein!

Was ich traure weiß ich nicht,
Es ist unbekanntes Wehe;
Immerdar durch Tränen sehe
Ich der Sonne liebes Licht.

Oft bin ich mir kaum bewußt,
Und die helle Freude zücket
Durch die Schwere, so mich drücket
Wonniglich[3] in meiner Brust.

Laß, o Welt, o laß mich sein!
Locket nicht mit Liebesgaben,
Laßt dies Herz alleine haben
Seine Wonne, seine Pein![4]

Withdrawal

Let, O world, O let me be!
Do not tempt with gifts of love,
Let this heart keep to itself
Its rapture, its pain!

Why I grieve, I do not know,
It is unknown grief;
Always through a veil of tears
I see the sun's dear light.

Often when I'm lost in thought,
Bright joy will flash
Through the oppressive gloom,
Bringing rapture to my breast.

Let, O world, O let me be!
Do not tempt with gifts of love,
Let this heart keep to itself
Its rapture, its pain!

Poem written 1832
Also set by Willy Burkhard, Distler, Franz, Fuchs and Lassen

1 Written in 1832, almost a decade after his first meeting with Maria Meyer (1823), the poem is an ardent plea to be spared the destructive eruptions of passion that bring nothing but pain: the insistent assonance, alliteration, sibilants and repetitions of the opening two lines eloquently suggest Mörike's resolve to steer clear of further emotional entanglements. Because of its melodic immediacy, this was the first Wolf song to become popular and has, for that reason, been belittled by some commentators, who consider it too sentimental. Unjustly so. Any sentimental rendering of 'Verborgenheit' has more to do with the performers' own lachrymose approach than the song itself, which treats the text with admirable control, particularly in the gradually deepening harmonic colour of the verse beginning „Oft bin ich mir kaum bewußt", which mirrors perfectly the heightening emotion of the poem.
2 'Verborgenheit' is sometimes wittily described as the Cowboy Song in German-speaking countries, because of the unfortunate propensity of non-German singers to sing the first two words without a glottal stop. ('Lasso' = 'lasso' in English.)
3 The adverb 'wonniglich' qualifies 'Freude zücket'.
4 The song was composed on Wolf's twenty-eighth birthday. Mörike's poem, with its blend of rapture and melancholy, would have appealed to the composer who suffered keenly from mood swings. He was delighted at the success of 'Verborgenheit', but later became disillusioned with this great song. He wrote to Karl Mayr that he considered it to be 'abgedroschen' – trite. See HW to Karl Mayr, 15 March 1897, p. 285. In a letter to Paul Müller of 16 May 1898, he referred to it, along with 'Fußreise' and 'Der Gärtner', as „Vorspeise leichtere[r] Kost" – a rather light hors d'œuvre. And Grohe, in a letter to Ernst Decsey (Wolf's first biographer) of 26 September 1904, described Wolf's fury at the way singers programmed 'Verborgenheit' rather than other songs of his: „Immer singen's, als wenn ich nix Anderes geschrieben hätte. Einstampfen laß ich das Lied noch." ('They always sing it, as though I had written nothing else. I shall have it pulped.')

13 Im Frühling[1]

Hier lieg' ich auf dem Frühlingshügel:
Die Wolke wird mein Flügel,
Ein Vogel fliegt mir voraus.
Ach, sag' mir, alleinzige Liebe,
Wo du[2] bleibst, daß ich bei dir bliebe!
Doch du und die Lüfte, ihr habt kein Haus.[3]

Der Sonnenblume gleich steht
    mein Gemüte offen,
Sehnend,
Sich dehnend
In Liebe und Hoffen.
Frühling, was bist du gewillt?
Wann werd' ich gestillt?

Die Wolke seh' ich wandeln und den Fluß,
Es dringt der Sonne goldner Kuß
Mir tief bis in's Geblüt hinein;
Die Augen, wunderbar berauscht,
Tun, als schliefen sie ein,
Nur noch das Ohr dem Ton der Biene
    lauschet.

Ich denke dies und denke das,
Ich sehne mich, und weiß nicht recht,
    nach was:
Halb ist es Lust, halb ist es Klage;
Mein Herz, o sage,

In spring

Here I lie on the springtime hill:
The clouds serve as my wings,
A bird flies ahead of me.
Ah tell me, one-and-only love,
Where you are, that I might be with you!
But you and the breezes, you have no home.

Like a sunflower my soul lies open,

Yearning,
Expanding
In love and hope.
Spring, what is your will?
When shall I be stilled?

I see the clouds drift by, the river too,
The sun kisses its golden glow
Deep into my veins;
My eyes, wondrously enraptured,
Close, as if in sleep,
Only my ears still catch the hum of the bee.

I muse on this, I muse on that,
I yearn, and yet for what I cannot say:

It is half joy, half lament;
Tell me, O heart,

---

1 Written in a single sitting at Scheer on 13 May 1828, Mörike sent the poem in a letter to his friend Johannes Mährlen in which he describes the setting and the gestation of the poem:

> Hier sitz' ich und schreib' ich in dem besonnten Garten des hiesigen katholischen Pfarrers. Die Laube, wo mein Tisch und Schreibzeug steht, läßt durch's junge Geißblatt die Sonne auf mein Papier spielen. Der Garten liegt etwas erhöht; über die niedrige Mauer weg, auf der man sich, wie einem Gesimse, setzen kann, sieht man unmittelbar auf den Wiesenplan. [. . .]

> Here I sit and write in the sunny garden of the local Catholic priest. The arbour, with my desk and writing things, allows the sun to filter through the young honeysuckle and play on my paper. The garden is situated rather high; over a low wall, on which one can sit like on a ledge, you have an unimpeded view onto the meadow. [. . .]

In *Maler Nolten*, Nolten feels „eine mächtige Sehnsucht [. . .] ein süßer Drang nach einem namenlosen Gute, das ihn allenthalben aus den rührenden Gestalten der Natur so zärtlich anzulocken und doch wieder in eine unendliche Ferne sich ihm zu entziehen schien" ('a mighty yearning [. . .] a sweet urge to reach a nameless good that seemed to beckon so gently through the moving forms of nature all around him and yet retreat into the infinite distance'). Mörike then quotes 'Im Frühling'.

2 First edition (1838): italicised 'd u'.
3 First edition (1838): Doch du und die Lüfte, sie haben kein Haus.

Was webst du für Erinnerung
In golden grüner Zweige Dämmerung?
– Alte unnennbare Tage![1]

What memories you weave
Into the twilit green and golden leaves?
– Past, unutterable days!

Poem written 13 May 1828

14 Agnes[2]

Rosenzeit! wie schnell vorbei,
    Schnell vorbei
Bist du doch gegangen!
Wär' mein Lieb nur blieben treu,
    Blieben treu,
Sollte mir nicht bangen.

Um die Ernte wohlgemut,
    Wohlgemut,
Schnitterinnen singen.
Aber, ach! mir krankem[3] Blut,
    Mir krankem Blut
Will nichts mehr gelingen.

Agnes

Time of roses! How swiftly by,
    Swiftly by
You have sped!
Had my love but stayed true,
    Stayed true,
I should feel no fear.

Cheerfully at harvest time,
    Cheerfully,
Reaping women sing.
But ah! I'm sick,
    Sick at heart
I fail at everything.

---

1   This famous line is fraught with biographical complexity. Does it refer to the still-persisting torment caused by the rupture with Maria Meyer? Or not? Mörike wrote another letter to Mährlen on 20 July 1828, in the postscript of which he stated in block capitals: „IN REBUS AMATORIIS HIC MULTUM, AT NEQUAQUAM PERICLITANDO PROFECI." ('In amorous matters I have, without risking anything, made good progress here.') It seems likely that he had an affair with Josephine, the daughter of the Catholic schoolmaster (mentioned in the letter above) in Scheer. Was it she who triggered the feeling of intense longing that we read in the poem? 'Unnennbare' has a double meaning, one positive ('inexpressible', 'ineffable') and one negative ('unutterable', 'unmentionable'); and the way Wolf sets the word (a *pianissimo crescendo* then *decrescendo* and descending phrase) suggests trauma, unutterable horror at the past (the spectre of Maria Meyer). Friedrich Eckstein wrote a famous book of memoirs, chronicling his encounters in the late nineteenth century with such figures as Bruckner, Chopin, Freud, von Hofmannsthal, Liszt, Mahler, Nietzsche, Twain, Wagner, Wolf and others. He called the volume „*Alte unnennbare Tage!*", where 'unnennbare' is best translated as 'ineffable'. The chapters on Wolf are required reading for anyone interested in his character.

2   The poem appears in *Maler Nolten* where it is sung by Agnes herself, who expresses her fear that Nolten might desert her. She is invited to sing and pointedly chooses a text as a plea to Nolten for fidelity. Mörike tells us that her voice was stronger in the lower than the upper register and that, having finished the song, she threw herself on Nolten's breast and cried, with quivering body and flooding tears: „Treu! Treu!" ('Fidelity! Fidelity!') We are also told that the prelude expressed 'the most profound and moving lament', and that the melody at the refrain 'took a turn impossible to describe, and seemed to express all the sadness and grief that could possibly lie concealed in the bosom of an unhappy creature'. Wolf's setting retains the folk-song-like flavour present in the original poem and, from the heavy minor ninths of the prelude on, expresses a wistfulness that can be overwhelming in a not too arty performance. Agnes, in addition to reciting a verse of 'Gebet', sings six songs in *Maler Nolten*, for which Wolf supplied titles: 'Agnes', 'Der Jäger', 'Lied vom Winde', 'Seufzer', 'Neue Liebe' and 'Wo find' ich Trost?' – see the notes to all these songs.

3   Mörike: kranken.

Schleiche so durch's Wiesental,	So I steal through the meadow vale,
So durch's Tal,	Meadow vale,
Als im Traum verloren,	As if lost in dreams,
Nach dem Berg, da tausendmal,	Up to where a thousand times,
Tausendmal	Thousand times,
Er mir Treu' geschworen.	He promised to be true.
Oben auf des Hügels Rand,	Up there on the hillside,
Abgewandt,	Turning away,
Wein' ich bei der Linde;	I weep by the lime tree;
An dem Hut mein Rosenband,	On my hat the rosy ribbon,
Von seiner Hand,	A gift from him,
Spielet in dem Winde.	Flutters in the wind.

Poem written 1831
Also set by Brahms, Distler, Franz, Hetsch, Ferdinand Hiller, E. F. Kauffmann and Viardot

15 Auf einer Wanderung[1]   On a walk

In ein freundliches Städtchen[2] tret' ich ein,	I arrive in a friendly little town,
In den Straßen liegt roter Abendschein.	The streets glow in red evening light.
Aus einem offnen Fenster eben,	From an open window,
Über den reichsten Blumenflor	Across the richest array of flowers
Hinweg, hört man Goldglockentöne schweben,	And beyond, golden bell-chimes come floating,
Und Eine[3] Stimme scheint ein Nachtigallenchor,	And *one* voice seems a choir of nightingales,

1   Mörike's 'Auf zwei Sängerinnen' (12 August 1841) introduces us to two travellers who wax lyrical about the beautiful voice of Marie Mörike, wife of cousin Karl. Three years later in 1845 Mörike wrote 'Auf einer Wanderung' which in lines 3–9 quotes a purple passage from the first poem. Marie's voice is referred to in line 6: „Und Eine Stimme scheint ein Nachtigallenchor". The second verse is new and describes how Mörike was affected by the intoxicating beauty of nature and music. Wolf took a fortnight to compose his song – a rarity with a composer who would often compose several songs a day; as in 'Im Frühling', he abandons the strophic form and lets the voice declaim the poem with a new-found freedom. The 6/8 rhythm of the piano's opening bar dominates the entire song in a series of miraculous transformations, while the vocal line weaves its way in and out of this texture, highlighting some phrases, musing on others. The unmistakable influence of Wagner is apparent – Wagner who once said that there were not „gesangliche oder deklamierte Stellen" in his operas, but that in his music 'declamation was song and song declamation'.
2   The town in question is Neuenstadt, close to Cleversulzbach where Mörike had been living since 1834 in the country parsonage. Wealthy cousin Karl lived in Neuenstadt with his musical wife Marie, whose voice Mörike celebrates in line 6 of 'Auf einer Wanderung'. Mörike and his sister Klara often walked the short distance from Cleversulzbach to Neuenstadt to attend social gatherings at his cousin's mansion, and it was perhaps during one of these outings that Mörike visited the Neuenstadt graveyard and guiltily picked a Christmas rose – see note 1 to 'Auf eine Christblume I'.
3   The capital letter denotes italics. Wolf, uncharacteristically, misses this and, instead of stressing 'Eine', which he sets to a quaver, stresses the unimportant 'und' at the beginning of the phrase by setting it to a crotchet.

Daß die Blüten beben,	Causing blossoms to quiver,
Daß die Lüfte leben,	Bringing breezes to life,
Daß in höherem Rot die Rosen leuchten vor.	Making roses glow a richer red.

Lang hielt ich staunend, lustbeklommen.	Long I halted, oppressed by joy.
Wie ich hinaus vor's Tor gekommen,	How I came out through the gate,
Ich weiß es wahrlich selber nicht.	I cannot in truth remember.
Ach hier, wie liegt die Welt so licht!¹	Ah, how bright the world is here!
Der Himmel wogt in purpurnem Gewühle,	The sky billows in a crimson whirl,
Rückwärts die Stadt in goldnem Rauch;²	The town lies behind in a golden haze;
Wie rauscht der Erlenbach, wie rauscht im Grund die Mühle!	How the alder brook chatters, and the mill below!
Ich bin wie trunken, irr'geführt –	I am as if drunk, led astray –
O Muse, du hast mein Herz berührt	O muse, you have touched my heart
Mit einem Liebeshauch!³	With a breath of love!

Poem written 1845

HEFT IV   **BOOK IV**

16 Elfenlied⁴   Elf-song

Bei Nacht im Dorf der Wächter rief: Elfe!	The village watch cried out at night: Eleven!
Ein ganz kleines Elfchen im Walde schlief –	An elfin elf was asleep in the wood –

---

1 There is a letter from Mörike to Wilhelm Waiblinger from February 1822 that describes how music [in 'Auf einer Wanderung' the voice of Marie Mörike] could transport him into a world of fantasy:

> Wirklich tut die Musik eine unbeschreibliche Wirkung auf mich [. . .] Da versink ich in die wehmütigsten Phantasien, wo ich die ganze Welt küssend voll Liebe umfassen möchte [. . .]
>
> Music truly has an indescribable effect on me [. . .] I sink into the most melancholy fantasies, and would fain kiss and embrace the whole world with love [. . .]

2 Mörike would have known Hölderlin's poem 'Patmos', which includes the phrase: „Im goldenen Rauche, blühte [. . .] mir Asia auf."

3 Richard Batka recounts how Wolf at a Liederabend, having recited 'Auf einer Wanderung', turned to the audience, exclaimed „Ist das Gedicht nicht zum Heulen schön?" ('Isn't the poem screamingly beautiful?'), and then began to sing.

4 The poem is a delightful piece of escapism that Mörike introduced into „Der letzte König von Orplid", scene 13, of his novel *Maler Nolten*, where it is sung by a trio of fairies: Talpe, Windigal and Malwy. The poem tells how a sleepy elf misinterprets the nightwatchman's cry of „Elfe": instead of thinking that he was calling out the time (eleven o'clock), the elf believes that he has been summoned ('Elfe' = elf); and drunk with sleep he totters away, mistakes the lights of a glow-worm for lamp-lit windows, and bumps his head on stone, as he tries to look in. 'Elfenlied' was one of Wolf's most popular songs in his lifetime – the reason, perhaps, why he called it 'abgeleiert' ('hackneyed'). See HW to Karl Mayr, 15 March 1897, p. 285.

Wohl um die Elfe! –	Just at eleven –
Und meint, es rief ihm aus dem Tal	And thinks the nightingale was calling
Bei seinem Namen die Nachtigall,	His name from the valley,
Oder Silpelit¹ hätt' ihm gerufen.	Or Silpelit had sent for him.
Reibt sich der Elf' die Augen aus,	The elf rubs his eyes,
Begibt sich vor sein Schneckenhaus,	Steps from his snail-shell home,
Und ist als wie ein trunken Mann,	Looking like a drunken man,
Sein Schläflein war nicht voll getan,	Not having slept his fill,
Und humpelt also tippe tapp	And hobbles down, tippety tap,
Durch's Haselholz in's Tal hinab,	Through the hazelwood to the valley,
Schlupft an der Mauer hin so dicht,	Slips right up against the wall,
Da sitzt der Glühwurm, Licht an Licht.²	Where the glow-worm sits, light on light.
„Was sind das helle Fensterlein?	'What bright windows are these?
Da drin wird eine Hochzeit sein:	There must be a wedding inside:
Die Kleinen sitzen bei'm Mahle	The little folk are sitting at the feast
Und treiben's in dem Saale;	And skipping round the ballroom;
Da guck' ich wohl ein wenig 'nein!"	I'll take a little peek inside!'
– Pfui, stößt den Kopf an harten Stein!	Shame! he hits his head on hard stone!
Elfe, gelt, du hast genug?	Elf, don't you think you've had enough?
Gukuk! Gukuk!³	Cuckoo! Cuckoo!

Poem written 1831
Also set by Hetsch

17 Der Gärtner⁴

The gardener

Auf ihrem Leibrößlein,	On her favourite mount,
So weiß wie der Schnee,	As white as snow,
Die schönste Prinzessin	The loveliest princess
Reit't durch die Allee.⁵	Rides down the avenue.
Der Weg, den das Rößlein	On the path that her horse
Hintanzet so hold,	Prances sweetly along,
Der Sand, den ich streute,	The sand I strewed
Er blinket wie Gold.⁶	Glitters like gold.

1 Silpelit is the name of a lady elf – and Wolf honours her with a respectful *poco rit*.
2 First edition (1838): Schlupft an der Weinbergmauer hin,/Daran viel Feuerwürmchen glühn.
3 Mörike writes 'Kuckuck' or 'Guckuck' in some versions. The 1878 edition, like the first edition, has 'Gukuk'.
4 See HW to Richard Sternfeld, 20 October 1892, p. 358, for Wolf's often expressed scorn for those singers who only ever perform such popular songs as 'Der Gärtner'. „Wozu habe ich an 200 Lieder veröffentlicht?" ('What is the point in my having published some 200 songs?') he exclaims. See also HW to Melanie Köchert, 23 September 1894, p. 360.
5 Wolf is not always the fastidious wordsetter he is claimed to be, and there are several examples of misaccentuation in his work. Here he unidiomatically stresses '*Leibrößlein*' and '*durch*'.
6 In a letter of 20 March 1843 to Wilhelm Hartlaub, Mörike describes how Agnes Schebest sang 'Der Gärtner', accompanied by Ernst Friedrich Kauffmann, the composer of the song. He was so

Du rosenfarbs Hütlein,	Little rose-coloured bonnet
Wohl auf und wohl ab,	Bobbing up and down,
O wirf eine Feder	O throw me a feather
Verstohlen herab!	Discreetly down!
Und willst du dagegen	And if you in exchange
Eine Blüte von mir,	Want a flower from me,
Nimm tausend für Eine,[1]	Take a thousand for *one*,
Nimm alle dafür!	Take all in return!

Poem written 1837
Also set by Distler, Kahn, E. F. Kauffmann,[2] Schumann and Viardot

---

overwhelmed by their performance that he quoted the last two lines of the second stanza, implying that his poem had been improved by their rendering. Mörike then describes how they performed other settings of his verse, before tackling Schubert's 'Erlkönig'. Mörike criticised the way in which Schubert set the child's cries: „Das Schreien des Kindes, wie es angefaßt wird, könnte Spiegel und Fenster zersprengen. Ich tadelte den Komponisten, fand aber wenig Beipflichtung." ('The screaming of the molested child could have smashed mirrors and windows. I blamed the composer but found little support.')

1 Mörike would have known Eichendorff's *Aus dem Leben eines Taugenichts* (1826) and the passage in Chapter 2 when a lady on horseback, who to the narrator/hero/gardener resembles the „schöne Magelone", rides on her horse along the avenue, with feathers in her hat. The besotted gardener stands 'drunk with anxiety, a beating heart and great joy' and addresses her: „Schönste gnädige Frau, nehmt auch diesen Blumenstrauß von mir und alle Blumen aus meinem Garten und alles, was ich habe." ('Fairest, gracious lady, accept this bouquet of flowers and all the flowers from my garden, and all that I possess.') Eichendorff's romantic, chivalrous scene is replaced by Mörike, the worldly priest, with an explicitly risqué scenario. All depends on the italicised 'Eine' for the lubricious innuendo to be grasped: that the *Lady Chatterley*-like gardener will give her all his flowers, if she in return will reward him with her maidenhead. Wolf repeats the final phrase to a *forte* dynamic.

2 Mörike, in a letter of 29 December 1842 to Wilhelm Hartlaub, writes: „Nun sang die Doktorin meinen Gärtner, von [E. F.] Kauffmann neuerdings ganz einfach komponiert. Er wird Dir gewiß auch gefallen. Die Begleitung ahmt einen sanften Galopp höchst angenehm nach, der neben der Melodie immer fortgeht und, wo dieselbe absetzt, besonders herausgehört wird." ('The doctor's wife sang my "Gärtner" that [E. F.] Kauffmann recently set quite simply. You too will certainly like it. The accompaniment imitates most pleasantly a gentle gallop, which keeps in step with the melody, and is especially conspicuous when the latter leaves off.')

Mörike expressed his gratitude to Julius Klaiber for giving a perceptive lecture on 'Der Gärtner' and other poems, by dedicating a poem to the critic ('An Julius Klaiber'):

Was du Gutes dem „Gärtner" erzeigt und der übrigen Sippschaft,
    Solches zu lohnen – was sind Rosen und Nelken für dich?
Hätt' ich nur Flaschen genug vom „Allarabestan" im Keller!
    Aber nun heißet es: nimm e i n e für tausend von mir!

The praise you lavished on 'Der Gärtner' and the rest
    Cannot be rewarded with roses and carnations.
If only I had enough bottles of champagne in my cellar!
    All I can say is: take *one* for a thousand of mine!

18 Zitronenfalter im April[1]

Grausame Frühlingssonne,
Du weckst mich vor der Zeit,
Dem nur im Maienwonne
Die zarte Kost gedeiht!
Ist nicht ein liebes Mädchen hier,
Das auf der Rosenlippe mir
Ein Tröpfchen Honig beut,
So muß ich jämmerlich vergehn
Und wird der Mai mich nimmer sehn
In meinem gelben Kleid.*[2]

Brimstone butterfly in April

Merciless spring sun,
You wake me before my time,
For only in blissful May
Can my delicate food flourish!
If there's no dear girl here
To offer me a drop of honey
From her rosy lips,
Then I must perish miserably
And May shall never see me
In my yellow dress.

Poem written *c.* 1852
Also set by Weingartner
* Wolf repeats the final phrase.

19 Um Mitternacht[3]

Gelassen stieg die Nacht an's Land,
Lehnt träumend an der Berge Wand,
Ihr Auge sieht die goldne Wage[4] nun
Der Zeit in gleichen Schalen stille ruhn;
    Und kecker rauschen die Quellen hervor,
    Sie singen der Mutter, der Nacht,
        in's Ohr
    Vom Tage,
    Vom heute gewesenen Tage.

At midnight

Night has serenely come ashore,
Leans dreaming against the mountain wall,
She watches now the golden scales of time
Quietly at rest in equipoise;
    And the springs babble more boldly,
    They sing in the ear of their mother,
        the night,
    Of the day,
    Of the day now ended.

1 It is the *Gonepteryx rhamni* who speaks as she emerges from hibernation. Mörike's seemingly sweet poem has symbolic import: the butterfly is the symbol, like Baudelaire's Albatros, of the poet living in an age that is out of sympathy with poetry and culture. See HW to Melanie Köchert, 12 October 1890, p. 120: „Im Ganzen gewann ich den Eindruck, daß ich nicht verstanden wurde." ('On the whole I got the impression that I was not understood.') Mörike's title was 'Citronenfalter im April'.
2 Wolf indicates that the final, repeated phrase should be sung *poco rit.* and *diminuendo*.
3 The poem concluded the first edition of Mörike's *Gedichte* (1838) where, as in the second edition (1847), it opens with the word 'Bedächtig' ('cautiously') – only later revised to 'Gelassen' ('serenely'). Mörike's poem, like 'Verborgenheit' and 'Gebet', speaks of balance – here the moment of ecstatic equipoise between night and memories of the past day. Stasis contrasts with movement, and this polarity is reflected in the change of metre. The first four lines of each stanza are iambic to suggest the dreamy and static character of Night; while lines 5–8 and 13–16 have a mixed iambic/anapaestic metre that conveys the rippling movement and the dynamic quality of the water. Wolf's darkly rocking triplets mirror the „uralt alte Schlummerlied", while brighter textures suggest the murmuring springs. His setting recalls Schubert's 'Nacht und Träume' in the way the voice floats over a low-lying accompaniment, most of which lies beneath middle C. Elisabeth Schwarzkopf told Graham Johnson that her biggest regret as a soprano was that she was unable to sing this low-lying song beloved of mezzo-sopranos.
4 In some other editions: Waage.

Das uralt alte Schlummerlied,	That old, that age-old lullaby,
Sie achtet's nicht, sie ist es müd';	She disregards, she is weary of it;
Ihr klingt des Himmels Bläue süßer noch,	The blue of the sky sounds sweeter to her,
Der flücht'gen Stunden gleichgeschwung'nes Joch.	The evenly curved yoke of the fleeting hours.
Doch immer behalten die Quellen das Wort,	But still the springs murmur on,
Es singen die Wasser im Schlafe noch fort Vom Tage,	Still the waters sing in their sleep Of the day,
Vom heute gewesenen Tage.	Of the day now ended.

Poem written October 1827
Also set by Max Bruch, Distler, Heimo Erbse, Franz, Ferdinand Hiller, E. F. Kauffmann, Lachner and Richard Trunk

20 Auf eine Christblume I[1]

On a Christmas rose I

Tochter des Walds, du Lilienverwandte,	Daughter of the forest, close kin to the lily,
So lang von mir gesuchte, unbekannte,	You whom I sought so long and never knew,
Im fremden Kirchhof, öd' und winterlich,	Now in a strange churchyard, bleak and wintry,
Zum erstenmal, o schöne, find' ich dich!	For the first time, O lovely one, I find you!
Von welcher Hand gepflegt du hier erblühtest,	Whose hand helped you to blossom here,
Ich weiß es nicht, noch wessen Grab du hütest;	I do not know, nor whose grave you guard;
Ist es ein Jüngling, so geschah ihm Heil,	If a young man lies here, he has found salvation,
Ist's eine Jungfrau, lieblich fiel ihr Teil.	If a young woman, a fair lot befell her.

1 'Auf eine Christblume I' was the last of the Mörike songs to be completed (26 November 1888), and Frank Walker in his biography of the composer aptly calls it 'an elegy, a nature picture, a religious meditation, a vision of elfland and a hymn to beauty all in one'. Writing to Wilhelm Hartlaub from Cleversulzbach on 29 October 1841, Mörike gives a detailed page-long prose description of the flower and how he found it in the graveyard at Neuenstadt. „So reizend fremd sah sie mich an, sehnsuchterregend!" ('It looked at me so strangely and charmingly, causing me such yearning!') His sister Klara, who had accompanied him on the walk, recognised the flower as a Christmas rose. They took it home with them (compare Goethe's 'Gefunden') and Mörike consulted his *Gartenbüchlein von Pastor Müller*, learning on page 116 that the flower blossoms early, appears in November, December and January (hence 'Christmas' rose), can endure freezing weather, thrives in sandy soil, favours shade or a wintry spot, but dies in a warm or sunny place. Following Pastor Müller's guidance not to place the rose in the house, Mörike set it in a glass outside the window „in den schönsten Mondenschein" ('in the most beautiful moonlight'). But a nocturnal wind blew it away and in the morning it could not be found. „Unrecht Gut soll nicht gedeihen," Mörike concludes; ill-gotten gain never thrives. Wolf, in a letter to Kauffmann of 24 November 1893, thanks his friend for sending him a 'poetic' account of the genesis of the poem, and refers to the poet in an ecstatic exclamation: „Göttlicher Mörike!" ('Divine Mörike!')

Im nächt'gen Hain, von Schneelicht
    überbreitet,
Wo fromm das Reh an dir vorüberweidet,
Bei der Kapelle, am krystall'nen Teich,
Dort sucht' ich deiner Heimat Zauberreich.

Schön bist du, Kind des Mondes,
    nicht der Sonne;
Dir wäre tödlich andrer Blumen Wonne,

Dich nährt, den keuschen Leib voll Reif
    und Duft,
Himmlischer Kälte balsamsüße Luft.

In deines Busens goldner Fülle gründet

Ein Wohlgeruch, der sich nur kaum
    verkündet;
So duftete, berührt von Engelshand,

Der benedeiten Mutter Brautgewand.

Dich würden, mahnend an
    das heil'ge Leiden,
Fünf Purpurtropfen schön und einzig
    kleiden:
Doch kindlich zierst du, um
    die Weihnachtszeit,[1]
Lichtgrün mit einem Hauch dein
    weißes Kleid.

Der Elfe, der in mitternächt'ger Stunde
Zum Tanze geht im lichterhellen Grunde,
Vor deiner mystischen Glorie steht
    er scheu
Neugierig still von fern und huscht vorbei.

Poem written 1841

In the darkling grove, overspread
    with snowy light,
Where the gentle deer grazes past you,
By the chapel, beside the crystal pool,
There I sought your enchanted realm.

How fair you are, child of the moon,
    not of the sun,
Fatal to you would be what is bliss
    to other flowers,

Your pure body, all rime and scent, feeds

On heavenly cold and balsam-scented air.

There dwells within the golden fullness
    of your chalice
A perfume so faint it can scarcely
    be perceived;
Such was the scent, touched
    by angelic hands,
Of the Blessed Mother's bridal robe.

Five crimson drops, portending
    the sacred Passion,
Would suffice as your sole and lovely
    ornament:
Yet child-like at Christmas time
    you adorn
Your white dress with a hint of
    palest green.

The elf, who at the midnight hour
Goes to dance in the glistening glade,
Stands awestruck from afar at your
    mystic glory,
Looks on in enquiring silence
    and scurries by.

---

1 Mörike: Weihnachtzeit.

21 Auf eine Christblume II[1]

Im Winterboden schläft, ein Blumenkeim,
Der Schmetterling, der einst um Busch und Hügel
In Frühlingsnächten wiegt den samt'nen Flügel;
Nie soll er kosten deinen Honigseim.

Wer aber weiß, ob nicht sein zarter Geist,
Wenn jede Zier des Sommers hingesunken,
Dereinst, von deinem leisen Dufte trunken,

Mir unsichtbar, dich blühende umkreist?

Poem written 1841

On a Christmas rose II

The butterfly that sleeps, a flower seed, in wintry earth,
Shall in spring nights to come

Flutter on velvet wing round hill and bush,
But never taste your honeyed dew.

But who knows if perhaps its gentle ghost,
When summer's loveliness has faded,
Might, some day, dizzy with your faint fragrance,
Unseen by me, circle you as you flower?

HEFT V

22 Seufzer[2]
(Crux fidelis)

Jesu benigne!
A cujus igne
Opto flagrare
Et Te amare:

BOOK V

Sigh
(Faithful cross)

Benign Jesus!
From whose fire
I long to burn
And to love Thee:

---

1 Wolf binds the song together with a figure in the accompaniment, repeated some twenty times, that represents the hovering butterfly of the poem.
2 The Latin poem is called 'Suspirium' in the first edition. Mörike came across the Latin original in an old songbook, published in the 1730s, that he discovered in a public house in a village between Nürtingen and Tübingen, *Geistreiches Gesangbuch, den Kern alter und neuer Lieder wie auch die Noten der unbekanten Melodeyen [. . .] in sich haltend*, edited by Joh. Anastas. Freylinghausen (1670–1739). He took only the first stanza and made four or five attempts at translating it, finally opting for the version that Wolf set. The 1876 edition of Mörike's *Gedichte* makes no mention of 'Crux fidelis'. The theme is related to his own 'Wo find' ich Trost?', the poem that follows it in *Maler Nolten*. A wonderful letter to his composer brother Karl (22 February 1832) shows how deeply the poem moved Mörike: „Der Ausdruck von religiösem Schmerz ist unnachahmlich groß und rührend in seiner Einfachheit." ('The expression of religious agony is inimitably great and moving in its simplicity.') He urges his brother to set it to music with the profound ardour that Mozart exhibited when he sat down to compose his Requiem. „Verstünde ich nur, Noten zu schreiben!!" ('If only I knew how to compose!!') he writes in the same letter.
    In *Maler Nolten* the song is sung as a duet by Henni and Agnes to the accompaniment of an organ. The narrative reads:

> Bald herrschte des Knaben und bald des Mädchens Stimme vor. Es schien altkatholische Musik zu sein. Ganz wundersam ergreifend waren besonders die kraftvollen Strophen eines lateinischen Bußliedes aus E-Dur.

Cur non flagravi?
Cur non amavi
Te, Jesu Christe?
–O frigus triste!
(aus der Passionshymne
  des Fortunatus)[1]

Why have I not burned?
Why have I not loved
Thee, Jesu Christ?
O sad coldness!
(from the Passion Hymn
  of Fortunatus)

Dein Liebesfeuer,
Ach Herr! wie teuer
Wollt' ich es hegen,
Wollt' ich es pflegen!
Hab's nicht geheget
Und nicht gepfleget,
Bin tot im Herzen –
O Höllenschmerzen![2]

The fire of your love,
O Lord,
How I longed to tend it,
How I longed to cherish it,
I have failed to tend it
And failed to cherish it,
Am dead at heart –
O hellish pain!

Poem written 1832
Also set by E. Kauffmann

23 Auf ein altes Bild[3]

On an old painting

In grüner Landschaft Sommerflor,[4]
Bei kühlem Wasser, Schilf und Rohr,
Schau, wie das Knäblein Sündelos
Frei spielet auf der Jungfrau Schoß!
Und dort im Walde wonnesam,
Ach, grünet schon des Kreuzes Stamm!

In the summer haze of a green landscape,
By cool water, rushes and reeds,
See how the Child, born without sin,
Plays freely on the Virgin's lap!
And there in the delightful wood
The Cross is already, alas, in leaf!

Poem written 1837
Also set by Kahn, E. Kauffmann and Reger

First the boy's voice, then the girl's voice predominated. It seemed to be ancient Catholic music. Wonderfully gripping in particular were the powerful verses of a Latin song of penitence in E major.

The same letter to his brother Karl discusses the difficulties of translating the Latin poem into German, particularly the last line. Mörike eventually decided to change the sense of the final line, from 'sad coldness' to 'hellish pain'.

1 Mörike: Altes Lied.   2 First edition (1838): War Eis im Herzen.
3 No one has yet identified the painting. Mörike, a more than competent draughtsman (see *Eduard Mörike. Zeichnungen*, edited by Herbert Meyer, published by Carl Hanser Verlag), was a great admirer of the Old Masters. Religious themes are surprisingly rare in a poet who was a vicar, but we must remember that Mörike was tormented by spiritual doubts and loathed writing sermons. For Wolf's reaction to his own setting, see HW to Edmund Lang, 14 April 1888, p. 352.
4 'Der Flor' has a number of meanings in German and Mörike perhaps intends a blend of 'riot of bloom', 'gauze' and 'mourning crape' ('Trauerflor').

24 In der Frühe[1]

Kein Schlaf noch kühlt das Auge mir,
Dort gehet schon der Tag herfür
An meinem Kammerfenster.
Es wühlet mein verstörter Sinn
Noch zwischen Zweifeln her und hin
Und schaffet Nachtgespenster.
– Ängste,[2] quäle
Dich nicht länger, meine Seele!
Freu' dich! schon sind da und dorten
Morgenglocken wach geworden.[3]

Poem written 1828
Also set by E. F. Kauffmann, Reger and Viardot

Early morning

Still no sleep cools my eyes,
The day's already dawning there
At my bedroom window.
My troubled mind still flounders,
Torn by doubts, to and fro,
Creating phantoms of the night.
– Frighten, torment
Yourself no more, my soul!
Rejoice! Already here and there
Morning bells have woken.

25 Schlafendes Jesuskind[4]
gemalt von Franc. Albani[5]

Sohn der Jungfrau, Himmelskind![6]
    am Boden
Auf dem Holz der Schmerzen eingeschlafen,
Das der fromme Meister sinnvoll spielend

Deinen leichten Träumen unterlegte;
Blume du, noch in der Knospe dämmernd
Eingehüllt die Herrlichkeit des Vaters!
O wer sehen könnte, welche Bilder
Hinter dieser Stirne, diesen schwarzen
Wimpern, sich in sanftem Wechsel malen!

Poem written 14 March 1862

The sleeping Christ-child
painted by Franc. Albani

Son of the Virgin, Heavenly Child!
    fallen asleep
On the ground, on the wood of suffering,
Which the pious master, in meaningful allusion,
Laid beneath Thy gentle dreams;
O flower, with the glory of God the Father,
Still hidden in the bud!
Ah, if one could but see the images
That pass in gentle succession
Behind this brow and these dark lashes!

---

1 The poem would have appealed to Wolf; throughout his life he suffered from insomnia.
2 The Peters edition of Wolf's song has 'Ängst'ge' instead of Mörike's 'Ängste', which should be restored. 'Ängste' here is not a plural noun but the archaic imperative form of the verb 'ängstigen'. Mörike used the metre of the Protestant hymn 'Wie schön leucht' uns der Morgenstern' by Philipp Nicolai (1556–1608).
3 The plethora of 'o's in the final two lines suggests the sound of bells.
4 The seasons would often dictate Wolf's choice of poem. 'Er ist's', 'Fußreise', 'Im Frühling' and 'Zitronenfalter im April', all spring songs, were composed in March and May, while the approach of Christmas inspired 'Auf eine Christblume I', 'Schlafendes Jesuskind' and 'Zum neuen Jahr'.
5 Francesco Albani (1578–1660) was an Italian baroque painter from Bologna whose *The Sleeping Christ Child with the Instruments of the Passion* can be seen at the Musée des Beaux-Arts d'Arras. Christ is depicted asleep literally on the Cross with His face towards the viewer.
6 The phrase is repeated by Wolf at the end of the song in hushed adoration: the singer is requested to sing *pp.*, *wie in tiefes Sinnen verloren* (*pp. as though lost in deep thought*); and pianists must within two bars effect a *diminuendo* from *ppp.* to *pppp*.

26 Karwoche[1]

O Woche, Zeugin heiliger Beschwerde!
Du stimmst so ernst zu dieser
    Frühlingswonne,
Du breitest im verjüngten Strahl der Sonne
Des Kreuzes Schatten auf die lichte Erde,

Und senkest schweigend deine Flöre nieder;
Der Frühling darf indessen immer keimen,
Das Veilchen duftet unter Blütenbäumen,
Und alle Vöglein singen Jubellieder.

O schweigt, ihr Vöglein auf den grünen
    Auen!
Es hallen[2] rings die dumpfen Glockenklänge,
Die Engel singen leise Grabgesänge;
O still, ihr Vöglein hoch im Himmelblauen!

Ihr Veilchen, kränzt[3] heut keine
    Lockenhaare!
Euch pflückt mein frommes Kind[4]
    zum dunkeln Straußes,
Ihr wandert mit zum Muttergotteshause,
Da sollt ihr welken auf des Herrn Altare.

Ach dort, von Trauermelodien trunken,
Und süß betäubt von schweren
    Weihrauchdüften,
Sucht sie den Bräutigam in Todesgrüften,
Und Lieb' und Frühling, alles ist versunken!

Holy week

O week, witness of sacred suffering!
You harmonise so gravely with this
    springtime rapture,
In the rekindled sunlight you spread
The Cross's shadow on the bright earth,

And silently lower your veils;
Spring meanwhile continues to bloom,
Violets smell sweet beneath blossoming
    trees,
And all the birds sing songs of praise.

Oh hush, you birds on green meadows!
Muffled bells are tolling all around,
Angels are singing their soft dirges;
Oh hush, you birds in the blue skies above!

You violets, adorn no maiden's hair today!

My devout child has picked you for
    the dark wreath:
You shall go with her to the church
    of the Virgin,
There you shall wither on the altar of
    our Lord.

Ah, there, dazed by the mourning melodies
And overcome by sweet and heavy incense,

She seeks the Bridegroom in vaults of death,
And love and spring – all is lost forever!

Poem written 1830

---

1 Immediately before Easter 1832, Mörike enclosed the poem in a letter to Luise Rau, where it is titled 'In der Charwoche'. Luise is addressed in the penultimate stanza. The title is spelt 'Charwoche' in the first edition and the 1876 edition; the poem appears, slightly altered, in *Maler Nolten*. It contrasts the joyous mood of spring with the solemnity of Passion Week. See also HW to Friedrich Eckstein, 8 October 1888, p. 353.
2 First edition (1838): schallen.
3 Mörike intends an imperative, since he places a comma after 'Ihr Veilchen'. Most modern editions of Wolf's score, which have no such comma, unhelpfully imply a present tense.
4 Luise Rau.

HEFT VI

27 Zum neuen Jahr
Kirchengesang[1]

Wie heimlicher Weise
Ein Engelein leise
Mit rosigen Füßen
Die Erde betritt,
So nahte der Morgen.
Jauchzt ihm, ihr Frommen,
Ein heilig Willkommen,
Ein heilig Willkommen!
Herz, jauchze du mit!

In Ihm sei's begonnen,
Der Monde und Sonnen
An blauen Gezelten
Des Himmels bewegt.
Du, Vater, du rate!
Lenke du und wende!
Herr, dir in die Hände
Sei Anfang und Ende,
Sei alles* gelegt!

Poem written 1832
Also set by Kahn and Weingartner
* 'Sei alles' is repeated joyfully.

BOOK VI

A poem for the New Year
A hymn

Just as a cherub,
Stealthily and softly
Alights on earth
With rosy feet,
So the morning dawned.
Cry out, you gentle souls,
A holy welcome,
A holy welcome!
O heart, rejoice as well!

May the New Year begin in Him,
Who moves
Stars and planets
In the blue firmament.
O Father, counsel us!
Lead us and guide us!
Lord, let all things,
Birth and death,
Be entrusted into Thy keeping!

---

1 Mörike wrote at the top of the poem: (Melodie aus *Axur*: Wie dort auf den Auen), thus explaining that the poem was meant to be sung to the melody of Artenio's aria in Salieri's opera *Axur, Re d'Ormus* (1787). Mörike might possibly have seen the 1828 production in Stuttgart. The amphibrachs of his poem were suggested by the text of Artenio's aria in the opera:

Wie dort auf den Auen	Just as there on the meadows
Beim Morgenlicht-Grauen	In the grey light of dawn
Die düstern Wolken	The sun breaks through
Die Sonne durchdringt,	The dismal clouds,
So steigt eines Kindes	So does a child's
Unschuldiges Flehen	Innocent pleading
Hinauf zu den Höhen,	Soar aloft
Wo Bramah ihm winkt.	From where Bramah beckons.

See also HW to Friedrich Eckstein, 8 October 1888, p. 353. Wolf responds to this seasonal poem in diatonic mode, using a succession of parallel thirds in contrary motion between the two hands to express the harmony of the text. Note how he handles the climax in verse 2, by giving such important words as 'Lenke', 'Herr', 'Anfang', 'Ende' and, above all, 'alles' ever longer note values, until the music, significantly marked *überströmend*, overflows with joy and praise. Wolf wrote the second verse on a card to Melanie Köchert on New Year's Eve 1891.

28 Gebet[1]

Herr! schicke was du willt,
Ein Liebes oder Leides;
Ich bin vergnügt, daß beides
Aus deinen Händen quillt.

Wollest mit Freuden
Und wollest mit Leiden
Mich nicht überschütten!
Doch in der Mitten*[2]
Liegt holdes Bescheiden.

Prayer

Lord! send what Thou wilt,
Pleasure or pain;
I am content that both
Flow from Thy hands.

Do not, I beseech Thee,
Overwhelm me
With joy or suffering!
But midway between*
Lies blessed moderation.

Stanza 1 written 1832, stanza 2 first published 1847
Also set by Bruch, Distler, Kahn, E. Kauffmann, Schoeck[3] and Weingartner
* „Doch in der Mitten" is repeated by Wolf.

29 An den Schlaf

Somne levis! quamquam certissima mortis imago,
Consortem cupio te tamen esse tori.
Alma quies, optata, veni! Nam sic sine vita

Vivere, quam suave est, sic sine morte mori![4]

To sleep

Light sleep! Though you be the most faithful image of death,
I still invite you as bedfellow to my couch!
Beautiful, longed-for silence, come! For without life

How sweet it is to live, dying thus without death!

1 The gestation of this famous poem is complex. Stanza 2 was the first to appear – in *Maler Nolten*, where it is spoken (not sung) by Agnes, shortly before she commits suicide. The novel was published in 1832. Eleven years later, Mörike copied out the poem with a new title ('In Demuth'/'In humility') and dated the manuscript 21 April 1843. The poem does not appear in the first edition of the *Gedichte* (1838). In the second (1847) and third (1856) editions, however, it appears with two verses, of which the original poem appears as verse 2 – the stanzas actually numbered as 'Gebet 1' and 'Gebet 2'. By the time of the *Ausgabe letzter Hand*, published in 1867, the poem appears as a single two-stanza prayer, as we know it from Wolf's setting. The second stanza, as spoken by Agnes in the original *Maler Nolten*, has a touch of madness about it, but the complete poem is no longer spoken by Agnes – instead, it appears as a calm disquisition on Lutheran doctrine: should one abandon oneself to God's will in true Lutheran fashion (verse 1) or should one reject orthodox doctrine and plead with God not to be overwhelmed by the extremes of emotion (verse 2). In the wake of the Maria Meyer episode, it is clear that Mörike rebelled against the dogma that had been taught him in the Tübinger Stift, from which he emerged as a clergyman in 1826.
2 Set at a higher pitch, the repeated words describe the poet's increased excitement that moderation might be possible: a wonderful effect.
3 'Gebet' is the fifteenth song of Schoeck's *Das holde Bescheiden* – the only one of the forty songs in the collection that was also set by Wolf.
4 The Latin poem above was written by Heinrich Meibom (1555–1625), a German historian and poet whose Latin verses were published in *Parodiarum horatianarum libri III et sylvarum libri II* (1588). Mörike, in a letter dated 10 March 1838 to Wilhelm Hartlaub, refers to Meibom's Latin poems as 'incomparably beautiful' („unvergleichlich schön") and explains how he had tried to translate them a decade previously – without success. Mörike found the lines quoted in a work on Hogarth's engravings by Georg Christoph Lichtenberg (1742–1799), one of his favourite authors.

Schlaf! süßer Schlaf! obwohl dem Tod wie du nichts gleicht,
Auf diesem Lager doch willkommen heiß' ich dich!
Denn ohne Leben so, wie lieblich lebt es sich!
So weit vom Sterben, ach, wie stirbt es sich so leicht![1]

Sleep! sweet sleep! though nothing so resembles death as you,
I bid you welcome to this couch!
For thus without life, how sweet it is to live!
So far from dying, ah, how easy it is to die!

Poem written *c.* 1837
Also set by Hanns Eisler and E. Kauffmann

30 Neue Liebe[2]

Kann auch ein Mensch des andern auf der Erde
Ganz, wie er möchte, sein?
– In langer Nacht bedacht' ich mir's,
und mußte sagen, nein!

So kann ich niemands heißen auf der Erde,
Und niemand wäre mein?
– Aus Finsternissen hell in mir aufzückt
ein Freudenschein:

Sollt' ich mit Gott nicht können sein,
So wie ich möchte, Mein und Dein?
Was hielte mich, daß ich's nicht heute werde?

Ein süßes Schrecken geht durch mein Gebein!
Mich wundert, daß es mir ein Wunder wollte sein,
Gott selbst zu eigen haben auf der Erde!

New love

Can one ever belong to another here on earth
Wholly, as one would wish to be?
Long I pondered this at night
and had to answer, no!

So can I belong to no one here on earth,
And can no one be mine?
– From the darkness a flame of joy
flashes bright within me:

Could I not be with God,
Just as I would wish, mine and Thine?
What could keep me from being so today?

A sweet tremor pervades my frame!
I marvel that it should have ever seemed a marvel
To have God for one's own on earth!

Poem written 1846

---

[1] The first edition (1838) has a different text:

Schlaf! sanfter Schlaf! obwohl dem Tod wie du Nichts gleicht:
Komm! theilen wir dies Lager brüderlich!
So ohne Leben, ach wie lieblich lebt es sich!
So ohne Tod, wie stirbt es sich so leicht!

[2] 'Neue Liebe', written by Mörike in 1846, was first published in the 1867 edition of his poems, appearing also in the second edition of *Maler Nolten*. The poem, one of half a dozen or so, is discovered in the novel by one of the characters at the back of a book, written „von einer kleinen, säuberlichen Hand, vermutlich eines Geistlichen" ('by a small neat hand, presumably a priest's'). The theme – the impossibility of sustaining a happy relationship with another human being – was a theme dear to Mörike. See 'Verborgenheit' and 'Gebet' among many other poems.

31 Wo find' ich Trost?[1]

Eine Liebe kenn' ich, die ist treu,
War getreu, solang ich sie gefunden,
Hat mit tiefem Seufzen immer neu,
Stets versöhnlich, sich mit mir verbunden.

Welcher einst mit himmlischem Gedulden

Bitter bittern Todestropfen trank,
Hing am Kreuz und büßte mein
    Verschulden,
Bis es in ein Meer von Gnade sank.

Und was ist's nun, daß ich traurig bin,
Daß ich angstvoll mich am Boden winde?
Frage: Hüter, ist die Nacht bald hin?
Und: was rettet mich von Tod
    und Sünde?

Arges Herze! ja gesteh' es nur,
Du hast wieder böse Lust empfangen;
Frommer Liebe, frommer Treue Spur,
Ach, das ist auf lange nun vergangen.

Ja, das ist's auch, daß ich traurig bin,
Daß ich angstvoll mich am Boden winde!
Hüter, Hüter, ist die Nacht bald hin?
Und was rettet mich von Tod und Sünde?

Where shall I find comfort?

I know a love that is true,
And has been true since first I found it,
Has, deeply sighing, ever afresh,
And always forgivingly espoused my cause.

He it was who once, with heavenly
    forbearance,
Drank death's bitter, bitter drops,
Hung on the cross and atoned for my sins,

Until they sank in a sea of mercy.

And why is it that I am now cast down,
That I writhe in terror on the ground?
That I ask: 'Watchman, what of the night?'
And: 'What shall save me from death
    and sin?'

Evil heart! why not confess it,
Once more you have felt wicked desires;
All trace of pious love, of pious faith,
Has vanished, alas, long ago.

Yes, that is why I am cast down,
Why I writhe in terror on the ground!
Watchman, watchman, what of the night?
And what shall save me from death
    and sin?

Poem written c. 1827
Also set by E. Kauffmann

---

[1] Written in his twenty-third year, unfulfilled emotionally, still raw from the Maria Meyer episode and distraught at the terminal illness of his older sister Luise, Mörike pours out his soul in 'Wo find' ich Trost?' His conscience was rarely clear when he failed to suppress erotic desires – see the Peregrina poems. The poet asks hysterically if he will be saved from death and sin. Wolf was an ardent admirer of Wagner (he had met him, aged fifteen, and remained a devotee throughout his life), and this is one of his most Wagnerian songs; perhaps he had the *Parsifal* theme in mind, which also deals with the struggle between lust and spiritual grace. The despairing cry, „Hüter, ist die Nacht bald hin?" scored for brass in the orchestral version, is from Isaiah 21:11: 'Watchman, what of the night?' Compare also Mendelssohn's *Lobgesang*. In *Maler Nolten*, 'Wo find' ich Trost?' follows on immediately after 'Seufzer'. Whereas 'Seufzer' is sung as a duet by Henni and Agnes, 'Wo find' ich Trost?' is sung by Agnes to Henni's accompaniment. Her despair, wonderfully caught by Wolf's music (the vocal range is from a high A flat to D below the stave), becomes too much for her, she runs away and is found the following morning – drowned in a forest well.

HEFT VII	BOOK VII
32 An die Geliebte[1]	**To the beloved**
Wenn ich, von deinem Anschaun tief gestillt,	When I, deeply calmed at beholding you,
Mich stumm an deinem heil'gen Wert vergnüge,[2]	Take silent delight in your sacred worth,
Dann hör' ich recht die leisen Atemzüge	Then I truly hear the gentle breathing
Des Engels, welcher sich in dir verhüllt.	Of that angel concealed within you.

1   Luise Rau, the vicar's daughter to whom Mörike was engaged from 1829 to 1833, inspired many of his most beautiful love poems, including 'An die Geliebte', whose gestation was described by the poet in a celebrated letter he wrote to her on 4 May 1830. Having received her letter, Mörike hurried to a wood to read it in romantic seclusion:

> Der Seitenweg, den ich mit Deinem Briefe machte, entdeckte mir ein vortrefflich angenehmes Örtchen, das ich bisher nicht gekannt hatte: ein kleiner, von Bäumen und Buschwerk besetzter, abhängiger Wiesenwinkel an der lebhaften Lauter, in die sich eine andre Quelle vom Berg her gießt. Dort saß ich nieder, las, dachte und fing mit Bleistift an zu schreiben, was Du hier als poetische Beilage erhältst. Dann stieg ich vollends den Wald hinan und spann die Verse so fort. Sie kamen recht aus meinem Innersten. Seitdem ist dieser Spaziergang mein Lieblingsweg. Ich machte ihn erst heute wieder und schnitt die Buchstaben L. E. in die Rinde einer jungen Erle dort am Bach. (Während des Eingrabens fiel mir ein, man könnte recht sinnreich ein i e b zwischen die beiden setzen.)

> The path on which I walked with your letter led me to a most delightful little place that was unknown to me: a sloping corner of a meadow, thick with bushes and trees, on the banks of the fast-moving Lauter, into which another stream flowed from the hills. I sat down there, read, thought and began with a pencil to compose the poem you will receive with this letter. I then climbed to the top of the wood and continued my poem. It came from the depths of my heart. This has since become my favourite walk. I set out on it again today and carved the letters L and E in the bark of a young alder tree by the stream. (As I did so, it occurred to me that one could meaningfully insert the letters OV between them.)

With the letter he enclosed five poems, including 'An die Geliebte' (Mörike's original title was 'Sonett an Luise'), which Wolf sets to a sort of rhythmically and harmonically heightened declamation. Luise, described as an angel in the octave, vanishes in the sestet, as Mörike contemplates the music of the spheres. In the final two lines and the postlude, Wolf – like Schubert before him in 'Freiwilliges Versinken' – depicts the stars in a series of softly repeated chords high above the stave; marked *sehr ausdrucksvoll*, they shine out ever more brightly, then fade in the *decrescendo*, before vanishing from view.

'An die Geliebte' appears towards the end of *Maler Nolten*. The poem, we are told, formed part of the posthumous papers of Theobald Nolten; and since they bore the title 'To L', Agnes claims them as her own, because one of her names was Luise. Although the deceased Nolten had been unfaithful to her, he still occupies the heart of the unhappy woman.

2   The line echoes a passage in a letter that Mörike wrote to Luise on 28 December 1829 at the very beginning of their four-year relationship:

> Nie tritt auch Deine Seele so rein und anschaulich aus ihrer Tiefe hervor, als wenn Du jene unvergeßlichen Lieder singst, unter denen sich mein Herz zum erstenmal zu Dir hinbewegte. Denk ich dieser Zeiten, jener Abende, weißt Du? so ist mir, ich träte in das innerste Heiligtum unserer Liebe, und ich müßte die Hände falten im glücklichsten Gefühle Deines Wertes.

Und ein erstaunt, ein fragend Lächeln quillt	And an amazed, a questioning smile
Auf meinem Mund, ob mich kein Traum betrüge,	Rises to my lips: does not a dream deceive me,
Daß nun in dir, zu ewiger Genüge,	Now that in you, to my eternal joy,
Mein kühnster Wunsch, mein einz'ger, sich erfüllt?	My boldest, my only wish is being fulfilled?
Von Tiefe dann zu Tiefen stürzt mein Sinn,	My soul then plunges from depth to depths,
Ich höre aus der Gottheit nächt'ger Ferne	From the dark distances of Godhead I hear
Die Quellen des Geschicks melodisch rauschen.	The springs of fate ripple in melody.
Betäubt kehr' ich den Blick nach oben hin,	Stunned I raise my eyes
Zum Himmel auf – da lächeln alle Sterne;	To heaven – where all the stars are smiling;
Ich kniee, ihrem Lichtgesang zu lauschen.	I kneel to listen to their song of light.

Poem written 7 May 1830
Also set by Weingartner

33 Peregrina I[1]
(Aus: *Maler Nolten*)[2]

Peregrina I
(from: *Maler Nolten*)

Der Spiegel dieser treuen, braunen Augen	The surface of these faithful brown eyes
Ist wie von innerm Gold ein Widerschein;	Is like a reflected gleam of inner gold;
Tief aus dem Busen scheint er's anzusaugen,	It seems to be drawn from deep within your breast –
Dort mag solch Gold in heil'gem Gram gedeihn.	There, in hallowed grief such gold may thrive.

Never does your soul emerge so purely and vividly from its depths as when you sing those unforgettable songs, during which my heart first went out to you. Are you aware that, if I recall that time and those evenings, it is though I were entering the innermost sanctum of our love, putting my hands together in prayer in the happiest feelings of your worth.

Mörike then mentions six songs that Luise used to sing – in whose settings he does not state: 'So laßt mich scheinen', 'Kennst du das Land', 'Freudvoll und leidvoll', 'Bleich flimmert in stürmender Nacht', 'Die Sonn er wacht' and 'Mir leuchtet die Hoffnung'. Graham Johnson points out that several of these songs appear in August Härtel's *Deutsches Liederlexicon: Eine Sammlung der besten und beliebtesten Lieder und Gesänge des deutschen Volkes*, which was extremely popular at the time, featuring songs by Himmel, Reichardt, Zumsteeg and others.

1 For the background to the Peregrina poems, see pp. 337–9 and HW to Melanie Köchert, 15 October 1890, p. 355. Ludwig Bauer, in a letter to Mörike's sister Luise of 6 September 1823, describes the shattering effect that Maria Meyer had on Mörike. Of the five Peregrina poems, familiar to us from the settings by Wolf and Schoeck, Wolf set the first and fourth, and Othmar Schoeck the second, third and fifth. All five songs have been often performed together in recent years by the German baritone Johannes Kammler and Roger Vignoles. The poems occur in *Maler Nolten*. 'Peregrina I', headed 'Warnung' ('Warning') in *Maler Nolten 1*, begins solemnly to a dotted-crotchet-and-quaver rhythm, but grows more impassioned and chromatic as the poet reflects on Peregrina's erotic charms and disloyalty. The melody of the postlude, which seems to express the pathological nature of sexual desire, becomes the main theme of the 'Peregrina II', which must number among the most disturbed

NO STANZA BREAK

In diese Nacht des Blickes mich zu tauchen,
Unwissend Kind, du selber lädst mich ein –
Willst, ich soll kecklich mich und dich entzünden,
Reichst lächelnd mir den Tod im Kelch der Sünden!

Also set by E. F. Kauffmann

To plunge into this dark night of your gaze,
Innocent child, you yourself invite me –
Want me boldly to consume us both in fire,
Smiling you offer me death in the chalice of sin!

34 Peregrina II
(Aus: *Maler Nolten*)[1]

Peregrina II
(from: *Maler Nolten*)

Warum, Geliebte, denk' ich dein
Auf Einmal nun mit tausend Tränen,
Und kann gar nicht zufrieden sein,
Und will die Brust in alle Weite dehnen?

Ach, gestern in den hellen Kindersaal,
Bei'm Flimmer zierlich aufgesteckter Kerzen,
Wo ich mein selbst vergaß in Lärm und Scherzen,
Tratst du, o Bildnis mitleid-schöner Qual;

Es war dein Geist, er setzte sich an's Mahl,
Fremd saßen wir mit stumm verhalt'nen Schmerzen;[2]
Zuletzt brach ich in lautes Schluchzen aus,
Und Hand in Hand verließen wir das Haus.

Why, beloved, do I now think of you
Suddenly and with a thousand tears,
And can find no fulfilment,
And yearn to unfurl my heart into infinity?

Ah, to the bright nursery yesterday,
In the gleam of decorative candles,
As I forgot myself amid noise and mirth,
You came, agony's image, lovely in compassion;

It was your ghost, it joined us at the feast,
Strangers we sat in mutely suppressed grief;
At last I broke out in loud sobbing,
And hand in hand we went from the house.

---

and overwrought love songs in the entire repertoire. Marked *sehr innig* (opposed to merely *innig* in 'Peregrina I'), the music veers towards the minor, the melodic line falters and falls apart, chromaticism increases as he recalls their relationship, until at „zuletzt brach ich . . ." the tempo quickens and the voice breaks out in loud sobbing, before the song limps to a close, as he remembers how, hand in hand, they left the house.

2 Wolf's 'Peregrina I' and 'Peregrina II' were his only Mörike settings to mention the novel in the song title.

1 Wolf's 'Peregrina I' and 'Peregrina II' were his only Mörike settings to mention the novel in the song title.

2 First edition (1838): Wir saßen fremd mit stumm verhaltnen Schmerzen.

35 Frage und Antwort[1]

Fragst du mich, woher die bange
Liebe mir zum Herzen kam,
Und warum ich ihr nicht lange
Schon den bittern Stachel nahm?

Sprich, warum mit Geisterschnelle
Wohl der Wind die Flügel rührt,
Und woher die süße Quelle
Die verborgnen Wasser führt?

Banne du auf seiner Fährte
Mir den Wind in vollem Lauf!
Halte mit der Zaubergerte
Du die süßen Quellen auf!

Poem written 1828
Also set by Distler and Felix Draeseke

Question and answer

You ask me where it came from,
This timid love that entered my heart,
And why I did not long ago
Draw its bitter sting?

Tell me, why with ghostly speed
The wind will whirr its wings,
And from whence hidden waters
Come to feed the sweet spring?

Just try halting a wind
In full career!
Or conjuring with a magic wand
The sweet springs to be still!

36 Lebe wohl[2]

„Lebe wohl" – Du fühlest nicht,
Was es heißt, dies Wort der Schmerzen;
Mit getrostem Angesicht
Sagtest du's und leichtem Herzen.

Farewell

'Farewell' – You do not feel
What it means, this word of pain;
With hopeful countenance
You said it, and a light heart.

---

[1] The poem, like 'Nimmersatte Liebe' and 'Erstes Liebeslied eines Mädchens', was inspired by Mörike's love for Josephine, a Catholic village schoolmaster's daughter in Scheer. Mörike would have known these lines from 'Lindamor an Cölinen' by Christian Ludwig Neuffer (1769–1839), a Swabian poet whom he read with pleasure:

Wer hält den Sturm, wenn er auf schwarzen Flügeln	Who can halt the storm, when on black wings
Durch bebende Gefilde fährt?	It passes through tremulous fields?
Wer kann den Lauf des schnellen Blitzes zügeln,	Who can tame the course of swift lightning,
Wenn sich die Wetterwolk' entleert?	When the thunder-cloud discharges its load?

[2] Mörike's passion for Luise Rau, though it yielded a great number of happy love poems such as 'An die Geliebte', also inspired one of his most tortured, 'Lebe wohl', which the poet included in a letter dated 8 August 1833 to his fiancée, shortly before they broke off their engagement. She was the daughter of the pastor at Plattenhardt, Württemberg, whose death caused the vacancy that Mörike was appointed to fill in May 1829. Luise was three years younger than Mörike, and after they had been engaged four years, he appears to have had a premonition that the relationship would not last. Mörike's anguish at Luise's decision to end the affair is clear from a letter dated 20 December 1833 he wrote to his fellow poet Friedrich Theodor Fischer, soon after the break. He begins by telling his friend that he had actually begun the letter at the beginning of November but had not sent it. He then explains the reason:

> Es hat sich inzwischen eine für mein ganzes Leben wichtige Katastrophe eingeleitet, deren schmerzhafte Entwicklung alles übrige bei mir verschlang.

Lebe wohl! – Ach tausendmal
Hab' ich mir es vorgesprochen,
Und in nimmersatter Qual
Mir das Herz damit gebrochen!

Farewell! – Ah, a thousand times
I have uttered it aloud,
And with never-ending anguish
Have broken my heart in doing so!

Poem written *c.* 1833
Also set by Distler, E. Kauffmann, Lachner and Lassen

37 Heimweh[1]

Longing for home

Anders wird die Welt mit jedem Schritt,
Den ich weiter von der Liebsten[2] mache;
Mein Herz, das will nicht weiter mit.
Hier scheint die Sonne kalt in's Land,
Hier däucht mir alles unbekannt,
Sogar die Blumen am Bache!
Hat jede Sache
So fremd eine Miene, so falsch ein Gesicht.
Das Bächlein murmelt wohl und spricht:
Armer Knabe, komm bei mir vorüber,
Siehst auch hier Vergißmeinnicht!
– Ja, die sind schön an jedem Ort,
Aber nicht wie dort.
Fort, nur fort!
Die Augen gehn mir über![3]

The world changes with every step
That takes me further from my beloved;
My heart is reluctant to follow.
Here the sun shines coldly on the land,
Here all seems unfamiliar,
Even the flowers by the brook!
Each thing
Has so foreign a look, so false a face.
The stream murmurs and says:
Poor boy, come to me,
Here too you'll see forget-me-nots!
Yes, they are lovely everywhere,
But not so lovely as there.
Onwards, onwards!
My eyes fill with tears!

Poem written *c.* 1830
Also set by E. Kauffmann

A momentous catastrophe has since occurred with consequences for my entire life, and the pain it caused means that I have ignored all else.

Though written around 1833, the poem does not appear in the first edition of Mörike's *Gedichte*, and yet from a poetic viewpoint it is as fine as any of his love poems. Perhaps the pain of parting from Luise was still too intense five years later in 1838 for Mörike to include the poem and thus be reminded of the trauma. Wolf captures Mörike's grief in the falling semitones of the opening bar, and every phrase thereafter ends in a drooping cadence, none greater in range and effect than in the closing climax, when the voice plummets from top A flat to D below the stave.

1 'Frage und Antwort', 'Lebe wohl' and 'Heimweh' appear consecutively on pp. 65–7 of the sixth edition of Mörike's *Gedichte* owned by Wolf, who set them one after the other on 29 March, 31 March and 1 April.
2 Luise Rau.   3 Cf. Goethe's 'Der König in Thule': „Die Augen gingen ihm über".

HEFT VIII

38 Lied vom Winde[1]

Sausewind, Brausewind!
Dort und hier!
Deine Heimat sage mir!

„Kindlein, wir fahren
Seit viel vielen Jahren
Durch die weit weite Welt,
Und möchten's erfragen,
Die Antwort erjagen
Bei den Bergen, den Meeren,
Bei des Himmels klingenden Heeren,
Die wissen es nie.*
Bist du klüger als sie,
Magst du es sagen.
– Fort, wohlauf!
Halt uns nicht auf!
Kommen andre nach, unsre Brüder,
Da frag' wieder!"

Halt' an! Gemach,
Eine kleine Frist!
Sagt, wo der Liebe Heimat ist,
Ihr Anfang, ihr Ende?

„Wer's nennen könnte!
Schelmisches Kind,
Lieb' ist wie Wind,
Rasch und lebendig,
Ruhet nie,
Ewig ist sie,
Aber nicht immer beständig.[2]
– Fort! Wohlauf![3]
Halt uns nicht auf!
Fort über Stoppel und Wälder und Wiesen!
Wenn ich dein Schätzchen seh',

BOOK VIII

Song of the wind

Storming wind, roaring wind!
Now here, now there!
Tell me where your homeland is!

'Child, we've travelled
For many many years
Through the wide wide world,
We too would fain ask this
And discover the answer
From the mountains, the seas,
The resounding legions of heaven:
They never know.*
If you're smarter than they,
You can tell us.
– Off, away!
Don't delay us!
Others follow, our brothers,
Ask them!'

Stop! Stay
A little while!
Say where love's home is,
Where it begins, where it ends?

'Who could say!
Mischievous child,
Love's like the wind,
Swift and brisk,
Never resting,
Everlasting,
But not always constant.
– Off, away!
Delay us no longer!
Away over stubble and forests and meadows!
If I see your sweetheart,

---

1 The song is sung in *Maler Nolten* by Agnes. She has been abandoned by her lover, the painter Nolten, who has left her for the aristocratic Countess Konstanze. In her ensuing madness Agnes has climbed to the top of a small bare hill above the forest and now sings „Sausewind, Brausewind!" What in the *Gedichte* is a zany colloquy between a girl and the winds is in the novel an emotional outpouring of an unhinged mind. „Sagt, wo der Liebe Heimath ist,/Ihr Anfang, ihr Ende?" becomes the desperate cry of a forsaken and deranged woman.
2 First edition (1838): Aber dein Schatz nicht beständig.
3 „Fort! Wohlauf! auf!" (Mörike) and „Frisch, wohlauf!" in the first edition (1838).

Will ich es grüßen.	I'll blow him a kiss.
Kindlein, Ade!"§	Child, farewell!'§

Poem written 1828
Also set by E. F. Kauffmann
* Wolf twice repeats the phrase.
§ 'Ade' is twice repeated by Wolf to a *pianissimo* dynamic as the wind gradually vanishes.

39 Denk' es, o Seele![1]   O soul, consider!

Ein Tännlein grünet wo,	A young fir is growing, where,
Wer weiß, im Walde,	Who knows, in the wood?
Ein Rosenstrauch, wer sagt,	A rosebush, who can say,
In welchem Garten?	In what garden?
Sie sind erlesen schon,	Already they are pre-ordained,
Denk' es, o Seele,	O soul, consider,
Auf deinem Grab zu wurzeln	To take root and grow
Und zu wachsen.[2]	On your grave.
Zwei schwarze Rößlein weiden	Two black colts are grazing
Auf der Wiese,	On the meadow,
Sie kehren heim zur Stadt[3]	At a brisk canter
In muntern Sprüngen.	They return to the town.
Sie werden schrittweis gehn	At a walking pace
Mit deiner[4] Leiche;	They will draw your coffin;

1 'Denk' es, o Seele!' ends Mörike's Novelle *Mozart auf der Reise nach Prag*, which describes the largely apocryphal events that befall Mozart and Constanze on their journey to Prague to stage *Don Giovanni*. They are invited to share in the festivities at Count von Schinzberg's castle, celebrating the engagement of his niece Eugenie to a nobleman. All appears to end happily. But then, in the epilogue, Eugenie closes the piano that Mozart had played, and jealously locks it lest the keys be touched by any hand other than Mozart's. She knows she has said farewell to a composer of genius. She senses that his days are numbered, that he is doomed to die a premature death. Pensively, she tidies away several volumes of songs and in doing so dislodges an old sheet of paper, which flutters to the ground. On it is written, we are told, an old Bohemian folk song. She reads it, and sensing the theme of transience and its relevance to Mozart, begins to weep. It is 'Denk' es, o Seele!', which is not of course a folk song at all but a wonderfully constructed lyric that describes the approach of death. Wolf's sepulchral D minor setting (the key of *Don Giovanni*) is permeated with tolling bells and ends in a funeral march that dies away in the final bars.

The manuscript of an earlier version of the poem, entitled 'Grabgedanken' ('Thoughts of the grave'), is dated September 1851. This version was first printed in 1852 in a Stuttgart ladies' magazine *Frauenzeitung für Hauswesen, weibliche Arbeiten und Moden mit vielen Modeblättern und dem Unterhaltungsblatte Salon*. It appears on p. 56 along with recipes for orange cake and Kartoffelpudding and advice on how to protect embroidery against moths. The revised version of the poem has no title at the end of *Mozart auf der Reise nach Prag*; but when Mörike included the poem in his *Gedichte*, he adopted the new sixth line ('Denk' es, o Seele!') as the title.
2 The version printed in the ladies' magazine ran: „Von beiden ist gewiß/Ein Reis erlesen,/Auf meinem Grab zu wurzeln/Und zu wachsen."
3 Version in the ladies' magazine: Sie tummeln sich zur Stadt.
4 Version in the ladies' magazine: Mit meiner Leiche.

Vielleicht, vielleicht noch eh'	Perhaps, perhaps even before
An ihren Hufen	Their hooves
Das Eisen los wird,	Shed the shoes
Das ich blitzen sehe!	That I see flashing!

Poem written before 1852
Also set by Distler, Dräseke, Franz, Kahn, E. Kauffmann and Pfitzner

40 Der Jäger[1,2] / The huntsman

Drei Tage Regen fort und fort,	Three days of endless rain,
Kein Sonnenschein zur Stunde;	No sunshine even now;
Drei Tage lang kein gutes Wort	Not one kind word for three whole days
Aus meiner Liebsten Munde!	From my beloved's lips!
Sie trutzt mit mir und ich mit ihr,	She's sulking and so am I –
So hat sie's haben wollen;	That's how she wanted it;
Mir aber nagt's am Herzen hier,	But it gnaws at my heart,
Das Schmollen und das Grollen.	This sulkiness and sullenness.
Willkommen denn, des Jägers Lust,	Welcome, then, to the hunter's delight,
Gewittersturm und Regen!	To thunderstorm and rain!
Fest zugeknöpft die heiße Brust	Button tight the ardent breast,
Und jauchzend euch entgegen!	And headlong with joy against the storm!
Nun sitzt sie wohl daheim und lacht	She'll be sitting at home and laughing now,
Und scherzt mit den Geschwistern;	And joking with her siblings;
Ich höre in des Waldes Nacht	I can hear the old leaves whispering
Die alten Blätter flüstern.	In the forest night.
Nun sitzt sie wohl und weinet laut	Now she'll be sitting and weeping aloud
Im Kämmerlein, in Sorgen;	For sorrow in her little room;
Mir ist es wie dem Wilde traut,	I feel at home like a deer,
In Finsternis geborgen.	Hidden in the darkness.
Kein Hirsch und Rehlein überall!	No stag or roe anywhere!
Ein Schuß zum Zeitvertreibe!	A shot will pass the time!
Gesunder Knall und Widerhall	The healthy crack and echo
Erfrischt das Mark im Leibe. –	Refresh the marrow in my bones.
Doch wie der Donner nun verhallt	But as the thunder now dies away
In Tälern, durch die Runde,[3]	In the valleys all around,

---

1 See HW to his mother, 19 April 1890, p. 354.
2 The poem, sung by Agnes in *Maler Nolten*, is chosen by Nolten; we are told that he liked the text, whereas Agnes did not. Agnes is described as singing „mit einer Stimme, die, kräftig und zart, sich doch stets lieber in die Tiefe als in die Höhe bewegte" ('with a voice that was strong and gentle, but always more inclined to move in the lower than in the higher register').
3 First edition (1838): In Thälern in die Runde.

Ein plötzlich Weh mich überwallt,	I'm assailed by sudden pain,
Mir sinkt das Herz zu Grunde.	My heart sinks like a stone.
Sie trutzt mit mir und ich mit ihr,	She's sulking and so am I –
So hat sie's haben wollen;	That's how she wanted it;
Mir aber frißt's am Herzen hier,	But it gnaws at my heart,
Das Schmollen und das Grollen.	This sulkiness and sullenness.
Und auf! und nach der Liebsten Haus!	So let's away to my love's house!
Und sie gefaßt um's Mieder!	And clasp her round the waist!
„Drück' mir die nassen Locken aus,	'Wring out these soaking locks of mine
Und küß' und hab' mich wieder!"	And kiss and take me back again!'

Poem written 1828

41 Rat einer Alten[1] / An old crone's advice

Bin jung gewesen,	I was young once,
Kann auch mit reden,	So I can talk,
Und alt geworden,	And now I'm old,
Drum gilt mein Wort.	What I say counts.
Schön reife Beeren	Lovely ripe berries
Am Bäumchen hangen:	Hang from the tree:
Nachbar, da hilft kein	Neighbour, it's no use
Zaun um den Garten;	Fencing the garden;
Lustige Vögel	Gleeful birds
Wissen den Weg.	Will find the way in.
Aber, mein Dirnchen,	But, young lady –
Du laß dir raten:	A piece of advice:
Halte dein Schätzchen	Make sure you treat your man
Wohl in der Liebe,	With love
Wohl im Respekt!	And respect!
Mit den zwei Fädlein	With those two threads
In Eins gedrehet.	Twined into *one*,
Ziehst du am kleinen	You'll lead him
Finger ihn nach.	By your little finger.
Aufrichtig Herze,	Be frank at heart,
Doch schweigen können,	Yet know when to keep quiet,
Früh mit der Sonne	Be up with the sun
Mutig zur Arbeit,	And work with a will,

---

1 This extraordinary song bristles with no fewer than 186 acciaccaturas, which convey the old woman's cantankerous, bossy and didactic manner. Compare Mozart's 'Die Alte', also in E minor, in which a similar termagant is instructed to sing „ein bißchen durch die Nase" ('slightly through the nose').

Gesunde Glieder,	A healthy body
Saubere Linnen,	And clean linen –
Das machet Mädchen	These things make a young woman
Und Weibchen wert.	And wife respected.
Bin jung gewesen,	I was young once,
Kann auch mit reden,	So I can talk,
Und alt geworden,	And now I'm old,
Drum gilt mein Wort.	What I say counts.

Poem written 1832

42 Erstes Liebeslied eines Mädchens[1]   A girl's first love song

Was im Netze? Schau einmal!	What's in the net? Take a look!
Aber ich bin bange;	But I'm afraid;
Greif' ich einen süßen Aal?	Is a sweet eel?
Greif' ich eine Schlange?	Is it a snake?
Lieb' ist blinde	Love's a blind
Fischerin;	Fisher girl;
Sagt dem Kinde,	Tell the child
Wo greift's hin?	What she's caught.
Schon schnellt mir's in Händen![2]	It's rearing up in my hands!
Ach Jammer! o Lust!	Ah misery, oh joy!
Mit Schmiegen und Wenden	Nestling and wriggling
Mir schlüpft's an die Brust.	It slithers to my bosom.

---

1   The twenty-four-year-old Mörike sent the poem as a bizarre wedding present to his bosom friend Ernst Friedrich Kauffmann, father of Emil, one of the foremost champions of Wolf's songs, enclosing it in a letter of 7 July 1828:

> Ein langes und breites Hochzeitlied schick ich Dir nicht, aber ein Liebesliedchen, das ich gestern auf der Steige von Weingarten vor mich hinbrummte, und zwar vom dritten Vers an nach der Melodie „Was zieht mir das Herz so". Setz es in Musik, gib Ihr am Brautmorgen einen Kuß und frag sie, wenn sie's nun absingt, ob das Lied nicht, auf ein Haar, alle die Seligkeit ausdruckt, die sie in den ersten Tagen Eurer Liebe empfunden.

> I shall not send you a long and extended wedding song but a little love ditty that I hummed to myself yesterday along the path to the vineyards, to the tune – from the third verse on – of „Was zieht mir das Herz so". Set it to music and give her a kiss on the morning after the wedding and ask her, as she chants it, whether the song does not, almost exactly, express all the rapture that she experienced in the first days of your love.

Wolf was well aware of the erotic side of Mörike's psyche – see HW to Emil Kauffmann, 5 June 1890, p. 355.

2   The rhythm of this stanza is that of Goethe's 'Sehnsucht' (p. 123), whose opening line is quoted in the letter above („Was zieht mir das Herz so") and whose rhythm Mörike continues in stanzas 4–6 of his own poem.

Es beißt sich, o Wunder!
Mir keck durch die Haut,
Schießt 's Herze hinunter!
O Liebe, mir graut!

Was tun, was beginnen?
Das schaurige Ding,
Es schnalzet da drinnen,
Es legt sich im Ring.

Gift muß ich haben!
Hier schleicht es herum,
Tut wonniglich graben
Und bringt mich noch um![1]

Incredible! It bites its way
Boldly through my skin,
Plunges down to my heart!
O Love, I shudder!

What can I do?
The gruesome thing's
Snapping in there,
Coiling into a ring.

Bring me poison!
Creeping about,
It burrows deliciously
And will be the death of me yet!

Poem written 1828
Also set by Hetsch

43 Lied eines Verliebten

A lover's song

In aller Früh, ach, lang vor Tag,
Weckt mich mein Herz, an dich zu denken,
Da doch gesunde Jugend schlafen mag.

Hell ist mein Aug' um Mitternacht,
Heller als frühe Morgenglocken:
Wann hätt'st du je am Tage mein gedacht?

Wär' ich ein Fischer, stünd' ich auf,
Trüge mein Netz hinab zum Flusse,
Trüg' herzlich froh die Fische zum Verkauf.

In der Mühle, bei Licht, der Müllerknecht
Tummelt sich, alle Gänge klappern;
So rüstig Treiben wär' mir eben recht!

Weh, aber ich! o armer Tropf!
Muß auf dem Lager mich müßig grämen,
Ein ungebärdig Mutterkind im Kopf.

At first dawn, ah! long before day,
My heart wakes me to think of you,
When healthy lads would love to sleep.

My eyes are bright at midnight,
Brighter than early morning bells:
Would you have thought of me even by day?

If I were a fisherman, I'd get up,
Carry my net down to the river,
Carry the fish to market with a happy heart.

The miller's lad, at first light,
Is hard at work, the machinery clatters;
Such hearty activity would suit me well!

But I, alas! poor wretch,
Must lie idly grieving on my bed,
Obsessed with that unruly girl.

Poem written c. 1837
Also set by Distler and Hetsch

---

[1] In a letter of 8 March 1894 to Potpeschnigg Wolf gives a vivid description of Frieda Zerny's performance of the song in Vienna's Saal Bösendorfer. Wolf himself was the accompanist, and given the erotic nature of the poem and his letters to Zerny, the performance must have been electric.

EDUARD MÖRIKE

HEFT IX **BOOK IX**

44 Der Feuerreiter[1]   Fire-rider

Sehet ihr am Fensterlein	See, at the little window
Dort die rote Mütze wieder?	There, his red cap again?
Nicht geheuer muß es sein,	Something must be wrong,
Denn er geht schon auf und nieder.	For he's pacing to and fro.
Und auf einmal welch Gewühle	And suddenly, what a seething throng
Bei der Brücke, nach dem Feld!	At the bridge, heading for the fields!
Horch! das Feuerglöcklein gellt:	Hark! how the fire bell shrills:
Hinter'm Berg,	Behind the hill,
Hinter'm Berg	Behind the hill,
Brennt es in der Mühle!	The mill's on fire!
Schaut! da sprengt er wütend schier	Look, there he gallops frenziedly
Durch das Tor, der Feuerreiter,	Through the gate, the fire-rider,
Auf dem rippendürren Tier,	Straddling his skinny mount
Als auf einer Feuerleiter!	Like a fireman's ladder!
Querfeldein! Durch Qualm und Schwüle	Across the fields! Through thick smoke and heat-haze
Rennt er schon und ist am Ort!	He rides and has reached his goal!
Drüben schallt es fort und fort:	The distant bell peals on and on:
Hinter'm Berg,	Behind the hill,
Hinter'm Berg	Behind the hill
Brennt es in der Mühle!	The mill's on fire!
Der so oft den roten Hahn	You who have often smelt a fire
Meilenweit von fern gerochen,	From many miles away,
Mit des heil'gen Kreuzes Span	And blasphemously conjured the blaze
Freventlich die Glut besprochen[2] –	With a splinter of the True Cross –

1 The poem originally comprised only four stanzas (1, 2, 4 and 5 of Wolf's song) and appeared as such in the first edition of the *Gedichte*, where it is titled 'Romanze vom wahnsinnigen Feuerreiter', and in the first version of *Maler Nolten* (see below). Ghost stories are being told and Christoph is telling the assembled company the tale of the fire-rider, when he is interrupted by one of the guests who urges him to sing it instead: „laut't ja viel besser so und hat gar eine schöne schauerliche Weise" ('it sounds much better that way and the melody has a haunting beauty'). Christoph is embarrassed but then sings the song „mit einer klangreichen, kraftvollen Stimme" ('in a strong, sonorous voice'). Mörike revised the poem in 1841 and added what is now the third stanza. The idea of the red cap bobbing up and down was, according to Mörike's friend Rudolf Lohbauer, suggested to Mörike by the sight of the insane poet Hölderlin pacing up and down in the room of his tower wearing a white cap. Wolf was fascinated by the poem and later arranged it for chorus and orchestra, a version that fails, however, to match the dramatic power of the piano-accompanied song, especially at „Da fällts in Asche ab", where the piano plays clumps of diminished seventh chords, marked *pppp*, that depict in wonderfully realistic fashion the ashes floating to the ground. The first verifiable performance of the piano-accompanied 'Der Feuerreiter' took place on 3 March 1892 in Berlin with Wolf singing to his own accompaniment.

2 'Besprochen' here means 'exorcised', 'extinguished through magic'. The idea of someone being punished for extinguishing fires by the use of black magic was found by Mörike in his friend Kerner's *Magikon* which, according to Friedrich Eckstein, Wolf also studied before composing his song.

Weh! dir grinst vom Dachgestühle	Look out! there, grinning at you from the rafters,
Dort der Feind im Höllenschein.	Is the Devil amid the flames of hell.
Gnade Gott der Seele dein!	God have mercy on your soul!
Hinter'm Berg,	Behind the hill,
Hinter'm Berg	Behind the hill
Ras't er in der Mühle!	He's raging in the mill!
Keine Stunde hielt es an,	In less than an hour
Bis die Mühle borst in Trümmer;	The mill collapsed in rubble;
Doch den kecken Reitersmann	But from that hour the bold rider
Sah man von der Stunde nimmer.	Was never seen again.
Volk und Wagen im Gewühle	Thronging crowds and carriages
Kehren heim von all' dem Graus;	Turn back home from all the horror;
Auch das Glöcklein klinget aus:	And the bell stops ringing too:
Hinter'm Berg,	Behind the hill,
Hinter'm Berg	Behind the hill
Brennt's! –	A fire! –
Nach der Zeit ein Müller fand	Some time after a miller found
Ein Gerippe samt der Mützen	A skeleton, cap and all,
Aufrecht an der Kellerwand	Upright against the cellar wall,
Auf der beinern Mähre sitzen:	Mounted on the fleshless mare:
Feuerreiter, wie so kühle	Fire-rider, how coldly
Reitest du in deinem Grab!	You ride in your grave!
Husch! da fällt's in Asche ab.	Hush – now it flakes into ash.

Mörike's original version ('Romance of the insane fire-rider') as it appeared in the first edition of 1838:

Romanze vom wahnsinnigen Feuerreiter

Sehet ihr am Fensterlein	Keine Stunde hielt es an,
Dort die rothe Mütze wieder?	Bis die Mühle borst in Trümmer;
Muß nicht ganz geheuer seyn,	Doch den wilden Reitersmann
Denn er geht schon auf und nieder;	Sah man von der Stunde nimmer;
Und was für ein toll Gewühle	Darauf stiller das Gewühle
Plötzlich auf den Gassen schwillt!	Kehret wiederum nach Haus;
Horch! das Jammerglöcklein grillt:	Auch das Glöcklein klinget aus:
Hinter'm Berg, hinter'm Berg	Hinter'm Berg, hinter'm Berg
Brennt's in einer Mühle!	Brennt's! –
Schaut! da sprengt er wüthend schier	Nach der Zeit ein Müller fand
Durch das Thor, der Feuerreiter,	Ein Gerippe sammt der Mützen
Auf dem rippendürren Thier,	Ruhig an der Kellerwand
Als auf einer Feuerleiter!	Auf der beinern' Mähre sitzen:
Durch den Qualm und durch die Schwüle	„Feuerreiter, wie so kühle
Rennt er schon wie Windesbraut!	Reitest du in deinem Grab!"
Aus der Stadt, da ruft es laut:	Husch! da fällt's in Asche ab.
Hinter'm Berg, hinter'm Berg	Ruhe wohl! Ruhe wohl
Brennt's in einer Mühle!	Drunten in der Mühle!

'Hinter'm Berg, hinter'm Berg' and 'Ruhe wohl! Ruhe wohl' are contained in one line, unlike in the revised version set by Wolf.

Ruhe wohl,
Ruhe wohl
Drunten in der Mühle!

Rest in peace,
Rest in peace
Down there in the mill!

Poem written 1823/24, revised 1841
Also set by Hetsch and E. F. Kauffmann

45 Nixe Binsefuß[1]

The water-sprite Reedfoot

Des Wassermanns sein Töchterlein
Tanzt auf dem Eis im Vollmondschein,
Sie singt und lachet sonder Scheu
Wohl an des Fischers Haus vorbei.

The merman's little daughter
Dances on the ice under a full moon,
Singing and laughing boldly
Past the fisherman's house.

„Ich bin die Jungfer Binsefuß,
Und meine Fisch' wohl hüten muß;
Meine Fisch' die sind im Kasten,
Sie haben kalte Fasten;
Von Böhmerglas mein Kasten ist,
Da zähl' ich sie zu jeder Frist.

'I am the maiden Reedfoot,
And I must look after my fish;
My fish are in this tank,
Having a cold Lent;
My tank's made of Bohemian glass,
So I can count them at any time.

Gelt, Fischermatz? gelt, alter Tropf,
Dir will der Winter nicht in Kopf?
Komm mir mit deinen Netzen!
Die will ich schön zerfetzen!
Dein Mägdlein zwar ist fromm und gut,
Ihr Schatz ein braves Jägerblut.

Not so, fisher fellow? Not so, old fool,
You cannot understand it's winter?
If you come near me with your nets,
I'll tear them all to shreds!
But your daughter's a good, devout girl,
And her sweetheart's an honest huntsman.

Drum häng' ich ihr, zum Hochzeitstrauß,
Ein schilfen Kränzlein vor das Haus,
Und einen Hecht, von Silber schwer,
Er stammt von König Artus her,
Ein Zwergen=Goldschmieds=Meisterstück,
Wer's hat, dem bringt es eitel Glück:
Er läßt sich schuppen Jahr für Jahr,
Da sind's fünfhundert Gröschlein bar.

That's why I'll hang, as a wedding bouquet,
A wreath of reeds outside her house,
And a pike of solid silver,
From King Arthur's time,
The masterpiece of a dwarf goldsmith,
Which brings its owner the best of luck:
Every year it sheds its scales,
Worth five hundred groschen in cash.

Ade, mein Kind! Ade für heut!
Der Morgenhahn im Dorfe schreit."

Farewell, child! Farewell for today!
The cock in the village cries morning.'

Poem written ?1828
Also set by Viardot

---

[1] 'Nixe Binsefuß' is the second of Mörike's four *Schiffer- und Nixen-Märchen*.

46 Gesang Weylas[1]

Du bist Orplid, mein Land!
Das ferne leuchtet;

Weyla's song

You are Orplid, my land!
That shines afar;

[1] During his adolescence Mörike would often spend summer nights in the woods with his friend Ludwig Bauer, seeking refuge from reality in his imagination and inventing the dream island of Orplid, Weyla, its tutelary goddess, and its strange inhabitants, including Ulmon the wizard and the female elf Silpelit – see 'Elfenlied'. Wolf told Emil Kauffmann that he imagined Weyla sitting on a moonlit reef, accompanying herself on the harp. The orchestral version increases the incantatory mood by adding clarinet and horn. Orplid is described in Part I of *Maler Nolten* by the actor Larkens, a porte-parole for Mörike himself who here recalls his youthful friendship with Bauer:

> Ich hatte in der Zeit, da ich noch auf der Schule studierte, einen Freund, dessen Denkart und ästhetisches Bestreben mit dem meinigen Hand in Hand ging; wir trieben in den Freistunden unser Wesen miteinander, wir bildeten uns bald eine eigene Sphäre von Poesie, und noch jetzt kann ich nur mit Rührung daran zurückdenken. [. . .] Wir erfanden für unsere Dichtung einen außerhalb der bekannten Welt gelegenen Boden, eine abgeschlossene Insel, worauf ein kräftiges Heldenvolk, doch in verschiedene Stämme, Grenzen und Charakterabstufungen geteilt, aber mit so ziemlich gleichförmiger Religion, gewohnt haben soll. Die Insel hieß O r p l i d, und ihre Lage dachte man sich in dem Stillen Ozean zwischen Neuseeland und Südamerika. Orplid hieß vorzugsweise die Stadt des bedeutendsten Königreichs: sie soll von göttlicher Gründung gewesen sein und die Göttin W e y l a, von welcher auch der Hauptfluß des Eilands den Namen hatte, war ihre besondere Beschützerin. Stückweise und nach den wichtigsten Zeiträumen erzählten wir uns die Geschichte dieser Völker. An merkwürdigen Kriegen und Abenteuern fehlte es nicht. Unsere Götterlehre streifte hie und da an die griechische, behielt aber im ganzen ihr Eigentümliches, auch die untergeordnete Welt von Elfen, Feen und Kobolden war nicht ausgeschlossen.
>
> Orplid, einst der Augapfel der Himmlischen, mußte endlich ihrem Zorne erliegen, als die alte Einfalt nach und nach einer verderblichen Verfeinerung der Denkweise und der Sitten zu weichen begann. Ein schreckliches Verhängnis raffte die lebende Menschheit dahin, selbst ihre Wohnungen sanken, nur das Lieblingskind Weylas, nämlich Burg und Stadt Orplid, durfte, obgleich ausgestorben und öde, als ein traurig schönes Denkmal vergangener Hoheit stehen bleiben. Die Götter wandten sich auf ewig ab von diesem Schauplatz, kaum daß jene erhabene Herrscherin zuweilen ihm noch einen Blick vergönnte, und auch diesen nur um eines einzigen Sterblichen willen, der, einem höheren Willen zufolge, die allgemeine Zerstörung weit überleben sollte.

I had, when still at school, a friend whose way of thinking and aesthetic aspirations went hand in hand with my own; in our free time, following our natural bent, we soon created a poetic world, which even today I cannot recall without emotion. [. . .] We invented for our literary purposes a realm lying beyond the known world, in complete seclusion, where allegedly a race of mighty heroes once lived, divided into various tribes, boundaries, and with differences of character, yet with a basically uniform religion. The island was called *Orplid*, and we imagined it to be located in the Pacific Ocean between New Zealand and South America. Orplid was also the chosen name of the city of the most important kingdom: it was said to have been founded by the gods, and the Goddess *Weyla*, after whom the island's main river was called, was its special patron. In fragmentary fashion, and following the order of the main epochs, we would tell each other the history of these peoples. There was no lack of remarkable wars and adventures. Our mythology had a few points in common with that of the Greeks, but on the whole retained its own character; it also included a subordinate world of elves, fairies and goblins.

Orplid, once the favourite of the immortals, ultimately had to suffer their wrath, when the ancient simplicity gradually gave way to a corrupting refinement of thought and morals. A

Vom Meere dampfet dein besonnter Strand[1]	Sea mists rise from your sunlit shore
Den Nebel, so der Götter Wange feuchtet.	And moisten the cheeks of the gods.
Uralte Wasser steigen	Ancient waters climb,
Verjüngt um deine Hüften, Kind!	Rejuvenated, child, about your waist!
Vor deiner Gottheit beugen	Kings, who attend you,
Sich Könige, die deine Wärter sind.	Bow down before your divinity.

Also set by E. Kauffmann

47 Die Geister am Mummelsee[2] / The ghosts on Mummelsee

Vom Berge was kommt dort	What's this winding down the midnight
um Mitternacht spät	mountain
Mit Fackeln so prächtig herunter?	With torches and such splendour?
Ob das wohl zum Tanze, zum Feste	Can they be going to a banquet or ball?
noch geht?	
Mir klingen die Lieder so munter.	Their singing sounds so joyful.
O nein!	Oh no!
So sage, was mag es wohl sein?	Then tell me what it can be?
Das, was du da siehest, ist Totengeleit,[3]	What you see is a funeral procession,
Und was du da hörest, sind Klagen.	And what you hear are lamentations.
Dem König, dem Zauberer, gilt es zu Leid,	They are mourning the king, the sorcerer,

---

    terrible fate snatched away all the human inhabitants, even their dwellings sank into oblivion, only Weyla's favourite creation, the castle and city of Orplid, was allowed to remain, extinct and desolate as it was, as a sad and beautiful monument to past grandeur. The gods turned from this scene for ever, and that noble goddess who ruled it rarely deigned to look at it, and only did so for the sake of a single mortal soul who by higher decree was long to survive the general destruction.

1   First edition (1838): Vom Meere dampfet dein erwärmter Strand. Mörike's 'Der letzte König von Orplid' owes much to Justinus Kerner's interest in the supernatural, especially his *Reiseschatten*. Like Kerner's *König Eginhart*, 'Der letzte König von Orplid' is written half in verse and half in prose.
2   The poem forms scene 7 of 'Der letzte König von Orplid' in *Maler Nolten*, where the stage directions read: 'Night. Moonlight. Wooded valley. Mummelsee. A large funeral procession of hovering wraiths winds its way down the mountainside. The King sits on a hill in the foreground, staring at the procession. Below, on the other side of the valley, unaware of the King, two young fairies.' It is the two young fairies who recite the verse (which has no title), and when they have finished, the wizard King Ulmon, who having claimed equality with the gods is condemned to live eternally until they release him from life, begs Weyla to let him die. He dreams that it is he who is lying in the crystal coffin, smiled over by his long deceased wife. What existed as a conversation between two fairies in *Maler Nolten*, published in 1832, appeared six years later in the first edition of Mörike's poems as 'Die Geister am Mummelsee'. The Mummelsee, a tarn in the Black Forest, features in a number of German poems, including Ludwig Hölty's 'Am Mummelsee', August Schnezler's *Mummelsee-Balladen* and Book 5, Chapter 10, of Hans Jakob Christoffel von Grimmelshausen's *Simplicissimus*.
3   Wolf's accompaniment here resembles Wagner's music for Titurel's funeral cortège in *Parsifal*, beginning „Geleiten wir".

Sie bringen ihn wieder getragen.[1]
>O weh!
So sind es die Geister vom See!

Sie schweben herunter[2] ins
>Mummelseetal –
Sie haben den See schon betreten –
Sie rühren und netzen den Fuß nicht
>einmal –
Sie schwirren in leisen Gebeten –

>O schau,
Am Sarge die glänzende Frau!

Jetzt öffnet der See das grünspiegelnde
>Tor;
Gib acht, nun tauchen sie nieder!
Es schwankt eine lebende Treppe hervor,
Und – drunten schon summen
>die Lieder.
>>Hörst du?
Sie singen ihn unten zur Ruh.

Die Wasser, wie lieblich sie brennen
>und glühn!
Sie spielen in grünendem Feuer;
Es geisten die Nebel am Ufer dahin,
Zum Meere verzieht sich der Weiher –
>Nur still!
Ob dort sich nichts rühren will?

Es zuckt in der Mitten – o Himmel!
>ach hilf!
Nun kommen sie wieder, sie kommen!
Es orgelt im Rohr und es klirret im Schilf;

Nur hurtig, die Flucht nur genommen!
>Davon!
Sie wittern, sie haschen mich schon!

They are bearing him back down again.
>Oh mercy!
They must be the ghosts of the lake!

They're gliding down to
>the Mummelsee valley –
Already they've alighted on the lake –
They move without ever wetting
>their feet –
They hover above while murmuring
>prayers –

>Oh look,
The glistening woman there by the coffin!

The lake now opens its mirror-green
>doors;
Look out, already they're cascading down!
A living staircase, wavering, rises,
And down in the depths they're droning
>their songs.
>>Can you hear?
They're singing him to rest below.

How sweetly the waters burn and glow,

Flickering in the green fire!
The mists swirling away on the shore,
The lake disappears into the sea –
>Hush now!
Will nothing ever move there again?

A swirl in the middle – O heavens!
>Ah help!
The ghosts – they're coming again!
There's a roar in the reeds and a wind
>in the rushes;
Quick now, run, take flight!
>Away!
They've caught my scent, they're
>catching me!

Poem written c. 1828
Also set by Karl Mörike

1 First edition (1838):

>Und Geister nur sind's, die ihn tragen.
>>Ach wohl!
>Sie singen so traurig und hohl.

2 First edition (1838): hernieder.

48 Storchenbotschaft[1]

Des Schäfers sein Haus und das steht auf zwei Rad,
Steht hoch auf der Heiden, so frühe wie spat;
Und wenn nur ein mancher so'n Nachtquartier hätt!
Ein Schäfer tauscht nicht mit dem König sein Bett.

Und käm' ihm zu Nacht auch was Seltsames vor,
Er betet sein Sprüchel und legt sich aufs Ohr;
Ein Geistlein, ein Hexlein, so lustige Wicht',
Sie klopfen ihm wohl, doch er antwortet nicht.

Einmal doch, da ward es ihm wirklich zu bunt:
Es knopert am Laden, es winselt der Hund;
Nun ziehet mein Schäfer den Riegel – ei schau!
Da stehen zwei Störche, der Mann und die Frau.

Das Pärchen, es machet ein schön Kompliment,
Es möchte gern reden, ach, wenn es nur könnt'!
Was will mir das Ziefer! – ist so was erhört?
Doch ist mir wohl fröhliche Botschaft beschert.

Ihr seid wohl dahinten zu Hause am Rhein?
Ihr habt wohl mein Mädel gebissen ins Bein?
Nun weinet das Kind und die Mutter noch mehr,
Sie wünschet den Herzallerliebsten sich her?

Und wünschet daneben die Taufe bestellt:
Ein Lämmlein, ein Würstlein, ein Beutelein Geld?

Stork-tidings

The shepherd's house stands on two wheels,
High on the moor, morning and night,
A lodging most would be glad of!
A shepherd wouldn't change his bed with a king.

And should by night any strange thing occur,
He prays a brief prayer and lies down to sleep;
A ghost, a witch, some airy creature –
They might knock, but he'll not answer.

But once it really became too much:
The shutters banged, the dog whined;
So my shepherd unbolts – lo and behold!
Two storks stand there, husband and wife.

The couple, they make a beautiful bow,
They'd like to speak, if only they could!
What do these fowl want? Whoever heard the like?
They must have joyful tidings for me.

I guess you live there, down by the Rhine?
I guess you've pecked my girl on the leg?
The child's now crying, the mother still more,
Wanting her sweetheart by her side?

And wanting the christening arranged:
A lambkin, a sausage, a purse of money?

---

1 See HW to Friedrich Eckstein, 27 March 1888, p. 351.

So sagt nur, ich käm' in zwei Tag' oder drei,	Well, tell her I'm coming in two days or three,
Und grüßt mir mein Bübel und rührt ihm den Brei!	Say hello to my boy, give his pap a stir!
Doch halt! warum stellt ihr zu zweien euch ein?	But wait! Why have two of you come?
Es werden doch, hoff' ich, nicht Zwillinge sein? –	It can't, I hope, be a case of twins? –
Da klappern die Störche im lustigsten Ton,[1]	The storks clap their beaks most merrily,
Sie nicken und knixen und fliegen davon.*	They nod and curtsey and fly away.*

Poem written 1838
Also set by Distler
* Wolf repeats the final line.

HEFT X

BOOK X

49 Zur Warnung[2]

By way of warning

Einmal nach einer lustigen Nacht	Once, after a convivial night,
War ich am Morgen seltsam aufgewacht:	I woke in the morning, feeling odd:
Durst, Wasserscheu, ungleich Geblüt;	Thirst, hydrophobia, unsteady pulse,
Dabei gerührt und weichlich im Gemüt,	Emotional and sentimental,
Beinah poetisch,[3] ja, ich bat die Muse um ein Lied.	Almost poetic, yes, I asked my Muse for a song.
Sie, mit verstelltem Pathos, spottet' mein,	With feigned pathos she mocked me,
Gab mir den schnöden Bafel ein:	Serving up this vile doggerel:
„Es schlagt eine Nachtigall Am Wasserfall;[4]	*Nightingale doth call By waterfall;*

---

1 The dactylic rhythm conveys the giggling storks' flapping wings, and the hilarious waltz tune ends on a merrily sustained B flat for the voice. Writing to Oskar Grohe on 3 March 1893, Wolf congratulates his friend on the birth of his son Helmuth, enclosing this doggerel that quotes from 'Storchenbotschaft' and puns on his son's name:

Heut klappert nur Einer „im lustigsten Ton",	Today only one claps its beak most merrily,
Hellmuthig er grüßet u. flieget davon.	Helmut greets you with bright eyes & flies away.

2 See HW to Marie Lang, 25 February 1888, p. 348.
3 Wolf quotes „Beinah poetisch" in a letter of 3 March 1894 to Frieda Zerny to describe how he was in the mood to compose.
4 Mörike would have known these lines from 'Des Schäfers Tageszeiten' in *Des Knaben Wunderhorn*:

Dort draus am Wasserfall	Out there by the waterfall
Schlaget die Nachtigall,	The nightingale's song
Giebt Wiederhall.	Is echoing.

Und ein Vogel ebenfalls,	*Another bird does the same –*
Der schreibt sich Wendehals,[1]	*Wryneck is his name,*
Johann Jakob Wendehals;	*Johann Jakob Wryneck;*
Der tut tanzen	*Who doth dance*
Bei den Pflanzen	*By the plants*
Obbemeldten Wasserfalls –"	*Of said waterfall –*
So ging es fort; mir wurde immer bänger.	And so it went on; I grew ever uneasier.
Jetzt sprang ich auf: zum Wein! Der war denn auch mein Retter.	Then I leapt up: Wine! That was my salvation.
– Merkt's euch, ihr tränenreichen Sänger,	– Mark well, you weepy bards:
Im Katzenjammer ruft man keine Götter!	Call not on the gods, when you're hung over!

Poem written 1836

50 Auftrag[2]

A commission

In poetischer Epistel	A desperate fellow calls for help
Ruft ein desperater Wicht:	In this poetic epistle:
Lieber Vetter! Vetter Christel!	My dear cousin, cousin Christel!
Warum schreibt Er aber nicht?[3]	Why do you not write?
Weiß Er doch, es lassen Herzen,	You know that hearts
Die die Liebe angeweht,	Smitten with love
Ganz und gar nicht mit sich scherzen,	Cannot be trifled with,
Und nun vollends ein Poet!	Least of all a poet's!
Denn ich bin von dem Gelichter,	For I am one of those creatures
Dem der Kopf beständig voll;	Whose head is always full;
Bin ich auch nur halb ein Dichter,	And though I'm only half a poet,
Bin ich doch zur Hälfte toll.	I am half demented.
Amor hat Ihn mir verpflichtet,	Cupid has pledged you to me,
Seinen Lohn weiß Er voraus.	You know what your reward will be.
Und der Mund, der Ihm berichtet,	And the lips that keep you informed
Geht dabei auch leer nicht aus.	Shall not go unrewarded.
Pass' Er denn zur guten Stunde,	So wait for the right moment
Wenn Sein Schatz durch's Lädchen schaut,	When your love looks from her window,
Lock' ihr jedes Wort vom Munde,	Go and find out every word
Das mein Schätzchen ihr vertraut.	My sweetheart confided to her.

1 Possibly a veiled reference to the poet Reinick ('Wendehals' = wryneck).
2 Wolf subtitles his song 'Couplet', thus implying that he has a French operetta style in mind.
3 First edition (1838) began:

In poetischer Epistel	In this poetic epistle
Ruft ein desperater Wicht	A desperate fellow cries
Aus dem Ton der höchsten Fistel:	In a thin, high-pitched voice:
Schurke, warum schreibt Er nicht?!	Rogue, why do you not write?!

Schreib' Er mir dann von dem Mädchen
Ein halb Dutzend Bogen voll
Und daneben ein Traktätchen,
Wie ich mich verhalten soll.*

Poem written 1828
* Wolf repeats the final line.

Then write me a six-page letter
All about the girl,
Enclosing a treatise of advice
On how I should respond!*

51 Bei einer Trauung

Vor lauter hochadligen Zeugen
Kopuliert man ihrer Zwei;
Die Orgel hängt voll Geigen,[1]
Der Himmel nicht, mein' Treu!
Seht doch! s i e weint ja greulich,
E r macht ein Gesicht abscheulich!
Denn leider freilich, freilich,
Keine Lieb' ist nicht dabei.

Poem written 1838

At a wedding

Before exclusively highborn witnesses,
Two exclusive people are being wed;
The organ pours forth joyful music,
But there'll be no joy in heaven, I vow!
Just look, *she's* crying her eyes out,
He's making a dreadful face!
For I'm very very sorry to say,
That love is wholly absent.

52 Selbstgeständnis

Ich bin meiner Mutter einzig Kind,
Und weil die andern ausblieben sind,
Was weiß ich wie viel, die sechs oder sieben,
Ist eben alles an mir hängen blieben;
Ich hab' müssen die Liebe, die Treue, die Güte
Für ein ganz halb Dutzend allein aufessen,
Ich will's mein Lebtag nicht vergessen.
Es hätte mir aber noch wohl mögen frommen,
Hätt' ich nur auch Schläg' für sechse bekommen.

Poem written 1837

Self-confession

I am my mother's only child,
And since the others failed to appear,
Who knows how many, six or seven,

Everything had to centre on me;
I've had to devour all by myself
The love, loyalty and kindness for
   a full half-dozen,
I'll never forget it, as long as I live.
I dare say it would have done me no harm,

If I'd been whipped for six as well.

---

1 Mörike is playing wittily with the idiom: „Der Himmel hängt voller Geigen" = 'the future is rosy'. The pedal point throughout the first half of the song simulates a funeral march.

Abschied[1]

Unangeklopft ein Herr tritt abends bei mir ein:
„Ich habe die Ehr', Ihr Rezensent[2] zu sein."
Sofort nimmt er das Licht in die Hand,
Besieht lang meinen Schatten an der Wand,
Rückt nah und fern: „Nun, lieber junger Mann,
Sehn Sie doch gefälligst mal Ihre Nas' so von der Seite an!
Sie geben zu, daß das ein Auswuchs is."
– Das? Alle Wetter – gewiß!
Ei Hasen! ich dachte nicht,
All mein Lebtage nicht,
Daß ich so eine Weltnase führt' im Gesicht!![3]

Der Mann sprach noch Verschied'nes hin und her,
Ich weiß, auf meine Ehre, nicht mehr;
Meinte vielleicht, ich sollt' ihm beichten.
Zuletzt stand er auf; ich tat ihm leuchten.
Wie wir nun an der Treppe sind,
Da geb' ich ihm, ganz froh gesinnt,
Einen kleinen Tritt
Nur so von hinten auf's Gesäße mit –
Alle Hagel! ward das ein Gerumpel,
Ein Gepurzel, ein Gehumpel!
Dergleichen hab' ich nie gesehn,

Goodbye

Without knocking a man one evening enters my room:
'I have the honour, sir, to be your critic.'
He instantly takes the lamp in his hand,
Surveys at length my shadow on the wall,
Moves back and forth: 'Now, young man,
Pray observe your nose in profile!
You'll admit that it's a monstrosity.'
– What? Good god – you're right!
Bless my soul! I never thought,
In all my life,
I had a nose of such cosmic size!!

The man said various other things,
What – I truly no longer recall;
Maybe he thought I should confess to him.
At last he got up; I lit his way.
As we stood at the top of the stairs,
I give him, in the best of spirits,
A little kick
On his derrière –
Goodness me! What a rumbling,
A tumbling, a stumbling!
I never saw the like,

---

[1] Mörike's 'Abschied' is the final poem of the sixth edition of his *Gedichte*. The copy of 'Abschied' that Mörike sent Hermann Kurz on 6 June 1837 was titled 'Der kommt nimmer'.
[2] Wolf had an acerbic side to his character, and would defend himself fiercely (see HW to his mother, 19 April 1890, p. 354) against hostile criticism and also attack his detractors – especially Eduard Hanslick, who had not only deigned to criticise Wolf's idol Wagner, but also revered the music of Johannes Brahms, whose songs Wolf abhorred, because of what he considered to be their insensitive prosody. The first edition of 'Abschied' bore the marking *diskret mauschelnd* ('to be sung in a discrete Yiddish manner'), and though this was deleted from subsequent editions, there can be little doubt that Wolf was thinking of Hanslick, whose mother was Jewish – a fact not lost on the Viennese society of the time. See HW to his parents, late June or early July 1883, p. 453, for Wolf's opinion of critics. Both Mörike and Wolf suffered from acerbic critics and neither enjoyed more than parochial recognition in their lifetimes. Ernst Decsey put it pithily and wittily when he wrote: „Der unbekannte Wolf hat den unbekannten Mörike entdeckt." ('The unknown Wolf discovered the unknown Mörike.') Cf. Goethe's 'Der Rezensent'.
[3] Mörike himself had a tiny nose.

All mein Lebtage nicht gesehn,
Einen Menschen so rasch die Trepp'
    hinabgehn![4]

In all my life never saw
A man go downstairs so fast!

Poem written 1837

---

4   At the end of 'Abschied' Wolf quotes music from Joseph Lanner's waltz 'Hoffnungs-Strahlen', Op. 158. Helene Gabillon, the close friend of Vally Franck, recounts in 'Erinnerungen an Hugo Wolf' how Wolf used to sit at the piano and play Lanner's waltzes with inimitable panache and romantic longing. Joseph Lanner (1801–1843) was an Austrian dance composer and violinist whose string band, which later developed into a full-size orchestra, played in taverns, coffee-houses and the Prater. He died of typhus at the pinnacle of his fame.

Paul Peitl
(1853–1917)

		page
Ein Grab	8–10 December 1876	421

POET

Poet, art critic, librettist and a friend of Wolf from his student years, Peitl furnished him with a libretto, *König Alboin*, which Wolf began to set in 1877 – completing a mere 21 bars. Peitl, who sometimes wrote under the pseudonyms of Paul Günther and Paul Mannsberg, also presented Wolf with another libretto, the details of which have not survived. On one of his many searches for accommodation in Vienna, Wolf visited Alleegasse 18, where a room had been advertised on the second floor, and he was amazed when Peitl opened the door. HW to his father, 24 November 1877, below, betrays Wolf's affection for the poet and admiration for his poetry.

COMPOSER

Wolf included 'Ein Grab' in a volume of songs with the title LIEDER *und* GESÆNGE. *1tes Heft. In Musik gesetzt von* HUGO WOLF that he sent in the summer of 1877 to the Ministry of Culture and Education; see p. 4.

LETTERS

HW to his father, Vienna, 24 November 1877

Heute bin ich besonders glücklich. Den ganzen Vor- und Nachmittag über suchte ich für mich eine passende Wohnung;¹ doch fand ich, soviel Mühe ich

---

1   Wolf had an extraordinary propensity for changing apartments. He hired rooms at well over thirty different addresses – for a variety of reasons. They were either too expensive or could not accommodate a piano. Or he quarrelled with the landlord or, more often than not, left because of noise: he could work only in absolute silence. If one also bears in mind the remarkable number of wealthy patrons who throughout his career invited him to stay for weeks or months on end, it becomes clear that Wolf led a nomadic existence in Vienna and the surrounding countryside. This unsettled existence is mirrored in the multiplicity of place names, printed at the head of each letter extract.

mir auch gab, nirgends das Rechte. Überall wurde für ein Zimmer 18–20 fl. verlangt. Der Zufall leitete mich in die Alleegasse N° 18, wo im 2. Stock links ein Zimmer angekündigt war. Ich läute an – wer öffnet mir nicht die Thür? G.[1] in höchsteigener Person, mit dem ich immer gewünscht zusammenzuwohnen, trat heraus und fragte nach meinem Begehren; er mußte mich nicht gleich erkannt haben, als ich ihm jedoch meinen Namen genannt, küßte er mich fast zu Tode und drückte mich so ab, daß ich schier erstickt wäre. Sogleich führte er mich in seine Behausung, zeigte mir seine schöne Bibliothek, las mir ein gutes Teil von seinem Drama, das nun schon vollendet und wirklich ergreifende Verse enthält, zeigte mir auch seine Gedichte und bat mich, selbe in Musik zu setzen, was ich denn auch bereitwillig versprach. Nun kam die Quartierfrage, aber da sah's gar jämmerlich aus, denn seine Mutter verlangte nicht weniger und nicht mehr als 23 fl. per Monat; das war mir denn doch zu bunt, und ich, der ich mir schon geschmeichelt, mit höchstens 15 fl. durchzukommen, fiel aus allen sieben Himmeln. Ich verabschiedete mich mit dem Versprechen, ihn bald zu besuchen.

Today I am especially happy. I spent all morning and afternoon looking for suitable accommodation; but however hard I tried I could find nothing that was right. Everyone was demanding 18–20 florins for a room. Chance led me to Alleegasse 18 where a room was advertised on the second floor to the left. I ring the bell – and who should open the door? None other than G. himself, with whom I'd always wished to share an apartment. He came out and asked me what I wanted; he cannot have recognised me to begin with, but when I told him my name, he almost kissed me to death and hugged me so violently that I all but suffocated. He led me at once into his home, showed me his beautiful library, read me a good portion of the play he had just finished and which contains some really moving lines, and also showed me his poems, asking me to set some to music – which I willingly promised to do. We then discussed the room, but my prospects there were pretty dismal, because his mother insisted on charging nothing less and nothing more than 23 florins a month; that was too much for me. I came down to earth with a bump, especially because I had flattered myself that I could get away with 15 florins a month. I said farewell and promised to visit him again soon.

---

1   Paul Günther, one of Peitl's pseudonyms.

HW to Käthe Wolf, Ober-Döbling, 7 December 1892

Die Skizze zum „König Alboin"[1] hat mir übrigens viel Spaß gemacht; man spürt schon das kleine Wölferl[2] darin; – es heult nicht mit den Andern, wenn schon auch sein eigenes Geheul noch lange nicht das richtige ist, aber es heult doch etwas apart u. das will auch was sein.

Composing the 'King Alboin' sketch was great fun. You can recognise the little wolf cub in the music; even though he doesn't yet howl with all the others, and though his own howl is still far from right, there is something special about it, & that must mean something.

LIED

Ein Grab

Wenn des Mondes bleiches Licht
Auf das dunkle Grab hier fällt,
Dann aus meinem Auge bricht
Die Trän', die keine Macht mehr hält.

Keine Blum am Grabe blüht,
Keine Seele denkt daran;
Kalter Wind vorüber zieht –
Was deckt das kühle Grab, sag an?

Was des Grabes Hülle deckt,
Kannst du dann nur ahnen,
Wenn dich gleicher Schmerz bewegt,
Der mag dich daran mahnen.

A grave

When the moon's pale light
Falls on the dark grave here,
A tear trickles from my eyes,
That nothing can restrain.

No flower blossoms by the grave,
Not a soul is aware of it;
Cold winds blow by –
Tell me what the cool grave conceals?

What lies beneath the grave's shroud,
You can divine only
When you too are moved by such grief –
That grief may then forewarn you.

---

[1] Wolf's sister had clearly forwarded him the sketch that he had left in Windischgraz during his last lengthy sojourn there. Peitl's libretto was based on *Der böse Geist*, a story by Franz Hoffmann, and Theodor Körner's *Alboin und Rosamunde*. See also letter to Anna Vinzenzberg, p. 296.
[2] To friends and relatives Wolf would often sign himself Wölfing, Wölferl, Wolferl, Wluhu and Lupusculus.

LUDWIG PFAU
(1821–1894)

			page
Im stillen Friedhof	10–28 May 1876	SATB with piano accompaniment	423

POET

Having finished school in Heilbronn, Pfau initially devoted himself to horticulture (his father's profession) but soon lost interest and went to Paris where he earned a living from portraiture and colouring botanical books. In 1841 compulsory military service caused him to return to Heilbronn, where he fell in love with Maria Widmann, who inspired many of his poems and songs. He matriculated at Heidelberg University in 1846 and became increasingly interested in politics. Editor of the satirical magazine *Der Eulenspiegel* at the time of the 1848 Revolution, he had to flee abroad as a result of his political activities. From 1852 he lived in Paris where he made a name for himself as translator and art critic. He met Heinrich Heine, translated Claude Tillier's *Mon Oncle Benjamin* (one of Wolf's favourite novels) and wrote a book on Belgian painting. His political verse was once extremely popular, especially poems such as 'Herr Biedermeier', 'Die deutschen Flüchtlinge', 'Zum 18. März 1848', 'Badisches Wiegenlied' and the 'Sonette für das deutsche Volk auf das Jahr 1850'. His *Gedichte*, first published in 1848, were reprinted in 1858 and his 'Schillerlied' was set to music by Meyerbeer in 1859. After the 1863 amnesty he returned to Württemberg, where he co-founded the Volkspartei – he was continually at loggerheads with the authorities and endured several periods of house arrest. At the outbreak of the Franco-Prussian War, he was banished because of his virulent attacks on Bismarck. When Mörike died in 1875, his family searched for a literary figure to finish the novel *Maler Nolten*, which he had left incomplete. Paul Heyse was approached but declined because of ill-health, and Pfau was also considered, but the task eventually fell to Julius Klaiber (see note 2 to Mörike, 'Der Gärtner', p. 384). Pfau attended Mörike's funeral, an honour accorded to very few of the poet's friends. He spent his old age in Stuttgart, where he became increasingly blind and deaf, and died there of a heart attack. His verse was much admired by the young Schoenberg, who set eleven of his poems in the early 1890s. There are also two charming settings of his verse by Alexander von Zemlinsky: 'O Blätter, dürre Blätter!' and 'O Sterne, goldene Sterne'.

COMPOSER

Wolf's source for 'Im stillen Friedhof' was probably the anthology *Dichtergrüße. Neuere deutsche Lyrik ausgewählt von Elise Polko*, which contained seven more poems that he was to set, see p. 205. 'Im stillen Friedhof' was one of Wolf's manuscripts that his sister Käthe sent him some five and a half years after their father's death. When Wolf saw that his father had written an inscription on the score, he was profoundly moved – see p. 519.

LIED

Im stillen Friedhof[1]

Wenn ich im stillen Friedhof geh',
    Wird mir so schwer zu Herzen,
    Daß man die treu'ste Menschenbrust,
    Die mitgetragen[2] Leid und Lust,
    So eilig kann verschmerzen.
Gras wächst darüber, ach wie bald!
    Das Grab wird selber heiter.
    Wie wenn ein Blatt vom Wipfel fällt,
    So geht ein Leben aus der Welt –
    Die Vögel singen weiter.
O Menschenherz mit deinem Stolz!
    Was flüstern die Cypressen?
    „Wir steh'n auf einem schmalen Raum,
    Darunter liegt ein Herze kaum,
    So ist es schon vergessen."*

In the silent cemetery

When I walk in the silent cemetery,
    I grow heavy at heart
    That you can forget so swiftly
    The most loyal of human beings
    With whom you shared joy and pain.
Grass grows over them, ah, how soon!
    The grave itself grows bright.
    Like a leaf falling from the treetop,
    A life departs this world –
    The birds continue to sing.
O hearts of men with your pride!
    What do the cypresses whisper?
    'We stand on a narrow plot of earth,
    No sooner does a heart lie underground
    Than it is forgotten.'*

* There are multiple repetitions of the final three lines.

---

1 The poem has no title in the *Gedichte von Ludwig Pfau* (Franckh'sche Verlagshandlung, 1858) where it is the second of ten poems of a cycle entitled *Lieder vom Herzen*. In a later edition, published by G. J. Göschen'sche Verlagshandlung in 1874, the poem stands alone with the title 'Im Friedhof'. In Elise Polko's *Dichtergrüße* anthology the title is 'Im stillen Friedhof'.
2 Pfau: mit getragen.

August von Platen
(1797–1835)

			page
Christnacht	24 December 1886– May 1889	for chorus, soloists and large orchestra	427

POET

Platen, in full Karl August Georg Maximilian, Graf von Platen-Hallermünde, suffered from a sense of isolation throughout his short life, as can be seen from his *Tagebuch*, a diary he kept assiduously from the age of thirteen until his death. Born of impoverished aristocratic parents, he abhorred Napoleon and his invasion of Germany, enlisted in the army in 1814 (a career quite unsuitable for a gay and eccentric dreamer), saw little action and in 1818 obtained indefinite leave of absence. He went to Würzburg to study law, botany and zoology but was soon spending more time indulging his love of languages. At his military boarding school in Munich he had learned Latin, Greek, Italian and English, and he now began studying Persian and Arabic, perhaps in emulation of Rückert, to whom he dedicated his *Lyrische Blätter* (1821) and Goethe, whose *West-östlicher Divan* he read in 1819. Although Goethe in *Über Kunst und Alterthum* praised Platen's poetry, he held that his verse was not suitable for singing („nicht für den Gesang bestimmt") – a statement he might have revised had he ever heard Schubert's 'Die Liebe hat gelogen' and 'Du liebst mich nicht' (1822), Loewe's 'Der Pilgrim vor St. Just' (1832) and Brahms's 'Wie rafft' ich mich auf in der Nacht' and 'Der Strom, der neben mir verrauschte' (1864). Platen turned his back on Germany in 1826, moved to Italy and returned home on only two occasions before he died almost a decade later.

In 1828 he became involved in one of the most infamous spats in German literary history. It all started when Heine published in his *Reisebilder* a poem by Karl Leberecht Immermann that mocked the trend of translating Persian poetry; Platen responded with *Der romantische Oedipus* (1829), a play in which he satirised Heine's Jewishness and enjoined Immermann ('Nimmermann' he's called in the play) to cut off his tongue and fingers; Heine then entered the fray in the next volume of his *Reisebilder* and, in prose that makes for unpleasant reading, poured scorn on Platen's aristocratic background, his homosexuality and his poetic pretensions. But Platen's finest poetry (he published *Ghaselen* in 1821 and *Sonette aus Venedig* in 1824) deserves a place in any anthology of German verse. He died in Syracuse on 5 December 1835 of an undefined gastric fever, exacerbated by overdosing on medicaments he hoped would cure the cholera he imagined, erroneously, that he had contracted.

COMPOSER

According to Ernst Decsey, it was Friedrich Eckstein who encouraged Wolf to write a work in the manner of Bach's *Christmas Oratorio* – and composition started, significantly, on Christmas Eve 1886. When Felix Weingartner expressed interest in performing some of Wolf's orchestral works, Wolf suggested a few of his orchestrated songs as well as *Penthesilea* and 'Christnacht'. The scores were duly dispatched, but when Arthur Nikisch also showed interest in the work, Wolf asked Oskar Grohe to retrieve the score from Weingartner, who had not yet responded. When Grohe confirmed that Weingartner was still interested, Wolf travelled to Mannheim and Mainz where he met Weingartner and Ludwig Strecker, the director of Schott's Söhne, who, although impressed by Wolf's playing of the piece on the piano, insisted that he would like to hear the oratorio in performance before starting negotiations with a view to publication. 'Christnacht' was premiered on 9 April 1891 in Mannheim in the presence of the composer, who asked Grohe to write an explanatory programme note based on Wolf's own analysis of the work – see HW to Oskar Grohe, 26 February 1891, p. 426. In a letter to Heinrich Rauchberg of 10 April 1891, Wolf described the performance as an 'Achtungserfolg' only – a *succès d'estime* – blaming the Mannheim orchestra but also his own heavy scoring. Schott's lost interest in the work, which was published only after the composer's death, with revised scoring by Ferdinand Foll and Max Reger.

LETTERS

HW to Oskar Grohe, Perchtoldsdorf, 16 April 1890

Ein anderes Werk, darauf ich große Stücke halte, wäre „Die Christnacht", eine Hymne von Platen für Chor und Soli und großes Orchester komponiert. Die Partitur ist ziemlich schwierig, dafür ist das Werk kurz und dürfte eine große Wirkung auf das Publikum nicht verfehlen. Ich kann es mit bestem Gewissen empfehlen.

Another work that I set great store by would be 'Die Christnacht', a hymn by Platen for choir, soloists and large orchestra. The score is somewhat complicated, but the work is short and shouldn't fail to produce a huge effect on audiences. I can recommend it with the clearest of consciences.

HW to Oskar Grohe, 26 February 1891

Das Werk wird durch zwei Motive eingeleitet, die in ihrer Durchführung – anschwellend bis zum höchsten Glanze und wiederum allmählich verklingend – die ganze Introduktion beherrschen. Diese zwei Motive bilden den Kernpunkt der Komposition, die Persönlichkeit Christi, des Kindes und Weltüberwinders, symbolisierend. Einem kindlich schlichten, von Holzbläsern getragenen Gesange: – einem wirklichen Volksgesange, den ich bei den in Steiermark üblichen, ländlich naiven Darstellungen der Heiligen Nacht selbst als Kind mitgesungen – antwortet das Horn – später Posaunen – in pathetischer Weise. Es ist das Motiv, worauf im Verlaufe des Stückes der Chor der Gläubigen die Worte singt: „Preis dem Geborenen bringen wir dar". Ich betone „Gläubigen" weil ich einen Sang der Hirten, nach des Dichters Angabe, mit dem feierlich pompösen Charakter dieser Stelle nicht für vereinbar hielt. In seiner vollkommenen und ursprünglichen Gestalt tritt das erste, schlichte Thema jedoch erst im Hirtengesange: „die Engel schweben, singend und spielend, durch die Lüfte" auf u. z. im Orchester, derweil der Chor im Kontrapunkt eine dem ganzen Charakter der Situation entsprechende Weise intoniert, wodurch, wie ich mir schmeichle, eine schöne Wirkung erzielt wird. Gegen den Schluß des Werkes, in der Weissagung des Engels der Verkündigung und dem antwortenden Doppelchor der Hirten und Gläubigen tauchen durchweg andere musikalische Gedanken auf, die erst beim vollkommenen Abschluß des Ganzen in das vorher erwähnte pathetische Thema einmünden, das, von dem ganzen Orchester getragen und umflutet, in Flammenzügen aufrollt das Dogma der menschgewordenen Gottheit und der Erlösung.

The work is introduced by two motifs, which in their development – swelling to the greatest brilliance, then gradually dying away – dominate the whole introduction. These two motifs form the core of the composition, and symbolise the personality of Christ, the Child and the World-conqueror. To a simple, childlike melody in the woodwind – a genuine folk song, which in the naively rustic representations of Christmas Eve traditional in Styria I myself joined in singing as a child – the horn, and later the trombones, reply, with an expressive phrase. It is the motif to which in the course of the piece the chorus of Believers sings the words, 'We sing praises to the new-born Child'. I stress the word Believers, because I did not consider a Shepherds song, as specified by the poet, to be compatible with the solemn and grandiose character of this passage. The initial simple theme in its complete and original form, however, first appears in the Shepherds' song ('the angels float through space, singing and playing') – but in the orchestra, while the chorus intones in counterpoint a melody wholly in keeping with the character of the scene – by which means, I flatter myself, a fine effect is achieved. Towards the end of the work, in the prophecy of the Angel of the Annunciation, and the answering double chorus of the Shepherds and Believers, entirely fresh musical material appears that only with the conclusion of the whole piece flows into the previously mentioned expressive theme, which, borne aloft and flooded around by the entire orchestra, reveals in flaming outlines the dogma of Divinity become Man, and of Redemption.

LIED

Christnacht
*Hymnus für Chor, Soli
und großes Orchester*

Der Engel der Verkündigung

Seraphimsche Heere,
Schwingt das Goldgefieder
Gott dem Herrn zur Ehre,
Schwebt vom Himmelsthrone
Durchs Gewölk hernieder,
Süße Wiegenlieder
Singt dem Menschensohne!

Ein Hirte

Was seh' ich? Umgaukelt mich Schwindel
    und Traum?
Ein leuchtender Saum
Durchwebt den azurenen, ewigen Raum,
Und[1] schreitet die Sterne des Himmels entlang,
Mit leisem Gesang,
Der seligen Schaaren musikischer Gang.

Chor der Hirten

Die Engel schweben singend
Und spielend durch die Lüfte,
Und spenden süße Düfte,
Die Liljenstäbe schwingend.

Christmas Eve
*Hymn for chorus, soloists
and large orchestra*

The Angel of the Annunciation

Seraphic throngs,
With your pinions of gold,
Honour the Lord God,
Float down from the throne of Heaven
Through the clouds,
Sing sweet lullabies
To the Son of man!

A shepherd

What do I behold? Do dreams and
    deception flit about me?
A gleaming seam
Shoots through the eternal blue air
And passes along the stars of Heaven,
Singing softly –
The musical path of the blessed throng.

Chorus of shepherds

The angels float through space,
Singing and playing,
Shedding sweet fragrances,
Waving fleur-de-lis.

---

1 Platen: Es.

Chor der Seraphim

Wohlauf, ihr Hirtenknaben,
Es gilt dem Herrn zu dienen,
Es ist ein Stern erschienen,
Ob aller Welt erhaben.

Chor der Hirten

Wie aus des Himmels Thoren
Sie tief herab sich neigen!
Laßt Eigentriebe schweigen,
Die Liebe ward geboren![1]

Der Engel der Verkündigung

Fromme Glut entfache
Jedes Herz gelind,
Eilt nach jenem Dache,
Betet an das Kind!

Jener heißerflehte
Hort der Menschen lebt,
Der euch im Gebete
Lange vorgeschwebt.

Traun! Die Nacht des Bösen
Sinkt nun fort und fort,
Jener wird erlösen
Durch das Eine Wort.

Chor der Gläubigen[2]

Preis dem Geborenen
Bringen wir dar,
Preis der erkorenen
Gläubigen Schaar.[3]

Engel mit Lilien
Stehn im Azur,
Fromme Vigilien
Singt die Natur:

Der den kristallenen
Himmel vergaß,
Bringt zu Gefallenen
Ewiges Maß!

Chorus of Seraphim

Come, you shepherd lads,
The time has now come to serve the Lord,
A star has appeared,
Raised above the whole world.

Chorus of shepherds

How far they float down
From the gates of Heaven!
Let selfishness be silent,
Love has been born!

The Angel of the Annunciation

Let a devout glow
Gently kindle every heart!
Hasten to the rooftop,
Worship the Child!

That fervently desired
Refuge of humanity lives,
He who has for many years
Appeared to you in prayer.

Indeed! The devil's power
Declines apace,
He will redeem us
Through a *single* word.

Chorus of believers

We sing praises
To the new-born Child,
Praises to the chosen,
Believing throng.

Angels with lilies
Hover in the blue,
Nature keeps a devout vigil,
Singing the while:

He who forgot
Crystalline Heaven,
Brings eternal moderation
To the fallen!

---

1 Platen: Laßt Eigentriebe schweigen,/Die Liebe ward geboren! These two lines are given to the *Chor der Seraphim*.
2 Platen: *Chor der Hirten*. 3 These four lines are repeated at the end of the chorus.

Der Engel der Verkündigung

Schon les' ich in den Weiten
Des künft'gen Tages bang,
Ich höre Völker schreiten,
Sie athmen Untergang.*

Es naht der müden Erde
Ein frischer Morgen sich,
Auf dieses Kindes „Werde"
Erblüht sie jugendlich.

Chor der Seraphim

Vergeßt der Schmerzen jeden,
Vergeßt den tiefen Fall,
Und lebt mit uns im Eden,
Und lebt mit uns im All!¹

The Angel of the Annunciation

Already I discern in the distance
Things that make me fear the future,
I hear peoples setting forth,
Breathing destruction.

A fresh morning draws near
The weary earth,
Responding to the Child's 'Become',
Earth now blossoms youthfully.

Chorus of Seraphim

Forget every pain,
Forget the deep fall,
And live with us in Eden,
And live with us in the universe!

* Wolf repeats these lines.

1   The final quatrain is reprised at the end of Wolf's Hymn by the Chorus of Seraphim and the Chorus of Believers.

ROBERT REINICK
(1805–1852)

		page
Wiegenlied im Sommer	17 December 1882	437
Wiegenlied im Winter	20 December 1882	438
Wohin mit der Freud'?	31 December 1882	439
	version for solo soprano, solo tenor, four-part mixed choir and piano, ?1883	
Laut und traut	late 1882/early 1883 fragment	
Ständchen	19 January 1883	442
Nachtgruß	24 January 1883	441
Frühlingsglocken	19 February 1883	441
Liebesbotschaft	18 March 1883	443
Liebchen, wo bist du?	12 April 1883	440
Dem Vaterland	12 May 1890	446
	arranged for male voices and orchestra May–4 June 1890 and May–June 1894, revised 1897 and 1898	
Frohe Botschaft	25 June 1890	447
Drei Gedichte von Robert Reinick		
Gesellenlied	24 January 1888	444
Skolie	1 August 1889	445
Morgenstimmung	8 September–23 October 1896; arranged for chorus and orchestra as 'Morgenhymnus', 12–17 December 1897	445
Dem Vaterland	vocal score of second orchestrated version, 1895	446

POET

Ach, was ist das für ein Grausen,	Alas, how horrible it is,
Wenn ein Maler und ein Dichter	When a painter and a poet
Beid' in e i n e r Seele hausen!	Dwell in the *selfsame* soul!
Nimmer gibt es schlimmre Wichter.	Impossible to imagine worse companions.

These opening lines of 'Gefährliche Nachbarschaft' ('Dangerous neighbours') are a neat summary of Reinick's predicament: was he to become a painter or a poet? Having passed his Abitur, he studied art at the Berliner Akademie under Gottfried Schadow and Karl Begas, but after a single term the twenty-year-old expressed his dissatisfaction in a letter to Friedrich Blech of 14 February 1826. It was only when he met the similarly versatile Franz Kugler that he began to consider literature more seriously as a career. Kugler introduced him to Berlin's „Mittwochsgesellschaft", a literary society that met every Wednesday, where he encountered such poets as Alexis, Chamisso, Eichendorff and Fouqué. It was not long before Reinick made a name for himself. *Drei Umrisse nach Holzschnitten von Albrecht Dürer. Mit erklärendem Text und Gesängen* was published in 1830, to be followed a year later by *Ritter, Tod und Teufel nach Holzschnitten von Albrecht Dürer. Mit erklärendem Text*. And together with Kugler he published the *Liederbuch für deutsche Künstler* in 1833, the year in which some of his poems appeared in the *Deutscher Musenalmanach*, edited by Adelbert von Chamisso and Gustav Schwab. Despite the joy of seeing his poems in print, he was aware of the minor nature of his talent, as can be seen from this letter of 25 January 1833 to Kugler, in which he compares himself to 'great' poets such as Lenau and Anastasius Grün:

> [. . .] da fühlt man sich mit seinem bißchen Lyrik wie eine Mücke dagegen. Nun die Mücken freuen sich auch des Sonnenscheins und die Leute, die solche kleine Mücken an schönen Frühlingsabenden lustig summen hören und hin und her spielen sehen, haben auch ihre Freude dran [. . .]

> [. . .] if one compares one's own modest verses with theirs, one feels rather like a midge. But midges also enjoy the sunshine, and the people who have heard such little midges cheerfully buzzing on beautiful spring evenings, and have seen them flying to and fro, also enjoy them [. . .]

Four years later he published the book of poems that has endeared him to lovers of Lieder, *Lieder eines Malers mit Randzeichnungen seiner Freunde*, a volume illustrated by himself and some thirty friends. A letter from Reinick to Franz Kugler of 9 March 1837 describes his joy at seeing his fledgling poems ('Gelbschnäbel') surrounded by the beautiful maidens, flowers, landscapes, etc., of these drawings. „Was doch ein reiches Gefolge und glänzend Kleider in der Welt nicht alles machen können!" ('What cannot be achieved in this world by a sumptuous entourage and glittering apparel!') Composers were perhaps drawn to the poems by the beguiling artwork: imagine Schumann's delight at seeing Jakob Fürchtegott Dielmann's idealised landscape of church, river and castle illustrating 'Sonntags am Rheine'. Schumann's *Sechs Lieder nach R. Reinick*,

Op. 36, date from the summer of 1840 and remain the finest set of Reinick Lieder in the repertoire. Schumann and Reinick became close friends: many reciprocal visits took place, and in 1848 Reinick became godfather to Ludwig Schumann. Reinick tried to interest the composer in setting Eichendorff's *Die Glücksritter* (see 'Der Schreckenberger' and 'Der Glücksritter', pp. 43–4) as an opera, but Schumann considered the Novelle to be unsuitable material. Reinick did, however, spend some time writing an opera libretto (*Genoveva*) for Schumann, based on Tieck's tragedy *Leben und Tod der heiligen Genoveva* (1799). When the work was well under way and Reinick had finished two-thirds of the libretto, Schumann chanced on Hebbel's drama *Genoveva* (1841), pp. 174–5, and felt this to be a much more appropriate source for his opera. Reinick was understandably disgruntled. Hebbel visited Schumann to discuss the libretto, but the meeting proved unfruitful, and Schumann subsequently decided to write the libretto himself.

From 1838 to 1841 Reinick lived in Italy, mostly in Rome, where he studied classical art and landscape painting. His landscapes, though they lack the visionary quality of a Karl Friedrich Schinkel (1781–1841), are attractive paintings and can be seen in a number of museums, especially the National Museum in Danzig. Aged thirty-nine, he became engaged to the twenty-year-old Marie Berendt, and when they married in 1844, they moved to Dresden, where he devoted himself to writing books for children. His *Lieder und Fabeln für die Jugend* (1844) and *Illustriertes ABC-Buch für kleine und große Kinder* (1845) met with great success. Unfortunately, Reinick was unable to enjoy his celebrity for long: he died of a ruptured artery a fortnight before his forty-seventh birthday.

COMPOSER

Wolf's source for all his Reinick songs were the *Lieder von Robert Reinick*, published in 1881 in Berlin by the G. Grote'sche Verlagsbuchhandlung. This late appearance of a revised edition of Reinick's verse more than twenty years after his death must have somehow convinced Wolf that Reinick was still very much a current poet. It is perhaps strange that he, normally so fastidious in his choice of texts, should have set Reinick so often: three times in 1882, six in 1883, once each in 1888 and 1889, twice in 1890, once in 1896 and once in 1897. Yet Reinick wrote charming, well-chiselled poetry – a mixture of Biedermeier, patriotism and folksong – that was both musical and syntactically not complex, and thus ideal for Lieder composition. Printed at the back of the 1844 edition of Reinick's poems is a useful list of all the – then – known settings of his poetry: *Verzeichniß der bisher im Druck erschienenen Compositionen der Lieder von R. Reinick*. The composers include Freudenberg, Krebs, Kücken, Kugler, Lindpaintner, Marschner,

Otto, Reißiger, Rietz, Schladebach, Schumann, Spohr, Stern, Taubert, Thrun and Tiehsen. Among composers born too late to be included in this list, mention should be made of Brahms ('Liebestreu', 'Juchhe!'), Loewe ('Der verliebte Maikäfer') and Pfitzner ('Kuriose Geschichte').

LETTERS

HW to Melanie Köchert, Perchtoldsdorf, 13 May 1890

Ich war gestern ungeheuer glücklich. Ein neues Lied ist mir wieder gelungen, aber, lieber Himmel! wie!!! Wenn der deutsche Kaiser dasselbe hört macht er mich schnurstraks zum Reichskanzler. Es ist von Reinick „dem Vaterland" betitelt u. schließt mit den Worten: „heil dir, heil dir, du deutsches Land!" Ja, da kann einer lang „heil dir" schreien, bis das so in's Mark geht wie mit meiner Musik. Wie ich zu diesem todesmuthig patriotischen Ton gelange ist mir selber räthselhaft. Ich fange nachgerade an zu glauben, daß ich eben alles kann. Na, Jäger[1] wird Purzelbäume schlagen! ist's doch für ihn geschrieben.

Yesterday I was over the moon. I managed to compose another song – but heavens above, what a song!!! If the German Kaiser hears it, he'll appoint me Imperial Chancellor on the spot. It's by Reinick, is called 'Dem Vaterland', & ends with the words: 'All hail, all hail, O German land!' Well, one can scream 'All hail!' for a long time before it enters one's very soul, as it does with my music. How I achieved this death-or-glory patriotic strain is a mystery even to me. I'm beginning to believe that I can do anything. Jäger will turn cartwheels – it's written for him!

HW to Emil Kauffmann, Perchtoldsdorf, 21 May 1890

Nun erlaube ich mir noch ein wichtiges Anliegen vorzubringen. Ich habe kürzlich ein Gedicht von Rob. Reinick „dem Vaterland" für Chor u. großes Orchester componirt, u., da sich dieses Stück wegen seines patriotischen Textes u. seiner Tauglichkeit für Männergesangvereine vorzüglich eignen dürfte, den Stuttgarter Gesangverein in Aussicht genommen, in der Voraussetzung, durch denselben anläßlich des bevorstehenden Sängerfests in Wien das Stück in sein Programm aufgenommen zu sehen. Sollten Sie, hochgeehrter Herr mit diesem Vereine irgendwie in Fühlung stehen, würde ich Ihnen äußerst verbunden sein,

---

1 Ferdinand Jäger (1838–1902), a Wagnerian tenor (the role of Parsifal was his calling card) who, tiring of the operatic stage, became fascinated by Wolf's songs and often performed them in concert. Schubert also favoured a former opera singer to perform his Lieder: Johann Michael Vogl.

wollten Sie einige empfehlende Worte für mich einfließen lassen. Leider bin ich mit der Instrumentation noch nicht zu Ende, weshalb ich die Composition zu Ihrer Einsicht noch nicht vorlegen kann. Ich erbitte mir eine baldige Antwort, ob überhaupt Aussichten vorhanden sind, dieses Projekt zu verwirklichen.

I now take the liberty of making an important request. I have recently composed a poem by Rob. Reinick, 'Dem Vaterland', for chorus & full orchestra; & since this piece, because of its patriotic text, is eminently suitable for men's choral societies, I have in mind the Stuttgart choral society, providing that the piece can be included in its programme for the upcoming song festival in Vienna. If, esteemed sir, you are in any way in touch with this society, I should be extremely grateful if you would put in a good word for me. I have unfortunately not yet finished the orchestration so that I cannot ask you for your opinion. Might I request that you let me know swiftly whether there is any likelihood of realising this project.

HW to Emil Kauffmann, Unterach, 5 June 1890

Die Partitur meines Hymnus'[1] ist beendet. [...] Ursprünglich, Freund Jäger[2] zulieb, für eine Singstimme u. Klavier geschrieben, empfand ich doch schon während des Niederschreibens die Unzulänglichkeit der auszuführenden Mittel. In seiner jetzigen Verfassung dürfte die Komposition einer großen Wirkung auf die Massen nicht verfehlen.

The score of my Hymn is complete. [...] Written originally for a single voice & piano, for our friend Jäger, I felt as I was writing it how inadequate these forces were. In its present form it shouldn't fail to impress the masses mightily.

HW to Oskar Grohe, Traunkirchen, 8 June 1893

Daß Ihnen mein Heinesches Lied[3] so gefällt, höre ich gern. Ich habe noch einiges aus derselben Zeit auszukramen wie z. B. das „Gesellenlied"[4] nach Reinick, das mich vielleicht am populärsten machen wird, eine Skolie[5] von demselben Poeten, einen transferierten Y – a schreienden Zettel und so Verschiedenes.[6]

Delighted that you so like my Heine song. I've also got a few other things to show you that were composed at the same time: the 'Gesellenlied' after Reinick that will perhaps make me most popular, a 'Skolie' by the same poet, and a translated hee-hawing weaver.

1 'Dem Vaterland'.   2 See note 1, p. 433.
3 'Wo wird einst'.   4 *Drei Gedichte von Robert Reinick*, No. 1, p. 444.
5 *Drei Gedichte von Robert Reinick*, No. 3, p. 445.   6 'Lied des transferierten Zettel', p. 467.

HW to B. Schott's Söhne in Mainz, Vienna, 31 December 1894

Der genaue Wortlaut für den Titel des Chores soll heissen: „dem Vaterland. Ein Hymnus für Männerchor u. grosses Orchester". – Unter dem Titel der Name des Dichters (Rob. Reinick). Ich erwarte einen nochmaligen Bürstenabzug des Klavierauszuges, vom Vaterland, den Sie mir baldigst zukommen lassen mögen. Förstler[1] in Stuttgart drängt mich ebenfalls um einen Klavierauszug des Hymnus; ich werde mich sehr freuen, wenn derselbe noch im Jahre 95 im Druck erscheinen soll.

The exact wording for the title of the chorus should read: 'Dem Vaterland. A Hymn for men's chorus & large orchestra'. The poet's name (Rob. Reinick) should appear beneath the title. I'm expecting another galley-proof of the piano arrangement of 'Dem Vaterland' – please send it to me as soon as possible. Förstler in Stuttgart is also pressing me for a piano arrangement of the Hymn; I should be delighted if this could appear in print during '95.

HW to Paul Müller, Vienna, 22 October 1896

Heute ist überhaupt ein glücklicher Tag für mich, da mir ein Lied, das mich Jahre hindurch schon verfolgt und für das ich absolut den richtigen Ton nicht finden konnte, endlich gelungen ist, zwar mit manchen Unterbrechungen und unter sehr viel Mühen (bei mir eine ganz ausnahmsweise Erscheinung), das aber grandios ausgefallen ist. Die Sache lag daran, daß das Gedicht von Rob. Reinick Morgenlied betitelt ist. Meiner Ansicht nach ist dieses Gedicht aber kein Lied. Daran nun lag's. Ich taufte den Titel in „Morgenstimmung" um und sofort änderte sich die Sache [...]

Dass mir dieses Lied („o dieses Lied" sage ich wie Freund Beckmesser[2]) endlich gelungen ist, versetzt mich in die erfreuliche Lage, einen Herzenswunsch von mir zu befriedigen, indem jetzt das Gesellenlied und die Skolie eine schöne trias bilden werden, die noch vor Weihnachten im Druck erscheinen soll. Das werden 3 prächtige „Lieder" sein. Aber weder die Morgenstimmung noch die Skolie sind Lieder im eigentlichen Sinn des Worts. Lied ist nur das Gesellenlied.

Today was such a happy day for me, as I finally managed to compose a song, albeit with many interruptions and with huge effort – a very rare occurrence with me – a song that has plagued me for years and years and for which I

---

1 Wilhelm Förstler (1851–1915), music director of the Stuttgart Liederkranz, welcomed Wolf with open arms during his first visit to Stuttgart in October 1890. Förstler conducted the first performance of 'Dem Vaterland' on 10 May 1891, which Wolf was unable to attend.

2 *Die Meistersinger von Nürnberg*, Act III, scene 5 – Beckmesser's cry of frustration at his inability to learn Stolzing's song.

simply couldn't find the right tone, but it has now turned out splendidly. The trouble was that this poem by Rob. Reinick was titled 'Morgenlied'. But in my opinion this poem is not a song. That was the problem. I re-christened it 'Morgenstimmung' ['Morning mood'], and that suddenly changed everything [. . .]

With this song now finally finished ('Oh this song' I can now say with Beckmesser), I am in the happy position of being able to fulfil a heartfelt wish: with 'Gesellenlied' and 'Skolie' I now have a beautiful trio that should appear in print before Christmas. 3 splendid songs. But neither 'Morgenstimmung' nor 'Skolie' are songs in the true sense of the word. 'Gesellenlied' is the only true song.

HW to Hugo Faisst, Vienna, 25 October 1896

Kürzlich habe ich ein Gedicht von Rob. Reinick, das mich schon lange beschäftigt, endlich ausgeführt. [. . .] Ich denke nun 3 Gedichte von Rob. Reinick demnächst in Druck zu geben. Als erstes kommt das „Gesellenlied", als zweites „Morgenstimmung" u. als drittes „Skolie", das 1889 componirt wurde. Leider tragen alle drei Lieder Tenorcharakter, daß also für Dich nichts dabei herrausschaut, was um so bedauerlicher ist, als Du mir versicherst jetzt besonders gut bei Stimme zu sein.[1]

I have recently finally finished setting a poem by Rob. Reinick that has occupied me for a long time. [. . .] I plan shortly to have the 3 songs published. First comes 'Gesellenlied', followed by 'Morgenstimmung' with 'Skolie', composed in 1889, as the third. Unfortunately all 3 songs are best sung by a tenor, so that there will be nothing for you – all the more regrettable since you assure me that you are in especially good voice.

HW to Karl Mayr, Vienna, 15 March 1897

Daß Ihnen meine jüngste Sendung Lieder[2] so wohl zusagt, darüber freue ich mich ausnehmend. Mit der Skolie, die allerdings an Ruppigkeit nichts zu wünschen übrig läßt, werden Sie sich schon noch befreunden, davor ist mir gar nicht bange –

> „Das kommt nur auf Gewohnheit an.
> So nimmt ein Kind der Mutter Brust
> Nicht gleich im Anfang willig an,
> Doch bald ernährt es sich mit Lust."[3]

---

1 Faisst was an amateur singer, a baritone.
2 *Drei Gedichte von Robert Reinick*.
3 Spoken by Mephistopheles to the Student in Goethe's *Faust* Part I, lines 1888–91.

Mein Freund Schalk z. B. zieht die Skolie den beiden andern Gesängen vor. Also nur Geduld.

I am delighted that my most recent consignment of songs pleases you so. And I have no doubt that you will soon like 'Skolie' – the embodiment of boorishness:

> 'It's a question of getting used to it.
> Just as a child does not at first
> Willingly accept its mother's breast
> But soon enjoys the nourishment.'

My friend Schalk, for example, prefers 'Skolie' to the other two songs. Therefore patience!

LIEDER

Wiegenlied im Sommer[1]

> Vom Berg hinabgestiegen
> Ist nun des Tages Rest;
> Mein Kind liegt in der Wiegen,
> Die Vögel all' im Nest,
Nur ein ganz klein Singvögelein
Ruft weit daher im Dämmerschein:
> „Gut' Nacht! gut' Nacht!
> „Lieb Kindlein, gute Nacht!" –

> Die Wiege geht im Gleise,
> Die Uhr tickt hin und her,
> Die Fliegen nur ganz leise
> Sie summen noch daher.
Ihr Fliegen, laßt mein Kind in Ruh!
Was summt ihr ihm so heimlich zu?
> „Gut' Nacht! gut' Nacht!
> „Lieb Kindlein, gute Nacht!"

> Der Vogel und die Sterne
> Und Alle rings umher,
> Sie haben mein Kind so gerne,
> Die Engel noch viel mehr.
Sie decken's mit den Flügeln zu
Und singen leise: „Schlaf in Ruh!

A summer cradle song

> The last traces of day
> Have slipped from the hillside;
> My child lies in its cradle,
> All the birds are in their nests.
Just one tiny little song-bird
Calls from afar in the gloaming:
> 'Good night! good night!
> Dear child, good night!' –

> The cradle rocks gently,
> The clock ticks to and fro,
> The flies still hum,
> But very softly now.
Leave my child in peace, you flies!
What are you humming him so secretly?
> 'Good night! good night!
> Dear child, good night!'

> The birds and the stars,
> And everything all around,
> Are so fond of my child,
> And the angels even fonder.
They cover him with their wings
And softly sing: 'Sleep in peace!

---

1 Reinick's title is 'Im Sommer', the second of *Vier Wiegenlieder*. Wolf omitted Reinick's second verse.

NO STANZA BREAK

„Gut' Nacht! gut' Nacht!
„Lieb Kindlein, gute Nacht!"

Good night! Good night!
Dear child, good night!'

Also set by Leo Blech

Wiegenlied im Winter[1]

    Schlaf ein, mein süßes Kind,*
    Da draußen geht der Wind,
Er pocht an's Fenster und schaut hinein,
Und hört er wo ein Kindlein schrein,
Da schilt und summt und brummt er sehr,
Holt gleich sein Bett voll Schnee daher,
Und deckt es auf die Wiegen,
Wenn's Kind nicht still will liegen.

    Schlaf ein, mein süßes Kind,*
    Da draußen geht[2] der Wind,
Er rüttelt an dem Tannenbaum,
Da fliegt heraus ein schöner Traum,
Der fliegt durch Schnee und Nacht
    und Wind
Geschwind, geschwind zum lieben Kind,
Und singt von Licht und Kränzen,
Die bald am Christbaum glänzen.

    Schlaf ein, mein süßes Kind,*
    Da draußen geht der Wind.
Doch ruft die Sonne: „Grüß euch Gott!"
Bläst er dem Kind die Backen roth,
Und sagt der Frühling: „Guten Tag!"
Bläst er die ganze Erde wach,
Und was er[3] still gelegen,
Springt lustig allerwegen.
    Jetzt schlaf, mein süßes Kind,
    Da draußen bläst der Wind.*

* The textual repetitions are Wolf's.

A winter cradle song

    Go to sleep, my sweet child!*
    Outside the wind is blowing,
It knocks at the window and peers in,
And if it hears a baby crying,
It scolds and moans and grumbles,
And fetches at once a bed of snow
And lays it on the cradle,
If the child will not lie still.

    Go to sleep, my sweet child!*
    Outside the wind is blowing,
It shakes the fir tree
And out flies a sweet dream
That flies through snow and night
    and wind,
Swiftly, swiftly to the dear child,
And sings of the lights and the wreaths
That soon will shine on the Christmas tree.

    Go to sleep, my sweet child!*
    Outside the wind is blowing,
But when the sun calls: 'God greet you!'
It blows the child's cheeks red,
And when springtime says: 'Good day!'
It blows till the whole earth wakes,
And all that he had quietened,
Leaps up for joy all around.
    Now go to sleep, my sweet child,
    Outside the wind is blowing.*

1   Reinick's title is 'Im Winter', the fourth of *Vier Wiegenlieder*.
2   Reinick: weht.   3   Reinick: erst.

Sechs Lieder von Robert Reinick
Six songs to poems by Robert Reinick

Between December 1882 and April 1883 Wolf composed eight songs to poems by Robert Reinick; a ninth, 'Laut und traut', exists only as a sketch. Two of them ('Wiegenlied im Sommer' and 'Wiegenlied im Winter') were published in 1888 as part of the *Sechs Lieder für eine Frauenstimme*. The *Sechs Lieder von Robert Reinick* were not published until 1936. 'Frohe Botschaft', composed much later than the others in 1890, did not originally form part of Wolf's collection.

1 Wohin mit der Freud'? How to express joy?

Ach du klarblauer Himmel	Ah, clear blue heavens,
Und wie schön bist du heut!	How lovely you are today!
Möcht' ans Herz gleich dich drücken	I'd like to press you straight to my heart,
Voll Jubel und Freud'.	Full of joy and happiness.
Aber's geht doch nicht an,	Yet it cannot be,
Denn du bist mir zu weit,	For you are too far from me,
Und mit all meiner Freud'	And what can I do
Was fang' ich doch an?	With all my joy?
Ach du lichtgrüne[1] Welt	Ah, you bright green world,
Und wie strahlst du voll Lust.	How you shine with pleasure.
Und ich möcht' gleich mich werfen[2]	I'd like to throw myself, full of love,
Dir voll[3] Lieb an die Brust;	Straight into your arms;
Aber's geht doch nicht an,	Yet it cannot be,
Und das ist ja mein Leid,	And that is what tortures me,
Und mit all meiner Freud'	And what can I do
Was fang' ich doch an?	With all my joy?
Und da sah ich mein Lieb	And then I saw my love
Am Kastanienbaum stehn,	By the chestnut tree,
War so klar wie der Himmel,	As bright as the sky,
Wie die Erde so schön,	As fair as the earth,
Und wir küßten uns Beid',	And we kissed each other
Und wir sangen voll[4] Lust,	And we sang full of joy,
Und da hab' ich gewußt:	And it was then I knew
Wohin mit der Freud'!	How to express my joy!

Also set by Friedrich Silcher

---

1 Reinick: lichte grüne. 2 Reinick: Und ich möcht' mich gleich werfen.
3 Reinick: vor. 4 Reinick: vor.

2 Liebchen, wo bist du?

    Zaubrer bin ich, doch was frommt es?
Denn mein Lieb ist eine Fei,
Höhnt mich mit noch ärgerm Zauber,
Ruf' ich freundlich sie herbei:
    Liebchen, wo bist du?

    Heute noch in Feld und Garten
Ging ich, sie zu suchen, aus:
Plötzlich lacht' aus einer Rose
Glühend roth ihr Mund heraus!
    Liebster, da bin ich!

    Ich nun ward ein schneller Zephyr,
Küßt' im Flug die Rose schon.
Ach! nur eine Rose küßt' ich,
Liebchen war daraus entflohn.
    Liebchen, wo bist du?[1]

    Horch, da sang am Waldes-Ufer
Plötzlich eine Nachtigall;
Wohlbekannt war mir die Stimme
Und sie sang mit süßem Schall:
    Liebster, da bin ich!

    Schnell zum Abendstern verwandelt,
Blickt' ich durch die grüne Nacht.
Ach, den leeren Busch erblickt' ich,
Liebchen hatt' sich fortgemacht.
    Liebchen, wo bist du?

    Und so treibt sie's alle Tage,
Läßt mir eben jetzt nicht Ruh',
Während dieses Lied ich singe,
Ruft sie unsichtbar mir zu:
    Liebster, da bin ich!

    Liebchen, mach' dem Spiel ein Ende!
Komm nun endlich selbst herbei!
Glaub', ein einz'ger Kuß ist schöner
Als die ganze Zauberei!
    Liebchen, wo bist du?

Also set by Heinrich Marschner

Sweetest, where are you?

    I am a magician, but to what purpose?
For my love is a fairy,
And she mocks me with more potent magic
When I tenderly call to her:
    Sweetest, where are you?

    Today I looked for her again
In field and garden:
Suddenly, from a rose,
Her glowing red lips laughed!
    Beloved, here I am!

    Then I turned into a swift breeze,
And kissed the rose as I blew by –
Alas, it was only a rose I kissed,
My sweetest had fled from it.
    Sweetest, where are you?

    Hark! Suddenly, at the edge of a wood,
A nightingale sang;
The voice was well known to me
And she sang in sweet tones:
    Beloved, here I am!

    Quickly becoming the evening star,
I gazed through the green night.
Ah, I saw the empty bush,
My sweetest had flitted away.
    Sweetest, where are you?

    And so she carries on, day after day,
Leaving me no peace at all,
While I am singing this song,
Invisibly she calls to me:
    Beloved, here I am!

    Sweetest, put an end to this game!
Once and for all appear in person:
Believe me – a single kiss
Is sweeter than all this sorcery!
    Sweetest, where are you?

---

1   Wolf omits verses 4 and 5 of Reinick's poem.

3 Nachtgruß[1]

In dem Himmel ruht die Erde,
Mond und Sterne halten Wacht,
Auf der Erd' ein kleiner Garten
Schlummert in der Blumen Pracht. –
Gute Nacht, gute Nacht!*

In dem Garten steht ein Häuschen,
Still von Linden überdacht;
Draußen vor dem Erkerfenster
Hält ein Vogel singend Wacht. –
Gute Nacht! gute Nacht!*

In dem Erker schläft ein Mädchen,
Träumet von der Blumenpracht;
Ihr im Herzen ruht der Himmel,
Drin die Engel halten Wacht. –
Gute Nacht! gute Nacht!*

* Wolf sets an extra „gute Nacht".

Goodnight greeting

Earth rests beneath the heavens,
Moon and stars are keeping watch,
On earth a little garden
Slumbers among the glittering flowers.
Good night! good night!*

In the garden there's a cottage
That lime-trees quietly shelter;
Before the oriel outside,
A bird keeps melodious watch.
Good night! good night!*

In the oriel a girl is sleeping,
Dreaming of the glittering flowers;
Heaven dwells within her heart,
Where the angels are keeping watch.
Good night! good night!*

4 Frühlingsglocken

S c h n e e=Glöckchen thut läuten!
Was hat das zu bedeuten?
Ei, gar ein lustig Ding!

Der Frühling heut geboren ward,
Ein Kind der allerschönsten Art;
Zwar liegt es noch im weißen Bett,
Doch spielt es schon so wundernett.
Drum kommt, ihr Vögel, aus dem Süd
Und bringet neue Lieder mit!
Ihr Quellen all,
Erwacht im Thal!
Was soll das lange Zaudern?
Sollt mit dem Kinde plaudern!

M a i-Glöckchen thut läuten!
Was hat das zu bedeuten?
Frühling ist Bräutigam!

Macht Hochzeit mit der Erde heut
Mit großer Pracht und Festlichkeit.
Wohlauf denn, Nelk' und Tulipan,
Und schwenkt die bunte Hochzeitfahn'!

Spring bells

*Snow*drop bells ring out!
What does this mean?
Such happy tidings!

Spring was born today,
A child of matchless beauty;
Though he still lies in his white bed,
He already plays so prettily.
So come, you birds, from the South
And bring new songs with you!
And all you streams,
Wake up in the valley!
Why this long delay?
You must chatter with this child!

Lily-of-the-valley bells ring out!
What does this mean?
Spring is a bridegroom!

Today he's marrying the earth
With great pomp and ceremony.
Come, then, carnations and tulips,
And wave your bright wedding banners!

---

1 Wolf changed Reinick's original title, which read, 'In dem Himmel ruht die Erde. Ständchen'.

NO STANZA BREAK

Du Ros' und Lilie, schmückt euch fein!	Roses and lilies, adorn yourselves!
Brautjungfern sollt ihr heute sein!	Today you are to be bridesmaids!
Ihr Schmetterling'	Nimble,
Sollt bunt und flink	Many-coloured butterflies
Den Hochzeitreigen führen,	Shall lead the wedding dance,
Die Vögel musizieren!	The birds shall provide the music!
B l a u-Glöckchen thut läuten!	*Blue*bells ring out!
Was hat das zu bedeuten?	What does this mean?
Ach, das ist gar zu schlimm!	Ah, that's truly too bad!
Heut Nacht der Frühling scheiden muß,	Spring must depart tonight,
Drum bringt man ihm den Abschiedsgruß,	So all have come to say goodbye.
Glühwürmchen ziehn mit Lichtern hell,	Glow-worms appear with bright lights,
Es rauscht der Wald, es klagt der Quell,	The forest rustles, the stream laments,
Dazwischen singt mit süßem Schall	And all the while from every bush
Aus jedem Busch die Nachtigall,	The nightingale sings sweetly,
Und wird ihr Lied	And does not quickly
So bald nicht müd',	Tire of singing,
Ist auch der Frühling schon so ferne,	Though spring's already far away,
Sie hatten ihn alle so gerne!	Each one of them loved him so!

Also set by Robert Schumann and Ludwig Spohr

5 Ständchen[1]

Serenade

Komm in die stille Nacht! –	Come into the silent night,
Liebchen, was zögerst du?	Why delay, my dearest?
Sonne ging längst zur Ruh',	The sun has set long ago,
Welt schloß die Augen zu.	The world has closed its eyes.
Rings nur einzig die Liebe wacht!	Love alone keeps watch around us!
Liebchen, was zögerst du?	Why delay, my dearest?
Schon sind die Sterne hell,	Already the stars are bright,
Schon ist der Mond zur Stell',	Already the moon has risen,
Eilen so schnell, so schnell!	They make such haste, such haste.
Liebchen, mein Liebchen! drum eil' auch du!	Dearest, my dearest, so make haste too!
Sonne ging längst zur Ruh'! –	The sun has set long ago! –
Traust wohl dem Schimmer nicht,	Do you not trust the shimmer
Der durch die Blüthen bricht?	That breaks through the blossom?
Treu ist des Mondes Licht.	The moonlight is faithful.
Liebchen, mein Liebchen, was fürchtest du?	Dearest, my dearest, what frightens you?
Welt schloß die Augen zu!	The world has closed its eyes!
Blumen und Blüthenbaum	Flowers and blossoming trees

---

1 Wolf changed Reinick's original title, which read, 'Komm in die stille Nacht! Ständchen'.

Schlummern in süßem Traum,
　Erde, sie athmet kaum,
Liebe nur schaut den Liebenden zu! –

Einzig die Liebe wacht,
　Ruft dich allüberall;
　Höre die Nachtigall,
　Hör' meiner Stimme Schall,
Liebchen, o komm in die stille Nacht!

Also set by Eduard Lassen and Schumann

6　Liebesbotschaft

Wolken, die ihr nach Osten eilt,
Wo die Eine, die Meine weilt,
All' meine Wünsche, mein Hoffen
　　und Singen
Sollen auf eure Flügel sich schwingen,
　Sollen euch Flüchtige
　Zu ihr lenken,
　Daß die Züchtige
Meiner in Treuen mag gedenken![1]

Und am Abend, in stiller Ruh'
Breitet der sinkenden Sonne euch zu!
Mögt mit Purpur und Gold euch malen,
Mögt in dem Meere von Gluthen
　　und Strahlen
　Leicht sich schwingende
　Schifflein fahren,
　Daß sie singende
Engel glaubt auf euch zu gewahren.

Ja, wohl möchten es Engel sein,
Wäre mein Herz gleich ihrem rein;
All' meine Wünsche, mein Hoffen
　　und Singen
Zieht ja dahin auf euren Schwingen,
　Euch, ihr Flüchtigen,
　Hinzulenken,
　Zu der Züchtigen,
Der ich einzig nur mag gedenken!

Also set by Schumann

A message of love

You clouds that hasten eastwards
To where my own love lives,
All my wishes, hopes
　　and songs
Shall go flying with you,
　Guiding you,
　To my sweetheart,
　That the chaste child
Shall faithfully think of me.

And at evening, in calm and silence,
Sail away to the setting sun!
Paint yourselves in purple and gold,
Immersed in the bright fires
　　of the sea,
　Skim its surface
　Like little ships,
　That she might think
You are singing angels.

And well might my thoughts be angels,
If my heart were as pure as hers;
All my wishes, hopes
　　and songs
Shall go flying with you,
　Guiding you
　To my sweetheart,
　The chaste child,
That I may think only of her!

1　Wolf omits verses 2 and 3 of Reinick's poem.

Drei Gedichte von Robert Reinick
Three Poems by Robert Reinick

These three songs, published in 1897 by Heckel, were dedicated to the tenor Ferdinand Jäger, a great champion of Wolf's songs, who sang 'Gesellenlied', from manuscript, at the composer's first public concert on 15 December 1888.

1 Gesellenlied[1]   The apprentice's song

„Kein Meister fällt vom Himmel!"[2] 'Masters don't fall from Heaven!'
Und das ist auch ein großes Glück! And it's a very good thing they don't!
   Der Meister sind schon viel zuviel;   There are far too many masters already,
   Wenn noch ein Schock   If another batch were to fall
      vom Himmel fiel',   from Heaven,
Wie würden uns Gesellen How all those masters
Die vielen Meister prellen Would thrash us apprentices,
Trotz unserm Meisterstück! Despite our masterly works!

„Kein Meister fällt vom Himmel!" 'Masters don't fall from Heaven!'
Gottlob, auch keine Meisterin![3] Nor masters' wives either, thank God!
   Ach, lieber Himmel, sei so gut,   Ah, dear Lord above, be so kind,
   Wenn droben eine brummen thut,   And if one's bleating away up there,
Behalte sie in Gnaden, Keep her, I beg you, where she is,
Daß sie zu unserm Schaden That she won't, to our detriment,
Nicht fall' zur Erden hin! Fall to earth as well!

„Kein Meister fällt vom Himmel!" 'Masters don't fall from Heaven!'
Auch keines Meisters Töchterlein! Nor masters' daughters either!
   Zwar hab' ich das schon lang' gewußt,   I've long been well aware of that.
   Und doch, was wär' das eine Lust,   And yet what a pleasure that would be,
Wenn jung und hübsch und munter If such a young, pretty and cheerful one
Solch Mädel fiel' herunter Were to fall from Heaven
Und wollt' mein Herzlieb' sein! And fall for me as well!

„Kein Meister fällt vom Himmel!" 'Masters don't fall from Heaven!'
Das ist mein Trost auf dieser Welt; That's my comfort here on earth;
   Drum mach' ich, daß ich Meister werd',   So I'm set on becoming one,
   Und wird mir dann ein Weib bescheert,   And if I'm also granted a wife,
Dann soll aus dieser Erden Then my life on earth

---

1   Reinick: 'Gesellen-Lied'. The *marcato* left-hand rhythm in bars 5–7 mirrors the opening bars of the overture to *Die Meistersinger von Nürnberg*. Wolf would almost certainly have had the young apprentice David from *Die Meistersinger* in mind when setting this poem.
2   Wolf would have appreciated the truth of this proverb at the beginning of 1888 after a decade or more of struggle – just as seven years later he would have appreciated the final line of 'Wohl denk' ich oft': 'And the entire world knows that I exist!' – see p. 327.
3   Wolf sets this line to a melody that echoes Sachs's „So mach' ich den Burschen gleich zum Gesell'" ('I'll forthwith make the lad a journeyman') from Act III, scene 4 of *Die Meistersinger von Nürnberg*.

Mir schon ein Himmel werden,	Shall become a Heaven
Aus dem kein Meister fällt.*	From which no master falls.*

* Wolf repeats the final line.

2 Morgenstimmung[1]   Morning mood

Bald ist der Nacht	Night will soon
Ein End' gemacht,	Be over;
Schon fühl' ich Morgenlüfte wehen.	Already I feel morning breezes stir.
Der Herr, der spricht:	The Lord says:
„Es werde Licht!"	'Let there be light!'
Da muß, was dunkel ist, vergehen. –	Then all that's dark must vanish. –
Vom Himmelszelt	Angels from
Durch alle Welt	Across the world
Die Engel Freude-jauchzend fliegen;	Come down from the skies, singing with joy;
Der Sonne Strahl	Sunlight blazes
Durchflammt das All. –	Across the globe. –
Herr, laß uns kämpfen, laß uns siegen!	Lord, let us fight, let us conquer!

Also set by Georg Henschel

3 Skolie   Banqueting song

Reich den Pokal mir schäumenden Weines voll,	Give me the goblet brimming with sparkling wine,
Reich mir die Lippen zum Kuße, die blühenden,	Give me your rosy lips in a kiss,
Rühre die Saiten, die Seelenberauschenden! –	Play the lyre that ravishes the soul! –
Feuer des Muthes brennt im Pokale mir,	The goblet's wine inflames my soul,
Gluthen der Liebe glühn auf der Lippe dir,	The ardour of love glows on your lips,
Flammen des Lebens rauschen die Saiten mir. –	The lyre kindles in me the flame of life. –
Woge des Kampfes, reiß in die Brandung mich!	Wave of battle, bear me into the breakers!
Wogen der Liebe, hebt zu den Wolken mich!	Waves of love, raise me to the clouds!
Schäumendes Leben, jubelnd* begrüß ich dich!	Surging life, I greet you with exultation!*

* Word repeated by Wolf.

1 See HW to Paul Müller, 22 October 1896, p. 435, for the difficulties Wolf experienced in composing this song. When he composed the *Drei Gedichte von Robert Reinick* clinical signs of incipient brain syphilis were already evident; within a year he was insane and interned in Dr Svetlin's asylum. It was there that he arranged the song for chorus and orchestra, renaming it 'Morgenhymnus'.

Dem Vaterland[1]
Ein Hymnus für Männerchor
  und großes Orchester

    Dem Vaterland!
Das ist ein hohes helles Wort,
Das hallt durch unsre Herzen fort
Wie Waldesrauschen, Glockenklang,
Drommetenschmettern, Lerchensang,
Das fällt ein Blitz in unsre Brust,
Zu heil'ger Flamme wird die Lust!
    Dem Vaterland!

    Dem Vaterland!
Das Wort giebt Flügel dir, o Herz.
Flieg auf, flieg auf, schau niederwärts
Die Wälder, Ströme, Thal und Höh'n:
O deutsches Land, wie bist du schön!
Und überall klingt Liederschall
Und überall ein Widerhall:
    Dem Vaterland!

    Dem Vaterland!
Das seinen Töchtern hat bescheert
Der keuschen Liebe stillen Heerd,
Das seinen Söhnen gab als Hort
Die freie That, das treue Wort,
Das seiner Ehren blanken Schild
Zu wahren allzeit sei gewillt,
    Dem Vaterland!

    Dem Vaterland!
O hohes Wort, o helles Wort,
Du tön' für alle Zeiten fort
Wie Waldesrauschen, Glockenklang,
Drommetenschmettern, Lerchensang!
Zu heil'ger Flamme weih' die Lust,
So lange schlägt die deutsche Brust
    Dem Vaterland!

Heil dir! heil dir* du deutsches Land!

* Wolf sets an extra 'heil dir'.

To the fatherland
A hymn for male choir
  and full orchestra

    Fatherland!
A bright and lofty word
That echoes through our hearts
Like rustling woods and ringing bells,
Blaring trumpets and lark song,
That flashes like lightning in our breast,
Changing joy into sacred flame!
    Fatherland!

    Fatherland!
The word gives you wings, O heart!
Fly up, fly up, look down
On forests, rivers, valleys and hills:
O German land, how fair you are!
And everywhere songs resound
And echo everywhere:
    Fatherland!

    Fatherland!
That gave its daughters
The silent hearth of love,
That gave its sons as sanctuary
Free deeds and loyal words –
That they might always strive to hold aloft
The shining shield of honour
    Of the fatherland!

    Fatherland!
O bright and lofty word,
Sound forth for evermore
Like rustling woods and ringing bells,
Blaring trumpets and lark song!
Dedicate all joy to this sacred flame,
As long as German hearts beat
    For the fatherland.

All hail! All hail,* O German land!

---

1   See HW to Melanie Köchert, 13 May 1890, p. 433, and to Emil Kauffmann, 21 May 1890, p. 433. That Wolf, who was usually so fastidious in his choice of poetry, should have waxed so lyrical about this jingoistic tub-thumping is surely a sign of mental instability.

ROBERT REINICK

Frohe Botschaft

   Hielt die allerschönste Herrin
Einst mein Herz so eng gefesselt,
Daß kein Wort es konnte sprechen
   Aus den engen Fesseln.

   Sandt' es ab als flinke Diener
Feurig schnelle Liebesblicke,
Zu besprechen sich im Stillen
   Mit der Herrin Blicken.

   Sandt' es Pagen, fein und listig:
Heimlich schlichen hin die Finger,
Schmiegten leise sich und bittend
   An die schönsten Finger.

   Sandt' es ab zwei kühne Boten:
Sind die Lippen gar verwogen
An der Herrin Mund geflogen,
   Botschaft sich zu holen.

   „Nun, ihr Boten, Pagen, Diener!
Welche Botschaft bringt ihr wieder,
Haben Augen, Finger, Lippen
   Nichts mir zu verkünden?"

   Und voll Freuden rufen Alle:
Juble, Herz! und laß das Zagen,
Deine Herrin sendet Gnade,
   Deine Bande fallen!

Glad tidings

   My fairest lady once held
My heart so closely fettered,
That it could utter no word
   In those tight chains.

   So it despatched as nimble servants
Swift and fiery loving glances
To converse in silence
   With my lady's glances.

   It despatched pages, elegant and artful;
Fingers slipped furtively
And pleadingly
   Between my fair one's fingers.

   It despatched two bold messengers;
And lips were brazen enough
To fly to my lady's lips,
   To return with messages.

   'Now, you messengers, pages
      and servants!
What tidings do you bring back,
Have eyes, fingers, lips
   Nothing to report to me?'

   And all of them cry with joy:
'Rejoice, heart, and fear no more,
Your lady pardons you,
   And unties your chains!'

OTTO ROQUETTE
(1824–1896)

Perlenfischer 3 May 1876 *page* 449

POET

Novelist, playwright, literary historian and university professor, Roquette was born in Krotoschin, the Prussian province of Posen, and after spending some time in Italy and Switzerland, moved to Berlin in 1852. Like Paul Heyse, Theodor Fontane, Franz Kugler, Theodor Storm and Adolph von Menzel, he was a member of Das Rütli, a German literary group named after the famous Swiss meadow immortalised in Schiller's *Wilhelm Tell* (1804). His lyric poetry, so different from the more ceremonial and public nature of 'Der Tunnel über der Spree', found favour with a number of Lieder composers, including Adolf Jensen, Max Reger, Franz Abt and, above all, Robert Franz.

COMPOSER

'Perlenfischer' was first published in the *Liederbuch von Otto Roquette* (1852) and subsequently appeared in an anthology, *Dichtergrüße. Neuere deutsche Lyrik ausgewählt von Elise Polko*, which seems likely to be the source for seven more poems that Wolf was to set, see p. 205.

Ernst Decsey in his biography of Wolf recounts how he and the composer discussed German poetry while walking through Munich in October 1890. Wolf fulminated against those literary critics who preferred the likes of Roquette and Bodenstedt to Mörike:

> Für den feinen zarten, goldigen Poeten Mörike hätte die Kritik keine Spur ernsthaften Verständnisses besessen, während sie einen Roquette, einen Bodenstedt oder gar den Stuttgarter Prälaten Gerok über den grünen Klee lobte. „Ach", seufzte er in komischer Betrübnis: „mit was für elendem Kraut hat nicht schon die Kritik ihre Öfen geheizt!"

> The critics had absolutely no serious understanding of the refined, sensitive, wonderful Mörike, while they praised the likes of Roquette, Bodenstedt

and even Gerok, the Stuttgart prelate, to the skies. 'Alas,' he sighed in mock sorrow, 'what wretched weeds the critics have used to heat their stoves!'

LIED

Perlenfischer

Du liebes Auge, willst dich tauchen
    In meines Aug's geheimster[1] Tiefe
    Zu späh'n,[2] wo in blauen Gründen
    Verborgen eine Perle schliefe.[3]
Du liebes Auge, tauche nieder,
    Und in die klare Tiefe dringe,
    Und lächle, wenn ich dir dies Bild[4]
    Als schönste Perle wiederbringe!

Pearl fisher

Dear eyes, will you dive
    Into my own eyes' most secret depths,
    To see where on a blue bed
    A hidden pearl is sleeping.
Dear eyes, dive down,
    Invade the clear depths
    And smile, when I bring you this image
    As the most lovely pearl!

1 Roquette: geheimste.   2 Roquette: spähen.   3 Roquette: schliefe?
4 Roquette: dein Bildniß.

Friedrich Rückert
(1788–1866)

		page
So wahr die Sonne scheinet	8 February 1878	454
Die Spinnerin	5–12 April 1878	455
Frühling Liebster	20 July 1878 fragment	

POET

Having studied law and philosophy at university, Rückert embarked on an academic career and spent some time in Vienna where, under the influence of Joseph von Hammer-Purgstall, he began to study Arabic, Turkish and Persian. He had learned Latin, Greek, Italian and medieval German at school, and later added Hebrew, Armenian, Ethiopian, Coptic, Finnish, Syrian, Sanskrit, Vedic and several Indian dialects to his remarkable store of languages. Few German poets were more prolific, and many of his poems are translations or adaptations of oriental literature. *Deutsche Gedichte*, a collection of his politically motivated writings, was published in 1814 under the pseudonym Freimund Reimar. The volume included *Geharnischte Sonette* (*Armour-clad Sonnets*) – patriotic poems that were inspired by Prussia's war against France. *Kranz der Zeit* followed in 1817, but his first significant collection was *Östliche Rosen* (1822), dedicated to Goethe, whose *West-östlicher Divan* had been published three years previously. Goethe's review recommended Rückert's verse to all composers, and also praised the musical verse of Hölty and Schulze, two poets favoured by Schubert.

Unlike Goethe, who studied translations of Hafiz's poetry for his own *Divan* verse, Rückert worked directly from the original languages – the reason, perhaps, for his astonishing rhythmic virtuosity. No other German poet displays such a dazzling variety of metres in his verse. *Ghaselen* appeared in 1822, *Weisheit des Brahmanen, ein Lehrgedicht in Bruchstücken* in six volumes between 1836 and 1839 and his *Gesammelte Gedichte* were published between 1834 and 1838. In December 1833 all six of his children fell ill with scarlet fever; four of them recovered but three-year-old Luise died on 31 December 1833, followed by five-year-old Ernst on 16 January 1834. Rückert was scarred for life and poured out his grief in a series of 428 poems, not intended for publication, that appeared posthumously in 1872 as *Kindertodtenlieder*.

Rückert led a generally uneventful life. In 1820 he settled in Coburg and the following year married his landlord's daughter, Luise Wiethaus, who inspired the four hundred or so love poems that were collected and published as *Liebesfrühling* in 1844 – treasure trove for many of the great Lieder composers. In 1827, on Platen's recommendation, he took up a chair of oriental languages at the University of Erlangen, and in 1841 was appointed professor of oriental languages in Berlin. Like so many poets, he had ambitions as a playwright, but neither *Saul und David* (1843) nor *Herodes der Große* (1844) met with any success. He retired from his Berlin professorship on half pay in 1848 and devoted the rest of his life to scholarship.

His poetry, with its elegance and rhythmic inventiveness, has inspired many of the finest Lieder in the repertoire by Berg, Brahms, Franz, Hensel, Loewe, Mahler, Pfitzner, Reger, Schubert, Clara Schumann, Richard Strauss and of course Robert Schumann, who set his verse some 40 times, including duets. Rückert wrote too much – over ten thousand poems – but the greatest of them deserve a place in any anthology of German verse.

COMPOSER

Wolf had for many years tried to interest publishers in his *Liederreihen*, when in 1883 he approached B. Schott's Söhne with his *Sechs Lieder für eine Frauenstimme*, comprising six songs he had written at various times during the preceding six years: 'Morgentau' (1877), 'Das Vöglein' (1878), 'Die Spinnerin' (1878), 'Wiegenlied im Sommer' (1882), 'Wiegenlied im Winter' (1882) and 'Mausfallen-Sprüchlein' (1882). After Schott's negative response (18 February 1883, p. 452), despite Mottl's support (HW to his parents, 10 April 1878, p. 452), Wolf now approached Breitkopf & Härtel (HW to Felix Mottl, 26 February 1883, p. 453). They declined to publish, so he decided to approach Simrock, having initially refused to do so (HW to Mottl, 26 February 1883). When they too turned him down (HW to his parents, late June or early July 1883, p. 453), he fell prey to a creative inertia that afflicted him on and off throughout his life. That the songs were finally published was due in no small measure to the kindness and generosity of Friedrich Eckstein – see p. 4.

LETTERS

HW to his parents, Vienna, 10 April 1878

Jetzt arbeite ich an zwei Liedern, wovon ich das eine, „Die Spinnerin" von Rückert, noch heute zu Ende schreibe, um es morgen Mottl[1] vorzuspielen, denn nur er sagt mir das Richtigste über den Wert oder Unwert meiner Arbeiten. Keinem vertraue ich so wie ihm.

I'm now working on two songs, one of which, Rückert's 'Die Spinnerin', I shall finish today to play it Mottl tomorrow – because he's the only one who really tells me whether my pieces are successful or worthless. I trust him more than anyone.

HW to Ludwig Strecker of B. Schott's Söhne, Vienna, 18 February 1883

Im Anschluß an den an Sie gerichteten Brief des Hofkapellmeisters Felix Mottl aus Carlsruhe, erlaube ich mir Ihnen beifolgend sechs Lieder zu übersenden. Es würde mir zur größten Ehre gereichen in Ihrem weltberühmten Verlag vertreten sein zu dürfen, u. ich würde Ihre Annahme dieser meiner Lieder zum Drucke als ein günstiges Omen für meine ganze Zukunft betrachten.

In connection with Hofkapellmeister Mottl's letter to you from Carlsruhe, I take the liberty of sending you these six songs. It would be the greatest honour for me to be represented by your world-famous publishing house, & I would consider it a favourable omen for my entire future, if you were to publish these songs of mine.

To HW from B. Schott's Söhne, Vienna, 24 February 1883

Ihr werthes Schreiben vom 18 et. haben wir nebst Manuscript erhalten und danken Ihnen zunächst für gefl. Uebersendung des Letzteren. Zugleich müssen wir Ihnen aber auch sagen, dass dasselbe um bei uns verlegt zu werden, zu einer äusserst ungünstigen Zeit gekommen ist, was wir umsomehr bedauern, als Herr Hofkapellmeister Mottl sich sehr günstig über Ihre Lieder ausliess. Unsere gesammte Arbeitskraft ist nämlich durch die Herausgabe einiger grösserer Werke ganz ausserordentlich angestrengt, wozu nun noch durch den Tod Meister Wagners das Drängen seiner Verehrer um Vollendung der Klavierauszüge, Transcriptionen und hauptsächlich der Partitur zu „Parsifal" kommt, so dass wir mit dem besten Willen unseren, ohnedies bedeutenden Vorrath von Manuscripten, die ebenfalls schon geraume Zeit der Veröffentlichung harren nicht noch mehr vermehren dürfen.

1 See p. 500.

We have received your esteemed letter of the 18th etc. together with the manuscript, and thank you for sending us the latter. But I have to inform you that this comes at a most unfavourable time for us, which we regret – all the more so since Herr Hofkapellmeister Mottl has expressed such a favourable opinion of your songs. Our entire staff are at the moment extraordinarily stressed in preparing for publication a number of substantial works. In addition, with the death of maestro Wagner, there has been pressure on us from his admirers to publish piano reductions, transcriptions and above all the score of *Parsifal* – so that we, with the best will in the world, cannot increase still further this pile of manuscripts which have already been waiting some time to be published.

HW to Felix Mottl, Vienna, 26 February 1883

Schott refüsirte in der höflichsten Weise die Herausgabe meiner Lieder u. bedauert die Ablehnung derselben umso mehr, als Sie ihm meine Sache so warm an's Herz gelegt. Ich will's nun auf gut Glück mit Breitkopf u. Härtl versuchen, da ich mich nicht entschließen kann, trotz Hanslick's Empfehlung, meine Compositionen Simrock anzubieten. Selbst die oberflächlichste Berührung mit der Brahmssippschaft möchte ich gern vermieden haben.

Schott's have declined in the politest possible way to publish my songs, & express their regret, especially as you had recommended them so warmly. I shall now try my luck with Breitkopf & Härtel, as I cannot bring myself, despite Hanslick's recommendation, to offer my compositions to Simrock. I should like to avoid even the slightest contact with the Brahms clique.

HW to his parents, Vienna, late June or early July 1883

Damit Sie übrigens nicht glauben sollen, als thäte ich für die Veröffentlichung meiner Compositionen nichts, sende ich Ihnen von einem Verleger (4. Ranges etwa) die Antwort auf meine Sendung. Aus dieser gedruckten Abfertigung dürften Sie wohl ersehen, wie schwer es ist einen Verleger zu finden, denn die meisten sehen das Manuskript gar nicht an, sondern legen zu dem ungesehenen Manuskript gleich die gedruckte Abfertigung u. schicken's zurück.

Ich könnte Ihnen Briefe von Simrock, Breitkopf u. Härtel etc. etc. zeigen, alle lehnen die Manuskripte ab, u. ich bin überzeugt, ohne dieselben vorher geprüft zu haben.

Sie können mir also keine Schuld beilegen, denn über das Herz eines Verlegers kann ich so wenig gebieten als über seinen Verstand. Es sind geizige, grausame Schufte; einer wie der Andere![1]

---

1 A view shared by Alfred Kerr and Richard Strauss in *Krämerspiegel* (1918) and Henry James

So that you do not believe that I am doing nothing to get my compositions published, I am sending you this reply from a publisher (fourth rate) to my consignment of music. You can appreciate from this <u>printed</u> snub how difficult it is to find a publisher, for most of them do not even look at the manuscript but immediately send back the unperused manuscript with the printed snub.

I could show you letters from Simrock, Breitkopf & Härtel, etc., etc., all of whom decline to accept my manuscripts – & I am convinced that they do so without having looked at them.

You cannot therefore blame me, for I have as little control over a publisher's heart as I do over his judgement. They are stingy, cruel scoundrels, every one of them!

LIEDER

So wahr die Sonne scheinet[1]

So wahr die Sonne scheinet,
   So wahr die Wolke weinet,
   So wahr das Feuer[2] sprüht,
   So wahr der Frühling blüht;
   So wahr hab ich empfunden,
   Wie ich dich halt umwunden:
   Du liebst mich, wie ich dich,
   Dich lieb' ich wie du mich.
Die Sonne mag verscheinen,
   Die Wolke nicht mehr weinen,
   Das Feuer[2] mag versprühn,
   Der Frühling nicht mehr blühn!
   Wir wollen uns umwinden
   Und immer so empfinden:
   Du liebst mich, wie ich dich,
   Dich lieb' ich wie du mich.

Truly as the sun shines

Truly as the sun shines,
   Truly as the cloud weeps,
   Truly as the flame flashes
   Truly as spring blossoms,
   As truly did I feel
   Holding you in my embrace:
   You love me, as I love you,
   I love you, as you love me.
The sun may cease to shine,
   The cloud may weep no more,
   The flame may flash and fade,
   The spring may cease to blossom!
   But we shall embrace
   And always feel:
   You love me, as I love you,
   I love you, as you love me.

Also set by Wilhelm Kienzl, Johanna Kinkel and Robert Schumann

---

in *The Aspern Papers* (1888) in which Miss Bordereau, addressing Jeremy Aspern, 'hisses out passionately, furiously: "Ah, you publishing scoundrel!"'
1   Rückert's poem was first published in *Urania. Taschenbuch auf das Jahr 1823* – a volume in which the first twelve songs of Wilhelm Müller's *Die Winterreise* also appeared for the first time.
2   Rückert: Die Flamme.

Die Spinnerin[1]

„O süße Mutter,
    Ich kann nicht spinnen,
    Ich kann nicht sitzen
    Im Stübchen[2] innen
    Im engen Haus;
    Es stockt das Rädchen,
    Es reißt das Fädchen,
    O süße Mutter,
    Ich muß hinaus.
„Der Frühling gucket
    Hell durch die Scheiben,
    Wer kann nun sitzen,
    Wer kann nun bleiben
    Und fleißig sein?
    O laß mich gehen,
    O laß mich sehen,
    Ob ich kann fliegen
    Wie Vögelein.
„O laß mich sehen,
    O laß mich lauschen,
    Wo Lüftlein wehen,
    Wo Bächlein rauschen,
    Wo Blümlein blühn.
    Laß sie mich pflücken,
    Und schön mir schmücken
    Die braunen Locken
    Mit buntem Grün.
„Und kommen Knaben
    In wilden Haufen,[3]
    So will ich traben,
    So will ich laufen,
    Nicht stille stehn;
    Will hinter Hecken
    Mich hier verstecken,
    Bis sie mit Lärmen
    Vorüber gehn.

The spinning girl

'O mother dear,
    I can spin no more,
    I can sit no longer
    In my little room
    In this cramped house;
    The wheel stops,
    The thread snaps,
    O mother dear,
    I must go out.
'Spring peers
    Brightly through the windows,
    Who can sit,
    Who can slave away
    Indoors?
    O let me go,
    And let me see
    If I can fly
    Like the birds.
'O let me watch,
    O let me listen,
    Where breezes blow,
    Where streams murmur,
    Where flowers bloom.
    Let me pluck them,
    And let me adorn
    My brown locks
    With bright green.
'And if boys come by
    In unruly bands,
    I'll make off,
    I'll run away
    And not stand still;
    Here I'll hide
    Behind the hedge,
    Till they and their noise
    Have gone away.

---

1 Rückert's original title was 'O süße Mutter!', set as such by Loewe. Frank Walker relates how Wolf showed his sister Modesta and her husband Josef Strasser a letter from Liszt to whom Wolf had sent a copy of 'Die Spinnerin', which he had played to the master during his interview. Liszt had written a gracious reply with a handwritten correction in the margin of the manuscript. See Jestremski, p. 135.
2 Rückert: Stüblein.   3 Rückert: Im wilden Haufen.

„Bringt aber Blumen
Ein frommer Knabe,
Die ich zum Kranze
Just nötig habe;
Was soll ich thun?
Darf ich wohl nickend,
Ihm freundlich blickend,
O süße Mutter,
Zur Seit' ihm ruhn?"

'But if a nice young man
Should bring me flowers
That I need just then
For a garland;
What shall I do?
Might I not nod
And smile at him,
O mother dear,
And lie by his side?'

Also set by Carl Loewe

Joseph Victor von Scheffel
(1826–1886)

		page
Biterolf	26 December 1886	462
Wächterlied auf der Wartburg	24 January 1887 arranged for men's chorus and orchestra, June–November 1894, unfinished	461

POET

Like Gottfried Keller, Franz Kugler and Robert Reinick, Scheffel was a promising painter. He inherited his artistic temperament from his mother Josephine, who was herself a talented poet, but was persuaded by his father to devote himself to law, which he studied between 1843 and 1847 in Munich. His career in the legal branch of the Baden civil service soon came to an end, however, and having worked in Säkkingen and Bruchsal, he obtained leave of absence to study painting in Italy. He finally left the civil service in 1853 and devoted himself to literature for the rest of his life. His most famous work, *Der Trompeter von Säkkingen* – begun in 1850 in Säkkingen, finished three years later on Capri and published in 1854 – became one of the most read German poems of the nineteenth century. Like Scheffel, its hero Jung Werner abandons his law studies and wanders south with his trumpet. Having fallen in love with the beautiful Margareta, he becomes her father's master of music. He defends his patron's castle with great bravery during a peasant revolt, but is denied Margareta's hand in marriage because of his lowly station. He then journeys to Italy, becomes a musician in the Pope's service in Rome, where he again encounters Margareta. Having been ennobled by the Pope, Werner returns with her to Säkkingen where they are married. The long poem (some six thousand lines) is written in unrhymed trochaic verse and contains the indestructible 'Alt-Heidelberg, du feine' and other popular poems.

Like Werner, Scheffel was raised to the nobility in recognition of his services to literature. His other works include the historical novel *Ekkehard* (1857), a short Novelle *Hugideo* (1878) and several volumes of poetry: *Frau Aventiure. Lieder aus Heinrich von Ofterdingens Zeit* (1863), *Gaudeamus, Lieder aus dem Engern und Weitern* (1868) and *Waldeinsamkeit* (1878). His collected works, *Werke*, appeared in ten volumes in 1917, and the six volumes of his correspondence were published between 1926 and 1967. Something of Scheffel's old-fashioned nature is captured in Anton von Werner's powerful 1878 drawing. Scheffel's star has now waned, but his blend of Romanticism and nationalism appealed to a huge swathe of the population in nineteenth-century Germany, thanks in part to the extraordinary success of Victor Nessler's *Der Trompeter von Säkkingen* (1884), the most successful of his eleven operas, which included such hits as 'Alt-Heidelberg, du feine' and 'Behüt dich Gott, es wär' zu schön gewesen', and was performed 900 times in Germany in 1888 – Wolf's annus mirabilis.

Another composer inspired by *Der Trompeter von Säkkingen* was Gustav Mahler, whose incidental music for a dramatic presentation of the poem was written in the same year as Nessler's opera. The music is now presumed lost, but we have some idea of how Mahler's *Trompeter* music sounded thanks to research carried out in the mid-1960s by Donald Mitchell. Max Steinitzer in an article of 1920 had quoted from memory (inaccurately in part) the opening bars of Mahler's trumpet tune from his *Trompeter von Säkkingen* music, and when Mitchell was shown a photocopy of the manuscript of the original version of Mahler's First Symphony, he recognised in the *Andante* movement of the symphony (a short C major piece entitled 'Blumine') the trumpet tune quoted by Steinitzer. Donald Mitchell completes the story in his programme note for the first performance since 1894 of the *Andante* given by the New Philharmonia Orchestra under Benjamin Britten on 18 June 1967 as part of the Aldeburgh Festival:

> It had long been presumed that the *Andante* was lost or destroyed, and I was greatly surprised a few months ago, on having the opportunity to inspect the manuscript of the symphony's original version (which itself has only come to light quite recently), to find the 'missing' movement still there and complete in every detail. One discovery often leads to another, and while the most important thing of all is the recovery of a complete symphonic movement by Mahler which has been lost sight of for something like seventy years or more, it is also my conviction that this *Andante* throws light on another early and lost work of Mahler's, some incidental music he wrote for the theatre. This was to accompany a series of 'living pictures', after Scheffel's once famous poem, *Der Trompeter von Säkkingen*, composed and first performed in 1884. Hence, without a doubt, the extensive and inspired melody for trumpet solo with which this beautiful movement begins.

COMPOSER

'Biterolf' (1886) and 'Wächterlied auf der Wartburg' (1887) are both taken from Scheffel's *Frau Aventiure. Lieder aus Heinrich von Ofterdingens Zeit*. Wolf owned a copy of the seventh edition (1876) and it seems likely that these two poems were set to music to commemorate the poet, who had died earlier in 1886. In the autumn of 1887 Friedrich Eckstein, at Wolf's request, approached the Viennese publishing house of Emil Wetzler with a proposal to publish Wolf's Lieder. Wolf then prepared two sets for publication: *Sechs Lieder für eine Frauenstimme* and *Sechs Gedichte von Scheffel, Mörike, Goethe und Just. Kerner.* Wolf declared his intention of dedicating the first set to his mother, and the second to his father – see HW to Edmund Lang, 15 February 1888, p. 292.

LETTERS

HW to Oskar Grohe, Döbling, 30 December 1890

Beim Herannahen des neuen Jahres gedenke ich der Verse in meinem „Wächterlied auf der Wartburg": rüstig mög ein jeder schreiten, wie's sich ziemt nach Recht und Fug.[1] Sie Glücklicher, der Sie immer in der Lage sind, Ihre Pflicht zu erfüllen, können das tun! Mir ist es leider versagt.

As the new year approaches, I think of those lines in my 'Wächterlied auf der Wartburg': 'So let everyone with vigour do his duty, as behoves him.' You are so lucky always to be in a position to do your duty. That is unfortunately denied me.

HW to Frieda Zerny, Vienna, 21 June 1894

Aus Graz erhielt ich dieser Tage eine Aufforderung mich mit einer Composition an einem dort zu veranstaltenden Musikfest, das Ende Juli stattfinden soll, zu betheiligen, wobei das Wächterlied mit Chor u. Orchester in Vorschlag gebracht wurde. Ich bin nun bereit diesem Wunsche zu entsprechen u. gehe soeben an die Arbeit, um damit bei Zeiten fertig zu werden. Da hierbei große Schwierigkeiten in punkto der Instrumentirung zu überwinden sein werden u. die Arbeit reiflich erwogen sein will, wirst Du mir's gewiß nicht übel nehmen, wenn ab u. zu eine Stockung meinerseits in unserer Correspondenz eintreten dürfte.

I recently received an invitation from Graz to take part with one of my compositions in a music festival there at the end of July – and a version of my 'Wächterlied' with chorus & orchestra was suggested. I'm ready now to oblige & have just started to work on it, in order to complete it on time. As the

---

[1] A misquotation; for correct wording, see the beginning of verse 3 of 'Wächterlied auf der Wartburg', p. 461.

orchestration will present huge difficulties & the whole work requires careful thought, I'm sure you won't take it amiss if, from my side, the flow of our correspondence is occasionally interrupted.

HW to Richard Sternfeld, Vienna, 14 July 1894

Hingegen würde mir ein großer Gefallen erwiesen, wenn es Ihnen möglich wäre, einen Männergesangverein in Berlin für meine Arbeiten zu interessieren. Ich verfüge gegenwärtig über zwei äußerst wirkungsvolle Chorstücke mit Orchester, davon eines, „Dem Vaterland" betitelt (Text von Rob. Reinick), vom hiesigen Männergesangverein zur Aufführung für die Konzertsaison angenommen wurde. Das andre: „Wächterlied auf der Wartburg" habe ich gerade auf dem Ambos, um die eine Barytonstimme, für die es ursprünglich gesetzt ward, in einen pompösen Männerchor mit großem Orchester umzuschmieden. [...] Ich hege die sichere Überzeugung, daß, wenn irgend eine meiner Kompositionen, diese zwei es sein werden, die im besten Sinne mich populär zu machen berufen sind. Ich trage mich nebstbei noch mit der verwegenen Idee herum, beide Stücke dem Deutschen Kaiser zu widmen – wüßte ich nur, wie das zu machen wäre? Vielleicht wissen Sie einen Rat dafür. –

You would on the other hand be doing me a great favour if it were possible to interest a male voice choir in Berlin in my works. I have at present two extremely effective choral pieces with orchestra, one of which, entitled 'Dem Vaterland' (text by Rob. Reinick), will be performed by the local men's choir during the concert season here. The other: 'Wächterlied auf der Wartburg', written originally for baritone, is currently on the anvil waiting to be forged anew into a grandiose piece for men's chorus and large orchestra. [...] I am utterly convinced that if any of my compositions are destined to make me popular in the best sense it will be these two. I am also toying with the outrageous idea of dedicating both pieces to the German Kaiser – if I only knew how to proceed. Perhaps you could advise? –

HW to Emil Kauffmann, Vienna, 16 July 1894

Gegenwärtig bearbeite ich das Wächterlied auf der Wartburg für Männerchor u. Orchester, wodurch ich mich genöthigt sehe, das Stück nach ges-dur zu transponiren, um den Tenören Gelegenheit zu geben nach ihrer glanzvollen Seite hin sich zu entfalten. Ich verspreche mir von dieser Arbeit einen ganz ungewöhnlichen Erfolg, wie auch das „Vaterland" ganz geeignet erscheint mir eine solide Popularität in weitesten Kreisen zu verschaffen.

I am at present arranging the 'Wächterlied auf der Wartburg' for men's chorus & orchestra, which means I shall have to transpose it to G flat major to give the tenors ample opportunity to display their brilliant sound. I'm counting on a resounding success, just as the 'Vaterland' also seems designed to spread my popularity far and wide.

LIEDER

Wächterlied auf der Wartburg[1]
('Neujahrsnacht des Jahres 1200')

Schwingt Euch auf, Posaunen-Chöre,
Daß in sternenklarer Nacht,
Gott der Herr ein Loblied höre
Von der Thürme hoher Wacht;
Seine Hand führt die Planeten
Sichern Laufs durch Raum und Zeit,
Führt die Seele nach den Fehden
Dieser Welt zur Ewigkeit.

Ein Jahrhundert will zerrinnen
Und ein neues hebt sich an,
Wohl dem, der mit reinen Sinnen
Stetig wandelt seine Bahn!
Klirrt sie auch in Stahl und Eisen,

Gold'ne Zeit folgt der von Erz,

Und zum Heil, das ihm verheissen,
Dringt mit Kampf ein männlich Herz.

Rüstig mög drum Jeder schaffen,[2]
Was sich ziemt nach Recht und Fug,
In der Kutte, in den Waffen,
In der Werkstatt wie am Pflug:
Dazu, Herr, den Segen spende
Deiner Burg, dem Berg, der Au ...
Netz' an des Jahrhunderts Wende
Sie mit deiner Saelde[3] Thau.

Watchman's song from the Wartburg
('New Year's night of the year 1200')

Soar on high, you serried ranks of trumpets,
That in the clear starry night
The Lord God might hear a song of praise
From the lofty watchtowers;
His hand guides the planets
Surely through space and time,
Guides the soul through the strife
Of this world into eternity.

A century is about to vanish,
And a new one is dawning;
Happy is he who with pure heart
Steadfastly pursues his path!
Though we now hear the clash of steel
      and iron,
A golden age will follow this one
      of base metal,
And a manly heart shall win its way through
To the promised salvation.

So let everyone with vigour
Do his duty, as behoves him,
In a cowl or in armour,
In the workshop or at the plough.
Therefore, Lord, pour out Thy blessing
On Thy castle, mountain and meadow ...
Bedew them, as this century turns,
With your beneficence.

---

1 The song was performed in an arrangement by Karl Sipek for eight trombones at the unveiling in 1905 of Wolf's commemorative plaque in Perchtoldsdorf. The Wartburg was the fortress of Landgraf Hermann of Thüringen that makes an appearance in Wagner's *Tannhäuser*. 'Wächterlied' (Scheffel's title) was the first of his *Wartburglieder* and opened *Frau Aventiure*. Scheffel dedicated his book to the Grand Duke Carl Alexander of Saxony, Burgherr auf Wartburg.
2 See HW to Oskar Grohe, 30 December 1890, p. 459.
3 An archaic word meaning 'bliss', 'beneficence'.

Biterolf[1]
('Im Lager von[2] Akkon 1190')

Kampfmüd und sonnverbrannt,
Fern an der Heiden Strand
Waldgrünes Thüringland,
Denk' ich an dich.
Mildklarer Sternenschein,
Du sollst mir Bote sein,
Geh', grüß' die Heimath mein
Weit überm[3] Meer!

Feinden von allerwärts
Trotzt meiner Waffen Erz;
Wider der Sehnsucht Schmerz
Schirmt mich kein Schild.
Doch wie das Herz auch klagt,
Ausharr' ich unverzagt:
Wer Gottes Fahrt gewagt,
Trägt still sein Kreuz.

Biterolf
('In camp at Acre, 1190')

Battle-weary and sun-scorched,
Far away on a heathen shore,
Green-forested Thuringia,
I think of you.
Soft bright starlight,
You shall be my messenger,
Go, greet my homeland
Far across the sea!

My weapons' steel defies
Enemies from every quarter;
Yet against the ache of longing
No shield protects me.
But however my heart complains
I shall endure undaunted:
He who has ventured forth on God's crusade
Bears his cross uncomplaining.

---

1 Scheffel's poem (Wolf omits the final verse) describes a crusader languishing in the camp at Acre during the campaign against Saladin waged by Philip Augustus of France and Richard I of England, whose forces retook the town in 1191. The poem, the first in a sequence of five, clearly moved Wolf, and the music with its slow minims and semibreves depicts with great sincerity the religious fervour of the soldier and his longing to see again his native Thuringia. Biterolf also appears as a knight in Wagner's *Tannhäuser*. The battle between Muslim and Christian worlds is also the theme of Schubert's 'Das Heimweh' (Johann Ladislaus Pyrker) in which a Christian soldier, languishing in the heat of North Africa, longs for home.
2 Scheffel: vor.   3 Scheffel: über.

WILLIAM SHAKESPEARE
(1564–1616)

		page
Lied des transferierten Zettel	11 May 1889	467
Elfenlied	11 May 1889 orchestrated October 1891 soprano, chorus (SSAA), small orchestra	468

POET

'The work of William Shakespeare has almost certainly given rise to a greater quantity of music than that of any other dramatist, or even of any other author.' These are the opening words of the Preface to *A Shakespeare Music Catalogue*, edited by Bryan N. S. Gooch and David Thatcher, a remarkable bibliographical achievement that lists over twenty thousand musical settings of Shakespeare's poems and plays. One of the reasons why Shakespeare's genius is recognised throughout the world is the role that music has played in the dissemination of his works. W. H. Auden, in an essay titled 'Music in Shakespeare' from *The Dyer's Hand*, distinguishes two kinds of songs in Shakespeare's plays, the 'called-for' and the 'impromptu', which, he writes, serve different dramatic purposes:

> A called-for song is a song which is sung by one character at the request of another who wishes to hear music, so that action and speech are halted until the song is over. Nobody is asked to sing unless it is believed that he can sing well and, little as we may know about the music which was actually used in performances of Shakespeare, we may safely assume from the contemporary songs which we do possess that they must have made demands which only a good voice and a good musician could satisfy.

> The impromptu singer stops speaking and breaks into song, not because anyone else has asked him to sing or is listening, but to relieve his feelings in a way that speech cannot do or to help him in some action. An impromptu song is not art but a form of personal behaviour. It reveals, as the called-for song cannot, something about the singer. On the stage, therefore, it is generally desirable that a character who breaks into impromptu song should not have a good voice. No producer, for example, would seek to engage Madame

Callas for the part of Ophelia, because the beauty of her voice would distract the audience's attention from the real dramatic point which is that Ophelia's songs are to the highest degree *not* called-for. We are meant to be horrified both by what she sings and by the fact that she sings at all. The other characters are affected but not in the way that people are affected by music.

'Elfenlied' is a called-for song – commanded by Titania; while 'Lied des transferierten Zettel' is an impromptu song, sung by Bottom to show the mechanicals that he is not afraid.

COMPOSER

Shakespeare played an important part in Wolf's life. During December 1878, while staying with the Gabillons, he received a complete Shakespeare as a Christmas present, and during a New Year's party there, at which members of the Burgtheater performed a parody on *Antony and Cleopatra*, he was called on to provide burlesque incidental music. In the spring of 1889 he seriously considered *A Midsummer Night's Dream* as an opera subject; a year later he was enthralled by *The Tempest*, expressing his rapture to Gustav Schur – see HW to Gustav Schur, 28 May 1890, p. 465 – and elaborating to his friend a detailed scenario of the three-act opera he had in mind. December 1889 saw him turn to *Hamlet*: vestigial sketches exist for what might be a symphonic piece or incidental music to the play. In a letter to Melanie Köchert of 15 January 1894 Wolf expresses his disgust at a performance of *A Midsummer Night's Dream* he had seen at the Burgtheater, and fulminates against the liberties taken by theatre directors and actors. His admiration for Shakespeare's play gave rise to two compositions, composed on the same day: 'Lied des transferierten Zettel' and 'Elfenlied'. There is good evidence that Wolf intended these two songs to form part of an opera based on *A Midsummer Night's Dream*. 'Elfenlied' is even supplied with stage directions: we are told that the two verses of the poem should be divided between the first and the second fairy, and shortly before the end of the song the score reads: „Die Elfen verschwinden" and „Titania schläft" ('The fairies vanish' and 'Titania sleeps'). Ernst Decsey recounts how Wolf one Sunday burst into Ferdinand Löwe's room and expatiated for half an hour on how Shakespeare's play was ideal material for an opera.

The publication of 'Elfenlied' was, typically for Wolf, fraught with difficulties. He first approached Schott's but when Ludwig Strecker hesitated, saying that he would like to attend a successful performance before committing his publishing house, Wolf discussed terms with Ries & Erler – see HW to Melanie Köchert, 9 January 1894, p. 466. When that came to nothing, the work was published by

Adolph Fürstner Verlag – a circumstance that Wolf communicated to Schott's in a letter of 19 January 1894, stating that they had refused it. Schott's (Ludwig Strecker) then pointed out in a letter of 22 January that the publishing house had not refused the work but merely wished to hear a performance.

The *Vier Gedichte nach H. Heine, Shakespeare und Lord Byron* were published in 1897 by Heckel in Mannheim. 'Lied des transferierten Zettel' is Wolf's only piano-accompanied setting of Shakespeare, a free translation by August Wilhelm von Schlegel of the second verse of Bottom's Act III song from *A Midsummer Night's Dream*. The end of the poem in Schlegel's very free translation mentions the cuckoo – the cue for Wolf to write a plethora of hee-haws (which had begun in the piano prelude) and cuckoo-calls for both the piano part and the voice. 'Elfenlied' was published in May 1894.

LETTERS

HW to Gustav Schur, Unterach, 28 May 1890

Etwas Überraschendes hab' ich aber doch auf Lager. Sie wissen, daß mich seit kurzem die Idee: Shakespeare's „Sturm" rein orchestral zu vertonen lebhaft in Unruhe versetzte. Nun habe ich neuerdings Shakespeare's „Zauber-Lustspiel" durchgenommen u. z. in Hinsicht auf eine symphonisch orchestrale Behandlung des Stückes. Aber je mehr ich bemüht war das Stück mir in seinen einfachsten Zügen zu veranschaulichen, desto lebhafter drängte sich die bunte Pracht dieser in ihren Contrasten ganz einzig dastehenden Bilderwelt vor meine Einbildungskraft. Heiliger Gott, denk ich mir, wenn <u>das</u> nicht ein von Himmel dir in den Schoß gefallener Opernstoff sein soll, auf was wohl könnte ich noch warten? Was sagen Sie Freund Schur? Prospero! welch ein majestätischer Bass! Fernando, Miranda – ein Liebespaar wie Adam u. Eva. Ariel! – ich höre schon die schönsten Coloraturen!?

But I have finished a work that will surprise you. You know that my recent idea of setting Shakespeare's *The Tempest* as a purely orchestral piece caused me great turmoil. I've just read through Shakespeare's 'magical comedy' again, with a view to composing a symphonic work. But the more I tried to reduce it to its simplest features, the more my imagination was struck by the multicoloured splendour of this world of images, utterly unique in all its contrasts. Good God, I think to myself, if <u>this</u> isn't heaven-sent material for an opera, I don't know what is! What do you say, my friend? Prospero – what a majestic bass! Fernando, Miranda – a pair of lovers like Adam & Eve. Ariel! – I'm already hearing the most beautiful coloratura music!?

HW to Emil Kauffmann, Traunkirchen, 12 October 1891

Meine einzige musikalische Arbeit in letzter Zeit war die Instrumentirung eines Elfenliedes aus Shakespeares Sommernachtstraum. Eine schöne leichte Sopranstimme u. ein wohlgeschulter Frauenchor unterstützt durch ein in duftigen Farben gehaltenes kleines Orchester dürften diesem Stücke einen unbestreitbaren Erfolg sichern.

My only recent musical activity was orchestrating an elf song from Shakespeare's *A Midsummer Night's Dream*. A beautiful light soprano voice & a well-trained women's chorus, supported by the delicate colours of a small orchestra – that should guarantee the piece certain success.

HW to Melanie Köchert, Berlin, 9 January 1894

Anakreons Grab aber wurde einfach verhetzt u. z. durch den Sänger, der das Ende nicht abwarten konnte. Sofort aber änderte sich die Situation während der Vorführung des Elfenliedes. Orchester, Solo (de Jong) u. Chor waren auf der Höhe ihrer Leistungen. Die Klangwirkung war noch krystallener als bei der Generalprobe, ein mondscheinartiger Duft schien über dem Ganzen zu schweben u. man konnte sich recht wohl einbilden die Silberglöcklein der Elfen zu hören, ihr feines Lachen, ihre drolligen Sprünge ... kurz es war ganz prächtig. <u>Das Stück mußte wiederholt werden.</u> [...] Heute Vormittag erhielt ich vom Verleger Ries u. Erler folgende Zeilen: „Sollte das gestern hier aufgeführte Elfenlied noch ungedruckt u. Sie geneigt sein dasselbe in userm Verlag erscheinen zu sehen, so bitten wir Sie in den Vormittagsstunden von 10–1 Uhr um Ihren Besuch." Endlich ein Verleger, der mich invitirt! Natürlich bin ich bereit ihm das Stück gegen ein entsprechendes Honorar zu verkaufen.

But 'Anakreons Grab' was simply rushed – because of the singer who was impatient to get to the end. But the situation changed immediately during the performance of 'Elfenlied'. Orchestra, soloist (de Jong) & chorus were in tiptop form. The sound was even more crystalline than in the dress rehearsal. A sort of moonlit haze seemed to hover over everything & it was easy to imagine hearing the little silver bells of the elves, their dainty laughter, their comical leaps ... in short, it was quite wonderful. <u>The piece had to be encored.</u> [...] This morning I received the following note from the publishers Ries & Erler: 'Should the "Elfenlied" performed last night not yet be published, and should you be inclined to have our publishing house do so, we ask that you call on us during the morning hours between 10.00 and 1.00.' Of course I'm prepared to sell him the piece, for a suitable honorarium.

WILLIAM SHAKESPEARE

LIEDER

Lied des transferierten Zettel[1]

Die Schwalbe, die den Sommer bringt,
    Der Spatz, der Zeisig fein,
  Die Lerche, die sich lustig schwingt
    Bis in den Himmel 'nein.
    Y-a, Y-a, Y-a![2]

Der Kuckuck, der der Grasemück'
    So gern ins Nestchen heckt,
  Und lacht darob mit arger Tück,
    Und manchen Ehmann neckt.
    Y-a, Y-a, Y-a!

Song of Bottom translated

The swallow, that brings in summer,
    The sparrow, the graceful siskin,
  The lark, that happily soars aloft
    Up into the sky.
    Hee-haw!

The cuckoo, who likes to hatch its eggs
    In the hedge-sparrow's nest,
  Laughing the while with wicked spite,
    Teasing many a married man.
    Hee-haw!

Translated, very freely, by August Wilhelm Schlegel

---

1   The relevant scene in Act III, scene 1 reads:

Quince
Bless thee, Bottom! bless thee! thou art translated.

Bottom
I see their knavery: this is to make an ass of me; to fright me, if they could. But I will not stir from this place, do what they can: I will walk up and down here, and I will sing, that they shall hear I am not afraid.

    The ousel-cock, so black of hue,
        With orange-tawny bill,
    The throstle with his note so true,
        The wren with little quill.

Titania [awaking]
What angel wakes me from my flow'ry bed?

Bottom

    The finch, the sparrow, and the lark,
        The plain-song cuckoo grey,
    Whose note full many a man doth mark,
        And dares not answer, nay;

For indeed, who would set his wit to so foolish a bird? Who would give a bird the lie, though he cry 'cuckoo' never so?

2   The 'Y-a's are Wolf's invention.

You spotted snakes with double tongue,[1]
   Thorny hedge-hogs, be not seen;
Newts, and blind worms, do no wrong;
   Come not near our fairy queen.

Philomel, with melody,[2]
Sing in our sweet lullaby;
Lulla, lulla, lullaby; lulla, lulla, lullaby:
Never harm,

Nor spell, nor charm,
Come our lovely lady nigh;
So, good night, with lullaby.

Weaving spiders come not here;
   Hence, you long-legg'd spinners, hence!
Beetles black, approach not near;
   Worm nor snail, do no offence.

Elfenlied

Bunte Schlangen zweigezüngt,
Igel, Molche, fort von hier!
Daß ihr euren Gift nicht bringt
In der Königin Revier!

Nachtigall mit Melodei,
Sing' in unser Eiapopei!
Daß kein Spruch, kein Zauberfluch
Der holden Herrin schädlich sei.
Nun gute Nacht mit Eiapopei!

Schwarze Käfer, uns umgebt
Nicht mit Summen,
Die ihr künstlich webt
An einem andern Ort!

Translated by August Wilhelm Schlegel

Elf-song

Coloured snakes with double tongue,
Hedgehogs, salamanders, avaunt!
That you do not bring your poison
Into the Queen's hunting-ground!

Nightingale – mingle your melody
With our lullaby!
That no decree, no spell
May harm our gracious lady.
So, good night, with a lullaby!

Black beetles – do not
Whirr around us,
Weave your webs
In another place!

---

1 Sung by the Fairies at the beginning of Shakespeare's *A Midsummer Night's Dream*, Act II, scene 2.
2 In Ovid's *Metamorphoses*, VI, Philomel was changed into a nightingale when pursued by Tereus, and her song henceforth was both sweet and sad.

Julius Sturm
(1816–1896)

		page
Über Nacht	23–24 May 1878	470

POET

Born at Köstritz in the principality of Reuss, Julius Sturm studied theology at Jena from 1837 to 1841, becoming pastor at Göschitz in 1851 and at Köstritz in 1857. His religious poems were once extremely popular, and *Fromme Lieder* (*Devout Hymns*) were published in three volumes between 1852 and 1892. In Elise Polko's anthology *Dichtergrüße*, Sturm, with 29 poems, is the third most represented poet, trailing behind Heine (34) and Geibel (32). Goethe appears a mere 24 times. Ferdinand Wilferth wrote a memoir of the poet in the *Deutsche Zeitung* of 16 December 1896, in which he mentions his 'noble profile, long, swept-back hair and the gentle expression of his eyes that were hidden behind spectacles'.

COMPOSER

Frank Walker describes the song in his biography of Wolf:

> Its chief significance lies in the first stanza, where the composer for the first time hit upon those uneasy, broken rhythms which he employed afterwards for identical purposes in *Alle gingen, Herz, zur Ruh* and in his setting of Byron's lines to the moon, 'Sun of the sleepless, melancholy star', to evoke the restless heartbeats, the unquiet throbbing of the pulses of those whom sleep has forsaken.

LIED

Über Nacht

Über Nacht, über Nacht
Kommt still das Leid,
Und bist du erwacht,
O traurige Zeit!
Du grüßest den dämmernden Morgen
Mit Weinen und mit Sorgen.

Über Nacht, über Nacht
Kommt still das Glück,
Und bist du erwacht,
O selig Geschick!
Der düstre[1] Traum ist zerronnen,
Und Freude ist gewonnen.

Über Nacht, über Nacht
Kommt Freud' und Leid,
Und eh' du's gedacht,
Verlassen dich beid'
Und gehen dem Herrn zu sagen,
Wie du sie getragen.

Overnight

Overnight, overnight
Grief comes silently,
And once you awake –
O mournful time!
You greet the dawn
With tears and sorrow.

Overnight, overnight
Happiness comes silently,
And once you awake –
O blessed fate!
The sombre dream has vanished
And joy is here.

Overnight, overnight
Come joy and grief,
And before you're aware,
Both leave you
And go to tell the Lord
How you have borne them.

[1] Sturm: düstere.

Heinrich Zschokke
(1771–1848)

		page
Nacht und Grab	by August 1875	472

POET

Zschokke was a writer and political journalist of German origin. Born in Magdeburg (one of his pseudonyms was Johann von Magdeburg), he ran away from school and joined a theatre troupe for which he wrote plays. In 1790 he began to study theology in Frankfurt an der Oder, and six years later emigrated to Switzerland where he earned his living as a teacher and took Swiss nationality – one of his most successful poems, 'Heimweh nach der Schweiz', written in Paris in 1796, expresses his longing to return to his adopted country. In 1804 he was a member of the Swiss Mining Board and Forestry Commission, and in 1814 he became a councillor in the canton of Aargau. Apart from travel books and historical novels, he wrote poems and Novellen, of which *Das Goldmacherdorf* (1817) is the best known, and published *Feldblumen. Eine andere Selbstschau in poetischen Gedenkblümlein*, which included 'Nacht und Grab', in 1850. Before the poems were printed, he copied them out in his own hand into a beautifully bound book which he presented to his wife on her birthday.

COMPOSER

Wolf composed 'Nacht und Grab' in the summer of 1875, no later than August. The song opened his Op. 3, which also contained four Goethe settings: 'Sehnsucht', 'Der Fischer', 'Wanderlied' and 'Auf dem See'; these songs were among his earliest compositions, written either at school or in the holidays before he enrolled at the Vienna Conservatoire. Zschokke's *Abenteuer einer Neujahrsnacht* was turned into a libretto by Franz Schaumann, a friend of Wolf, and set to music by Richard Heuberger. Wolf almost certainly knew this work, since he seriously considered Schaumann as librettist for his own *Der Corregidor*.

LETTER

See HW to Alexander Pöch, August 1875, p. 117.

LIED

Nacht und Grab[1]

Sei mir gegrüßt, o schöne Nacht,[2]
In deiner hehren Sternenpracht!
Mit weichen Händen bietest du
Des Staubes Kindern deine Ruh'.
O Brüder, schlummert sanft den süßen
    Schlummer;
Ein neuer Tag[3] weckt euch zu neuem
    Kummer.

Auch in den stummen Gräbern Ihr,
Ruht sanft von eurer Arbeit hier.
Vergessenheit ist euer Loos
Und euer Obdach dieses Moos.
O Brüder, schlummert sanft des Todes
    Schlummer,
Kein neuer Tag weckt euch zu neuem
    Kummer.

Night and grave

Welcome, o beautiful night,
In your sublime star-spangled splendour!
With tender hands you offer
Repose to the children of dust.
O brothers, sleep in peace
    this sweet sleep;
A new day wakens you to new sorrow.

And you, in your silent graves,
Rest in peace from your earthly toil;
Oblivion is your destiny,
And this moss your shelter.
O brothers, sleep in peace
    the sleep of death,
No new day will waken you
    to new sorrow.

---

1   The original poem bears the subtitle (Biberstein 1803). Biberstein is a municipality in the canton of Aargau in Switzerland.
2   Zschokke: o stille Nacht.   3   Zschokke: Der neue Tag.

Vincenz Zusner
(1803–1874)

		page
Abendglöcklein	18 March–24 April 1876	474

POET

Zusner earned a great fortune as a manufacturer and bequests in his will funded two scholarships a year, to be administered by the Vienna Conservatoire and the Gesellschaft der Musikfreunde for the best settings of his own poems. Among the many prize-winners was Alexander Zemlinsky. 'Das Abendglöcklein' was first published in *Gedichte von Vincenz Zusner* (1842).

COMPOSER

Wolf originally intended 'Abendglöcklein' to form part of his Op. 9, along with 'Meeresstille' and 'Liebesfrühling' (both Lenau), 'Erster Verlust' and 'Mai' (both Goethe), and 'Der goldene Morgen' (Anon.), but later withdrew it in order to include it in another collection of songs – see the manuscript in the Wienbibliothek im Rathaus, meticulously worded: *Op 14 Abendglöcklein. Zusner Vinzenz*, and dated *Samstag den 18/3 bzw. Fine Montag den 24 April ¾7 Abends*.

LETTER

HW to his father, Vienna, 18 December 1877

Am 1. Jänner wird entschieden, wer den Preis[1] erhaltet: ich habe große Hoffnungen. Das Scherzo aus der Symphonie gefällt allgemein, ein Lied „An***" von Lenau, das ich bei Goldschmidt vorgespielt, entzückte die Zuhörer, und so glaube ich, mit Recht große Hoffnungen auf den Preis setzen zu dürfen.

---

1 Possibly the Zusner-Preis, although by the spring of 1877 Wolf had left the conservatoire.

The winner of the prize will be decided on 1 January; I have high hopes. The Scherzo from my Symphony is liked by all; a setting of Lenau's 'An***' that I played at Goldschmidt's entranced the audience, and so I am justified in harbouring great hopes of winning the prize.

LIED

Abendglöcklein[1]

Des Glöckleins Schall
Durchtönt das Thal,
Mir[2] Ruhe zu verkünden;*
Nur ich allein
Mit meiner Pein
Vermag sie nicht zu finden.*

Wann läutest du
Denn mir zu Ruh'
Von deinem Kirchlein droben? –
Sey ruhig, Herz!
Ein jeder Schmerz
Hört einmahl auf zu toben.

Einst wird dich schon
Des Glöckleins Ton
Mit deiner Qual versöhnen.
Und schweigt der Klang
Auch noch so lang,
Er muß doch endlich tönen!

Little evening bell

The little bell rings
Through the valley,
Announcing peace to me;*
Only I,
Alone with my torment,
Am unable to find such peace.*

When will you
Ring me to rest
From your little church up there?
Be calm, O heart!
Every pain
Finally ceases to throb.

The little bell
Will one day
Finally assuage your pain.
And though the bell
Has long been silent,
It will sound in the end!

* These lines are repeated by Wolf.

1 Zusner: 'Das Abendglöcklein'. The text contrasts the serenity of the church-bell-pealing valley with the poet's loneliness, and inspired Wolf to write an attractive song in which the bright bells, first heard in the right-hand quavers of the prelude, ring out more plaintively in the postlude, anticipating the time when they will toll at the poet's funeral.
2 Zusner: Um.

Correspondents

HW to Josef Strasser, June 1886

Ich bin steinunglücklich und zugleich wütend auf mich. Bedauert mich, denn ich weiß nun sicher, daß mein Los ist, alle die zu kränken, die mich lieben und die ich liebe.

I am wretchedly unhappy and at the same time furious with myself. Pity me, for I am now convinced that it is my fate to hurt all those people who love me and whom I also love.

The usual form of address, formal (Sie) or informal (Du), is shown in the heading for each correspondent. Page references to displayed extracts from Wolf's letters to each correspondent are listed following each entry.

FRIEDRICH ECKSTEIN (Du)
(1861–1939)

Philosopher, polymath, scholar and mystic, this music-lover was able to indulge his multifarious hobbies through the fortune he inherited from his father's vellum business. He studied music with Bruckner and came into contact with a glittering array of musicians, artists, poets, architects, scientists and philosophers including Gustav Mahler, Adolf Loos, Karl Kraus, Hugo von Hofmannsthal, Franz Liszt, Frederic Chopin, Friedrich Nietzsche, Hans Makart, Mark Twain, Rudolf Steiner, Richard Wagner and Sigmund Freud, all of whom figure prominently in his autobiographical „*Alte unnennbare Tage!*", a rich source of Wolf anecdotes and required reading for anyone interested in Wolf's character. Eckstein worshipped Wagner and made the journey from Perchtoldsdorf (his birthplace) to Bayreuth on foot.

Wolf first met him in 1882 in Café Griensteidl and did not initially warm to him, but it was not long before he became a close friend (Wolf was soon using the 'Du' form of address in his letters, though not in those included here) and one of his most generous champions and benefactors. Eckstein acted as a sort of amanuensis to Wolf, as he had done with Bruckner, and it was largely through his influence and generosity that the *Sechs Lieder für eine Frauenstimme* were published by Wetzler in 1888 – he contributed to the costs and continued to help Wolf in times of need. He also put Wolf up for long periods at his homes in the Siebenbrunnengasse (which Wolf loved for its library and hated for its lack of cleanliness) and also at his villa in Unterach am Attersee. Eckstein – known affectionately by Wolf's friends as 'Eck', 'Samiel', 'Sami' or 'Proteus' (because of his many interests) – was a vegetarian for a while, dressed eccentrically, sported a luxuriant black beard and wore a black horn-rimmed pince-nez. Rosa Mayreder, the librettist of *Der Corregidor*, describes in *Mein Pantheon* how Eckstein's sartorial habits changed dramatically when he distanced himself from Vienna's Wagner-Verein, whose anti-Semitic tendencies he abhorred. He now renounced vegetarianism, dressed elegantly, wore patent-leather shoes, a variety of colourful cravats and had his hair cut short. It seems that his attendances at Wolfiaden were always keenly anticipated.

Anecdotes abound in „*Alte unnennbare Tage!*" We learn how Wolf used to wake his friend by playing Bach's *Italienisches Konzert* on the piano; and how once, shortly before he lost his mind, Wolf woke him with screams, curses and grimaces, as he ripped out the hairs of his beard. We hear how he would play and sing his Lieder with imperfect vocal and piano technique and yet with overwhelming emotional impact; how he loved Chopin's song 'Poland's Funeral Hymn' in E flat minor, Op. 74/17, inspired by the Russian suppression of the

1830 Polish insurrection; and how he adored Bizet's *Carmen*, which he would play again and again at the piano. Among Wolf's favourite books were Laurence Sterne's *Tristram Shandy*, Mark Twain's *Huckleberry Finn*, Jean Paul's *Der Titan*, and Claude Tillier's *Mon Oncle Benjamin*. A private recital in Bayreuth in the drawing room of the American philanthropist Mrs Elizabeth Fairchild is described in detail: Wolf pulling the tuning key from his hip pocket and retuning the already tuned Steingräber grand piano, and Eckstein, at Wolf's request, reciting the poems clearly and distinctly before the songs were played. Other anecdotes also deal with Wolf's propensity for tuning pianos. Eckstein tells us how Wolf always went out with a tuning key and a tuning fork in his back pocket, and how, if pressed by his hosts to perform his songs after supper, he would often either brusquely refuse or leave the room. Occasionally, however, he adopted another method: he would feign compliance, sit down at the piano, play a few chords, insist that the recently tuned piano was out of tune and proceed to tune it for an hour or more. Small dinners in Eckstein's home were a different matter, and there is a charming description of an evening *à trois* with Hugo von Hofmannsthal during which they discussed opera and opera libretti.

Wolf's acute sense of humour is revealed in the way he and Eckstein would laugh themselves helpless reading episodes from *Huckleberry Finn*. And Eckstein tells us how the composer would often greet him with the hellish words from Berlioz's *La Damnation de Faust*: 'Marexil burrudixe formy Dinkorlitz, Tradium, Merondor, Irkymur, Irimirikarabrao!' (*sic*), and how during a performance of the work in the opera house, when the words had been replaced by tame circumlocutions, Wolf had stood up, screamed his indignation and stormed out.

See pp. 59, 347, 351, 353, 362.

HUGO FAISST (Du)
(1862–1914)

Lawyer, amateur singer. Like Richard Strauss, he abhorred an 'ß' at the end of his name, and always signed himself 'Faisst', although his name was spelt 'Faißt' in the Stuttgart address book. He studied chemistry, spent some time in North America and then settled down in Stuttgart as a lawyer.

Following advice by Emil Kauffmann, Faisst wrote to Wolf in July 1893, declaring himself a champion of his songs. Wolf, writing to Kauffmann on 5 August 1893, refers to this letter, stating that Faisst as a baritone would find few songs to suit him. The first time he sang Wolf Lieder in public was at a concert that Kauffmann had arranged in Tübingen, in which his rendering of several *Goethe-Lieder* had been well received by the critics. Wolf and Faisst first met in late January 1894, and by February 1895 Wolf was living as a guest at Faisst's home in Stuttgart (Archivstraße 5).

On 7 February 1894 Wolf accompanied Faisst in a soirée of songs that included *Harfenspieler* (1–3), 'Anakreons Grab', 'Cophtisches Lied I and II', 'Ob der Koran von Ewigkeit sei?' and 'Erschaffen und Beleben'. A succession of Liederabende followed, not always with Wolf at the piano, in Mannheim (8 February 1894), Tübingen (18 February), Vienna (3 April), and several in Stuttgart during 1897, 1898, 1899 and 1900. In early 1898 Faisst founded the Stuttgart Hugo-Wolf-Verein, where he was to give many recitals. On 26 April 1903 he arranged a commemorative Wolf recital in which, according to Vienna's *Neue musikalische Presse*, he 'performed some of Wolf's most beautiful songs', and in December of the same year he sang all of Wolf's orchestral songs.

Faisst's hagiographical affection for Wolf occasionally irked the composer. In a letter to Frieda Zerny (6 July 1894) he referred to Faisst's „überschwängliche Verehrung meiner Person" ('over-exuberant veneration of my person') and how his unseemly praise („unschicklich vorgebrachtes Lob") hurt him more than the most unjustified censure. Yet Wolf, with typical inconsistency, fully appreciated Faisst's kindness, which he described to Karl Mayr (15 March 1897), referring to his „lieben Freund" and his „äußerst zart gestimmte Seele" ('extremely tender soul') inside his 'robust frame' („robusten Corpus"). Wolf's affection for Faisst is revealed in many of the letters in which he refers to his friend as „Kurwenal" (Faisst was a passionate Wagnerian) and „Faischti". When Wolf finally possessed a home of his own in the Schwindgasse, it was Faisst who largely financed the move with a gift of 1000 marks. And when Wolf was committed to the Niederösterreichische Landesirrenanstalt on 4 October 1898 as a 'first-class' patient, Faisst and his mother covered the expense with a yearly contribution of 2000 kronen. It was from this asylum that Wolf sent Faisst in early 1899 one of his last and most heartrending letters:

> Liebster Freund! Es wäre sehr lieb von Dir, wenn Du mir nach so langer Pause wiedereinmal ein Lebenszeichen zukommen ließest. Wie Du aus diesen Zeilen entnehmen könntest geht es mir gerade nicht am besten. Vielleicht treffen wir uns dießmal irgendwo in Tirol od. in der Schweiz, wohin ich am liebsten ginge. Leider werde ich hier in einer Anstalt, in der ich untergebracht bin noch zurückgehalten u. fürchte sehr überhaupt nicht mehr hinauszukommen. Sollte mir's dennoch beschieden sein wieder der menschlichen Gesellschaft anzugehören werde ich mich neuerdings an Dich wenden.

> Dearest friend! It would be very kind if after such a long silence you would once again let me have a sign of life. As you will see from these lines, things are not exactly going well for me. Perhaps we'll meet next time in the Tyrol

or in Switzerland, where I would most like to go. Unfortunately I am still confined in an asylum, & I fear very much that I shall never get out again. If, however, it be granted me once more to belong to human society, I shall turn to you again.

See pp. 195, 229, 231, 325, 363, 436.

VALENTINE (VALLY) FRANCK (Du)
(1856–?)

Born in Paris as the daughter of the learned Professor Adolph Franck (1809–1893), who taught philosophy at various French universities, Vally grew up in a highly cultured environment. She spoke fluent Czech, English, French, German and Italian and was a competent pianist. After the early death of her mother, she spent much of her childhood and adolescence at the houses of her uncle in Roskosch or Vienna, where she met Helene Gabillon, daughter of the celebrated German actor Ludwig Gabillon (1825–1896). Together they founded a reading society, Eulonia, to which Wolf was occasionally invited. It was there or at the house of Adalbert von Goldschmidt that Wolf first met Vally, who was four years older, in the spring of 1878, and by the end of the year they were deeply in love.

The relationship lasted almost three years, ending in the spring of 1881, causing Wolf untold anguish (see HW to Max Wolf, p. 25). None of their letters survive, but Vally's correspondence with Helene provides tantalising glimpses of their life together. In July 1878 she writes to her friend:

> Es war ohnehin ein schmerzlicher Tag, mein kleiner Freund schied [. . .] Die letzten Tage in Wien waren unerträglich, heiß, einsam, krank, sehnsüchtig – es war kein Leben mehr [. . .] Der erste Brief, den ich gleich am Tag meiner Ankunft erhielt, war ein 6 Seiten langer von Hugo, – ist das nicht schön?

> It was moreover a painful day when my little friend departed [. . .] These last days in Vienna were unbearable, hot, lonely, sick and full of longing [. . .] Life had ceased to exist. The first letter from Hugo that I received on the very day of my arrival was 6 pages long – is that not beautiful?

Recuperating in Roskosch from an illness that immobilised one side of her face (it eventually responded to medical treatment), Vally wrote to Helene on 25 July 1879:

> Wie kannst Du glauben, ich würde Dir etwas so Wichtiges wie Hugos Hiersein verschweigen [. . .] Ich wäre nur zu froh, ihn hier zu haben, aber das findet meine Tante auch (daß ich zu froh wäre!) und legt ihr wohlweises Veto ein.

How can you believe that I would not inform you about something as important as Hugo's presence here? [. . .] I should be only too glad to have him here, but that is also my aunt's opinion (that I should be *too* glad!), and she applies her most prudent veto.

And on 25 August 1879 she writes:

Das liebe Geschöpf ist mir und sich treu geblieben, ich erhalte viele und liebe Briefe, ab und zu auch Compositionen. Nicht verhehlen kann ich Dir, daß ich die Briefe beantworte, die Compositionen spiele und die mir geschickten Bücher lese. Wie das enden soll, wissen die Götter, einstweilen geht die Selbstständigkeit und Originalität meines Styles verloren, denn ich schreibe schon ganz so wie Hugo.

The dear creature has remained loyal to me and to himself, I receive many loving letters and occasionally compositions. I cannot hide from you the fact that I answer the letters, play the compositions and read the books sent to me. Only the gods can tell how it will all end; meanwhile I have lost the independence and originality of my style, for I write now exactly like Hugo.

Less than two months later, a quarrel nearly ended their relationship, as we learn from this letter that Vally wrote to Helene on 4 October 1879:

Ich bin steinunglücklich [. . .] Ich habe mich mit meinem einzigen, besten, liebsten Freunde Hugo entzweit. Und warum? Aus verwünschter dummer Tugend und Vernunft meinerseits! Er schrieb mir nämlich immer heißer und heißer werdende Briefe, die Flammen loderten immer höher und mir ward endlich gruselich. Was soll bei diesem leidenschaftlichen Temperament aus s o einer Liebe werden? dachte ich und da ich bei meiner herzlichen Neigung zu dem Kleinen es ohnehin hatte zu weit gedeihen lassen, schrieb ich in einer Anwandlung von Tugend einen harmlos heiteren, etwas kühleren, n i c h t v e r s t e h e n w o l l e n d e n Brief. Ich wollte ihn nur nach und nach wieder in venünftigere Regionen bringen. Diese sensitive Pflanze verstand es aber sogleich und wie erschrak ich, als ich einen Brief erhielt, worin er mitteilte, in Folge meines Schreibens hätte er anfangs mich gar nie mehr wiedersehen wollen, dann aber hätte er den goldenen Mittelweg ergriffen, wie ich es wünsche wolle er mein Freund sein, künftigen Winter wolle er nach Nußdorf oder Währing ziehen (so weit als möglich von uns!) und einmal der Woche zu uns kommen, mir einiges vorzuspielen. Und wie viel Schmerz und Bitterkeit zwischen den Zeilen zu lesen war! – ich war zu unglücklich und weinte einen ganzen Nachmittag lang die bittersten Tränen und kann mich noch immer nicht an den Gedanken gewöhnen, Hugo, meine einzige Freude verloren zu haben. Ich glaube es auch noch nicht, daß wir so leicht auseinanderkommen. Nun erhielt ich noch eine Karte mit der Bemerkung, er reise nun nach Wien, ich möge den Oktober angenehm in Roskosch verbringen. Seine Adresse in Wien gab er nicht, heißt das, daß er diesen ganzen Monat nichts mehr von sich hören lassen wird? Vielleicht hörst Du was, solltest Du seine Adresse wissen, so vorenthalte sie mir nicht.

I am wretchedly unhappy [. . .] I have quarrelled with my only, my best and my dearest friend Hugo. And why? Due to cursed, stupid virtue and reason on my part! He was writing me ever more passionate letters; the flames blazed higher and higher and at length it gave me an eerie feeling. I asked myself how *such* a passionate love as his would end; and since, because of my heartfelt affection for the little one, I had already let the affair go too far, I wrote in a fit of virtue an innocently cheerful letter, rather cooler in tone, that professed *not to understand*. I only wanted to bring him back gradually into the realm of reason. But this sensitive plant understood at once; how shocked I was when I then received a letter in which he informed me that, as a result of my writing, he had at first never wished to see me again, but had then discovered a middle way and would be my friend as I wished; in the coming winter he would move out to Nußdorf or Währing (as far as possible from us!) and visit us once a week in order to play something for me. The pain and bitterness that was to be read between the lines! I was so unhappy and wept the most bitter tears throughout a whole afternoon, and still cannot get used to the thought that I have lost Hugo, my only joy. But I don't yet believe that we can be parted so easily. I've now received another card, saying that he is now travelling back to Vienna and wishing me a pleasant October in Roskosch. He did not give his address in Vienna – does this mean that I shall not hear from him for this entire month? Perhaps you will hear something from him? Should you discover his address, please don't withhold it from me.

They made their peace (perhaps this experience resonated with Wolf when he came to compose 'Nun laß uns Frieden schließen' from the *Italienisches Liederbuch*) and the affair lasted a little longer. But Wolf idolised her with a romantic ardour that she, despite her fondness for him, could not reciprocate. Helene Bettelheim-Gabillon, in a portrait-sketch of Vally written specifically for Frank Walker's *Hugo Wolf. A Biography*, depicts her as an independent being who enjoyed a number of courtships during the years that she was with Wolf. Helene recalls in her published reminiscences (see BIBLIOGRAPHY) that Wolf, suspecting Vally's infidelities, used to give vent to his despair by singing Schumann's 'Ein Jüngling liebt ein Mädchen', and also by rendering his own 'Aus meinen großen Schmerzen' in a 'toneless, veiled voice' – see note 2 to 'Aus meinen großen Schmerzen', p. 198. Wolf's Heine songs almost all touch on the theme of infidelity or unhappy love, and it seems likely that they were inspired by his beloved but errant Vally. It was to Vally, incidentally, that he originally dedicated eight songs to texts by Lenau and Eichendorff – a sheet of paper has been preserved with the heading: 'Lieder und Gesänge von N. Lenau and J. von Eichendorff. Fräulein V ... F ... geweiht, von Hugo Wolf'. Vally's full name has been erased, presumably after the couple went their separate ways.

It was after she had visited Wolf in Maierling that their affair came to an end. Wolf was living in the summer of 1880 at the Marienhof in Maierling as the guest of Dr Joseph Reitzes (see note 1 to 'Mausfallen-Sprüchlein', p. 365), and Vally, breaking with the strict conventions of the time, travelled clandestinely to Alland, a village just a few miles from Maierling, to be near her beloved. The information that we have about Vally's stay is provided in *Hugo Wolf in Maierling* by Heinrich Werner who, as a young boy, witnessed the goings-on: Hugo and Vally were observed through a telescope, kissing on a hilltop; a Rastelbinder (itinerant tinker), plying between Alland and Maierling, delivered their love letters. The idyll was of short duration; Vally returned in the autumn to Paris. It was she who ended their relationship – there was little prospect of Wolf ever being able to support himself financially, and it seems likely that she transferred her affections to one of her many suitors mentioned by Helene Gabillon. Wolf was distraught, poured out his feelings in a flurry of letters to family and friends and drowned his sorrow in composition: between 31 March and 30 April 1881 he composed the *Sechs geistliche Lieder nach Gedichten von Joseph von Eichendorff*. The memory of Vally continued to haunt him. In a letter to Melanie Köchert of 10 September 1897, more than fifteen years later, he describes how he had received a parcel from Paris containing two bottles of marsala; having opened the package, he noticed that the address had been written by Vally. And he tells Melanie, „Hätte ich diesen Umstand rechtzeitig bemerkt, würde ich die Kiste unfehlbar abgelehnt haben." ('Had I noticed this circumstance in time, I would without any doubt have declined to accept the case of wine.')

OSKAR GROHE (Du)
(1859–1920)

District judge and amateur composer who grew up in a musical family. Having retired early because of poor eyesight, he spent much of his time championing such composers as Strauss, Weingartner, Furtwängler and Wolf. It was Joseph Schalk's influential article, 'Neue Lieder, neues Leben', published in Munich's *Allgemeine Zeitung* on 22 January 1890, that alerted Grohe to Wolf's songs. They began to correspond in April 1890 and their last letters date from 1898 – an invaluable source of information on the man and his music. Grohe kept inviting the composer to his home in Mannheim and Wolf eventually visited him in October 1890. In April 1891 he stayed with his new friend for a whole week, and played four-handed versions of the *Siegfried Idyll* and Bruckner's symphonies with Grohe and his wife Jeanne, who used her influence to introduce Wolf to important figures in the musical world. Wolf discussed his latest compositions with Grohe, who was often quick to criticise – especially regarding *Der Corregidor* and *Manuel Venegas* – which led to tensions. That was probably the reason why Grohe hesitated to become a member of the Hugo-Wolf-Verein. Grohe's flirtation with Frieda Zerny (Wolf dubbed him a 'Don Juan') also put a temporary strain on their relationship. Despite these differences, Grohe remained an ardent supporter and dedicated one of his own songs, 'Julinacht' to a text by Hermann Lingg: „Dem Meister des deutschen Liedes" ('To the Master of German Song').

See pp. 10, 59, 122, 177, 192, 193, 194, 217, 223, 269, 323, 326, 355, 362, 425, 426, 434, 459, 537, 538, 539, and, for a letter to Jeanne Grohe, p. 223.

MICHAEL HABERLANDT (Du)
(1860–1940)

Indologist and folklorist, Haberlandt studied Sanskrit, for which he was awarded a D. Phil., and subsequently headed the Ethnographical Department at the Natural History Museum in Vienna. He first met Wolf on 3 December 1896 but it was only after the concert on 22 February 1897 – Wolf's last appearance as accompanist in public – that Haberlandt resolved to found the Hugo-Wolf-Verein, and that their friendship began. It was due largely to Haberlandt's energy that over a hundred members joined the HWV and it was he who administered the funds that contributed 200 florins each year towards Wolf's living expenses and his upkeep in Dr Svetlin's asylum. Haberlandt accompanied Wolf to the asylum on 20 September 1897 and collected him on 24 January 1898 on the day of his release. In his little book on the composer, Haberlandt describes how Wolf, in his haste to get away from the dreaded institution, bounded out of the asylum 'with large strides, taking two or three steps at a time' („mit großen Sätzen, zwei, drei Stufen auf einmal nehmend"). Haberlandt also organised Wolf's transfer to the Niederösterreichische Landesirrenanstalt when the composer's mind finally gave way. He shouldered much of the responsibility involved in caring for Wolf after his mental collapse, and spent hours at his bedside with Melanie Köchert and Heinrich Werner as he lay dying. After Wolf's death, he continued to champion his Lieder, writing articles and editing letters. The funeral oration that he delivered over his friend's open grave at the Zentralfriedhof (see APPENDIX 2) moved all who were present. In a letter to his sister Modesta, Wolf describes Haberlandt as 'a true jewel, a paragon of action, energy and resilience, [. . .] and yet straightforward and incomparably modest and devoted' („ein wahres Juwel und von einer Tatkräftigkeit, Energie und Ausdauer, [...] dabei durchaus schlicht und von einer beispiellosen Bescheidenheit und Hingebung").

AUGUST HALM (Sie)
(1869–1929)

Composer, conductor, musicologist and critic. Wolf first met him in October 1890 at the house of Emil Kauffmann. Ernst Decsey (vol. III, p. 128) describes him thus: „Ein kleiner Mann mit einer mächtigen Denkerstirne, ungeheuer belesen, ungeheuer musikalisch, ungeheuer vielseitig, künstlerisch und fein, beredt und witzig, das Ganze zusammengehalten von echt schwäbischem Humor." ('A small man with a mighty thinker's brow, hugely wide read, hugely musical, hugely versatile, artistic and refined, eloquent and witty – all this held together by genuine Swabian humour.'). Like Wolf, he had a passion for hiking. He championed Wolf's songs and wrote a review of a Liederabend in Tübingen for the *Schwäbische Kronik* of 2 November 1893. Attended the premiere of *Der Corregidor* and criticised the tempi of the conductor Hugo Röhr, a view shared by Wolf. Halm much preferred the performance of *Der Corregidor* conducted by Bruno Walter in January 1906 at the Städtische Oper in Berlin.

KARL HECKEL (Sie)
(1868–1923)

Playwright and music publisher, the son of Emil Heckel. Wolf first encountered Karl Heckel during his search for a new publishing house to replace Schott's. Oskar Grohe, a friend of Heckel, suggested K. Ferd. Heckel, but Wolf had set his sights on a more prestigious firm. Grohe then urged Wolf to consider Heckel's drama about Buddha for a possible opera, which drew from Wolf a remarkable letter to Grohe (28 June 1890):

> Ich für mich will heiter sein, und wenn hundert Leute mit mir lachen können, bin ich's zufrieden. Ich strebe auch keine „welterlösende" Heiterkeit an. Nichts weniger als das. Das überlassen wir billig den großen Genies.
>
> I for my part will be merry, and if a hundred people can laugh with me, I shall be content. Nor do I strive for any 'world-redeeming' merriment. Anything but that. That we can justly leave to the great geniuses.

Wolf wrote a charming letter to Heckel of 23 July 1890 wishing him good fortune in his search for an opera composer for his Buddha. Wolf was also to decline another of Heckel's libretti, *Prospero*, based on *The Tempest*. In 1895, dissatisfied with Schott's, Wolf decided to entrust *Der Corregidor* to Heckel's publishing firm. Heckel published the work on commission for Wolf, who retained ownership of the copyright but had to pay the printing costs. Heckel, who received 20 per cent of the net profits, also took on all of Wolf's other published works, except for Shakespeare's 'Elfenlied'. At the time of *Manuel Venegas*, Wolf considered Heckel as a possible librettist, as we see from this letter to Melanie Köchert of 8 June 1897.

> Vielleicht ist doch Heckel der Mann, der berufen wäre, mir den richtigen Text zu schreiben. [. . .] Jedenfalls hat es bei ihm noch das Gute, daß er sehr musikalisch ist u. ganz genau weiß, was für einen Musiker taugt [. . .] Hoernes ist verteufelt unmusikalisch.

> Perhaps Heckel is after all destined to write the perfect libretto for me. [. . .] At least he has the merit of being very musical, & he knows exactly what a composer needs [. . .] Hoernes is devilishly unmusical.

But it was Hoernes who won the day.

See pp. 10, 323.

THEODOR HELM (Sie)
(1843–1920)

Wolf's immediate predecessor in the pages of the *Salonblatt*, Helm was a music critic who always championed Wolf's Lieder. The composer's letter of advice to Helm in March 1888 on how to review his songs in the *Deutsche Zeitung* speaks eloquently of Wolf's manipulative side. It is to Helm that we owe the first verifiable review of Wolf's songs, when he wrote about Rosa Papier's recital in the Saal Bösendorfer on 2 March 1888. The same review also mentioned the two volumes of 12 songs that had recently been published by Wetzler. Although Wolf in a letter to Helm of 15 November 1892 had expressed his profound gratitude for the critic's efforts on his behalf – „Sie haben stets ein so herzliches Interesse u. eifriges Wohlwollen meinen künstlerischen Bestrebungen entgegengebracht" ('You have always manifested such a keen interest in my creative endeavours & shown me such enthusiastic goodwill') – he was equally capable of pouring scorn on him. When Helm, in an article of 7 April 1894, compared Wolf's songs with those of another composer, one Martin Plüddemann, Wolf's fury knew no bounds: in a letter to Hugo Faisst of 13 September 1894, he calls Helm an „Idiot" and worse. Despite such outbursts of anger, Helm remained faithful to his idol, and continued to write articles on his songs.

See p. 292.

ENGELBERT HUMPERDINCK (Du)
(1854–1921)

It was in his capacity as reader for Schott's that Humperdinck first encountered Wolf's Lieder. According to Humperdinck's diaries, he received a bulky packet of songs on 1 April 1890 by one Hugo Wolf, a name hitherto unknown to him, and was astonished at the quality. He conveyed his opinion to Ludwig Strecker of Schott's who shared his enthusiasm. Humperdinck and Wolf then met at Schott's in October 1890, and after Wolf had visited Humperdinck in Frankfurt, their friendship was sealed. „Humpi" showed him the Goethe sights, they played a piano reduction of Bruckner's Third Symphony together, and Wolf asked Humperdinck for a letter of introduction to Bruckner. Wolf later wrote to Hermann Wette: „Wir schieden als die besten Freunde" ('We departed the best of friends'). Humperdinck also tried to interest the baritone Julius Stockhausen in Wolf's songs. When Humperdinck was planning to pen an article on Wolf's Lieder, he received, as Helm had done, detailed suggestions on what to write – see p. 27. Humperdinck wrote a generous review in the *Frankfurter Zeitung* on 10 April 1891 of the premiere of 'Christnacht'. During a further visit to Frankfurt in April 1891, Wolf played through the entire *Spanisches Liederbuch*, while Humperdinck introduced his new friend to scenes from *Hänsel und Gretel*. When Humperdinck informed Wolf that he intended to write only incidental music to his sister's libretto, Wolf urged him to compose a complete opera – see Ernst Decsey, vol. III, p. 73. Wolf, therefore, played a crucial part in the success of the 'Märchenoper' when the premiere was conducted by Richard Strauss in December 1893. Wolf attended the dress rehearsal and two performances, and although he wrote to Faisst (30 December 1894) that the music did not add up to much („An der Musik ist wohl nicht viel daran"), he was delighted at the opera's success, which was to make Humperdinck a rich man. Their relationship cooled, however, when in April 1897 Wolf played *Der Corregidor* to Humperdinck on the piano; in a letter of 4 April 1897 to Karl Heckel, Wolf gave vent to his feelings: „[Er] zeigte absolut kein Verständniß für mein Werk, so daß ich in der Mitte desselben meinen Vortrag abbrach." ('[He] showed absolutely no understanding for my work, so that I broke off in the middle of my performance.')

See pp. 27, 61, 269.

EMIL KAUFFMANN (Sie)
(1836–1909)

University music director, teacher, conductor and composer. His father, a schoolteacher and amateur composer, was a close friend of Eduard Mörike. Emil, who was appointed first violinist of the Stuttgart Hofkapelle in 1862, wrote critical reviews of concerts in Stuttgart, directed the Polytechniker-Liederkranz, and then in 1868 moved to Basel where he taught violin and piano. A decade later he became extremely active in the musical life of Tübingen, where he gave organ lessons and took charge of the Akademische Musiktafel, as well as the orchestral and oratorio societies. In 1880 he began to lecture widely on music. As a conductor, he championed Palestrina, Schütz, Bach, Gluck, Mozart, Beethoven, Brahms and Bruckner.

It was through Joseph Schalk's 1890 article in Munich's *Allgemeine Zeitung*, 'Neue Lieder, neues Leben', that Kauffmann became aware of Wolf's songs. Astonished at their originality, he wrote to Wolf in 1890, enclosing the original manuscript of Mörike's poem 'An Longus'. Wolf replied on 17 March, informing Kauffmann that 'An Longus', though uncomposable („Componierbar ist es nun freilich nicht"), was one of his favourite poems. Kauffmann responded by writing a piece, 'Eduard Mörike und Hugo Wolf', in the *Schwäbische Kronik* that appeared on 12 April 1890 – an article of remarkable insight that contains the prescient comment:

> Nur langsam werden seine Werke sich verbreiten; sie zeigen sich in ihrer Originalität dem gewöhnlichen Ohr spröde, verlangen eine gesammelte Stimmung, ein inniges sich Vertrautmachen mit der Eigenart des Komponisten, vorzügliche Sänger und nicht minder treffliche Begleiter.

> His songs will become known only slowly; to ears not used to such originality, these songs will sound harsh – they require concentration, an intimate knowledge of the composer's idiom, excellent singers and no less excellent accompanists.

Kauffmann and Wolf corresponded until August 1898, and the 77 extant letters that Wolf sent him contain much information about his South German circle of friends, and the creation and performances of his works. Kauffmann received free copies of all Wolf's works and was kept informed by the composer of the many highs and lows in his life, his plans for future works, especially *Der Corregidor* and *Manuel Venegas*. Wolf arrived unannounced at Kauffmann's home in Tübingen in the autumn of 1890 and stayed for several days. In a letter to Melanie Köchert, dated 14 October 1890, Wolf described how Kauffmann had introduced him to many of his influential friends at a soirée in his home during which he sang a number of his songs and, although he was very hoarse, the guests had all been entranced („entzückt"). The next day he wrote again, telling Melanie that he sang the *Keller-Lieder* and extracts from the *Spanisches Liederbuch* – 'Das Köhlerweib ist trunken' was especially applauded. And he added, with touching self-awareness and frightening prescience, „Der hingebende Enthusiasmus dieser lieben Menschen könnte mich wirklich größenwahnsinnig machen." ('The unstinting enthusiasm of these dear people could make me truly megalomanic.') The same letter describes how Kauffmann at breakfast read aloud to him some of Mörike's letters to his father. On 22 November 1890, Kauffmann published another article in the *Allgemeine Zeitung*, this time on Wolf's *Goethe-Lieder*. Again Wolf was delighted.

Wolf stayed with Kauffmann again in April 1891, and in a letter to his mother (27 April 1891) he describes the success of the songs performed at the musical soirées at Kauffmann's house. Although Kauffmann was unsuccessful in his efforts to promote Wolf's orchestrated songs, he continued to sing Wolf's praises in a succession of important articles. After his piece on the *Alte Weisen* and the *Spanisches Liederbuch* had appeared in Leipzig's *Musikalisches Wochenblatt*, Wolf thanked him in a letter, dated 12 October 1891: „Unter allen meinen Freunden sind Sie wohl der einzige, welcher stets den innigsten u. herzlichsten Antheil an meinem Ringen u. Streben nimmt." ('Of all my friends, you are, I think, the only one who always takes the most passionate and heart-warming interest in my struggles and striving.') Kauffmann wrote another article in 1893, this time on the *Italienisches Liederbuch*, in the same *Musikalisches Wochenblatt*, and a delighted Wolf wrote to Kauffmann (10 July 1893), „Sie haben mich voll u. ganz verstanden." ('You have utterly and fully understood me.')

Equally important in promoting Wolf's Lieder were the concerts arranged by Kauffmann. On 31 October 1893 in Tübingen, Karl Diezel (tenor), Emma Dinkelacker (soprano), Hugo Faisst (baritone) and Kauffmann's son-in-law Wilhelm Schmid (piano) performed 22 songs, of which more than half were encored. Kauffmann arranged another concert in Tübingen on 18 February 1894, in which Diezel and Frieda Zerny were the soloists.

Kauffmann could also be critical: in the 'Eduard Mörike und Hugo Wolf' article, he found Wolf guilty of composing „ungelöste Dissonanzen" ('unresolved dissonances') – which irked the composer. And when Kauffmann reviewed the premiere of *Der Corregidor* in the *Musikalisches Wochenblatt*, finding fault with the libretto for its plethora of farcical and burlesque moments, Wolf wrote to Oskar Grohe (24 September 1896) in high dudgeon, „Ich glaube der gute Altersgraue leidet an Gehirnerweichung." ('I think the good old man is going soft in the head.') But the friendship remained intact, and Wolf later sent Kauffmann his new volume of songs to texts by Heine, Shakespeare and Byron, as well as the libretto of *Manuel Venegas*. And Kauffmann remained loyal to the very last, donating a considerable sum of money towards Wolf's upkeep in Dr Svetlin's asylum.

Both Emil Kauffmann and his father Ernst Friedrich (1803–1856) composed a number of songs on Mörike poems; indeed, Ernst Friedrich's were among the very first *Mörike-Lieder*. They include: 'Die Soldatenbraut', 'Ein Stündlein wohl vor Tag', 'Rosenzeit, wie schnell vorbei', 'Die traurige Krönung', 'Der Frühling', 'Der Gärtner', 'Schön Rohtraut', 'Lied vom Winde', 'Um Mitternacht',

'Der Feuerreiter', 'Lammwirts Klagelied', 'Peregrina' ('Der Spiegel dieser treuen braunen Augen'), 'In der Frühe', 'Begegnung', 'Jägerlied', 'Der König bei der Krönung', 'Die Schwestern' and 'Kirchengesang zu einer Trauung'.

Emil Kauffmann's Mörike songs include: 'Denk' es, o Seele!', 'Wo find' ich Trost?', 'Auf ein altes Bild', 'An den Schlaf', 'Seufzer', 'Du bist Orplid, mein Land', 'Heimweh', 'Lebe wohl', 'An eine Äolsharfe', 'Mausfallen-Sprüchlein' and 'Früh im Wagen'.

See pp. 27, 28, 29, 121, 218, 219, 221, 225, 227, 228, 326, 355, 357, 360, 433, 434, 460, 466, 538.

MELANIE KÖCHERT (Sie and Du)
(1858–1906)

In 1878 Melanie Lang married Heinrich Köchert, an extremely wealthy Viennese court jeweller. They and their three children – Ilse (born 1879), Hilde (1880) and Irmina (1882) lived on the fourth floor of a magnificent villa in the Mehlmarkt (now Neuer Markt 15). Wolf probably first met her in 1879 at the house of Adalbert von Goldschmidt, and at the suggestion of her husband she began piano lessons with Wolf. Heinrich, who owned houses in Vienna, Döbling and Rinnbach am Traunsee, became one of Wolf's most generous benefactors, accommodating him for long periods at all these addresses. Wolf had a special fondness for the villa in Döbling with its beautiful garden, which boasted a classical temple – within a stone's throw of the Leidesdorf Psychiatric Clinic in Ober-Döbling where the insane Nikolaus Lenau had ended his days. It was largely due to Heinrich Köchert that Wolf was appointed music critic for the *Wiener Salonblatt* – as court jewellers, the Köchert family were important advertisers in the journal and wielded considerable influence. Wolf was soon accepted as a member of the Köchert family and had a touching relationship with the children. He composed 'Epiphanias' for Melanie, and it was performed by her three children on 6 January 1889 to celebrate her thirty-first birthday. They all dressed up as the Three Kings, with Wolf providing the accompaniment from behind a screen – see p. 149.

In the summer of 1883, having seen *Parsifal* in Bayreuth, Wolf spent seven weeks with the Köchert family in Rinnbach. His relationship with Melanie deepened. Two years older than Wolf, she had gleaming brown eyes and a rather melancholy face – the reason, perhaps, why Wolf often called her Mignon. They shared an intense love of poetry, and it was not long before they became clandestine lovers. They began to correspond. Wolf would often write daily to his beloved, informing her about events in his life, his hopes, his traumas. In not one of the 245 published letters does Wolf use the intimate 'Du' form of address: they exercised extreme caution when writing letters that might have been seen by others. And Frank Walker, having interviewed Melanie's children for his biography of the composer, tells us that they never once heard Wolf or their mother call each other 'Du' in their conversations. In the early years of their relationship, however, they corresponded under assumed names, often via Wolf's publisher Lacom or in the personal columns of the *Neue Freie Presse*, writing each other passionate letters and notes that use the intimate 'Du' – examples can be found among Walter Legge's unpublished papers, quoted in part in Fischer-Dieskau's *Hugo Wolf. Leben und Werk*. Walker, when he saw the letters, remarked that Melanie's handwriting 'seemed to exhibit positively pathological symptoms'. To cover their tracks, all intimate letters were later burned, though Frank Walker saw them in Vienna and Traunkirchen as late as 1946 before they were destroyed according to the wishes of the Köchert family. Their passionate nature reveals Melanie as a tormented woman on the brink of a nervous breakdown, especially in phrases such as „Rette mich! Rette mich!" ('Save me! Save me!'); „Du weißt nicht, was ich gelitten habe!" ('You have no idea what I have suffered!'); and „Ich habe nur noch einen Wunsch, Dich wieder einmal ganz zu besitzen und dann sterben" ('I have only one wish: to possess you wholly once more and then die') – all quoted in Fischer-Dieskau: *Hugo Wolf. Leben und Werk*.

How long was Melanie's husband kept in the dark? It was probably not until 1893 that he stumbled on the truth. In a letter to Marie Lang of 19 June, Wolf writes:

> K... scheint bis dato nichts unternommen zu haben. Ich sah seine Flagge vom Ebenseer-Bahnhof lustig im Winde wehen. Möge auch unsere einstige „Freundschaft" verwehen, lustig, ohne stürmische Epiloge. Ich fühle mich so leicht u. froh, seit ich mir diese böse Sache vom Halse geschafft. Es war aber auch hohe Zeit. –

> K... [Heinrich Köchert] seems so far to have taken no action. From the Ebensee station I saw his flag blowing merrily in the breeze. May our former 'friendship' likewise blow away, merrily, without a stormy epilogue. I feel so happy & relieved, since I have rid myself of this bad business. But it was high time. –

It seems that Köchert magnanimously accepted the situation, remained Wolf's friend and continued to act as his generous benefactor.

Wolf's letters to Melanie reveal how dependent he was on her love. She saw it as her life's work to support this wayward genius through thick and thin. She was always there for him, buying him crates of beer, eggs, white bread, new handkerchiefs, winter stockings, and arranging for the repair of his beloved coffee machine. She is consulted whenever Wolf has a difficult letter to write to publishers or impresarios, and although she played no instrument, he often sought her opinion on musical matters. Shaken by his affair with Frieda Zerny (see pp. 520–22), she still stood by him. They read books together and shared a love of nature. Phrases such as „Wenn Sie nur hier wären! Wenn Sie meine Freude nur mit mir teilen könnten!" ('If only you were here! If only you could share my joy!') surface again and again in the letters. She furnished his apartment at Schwindgasse 3 and, when he was released from Dr Svetlin's asylum on 24 January 1898, at Mühlgasse 22. During this brief period of remission, she and his sister Käthe accompanied him on a voyage that took in Trieste, Duino, Miramare, Pirano, Portorosa, Rovigno, Lussin and Lovrana. When he then experienced a relapse and was taken to the mental home at the Niederösterreichische Landesirrenanstalt, she regularly visited him three times a week. Deeply depressed after his death in 1903, Melanie committed suicide three years later by hurling herself from the fourth floor of the Köchert villa in the Mehlmarkt. She lies buried in the family grave at Hietzing. Wolf dedicated to her all his songs and fittingly wrote this inscription – later removed by another hand – in one of his Lieder volumes:

> An Frau Melanie.
> Von allen, die der Tonkunst Zauber tief empfanden
> Hat niemand mich so ganz wie Du verstanden.

> To Frau Melanie.
> No one who has felt deeply the magic of music
> Has ever understood me quite like you.

See pp. 59, 60, 62, 120, 216, 219, 228, 229, 230, 270, 280, 281, 282, 283, 284, 355, 359, 360, 361, 433, 466, and for Ilse Köchert, p. 280.

BERTHA VON LACKHNER (Sie)
(dates unknown)

She was the sister of Therese Preyss, whose husband Viktor Preyss rented the 'Marienhof' in Maierling, where she and Wolf met in 1880. Wolf usually addressed her as „Tante Bertha" and once as „Mama" (letter of 3 April 1883). She treated him as an adopted son and lavished all her motherly care on him whenever he stayed in Maierling. Wolf's letters to her are extremely affectionate, and the zaniest he ever wrote. He delighted in her cooking and expressed his gratitude in charming doggerel – see p. 318. When a piano was installed at the 'Marienhof', Wolf used to treat her and her family to lengthy extracts from *Der Ring des Nibelungen*, *Die Meistersinger von Nürnberg* and *Tristan und Isolde*. She bought Wolf the piano reduction of *Parsifal* that gave him such pleasure, even though he later wrote to Henriette Lang (31 August 1882) that she had only 'feigned interest' in the opera. Wolf's impetuous nature meant that they occasionally fell out – as he did with most of his friends – but she never bore a grudge. And though her knowledge of music was limited, Wolf would often keep her abreast of his progress with the *Mörike-Lieder*.

See pp. 345, 349.

EDMUND LANG (Du)
(1861–1918)

The brother of Melanie Köchert, Lang studied law at the University of Vienna. He married Mitzi Werner and was widely recognised in Wolf's circle as an authority on literature and art. Although he and Wolf first met in 1879, it was not until well over a decade later that they exchanged the 'Du'. In late 1887/ early 1888, Wolf stayed with the Langs in the Belvederegasse, before moving to the Werner residence at Brunnergasse 26 in Perchtoldsdorf, where he composed many of the *Mörike-Lieder*, the entire *Spanisches Liederbuch*, and Book II of the *Italienisches Liederbuch*. Wolf kept Lang regularly informed about his progress – see the entry for MÖRIKE, in particular, pp. 345–52 – and played through some of the songs to his friend in February; and seven years later Lang was present at the run-through of some of the *Der Corregidor* music. As a lawyer, he helped Wolf in his dealings with Wetzler, when the publishing house went bankrupt in 1890. Wolf, in his madness, fell out with most of his friends, Lang included, but made peace with him in one of his last letters from the asylum, undated but probably from 1899:

> Liebster Edmund! Würdest Du wohl die große Freude mir anthun u. mich hier durch Deinen Besuch beglücken?
>
> Dearest Edmund! It would give me such great joy if you came to visit me here.

See pp. 292, 345, 346, 347, 349, 350, 352.

HENRIETTE LANG (Sie)
(1856–1936)

Wolf met Henriette Lang, the sister of Melanie Köchert, in 1878, and it was in her parents' house that he gave piano lessons to Vally Franck. Vally and Henriette were intimate friends, and „Hansi" soon became Wolf's confidante. He kept her informed about his affair with Vally, and because she lived at a variety of addresses far distant from Vienna, he maintained a lively correspondence with her. It was through Henriette that Wolf met other members of her family: brother

Edmund who was to become his closest male friend, and sisters Marie and Melanie. We learn from a letter to Henriette of 26 January 1881 that Wolf gave piano lessons to Melanie, and it was not long before they became clandestine lovers. When Henriette married Baron Schey, she and Wolf corresponded less but remained good friends. Henriette and her husband then did all they could to support Wolf, bought him a secondhand Bösendorfer piano in 1890 and invited him to their summer residence in Traunkirchen.

See p. 192.

MARIE LANG (Sie)
(1858–1934)

Theosophist, much influenced by the teachings of Rudolf Steiner, she was what we would now call a feminist, and active as such in Vienna, where she co-founded the 'Allgemeiner Österreichischer Frauenverein'. She first met Wolf around 1880, when he was spending much time with her brother Edmund Lang. She was married at that time to Theodor Köchert, brother of Heinrich, and lived in the same house as her brother-in-law in the Mehlmarkt (now Neuer Markt 15). In an article published in *Die Zeit* on 3 January 1904, 'Hugo Wolfs Entwicklungszeit', she describes her first meeting with the composer. No sooner had they been introduced than she was called away to see to her child on the floor below. When she returned fifteen minutes later, the following incident took place:

> Als ich aber auf die enge Wendeltreppe hinaustrat, stürzte mit lautem Gepolter, wild wie ein angeschossener Eber, Wolf an mir vorbei, fällt, rafft sich blitzschnell wieder auf und die Treppe hinunter. Der Gastgeber und andere hinter ihm her, rufend und schreiend: „Dableiben, halt, Wolf zurück!" – Es half nichts, er war davon. In wilder Hast davon, ohne Rock, den hielt der Hausherr in den Fäusten, mit denen er ihn festzuhalten getrachtet hatte.

> But as I set foot on the narrow winding staircase, Wolf stormed headlong past me, making a terrible racket, wild as a wounded boar, fell, picked himself up in a flash and hurtled down the stairs. The host and others followed him, calling and shouting: 'Stop there! Wolf, come back!' To no avail, he was gone, gone in wild haste without his jacket, which the head of the household held in the hands that had attempted to stop him.

Wolf's panicked retreat had been caused by the unexpected presence of Vally Franck, who had recently ended her relationship with him. Marie Lang's article also reveals how much Wolf suffered from the genius of Wagner. Despite his intense admiration of the Bayreuth master, he felt powerless to achieve anything significant in the operatic world. Marie Lang records Wolf's words:

> Er hat mir keinen Raum gelassen, gleich einem mächtigen Baume, der mit seinem Schatten das unter seinen weithinragenden Ästen aufsprießende Jungholz erstickt.

> He has left me no room, like a mighty tree that with its shade suffocates the sprouting young growth beneath its widely spreading branches.

She then goes on to describe the creative paralysis that overcame Wolf on occasions:

> Tiefste Niedergeschlagenheit ergriff ihn. Die Erkenntnis von Wagners übermäßiger Größe, seines ungeheuren Reichtums, der Universalität seines Genius übten eine zermalmende Wirkung auf Wolf aus.

> Deepest despondency would seize him. The realisation of Wagner's immeasurable greatness, his monstrous wealth, the universality of his genius exerted a crushing effect on Wolf.

Marie Lang first corresponded with Wolf in 1886. Wolf lodged with Edmund and Marie Lang in the summer of 1887 after he had broken the fibula of his right leg and was unable to fend for himself in his Kumpfgasse apartment.

Wolf would often inform Marie about his song-writing progress. She encouraged Rosa Mayreder to finish the *Corregidor* libretto, furnished Wolf with her own scenario to *Manuel Venegas* (which Wolf secretly despised), was present at the first private run-through of *Der Corregidor*, and helped him move into his Schwindgasse lodgings.

See pp. 25, 348.

RUDOLF VON LARISCH (Du)
(1856–1934)

A government official and calligraphy artist, who first met Wolf around 1888. Influenced by the Viennese Secession and the Wiener Werkstätte, Larisch promoted the revival of calligraphy, and lectured on lettering and typography in Vienna. His most important work, *Unterricht in ornamentaler Schrift* (*Instruction in Ornamental Lettering*), was published in 1905 and by 1934 had run to eleven editions. He had a summer residence in Perchtoldsdorf and from 1896 lived for a while at the same address as Wolf in the Schwindgasse; he was a co-founder of the Vienna Hugo-Wolf-Verein, and as a committee member contributed a minimum of 50 florins to the funds of the society (ordinary members contributed 5 florins). It was Larisch who handed Wolf 50 florins living expenses every quarter, for which Wolf always gave a receipt. In a letter to Josef Strasser of 14 July 1889, Wolf calls Larisch „einer meiner besten Freunde" ('one of my best friends') but warns his brother-in-law that he was „ein wüthender Antisemit" ('a raging anti-Semite'). Larisch was one of Wolf's most loyal friends: he contacted many potential Wolf singers, supplied him with manuscript paper and dealt with impresarios. It was Larisch who was entrusted with the task of arranging Wolf's removal to Dr Svetlin's asylum and he was the recipient of one of Wolf's last letters, dated 4 August 1898, before he was interned in the Niederösterreichische Landesirrenanstalt.

See pp. 120, 280.

DETLEV VON LILIENCRON (Sie)
(1844–1909)

Friedrich Adolf Axel Freiherr von Liliencron (he called himself Detlev only after 1883) was born in Kiel on 3 June 1844. His father came from landed gentry stock, his mother was an American who had been brought up in England. Liliencron joined the Prussian army in 1863, fought in the wars against Austria and France, was discharged in 1875 for incurring debts and was sent by his family to America. On his return in 1877 he embarked on a literary career and soon won the recognition of Theodor Storm and Emanuel Geibel. His first two marriages ended in divorce, but his third (1900) was a success, and he settled down in Alt-Rahlstedt near Hamburg. His final years were arguably the happiest of his life but he was often short of funds despite an annual allowance of 2000 marks from the Emperor's privy purse, as can be seen from a letter of 23 October 1901 to a friend in which he explains how he had to miss a recital given by Eugen Gura that featured settings of his own poems, because he lacked the money for a ticket. In the final years of his life he struck up a close friendship with Richard Dehmel who, in his funeral oration, praised the variety of Liliencron's poetry which could be „liebenswürdig" ('charming') and „leichtsinnig" ('frivolous') but also serious: „Er war auch der Mann der schweren Stunden, der einsamen Fragen und Gedanken." ('He was also a man who suffered troubled hours, consumed by lonely questions and thoughts.') Liliencron's autobiographical novel, *Leben und Lüge* (*Life and Lies*) was published in 1908, a year before his death.

Liliencron, like many poets passionate about art song, tried tenaciously to interest composers in his poems. When he sent Wolf two volumes of his verse in the hope that he would find poems suitable for musical composition, Wolf replied on 9 June 1890 that he was unable to do so, suggesting instead that Liliencron write for him an opera libretto based on Shakespeare's *The Tempest*. Several months later

Wolf received a copy of *Der Haidegänger* from Liliencron's publishers, but again he regretted that he could find nothing 'lyrical' enough. Despite finding much of Liliencron's poetry repellent (as he wrote to Emil Kauffmann on 22 December 1890), he was touched by the poem 'An Hugo Wolf' (see APPENDIX 1) and expressed his gratitude to the poet. Liliencron had better fortune with Brahms who, when sent a copy of *Adjutantenritte* (1883), set 'Maienkätzchen' and 'Auf dem Kirchhofe', one of his greatest songs. Liliencron also approached Hans Pfitzner, Richard Strauss and Eugen d'Albert, but it was with Oscar Straus that he achieved the popularity that he always craved. Straus's setting of Liliencron's 'Die Musik kommt', a poem written at Plön in 1881, which the poet later described as „ziemlich dummes Zeug" ('pretty inane nonsense'), soon became a „Gassenhauer" (a popular song) that was sung on the streets of Berlin.

Liliencron's *Kampf und Spiele* contains poems on a number of nineteenth-century literary figures who loom large in the history of Lieder: Otto Julius Bierbaum, Goethe, Klaus Groth, Karl Henckell, Keller, Conrad Ferdinand Meyer, Mörike and Storm.

See also APPENDIX 1, and pp. 218, 283.

FRIDA (FRIEDA) VON LIPPERHEIDE (Sie)
(1840–1896)

Baron Franz Josef von Lipperheide and his wife Baronin Frida von Lipperheide were two of Wolf's most wealthy patrons and put several of their residences at the composer's disposal. They first met Wolf at a concert of his songs on 5 March 1892, after which they invited him to stay at Matzen, near Brixlegg, in Tyrol. Wolf lived in the „Jägerhäusl" ('hunting lodge') attached to their castle at Matzen for ten days in early 1894, returned on 17 September and stayed till the middle of October. The Baron and Baroness paid Wolf's travel expenses and did all they could to make his stay as pleasant as possible while he worked on *Der Corregidor*. He returned on 16 May 1895 and three days later described his elation in a letter to Kauffmann:

> Im ersten Stock ist mein Schlafzimmer, parterre mein Arbeitszimmer. Ein sehr gutes Pianino – freilich nur ein Pianino – unterstützt mich in meinen Arbeiten. Ich wohne völlig isoliert von Allen, ja, nicht einmal ein dienstbarer Geist wohnt in dem Häuschen. Eine schönere Einsamkeit kann selbst die ausschweifendste Phantasie sich nicht erträumen. Keine Menschenseele stört mich hier, nur die Finken u. Grillen, zuweilen auch die Spechte mit ihrem höllischen Gekreisch bringen mich manchmal aus meiner Gemütsruhe. Ein paar Flintenschüße werden hoffentlich die gewünschte Wirkung thun u. mir diese unholden Gesellen vom Halse schaffen.

My bedroom is on the first floor, my study on the ground floor. A very good upright piano – but only an upright – helps me in my work. I live completely cut off from everything – there is not even a ministering angel here. It is impossible to imagine or dream up a more beautiful solitude. Not a soul disturbs me, only the finches & crickets and occasionally the woodpeckers with their hellish screeching upset my peace of mind. A few rounds from my shotgun will, I hope, have the desired effect & rid me of these devils.

During the two summer months, when his hosts were absent, Wolf was allowed to live in the castle, use the Bechstein grand and invite his friends to stay. He remained at Matzen until 28 December 1895, by which time the opera and the orchestration were finished. He wrote in the guest book:

In dankbarer Erinnerung an die schönste und glücklichste Zeit meines Lebens. Vom 16. Mai bis 28. Dezember, meinen lieben hochverehrten Gastgebern Freiherrn und Freifrau v. Lipperheide zu Ruhm und Heil!

In grateful remembrance of the loveliest and happiest time of my life, from 16 May to 28 December, to my dear hosts, Baron and Baroness von Lipperheide, with salutations and praise!

He also showed his gratitude by dedicating his Shakespearean 'Elfenlied' to the Baroness: 'Freifrau Frida von Lipperheide zugeeignet'. Karl Mayreder executed a watercolour drawing of Wolf at work in the hunting lodge (reproduced in Dietrich Fischer-Dieskau's *Hugo Wolf. Leben und Werk*, p. 321). The Lipperheides also accommodated Wolf in their Berlin home where he lived 'like a prince in a fairy tale, who has only to utter a wish to see it at once fulfilled' („wie ein Märchenprinz, der nur einen Wunsch zu äußern braucht, um ihn allsogleich erfüllt zu sehen"). The Baron also made Wolf an annual grant of 1000 marks to relieve him from financial cares. The Baroness was convinced of Wolf's greatness and wrote in a letter to Oskar Grohe, „Seine Musik muß ja die Welt erobern." ('His music will conquer the world.') When she died unexpectedly and suddenly from a heart attack in September 1896, Wolf was devastated and wrote to Potpeschnigg (15 September 1896), „Ich verliere an der Verstorbenen eine meiner besten Freundinnen, ja ich darf wohl sagen eine zweite Mutter." ('With her death I lose one of my dearest female friends, I might even say a second mother.') He never returned to Matzen.

See p. 230.

KARL MAYR (Sie)
(1864–1917)

In September 1896, the historian Karl Mayr paid an unannounced visit to Wolf at Schwindgasse 3, as Wolf explained in a letter to Hugo Faisst of 26 September 1896:

> Ein Münchener Privatdozent für Geschichte Dr. Karl Mayr hat mich heute aufgesucht um den Componisten „so vieler schöner Lieder", wie er sich ausdrückte kennen zu lernen. Ich habe meine manirlichsten Seiten hervorgekehrt. Nächstens will er mich mit seiner Braut, die meine Lieder singt, bekannt machen.

> A history lecturer from Munich paid me a visit today in order to make the acquaintance of, as he put it, the composer 'of so many beautiful songs'. I was on my best behaviour. In the near future he will introduce me to his fiancée who sings my songs.

The singer in question was Clementine Schönfield who, when they met, sang many of Wolf's songs including 'Herr, was trägt der Boden hier', which Wolf had allegedly never heard live before. Schönfield subsequently gave many recitals of Wolf's Lieder and did much to make his music known.

See pp. 11, 63, 285, 436.

EDWIN MAYSER (Sie)
(1859–1937)

Classical scholar, teacher at Stuttgart's Karlsgymnasium and gifted amateur musician, Mayser became the regular pianist at Hugo Faisst's Hugo-Wolf-Verein concerts. He first met Wolf at the house of Faisst's parents in Heilbronn in 1894, and two years later Mayser was present at the premiere of *Der Corregidor*, sitting close to Wolf himself in the central box. Frank Walker tells us that when Mayser and his wife visited Wolf the following day, Wolf sang and played the still unpublished songs from Book II of the *Italienisches Liederbuch*. According to Walker, Wolf told Mayser that Book II contained more absolute music than Book I. Many things in it, he said, could be played equally well by a string quartet. In 1898 Wolf gave Mayser a presentation copy of the *Michelangelo-Lieder*.

See p. 363.

FELIX MOTTL (Sie)
(1856–1911)

Conductor and composer, Mottl co-founded (aged sixteen!) Vienna's Wagner-Verein, having personally asked Wagner's permission for starting the society. For a short time he was Kapellmeister of the Ring-Theater, which burned down in 1881, and from 1886 to 1906 he conducted regularly at the Bayreuth Festival. Wolf first met him in 1877, and a friendship soon developed. Mottl advised him on his compositions, enthused for his Symphony and String Quartet, gave him twice weekly piano lessons at which Wolf played sonatas by Beethoven and others, and also piano reductions of *The Ring* in order to be able to earn money as a répétiteur (HW to his father, 15 November 1877). Mottl also tried (unsuccessfully) to persuade Schott's to publish a volume of Wolf's Lieder (see p. 452). Together with Wolf, Mottl attended some sessions of the Eulonia Chorus, which had been founded by Vally Franck and Helene Gabillon, singing hoarsely and conducting the choir, while Wolf remained silent. Although he and Wolf visited Bayreuth together in 1883, their relationship soured in later years – possibly because Mottl's resolve to conduct *Der Corregidor* in Karlsruhe was never realised. Mottl also showed interest in *Manuel Venegas*, but Wolf insisted that he should conduct *Der Corregidor* first. He did, however, conduct the orchestral version of 'Prometheus' on 14 April 1903, almost two months after Wolf's death.

See p. 453.

PAUL MÜLLER (Sie)
(1848–1917)

Berlin schoolmaster, musician and pianist, Müller first met Wolf on 3 March 1892 during a recital of Wolf Lieder in Berlin's Richard-Wagner-Verein. Wolf in a letter to Hugo Faisst called him „ein ganz charmanter Herr" ('a most charming gentleman'), though he suspected him of feigning interest in his songs. Three years later Müller founded the Hugo-Wolf-Verein in Berlin, after which he served Wolf in a variety of ways, especially proofreading with an eagle eye new editions of his songs, informing Wolf of all the errors and commenting on passages that he deemed would be difficult to play. He attempted in vain to organise the premiere of *Der Corregidor* in Berlin, and was present at the first performance in Mannheim. He visited Wolf in Matzen during the summer of 1896 and proofread with Heinrich Potpeschnigg Book II of the *Italienisches Liederbuch*. In a letter to Müller, dated 22 August 1896, Wolf hoped for „gute dauernde Freundschaft" ('a good lasting friendship') but, as with most of Wolf's relationships, there was to be the inevitable falling out – occasioned this time by the admiration of Brahms that Müller expressed to Wolf when he visited him in the Schwindgasse during Easter 1897. Wolf gave vent to his displeasure in a letter to Faisst of 23 April 1897, in which he branded Müller a mediocre character with little personality, and intellectually limited. Four months earlier Wolf had written to Müller in the most glowing terms to thank him for the Christmas gift of Michelangelo's poems (see HW to Paul Müller, 25 December 1896, p. 322). Wolf continued to seek Müller's opinion, and sent him the libretto to *Manuel Venegas*; Müller replied immediately, praising it to the skies (letter of 19 September 1897). In 'Erinnerungen an Hugo Wolf', an essay published in *Die Musik*, Müller recalls how Wolf, referring to Schubert's settings of the *Harfnerlieder*, had exclaimed: „Da hat Schubert den Goethe halt nicht verstanden." ('Schubert failed to understand the Goethe of these poems.')

See pp. 63, 122, 228, 322, 323, 325, 435.

SIEGFRIED OCHS (Sie)
(1858–1929)

German conductor and composer who was expelled from his Berlin conservatoire for expressing the view to Ernst Rudorff, head of the piano faculty at the Hochschule, that he would exchange all of Mendelssohn's piano music for Wagner's prelude to *Die Meistersinger*. The greatest choral conductor of his time, he set extremely high standards, conducted Bach's *Matthäuspassion* without cuts and insisted on 117 rehearsals for a performance of Beethoven's *Missa solemnis*. It was during Wolf's stay in Berlin in March 1892 that Ochs met the composer, who was delighted that he had expressed a wish to conduct the Shakespearean 'Elfenlied'. Ochs recalled in his 'Persönliche Erinnerungen', published in the *Allgemeine deutsche Musikzeitung* in 1903, that he had to read only a few bars of the scores that Wolf had sent him ('Elfenlied', 'Der Feuerreiter' and incidental music to *Das Fest auf Solhaug*) to realise that Wolf was an exceptional talent. When in 1894 Ochs rehearsed these works in the Philharmonie in preparation for a concert there, Wolf flew into a rage when Ochs chose a tempo in a number from *Das Fest auf Solhaug* that he considered to be far too slow. Ochs gave the following account of the debacle in *Geschehenes, Gesehenes*, pp. 309–10, that illustrates Wolf's tempestuous and sporadically contradictory nature:

> In dem Korridor, in welchen die Ausgänge des großen Philharmoniesaales münden, stand zwischen einigen leeren Bierfässern, gleichsam hinter einer Barrikade, Hugo Wolf, tobend, gestikulierend, bleich im Gesicht. Seine Rede war eine Flut von Gehässigkeiten, nicht wiederzugebenden Schimpfworten und Verdächtigungen über uns alle, die wir seine Werke aufzuführen

bestrebt waren. Es gelang keinem von uns, ihn zu beruhigen, bis er endlich, von seiner Erregung übermannt, wie ein Halbtoter zusammenbrach und nur noch die Worte murmelte: „Macht's, wie Ihr wollt."

In the corridor, into which all the exits of the large auditorium of the Philharmonie lead, between empty beer barrels that seemed to serve as a barricade, stood Hugo Wolf, raging, gesticulating, pale, letting loose a torrent of spiteful remarks, unrepeatable foul language full of contempt for all of us who were striving to perform his works. Not one of us managed to calm him, until, finally exhausted, he collapsed like one half-dead, muttering: 'Do as you want.'

When Ochs pointed out that the score was marked *äußerst langsam*, Wolf explained that anyone could see that this was an „Eselei" ('stupidity') on his part. Ochs concluded his description with the observation that such an outburst was, in retrospect, an early manifestation of Wolf's incipient insanity. Despite Wolf's outbursts, Ochs remained a devotee of his music, and on 5 December 1904 gave a concert in the Philharmonie to honour the late composer. The concert featured 'Der Feuerreiter', which had to be encored, 'Christnacht' and the orchestral versions of 'Auf ein altes Bild', 'Der Rattenfänger', 'Gebet', 'In der Frühe', 'Mignon' ('Kennst du das Land') and 'Wo find' ich Trost?'

See pp. 223, 358.

HEINRICH POTPESCHNIGG (Du)
(1847–1932)

Dentist in Graz, pianist, composer. Potpeschnigg gave up his dental practice to devote his life to music, and became a much sought-after song accompanist. Having been introduced to Wolf's Lieder in 1890 through the architect Friedrich Hofmann, he lost no time in arranging a Wolf Liederabend at the Richard-Wagner-Verein in Graz. He accompanied Ferdinand Jäger (1838–1902) on 12 April 1890 in a programme that included 'Der Tambour', 'Der Gärtner', 'Der Jäger', 'Frühling übers Jahr', 'Hätt ich irgend wohl Bedenken', 'Der Rattenfänger', 'Der Freund', 'Anakreons Grab', 'Gebet' and 'Verschwiegene Liebe'; and in the *Grazer Wochenblatt* of 20 April 1890 he was praised as a pianist of technical and interpretative prowess. The ensuing friendship between Wolf and Potpeschnigg flourished over the next decade, and there are some 230 extant letters and cards from Wolf to his friend written between May 1890 and September 1898. Other concerts in which Potpeschnigg accompanied singers in Wolf songs took place on 6 January 1891 (Jäger), 22 March 1891 (Friederike Mayer), 13 May 1892 (August and Marie Krämer) and 11 March 1897 (Marie Krämer-Wild). After a huge success in the Saal Bösendorfer on 3 April 1894, Wolf wrote to Potpeschnigg, begging him to arrange a Wolf Liederabend in the Grazer Wagner-Verein in which he, Wolf, would accompany Frieda Zerny and Hugo Faisst. Potpeschnigg did indeed arrange the concert, which took place on 14 April. It was poorly attended and received almost in silence by the audience. Wolf stormed offstage after the first group of songs, seized his hat and coat and was about to leave when Potpeschnigg exclaimed, „Herr Wolf, Sie werden uns doch nicht verlassen wollen!" ('But Herr Wolf, you are not going to leave us!') Wolf, seeing the tears in Potpeschnigg's eyes, asked, „Sie weinen?" ('You are crying?') To which Potpeschnigg replied, „Soll man denn nicht weinen, wenn Ihr beide so schön musiziert?" ('And why shouldn't one weep, when you both perform so beautifully?') Whereupon Wolf took off his coat and exclaimed, „Jetzt will ich bleiben – für Sie spiel' ich weiter!" ('I shall now stay – I shall continue to play for *you*.') After the concert they exchanged the 'Du' for the first time; and in future letters Wolf would often address his friend as 'Liebster Enrico'.

Potpeschnigg also served Wolf assiduously in the arduous task of copying and proofreading, especially the manuscript to *Der Corregidor*. Wolf was astonished that Potpeschnigg could spot mistakes that he himself had overlooked, writing to him on 17 March 1896, „Mensch, was hast Du nur für Augen! Ich komme aus dem Staunen gar nicht heraus [. . .] Mit Dir verglichen, bin ich ja ein völlig Blinder." ('Good Lord, you've eyes like a hawk! I can't get over it [. . .] Compared with you, I'm utterly blind.') And Potpeschnigg helped Wolf in many other ways: it was he who persuaded him to take a bow on stage after Act III of *Der Corregidor*; he gave Wolf his valuable desk to help him furnish his first home in the Schwindgasse; he accompanied him on a journey from Brixlegg to Cortina; and he housed Wolf in his Graz home during August 1896. It was about this time that Wolf, travelling to Potpeschnigg by train, had the misfortune to get a cinder lodged in his eye. When Potpeschnigg took him to Dr Anton Elschnig (1863–1939) to get it removed, the latter, having examined Wolf, took Potpeschnigg aside and told him that the pupils of Wolf's eyes showed, in their inability to expand and contract, symptoms of the incipient general paralysis of tertiary syphilis.

Writing to Potpeschnigg on 15 December 1897 from Dr Svetlin's asylum, Wolf talks in touching terms about their friendship: „Wie froh bin ich, alle meine bisherigen sogenannten „Freunde" durch mein Unglück losgeworden zu sein. Ich habe nunmehr niemanden in der Welt, als nur Dich und Mayreders." ('How happy I am in my misfortune to have got rid of all previous so-called "friends". I now have no one in the world but you and the Mayreders.'). Sixteen days later, however, on 31 December 1897, he writes to his sister, Modesta Strasser, that he is relieved that his friendship with Potpeschnigg is at an end: „So bin ich glücklicherweise wiederum einen sogenannten Freund losgeworden." ('And so I have fortunately got rid of another so-called friend.') This came about, he writes, because Potpeschnigg had written him a „blitzdummen Brief" ('an idiotic letter') that had depressed him. A flurry of thirteen cards and letters in 1898 and 1899 shows that the friends were soon reconciled. When Wolf had been transferred from Dr Svetlin's mental asylum to the Niederösterreichische Landesirrenanstalt, the loyal Potpeschnigg visited Wolf, who begged his friend to get him out of the place. After a painful scene (described by Ernst Decsey), they embraced and Potpeschnigg departed. They never met again. In 1902 Potpeschnigg gave a succession of Wolf recitals in Cilli, Laibach and Graz, and the reviews sang his praises, not just as a masterful accompanist but as the person who had done more than anyone else to popularise Wolf's songs. After Wolf's death, Potpeschnigg continued to champion his friend's Lieder.

See pp. 10, 64, 228, 229, 284, 326, 539.

JOSEPH SCHALK (Du)
(1857–1900)

Pianist and conductor, Schalk studied at the Vienna Conservatoire under Bruckner, whose music he championed. He first met Wolf at the house of Adalbert von Goldschmidt and became interested in his songs after hearing the two Reinick 'Wiegenlieder' in 1888 – which is when their correspondence begins. They often met at Schalk's residence in the Jordanstraße. When Schalk became artistic director of the Vienna Wagner-Verein, he insisted on programming Wolf's Lieder in the Thursday Evening concerts, which helped to make his songs better known. But the critics and some of the members of the Wagner-Verein felt that he had gone too far when on 15 December 1888 Schalk presented a Beethoven-Wolf-Abend at which Ferdinand Jäger sang nine Wolf songs accompanied by the composer (it was the first time Wolf had accompanied his songs in public), the rest of the recital consisting of two Beethoven piano sonatas and the Variations, Op. 35, played by Schalk himself. Wolf vowed never to perform at the Wagner-Verein again, but Schalk stood by him and persuaded him to change his mind.

Their correspondence is full of warmth and affection. Although Schalk's Christian name was usually spelt Josef, Wolf insisted on Joseph, often addressing his friend as Josephus and signing off as Lupusculus. Wolf kept him informed about all his composing plans and rewarded him for his unswerving loyalty by dedicating to him and his brother Franz the *Eichendorff-Lieder*. He also wrote him a touching letter of gratitude, which ends with an adapted quotation from Eichendorff's poem 'Der Freund': see HW to Joseph Schalk, 7 September 1889, p. 26. Schalk's perceptive and pioneering article on Wolf's *Mörike-Lieder*, 'Neue Lieder, neues Leben' (a pun on Beethoven's Goethe song) that appeared on 22 January 1890 in the *Münchener Allgemeine Zeitung*, spawned many others, for which Wolf was eternally grateful. Schalk also wrote about the *Goethe-Lieder* and the *Spanisches Liederbuch*. It was Schalk who conducted the premiere of *Das Fest auf Solhaug* – a performance that was, according to Wolf, ruined by poor soloists and an inadequate orchestra; elsewhere, however, he was criticised for not tailoring the vocal music to suit singing actors. Schalk was also heavily involved with *Der Corregidor*: Wolf asked for his advice concerning the tempo markings. Despite ill-health (asthma), Schalk worked tirelessly to get the opera both published and performed. In the Wagner-Verein alone, he accompanied singers in Wolf songs on more than twenty occasions. He died two years before Wolf, and Marie Lang recalls that Wolf was profoundly upset at his friend's passing.

See pp. 25, 26 and, for Franz Schalk, pp. 348, 349, 350.

JOSEPH VON SCHEY (Sie)
(1853–1938)

A distinguished patron of the arts, Baron Joseph von Schey took a keen interest in Wolf and his music. In a letter to Oskar Grohe of 26 July 1898, Wolf calls him one of his „ältesten Bekannten" ('oldest acquaintances'), and always sent him the first editions of his works. Having married Henriette Lang in 1884, Schey lived with his wife in Graz. Wolf was a guest on several occasions at the Baron's summer residences in Rinnbach and Traunkirchen, and he spent a week in September 1890 with Joseph and Henriette at their property in Kövecses in Hungary. Wolf also visited the couple in Graz during December 1893 and April 1894. Wolf expressed his gratitude to Schey who had recommended him for a vacant conducting post in Graz, but eventually decided not to apply.

See p. 537.

WILHELM SCHMID (Sie)
(1859–1951)

It was during Wolf's stay in Tübingen at the home of Emil Kauffmann that he met the latter's son-in-law, Wilhelm Schmid. Together they embarked on a tour of Mörike sights in the region, and it was not long before a friendship developed, as can be seen from a letter Wolf wrote to Schmid on 8 November 1890, in which he thanked him for his intuitive understanding of his art, which boosted his own self-confidence as a composer. Schmid was a fine amateur pianist who, together with Kauffmann, accompanied Hugo Faisst in a Wolf matinée in Tübingen on 31 October 1893. In anticipation of this concert, Schmid published in the *Tübinger*

Chronik of 28 October 1893 a remarkably prescient article on Wolf's Lieder, in which he describes the composer as „einer der größten, wo nicht der größte musikalische Lyriker dieser Zeit. [. . .] Was Wagner für die Oper, ist für das Lied Hugo Wolf." ('One of the greatest, if not the greatest songwriter of the age. [. . .] What Wagner is for opera, Hugo Wolf is for song.') Schmid's enthusiasm for *Alte Weisen* and the *Spanisches Liederbuch* caused Wolf to write him a charming letter (20 March 1891), beginning „Mein lieber Freund", in which he expresses heartfelt thanks for his friend's interest in his songs. Schmid was a distinguished philologist with a strong interest in Greek and Latin, and knowing of Wolf's search for a good opera libretto, he sent him a German translation of Aristophanes' *The Birds* which Wolf in a letter of 8 November 1890 found „entschieden zu satyrisch" ('decidedly too satirical').

See p. 268.

GUSTAV SCHUR (Du)
(?–1919)

Bank official, amateur poet and treasurer of the Wagner-Verein in Vienna. In 1890, at Schur's instigation, a group was formed, consisting mainly of his friends, to help Wolf financially. A fund was established and in the following years was used to contribute towards publication costs and also provide Wolf with travelling expenses. Schur had a happy knack of interesting influential and wealthy sponsors in Wolf's Lieder. He also introduced Wolf to singers, including Friederike Mayer, and negotiated on Wolf's behalf with publishers such as Breitkopf & Härtel and Schott's. When Schott's published the *Spanisches Liederbuch*, Wolf sent Schur an accompanying letter of gratitude on 7 March 1891:

> Ist es doch zum guten Teile das Werk Deiner redlichen Bemühungen, was mich jetzt so vertrauensvoll in die Zukunft blicken läßt. Du hast mit kühner und glücklicher, mit echter Freundeshand das Steuer meines Lebensschiffleins gegen Wind und Wetter gerichtet, über manche Klippe mir hinweggeholfen und mich in den Hafen eines ersten Verlegers gebracht.

> It is due in no small measure to your noble efforts that I can face the future with such confidence. You have bravely and successfully and in true friendship steered the little ship of my life in all weathers, and helped me to navigate over many rocks into the harbour of my first publisher.

When Wolf heard of his friend's literary activities, he urged him to fashion a scenario of *Manuel Venegas*, which did not meet with his approval. Schur also encouraged Franz Schaumann to make a libretto of Pedro de Alarcón y Ariza's

The Three-cornered Hat, which Wolf likewise rejected. From October 1890, Wolf and Schur used the 'Du' form of address. His *Erinnerungen an Hugo Wolf, nebst Hugo Wolfs Briefen an Gustav Schur*, edited by Heinrich Werner, were published in 1922.

See pp. 61, 215, 216, 279, 280, 465.

RICHARD STERNFELD (Sie)
(1858–1926)

Sternfeld – historian, musicologist, amateur pianist and composer – was an important champion of Wolf's music in Berlin, especially in the Wagner-Verein. He met Wolf in Berlin towards the end of February 1892, and later provided Ernst Decsey (vol. III, p. 91) with a detailed description of the composer:

> Eine kleine schmächtige Gestalt, ein schmales Gesicht, das von Enttäuschungen und Entbehrungen sprach, sonst kaum auffiel. Nur die Augen waren von wunderbarem Ausdruck; ganz dunkle Sterne, prüfend und spähend wie Jägeraugen, die blitzen und zürnen konnten, aber auch lachen oder zuweilen tieftraurig in sich hineinschauen.

> A small, delicate figure, a narrow face that spoke of disappointments and deprivations, but was otherwise hardly striking. His eyes, on the other hand, were wondrously expressive; utterly dark stars, searching and peering like a hunter's, that could flash and rage but also laugh and at times gaze most sadly into his own soul.

Initially, however, Sternfeld was appalled at the composer's manners: „Er konnte grob sein wie Beethoven, aufbrausend wie Wagner, rücksichtslos wie Brahms." ('He could be as coarse as Beethoven, as hot-tempered as Wagner and as insensitive as Brahms.') He arranged a private concert on 5 March 1892 of Wolf's songs in Berlin's Wagner-Verein, after which he wrote one of the first serious articles on Wolf's Lieder, 'Ein neuer Liederfrühling', published on 12 March 1892 in Fritz Mauthner's *Magazin für Litteratur*, in which he heaped praise on the *Mörike-Lieder*, claiming that it was through Wolf's settings that Mörike was now enjoying a renaissance. Wolf kept Sternfeld informed about his (eventually unsuccessful) plans to settle in Berlin, and wrote him euphoric letters about *Der Corregidor* and *Manuel Venegas*. Together they visited Kleist's grave on the Wannsee in Berlin – an experience that shook Wolf to the core, as he explained in a letter to Melanie Köchert of 24 January 1894. He was, after all, a great admirer of Kleist's plays, especially *Der Prinz von Homburg* and *Penthesilea*, for both of which he composed music, and *Der zerbrochene Krug* – see HW to his father, 5 September

1880, p. 191. After Wolf's death, Sternfeld published a perceptive and passionate article on the composer („Zum Gedächtnis eines Meisters des deutschen Liedes", which appeared in the *Deutsche Revue* edition of July–September 1903.

See pp. 358, 460.

JOSEF STRASSER (Du)
(1856–1915)

Wolf's sister Modesta married Strasser in 1876 and though he, a tax inspector, had little interest in music, he soon became one of Wolf's closest friends. In a letter to him of 9 June 1885, Wolf writes:

> Du bist der einzige Mensch, dem ich auch von ganzem Herzen zugetan bin, den ich liebe, achte und verehre. Du bist der einzige, der mich noch glauben macht, der Mensch sei nicht ganz Bestie, und in diesem „ganz" liegt schon ein großes Lob für Dich, denn gemeinhin fand ich die Menschen noch tief unter der Bestie. Kurzum und ohne viel Umschweife: ich liebe Dich.

> You are the only human being to whom I am devoted with my whole heart, whom I love, esteem and admire. You are the only person who makes me still believe that man is not entirely beast, and in this 'entirely' lies great praise for you, for in general I have found mankind far inferior to beasts. In short, and without beating about the bush: I love you.

Wolf spent the summer of 1884 at the home of Josef and Modesta in Schloss Gstatt, near Öblarn in Northern Styria, where he worked on his String Quartet in D minor, and the music to *Prinz von Homburg* and *Penthesilea*. In a thank-you letter to Strasser of 23 July 1885 Wolf described his stay as the „schönste Zeit" ('loveliest time') of his life. Wolf kept Strasser informed about a multiplicity of matters, his health, his compositions (especially the *Mörike-Lieder*, the *Goethe-Lieder* and the *Spanisches Liederbuch*), his dealings with publishers and his constant search for accommodation. In the summer of 1885, the Strassers moved to Murau where Wolf joined them from June to October 1886. Strasser was also active as impresario and arranged a concert of Wolf's works in September 1887 in Arnfels near Leibnitz. When Strasser moved to Bruck in 1888, Wolf joined him for long walks in Upper Styria and Carinthia. Their relationship cooled somewhat after 1891 when Strasser's marriage to Modesta broke down, and in a letter to Melanie Köchert he confessed: „Gegenüber meinem Schwager bin ich freundlich, aber gemessen, sehr gemessen, und weiche ihm auch gern aus". ('Towards my brother-in-law I am friendly but reserved, very reserved, and like to avoid him.')

See pp. 59, 293 (and Modesta), 351, 537.

LUDWIG STRECKER (Sie)
(1853–1943)

Alfred Kerr's malicious lampoon in Richard Strauss's *Krämerspiegel* has given Ludwig Strecker a bad name. Punning on the phrase „Auf das Streckbett legen" ('to put on the rack'), Kerr had characterised the publisher as a „Strecker" – a torturer, someone who operates the rack. In fact, Strecker was a man of culture and refinement, as Wolf discovered when he visited him on 20 October 1890. Strecker had inherited the publishing business of Schott's in 1874, and it was not long before the firm had published the *Siegfried Idyll* (1877) and *Parsifal* (1882). Wolf first approached Schott's in 1883, but the firm was too busy coping with the recent death of Wagner, publishing piano reductions, transcriptions of his works and also the score of *Parsifal*, to consider his own songs (see B. Schott's Söhne to HW, 18 February 1883, p. 452). Wolf renewed contact with Schott's in March 1890 but soon became exasperated with Strecker's way of doing business, as can be seen from his letter to Gustav Schur on 16 June 1890: „Ja, ich will lieber fortwursteln, als mit diesem Käsekrämer ein Geschäft machen. Ich bin des Feilschens nun satt." ('I'd sooner muddle through on my own than do business with this cheese-parer. I'm finally fed up with bargaining.') However, thanks to his friend Oskar Grohe's determination to find a celebrated publishing house to replace the small Viennese firms such as Wetzler who had now gone bankrupt, and thanks also to the recommendation of Felix Mottl (see HW to Ludwig Strecker, 18 February 1883, p. 452) and of Engelbert Humperdinck, who had recommended Wolf's Lieder when working for Schott's as reader, Wolf eventually succeeded in impressing the publishers. He travelled to Mainz to meet Strecker in person and was beguiled by his charming personality. He was treated royally to a banquet of many courses and choice wines, shown Wagner's 1861 draft of the *Meistersinger* libretto and got on famously with Strecker's wife (see HW to Gustav Schur, 22 October 1890, p. 61), winning her over as an ally. Strecker himself was not so convinced by some of the *Spanisches Liederbuch* that Wolf performed for him but by the end of his stay he had agreed to publish on commission not only the *Spanisches Liederbuch* and the *Alte Weisen*, but also to take over the Mörike, Eichendorff and Goethe volumes. He was later to publish Book I of the *Italienisches Liederbuch*, 'Der Feuerreiter' for men's chorus and orchestra, and the piano reduction of 'Dem Vaterland' (but not the score). Despite Wolf's efforts, Strecker rejected 'Christnacht' and, subsequently, *Der Corregidor*.

Disappointed at Strecker's lack of success in selling his works, Wolf parted company with Schott's in October 1895, bought back the *Italienisches Liederbuch* and eventually found a new publishing house in the Karl Heckel Verlag. Strecker defended his record in a letter to Ernst Decsey of 19 August 1903:

Die letzte Enttäuschung, jene über das schlechte Resultat des Verkaufs seiner Lieder, welche zur Auflösung unserer Beziehungen führte hätte ich ihm weniger übel nehmen sollen als ich es that; ich mag aber damals selbst etwas nervös gewesen sein & so ging ich nur zu bereitwillig auf seinen mich kränkenden Vorschlag der Auslieferung seiner Werke an Heckel ein. Wenn Sie die Correspondenz gelesen haben, werden Sie mir zugeben, daß oft große Geduld dazu gehörte, Alles ruhig hinzunehmen, was er im ersten Gefühlsausbruch niederschrieb [. . .] Nichts versäumt worden ist, was einem Bekanntwerden nützlich & dienlich sein konnte.

I should not have been so hard on him concerning the final disappointment, namely the poor sales of his Lieder – which led to the end of our business relationship; it could be that I too was rather nervous at that time & agreed only too readily to his insulting suggestion that his works should be taken on by Heckel. When you have read the entire correspondence [there are some 87 existing letters], you will agree with me that great patience was often required to accept with equanimity everything that he wrote in the first outburst of emotion [. . .] Everything was done to get his songs known.

See p. 222, and, for B. Schott's Söhne, 60, 62, 221, 222, 224, 226, 435, 452.

KATHARINA VINZENZBERG (Du)
(1830–1892)

Wolf's aunt (Katharina was his father's sister) played a crucial role in launching his career. When Wolf wrote to his father on 29 June 1875 that he would reluctantly follow his parents' advice and not embark on a musical career – „Denn in Ihrem letzten Brief sah ich, daß der Musiker in Ihren Augen ein fast verächtliches Individuum ist" ('For your last letter makes it clear that a musician is in your eyes an almost despicable individual') – it was Katharina who came to the rescue. She persuaded his parents to give him a chance at the Vienna Conservatoire, where her own daughters Anna (piano) and Ida (singing) were already studying. She accommodated him in her family home at Mayergasse 14 in the second Bezirk, and charged his parents a mere 16 florins a month for full board. There was much music-making in the Mayergasse and Hugo would get Ida to sing arias from a number of operas, criticising her severely when her intonation was faulty. When the Vinzenzberg family moved to Hetzendorf in May 1876, Wolf went with them, only to part company five months later when he set up on his own at Margaretenstraße 7 in the fourth Bezirk, a district where he always felt at ease.

For Anna Vinzenzberg, see p. 296.

FAMILIE WERNER

Hugo Werner (1838–1902) (Sie)
Marie Werner (1845–1914) (Sie)
Mitzi Werner (1861–1939) (Du)
Hugo Werner (1863–1940) (Du)
Heinrich Werner (1873–1927) (Du)

Wolf first met the Werner family in the summer of 1880 in Maierling. Heinrich's parents were visiting their relatives, the Preyss family, at the 'Marienhof', where Wolf was staying as a guest – see Bertha von Lackhner, p. 492. Wolf immediately struck up a good relationship with Marie Werner, the mother of Mitzi, Hugo and Heinrich; she always took a keen interest in Wolf's career and, crucially, put the family house in Perchtoldsdorf at Wolf's disposal, where he was to compose 44 of the 53 *Mörike-Lieder*, all of the *Spanisches Liederbuch*, 24 of the *Italienisches Liederbuch*, and Act I and most of Act II of *Der Corregidor*. Wolf did not initially take to Hugo Werner senior because of his anti-Wagner sentiments, but their relationship improved and Hugo eventually came to adore Wagner's music. It was in the 'Marienhof' that Wolf composed 'Mausfallen-Sprüchlein' for Mitzi Werner, whose 'bell-like' voice he greatly admired – see HW to Bertha von Lackhner, 21 October 1882, p. 345 – and to whom the song is dedicated. She, however, declared in a letter to Lackhner that the song was „nicht des Ansehens wert" ('not worthy of consideration'). He nonetheless continued to encourage her in her career and advised her on how to train her voice. He accompanied her many times, but Wolf was a hard taskmaster and she eventually sought out other pianists – to Wolf's disappointment.

It was to the youngest member of the family, Heinrich, that Wolf felt closest. They were soon using the intimate 'Du', and Wolf would often address his friend affectionately as 'Enrico No. 2' ('Enrico No. 1' was Heinrich Potpeschnigg) or 'Signor Enrico'. From 1895 Heinrich kept a diary, which contains many valuable vignettes of Wolf, especially of him playing and singing through the whole of *Der Corregidor* to a large group of his friends at Schwindgasse 3 on 13 March 1897. The diary also gives vivid and painful descriptions of Wolf's madness. When the stricken composer was allowed to make daily excursions from the asylum in the summer of 1899, it was Heinrich who accompanied him to Perchtoldsdorf and other familiar places. He was instrumental in founding Vienna's Hugo-Wolf-Verein and later became its secretary. After Wolf's death, Heinrich wrote many articles on his friend and edited volumes of his correspondence. Of especial interest is the beautifully presented *Hugo Wolf in Perchtoldsdorf*, which includes detailed descriptions of Perchtoldsdorf, the family house at Brunnergasse 26, which opened as a Wolf Museum in 1973, Wolf's study and his daily routine. The book also contains a facsimile of Wolf's handwriting and photos of the house, the study and the „Häuslein Windebang" where he would often relax and find inspiration, and the unveiling of a commemorative plaque in 1905 that reads: „In diesem Hause schuf Hugo Wolf viele unsterbliche Lieder" ('In this house Hugo Wolf composed many immortal songs'). Other publications include *Hugo Wolf in Maierling: Eine Idylle* and *Hugo Wolf und der Wiener akademische Wagner-Verein*.

Something of Wolf's gratitude to the Werner family can be gleaned from a poem that he wrote in their honour and which he sent them on 6 June 1882 from Maierling to the family home in Perchtoldsdorf. It was six years later that the family offered him accommodation at Brunnergasse 26 where he was to compose 112 of his most celebrated Lieder, but Wolf's indebtedness to the whole family already leaps from every line of this modest little poem:

Meinen liebenswürdigen Gastgebern Herrn u. Frau Werner	**To my kind hosts Herr & Frau Werner**
„Reichthum allein thut's nicht auf Erden Das ist nun einmal weltbekannt,"[1] – Dießmal doch macht's mir ein wenig Beschwerden, Daß ich nur ein armer Musikant.	'Wealth is not everything on earth, That is known throughout the globe,' – But on this occasion I rather regret That I am just a poor musician.
Mir wär's sehr lieb hätt ich mehr auf Erden, Als nur das bischen, bischen Talent, <u>Ich</u> kann dabei nicht recht glücklich werden, Und <u>andern</u> ist damit auch nichts gegönnt.	I would greatly prefer to have more on earth Than my teeny weeny bit of talent, This will never make <u>me</u> truly happy, And <u>others</u> do not profit either.
Muss ich als Schuldner von Petersdorf scheiden, Nehmt guten Willen hin für die That, Könnt ich's vergelten, ich thät es mit Freuden, Aber „ein Schelm, der mehr gibt als er hat."	If I must leave Petersdorf as a debtor, Accept my goodwill for your kindnesses, If I could reward you, I would do so with pleasure, But only 'a rogue gives more than he possesses'.
Für alles Gute, das ich genoßen, Stehen mir Worte nur zu Geboth, Aber aus tiefster Seele gefloßen Ist mir ein herzliches „vergelt es Gott."	For all the good things that I have enjoyed, I only have words to express what I feel, But I offer you a hearty 'God bless you' From the very depths of my soul.

---

1 Wolf quotes from Marie's recitative and aria in Albert Lortzing's *Der Waffenschmied* (1846). Wilhelm Schmid recalled in 1925 how he once found Wolf singing the simple melody at the piano with great fervour.

ADRIENNE WOLF (Du)
(1867–1923)

Wolf's sister. Named after Philipp and Katharina Wolf's second daughter, who died of typhus in 1858, the younger Adrienne was a vivacious young girl with a passion for music. She studied piano and became a talented dancer. When her mother died, she married and had three children; according to her daughter Ilse, Adrienne sang Lieder by Schubert, Schumann and Wolf. She had a close and loving relationship with Wolf who would often write to her about his music and play her his most recent compositions. She collected newspaper reviews of his concerts and looked after many manuscripts of his music. Thirty-nine letters from Wolf to 'Jenny', as he affectionately called her, have been preserved, among them two of the most heartrending. In Vienna's Austrian National Library there is a letter that Wolf wrote to his sister on 18 September 1897 which contains this megalomanic claim:

> Jetzt ist Mahler provisorischer Director. Der definitive Director aber werde – erschrick nicht – ich – sein. Also 12.000 Gulden Gehalt u. meine Opern kann ich nach Herzenslust aufführen.

> Mahler is now caretaker director [of the Vienna Hofoper]. The actual director – don't be frightened – is what I shall become. 12,000 florins salary, & I shall be able to perform my operas to my heart's content.

The other letter was one of the last to be written by her brother, from the Niederösterreichische Landesirrenanstalt on 17 July 1899:

> Liebe Jenny! Vielleicht könntest Du mit Käthi u. Modesta mich besuchen. Es wäre schön, wenn auch die Mutter käme. Vielleicht nimmt mich die Mutter nach Windischgraz. Ich gehe überall hin, wenn ich nur von hier fortkomme.

> Dear Jenny! Perhaps you could visit me with Käthi & Modesta. It would be lovely if mother came too. Perhaps mother will take me with her to Windischgraz. I'll go anywhere, as long as I can get out of here.

GILBERT WOLF (Du)
(1862–1938)

Wolf's brother. Although Gilbert played violin, piano and guitar competently, and the Jew's harp expertly, he showed little interest in Hugo's music, as Wolf suggests in a letter to his mother of 13 January 1897:

> Es ist nicht möglich mit ihm irgend ein anregendes Gespräch zu führen, so daß ich es gar nicht begreife, warum er überhaupt zu mir kommt, denn wir sprechen fast nie ein Wort zueinander. Der einzige Zweck, der ihn zu mir führt ist, daß er mich schließlich anpumpt.
>
> It is not possible to have any stimulating conversation with him, so I simply do not understand why he comes to me, since we hardly ever speak to one another. The only reason he visits is to touch me for money.

Despite such incompatibility, Gilbert kept urging Wolf to join him in America, as he wrote in a letter to Frieda Zerny of 1 March 1894. Wolf was excited by the idea and planned to give concerts there with Frieda who would also, he hoped, make a name for herself on the operatic stage – he even encouraged her to learn the role of Sieglinde in *Die Walküre*. Nothing came of the plan, although Wolf had a watercolour caricature made of himself by Anton Katzer with the title: „Mr. Wolf in Amerika, Golddollars gewinnend" ('Mr Wolf in America, earning golden dollars'). Gilbert spent some four years in America and returned a wealthy man, and then became fairly prosperous in the leather business on his return to Vienna. He visited Hugo in both asylums and was, according to Fritz Zangger in *Das ewige Feuer im fernen Land. Ein deutsches Heimatbuch aus dem Südosten*, „voll stolz auf seinen Bruder" – very proud of his brother. And it was Gilbert who at the end of his life established the first Wolf Museum in Windischgraz, which was disbanded at the end of the Second World War.

KATHARINA WOLF (Sie)
(1824–1903)

Wolf's mother Katharina, née Nußbaumer, came from Wolfsbach, near Malborghet in Carinthia, an area where Italian influence was strong – hence her lifelong interest in Italy and the South. She married Philipp Wolf, who was four years younger, in 1851, and bore him eight children: Modesta (1852), Adrienne (1854), who died in childhood, Max (1858), Hugo (1860), Gilbert (1862), Cornelia (1863), Katharina (1865) and Adrienne (1867). According to Frank Walker, she was kindly, homely, but also strong-willed with a sharp temper, something that Hugo inherited. Her dominant personality contributed to the rift in her marriage – see Philipp Wolf, p. 517. She was, like Hugo, extremely well read. Although Wolf always addressed her formally, he was a devoted son and dedicated to her his *Sechs Lieder für eine Frauenstimme*. The bond between them grew even closer after his father's death, and Wolf was at pains in his letters to convince her that he was making a great success of his career, although at the same time he never hid from her his problems. On several occasions she helped him financially and regularly sent him supplies of her home-made smoked sausages, which Wolf adored. Wolf harboured hopes of living with his mother on his discharge from the asylum – something that never happened. She visited him at least twice in the Niederösterreichische Landesirrenanstalt, the last time in 1901 when she was seventy-seven.

See pp. 4, 118, 119, 176, 177, 220, 230, 268, 270, 283, 302, 304, 305, 354, 357, 452, 453, 536.

KATHARINA (KÄTHE) WOLF (Du)
(1865–1944)

Wolf's sister. Käthe, like her sister Adrienne, was extremely well read, and had a predilection for the works of Turgenev. Wolf was very fond of her and on her death she was laid to rest in his own cenotaph. Wolf kept her informed by letter about many of the events in his life and would send her galley proofs of his songbooks to correct. In 1894 she was employed as a companion to Oberbergrat Riedl at Cilli in southern Styria not far from Windischgraz, and in 1901 she married a mining official, Josef Salomon. When she was widowed, she retired to Vienna. Käthe played a major part in obtaining Wolf's discharge from Dr Svetlin's asylum on 24 January 1898, as is apparent from Wolf's letter to his sister, dated 10 January 1898:

> Dieser Brief wird nicht offiziell durch die Leitung der Anstalt abgeschickt, sondern wandert als Schmuggelwaare in den Briefschalter. Meine Freundin Frau Köchert besorgt diese Angelegenheit. Mir schreibe offiziell an die Anstalt H.W. III. Leonhardgasse 3–5 [. . .] Der Zweck Deiner Beantwortung soll darin bestehn, mich möglichst bald aus den Klauen der Anstalt zu befreien [. . .] Über diesen Gegenstand darfst Du natürlich kein Jota in Deiner Antwort erwähnen, denn die Leute hier müssen glauben, daß ich zu Dir nach Cilli mich begebe, sonst lassen sie mich nicht los. [. . .] Wenn Du vorgibst mich bei Dir zu beherbergen hat die Behörde nichts mehr dreinzureden.

> This letter is not being officially dispatched by the management of the asylum but is being smuggled out by my friend Frau Köchert. Write to me, however, officially at the asylum: H.W. III. Leonhardgasse 3–5 [. . .] The purpose of your reply is to free me as soon as possible from the clutches of this asylum [. . .] Of course, absolutely no mention of this should be made in your reply, for the people here must believe that I am going to you in Cilli, otherwise they will not release me. [. . .] If you pretend to them that you will receive me in your home, the authorities can have no further objection.

After Michael Haberlandt had collected him from the asylum on the day of his release, Wolf spent some time in and around Cilli, before embarking with Käthe and Melanie Köchert on a tour of the Istrian peninsula, travelling through Trieste and visiting Graz and Salzburg.

See pp. 61, 225, 421.

MAX WOLF (Du)
(1858–1915)

Despite pouring out his heart to Max after the break with Vally Franck (see HW to Max Wolf, 3 April 1881, p. 25), Wolf had little in common with his older brother. More interested in business ventures and mountain-climbing than music or the arts (although he did play the cello when the family made music together), Max disapproved of his younger sibling, while Hugo criticised his brother's mercenary tendencies in a sketch entitled *Bruder Maxens Höllenfahrt: ein dramatischer Scherz* (*Brother Max's Journey to Hell: a dramatic joke*) that he wrote in 1881, contained in an exercise book with other poetical effusions. The plot features Max and the Devil: Max, wishing to become a merchant, offers his soul to the Devil to achieve his aim. After Wolf's death, it was Max who on 1 March 1903 expressed the family's thanks to the Vienna Wagner-Verein for all they had done to support Hugo in his career.

See p. 25.

MODESTA WOLF (Du)
(1852–1922)

Wolf's sister. A needleworker by profession, Modesta married tax inspector Josef Strasser against the wishes of her parents. Wolf, who often addressed her in jest as 'Frau Finanzräthin', would often visit the couple in their various homes (see Josef Strasser, p. 508), and he always enjoyed their company. She gave birth to five children, and when she and her husband divorced, she lived in straitened circumstances. Wolf often wrote to Modesta about important events in his life, and in one of his last letters (15 July 1899) he begged her to write to the chief surgeon of the Niederösterreichische Landesirrenanstalt to release him into her care. At the end of her life, she quarrelled with Rosa Mayreder over *Der Corregidor*, maintaining that she should receive a quarter of the royalties.

PHILIPP WOLF (Sie)
(1828–1887)

Wolf's father. Philipp inherited his father's leather business without much enthusiasm, and tried hard in his leisure hours to better himself, learning to play the piano, violin, flute and harp, and singing in a men's choir. His love of music inspired him to teach his own children a variety of musical instruments, and Hugo began to learn both piano and violin before he was five. Hugo was also taught to tune a piano, an art that became a passionate hobby – see p. 478. Of all his children, Hugo was his father's favourite, and in the little household orchestra that Philipp formed, he and Hugo played the violin, Max the cello and Uncle Ruess the horn. The family home and leather warehouse was burned to the ground in 1867, and Philipp suffered financially in the following years. In November 1868, he took his son to hear Donizetti's *Belisario* in Klagenfurt, where Modesta was taking a domestic science course. Wolf was entranced. Despite his love of music, Philipp was loath to permit his son to embark on a musical career, but eventually relented – see HW to Alexander Pöch, August 1875, p. 117, and Katharina Vinzenzberg, p. 510. Wolf assiduously kept his parents informed about his progress and achievements throughout his life, in letters that always use the 'Sie' form of address. Although Wolf's childhood was relatively happy, his parents were constantly at each other's throats, and his mother had affairs with a major from the local garrison and a chaplain. Something of the tense atmosphere can be gleaned from this extract from a letter Philipp wrote to Hugo on 2 March 1879, quoted in Dietrich Fischer-Dieskau, *Hugo Wolf. Leben und Werk,* pp. 67–8:

> Während ich hier schreibe im 2. Stock schimpft die Mutter schon über eine Stunde ununterbrochen über mich zu Kathi und Jenni [. . .] Gilbert soll froh sein, dass er in Wien ist, wie nachtheilig wirkt das ewige Schimpfen und Heruntersetzen auf das Gemüth der Kinder, wenn die unfehlbare Engelsmutter den Vater als ein verworfenes liederliches Individuum hinstellt.

> As I write this on the second floor, your mother has for over an hour been complaining about me in foul language to Kathi and Jenni [. . .] Gilbert should count himself lucky that he's away in Vienna. Such cursing and vilification has a bad effect on the children when the infallible angel of a mother dismisses your father as a depraved and slovenly individual.

And two months later, on 22 May 1879, he writes to Hugo:

> Die Mutter hat ihr Ziel erreicht, mich in den Augen der Kinder als Scheusal hinzustellen.

> Your mother has achieved her goal, depicting me as a monster in the eyes of her children.

Nor was Philipp's relationship with Hugo always easy. There were times in Wolf's life, as in 1879, when he constantly begged his father for money and received such broadsides as:

> Ich habe heute kein Geld, werde Dir morgen 30 fl. senden, Gott weiß es wo die noch ruhen! Du mußt übrigens meine Verhältnisse schlecht kennen, daß Du in so kurzer Zeit nacheinander solche Summen verlangst, und bei Ankauf der Kleider so unpraktisch zu Werke gehst, denn heutzutage lassen sich nur solche Leute vom Schneider anmessen, die Geld zum Wegwerfen haben, ein sparsamer Mensch kauft sich fertige Waare.

> I have no money today. I shall send you 30 florins tomorrow, God only knows where it's coming from! You must, moreover, be wholly ignorant of my circumstances that you keep asking for such sums within such a short space of time, and in buying clothes in such an unpractical manner, for these days only people who have money to throw away allow themselves to be measured by a tailor. A thrifty man buys ready-made clothes.

At other times Philipp criticises Hugo for wasting his time with music and other cultural pursuits, as in this letter of 9 October 1880:

> Dein letztes Schreiben hat mich sehr betrübt und niedergeschlagen – und Du magst nun sagen was Du willst, Dein Ziel ist ein verfehltes! [. . .] Du liest Schopenhauer und dergleichen – anstatt Musik, cultivirst Selbstmord-gedanken, trinkst den stärksten Kaffee – der Dein ganzes Nervensistem aufreibt – bewunderst Wagner als ganz unerreichbar. Warum an einer Idee festhalten, die Du nie zu realisieren Dir getraust, woran Du selbst verzweifelst! Was thatest Du in Mayerling? [. . .] Wäre es nicht wegen der Stellung ich würde sagen, gehe nach Hause und fang was Anderes an, da es mit der Musik nicht geht.

> Your last letter has very much saddened and depressed me – and, say what you like, you have failed! You read Schopenhauer and the like – instead of music you cultivate thoughts of suicide, you drink the strongest coffee which undermines your entire nervous system, you worship Wagner as something utterly unattainable. Why cleave to an idea that you will never be confident of realising, of which you yourself despair? What were you doing in Maierling? [. . .] If it weren't for the military service, I'd say: go home and start something else, since music is getting you nowhere.

Nor does he approve of his son's conversion to vegetarianism, as this letter from early 1883 makes clear:

> Mir gefällt Dein ganzes Gebahren nicht – starker Kaffee (Gift), dann Hülsenfrüchte – da mußt Du ja zu Grunde gehen – da hat Dir ein Esel

was in den Kopf gesetzt der es nicht verstanden hat. [. . .] Die Kost welche man von Jugend auf gewöhnt ist ist die richtige, alles andere ist Dummheit u. Schwindel.

Your whole behaviour displeases me – strong coffee (poison), and then legumes! That's the best way to come to grief – the suggestion of an idiot you haven't understood. [. . .] The correct diet is the one you were brought up on, all else is folly & humbug.

But Philipp was also proud of his son. Congratulating Hugo on his twenty-seventh birthday, he writes:

Meine und Deine Wünsche sind die gleichen, sie gipfeln in Deinen Erfolgen, es ist eine Sysiphusarbeit an der Du Dich abmühst – Dein Ringen spiegelt sich an Deinen kritischen Aufsätzen – doch verzage nicht – auch Dir wird noch die Sonne der Anerkennung leuchten . . .

My wishes are the same as your own, culminating in your successes. You have given yourself a laborious Sisyphean task; your struggle is mirrored in your critical essays – but do not despair, the sun of recognition will shine on you yet . . .

Wolf was inconsolable after his father's death, and he mourned for a great many years. When his sister Käthe forwarded him a parcel of his music manuscripts some five and a half years later, Wolf wrote to her on 7 December 1892 how touched he had been to see his father's comments on one of his songs, 'Im stillen Friedhof', a setting of a poem by Ludwig Pfau (see p. 423) for mixed chorus and piano that Wolf had composed in May 1876:

Und die Aufschrift von so lieber unvergeßlicher Hand!! Du kannst's nicht ermessen, wie unbeschreiblich dieser Anblick mich gerührt u. mich im Tiefsten erschüttert. 'Im stillen Friedhof' – – es war das einzige Lied, das die liebe Hand des Vaters mit einer Aufschrift versehen. Und nun liegt Er im stillen Friedhof u. keines meiner Lieder dringt zu ihm. Ach, wozu componire ich wohl noch, da Er sie nicht mehr hört.

And the inscription written by such a dear and unforgettable hand!! You cannot conceive how the sight of it touched & moved me to the depths of my being. 'Im stillen Friedhof' – – it was the only song that Father's dear hand provided with an inscription. And now he lies in the silent cemetery & none of my songs can reach him. Ah, why do I go on composing when he can no longer hear them.

See pp. 4, 10, 118, 119, 176, 177, 191, 263, 302, 304, 305, 419, 452, 453, 473, 536.

FRIEDA ZERNY (Du)
(1864–1917)

Mezzo-soprano (with the family name Zimmer) who studied with Julius Stockhausen, for whom Brahms wrote many of his songs. She sang in numerous opera houses before retiring from the stage to devote her life to recital work and poetry. Wolf had been informed by a Darmstadt friend that a certain Fräulein Zimmer, a young opera singer of striking beauty, was an ardent admirer of his songs. Having heard her sing in Darmstadt in early 1894, he wrote a letter to Frida von Lipperheide (2 February 1894), informing her that he had been so won over by her 'beautiful, warm voice', her rare physical beauty („seltene körperliche Schönheit") and her great understanding of his songs that he feared he would fall in love with her. Her wish was to excel on the operatic stage, but at Wolf's request she now terminated her contract at the opera house in Mainz to devote herself to recital work. Later, however, also on Wolf's advice, she resumed her operatic career and scored a great triumph as the Witch in Humperdinck's *Hänsel und Gretel*. In a letter to Frieda of 19 September 1894, Wolf congratulated her on her engagement at the Dresden Opera, while expressing regret that she would now not be available to sing his Lieder. After he had accompanied her at Liederabende in Stuttgart (arranged by Kauffmann) and Tübingen, they spent several days together. On 1 March 1894 he wrote to his mother that he had fallen in love with a „reizende junge Sängerin" ('a charming young singer') who sings his songs with deep understanding. And he closed the same letter with a hint that his mother might soon receive a „Heiratsanzeige" (announcement of a forthcoming marriage). On the same day he wrote a letter to Frieda in Mainz, telling her how Melanie Köchert knew their secret. She had interrupted him writing this long letter and there had been a terrible scene. He confessed everything, telling Frieda how much he loved her and how much Melanie loved him and hated her. And in the same breath he described Melanie as „ein göttliches Weib" ('a divine woman'):

> Ach Frieda, sie liebt mich mehr denn je u. doch – sie ahnt Alles. Ja, trotzdem ich läugnete u. sie beruhigen wollte – sie weiß Alles. [. . .] Sie weiß, daß Du mich liebst, weiß, daß auch ich Dich liebe. [. . .] Ich schilderte Dich ihr in den glühendsten Farben – sie hasst Dich, sie bedauert mich, aber sie liebt mich nur umsomehr. Dennoch wirkte mein Geständniß beruhigend auf sie ein, denn nichts ist qualvoller als der Zustand der Ungewißheit. O sie ist ein göttliches Weib, heroisch vom Wirbel bis zur Zehe.

> Ah Frieda, she loves me more than ever – and yet she suspects *everything*. Despite my denials & attempts to calm her, she knows *everything*. [. . .] She knows that you love me, knows also that I love you. [. . .] I described you to

her in the most glowing colours – she hates you, she pities me, and she loves me all the more. My confession had a calming effect on her, for nothing is more painful than uncertainty. Oh she is a divine woman, heroic through and through.

When he next wrote to Frieda on 7 March 1894, he mentions their plan to emigrate to America, where Friedrich Eckstein would establish contact with a Boston impresario – and to this end Wolf urged her to study the role of Sieglinde for a possible performance of *Die Walküre* in Mainz. This, he declared, would considerably enhance the possibility of earning their keep in America. Wolf had already begun learning English with Miss Agnes Park, a former governess of the Köchert children.

After Lieder recitals in Vienna and Graz, he was convinced that he had found the ideal singer for his Lieder – a feeling he expressed in a letter to his sister Käthe (14 March 1894):

Fräulein Zerny ist übrigens eine ganz ungewöhnliche Erscheinung, abgesehen von ihren enormen künstlerischen Qualitäten – sie verfügt über einen herrlichen Mezzosopran – zeichnet sie sich auch durch eine ganz hervorragende Bildung und einen energischen Charakter aus, der seinesgleichen in der Welt sucht. Außerdem ist sie jung und schön – nicht hübsch sondern schön, und singt meine Sachen mit einer Hingebung und einem Verständnis, wie man sich dergleichen im Traum nicht schöner vorstellen kann.

Fräulein Zerny is, moreover, a wholly exceptional phenomenon. Quite apart from her enormous artistic qualities – she possesses a splendid mezzo-soprano voice – she is highly educated and has an energetic character quite unmatched in the entire world. She is also young and beautiful – not pretty but beautiful, and sings my things with a devotion and understanding that could not be bettered even in a dream.

Despite rumours about their affair (see letter to Oskar Grohe of 16 March 1894), they continued to give concerts together. On 3 April 1894 they performed in Vienna's Saal Bösendorfer a programme that Wolf himself had chosen: 'Tretet ein, hoher Krieger', 'Du milchjunger Knabe', 'Wie glänzt der helle Mond', 'Die Zigeunerin', 'Herr, was trägt der Boden hier?', 'In dem Schatten meiner Locken', 'Mögen alle bösen Zungen' (!), 'Alle gingen, Herz, zur Ruh'', 'Peregrina I', 'Erstes Liebeslied eines Mädchens', 'Gesang Weylas' and 'Um Mitternacht'. This was followed on 5 April by a concert devoted to songs from the *Spanisches Liederbuch*; and just over a week later they gave a recital in Graz.

Several hours before this concert began on 13 April 1894, Wolf sent an astonishing, duplicitous note to Melanie Köchert:

> Sie haben vollkommen recht. Sie ist eine Egoistin u. kann Alles, nur nicht lieben. Wenn Sie wüßten, wie kühl u. gleichgiltig ich mich gegen sie verhalte! Kaum, daß ich ihr einen Blick schenke. Geradezu widerwärtig wird sie mir. Glücklicherweise scheint ihr meine sichtliche Abneigung keinen besonderen Eindruck zu machen u. so hoffe ich sie demnächst auf gute Manier loszukriegen.
>
> You are quite right. She is an egotist & can do everything but love. If you knew how coolly & indifferently I behave towards her! I scarcely look at her. She's becoming downright repugnant to me. Fortunately, my obvious aversion seems to make no particular impression on her, & so I hope shortly to be rid of her with good grace.

Wolf continued to write passionate letters to Frieda, beginning one on 24 April 1894 with a quote from Heine's 'Mein Wagen rollet langsam': „Ich sitze u. sinne u. sinne und träume – und denk an die Liebste mein." ('I sit & muse & muse and dream – and think of my dear love.')

By the time they met again in June 1894 in Munich, the nature of their relationship had changed – Wolf wrote to her on 26 June, mentioning the „Veränderung" ('change') in his feelings. Two months later Frieda offered to release him from any obligation – which he accepted. They continued to correspond; and she occasionally sent him her poems. Twice she suggested in letters that they resume their relationship in some form. Wolf declined. On 10 October 1894, he wrote her a letter which makes it quite clear that, though he still found her physically attractive, there was no way back:

> Ich kann es nicht läugnen, daß es mich siedend heiss überkam bei dem Gedanken neuerdings wieder an Deinem Busen zu erwarmen. Ganz im Geheimen willst Du mein Liebchen, meine Philine sein, ja sogar die Altjungfernschaft (Schelm!) willst Du Dir aufladen, um ganz wieder mir anzugehören? Nein, mein artiges Philinchen, das ist zuviel, zuviel der Liebe und Güte . . . Du weißt gar nicht, was Du da in einem Athem sprichst. [. . .] Du wirst wieder besonnen werden, wirst eine berühmte Sängerin, vergißt mich armen Teufel u. heirathest einen Marquis, wenn nicht gar einen Reichsbaron. Das soll die Lösung des Romanes sein, den wir so schön begonnen haben, leider jedoch nicht zu Ende führen dürfen.
>
> I cannot but deny that I was overcome with seething desire when I recently thought of warming myself once more against your bosom. Is it your secret wish, my love, to be my Philine and even embrace spinsterhood (you minx!) in order to belong to me again entirely? No, my pretty little Philine, that would be too loving, too kind . . . You have no idea what you are saying. [. . .] You will come to your senses, become a famous singer, you will forget this poor devil & marry a marquis or even a baron. That will be the denouement

of the novel that began so beautifully but which, unfortunately, we were unable to see through.

In the summer of 1894 she performed the roles of a squire and a flowermaiden in the Bayreuth production of *Parsifal*; and she continued to sing Wolf's Lieder when they had gone their separate ways.

Scholars have yet to come up with any convincing single reason for the break with Frieda. Fischer-Dieskau suggests that Wolf, fearful of infecting her with his syphilis, did not consummate his relationship with Frieda – which led to irreconcilable tensions. But the language that Wolf uses in his letters scarcely tallies with this interpretation. Perhaps it had become too difficult for Wolf to play one mistress off against the other; perhaps, like Brahms, he was incapable of committing – the latter's devastating letter to Agathe von Siebold springs to mind: „Ich liebe Dich! ich muß Dich wiedersehen! Aber Fesseln tragen kann ich nicht!" ('I love you! I must see you again! But I cannot be fettered!') But the most likely reason remains the impossibility of sustaining a relationship at the same time as composing music. At the end of his affair with Vally Franck, Wolf had written to his father (14 May 1881), „Mir muß die Kunst die untreue Geliebte ersetzen." ('My art must replace my faithless beloved.') Frieda was not unfaithful, but Wolf could compose only in isolation, and in a letter written to her on 21 June 1894, shortly after their final meeting in Munich, he declares:

> Auch die Tage von München waren nur ein trügerischer Sonnenschein, der sich nur zu bald verflüchtigte. Ich fürchte wirklich, daß ich nur für die Einsamkeit tauge, zumindest fühle ich mich am wohlsten fern von aller Welt, in stiller Abgeschiedenheit, nur meinen Grillen nachhängend.

> And the sunny days spent in Munich were merely deceptive and dispersed all too quickly. I really fear that I am suited only for solitude, at least I feel most comfortable when I am far distant from the world, quiet and isolated, and can immerse myself in my own ideas.

Five days later he is even more explicit:

> Ihr Frauen freilich habt es leicht. Euch ist die Liebe schon Beruf. [...] Aber Liebe <u>allein</u>, als Beruf für den Mann, mag vielleicht im Roman od. auf der Bühne am Platze sein; dort vermag sie etliche Bände od. auch fünf Akte auszufüllen, aber als Beruf für ein ganzes Menschenleben in Wohligkeit taugt sie gewiß nicht.

> It's easy for you women. Love, for you, is a vocation in itself. [...] But love <u>alone</u> as a vocation for a man may perhaps be appropriate in a novel or on the stage; there it may suffice to fill out several volumes or five acts, but in reality it in no way serves as a calling for man's whole life.

Frieda Zerny was not only a brilliant interpreter of Wolf's songs, she was also a gifted writer, which makes it doubly regrettable that her letters to Wolf have not survived. There are a few poems that have come down to us, and here she remembers her lover:

In memoriam
Für Hugo Wolf

Uns zog das Leben fort von deiner Seite.
Du winktest still: Laßt einsam mich
    nur gehn!
Auf deiner Stirn, der bleichen,
    tief gesenkten,
Sahn wir des Leidens dunkle Male stehn.

Du starbst uns hin – allein in unserer Seele
Lebt unverlöscht dein tiefer Flammenblick.

Erinnrung führt uns zu den fernen Pfaden,
Die einst mit dir wir wandelten, zurück.

In deinen Liedern lacht das hellste Leben,
Die „tiefsten Nächte" glühn in deinem Sang.
Und aller Lenze wonnigstes Entzücken

Und aller Schmerzen schärfster Weheklang.

All deinen Reichtum hast du uns gelassen. –
Wir sehn im Wechsel fliehen Tag und Nacht,
Doch selbst die Frühlingssonne birgt sich
    trauernd
Vor deines unerhörten Schicksals Macht.

In memoriam
For Hugo Wolf

Life ripped you from our side.
Silently, you made a sign: Let me go, alone!
On your brow, pale and lowered
    to your breast,
We saw the dark signs of suffering.

You passed away from us – but in our soul
Your deep fiery gaze lives on,
    unextinguished.

Memory leads us back to distant paths,
On which we once walked with you.

Brightest life laughs in your Lieder,
'Deepest nights' glow in your song –
And the most blissful rapture of
    every spring

And the sharpest pangs of every pain.

You have left us your abundance –
We see day and night flee in turn,
But even the spring sun hides in mourning

Before the might of your outrageous destiny.

See pp. 194, 459.

APPENDIX 1

DETLEV VON LILIENCRON'S 'AN HUGO WOLF'

On 11 October 1890, Wolf wrote a letter to Melanie Köchert from Munich, where he had travelled to meet Detlev von Liliencron who had sent him two volumes of verse in the hope that he might find poems suitable for song setting. The letter to his mistress brims with excitement:

> Heute spielte ich Conrad u. Liliencron meine Sachen vor. Die Beiden waren im buchstäblichsten Sinne des Wortes
> niedergedonnert.
> Der Eine weinte u. der andere schrie. Es war zum toll werden.
> Liliencron will mich um jeden Preis andichten. Vielleicht bin ich der Held seiner nächst erscheinenden Novelle. Der Eine schrie das gienge über Wagner, der andere brüllte, daß der Teufel selber nicht die Dinge zusammenbrächte; kurz – die Kerle sind rasend geworden.

> Today I played my things to Conrad & Liliencron. Both were quite literally
> thunderstruck.
> One wept & the other screamed. It was enough to send you insane.
> Liliencron wants at all costs to write about me. Perhaps I shall be the hero of his next Novelle. One bawled: 'That's better than Wagner', the other roared that even the Devil could not concoct anything comparable; in short – they have both gone raving mad.

The scene is easy to imagine. Liliencron, having heard about Wolf's Lieder through Joseph Schalk's 'Neue Lieder, neues Leben' article, had written enthusiastically to the composer, who was keen to collaborate with him on a new opera. And although they could not agree on a subject, and although Wolf could find no suitable poem for song setting in the two volumes of verse that Liliencron had sent him, he saw in the poet an important ally. Indeed, Liliencron had written to Wolf on 26 August 1890, promising that he would do everything in his power to popularise his Lieder.

Knowing that Liliencron was a keen amateur singer, well acquainted with the great Lieder of the past, Wolf set out for Munich with great hopes, confident of finding in the German poet a new friend and supporter. The private performance of the 53 Mörike songs mentioned in 'An Hugo Wolf' took place at the home of Liliencron's friend Michael Georg Conrad, a peripheral figure in the Naturalismus movement in German literature who wrote short stories and novels. At midday on 11 October Conrad returned from a walk to discover his house resounding with music. Wolf introduced himself as 'Hugo Wolf from Vienna' and insisted that Munich must get to know him. To this end, several important musical figures were invited the next day to hear Wolf play his songs at the piano sale rooms of Alfred Schmied – but in a letter to Gustav Schur, penned later that day, Wolf admitted that he had been understood 'only by a few'.

Liliencron, whose poem 'An Hugo Wolf' appears in *Der Haidegänger*, asked his publisher to send Wolf a copy. Wolf was delighted; privately, however, in a letter to Emil Kauffmann of 22 December 1890, he poured scorn on Liliencron's new volume, which he regarded as vastly inferior to his earlier poetry. As for Liliencron, he remained a loyal devotee and did all he could to champion Wolf's Lieder. In a letter to an admirer, dated January 1891, he displayed extraordinary prescience when he predicted that it would take fifty years for Wolf's Lieder to be accepted by the German public:

Kennen Sie Hugo Wolf, den jungen Komponisten, in Wien? 50 Jahre wird's dauern, bis er, nach der bekannten „Eigentümlichkeit" der Deutschen, durchgedrungen ist. Das ist einfach phenomenal. Er schrieb (spielte und sang sie mir vor) 53 Mörike-Lieder und 51 Goethe-Lieder. Lassen Sie bitte sich diese Lieder ja aus Wien kommen; aber erwähnen Sie bitte seinen Namen nicht dem lieben Johannes. Der ist, glaub ich, rasend auf ihn.[1]

Do you know Hugo Wolf, the young composer from Vienna? It will take 50 years for him to make a name for himself, given the well-known German

---

[1] Brahms did not on the whole appreciate Wolf's music – partly, perhaps, because of Wolf's public vilification of him. When the young Wolf visited Brahms in the Karlsgasse in March 1879 with a volume of recently composed songs, Max Kalbeck tells us in his article first published in *Musikbuch aus Österreich* on 9 March 1904 that Wolf 'kept on kissing the latch of Brahms's study door in reverence' („aus Verehren") – Wolf was at this stage of his career an admirer of Brahms's music, and when he took some of the latter's *Volks- und Kinderlieder* to play at the Gabillons, Helene later described in *Im Zeichen des alten Burgtheaters* how Brahms's music 'sent him into ecstasies' („in glühender Ekstase"). And Wolf wrote in a letter to his parents of 15 December 1878 that he was „sehr begierig" ('very eager') to hear Brahms's Symphony in C minor in Vienna that evening. Wolf was greatly discouraged by his interview with the great man, and Kalbeck tells us that Brahms advised him to study counterpoint with Gustav Nottebohm. Wolf, despite his disappointment, approached Nottebohm but was not prepared to pay the 3 florins that the celebrated musicologist charged for a lesson. From that moment on, Wolf seems to have acquired a deep loathing of Brahms. According to Brahms, quoted by Kalbeck in Volume 3 of his *Johannes Brahms*, Wolf from now on 'spat poison and gall' („Nun speit er Gift und Galle"). His reviews of Brahms's music in the *Wiener Salonblatt* are outrageously vitriolic, fuelled to a large degree by personal animosity. Let three examples suffice. The Symphony in D major ('An air so icy, dank and misty blows through this composition that your heart could freeze and you struggle for breath; you could catch a cold') („Durch diese Komposition geht eine Luft, so eisig, naßkalt und neblig, daß einem das Herz erfrieren, der Atem benommen werden möchte; 'nen Schnupfen könnt' man sich dabei holen"); the Violin Concerto he found „widerwärtig" ('repellent') – 'full of platitudes and meaningless profundity' („voll Platitüden und nichtssagendem Tiefsinn"); while the Symphony in E minor is characterised by 'nullity, emptiness and hypocrisy' („Nichtigkeit, Hohlheit und Duckmäuserei").

character. He is simply phenomenal. He has composed 53 Mörike Lieder and 51 Goethe – which he played and sang to me. Send to Vienna for these songs; but don't mention his name to dear Johannes who is, I think, mad at him.

An Hugo Wolf

Erinnerst du dich der Tage:
Hinter dir saßen
Conrad,[1] der Hüne, und ich.
Du sangst uns
Deine 53,
Drei-und-fünf-zig!
Mörike-Lieder vor
Und deine ungezählten Wunderweisen
Aus Goethe und Eichendorff.
Wie war das Alles neu!
Zum Erstarren neu!
Vorn im Mörike-Heft,
Auf erster Seite,
Hattest Du, Bescheidener,
Des Dichters Bild verehrend aufgestellt.
Welcher Tonsetzer that je so?

Und während du glühend sangst,
Gingen draußen die Deutschen vorüber.
Sie trugen in ihren Taschen
Billete zu „Mamsell Nitouche".[2]
Und die Schamröte flog mir in's Gesicht

To Hugo Wolf

Do you remember those days:
Sitting behind you were
Conrad the Colossus and me.
You sang to us
Your 53,
Fif-ty-three!
Mörike-Lieder
And the countless wondrous melodies
From your Goethe and Eichendorff volumes.
How new it all was!
Numbingly new!
In the Mörike volume,
On the first page,
You, modest man,
Had set the poet's portrait in admiration.
What composer ever did that?

And while you sang with fervour,
The Germans passed by outside
With tickets for *Mam'zelle Nitouche*
In their pockets.
And my face flushed red
    with embarrassment

Despite the puerile hyperbole and the ubiquitous sneers and jibes, Wolf was a perceptive and generally well-informed critic, and it is not always realised that he greatly appreciated some of Brahms's compositions, including his folk songs and *Die schöne Magelone*. His sporadic appreciation of Brahms is also clear from his reviews of the String Sextet in G (2 March 1884), the 'Alto Rhapsody' (11 April 1886), 'Von ewiger Liebe' (3 April 1887) and especially the String Quintet in F (23 March 1884) which drew from him some purple prose rarely encountered in his other reviews. Brahms was present at the Gesellschaft der Musikfreunde concert on 2 December 1894, and was seen to applaud warmly the choral 'Elfenlied' and 'Der Feuerreiter'. Eduard Hanslick too was impressed, writing in his review of the concert that Wolf was „Unzweifelhaft ein Mann von Geist und Talent" ('Without doubt a man of intellect and talent'). And Heinrich Werner (in „Hugo Wolf. Zur zwanzigsten Wiederkehr des Todestags", published in the *Neues Wiener Tagblatt* of 20 February 1923), tells us that Kalbeck, shortly before Wolf's death, visited the house in Perchtoldsdorf where he had composed so many masterpieces and admitted: „Ich hab' ihm unrecht getan." ('I did him wrong.')

1 Michael Georg Conrad (1846–1927), founder of a literary journal, *Die Gesellschaft*, in which during 1890 he published an essay on Wolf's *Mörike-Lieder*. Liliencron's *Kampf und Spiele* contains a poem about Conrad, titled 'An M. G. Conrad'.
2 *Mam'zelle Nitouche* is a vaudeville-operetta by Hervé (1825–1892) to a libretto by Henri Meilhac and Albert Millaud. The title translates approximately as *Little Miss Hypocrite* ('nitouche' = 'never touch [it]'). First performed at the Théâtre des Variétés on 26 January 1883, it remained in

Für unsre Landsleute,	For our compatriots,
Daß sie dir nicht horchten;	Because they were not listening to you,
Daß sie ihren großen, lieben	Because they did not know their great,
Dichter Mörike nicht kennen.	Dear poet Mörike.
Wir erhoben uns.	We rose.
Auf der Straße	On the street
Nahm Conrad, der Hüne, dich	Conrad the Colossus
Auf seine Athletenschultern,	Lifted you onto his athlete's shoulders
Und trug dich durch die Menge,	And carried you through the crowd,
Wie einst der heilige Christoph das Jesulein	As Saint Christopher once carried little Jesus
Durch das tosende Wildwasser brachte.	Across the raging torrent.
Einer Spielzeugtändlerin	I bought a little flag
Kauft' ich ein Fähnchen ab.	From a woman selling toys,
Und das Fähnchen wuchs schnell	And the little flag quickly turned into
Zur mächtigen, prunkenden Fahne.	A mighty, magnificent banner.
Einem Flötenbläser winkt' ich,	I beckoned to a flute-player
Der einsam im Kinderkreise blies;	Playing alone to a circle of children,
Und er kam und ging mit:	And he rose and went with us:
Duidldidum, duidldidum.	Rum-ti-tum, rum-ti-tum.
Einem Zinkenisten winkt' ich	I beckoned to a bugler
Aus einer Gassenmusik;	In a street band,
Und er kam und ging mit:	And he rose and went with us:
Tatara ta, Tatara ta.	Rata-tat-ta, rata-tat-ta.
Einem Beckenschläger winkt' ich,	I beckoned to a cymbal-player
Der einem Bärenzeiger gesellt stand;	Who kept a bear-trainer company,
Und er kam und ging mit:	And he rose and went with us:
Dschingdada, Dschingdada.	Dschingdada, Dschingdada.
Die drei machten Bocksprünge, während sie spielten,	The three of them capered as they played,
Und tanzten wie trunkene Derwische.	And danced like drunken dervishes.
Vor dem Zuge schwang ich	At the head of the procession
Die mächtige Prunkfahne hin und her,	I waved the mighty magnificent banner,
Und ich rief:	And I cried:
Platz da, Platz da, Gesindel,	Make way! Make way, you rabble!
Ein junger Germanenkönig kommt,	A young German king is coming,
Ein König der neuen Kunst!	A king of the new art!
Platz da, Platz da, Gesindel,	Make way! Make way, you rabble!
Ein König kommt!	A king is coming!
Und die Deutschen	And the horrified Germans

---

the repertoire for many years. Hervé was organist at Saint-Eustache in Paris during the day, where he was known by his real name, Florimond Ronger, and at night transformed himself into Hervé, composer of operettas.

Griffen entsetzt in ihre Taschen	Felt in their pockets
Und fühlten nach den Billeten	For their tickets
Zu „Mamsell Nitouche".	To *Mam'zelle Nitouche*.
Und sie rannten schleunig	And ran as fast as they could
Zu „Mamsell Nitouche".[1]	To *Mam'zelle Nitouche*.

1   Marcell Salzer (1873–1930), a member of Wedekind's 'Überbrettl', recorded the poem in July 1906 – it can be heard on YouTube. The poem was written between 10 and 12 October 1890, immediately after Liliencron had heard Wolf perform the *Eichendorff-*, *Goethe-* and *Mörike-Lieder* at the house of Michael Georg Conrad in Munich.

APPENDIX 2

FROM MICHAEL HABERLANDT'S FUNERAL ORATION, SPOKEN AT HUGO WOLF'S GRAVESIDE ON 24 FEBRUARY 1903

So versammelst du, großer entschlafener Freund, wieder wie einst, wenn du uns in engem Kreise mit deiner Kunst entzücktest, die Schar deiner Freunde um dich, aber es ist heute zum letztenmal, und es gilt Abschied auf immer zu nehmen.

Aber seht, – aus dem kleinen Häuflein der Getreuen, die dir im Leben nahe stehen durften, ist eine große Trauergemeinde geworden, – diese ganze große Stadt, ein ganzes Volk, weit über die Grenzen des Vaterlandes hinaus reichend, das heute diese Stunde des letzten Abschiedes trauernd mit uns verlebt, und das sich in Ehrfurcht beugt vor der Schwere deines Schicksals, der Reinheit deines armen, stolzen Lebens und dem Adel deiner himmlischen Kunst.

Ja, ein schweres Schicksal haben dir die ewigen Mächte, die über diesem Leben walten, auferlegt. Kurz war dein Dasein, arm an kleinem Menschenglück und Freuden; von den Ehren und Gütern dieser Welt hast du nichts, fast nichts genossen. In Armut nur deiner Kunst lebend, bist du, fast unbekannt, von vielen verkannt, verspottet, geschmäht, wie so mancher Genius, durch dein kurzes Leben in ein langes, schauerliches Reich der Leiden und endlich in den frühen Tod gegangen. [. . .]

Und wir danken dir am tiefsten für die edlen Gaben deiner Kunst. Was du, ein königlich Schenkender, uns gegeben, spät haben wir es erkannt, und vielen ist das Ohr noch taub und das Herz noch verschlossen für deine neue, tiefinnerliche Sprache, in der du Herz und Geist unserer Zeit zum Erklingen gebracht hast. [. . .]

Und nun, wie du in einem deiner schönsten Lieder sangest:

Zur Ruh, zur Ruh

Zur Ruh, zur Ruh
Ihr müden Glieder!
Schließt fest euch zu,
Ihr Augenlider!
Du bist allein,
Fort ist die Erde;
Nacht muß es sein,
Daß Licht dir werde.[1]

---

1 Haberlandt, cleverly and movingly, adapts lines 5 and 8 of Kerner's poem that had originally run (see p. 292):

And so once more you gather the host of your friends about you, dearest, departed friend – just as when you delighted those closest to you with your art – but today is the last time, and we must now bid you farewell for ever.

But look – the small number of loyal friends who were close to you in life has become a great congregation of mourners: this entire city, an entire people, stretching far beyond the borders of the fatherland, mourns with us at this final hour, and bows its head out of respect for your tragic fate, the purity of your poor, proud life and the nobility of your heavenly art.

The eternal powers that control our lives have imposed upon you a grim fate. Your life was short, lacking human happiness and joy; of the honours and blessings of this world, you have enjoyed nothing, almost nothing. Living in poverty exclusively for your art, you have, almost unknown, been misunderstood by the multitude, mocked, reviled like many a genius, passing in your short life through a long and terrible realm of suffering before finally experiencing an early death. [. . .]

We thank you from the depth of our hearts for the noble gifts of your art. What you have given us so royally – we were slow to recognise, and many there are who still do not hear or feel your new, deeply spiritual language, in which you have captured in music the heart and spirit of our times. [. . .]

And now, as you sang in one of your most beautiful songs:

To rest, to rest

To rest, to rest,
You weary limbs,
Close tight,
You eyelids!
You are alone,
The world is left behind;
Night must come
That you may find light.

Zur Ruh, zur Ruh
Ihr müden Glieder!
Schließt fest euch zu,
Ihr Augenlider!
Ich bin allein,
Fort ist die Erde;
Nacht muß es sein,
Daß Licht **mir** werde.

APPENDIX 3

ORCHESTRATED SONGS

Wolf never composed an orchestral song, but he did orchestrate some thirty of his existing piano-accompanied songs. He seems to have done so for a variety of reasons. Firstly to reach a larger audience, those concert-goers who relished orchestral works; secondly, he tended to orchestrate already existing songs when he was suffering from creative inertia; and thirdly, he clearly harboured megalomanic ambitions to become a great opera composer.

Auf ein altes Bild (?May 1889)
Seufzer (28 May 1889)
Karwoche (29 May 1889)
Der Rattenfänger (5 February 1890)
Er ist's (20 February 1890)*
Gesang Weylas (21 February 1890)
Schlafendes Jesuskind (?May 1889)
Mignon ('Kennst du das Land') (1890)*
Anakreons Grab (1890)*
Ganymed [lost] (before April 1890)*
Prometheus (1890)
In der Frühe (6 May 1890)
An den Schlaf (4 September 1890)
Gebet (4 September 1890)
Neue Liebe (5 September 1890)
Wo find' ich Trost? (6 September 1890)
Auf eine Christblume I [fragment] (25 September 1890)
Harfenspieler I (2 December 1890)
Harfenspieler II (4 December 1890)
Harfenspieler III (4 December 1890)
Denk es, o Seele! (4 May 1891)
Geh, Geliebter, geh jetzt! [lost] (May 1892)*
Der Feuerreiter (October–November 1892)
Mignon ('Kennst du das Land') (31 October 1893).
   New version after loss of the first.*
Anakreons Grab (13 November 1893). New version after loss of the first.*
Epiphanias [fragment] (25 April 1894)
Wächterlied auf der Wartburg [fragment] (June/July 1894)

In dem Schatten meiner Locken (summer 1895, orchestrated
  for *Der Corregidor*)
Herz, verzage nicht geschwind (autumn 1895, orchestrated
  for *Der Corregidor*)
Wer sein holdes Lieb verloren (1–4 December 1897, orchestrated
  for *Manuel Venegas*)
Wenn du zu den Blumen gehst (5–6 December 1897, orchestrated
  for *Manuel Venegas*)
Morgenstimmung (12–17 December 1897, as 'Morgenhymnus',
  arranged for chorus and orchestra)

* 'Ganymed', 'Geh, Geliebter, geh jetzt!', 'Anakreons Grab', 'Er ist's' and 'Mignon' were all orchestrated by Wolf for a performance by the Philharmonic Chorus in Berlin on 8 January 1894. Unfortunately, as he told Oskar Grohe in a letter of 17 November 1893, he left them in a Viennese tramcar while going to post them to Berlin. He managed to re-orchestrate 'Mignon' and 'Anakreons Grab' in time for the concert, but 'Ganymed', 'Geh, Geliebter, geh jetzt!' and the first version of 'Anakreons Grab' were never recovered. 'Er ist's' and the first version of 'Mignon' were later found and published posthumously.

APPENDIX 4

OPERA

Wolf's interest in opera dates from November 1868 when his father took the eight-year-old boy to hear Donizetti's *Belisario* in the opera house at Klagenfurt. Hugo was mesmerised. Three years later, while at school in the Konvikt at the Benedictine monastery in the Lavant valley in Carinthia, one of the teachers, Father Sales Pirc, ordered a pot-pourri of operas by Bellini, Donizetti, Gounod and Rossini to fuel his pupil's passion. And the little diary that Wolf kept during his adolescence teems with excited references to the operas that he heard from his Stammplatz in the gods of the Hofoper: *Don Giovanni, Der fliegende Holländer, Lohengrin, Tannhäuser, Der Freischütz, Lucia di Lammermoor*. No opera made a greater impression than *Tannhäuser*, which he saw in November 1875 – see HW to his parents, 23 November 1875, p. 536. His ambition to compose a successful opera runs through the correspondence like a *leitmotiv*.

As music critic of the *Wiener Salonblatt*, Wolf reviewed a vast number of operas, including, in 1884 alone, performances of the following: *Die Stumme von Portici* (Auber), *Zar und Zimmermann, Der Waffenschmied* (Lortzing), *Die heimliche Ehe* (Cimarosa), *Der Troubador, Aida* (Verdi), *Die Hugenotten, Der Prophet, Die Afrikanerin* (Meyerbeer), *Lucrezia Borgia, Die Regimentstochter, Lucia di Lammermoor* (Donizetti), *La Gioconda* (Ponchielli), *Mefistofele* (Boito), *Die Jüdin* (Halévy), *Lohengrin, Tristan und Isolde, Das Rheingold, Die Meistersinger von Nürnberg* (Wagner), *Fidelio* (Beethoven), *Der Vampyr* (Marschner), *Martha* (Flotow), *Iphigenie in Tauris* (Gluck), *Die Entführung aus dem Serail, Figaros Hochzeit, Don Giovanni* (Mozart), *Der Barbier von Sevilla, Wilhelm Tell* (Rossini), *Hamlet* (Thomas), *La sonnambula* (Bellini), *Der Trompeter von Säkkingen* (Nessler), *Euryanthe, Oberon, Der Freischütz* (Weber). Small wonder that Wolf wished to make his own name in the world of opera.

Der Corregidor was the only opera that he finished. Rosa Mayreder-Obermayer fashioned the libretto from *El sombrero de tres picos* (1874) by Pedro Antonio de Alarcón y Ariza. The opera, composed from 12 March to 25 December 1895, was premiered in Mannheim on 7 June 1896 and received its first UK performance at the Royal Academy of Music on 13 July 1934; it was revised from the summer of 1896 to the spring of 1897. Two newly orchestrated songs from the *Spanisches Liederbuch* were incorporated by Wolf into the score, contrary to the advice of his publisher, Ludwig Strecker of Schott's: 'In dem Schatten meiner Locken' and 'Herz, verzage nicht geschwind'. On 13 March 1897, his thirty-seventh birthday, Wolf invited many of his friends to his home in the Schwindgasse to hear him perform the revised version of *Der Corregidor*, from beginning to end. He was in exalted mood and fine voice, and many of those present (including the Mayreders, the Langs, Haberlandt, Joseph Schalk and Heinrich Werner) wrote about the occasion. In Thomas Mann's novel *Doktor Faustus*, the syphilitic composer Adrian Leverkühn likewise invites some of his friends to hear himself play extracts from his semi-operatic Symphonische Kantate *Dr. Fausti Weheklag (The Lamentation of Dr Faustus)*. We know from several remarks in Mann's *Die Entstehung des Doktor Faustus* that he studied Wolf's letters (and also Ernest Newman's biography of Wolf) while planning and writing the novel, and there are phrases in the novel that Mann lifted from Wolf's own correspondence – „Möge sich die Hölle meiner erbarmen" from Chapter 43 being one of several. See HW to Oskar Grohe, 30 December 1890, p. 217.

Manuel Venegas remains a fragment, but one that contains passages of fine music. Some 50 pages of Act I exist in vocal score, and it was composed from 29 July to 5 December 1897 to a libretto by Moriz Hoernes from the novel *El niño de la bola* by Pedro Antonio de Alarcón y Ariza. Wolf wrote to Potpeschnigg (2 and 6 December 1897) that he hoped to incorporate into *Manuel Venegas* six to ten orchestrated songs from the *Spanisches Liederbuch*, mostly at the beginning of Act I. Only two songs, however, found their way into the opera: 'Wer sein holdes Lieb verloren' and 'Wenn du zu den Blumen gehst'. It was during Hartmut Höll's first year as artistic director of the Stuttgart Hugo-Wolf-Verein in 1985 that the *Manuel Venegas* fragment received its first complete performance.

Some libretti, mentioned in his correspondence, to which Wolf gave serious consideration as operatic subjects:

Alboin und Rosamunde (Körner) [1876/7]
Prinzessin Ilse (Heine) [1882]
Ein Sommernachtstraum (Shakespeare) [1888][1]
Der Sturm (Shakespeare) [1890 and 1894][2]
Das öffentliche Geheimnis (Gozzi) [1890]
Buddha (Heckel) [1890]
Das Fest auf Solhaug (Ibsen) [1890]
Hermann und Dorothea (Goethe) [1892]
Actéon (Scribe) [1893]
Weh dem, der lügt! (Grillparzer) [1893][3]
Hannele (Hauptmann) [1893]

---

1   Seven pages of sketches plus a scenario are extant. Though nothing came of the venture, Wolf did compose two poems from *A Midsummer Night's Dream*: 'Lied des transferierten Zettel' and 'Elfenlied' for solo voices, women's chorus and piano – both composed on 11 May 1889.
2   Wolf sketched a scenario to *Der Sturm*.
3   Wolf fashioned a complete scenario to *Weh dem, der lügt!* on a single page.

Phöbus Apollo (Anon.) [1893]
Schloß Dürande (Eichendorff) [1894]
Königskinder (Ernst Rosmer – pseudonym for Elsa Bernstein-Porges) [1894]
Gyges und sein Ring (Hebbel) [1894]
Die Bernsteinhexe (Mayreder, after Meinhold) [1895]
Eldas Untergang (Mayreder) [1895]
Die heilige Cäcilie (Backmeister) [1896]
Die versunkene Glocke (Hauptmann) [1897]
Amphitryon (Kleist) [1897][1]

Friedrich Eckstein tells us in „*Alte unnennbare Tage!*" that Wolf spent an evening with Hugo von Hofmannsthal, during which he sang some of his own songs to the Austrian poet, and discussed ideas for opera libretti.

LETTERS

HW to his parents, Vienna, 23 November 1875

Ich hatte meinen alten guten Platz auf der IV. Gallerie. Schon die Ouverture war wundervoll u. erst die Oper [*Tannhäuser*] – ich finde keine Worte dazu – dieselbe zu beschreiben. Ich sag Ihnen nur, daß ich ein Narr bin. Nach jedem Akte wurde Wagner stürmisch hervorgerufen u. ich applaudirte so, daß mir die Hände wund wurden. Ich schrie nur immer Bravo Wagner, Bravissimo Wagner, u.z. so, daß ich fast heiser geworden bin u. die Leute mehr auf mich als auf Richard Wagner schauten.

I sat in my usual good seat in the uppermost gallery. The overture was wonderful, & as for the opera [*Tannhäuser*] – I have no words to describe it. I can only say that I am infatuated. There was wild applause at the end of each act when Wagner took a bow, & I applauded till my hands were sore. I kept screaming Bravo Wagner, Bravissimo Wagner until I was almost hoarse, & people looked at me more than Richard Wagner.

See **HW to Edmund Lang, Perchtoldsdorf, 22 February 1888**, p. 345.

---

1   Wolf wrote to Potpeschnigg (3 March 1897) that he regarded the play to be „eine geradezu idealische komische Oper" ('an almost ideal comic opera').

HW to Josef Strasser, Perchtoldsdorf, 15 April 1890

Ich bin jetzt wieder fleissig. Habe bereits 41 Spanische am Lager. 44 müssen's werden. Dann wird noch wie bisher in Liedern „gemacht" und dann ... ja dann ... ja dann will's gar hoch hinaus! Dann schreib' ich nur mehr Tetralogien.

Am now working hard again. 41 Spanish songs finished. The total must reach 44. That will then be the end of song composition. Then ... then ... then the sky will be the limit! Then I shall only write tetralogies.

See **HW to Gustav Schur, Unterach, 28 May 1890**, p. 465.

See **HW to Karl Heckel, Unterach, 28 June 1890**, p. 485.

HW to Joseph von Schey, Döbling, 18 August 1890

Ich befinde mich jetzt in sehr gedrückter Stimmung, da ich vom Schicksal ausersehen zu sein scheine <u>keine</u> Oper zu schreiben. Alle meine darauf bezüglichen Pläne haben Schiffbruch erlitten u. ich fange nachgerade an allen Muth zu verlieren.

I feel very depressed, because it seems that I have been singled out by Fate <u>not</u> to write an opera. All my plans to do this have failed & I'm beginning to lose all courage.

HW to Oskar Grohe, Vienna, 4 November 1890

Einstweilen bin ich beauftragt zu dem Ibsen'schen Stück „Das Fest auf Solhaug" eine Musik zu schreiben, bestehend aus Melodramen Liedern u. Chören u. z. für das Wr. Hofburgtheater. Wie gefall ich Ihnen als Hoftondichter u. Gelegenheitskomponist? Sehen Sie sich das Ibsen'sche Stück an; es ist in der Universalbibliothek erschienen u. dürfte Ihnen einen großen Eindruck machen. Ich hätte gar nicht übel Lust eine Oper daraus zu machen.

Meanwhile, I have been commissioned to write incidental music to Ibsen's play *The Feast at Solhaug*, consisting of melodrama, songs & choruses for Vienna's Burgtheater. How do you like me as Court composer and occasional composer? Read Ibsen's play, it has been published by Universal and should make a great impression on you. I wouldn't at all mind turning it into an opera.

See **HW to Oskar Grohe, Döbling, 18 December 1890**, p. 269.

HW to Emil Kauffmann, Unterach, 1 June 1891

Also ist die leidige u. wiederum brennend gewordene Frage um den Operntext zu Schanden gekommen! Dacht' ich mir's doch! Ich fange bereits an Operntexte als Fata morgana zu betrachten, als Dinge von realer Unmöglichkeit. „Wahn! Wahn! Überall Wahn!"[1] Ich will gar nichts mehr davon hören. Fast möchte ich glauben, daß ich am Ende meines Lebens angelangt bin. Unmöglich kann ich doch 30 Jahre hindurch noch Lieder od. Musiken zu Ibsen'schen Dramen schreiben. Und doch wird es nie zur heissersehnten Oper kommen. Ich bin eben am Ende. Möge es bald ein vollständiges sein – ich wünsche nichts sehnlicher.

So – once again the tiresome & urgent search for an opera text has come to nothing! I thought as much! I'm beginning to think of opera libretti as a fata morgana, something that can never be. 'Madness! Madness! Everywhere madness!' I'll hear no more of it. I almost believe I've reached the end of my life. There's no way that I can spend the next 30 years writing songs and incidental music to Ibsen's plays. And yet the fervently longed-for opera will never materialise. I've reached the end – may it come soon and completely. That is my most ardent wish.

See **HW to Emil Kauffmann, Traunkirchen, 12 October 1891**, p. 218.

HW to Oskar Grohe, Döbling, 9 January 1892

Ich besitze schon eine kleine Bibliothek der scheußlichsten, viehischesten, mörderischsten, trottelhaftesten, haarausreißendsten, leichenschänderischsten Operntexte.

I already own a small library of the most abominable, terrible, murderous, idiotic, frustrating, necrophilic opera libretti.

HW to Oskar Grohe, Döbling, 22 December 1892

In letzter Zeit bin ich glücklich einigen Fallen, die mir Librettisten von Profession stellen wollten, entgangen. [. . .] Die Grundidee ihres Denkens u. Dichtens ist immer der Cassaerfolg. [. . .] Zwei von diesem Gelichter [. . .] hab' ich mir nun glücklich vom Halse geschafft, nachdem ich ihnen rundweg erklärte, daß ich mit dem Operncomponiren ein für allemal nichts zu schaffen haben wolle. Und doch, fände sich endlich der Rechte! der Echte! Mit welchem Jubelrausch

---

[1] 'Wahn' translates as 'madness', 'delusion' – a frighteningly prescient noun in this connection. The phrase is sung by Hans Sachs in *Die Meistersinger von Nürnberg*, Act III.

würde ich in seine Arme stürzen und mich ihm vermählen, um das zu gebären, was nur ein Dichter zu zeugen vermag.

I have recently managed to avoid several traps that professional librettists have wished to set me. [...] Box-office success is all they think about. [...] I've managed to get rid of two of this rabble by roundly declaring that I've finished with composing operas and will have nothing further to do with it. And yet, if only the right librettist would appear, the authentic one! With what rapture would I throw myself into his arms and wed myself to him and give birth to something that only a poet can engender.

See **HW to Emil Kauffmann, Vienna, 7 March 1894**, p. 28.

HW to Oskar Grohe, Vienna, 18 January 1895

Ein Wunder, ein unerhörtes Wunder ist geschehen. Der lang ersehnte Operntext hat sich endlich gefunden; Fix u. fertig liegt derselbe vor mir u. ich brenne nur so vor Begierde mich an die musikalische Ausführung zu machen. Sie kennen doch die Novelle „der Dreispitz" von Pedro de Alarcon. Dieselbe ist bei Reclam erschienen. Frau Rosa Mayreder, eine, mir seit Jahren bekannte, geniale Frau, hat das Kunststück fertig gebracht die Novelle in ein äußerst wirkungsvolles Opernbuch umzuwandeln. [...]

A miracle, an incredible miracle has occurred. The libretto, which I have long yearned for, has been found; there it lies in front of me, utterly ready, & I am now burning with desire to write the music. You know the Novelle *The Three-cornered Hat* by Pedro de Alarcón. It has been published by Reclam. Frau Rosa Mayreder, a brilliant woman whom I have known for many years, has done the trick and turned the Novelle into a highly effective libretto. [...]

See **HW to Melanie Köchert, Vienna, 8 June 1897**, p. 486.

See **HW to Melanie Köchert, Vienna, 31 July 1897**, p. 270.

See **HW to Adrienne Wolf, Vienna, 18 September 1897**, p. 513.

HW to Heinrich Potpeschnigg, Vienna, 6 December 1897

Nach meiner Freilassung[1] (vermutlich am 15. d. M.) übersiedle ich sofort nach Luzern, wo ich meine ständiges Quartier aufschlagen werde. Von dort aus will ich mich umsehen, um ein Opernpersonal samt Orchester zusammenzutrommeln, das unter meiner Fahne alle Staaten (ausgenommen Österreich) bereisen soll, und zwar zum Behufe von Opernvorstellungen und Konzerten, wobei natürlich nur meine Werke, die Opern: Corregidor, Venegas und Penthesilea, Fest auf Solhaug, Prinz von Homburg etc. aufgeführt werden. [...] Gegenwärtig arbeite ich an der Instrumentation von zehn Liedern aus dem spanischen Liederbuch, die größtenteils zu Beginn des ersten Aktes Venegas vorkommen.

After my release (presumably on the 15th of this month), I shall move at once to Lucerne, where I shall set up my permanent headquarters. From there I shall set about drumming up an opera company, with orchestra, that shall under my banner tour every country (except Austria), giving concerts and operatic performances, devoted exclusively to my works: the operas *Corregidor*, *Venegas* and *Penthesilea*, *Das Fest auf Solhaug*, *Prinz von Homburg*, etc. [...] I am at present orchestrating ten songs from the *Spanisches Liederbuch*, which mostly occur at the beginning of the first act of *Venegas*.

See also p. 495, under Marie Lang.

---

1   Wolf was released from Dr Svetlin's asylum on 24 January 1898. After a period of convalescence, which included a journey through Istria with Melanie Köchert, he was admitted on 4 October 1898 to the Niederösterreichische Landesirrenanstalt, where he remained for the rest of his life.

APPENDIX 5

SKETCHES AND FRAGMENTS

Stephen Spender, in an essay titled 'The Making of a Poem' (first published in *Partisan Review* in the summer of 1946), describes two different ways of creating a poem:

> Some poets write immediately works which, when they are written, scarcely need revision. Others write their poems by stages, feeling their way from rough draft to rough draft, until finally, after many revisions, they have produced a result which may seem to have very little connection with their early sketches.
>
> These two opposite processes are vividly illustrated in two examples drawn from music: Mozart and Beethoven. Mozart thought out symphonies, quartets, even scenes from operas, entirely in his head – often on a journey or perhaps while dealing with pressing problems – and then he transcribed them, in their completeness, onto paper. Beethoven wrote fragments of themes in note books which he kept beside him, working on and developing them over years. Often his first ideas were of a clumsiness which makes scholars marvel how he could, at the end, have developed from them such miraculous results.

Although one might cavil at some of the detail in the above paragraph, the generalisation holds good: geniuses work in different ways to achieve their ends. Until fairly recently, it was generally felt that Wolf's Lieder were composed almost spontaneously in bouts of feverish inspiration, and his own letters to friends have lent credence to that view – see HW to Edmund Lang on 22 February 1888 (p. 345) and 24 February 1888 (p. 347), and to Josef Strasser on 23 March 1888 (p. 351). The truth is rather different, and thanks to scholars such as Margret Jestremski (*Hugo Wolf. Skizzen und Fragmente*), we now know that Wolf often struggled to find the final form of his Lieder.

Most of these sketches and fragments are housed in two famous Viennese libraries: the Österreichische Nationalbibliothek (ÖNB) and the Wiener Stadt- und Landesbibliothek (WStB). The following list contains all the known sketches and fragments (some brief, some highly developed) that eventually led to the definitive version of a song.

Anon.
Der Morgentau (ÖNB)

Eichendorff
Aufblick (WStB)
Das Ständchen (ÖNB)
Der Freund (ÖNB)
Der Glücksritter (ÖNB)
Der Schreckenberger (ÖNB)
Der Soldat I (ÖNB)
Der Soldat II (ÖNB)
Die Kleine (ÖNB)
Die Zigeunerin (ÖNB)
Heimweh (ÖNB)
In der Fremde II (ÖNB)
Nachtzauber (ÖNB)
Seemanns Abschied (ÖNB)
Unfall (ÖNB)
Waldmädchen (ÖNB)

Goethe
Anakreons Grab (ÖNB)
Beherzigung ('Ach, was soll der Mensch verlangen?') (ÖNB)
Beherzigung ('Feiger Gedanken') (ÖNB)
Blumengruß (ÖNB)
Cophtisches Lied II (ÖNB)
Der Sänger (ÖNB)
Die Spröde (ÖNB)
Epiphanias (ÖNB)
Gutmann und Gutweib (ÖNB)
Harfenspieler II (ÖNB)
Harfenspieler III (ÖNB)
Mignon (ÖNB)
Philine (ÖNB)
Prometheus (ÖNB)
Prometheus (orchestral version) (ÖNB)
Ritter Kurts Brautfahrt (ÖNB)
Spottlied aus *Wilhelm Meister* (ÖNB)
Wanderers Nachtlied (ÖNB)

Heine
Mir träumte von einem Königskind (WStB)
Wo wird einst (ÖNB)

SKETCHES AND FRAGMENTS

Hoefer
Fröhliche Fahrt (WStB)

Italienisches Liederbuch
Hoffärtig seid Ihr (ÖNB)
Nein, junger Herr (ÖNB)

Lenau
Frühlingsgrüße (WStB)
Nächtliche Wanderung (ÖNB)

Matthisson
Andenken (ÖNB)

Mörike
Agnes (ÖNB)
An eine Äolsharfe (ÖNB)
Auf eine Christblume I (ÖNB)
Auf eine Christblume I (orchestral version) (WStB)
Der Feuerreiter (ÖNB)
Der Knabe und das Immlein (ÖNB)
Die Geister am Mummelsee (ÖNB)
Elfenlied (ÖNB)
Karwoche (ÖNB)
Karwoche (orchestral version) (WStB)
Lebe wohl (ÖNB)
Lied eines Verliebten (ÖNB)
Mausfallen-Sprüchlein (ÖNB)
Nixe Binsefuß (ÖNB)
Peregrina II (ÖNB)
Schlafendes Jesuskind (ÖNB)
Selbstgeständnis (ÖNB)
Suschens Vogel (WStB)
Verborgenheit (ÖNB)
Verschwiegene Liebe (ÖNB)
Wo find' ich Trost? (ÖNB)
Zitronenfalter im April (ÖNB)

Platen
Christnacht (ÖNB)

Reinick
Dem Vaterland (ÖNB)
Frohe Botschaft (ÖNB)
Frühlingsglocken (ÖNB)
Gesellenlied (ÖNB)
Wiegenlied im Sommer (ÖNB)
Wiegenlied im Winter (ÖNB)
Wohin mit der Freud'? (ÖNB)

Scheffel
Biterolf (ÖNB)
Wächterlied auf der Wartburg (ÖNB)
Wächterlied auf der Wartburg (orchestral version) (ÖNB)

Spanisches Liederbuch
Ach, des Knaben Augen (WStB)
Die ihr schwebet (ÖNB)
Geh, Geliebter, geh jetzt! (WStB)
Geh, Geliebter, geh jetzt! (orchestral version) (ÖNB)
Ich fuhr über Meer (ÖNB)
Klinge, klinge, mein Pandero (WStB)
Mühvoll komm ich und beladen (WStB)
Sagt, seid Ihr es (WStB)
Wer sein holdes Lieb verloren (ÖNB)
Wunden trägst du, mein Geliebter (WStB)

The titles of other sketches and fragments, which did not lead to a successfully completed song, are listed under each poet ('Wanderlied', for example, under Goethe, and 'Der Raubschütz' under Lenau).

There are some sketches and fragments of settings of poems by poets who do not feature in this book:

Friedrich Halm
Das taube Mütterlein (Prokrajinski Archive, Maribor)

Ludwig Hölty
Mailied (WStB)
Trinklied im Mai (WStB)

Friedrich von Sallet
Der Morgen (Prokrajinski Archive, Maribor)

Friedrich Steinebach
Das Lied der Waise (WStB)

BIBLIOGRAPHY

Auden, W. H., *The Dyer's Hand* (Faber and Faber, 1962)
Baechtold, Jakob (ed.), *Briefwechsel zwischen Moritz von Schwind und Eduard Mörike* (Verlag des Litterarischen Jahresberichts, 1890)
—, *Gottfried Kellers Leben. Seine Briefe und Tagebücher*, 3 vols (Berlin, 1894–7)
Batka, Richard and Heinrich Werner (eds), *Hugo Wolfs Musikalische Kritiken* (Breitkopf & Härtel, 1911)
Bettelheim-Gabillon, Helene, *Im Zeichen des alten Burgtheaters* (Wiener Literarische Anstalt, Vienna, 1921)
Böhm, Hans, *Heinrich Heine. Gedichte 1812–1827. Kommentar* (Akademie-Verlag, Berlin, 1982)
Browne, Lewis, *That Man Heine* (Literary Guild of America, 1927)
Byrne, Lorraine, *Schubert's Goethe Settings* (Ashgate, 2003)
Canisius, Claus, *Goethe und die Musik* (Piper Verlag, 1998)
Carner, Mosco, *Hugo Wolf Songs* (BBC Music Guides, 1982)
Cervantes, Miguel de, *The Complete Exemplary Novels*, edited by Barry Ife and Jonathan Thacker (Aris and Phillips, 2013)
Challier, Ernst, *Großer Lieder-Katalog* (Ernst Challier's Selbstverlag, Berlin, 1885)
Davies, Gareth A., *Variations on Spanish Themes* (Leeds Philosophical and Literary Society, 1982)
Decsey, Ernst, *Hugo Wolf*, 4 vols (Schuster & Loeffler, 1903–6)
Deutsch, Helmut, *Gesang auf Händen tragen* (Henschel, 2019), translated by Richard Stokes as *Memoirs of an Accompanist* (Kahn & Averill, 2020)
Eckstein, Friedrich, *„Alte unnennbare Tage!"* (Herbert Reichner Verlag, 1936)
Elster, Ernst, *Heines Werke*, 7 vols (Leipzig, 1887–90)
Embden-Heine, Maria, *Erinnerungen an H. Heine* (Hamburg, 1881)
Fischer-Dieskau, Dietrich, *Töne sprechen, Worte klingen* (Deutsche Verlags-Anstalt/Piper, 1985)
—, *Der Nacht ins Ohr* (Carl Hanser Verlag, 1998)
—, *Hugo Wolf. Leben und Werk* (Henschel Verlag, 2003)
Friedlaender, Max, *Brahms' Lieder* (Berlin–Leipzig, 1922)
Glauert, Amanda, *Hugo Wolf and the Wagnerian Inheritance* (Cambridge University Press, 2009)
Goes, Albrecht, *Mit Mörike und Mozart* (S. Fischer Verlag, 1988)

Gooch, Bryan N. S., and David Thatcher (eds), *Musical Settings of British Romantic Literature* (Garland Publishing, 1982)
—, *A Shakespeare Music Catalogue* (OUP, 1991)
Grappin, Pierre, *Heine. Buch der Lieder* (Hoffmann und Campe, 1975)
Grasberger, Franz (ed.), *Briefe an Melanie Köchert* (Hans Schneider, 1964)
Haberlandt, Michael, *Hugo Wolf* (Darmstadt, 1911)
Hebbel, Friedrich, *Weltgericht mit Pausen*, selected and introduced by Alfred Brendel (Hanser, 2008)
Hellmer, Edmund, *Hugo Wolf. Erlebtes und Erlauschtes* (Wiener Literarische Anstalt, 1921)
Heyse, Paul, *Italienisches Liederbuch* (Wilhelm Hertz, 1860)
Hilmar, Ernst, *Hugo Wolf Enzyklopädie* (Hans Schneider, 2007)
Hirth, Friedrich (ed.), *Heinrich Heines Briefwechsel*, 3 vols (Georg Müller and Propyläen-Verlag, 1914–20)
Hofmannsthal, Hugo von, 'Goethe's Opern und Singspiele' (Verlag Ullstein, n.d.)
Höll, Hartmut, *WortMusik* (Staccato Verlag, 2012)
Honolka, Kurt, *Hugo Wolf. Sein Leben, sein Werk, seine Zeit* (Knaur, 1990)
Jancik, Hans (ed.), *Kleine Chöre* (Musikwissenschaftlicher Verlag, Wien, 1980)
—, *Nachgelassene Lieder I* (Musikwissenschaftlicher Verlag, Wien, 1980)
—, *Nachgelassene Lieder II* (Musikwissenschaftlicher Verlag, Wien, 1969)
—, *Nachgelassene Lieder III* (Musikwissenschaftlicher Verlag, Wien, 1976)
—, *Lieder nach verschiedenen Dichtern* (Musikwissenschaftlicher Verlag, Wien, 2010)
Jestremski, Margret, *Skizzen und Fragmente* (Georg Olms Verlag, 2002)
—, *Hugo Wolf Werkverzeichnis* (Bärenreiter, 2011)
Johnson, Graham, 'The Italian Song Book of Hugo Wolf' (Hyperion Records, 1994)
—, 'Goethe Lieder' (Hyperion Records, 2000)
—, *Franz Schubert: The Complete Songs* (Yale University Press, 2014)
Kalbeck, Max, *Johannes Brahms*, 4 vols (Hans Schneider, 1976)
Kerner, Theobald, *Das Kernerhaus und seine Gäste* (Wilhelm Röck Verlag, 1894)
Klinckerfuß, Margarethe, *Aufklänge aus versunkener Zeit* (Port-Verlag, 1947)
Kneisel, Jessie Hoskam, *Mörike and Music* (D.Phil thesis, Columbia University, 1949)
Kravitt, Edward F., *The Lied: Mirror of Late Romanticism* (Yale University Press, 1996)
Krek, Gojmir, 'Hugo Wolf in Slovenci', *Novi Akordi*, IX, 1910
Kuh, Emil, *Friedrich Hebbel*, 2 vols (Vienna, 1877)
Liedtke, Christian, *Heinrich Heine: Ein ABC* (Hoffmann und Campe, 2015)

Loges, Natasha, *Brahms and his Poets* (The Boydell Press, 2017)
Luke, David (ed.), *Eduard Mörike: Mozart's Journey to Prague* (Libris, 1997)
McFarlane, James Walter, and Graham Orton (trans. and eds), *The Oxford Ibsen*, vol. 1 (OUP, 1970)
Mahler, Alma, *Erinnerungen an Gustav Mahler* (Ullstein, 1971; Vienna, 1980)
Mare, Margaret, *Eduard Mörike: The Man and the Poet* (Methuen, 1957)
Mayreder, Rosa, *Erinnerungen an Hugo Wolf* (Rikola Verlag, 1921)
—, *Mein Pantheon* (Verlag am Goetheanum, 1988)
Meyer, Herbert (ed.), *Eduard Mörike. Zeichnungen* (Carl Hanser Verlag, 1952)
Mitchell, Donald, *Gustav Mahler: The Wunderhorn Years* (Faber and Faber, 1975)
Müller, Paul, 'Erinnerungen an Hugo Wolf', *Die Musik* (Berlin, 1903)
Muschg, Adolf, *Gottfried Keller* (Kindler Verlag, 1977)
Newman, Ernest, *Hugo Wolf* (Methuen, 1907)
Ochs, Siegfried, 'Persönliche Erinnerungen', *Allgemeine deutsche Musikzeitung* (1903)
Ormsby, Eric, *Johann Wolfgang von Goethe. West-Eastern Divan* (Gingko, 2019)
Prawer, S. S., *Mörike und seine Leser* (Ernst Klett, Stuttgart, 1960)
Prochnik, George, *Heinrich Heine. Writing the Revolution* (Yale University Press, 2020)
Quarrie, Paul (ed.), *Poems from Greek Antiquity* (Alfred A. Knopf, 2020)
Rose, William, *The Early Love Poetry of Heinrich Heine* (Oxford University Press, 1962)
Sammons, Jeffrey L., *Heinrich Heine: A Modern Biography* (Princeton University Press, 1979)
Sams, Eric, *The Songs of Hugo Wolf*, 2nd edn, rev. and enlarged (Eulenburg Books, 1983)
Schiwy, Günther, *Eichendorff. Eine Biographie* (C. H. Beck, 2000)
Schur, Gustav, *Erinnerungen an Hugo Wolf* (Gustav Bosse Verlag, 1922)
Sleeman, Margaret G., *Variations on Spanish Themes* (Leeds Philosophical and Literary Society, 1982)
Snyder, Lawrence D., *German Poetry in Song: An Index of Lieder* (Fallen Leaf Press, 1995)
Spitzer, Leopold (ed.), *Gedichte von Joseph v. Eichendorff* (Musikwissenschaftlicher Verlag, Wien, 1993)
—, *Spanisches Liederbuch* (Musikwissenschaftlicher Verlag, Wien, 1994)
—, *Gedichte von J. W. v. Goethe* (Musikwissenschaftlicher Verlag, Wien, 1996)
—, *Italienisches Liederbuch* (Musikwissenschaftlicher Verlag, Wien, 1997)
—, *Nachgelassene Lieder IV* (Musikwissenschaftlicher Verlag, Wien, 1998)
—, *Hugo Wolf Briefe*, 4 vols (Musikwissenschaftlicher Verlag, Wien, 2010)

—, *Hugo Wolf – Werk und Leben* (Musikwissenschaftlicher Verlag, Wien, 2017)
Staiger, Emil, *Musik und Dichtung* (Atlantis Musikbuch-Verlag, 1947)
Sternfield, Richard, „Zum Gedächtnis eines Meisters des deutschen Liedes", *Deutsche Revue* (July–September 1903)
Thomas, Lionel (ed.), *Eduard Mörike. Poems* (Basil Blackwell, Oxford, 1970)
Unterberger, Rose, *Die Goethe Chronik* (Insel Verlag, 2002)
Vignoles, Roger, *Hugo Wolf. Mörike-Lieder* (Hyperion Records, 2001)
—, *Hugo Wolf. Lieder nach Heine und Lenau* (Hyperion Records, 2002)
Walker, Frank, *Hugo Wolf: A Biography* (Dent, 1951; 2nd edn, 1968)
Walwei-Wiegelmann, Hedwig (ed.), *Goethes Gedanken über Musik* (Insel Verlag, 1985)
Werba, Erik, *Hugo Wolf und seine Lieder* (Österreichischer Bundesverlag, 1984)
Werner, Heinrich, *Hugo Wolf in Maierling: Eine Idylle* (Breitkopf & Härtel, 1913)
—, *Hugo Wolf in Perchtoldsdorf* (Gustav Bosse Verlag, 1925)
—, *Hugo Wolf und der Wiener akademische Wagner-Verein* (Gustav Bosse Verlag, 1926)
Werner, Michael (ed.), *Begegnungen mit Heine. Berichte der Zeitgenossen* (Hoffmann und Campe, 1973)
Wiese, Benno von, *Eduard Mörike* (Rainer Wunderlich Verlag, 1950)
Youens, Susan, *Hugo Wolf: The Vocal Music* (Princeton University Press, 1992)
—, *Hugo Wolf and his Mörike Songs* (Cambridge University Press, 2000)
—, *Heinrich Heine and the Lied* (Cambridge University Press, 2007)
—, '"The problem of solitude" and critique in song: Schubert's loneliness', in Lorraine Byrne Bodley and Julian Horton (eds), *Schubert's Late Music: History, Theory, Style* (Cambridge University Press, 2016), pp. 309–30
Zangger, Fritz, *Das ewige Feuer im fernen Land. Ein deutsches Heimatbuch aus dem Südosten* (Celje, 1937)

Index of Titles and First Lines

References to the texts of the songs and main entries are indicated in **bold** type. HWW numbers are shown for song titles but not for first lines, except when they are the same.

6 *Alte Weisen* xxxii, xxxiii, xxxviii, xlv, 276–89, 489, 506, 509
10 Variations on an Original Theme 117–18

Abendbilder (HWW 43) xvii, xlvii, 298, **309**
Abendglöcklein (HWW 23) xlvi, 473, **474**
Abschied (HWW 119/53) l, 330, 340, 367, **417**
Ach, des Knaben Augen (HWW 129/6) liii, 53, 56, 67n, **70**
Ach du klarblauer Himmel **439**
Ach im Maien war's, im Maien (HWW 129/30) liii, 53, 57, **93**
Ach neige **127**
Ach, was soll der Mensch verlangen? **148**
Ach! wer bringt die schönen Tage **125**
Ach, wie lang die Seele schlummert! (HWW 129/8) liii, 52, **72**
Ade, mein Schatz, du mocht'st mich nicht **48**
Agnes (HWW 119/14) l, 331, **380**, 380n, 543
Alle gingen, Herz, zur Ruh (HWW 129/31) lii, 52, 58, **94**, 469, 521
Alles endet, was entstehet (HWW 162/2) lvii, 320, 322, **328**
Alles wiegt die stille Nacht **297**
Als ein unergründlich Wonnemeer **308**
Als ich auf dem Euphrat schiffte (HWW 120/41) lii, 108, 116, 120–21, 163, **164**
Als ich noch ein Knabe war **152**
Am frischgeschnittnen Wanderstab **375**
Am Kreuzweg, da lausche ich, wenn die Stern' **41**
Amour modeste, *see* Bescheidene Liebe
An dem reinsten Frühlingsmorgen **154**
An den Schlaf (HWW 119/29) l, 331, 353, **393**
   orchestration (HWW 140) liv, 331, 355, 532
An die Geliebte (HWW 119/32) xvii, li, 331, 353n, **396**
An die Türen will ich schleichen **131**
An die Wolke (fragment) **298**
An eine Äolsharfe (HWW 119/11) xvii, l, 331, 372n, **376**, 376n, 543
An Himmels Höh'n **315**
An* (HWW 46) xlvii, 3, 4, 190, 298, 300, 301, 302, **313**, 473–4
Anakreons Grab (HWW 120/29) li, 107, 130n, **156**, 336, 466, 479, 502, 542
   orchestration (HWW 131) xlvi liii, 107, 532, 533n
   orchestration (second version) (HWW 154) lv, 107, 532, 533n
Andenken (HWW 45) xlvii, 4, 316, **318**, 543
Anders wird die Welt mit jedem Schritt **400**

Angelehnt an die Epheuwand 377
Auch kleine Dinge können uns entzücken (HWW 159/1) xviii, lv, 208, 214, 215, **232**
Auf dem grünen Balkon (HWW 129/15) liii, 52, 57, **78**
Auf dem See (HWW 7) xlvi, 107, 116, **124**, 471
Auf der Wanderschaft (HWW 59) xlvii, 13, **15**, 376n
Auf der Wanderung (HWW 73) xlvii, 261, 262, **264**, 376n
Auf die Dächer zwischen blassen 39
Auf ein altes Bild (HWW 119/23) l, 331, 344, 352, **389**
    orchestration (HWW 124) lii, 331, 502, 532
Auf eine Christblume I (HWW 119/20) li, 331, 344, 353n, **386**, 390n, 543
    orchestration (HWW 143) liv, 331, 532, 543
Auf eine Christblume II (HWW 119/21) l, 331, **388**
Auf einer Wanderung (HWW 119/15) xvi, xvii, xviii, xxxviii, l, 120–21, 330, 349n, 376n, **381**
Auf ihrem Leibrößlein 383
Aufblick (HWW 98/1) xlviii, 16, 22, **31**, 542
Auf's Wohlsein meiner Dame 43
Auftrag (HWW 119/50) xlix, 330, 340, 348n, **415**
Aus meinen großen Schmerzen (HWW 69/4) xlvii, 181, 188, 189, 190-91, **198**, 198n, 482

Bald ist der Nacht 445
Ballade. Gesang Margits (HWW 150/1) liv, 266, **272**
Bedecke deinen Himmel, Zeus 169
Bedeckt mich mit Blumen (HWW 129/36) lii, 52, 58, 64n, **97**
Begegnung (HWW 119/8) xvii, l, 141n, 330, **374**
Beherzigung (Goethe) (HWW 114/4) xlix, 107, **128**, 129n, 542
Beherzigung (*Goethe-Lieder*) (HWW 120/18) li, 108, **148**, 542
Bei dem angenehmsten Wetter 46
Bei dem Glanz der Abendröte 154
Bei einer Trauung (HWW 119/51) xlix, 330, **416**
Bei Nacht im Dorf der Wächter rief 382
Benedeit die sel'ge Mutter (HWW 159/35) xxvi, lvi, 209, 237n, **252**
Bergkönig ritt in die Lande weit 272
Bescheidene Liebe (HWW 53) xlvii, 3, **5**
Bin ein Feuer hell, das lodert 50
Bin jung gewesen 404
Bin mit dir im Wald gegangen 310
Biterolf (HWW 114/3) xxxii, xlix, 129n, 457, 458, **462**
Bitt' ihn, o Mutter (HWW 129/26) liii, 52, **89**
Blindes Schauen, dunkle Leuchte (HWW 129/19) liii, 52, **82**
Blumengruß (HWW 120/24) li, 108, **153**, 203n, 542
Bunte Schlangen zweigezüngt 468

Christnacht (HWW 121) xix, xxxii, xxxiii, lii, 282, 424, 425–7, **427**, 487, 502, 509, 543
Cophtisches Lied I (HWW 120/14) li, 108, 120–21, **145**, 479
Cophtisches Lied II (HWW 120/15) li, 108, 120–21, **146**, 479, 542

INDEX OF TITLES AND FIRST LINES

Da fahr' ich still im Wagen 33
Da nur Leid und Leidenschaft (HWW 129/42) liv, 53, **103**
Dank des Paria (HWW 120/30) li, 107, **157**, 158n
Das Beet, schon lockert **155**
Das Fest auf Solhaug xxi, xxxiii, 217n, **267–73**, 501, 505, 537
Das gelbe Laub erzittert (fragment) 181, 190
Das ist ein Brausen und Heulen (HWW 69/3) xlvii, 181, 188, 189, 190, **198**
Das Kind am Brunnen (HWW 62) xlvii, 174, 175, 176, **178**, 190
Das Köhlerweib ist trunken (HWW 137/5) liv, 276, 279, 280n, **288**
Das Lied der Waise (fragment) 3, 544
Das Ständchen (HWW 118/4) l, 17, 21, 34n, **39**, 371n, 542
Das taube Mütterlein (sketch) 205, 544
Das verlassene Mägdlein (HWW 119/7) xviii, l, 330, 352, **373**
Das Vöglein (HWW 101/2) xlvii, 4, 174, 176, **179**, 451
Das Wasser rauscht', das Wasser schwoll 124
Das zerbrochene Ringlein (lost) 16, 17–18, 22
Daß doch gemalt all deine Reize wären (HWW 159/9) lv, 207, 212, **236**
Dein Liebesfeuer **389**
Dein Wille, Herr, geschehe! xlvi, **32**
Deine Mutter, süßes Kind (HWW 129/41) xvii, liii, 53, 57, **102**
Dem Vaterland (HWW 135) liv, 430, 433–5, 460–61 **446**
 arrangement (HWW 136) liv, 430, 460–61, 509
Denk' es, o Seele! (HWW 119/39) l, 330, 349n, **402**
 orchestration (HWW 147) lv, 330, 532
Der Corregidor xx–xxi, xxxi, xxxiii, xxxiv, xxxvii, xxxviii, xlvi, 55, 56, 62n, 75–6n, 84n, 213, 228, 471, 477, 484, 485, 486, 488–9, 493, 495, 497–8, 499, 500, 503, 505, 507, 509, 516, 533, 534–5, 540
Der du von dem Himmel bist **129**
Der Feuerreiter (HWW 119/44) xxxviii, li, 214, 331, 353, 358, **407**, 543
 orchestration (HWW 151) xxxiii, xlvi, lv, 331, 501–2, 509, 527n, 532
Der Fischer (HWW 5) xlvi, 107, 116–18, **124**, 471
Der Freund (HWW 118/1) l, 17, 24, 26n, **37**, 371n, 502, 542
Der Frühhauch hat gefächelt **6**
Der Gärtner (HWW 119/17) xv, xviii, xlix, 141n, 330, 359, 360, 378n, **383**, 502
Der Genesene an die Hoffnung (HWW 119/1) xlix, 330, 367, **368**, 368n
Der Glücksritter (HWW 118/10) l, 16, 27, **43**, 542
Der goldene Morgen (HWW 25) xlvi, 3, **5**, 473
Der Jäger (HWW 119/40) xvii, xlix, 330, 348, 354–5, 380n, **403**, 502
Der Kehraus (lost) 16, 22
Der Knabe und das Immlein (HWW 119/2) xvii, xlix, 154–5n, 330, 342, 346, 348n, 361, **368**, 370n, 543
Der König bei der Krönung (HWW 114/2) xxxii, xlix, 129n, 158n, 330, 342, **367**, 367n
Der kriegslustige Waffenschmied (fragment) 298
Der Mond hat eine schwere Klag' erhoben (HWW 159/7) liv, 207, 213, 216, 217n, **235**
Der Morgen (fragment) 544
Der Musikant (HWW 118/2) l, 16, 24, 29, **38**, 228n

Der neue Amadis (HWW 120/23) lii, 109, **152**
Der Rattenfänger (HWW 120/11) li, 107, 120–21, **141**, 502, 532
  orchestration (HWW 126) liii, 107, 502
Der Raubschütz (fragment) 298
Der Sänger (HWW 120/10) li, 108, **139**, 542
Der Schäfer (HWW 120/22) li, 107, 110, **151**
Der Scholar (HWW 118/13) l, 17, 27, 29, **46**
Der Schreckenberger (HWW 118/9) l, 16, 27, **43**, 542
Der Schwalben Heimkehr (HWW 55) xlvii, 205, **205**
Der schwere Abend (lost) 298
Der schwere Traum (fragment) 3
Der Soldat I (HWW 118/5) xvii, xlv, xlix, 16, 23, 24, 27, **40**, 542
Der Soldat II (HWW 118/6) xxxii, xlv, xlix, 16, 23, **41**, 542
Der Spiegel dieser treuen, braunen Augen 397
Der Strauß, den ich gepflücket **153**
Der Tambour (HWW 119/5) xxxii, xlv, xlix, 330, 342, **371**, 371n, 502
Der traurige Jäger (lost) 16, 22
Der verzweifelte Liebhaber (HWW 118/14) l, 17, **46**
Dereinst, dereinst, Gedanke mein (HWW 129/32) liii, 53, 58, **94**
Derweil ich schlafend lag **370**
Des fahrenden Schülers Lieben und Leiden 262, 263
Des Glöckleins Schall **474**
Des Schäfers sein Haus und das steht auf zwei Rad **413**
Des Wassermanns sein Töchterlein **409**
Dichterleben 262, 263
Die Bekehrte (HWW 120/27) lii, 109, **154**, 370n
Die du Gott gebarst, du Reine (HWW 129/2) lii, 52, **66**
Die Flucht (fragment) 181
Die Geister am Mummelsee (HWW 119/47) l, 175, 331, **411**, 543
Die heiligen drei König' mit ihrem Stern **149**
Die ihr schwebet (HWW 129/4) lii, 52 57, 61, **68**
Die Kleine (HWW 115) xlix, 16, 24, **36**, 542
Die Nacht (HWW 89) xlv, xlviii, 16, 22, 24, 29, 29n, 37, **50**
Die Nacht ist finster, schwül und bang **311**
Die Nachtigallen schweigen (fragment) 261
Die schöne Nacht (lost) 118n, 303n
Die Schwalbe, die den Sommer bringt **467**
Die Spinnerin (HWW 101/3) xvii, xlvii, 4, 176, 205, 450, 451, 452, **455**
Die Spröde (HWW 120/26) lii, 107, 109, **154**, 155n, 203n, 370n, 542
Die Spröde (fragment) 107
Die Stimme des Kindes (HWW 20) xlvi, 205, 298, 303, **307**
Die Tochter der Heide (HWW 109) xxxi, xlix, 330, 342, **366**
Die Verlassene (fragment) 3
Die Zigeunerin (HWW 118/7) xviii, xlix, 16, 24, 28, **41**, 521, 542
Dies zu deuten, bin erbötig! (HWW 120/42) lii, 108, 120, **165**
Dichterliebe (proposed song-cycle) xxxviii

Dir angetrauet am Altare 367
Drei Gedichte von Michelangelo xxxiv, xlvi
Drei Gedichte von Robert Reinick 430, 434, 436, **444–5**
Drei Tage Regen fort und fort **403**
Du bist Orplid, mein Land! **410**
Du bist wie eine Blume (HWW 39) xlvii, 181, 188, **196**, 205
Du denkst mit einem Fädchen mich zu fangen (HWW 159/10) xxvi, lv, 207, 219n, **237**
Du giebst mir Licht! (planned but uncomposed) 322
Du liebe, treue Laute **29**
Du liebes Auge, willst dich tauchen **449**
Du milchjunger Knabe (HWW 137/3) liv, 276, 278–9, 285, **287**, 521
Du sagst mir, daß ich keine Fürstin sei (HWW 159/28) lvi, 208, **247**
Dunkel sind nun alle Gassen **265**
Durch Liebestreue glaubt (planned but uncomposed) 322

Eichendorff-Lieder xviii, xxxii, xxxiv, xxxviii, xlviii, xlix, l, **16–51**, 58, 228n, 281n, 371n, 504, 509, 529n
Eide, so die Liebe schwur (HWW 129/20) liii, 53, 59, **83**
Ein Blumenglöckchen **153**
Ein Grab (HWW 37) xlvii, 419, **421**
Ein schlafend Kind! o still! in diesen Zügen **307**
Ein Ständchen Euch zu bringen kam ich her (HWW 159/22) lv, 34n, 208, **244**
Ein Stündlein wohl vor Tag (HWW 119/3) xlix, 155n, 330, 347, 348n, **370**, 370n
Ein Tännlein grünet wo **402**
Eine Liebe kenn' ich, die ist treu **395**
Einkehr (HWW 98/2) xlviii, 16, 22, **31**
Einmal nach einer lustigen Nacht **414**
Elfenlied (*Mörike-Lieder*) (HWW 119/16) xlix, 330, 358n, **382**, 382n, 543
Elfenlied (Shakespeare) (HWW 148) xix, xxxii, xxxiii, lii, 30, 358, 463, 464–6, **468**, 486, 498, 535n
  orchestration (HWW 148) xxxiii, lv, 463, 501, 527n
Epiphanias (HWW 120/19) li, 108, **149**, 490, 532, 542
Er ist's (HWW 119/6) l, 141n, 331, **372**, 390n
  orchestration (HWW 127) liii, 331, 532, 533n
Ergebung (HWW 98/5) xlviii, 16, 22, **32**
Erhebung (HWW 98/6) xlviii, 16, 22, **33**
Ernst ist der Frühling (HWW 82) xlviii, 181, 190, 191, **202**
Erschaffen und Beleben (HWW 120/33) li, 108, 116, **159**, 479
Erster Verlust (HWW 16) xlvi, 107, **125**, 473
Erstes Liebeslied eines Mädchens (HWW 119/42) l, 330, 349–50, **405**, 521
Erwartung (HWW 88) xliii, xlvi, 16, 22, 24, 29, 29n, 37, **49**
Es blasen die blauen Husaren (HWW 69/7) xlvii, 181, 188, 189–90, **200**
Es segeln die Wolken, weiß niemand wohin? **6**
Es war ein alter König (HWW 79) xlviii, 181, 190, 191, 191n, **201**
Es war ein fauler Schäfer **151**

Feiger Gedanken 128
Frage nicht (HWW 85) xlviii, 298, 302, **312**
Frage und Antwort (HWW 119/35) l, 331, **399**
Fragst du mich, woher die bange 399
Frau Amme, Frau Amme, das Kind ist erwacht! 178
Frech und froh I (HWW 120/16) li, 107, **147**
Frech und froh II (HWW 120/17) lii, 108, **148**
Friedlicher Abend senkt sich aufs Gefilde 309
Frohe Botschaft (HWW 138) liv, 430, 439, **447**
Fröhliche Fahrt (HWW 27) xlvi, 259, **259**, 543
Früh, wann die Hähne krähn 373
Frühling läßt sein blaues Band 372
Frühling Liebster (fragment) 450
Frühling übers Jahr (HWW 120/28) li, 108, **155**, 502
Frühlingsglocken (HWW 104/4) xlix, 430, **441**
Frühlingsgrüße (HWW 11) xlvi, 298, **306**, 543
Fühlt meine Seele (HWW 162/3) lvii, 320, 322, 342, **329**
Führ mich, Kind, nach Bethlehem! (HWW 129/5) liii, 52, 63, 64n, 67n, **70**
Fußreise (HWW 119/10) xv, l, 330, 350, 360, 363, **375**, 375n, 376n, 390n

Ganymed (HWW 120/50) li, 108, 116, 121, **171**, 172n
    orchestration (HWW 132) liii, 108, 532, 533n
Gebet (HWW 119/28) xvii, xviii, l, 130n, 330, 349n, **393**, 502
    orchestration (HWW 139) liv, 330, 355, 502, 532
Gedichte von Eduard Mörike ... 330, 354n, **367–418**
Gedichte von J. W. v. Goethe 116, **130–73**
Gedichte von Joseph v. Eichendorff **37–51**
Geh! gehorche meinen Winken 146
Geh, Geliebter, geh jetzt! (HWW 129/44) xviii, liii, 53, **105**, 532, 533n
Geistesgruß (HWW 22/2) xlvi, 107, 118n, **126**, 303n
Geistliche Lieder 22
Gelassen stieg die Nacht an's Land 385
Genialisch Treiben (HWW 120/21) lii, 109, **151**
Gesang Weylas (HWW 119/46) xvii, li, 331, 353n, **410**, 521
    orchestration (HWW 128) liii, 331, 532
Gesegnet sei das Grün und wer es trägt! (HWW 159/39) lvi, 209, **254**
Gesegnet sei, durch den die Welt entstund (HWW 159/4) liv, 207, 213, 216n, **233**
Geselle, woll'n wir uns in Kutten hüllen (HWW 159/14) lv, 208, **239**
Gesellenlied (HWW 160/1) xlix, 195, 430, 434, 435–6, **444**
Gleich und gleich (HWW 120/25) li, 107, **153**
Glücklich wer zum Liebchen zieht 259
Goethe-Lieder xvii, xviii, xxii, xxxii, xxxiii, xxxvii, li, lii, 21, 58, **107–73**, 281n, 367n, 478, 489, 505, 508, 509, 527, 529n
Golden lacht und glüht der Morgen 5
Gottvertrauen (HWW 33) xlvi, 259, 315, **315**
Grablied (HWW 32) xlvi, 314, **314**

INDEX OF TITLES AND FIRST LINES 555

Grausame Frühlingssonne **385**
Grenzen der Menschheit (HWW 120/51) li, 108, 116, **172**
Gretchen vor dem Andachtsbild der Mater Dolorosa (HWW 76) xxxviii, xlvii, 107, 119, **127**, 176
Großer Brahma! nun erkenn' ich 157
Grüß' euch aus Herzensgrund 49
Gudmunds erster Gesang (HWW 150/2) lv, 266, **272**
Gudmunds zweiter Gesang (HWW 150/3) liv, 266, **273**
Gutmann und Gutweib (HWW 120/13) li, 108, **143**, 542

Ha, ich bin der Herr der Welt! mich lieben **158**
Hans Adam war ein Erdenkloß **159**
Harfenspieler I (HWW 120/1) xvi, li, 107, 114–15, 120–21, **130**, 172n, 214, 479
    orchestration (HWW 144) liv, 107, 532
Harfenspieler II (HWW 120/2) xvi, li, 107, 114–15, 120–21, **131**, 172n, 214, 479, 542
    orchestration (HWW 145) liv, 107, 532
Harfenspieler III (HWW 120/3) xvi, li, 107, 114–15, 120–21, **131**, 172n, 214, 479, 542
    orchestration (HWW 146) liv, 107, 532
Hätt ich irgend wohl Bedenken (HWW 120/43) lii, 108, **165**, 502
Heb' auf dein blondes Haupt und schlafe nicht (HWW 159/18) lv, 208, **242**
Heimweh (*Eichendorff-Lieder*) (HWW 118/12) l, 17, 24, 25n, **45**, 542
Heimweh (*Mörike-Lieder*) (HWW 119/37) xvii, l, 331, **400**
Heine-Lieder 185, 190
Heiß mich nicht reden, heiß mich schweigen **133**
Herbst (HWW 86) xlviii, 298, 302, **313**
Herbstentschluß (HWW 84) xlviii, 298, 302, **311**
Herbstklage (HWW 87) xlviii, 298
Herr! schicke was du willt **393**
Herr, was trägt der Boden hier (HWW 129/9) liii, 52, **73**, 499, 521
Herz, verzage nicht geschwind (HWW 129/21) lii, 52, 56, **84**, 85n
    orchestration (*Der Corregidor*) 533, 534
Heut' Nacht erhob ich mich um Mitternacht (HWW 159/41) lvii, 34n, 209, 214, **255**
Hielt die allerschönste Herrin **447**
Hier lieg' ich auf dem Frühlingshügel **379**
Hoch auf dem alten Turme steht **126**
Hochbeglückt in deiner Liebe (HWW 120/40) lii, 108, 163, **164**
Hoffärtig seid Ihr, schönes Kind (HWW 159/13) lv, 208, **238**, 543
Horch, wie still es wird im dunkeln Hain **308**
Hörst Du nicht die Quellen gehen **42**

Ibsen-Lieder xlvi, liv, lv
Ich armer Teufel, Herr Baron **132**
Ich bin der wohlbekannte Sänger **141**
Ich bin meiner Mutter einzig Kind **416**
Ich bin wie and're Mädchen nicht **5**
Ich denke Dein **318**

Ich esse nun mein Brot nicht trocken mehr (HWW 159/24) lvi, 208, **245**
Ich fuhr über Meer (HWW 129/18) lii, 52, **81**
Ich fuhr wohl über Wasser **273**
Ich geh' durch die dunklen Gassen **35**
Ich ging bei Nacht einst über Land **47**
Ich hab' ein Liebchen lieb recht von Herzen **47**
Ich hab' in Penna einen Liebsten wohnen (HWW 159/46) lvii, 209, 214, 231, **258**
Ich hatt' ein Vöglein, ach wie fein! **364**
Ich ließ mir sagen und mir ward erzählt (HWW 159/26) lvi, 208, **246**
Ich sah den Lenz einmal **307**
Ich stand in dunkeln Träumen (HWW 69/2) xlvii, 181, 188, 189, 190, **197**
Ich wandelte sinnend allein auf der Halde **272**
Ihr jungen Leute, die ihr zieht ins Feld (HWW 159/16) lv, 189, 208, **241**
Ihr seid die Allerschönste weit und breit (HWW 159/3) liv, 207, 216n, **233**
Im Frühling (HWW 119/13) xvi, l, 202n, 331, 381n, **379**, 390n
Im Sommer (HWW 22/1) xlvi, 116, 274, **275**, 303, 303n
Im stillen Friedhof (HWW 28) xlvi, 205, 422, **423**, 519
Im Weinberg auf der Höhe **368**
Im Winterboden schläft, ein Blumenkeim **388**
In aller Früh, ach, lang vor Tag **406**
In dem Himmel ruht die Erde **441**
In dem Schatten meiner Locken (HWW 129/12) lii, 52, 56, 62, **75**, 521
    orchestration (*Der Corregidor*) 533, 534
In der Fremde I (HWW 99) xlviii, 16, 18, 22, 29, **33**, 33–4n
In der Fremde II (HWW 105) xlix, 16, 18, 23, **35**, 542
    (first setting; fragment) 16
In der Fremde VI (HWW 103) xlviii, 16, 18, 23, **34**
In der Frühe (HWW 119/24) xvii, l, 331, **390**
    orchestration (HWW 134) liv, 331, 502, 532
In ein freundliches Städtchen tret' ich ein **381**
In grüner Landschaft Sommerflor **389**
In poetischer Epistel **415**
Irdische und himmlische Liebe (destroyed) 322, 325
Ist auch schmuck nicht mein Rößlein **40**
Italienische Serenade für kleines Orchester xxxiii, 23, 222
Italienisches Liederbuch xv, xvii, xviii, xx, xxii, xxvi, xxxii, xxxiii, xxxiv, xxxvii, xxxviii, xlv, xlvi, lv, lvi, lvii, 3, 21, 38n, 58, 63n, 189, 190, **212–58**, 371n, 482, 489, 493, 499, 500, 509

Ja, die Schönst'! ich sagt' es offen (HWW 74) xxxviii, xlvii, 261, 262, **265**
Jägerlied (HWW 119/4) xlix, 330, 347, 348n, **370**

Kampfmüd und sonnverbrannt **462**
Kann auch ein Mensch des andern auf der Erde **394**
Karwoche (HWW 119/26) xvii, li, 243n, 331, 344, 353, **391**, 543
    orchestration (HWW 123) lii, 331, 355, 532, 543
„Kein Meister fällt vom Himmel!" **444**

INDEX OF TITLES AND FIRST LINES

Kein Schlaf noch kühlt das Auge mir **390**
Keine gleicht von allen Schönen (HWW 161/4) lvii, 8, 9, 10, **11**, 194n
Keine gleicht von allen Schönen, Zauberhafte, dir! **11**
Keller-Lieder liv, 61, 488
Kennst du das Land, wo die Zitronen blühn **137**, 342–3
Kleine Gäste, kleines Haus **365**
Klinge, klinge, mein Pandero (HWW 129/11) xvii, liii, 52, 57, **75**
Knabentod (HWW 64) xlvii, 174, 175, 177, **180**
Komm in die stille Nacht! **442**
Komm, Liebchen, komm! (HWW 120/44) lii, 108, 120–21, **166**
Komm, o Tod, von Nacht umgeben (HWW 129/34) liv, 53, 58, **96**
Komm, Trost der Welt, du stille Nacht! **31**
König Alboin (sketch) 419, 420
Königlich Gebet (HWW 120/31) li, 108, **158**

Laß, o Welt, o laß mich sein! **378**
Laß sie nur gehn, die so die Stolze spielt (HWW 159/30) lvi, 208, **248**
Lasset Gelehrte sich zanken und streiten **145**
Laut und traut (fragment) 430, 439
Lebe wohl (HWW 119/36) l, 331, **399**, 543
Letzte Bitte (HWW 98/4) xlviii, 16, 22, **32**
Lichtlein schwimmen auf dem Strome **150**
Liebchen, wo bist du? (HWW 104/2) xlix, 430, **440**
Liebe mir im Busen zündet (HWW 129/27) liii, 53, **90**
Lieber alles (HWW 118/11) l, 17, **44**
Liebesbotschaft (HWW 104/6) xlix, 430, **443**
Liebesfrühling (Hoffmann von Fallersleben) (HWW 72) xxxviii, xlvii, 261, 262, **263**
Liebesfrühling (Lenau) (HWW 15) xlvi, 298, 301, **307**
Liebesglück (HWW 118/16) l, 17, 29, **47**
Liebesqual verschmäht mein Herz **148**
Lied des transferierten Zettel (HWW 161/2) xvii, xviii, lii, 194, 434, 463, 464–5, **467**, 535n
Lied eines Verliebten (HWW 119/43) l, 330, **406**, 543
Lied vom Winde (HWW 119/38) xlix, 141n, 330, 342, 380n, **401**
Lieder aus der Jugendzeit 190
LIEDER und GESÆNGE. 1stes Heft. In Musik gesetzt von HUGO WOLF 4, 296, 301, 318, 419
Lieder und Gesänge von N. Lenau und J. Eichendorff. Fräulein V . . . F . . . geweiht, von Hugo Wolf 22, 302, 313n, 483
Liederstrauß (Heine settings) xxx, xxxi, 188, 189, 192n, **197–200**
Locken, haltet mich gefangen (HWW 120/47) lii, 108, **168**

Mädchen mit dem roten Mündchen (HWW 38) xlvii, 181, 188, **195**, 205
Mai (fragment) 107, 473, 544
Mailied (HWW 22/3) xlvi, 107 118n, **126**, 303n
Man sagt mir, deine Mutter woll' es nicht (HWW 159/21) lv, 208, **243**
Manch Bild vergessener Zeiten (fragment) 181, 190

Manuel Venegas xxi, xxxiii, xxxiv, lvii, 56, 63n, 64, 79n, 80n, 267, 270, 484, 486, 488–9, 495, 500, 501, 506, 507, 533, 535, 540
Mausfallen-Sprüchlein (HWW 101/6) xxxi, xlv, xlviii, 203n, 330, 340, 342, 345, **365**, 451, 483, 543
Meeresstille (HWW 14) xlvi, 117–18, 298, **306**, 473
Mein Liebchen, wir saßen beisammen (HWW 69/6) xlvii, 181, 188, 189, **199**, 243n
Mein Liebster hat zu Tische mich geladen (HWW 159/25) 208, 214, **246**
Mein Liebster ist so klein (HWW 159/15) lv, lvi, 207, 214, 219n, **240**
Mein Liebster singt am Haus im Mondenscheine (HWW 159/20) lv, 34n, 208, **243**
Michelangelo-Lieder lvii, 499
Mignon (HWW 120/9) li, 108, 120, **137**, 214, 542
    orchestration (HWW 133) xlvi, liii, 108, 502, 532, 533n
    orchestration (second version) (HWW 153) lv, 108, 532, 533n
Mignon I (HWW 120/5) li, 108, **133**, 172n
Mignon II (HWW 120/6) li, 108, 120, **133**, 172n
Mignon III (HWW 120/7) li, 108, **134**, 172n
Mir träumte von einem Königskind (HWW 69/5) xlvii, 181, 188, 189, **199**, 200n, 542
Mir ward gesagt, du reisest in die Ferne (HWW 159/2) liv, 207, 212, 215, 216, **232**
Mit des Bräutigams Behagen **142**
Mit Mädchen sich vertragen **147**
Mit meinem Saitenspiele **34**
Mit schwarzen Segeln (HWW 80) xlviii, 181, 190, 191n, **201**
Mögen alle bösen Zungen (HWW 129/23) liii, 53, **86**, 521
Morgenhymnus *see* Morgenstimmung
Morgenstimmung (HWW 160/2) xxxiv, lvii, 430, 435–6, **445**
    version for chorus and orchestra (as 'Morgenhymnus') (HWW 168) xxxiv, lvii, 430, 445n, 533
Morgentau (HWW 101/1) xxxii, xlvii, 3, 4, 5, **6**, 291, 304, 451, 542
Mörike-Lieder xvii, xviii, xx, xxvi, xxxii, xxxiii, xxxviii, xlix, l, li, 14, 15, 21, 24, 58, 175, 188, 193, 228, 341–2, 344–5, 493, 504, 507, 508, 509, 525, 527, 527n, 529
Mühvoll komm' ich und beladen (HWW 129/7) liii, 53, 57, **71**

Nach dem Abschiede (HWW 75) xlviii, 261, 262, **265**
Nach langem Frost, wie weht die Luft so lind! **306**
Nachgelassene Lieder 302
Nachruf (HWW 92) xvii, xlviii, 16, 22, **29**, 49n, 51n
Nacht ist wie ein stilles Meer **50**
Nacht und Grab (HWW 3) xlvi, 117–18, 471, **472**
Nachtgruß (HWW 104/3) xlviii, 430, **441**
Nachtgruß (Eichendorff; fragment) 16
Nächtliche Wanderung (HWW 58) xlvii, 4, 190, 298, 301, **311**, 376n, 543
Nachtzauber (HWW 118/8) xviii, xlv, xlix, 16, 22, 24, **42**, 542
Nein, junger Herr, so treibt man's nicht, fürwahr (HWW 159/12) lv, 208, **238**, 543
Neue Liebe (HWW 119/30) l, 331, 344, 353, 380n, **394**
    orchestration (HWW 141) liv, 331, 355, 532
Nicht Gelegenheit macht Diebe (HWW 120/39) li, 108, **163**

INDEX OF TITLES AND FIRST LINES 559

Nicht länger kann ich singen (HWW 159/42)　lvi, 34n, 209, 214, 229n, **256**
Nimmer will ich dich verlieren! (HWW 120/48)　lii, 108, **169**
Nimmersatte Liebe (HWW 119/9)　xlix, 330, 348, **374**
Nixe Binsefuß (HWW 119/45)　l, 141n, 175, 331, **409**, 543
Nun bin ich dein (HWW 129/1)　liii, 53, 57, 58, **65**
Nun ist es Herbst, die Blätter fallen　**313**
Nun laß uns Frieden schließen, liebstes Leben (HWW 159/8)　liv, 207, 213, 217n, 236n, **235**, 482
Nun wandre, Maria (HWW 129/3)　lii, 52, 56, 59, **67**, 141n
Nur wer die Sehnsucht kennt　**133**

O süße Mutter　**455**
O, wag' es nicht, mit mir zu scherzen　**313**
O wär' dein Haus durchsichtig wie ein Glas (HWW 159/40)　lvi, 190, 203n, 209, **254**
O Woche, Zeugin heiliger Beschwerde!　**391**
O wüßtest du, wie viel ich deinetwegen (HWW 159/44)　lvii, 209, **257**
Ob auch finstre Blicke glitten (HWW 129/35)　liv, 53, **96**
Ob der Koran von Ewigkeit sei? (HWW 120/34)　li, 108, **160**, 479

Penthesilea　xxi, xxxi, xxxii, xxxiv, 118n, 122n, 354n, 425, 508
Peregrina I (HWW 119/33)　l, 331, **397**, 398n, 521
Peregrina II (HWW 119/34)　l, 331, **398**, 543
Perlenfischer (HWW 26)　xlvi, 205, 448, **449**
Phänomen (HWW 120/32)　li, 108, 116, 120, 122, **158**
Philine (HWW 120/8)　li, 107, **136**, 542
Piano Sonata　xxix, 116–18, 117n
Preciosas Sprüchlein gegen Kopfweh (HWW 129/24)　lii, 52, **87**
Prinz Friedrich von Homburg (incidental music)　xxxi
Prinz von Homburg　xxi, 508
Prometheus (HWW 120/49)　li, 108, 116, 121, **169**, 172n, 214, 542
　orchestration (HWW 130)　liii, 108, 355, 500, 532

Rat einer Alten (HWW 119/41)　l, 330, **404**
Reich den Pokal mir schäumenden Weines voll　**445**
Resignation (HWW 98/3)　xlviii, 16, 22, **31**
Ritter Kurts Brautfahrt (HWW 120/12)　li, 108, **142**, 542
Romanzen von J. von Eichendorff (lost)　22
Rosenzeit! wie schnell vorbei　**380**
Rückkehr (HWW 102)　xlviii, 16, 18, 23, **34**

Sagt ihm, daß er zu mir komme (HWW 129/25)　liii, 53, **88**
Sagt, seid Ihr es, feiner Herr (HWW 129/22)　lii, 52, **85**
St. Nepomuks Vorabend (HWW 120/20)　li, 107, **150**, 203n
Sausewind, Brausewind!　**401**
Scheideblick (HWW 35)　xlvii, 298, **308**
Schlaf ein, mein süßes Kind　**438**

Schlaf! süßer Schlaf! obwohl dem Tod wie du nichts gleicht **394**
Schlafendes Jesuskind (HWW 119/25) l, 331, 344, 353, **390**, 390n, 543
    orchestration (HWW 125) lii, 331, 532
Schmerzliche Wonnen und wonnige Schmerzen (HWW 129/28) liii, 53, **91**
S ch n e e=Glöckchen thut läuten! **441**
Schön Hedwig (lost) 174
Schon streckt' ich aus im Bett die müden Glieder (HWW 159/27) lvi, 208, **247**
Schon zerfließt das ferne Gebirg mit Wolken **309**
Schweig' einmal still, du garst'ger Schwätzer dort! (HWW 159/43) xvii, lvi, 34n, 209, 229n, **256**
Schwingt Euch auf, Posaunen-Chöre **461**
Sechs Gedichte von Scheffel, Mörike, Goethe und Just. Kerner xxxii, 128–9n, 291, 367n, 459
Sechs geistliche Lieder nach Gedichten von Eichendorff xxxi, xlv, 16, **30–33**, 371n, 483
Sechs Lieder für eine Frauenstimme xxxi, xxxii, 4, 128–9n, 176, 291, 367n, 439, 451, 459, 477, 514
Sechs Lieder von Robert Reinick **439–43**
Seemanns Abschied (HWW 118/17) l, 16, 27, **48**, 542
Sehet ihr am Fensterlein **407**
Sehnsucht (HWW 4) xlvi, 107, 116–18, **123**, 471
Sei mir gegrüßt, o schöne Nacht **472**
Selbstgeständnis (HWW 119/52) l, 330, 340, **416**, 543
Selig ihr Blinden (HWW 159/5) liv, 207, 216n, **234**
Seltsam ist Juanas Weise (HWW 129/13) lii, 52, 57, **76**
Seraphimsche Heere **427**
Serenade for string quartet xxxii
Seufzer (HWW 119/22) l, 331, 344, 357 380n, **388**
    orchestration (HWW 122) lii, 331, 532
Sie blasen zum Abmarsch (HWW 129/38) liii, 52, **99**, 189
Sie haben heut' abend Gesellschaft (HWW 69/1) xlvii, 181, 188, 189, **197**
Sie haben wegen der Trunkenheit (HWW 120/37) li, 108, **162**
Singet nicht in Trauertönen **136**
Singt mein Schatz wie ein Fink (HWW 137/2) liv, 276, 278, 280, **287**
Skolie (HWW 160/3) lii, 430, 434, 435–6, **445**
So ist die Lieb'! So ist die Lieb'! **374**
So lang man nüchtern ist (HWW 120/36) li, 108, 122, **161**
So laß herein nun brechen **33**
So laßt mich scheinen, bis ich werde **134**
So wahr die Sonne scheinet (HWW 57) xlvii, 450, **454**
So wälz' ich ohne Unterlaß **151**
Sohn der Jungfrau, Himmelskind! am Boden **390**
Soldat sein ist gefährlich **44**
Sonne der Schlummerlosen (HWW 161/3) lvii, 8, 9, 10, **12**, 194n, 469
Sonne der Schlummerlosen, bleicher Stern! **12**
Spanisches Liederbuch xvii, xxxii, xxxiiii, xxxiv, xxxviii, xlv, lii, liii, liv, lvii, 3, 21, **52–106**, 189, 214, 222, 228, 267, 283, 371n, 487, 488–9, 493, 505, 506, 508, 509, 521, 534–5, 537, 540
Spätherbstnebel, kalte Träume (HWW 81) xlviii, 181, 190, 191n, **201**

INDEX OF TITLES AND FIRST LINES 561

Spottlied aus *Wilhelm Meister* (HWW 120/4) li, 107, **132**, 542
Ständchen (Körner) (HWW 44) xlvii, 4, 34n, 295, 296, **297**
Ständchen (Reinick) (HWW 104/5) xlviii, 34n, 430, **442**
Sterb' ich, so hüllt in Blumen meine Glieder (HWW 159/33) lvi, 209, 229n, **250**, 371n
Sterne mit den goldnen Füßchen (HWW 94) xlviii, 181, 190, **203**
Stille Sicherheit (HWW 36) xlvii, 298, **308**
Stille wird's im Walde; die lieben kleinen **309**
Storchenbotschaft (HWW 119/48) l, 330, 340, 351–2, **413**
String Quartet in D minor xxx, xxxi, xxxii, xlv, 351n, 500, 508
Studieren will nichts bringen **46**
Sturm mit seinen Donnerschlägen **306**
Suschens Vogel (HWW 96) xxxi, xlv, xlviii, 330, 342, **364**, 543
Symphony in B major xxx, xlv, 304, 474, 500
Symphony in F minor xxx
Symphony in G minor xlv

The Corsair overture (sketch; lost) 9, 10
Tief im Herzen trag' ich Pein (HWW 129/33) liv, 53, **95**, 243n
Tochter des Walds, du Lilienverwandte **386**
Tödlich graute mir der Morgen **368**
Trau nicht der Liebe (HWW 129/29) liii, 53, **92**
Traurige Wege (HWW 56) xlvii, 3, 5, 190, 298, 301, 304, 305, **310**
Treibe nur mit Lieben Spott (HWW 129/14) lii, 52, 57, **78**
Tretet ein, hoher Krieger (HWW 137/1) liv, 276, 278, 279, 285, **286**, 521
Trinklied im Mai (fragment) 544
Trübe Wolken, Herbstesluft **311**
Trunken müssen wir alle sein! (HWW 120/35) li, 108, 120–21, **161**

Über die Hügel und über die Berge hin **264**
Über Nacht (HWW 67) xlvii, 190, 469, **470**
Über Wipfel und Saaten **38**
Um Mitternacht (HWW 119/19) l, 331, **385**, 521
Unangeklopft ein Herr tritt abends bei mir ein **417**
Und frische Nahrung, neues Blut **124**
Und morgen fällt Sankt Martins Fest **143**
Und schläfst du, mein Mädchen (HWW 129/37) lii, 52, **98**
Und steht Ihr früh am Morgen auf vom Bette (HWW 159/34) lvi, 208, **251**
Und willst du deinen Liebsten sterben sehen (HWW 159/17) lv, 207, **241**, 371n
Unfall (HWW 118/15) xvii, l, 17, 27, **47**, 542

Verborgenheit (HWW 119/12) xv, l, 285, 289n, 330, 349n, **378**, 543
Vergeht mir der Himmel **31**
Verschling' der Abgrund meines Liebsten Hütte (HWW 159/45) xvii, lvii, 209, 230n, **257**
Verschwiegene Liebe (first setting; fragment) 16, 22
Verschwiegene Liebe (HWW 118/3) l, 16, 21, **38**, 502, 543
Vier Gedichte nach H. Heine, Shakespeare und Lord Byron xxxiv, 9, 190, 465

Vöglein vom Zweig 179
Vom Berg der Knab' 180
Vom Berg hinabgestiegen 437
Vom Berge was kommt dort um Mitternacht spät 411
Vor lauter hochadligen Zeugen 416

Wach' auf, erwache wieder 314
Wächterlied auf der Wartburg (HWW 114/1) xlix, 129n, 457, 458–61, **461**
    arranged for men's chorus and orchestra (unfinished) (HWW 157) lvi, 457, 460, 532
Wagen mußt du und flüchtig erbeuten 41
Wahlspruch 3
Waldmädchen (HWW 116) xlix, 16, 24, 37, **50**, 542
Wanderers Nachtlied (HWW 114/5) xxxii, xlix, 107, **129**, 376n, 542
Wanderlied (Anon.) (HWW 48) xlvii, 3, **6**, 190, 304, 376n, 471
Wanderlied (Goethe; fragment) 107, 116–18
Wandern lieb' ich für mein Leben 38
Wandl' ich in dem Morgentau (HWW 137/4) liv, 276, 279, 280n, 285, **288**
Warum, Geliebte, denk' ich dein **398**
Was doch heut Nacht ein Sturm gewesen 374
Was für ein Lied soll dir gesungen werden (HWW 159/23) lvii, 209, 230n, **244**
Was hör' ich draußen vor dem Tor **139**
Was im Netze? Schau einmal! **405**
Was in der Schenke waren heute (HWW 120/38) li, 108, **162**
Was soll der Zorn, mein Schatz, der dich erhitzt? (HWW 159/32) lvi, 209, **249**
Was soll ich sagen? (fragment) 13, 15
Was zieht mir das Herz so? **123**
Wasch' dich, mein Schwesterchen, wasch' dich! **366**
Wehe der, die mir verstrickte (HWW 129/43) liv, 53, **104**
Weil jetzo alles stille ist 31
Weint nicht, ihr Äuglein (HWW 129/39) liii, 53, **100**
Wenn der uralte 172
Wenn des Mondes bleiches Licht **421**
Wenn du, mein Liebster, steigst zum Himmel auf (HWW 159/36) lvi, 209, **252**
Wenn du mich mit den Augen streifst und lachst (HWW 159/38) lvi, 209, **253**
Wenn du zu den Blumen gehst (HWW 129/16) xxxiv, lii, 52, 56, 57, 63, **79**
    orchestration (*Manuel Venegas*) (HWW 167) lvii, 52, 64n, 533, 535
Wenn Fortuna spröde tut 43
Wenn ich dein gedenke (HWW 120/46) lii, 108, 120–21, 167n, **168**
Wenn ich im stillen Friedhof geh' **423**
Wenn ich in deine Augen seh (HWW 40) xlvii, 181, 188, **196**
Wenn ich, von deinem Anschaun tief gestillt 396
Wenn meine Mutter hexen könnt' 371
Wenn zu der Regenwand 158
Wer auf den Wogen schliefe 37
Wer in die Fremde will wandern 45
Wer nie sein Brot mit Tränen aß xiv, **131**

Wer rief dich denn? Wer hat dich herbestellt? (HWW 159/6) liv, 207, 213, 216, 217n, **234**
Wer sein holdes Lieb verloren (HWW 129/17) lii, 52, 56, 61, **80**
　　orchestration (*Manuel Venegas*) (HWW 166) xxxiv, lvii, 52, 64n, 533, 535
Wer sich der Einsamkeit ergibt **130**
„Wer tat deinem Füßlein weh?" (HWW 129/40) liii, 52, **101**
Wie des Mondes Abbild zittert (HWW 90) xlviii, 181, 190, **202**
Wie ein todeswunder Streiter **32**
Wie Feld und Au **275**
Wie glänzt der helle Mond (HWW 137/6) liv, 276, 279, 280n, 285n, **289**, 289n, 521
Wie heimlicher Weise **392**
Wie im Morgenglanze **171**
Wie lange schon war immer mein Verlangen (HWW 159/11) xvii, lv, 38n, 207, 214, 228n, **237**, 256n
Wie oft schon ward es Frühling wieder **263**
Wie sehr ich dein, soll ich dir sagen? **312**
Wie soll ich fröhlich sein und lachen gar (HWW 159/31) lvi, 208, **249**
Wie sollt' ich heiter bleiben (HWW 120/45) lii, 108, 120-21, **167**
Wie viele Zeit verlor ich, dich zu lieben! (HWW 159/37) lvi, 208, 228n, **253**
Wiegenlied im Sommer (HWW 101/4) xxxi, xlviii, 4, 430, **437**, 439, 451, 504
Wiegenlied im Winter (HWW 101/5) xxxi, xlviii, 4, 430, **438**, 439, 451, 504
Wir haben beide lange Zeit geschwiegen (HWW 159/19) lv, 208, 213, **242**
Wo die Rose hier blüht, wo Reben um Lorbeer sich schlingen **156**
Wo find' ich Trost? (HWW 119/31) li, 331, 344, 353, 363, 380n, **395**, 543
　　orchestration (HWW 142) liv, 331, 355, 502, 532
Wo ich bin, mich rings umdunkelt (HWW 68) xlvii, 181, 189, 190, **200**, 200n
Wo wird einst (HWW 161/1) xlix, 181, 190,192n, 193n, 194n, 195n, **203**, 435, 542
Wohin mit der Freud'? (HWW 104/1) xlviii, xlix, 430, **439**
　　second version (HWW 107) 430
Wohl denk' ich oft an mein vergang'nes Leben (HWW 162/1) lvii, 320, 322, 323, 325, **327**, 444
Wohl kenn' ich Euren Stand, der nicht gering (HWW 159/29) lvi, 208, 232n, **248**
Wohl wandert' ich aus in trauriger Stund' **15**
Wolken, die ihr nach Osten eilt **443**
Wolken, wälderwärts gegangen **34**
Wunden trägst du, mein Geliebter (HWW 129/10) liii, 52, 73n, **74**
Wunsch (fragment) **298**

Zaubrer bin ich, doch was frommt es? **440**
Zierlich ist des Vogels Tritt im Schnee **370**
Zitronenfalter im April (HWW 119/18) xlix, 330, **385**, 390n, 543
Zum neuen Jahr (HWW 119/27) xvii, l, 203n, 331, 344, 353, 390n, **392**
Zur Ruh, zur Ruh! (HWW 114/6) xxxi, xxxii, xxxv, xlix, 4, 129n, 290, 291, **294**
Zur Warnung (HWW 119/49) xlix, 161n, 330, 340, 348, **414**
Zwischen Bergen, liebe Mutter **36**
Zwischen Weizen und Korn **126**

GENERAL INDEX

Main entries are indicated in **bold**.

For references to the individual parallel texts and translations of poems set by Hugo Wolf, see INDEX OF TITLES AND FIRST LINES (pp. 549–63). Poems set by Wolf are not included in the GENERAL INDEX under their authors unless they are mentioned separately from their texts.

For references to texts and translations of displayed extracts from the letters of Hugo Wolf, see also CHRONOLOGY: LETTERS (pp. xxxvii–xliv) and CORRESPONDENTS (pp. 475–524).

1848 Revolution 20, 261, 422

Aargau 471, 472n
Abbas, Shah 166n
Aberdeen 8
Abt, Franz Wilhelm 448
  'Agathe' 205, 206
  'Mir träumte von einem Königskind' 199
Acre 462
Adolph Fürstner Verlag (publisher) 465
Adriatic xxxiv
Afghanistan 165n
Aix-en-Provence 146n
Alarcón y Ariza, Pedro Antonio de
  El niño de la bola 56, 535
  El sombrero de tres picos (The Three-cornered Hat) 62n, 506–7, 534, 539
Albani, Francesco: *The Sleeping Christ Child* ... 390n
Albert, Eugen d' 497
  'Er ist's' 372
  'Nimmersatte Liebe' 374
  'Ein Stündlein wohl vor Tag' 370
Aldeburgh Festival 458
Alexander of Macedon (Alexander the Great) 166n
Alexis, Willibald 431
Alland 483
Allgemeine deutsche Musikzeitung 501
Allgemeine Zeitung xxxii–xxxiii, 483, 488, 489
Allgemeiner Österreichischer Frauenverein 494

Allmers, Hermann 212
Almeida, Alvaro Fernandez de
  'Tango vos, el mi pandero' 74
Alsace 109
Alt-Rahlstedt 496
Alto Adige 161n
Amadis de Gaul 152n
America 262, 299, 478, 496, 514, 521
Anacreon 156–7n, 274
Ancient and Modern Scots Songs 143n, 145
Andalusia 98n
André, Johann 110, 304
  Erwin und Elmire 110
anti-Semitism 184
Aristophanes: *The Birds* 506
Arnfels 508
Arnim, Achim von 13, 18
Arnim, Achim von, and Clemens Brentano
  Des Knaben Wunderhorn 17, 31n, 39n, 141n, 213, 291, 374n
  'Der ernsthafte Jäger' 370n
  'Icarus' 291
  'Lied des Verfolgten im Turm' 39n
  'Der Rattenfänger von Hameln' 141
  'Des Schäfers Tageszeiten' 414n
  'Schall der Nacht' 31n
  'Das Wiedersehen am Brunnen' 374n
Arnim, Bettina von 53
  'Wanderers Nachtlied' 130
Arno, River 213, 248n
Arras: Musée des Beaux-Arts 390n
Aspern 45n
Athens 53

GENERAL INDEX

Attersee xxviii
Auber, Daniel: *La Muette de Portici* (*Die Stumme von Portici*) 534
Auden, W. H.
 The Dyer's Hand 463
 'Music in Shakespeare' 463-4
Aulnoy, Marie Catherine d'
 'The Dolphin' 152n
Austria xxi, xxiii, xxxvii, 45n, 261, 290, 299, 496, 541
 Civil Service 299

B. Schott's Söhne (publisher) xxxi, xxxiii, 27n, 30, 58, 61, 207, 212, 268, 282-3, 425, 451, 452-3, 464-5, 485-6, 487, 500, 506, 509, 534
 correspondence xxxix, xli, xlii, 60, 62-3, 221-7, 435, 452
Bach, Johann Sebastian 488
 chorales 112
 Christmas Oratorio 425
 Italian Concerto 477
 St Matthew Passion 501
Backmeister, Lucas: *Die heilige Cäcilie* 536
Bad Mergentheim 336
Baden xxxvii, 457
Baechtold, Jakob (ed.): *Gottfried Kellers Leben . . .* 277, 285
Bahr, Hermann xxxi
Balakirev, Mily Alexeyevich 9, 182
Balkh 165n
Balsamo, Giuseppe (Count Cagliostro) 146n
Balsamo, Lorenza Feliciana (Countess Serafina di Cagliostro) 146n
Barcelona 146n
Barenboim, Daniel 302
Bartók, Béla 109
Basedow, Johann Bernhard 126n
Basel 488
Bastille 146n
Batka, Richard 343, 382n
Baudelaire, Charles 385n
 'Enivrez-vous' 161n
 Le Spleen de Paris 161n
Bauer, Ferdinand Christian 341

Bauer, Ludwig 334, 340, 397n, 410n
Baumgartner, Wilhelm 277
Bayreuth xxxi, xxxii, xxxvii, 13, 120n, 176n, 210, 212, 225n, 477, 478, 490, 495, 500
Bayreuth Festival 118n, 500, 523
Beecham, Thomas xxiii
Beethoven, Ludwig van xv, xviii, xxi, xxix, xxxii, xxxv, 25n, 109, 110, 116, 333, 488, 504, 507, 541
 'Adelaide' 299, 316-17
 'Andenken' 319
 Fidelio 130n, 301, 534
 'Frech und froh I' 147
 Grosse Fuge 169n
 'Kennst du das Land' 137-8n, 139
 Late Quartets 301
 'Mailied' 111
 Missa solemnis 501
 'Neue Liebe, neues Leben' 111
 'Nur wer die Sehnsucht kennt' 134, 134n
 Piano Sonata Op. 90 xxxiv
 piano sonatas 500, 504
 'Sehnsucht' 123
 Symphony No. 5 333
 Symphony No. 9 ('Choral') 300-301
 Variations, Op. 35 504
 'Wonne der Wehmut' 112
Begas, Karl 431
Behrends, Marie 300
Bellini, Vincenzo 534
 La sonnambula 534
Berendt, Marie 432
Berg, Duchy of 181
Berg, Alban 54, 175, 301, 451
 'Auf geheimem Waldespfade' 299
 'Erster Verlust' 126
 'Ernst ist der Frühling' 202
 'Grenzen der Menschheit' 173
 'Kennst du das Land' 139
 'Schlafen, Schlafen, nichts, als Schlafen!' 175
 'Spätherbstnebel, kalte Träume' 202
Berge, Ida zum 262
Bergen 266

Berka 159n
Berlin xxxi, xxxiv, xxxvii, xli, xlii, 13, 18, 20, 53, 210, 211, 224, 225, 227, 261, 285, 358n, 407n, 432, 448, 460, 498, 500, 501, 507
   Botanical Gardens 14
   Hochschule 501
   Hugo-Wolf-Verein 500
   Nationalgalerie 19, 295
   Philharmonic Chorus 533
   Philharmonie 501–2
   Richard-Wagner-Verein 500, 507
   Städtische Oper 485
   University 210, 321
Berliner Akademie 431
Berlioz, Hector 184
   La Damnation de Faust 478
Berner, Christoph 258n
Berners, Lord
   'Du bist wie eine Blume' 196
Berry, Walter 326n
Bettelheim-Gabillon, Helene 198n, 302, 305, 312n, 313n, 480–83, 500, 526n
   correspondence 480–82
   'Erinnerungen an Hugo Wolf' 418n
   Im Zeichen des alten Burgtheaters 526n
Biberstein 472n
biblical references
   Genesis 159n
   I Kings 375n
   Isaiah 395
   Matthew 373n
   Luke 67n
   I Corinthians 148n
Biedermeier 337, 432
Bierbaum, Otto Julius 497
Bismarck, Otto von 422
Bizet, Georges: *Carmen* 478
Blech, Friedrich 431
Blech, Leo: 'Wiegenlied im Sommer' 438
Bodenstedt, Friedrich von 54, 210, 448
   'Mir träumte einst ein schöner Traum' 54
Bohemia 17, 151n

Böhl de Faber, Juan Nicolás 54, 56
   Floresta de Rimas Antiguas Castellanas (ed.) 54, 65–70, 72–7, 79–89, 92–100, 102, 104–5
Bohm, Carl
   'Er ist's' 372
   'Mädchen mit dem roten Mündchen' 195
Boïeldieu, François-Adrien 110
Boisserée, Sulpiz 166n, 169n
Boito, Arrigo: *Mefistofele* 534
Bologna 390n
Boncourt 13
Bonn 185–6
   University 261
Boosey & Hawkes (publisher) 73n, 74n
Borg, Kim 326n
Borodin, Alexander 182
Bos, Coenraad van xxii, 130n
Boston, US 122n, 521
Bote & Bock (publisher) 5n, 191
Brahms, Johannes xv, xviii, xxx, xlv, 54, 55, 118n, 175, 182, 189, 209–10, 212, 262, 267, 269, 276, 281, 282, 291, 341, 345, 417n, 451, 453, 488, 497, 500, 507, 520, 523, 526–7, 526–7n
   'Agnes' 381
   Alto Rhapsody 527
   'Am Sonntag Morgen' 215
   'An eine Äolsharfe' 377, 377n
   'Auf dem Kirchhofe' 497
   'Es rauschet das Wasser' 151n
   'Die ihr schwebet' 57, 68–9
   'In dem Schatten meiner Locken' 76
   Fünf Gedichte, Op. 19 xvi
   'Juchhe!' 433
   'Liebestreu' 433
   Mädchenlieder 278
   'Maienkätzchen' 497
   'Meerfahrt' 189
   'Mein Liebchen, wir saßen zusammen' 200
   'Phänomen' 116, 159, 159n
   'Salome' 278, 281, 287
   Die schöne Magelone 527n
   'Singt mein Schatz wie ein Fink' 278
   String Quintet No. 1 in F 527n

String Sextet No. 2 in G 527n
'Der Strom, der neben mir
  verrauschte' 424
Symphony No. 1 in C minor 526n
Symphony No. 2 in D 526n
Symphony No. 4 in E minor 526n
'Therese' 278, 281, 287
Violin Concerto in D 526n
Volks- und Kinderlieder 526n
'Von ewiger Liebe' 527n
'Wie rafft' ich mich auf in der Nacht'
  424
'Wiegenlied' 359n
Brandes, Georg 266–7
Braunschweig 261–2
  Katharineum school 261
Breitkopf, Bernhard Theodor 110
Breitkopf & Härtel (publishing house) xl,
  xlv, 4, 21, 23, 190, 280–81, 301, 451,
  453–4, 506
Brendel, Alfred 46n, 175
Brentano, Clemens 18
  see also Arnim, Achim von
Breslau 17, 20, 261
  University 261
Breuer, Bertha 176
Breuer, Dr Josef 176, 176n, 190
Breuer, Robert 176
Breuer family xxxviii, 176, 190
Bridge, Frank
  'Wenn ich in deine Augen seh' 197
Brion, Friederike 111
Britten, Benjamin 458
  Schubert: 'Gretchens Bitte'
    (completion) 128n
Brixlegg xxxvii, 497, 503
Browne, Lewis: *That Man Heine* 196n
Browning, Robert: 'The Pied Piper of
  Hamelin' 141n
Bruch, Max 54, 212
  'Cophtisches Lied I' 146
  'Cophtisches Lied II' 147
  'Gebet' 393
  'Um Mitternacht' 386
Bruchmann, Franz von 157n
Bruchsal 457

Bruck 508
Bruckner, Anton xxii, xxxii, xxxiii, 4, 48n,
  54, 360, 380n, 477, 487, 488, 504
  symphonies 116, 484
  Symphony No. 3 xxx, 487
  Symphony No. 7 26n, 32n
Brun, Friederike 317
Büchmann, Georg 321
  Geflügelte Worte 321
Bülow, Cosima von 174
Bülow, Hans von 174
  'Ernst ist der Frühling' 202
Buonarroti the Younger 320, 329n
Burckhardt, Jacob 211
Bürger, Gottfried August 186
Burgmüller, Norbert
  'Du bist wie eine Blume' 196
  'Harfenspieler II' 130
  'Harfenspieler III' 131
Burkhard, Willy: 'Verborgenheit' 378
Busoni, Ferruccio 9
  'Die Bekehrte' 155
  'Du bist wie eine Blume' 196
Byron, Allegra 8
Byron, George Gordon, Lord xxxiii, lvii,
  8–9, 10–12, 194–5, 284n, 363n, 489
  Childe Harold 8
  The Corsair 10
  'Harmodia' 12n
  Hebrew Melodies 9, 12n
  Hours of Idleness 8
  'I saw thee weep' 9
  The Lament of Tasso 9
  Manfred 9
  'Sun of the sleepless, melancholy star'
    469
  'Thyrza' cycle 8, 11n

C. Lacom (publisher) xxxii, 281, 281n, 491
Cadiz 98n
Calderón de la Barca, Pedro 53, 55
Cambridge 8
Camões, Luis de 95n
  'De dentro tengo mi mal' 95
  Os Lusiadas 95n
Campe (publisher) 261

Campe, Julius 185, 186
Capri 457
Carbonari 8
Carinthia 377n, 508, 514, 534
Carl Alexander, Grand Duke of Saxony, Burgherr auf Wartburg 461n
Carl August, Duke of Saxe-Weimar-Eisenach 124n, 129n, 156n
Carl Hanser Verlag (publisher) 175
Carlsruhe 452
Carlyle, Thomas 114, 143n
Carroll, Lewis 340
Cary, Stephen: 'A. E. Housman and the Renaissance of English Song' 182
Casanova 8
Castelnuovo-Tedesco, Mario: 'There be none of Beauty's daughters' 11
Castillejo, Cristóbal de: 'Alguna vez' 94
Cavalieri, Tommaso 321, 322, 329n
Cephalonia 8
Cervantes, Miguel de 56, 87
   Don Quixote 96n
   La Gitanilla 87n
   Novelas ejemplares 87n
Chabrier, Emmanuel 225n
   'Toutes les fleurs' 225n
Challier, Ernst: *Großer Lieder-Katalog* 24, 53, 116, 137n, 141n, 147n, 153n, 196n, 207, 317
Chamisso de Boncourt, Louis Charles Adelaïde de (Adelbert von Chamisso) xlvii, **13–14**, 15, 22, 53, 212, 290, 431
   'Die alte Waschfrau' 14
   Collected Works 14
   Frauen-Liebe und Leben 14
   'Noch hallt nur aus der Ferne' 15
   Peter Schlemihls wundersame Geschichte 14, 15
   'Der Regen strömt, die Sonne scheint' 15
   Reise um die Welt in den Jahren 1815–1818 14
   'Salas y Gomez' 14
   'Das Schloß Boncourt' 13, 14
   'Tragische Geschichte' 14
   'Traum und Erwachen' 14

'Das Vermächtnis' 14
'Was soll ich sagen?' 14
Les yeux de mon imagination . . . 13
Chaworth, Mary 8
Cherubini, Luigi 110
Chopin, Frédéric 189, 243n, 380n, 477
   'Poland's Funeral Hymn', Op. 74/17 243n, 477
   'Two corpses', Op. 74/11 243n
Christian VIII of Denmark 174
Christliches Magazin 129n
Cilli 504, 515–16
Cimarosa, Domenico 110
   'Die Bekehrte' 155
   Die heimliche Ehe 534
   L'impresario in angustie 154n
   'Die Spröde' 154
Clairmont, Claire 8, 11n
Clark, Kenneth 321
Claudius, Matthias 17, 316
Cleversulzbach 290, 335–7, 381n, 386n
Coburg 451
Cologne xxxvii, 142n
Colonna, Vittoria 321
Condivi, Ascanio 321, 328n
Conrad, Michael Georg xxxiii, 525, 527n, 529n
Conz, Karl Philipp 290
Copenhagen 174, 266
Cornelius, Peter 175, 210, 212
   'Es war ein alter König' 201
   'Preciosas Sprüchlein gegen Kopfweh' 88
   'Der Soldat' 41
Cortina 503
Corvey 262
Cota, Rodrigo de 82
Cotta (publisher) 336, 341
Cui, César
   'Es blasen die blauen Husaren' 200
Culture and Education, Ministry of 4, 295, 302, 318, 419
Czerny, Karl 223

Da Ponte, Lorenzo: *Don Giovanni* (libretto) 56

GENERAL INDEX

Dahn, Felix 54, 210
  'Du meines Herzens Krönelein' 54
Dalmedico, Angelo, 231
  Canti del popolo Veneziano 211, 215, 239, 245–6, 252n, 254, 257
  'Cenni sulle Vilote' 254n
Damrosch, Leopold
  'Bedeckt mich mit Blumen' 97
  'Dereinst, dereinst, Gedanke mein' 95
  'Geh, Geliebter, geh jetzt!' 105
  'Mädchen mit dem roten Mündchen' 195
Danube, River 339
Danzig 20
  National Museum 432
Darmstadt 520
Davies, Gareth A., *see* Sleeman, Margaret G., and Gareth A. Davies
Debussy, Claude 24
Decsey, Ernst xv, xxii, 39n, 55, 142n, 378n, 417n, 425, 448, 464, 504, 507, 509–10
  Hugo Wolf xxii, 485, 487
Dehmel, Richard 496
Delius, Frederick
  A Village Romeo and Juliet 279
Denmark 315
Dessauer, Josef 19
Deutsch, Helmut xv, 43n
  Gesang auf Händen tragen 43n
Deutsche Revue 508
Deutsche Zeitung 37n, 291–2, 293, 322, 469, 486
Deutscher Dichterwald 18
Deutscher Musenalmanac 14, 431
Diabelli, Antonio 223
Diana (dog) 346–7
Dichtergrüße. Neuere deutsche Lyrik ausgewählt von Elise Polko 205, 423, 448, 469
Dickens, Charles: *Pickwick Papers* 284n
Dielmann, Jakob Fürchtegott 431
Dieren, Bernard van: 'Epiphanias' 150
Diezel, Karl 489
Dinkelacker, Emma 489
Diogenes 151n
Distler, Hugo 365–6n
  'Agnes' 381
  Chorliederbuch 365n

'Denk' es, o Seele!' 403
'Er ist's' 372
'Frage und Antwort' 399n
'Der Gärtner' 384
'Gebet' 393
'Jägerlied' 371
'Der Knabe und das Immlein' 369
'Lebe wohl' 400
'Lied eines Verliebten' 406
'Mausfallen-Sprüchlein' 365
'Nimmersatte Liebe' 374
'Storchenbotschaft' 414
'Ein Stündlein wohl vor Tag' 370
'Der Tambour' 372
'Die Tochter der Heide' 367
'Um Mitternacht' 386
'Verborgenheit' 378
'Das verlassene Mägdlein' 373
Dittersdorf, Carl Ditters von 110
Döbling xxxii, **xxxvii**, xl, xli, xlii, 217, 490
Doceo, Mari (attrib.): 'Cubridme de flores' 97
Donizetti, Gaetano 534
  Belisario xxix, 517, 534
  La Fille du régiment (Die Regimentstochter) 534
  Lucia di Lammermoor 534
  Lucrezia Borgia 534
  Marino Faliero 9
  Parisina 9
Donne, John 374n
Döring, Heinrich 318
Dräseke, Felix
  'Denk' es, o Seele!' 403
  'Frage und Antwort' 399
Dresden 171n, 174, 184, 432
Dresden Opera 520
Duino xxxiv, 492
Düntzer, Heinrich 148n
Düsseldorf 181, 200n
Dyck, Ernest van 225–7

Ebensee xli
Eckermann, Johann Peter 111, 124n, 143n
  J. P. Eckermanns Gespräche mit Goethe 139n

Eckstein, Friedrich xxiii, xxxi, xxxii,
　　xxxviii, 4, 24, 37n, 38n, 39n, 55, 128–9n,
　　291, 367n, 380n, 407n, 425, 451, 459,
　　477–8, 521
　correspondence xl, xliii, 59, 347, 351, 353,
　　362
　„*Alte unnennbare Tage!*" 55, 380n, 477, 536
Edinburgh 317
Edleston, John 8, 11–12n
Egk, Werner: *Peer Gynt* 266
Ehmann, Friederike 290
Eichendorff, Agnes von 21
Eichendorff, Aloysia von, *see* Larisch,
　　Aloysia (Louise) von
Eichendorff, Anna von 21
Eichendorff, Hermann von 29
Eichendorff, Joseph, Freiherr von xxvii,
　　xxxii, xlviii, xlix, l, 16–51, **17–21**, 53, 55,
　　87n, 175, 210, 212, 276, 295, 316, 336, 431,
　　483, 509
　death 20
　as Florens 18
　Ahnung und Gegenwart 19, 20, 36n, 49n,
　　342
　'An die Lützowschen Jäger' 18
　Auf meines Kindes Tod 21
　Aus dem Leben eines Taugenichts 20, 23,
　　24, 36n, 38n, 45n, 384n
　'Bist du manchmal auch verstimmt' 38n
　'Dein Wille, Herr, geschehe' xlvi
　Dichter und ihre Gesellen 20, 41n, 46n,
　　50n
　'Der Einsiedler' 22, 31n
　Ezelin von Romano 20
　Die Freier 20
　'Der Freund' 504
　Die Freunde 37n
　'Die Fröhliche' 36n
　'Durch Feld und Buchenhallen' 38n
　Gedichte von Joseph Freiherrn von
　　Eichendorff 22, 24, 29, 36–7n, 41n, 50n
　'Der Glückliche' 29
　Die Glücksritter 43n, 432
　'Gruß' 38n
　Joseph von Eichendorff's sämmtliche
　　Werke 29

　Julian 20, 42n
　Krieg den Philistern! 20
　Der letzte Held von Marienburg 20, 47n
　'Lieber alles' xxvii
　Das Marmorbild 20
　Eine Meerfahrt 31n, 48n, 50n
　'Mittag' 22
　'Die Nachtblume' 29, 50n
　'Nachtgruß' 22
　'O Täler weit, o Höhen' 18
　Robert und Guiscard 20, 38n
　Das Schloß Dürande 20, 27–8, 536
　'Der Soldat I' 19
　'Der Soldat II' 19
　'Steckbrief' 29
　'Tamburinschlägerin' 75n
　'Der Tiroler Nachtwache' 45n
　Der verliebte Reisende 18, 34n, 35n
　'Der verliebte Reisende' 29
　'Von fern die Uhren schlagen' 21
　'Wandern lieb' ich für mein Leben' 38n
　'Der wandernde Musikant' 29
　'Der wandernde Student' 29
　'Was ist mir denn so wehe?' 21
　'Wenn die Sonne lieblich schiene' 38n
　'Wer in die Fremde will wandern' 23
　'Das zerbrochene Ringlein' 17
　Der zufriedene Musikant/
　　Der wandernde Musikant 38n
Eichendorff, Wilhelm 17, 18, 19, 354n
Eisler, Hanns: 'An den Schlaf' 394
Elgar, Edward 130n
Elschnig, Anton 503
Elster, Ernst 196n, 203n
Eltingen 335
Embden-Heine, Maria: *Erinnerungen an*
　　H. Heine 196n
Emichsburg 377n
Emil Wetzler (publisher) xxxii, 4, 129n,
　　291, 354n, 367, 367n, 459, 477, 486, 493,
　　509
Ems 126n
Ende, Richter 263
Endenich xxxv
Enghaus, Christine 174
England 182

Ense, Varnhagen von 13
Erb, Karl xxii
Erbse, Heimo: 'Um Mitternacht' 386
Erk, Ludwig 262
  Deutscher Liederschatz 205
Erlangen, University of 451
Escrivá, Comendador: 'Ven muerte tan escondida' 95
Eulenspiegel, Der (magazine) 422
Eulonia (reading group) 480
Eulonia Chorus 500

F. R. Schoch (publisher) 318
Fackel, Die 152n
Fairchild, Elizabeth 478
Faisst, Hugo xxxiii, xxxiv, 285, 328n, 360–61, 436, **478–80**, 489, 499, 503, 505
  correspondence xliii, 195, 195n, 229, 230–31, 231n, 289n, 325, 358n, 362, 363, 436, 486, 487, 499, 500–501
Faißt, Immanuel 341
Fenby, Eric 130n
Fichte, Johann Gottlieb 13
Fischer, Friedrich Theodor 399n
Fischer-Dieskau, Dietrich xv, xxiii, 3, 20, 302, 523
  Hugo Wolf. Leben und Werk xv, xxiii, 3, 12n, 33n, 491, 498, 517
  Töne sprechen, Worte klingen 20
Florence: Santa Croce 320
Flotow, Friedrich von: *Martha* 534
Foll, Ferdinand 190, 425
Fontane, Theodor 210, 345, 448
Förster, Katharina Barbara 17
Förstler, Wilhelm 435, 435n
Foulds, John: 'There be none of Beauty's daughters' 11
Fouqué, Friedrich de la Motte 290, 431
France 13, 182, 187, 261, 496
Franck, Adolph 480
Franck, Valentine (Vally) xxx, xxxi, xxxvii, xlv, 18, 22, 25, 29n, 30, 33n, 176, 190, 192, 198n, 301, 302, 312n, 313n, 418n, **480–83**, 493, 494, 500, 516, 523
  correspondence 305, 480–82, 523
Franco-Prussian War 422

Frankfurt xxxiii, xxxvii, 27, 109, 110, 113, 130n, 166n, 487
Frankfurt an der Oder 471
Frankfurter Zeitung 487
Franz, Robert 54, 182, 187, 295, 301, 334, 341, 345, 448, 451
  'Agnes' 381
  'Aus meinen großen Schmerzen' 189, 199
  'Das ist ein Brausen und Heulen' 198
  'Denk' es, o Seele!' 403
  'Er ist's' 372
  'Frage nicht' 313
  'Liebesfrühling' 307
  'Mädchen mit dem roten Mündchen' 195
  'Mailied' 127
  'Mein Liebchen, wir saßen zusammen' 200
  'Mit schwarzen Segeln' 201
  'Sterne mit den goldnen Füßchen' 203
  'Stille Sicherheit' 308
  'Ein Stündlein wohl vor Tag' 370
  'Um Mitternacht' 386
  'Verborgenheit' 378
  'Das verlassene Mägdlein' 373
  'Wenn ich in deine Augen seh' 197
  'Wie des Mondes Abbild zittert' 203
Frauenzeitung für Hauswesen . . . (magazine) 402n
Frauscher, Moritz 326, 326n
Freiburg University 274
Freiligrath, Ferdinand von 290, 340
Freitagsgesellschaft 146n
French Revolution 13
Freud, Sigmund 176n, 380n, 477
  Studien über Hysterie 176n
Freudenberg, Wilhelm 432
Frey, Carl 320
Freya (magazine) 366n
Freylinghausen, Joh. Anastas.: *Geistreiches Gesangbuch . . .* 388n
Friedlaender, Max 277
  Brahms' Lieder 277–8
Friedrich, Caspar David 295
Friedrich III, Kaiser 321
Friedrich Wilhelm III of Prussia 18

Friedrich Wilhelm IV of Prussia 54
Friesen, Karl Friedrich 295
Fuchs, Marta xxii
Fuchs, Robert xxii
  'Verborgenheit' 378
  'Das verlassene Mägdlein' 373
Furtwängler, Wilhelm 483

G. Grote'sche Verlagsbuchhandlung (publisher) 432
Gabillon, Helene, *see* Bettelheim-Gabillon, Helene
Gabillon, Ludwig 480
Gabillon family 464, 526n
Gadebusch, battle of 295
Gaisberg, Fred xxii
Ganymede 171n
Ganges, River 157n
Gartenbüchlein von Pastor Müller 386n
Geibel, Emanuel 52–106, **53–4**, 210, 212, 290, 340, 341, 469, 496
  as Don Manuel del Rio 71, 71n
  'Dunkler Sichtglanz' 82n
  'Mühvoll komm' ich und beladen' 71, 71n
  'Schmerzliche Wonnen und wonnige Schmerzen' 91n
  Volkslieder und Romanzen... 54
Geibel, Emanuel, and Paul Heyse
  Spanisches Liederbuch 54, 56–8, 60, 212
Genée, Richard 62, 62n
Geneva 217n
Georgii, Eberhard von 332
Gerhardt, Elena xxii, 122n
Germany xxxiii, xxxvii, 13, 14, 45n, 276, 290, 424
  unification of 261, 340
Gerok, Karl 448–9
Gesellschaft, Die 527n
Gesellschaft der Musikfreunde 473, 527n
'Get up and bar the door' 143n, 145
Gibbs, Armstrong: 'There be none of Beauty's daughters' 11
Gildemeister, Otto 11, 12
  'Ich sah dich weinen' 9
Ginster, Ria xx

Girardi, Enzo Noè 320
Giuliani, Mauro 316
Glafey, Annette von 316
Glazunov, Alexander: 'Wenn ich in deine Augen seh' 197
Gleim, Johann Wilhelm Ludwig 157n
Gluck, Christoph Willibald 110, 333, 488
  Iphigenie in Tauris 534
Glück, Friedrich 17
  'Das zerbrochene Ringlein' 17
Gmelin, Lotte 299
Gmunden 376n
Gnesin 196n
Goethe, Christiane von 156n
Goethe, Cornelia von 109
Goethe, Johann Wolfgang von xvi, xxvii, xxxii, xxxiii, xlv, xlvi, xlviii, xlix, lii, liii, lv, 14, 17, 20, 47n, 55, 107–73, **109–15**, 175, 182, 186, 274, 276, 284, 302–3, 317, 332, 335, 341, 354n, 362n, 365n, 424, 450, 469, 471, 473, 487, 497, 501, 504, 509, 527
  family 109
  and opera 110–11
  12 Lieder des Volkes 110
  'An den Mond' 130n, 156n, 335
  'An die Entfernte' 125n
  'An Schwager Kronos' 169n
  Annals 111
  'Auf dem See' 124n
  'Auf Miedings Tod' 110
  'Celebrität' 151n
  Claudine von Villa Bella 147n
  Complete Works 141n
  'Dank des Paria' 157n
  'Der du von dem Himmel bist' 335
  'Des Paria Gebet' 157n
  Dichtung und Wahrheit 109, 111, 124n, 126n, 130n
  Egmont 112
  'Erster Verlust' 125n
  Erwin und Elmire 110
  Faust xxviii, 109, 112, 118–19, 127n, 134n, 156n, 169n, 191n, 436n
  'Frühling übers Jahr' 156n
  'Ganymed' 172n

GENERAL INDEX 573

'Gefunden' 156n, 386n
'Geistesgruß' 126n, 303n
'Gesang der Geister über den Wassern' 172n
'Goethe's Gartenhaus am untern Park bei Weimar' 156n
Goethes Opern und Singspiele 110
'Grenzen der Menschheit' 172n
Der Groß-Cophta 145–6n
Hermann und Dorothea 224n, 535
Iphigenia auf Tauris 130n, 156n
Italienische Reise 146n
'Jägers Abendlied' 130n, 156n
'Komm, Liebchen, komm!' 165n
'Der König in Thule' 400n
'Königlich Gebet' 367n
'Legende' 157–8n
Lila 129n
'Locken, haltet mich gefangen' 113
'Mailied' 303n
'Meine Göttin' 172n
'Der Musensohn' 111
Die Mystifizierten 146n
'Nicht Gelegenheit macht Diebe' 164n
Paria 157n
'Phänomen' xxvii
'Prometheus' 172n, 214
'Rastlose Liebe' 130n, 156n
'Der Rezensent' 417n
'Der Sänger' 141n
Scherz, List und Rache 125n
'Die schöne Nacht' 303n
Schriften 125n
'Sehnsucht' 405n
La sposa rapita (libretto) 109
Torquato Tasso 130n, 156n, 183
Trilogie der Leidenschaft 112, 125n
'Trost in Tränen' 290
Über Kunst und Alterthum 424
Die ungleichen Hausgenossen 125n
Venetian Epigram 374n
'Wandrers Nachtlied' 129n, 156n
'Warum gabst du uns die tiefen Blicke' 117, 335
West-östlicher Divan 112–14, 116, 158–69, 424, 450

Wilhelm Meisters Lehrjahre xvi, 20, 112, 116, 131–9nn, 172n, 342
Wilhelm Meisters Theatralische Sendung 134n, 139n
'Wonne der Wehmut' 112, 125n
'Zwischen Lavater und Basedow' 126n
Goetz, Hermann: 'Wie lange schon war immer mein Verlangen' 207, 237
Goldmark, Karl 9
Die Königin von Saba 142n
Goldschmidt, Adalbert von xxx, 342, 365n, 474, 480, 490, 504
Die sieben Todsünden 142n
Goldschmidt, Paula von 243n, 345, 365n
Goldschmidt family xxx, 304
Gooch, Bryan N. S, and David Thatcher
Musical Settings of British Romantic Literature 9
A Shakespeare Music Catalogue 463
Görres, Joseph 17
Göschitz 469
Gottfried, Johann Ludwig: *Chronika* 141n
Gotthelf, Jeremias 369n
Der Bauernspiegel 369n
Göttingen 262
Burschenschaft 184
University 261
Gounod, Charles 534
Gozzi, Carlo: *Das öffentliche Geheimnis* 535
Graener, Paul: 'Blumengruß' 153
Gramophone (periodical) xii
Gramophone Company xxii, xxiii
Grasberger, Franz 329n
Briefe an Melanie Köchert (ed.) 329n
Graz xxxi, xxxv, 61, 117, 228n, 301, 365n, 459, 502–4, 505, 516, 521
Gymnasium xxix
Richard-Wagner-Verein 502–3
Stadttheater 267
University 304n
Grazer Tagespost xxii, 354n
Grazer Wochenblatt 354n, 502
Greece 53
independence of 340
Greif, Martin 210

Grieg, Edvard 54, 182
    'Borte!' 266
    'Dereinst, dereinst, Gedanke mein' 95
    'En Fuglevise' 266
    'En Svane' 266
    'Es war ein alter König' 190, 201
    'Ich stand in dunkeln Träumen' 198
    'Med en Vandlilje' 266
    Peer Gynt 266
    Seks Digte af Henrik Ibsen 266
    'Spillemænd' 266
    'Stambogsrim' 266
    'Zur Rosenzeit' 110
Griensteidl, Café 477
Griffes, Charles 54, 182
    'Das ist ein Brausen und Heulen' 198
    'Mit schwarzen Segeln' 201
    'Wo bin ich, mich rings umdunkelt' 200
Grillparzer, Franz: Weh dem, der lügt! xxxi, 535, 535n
Grimm, Herman 164n
    'Goethe und Suleika' 113
Grimm, Jacob 261, 345
Grimm, Wilhelm 261
Grimma 315
    Fürstenschule 315
Grimmelshausen, Hans Jakob Christoffel von: *Der abentheuerliche Simplicissimus* 31n, 411n
Grohe, Helmuth 414n
Grohe, Jeanne (Jeanette) 194n, 484
    correspondence xlii, 223
Grohe, Oskar 45n, 94n, 357, 425, **483–4**, 485, 509
    correspondence xv, xvii, xix–xx, xl, xli, xlii, xliii, 10, 55, 56–61, 122, 177, 192–3, 194–5, 212, 217–18, 223, 269, 323, 326, 355, 362, 378n, 414n, 425, 426, 434, 459, 485, 489, 498, 505, 533, 537, 538, 539
    'Julinacht' 484
Groth, Klaus 497
Grün, Anastasius 431
Gstatt, Schloß 376n, 508
Guadalquivir, River 98n
Guasti, Cesare 320
Guiccioli, Teresa 8

Gura, Eugen 120–21, 120n, 496
Güra, Werner 258n

Haberlandt, Michael xxxiv, xxxv, xxxviii, 292, **484–5**, 516, 535
    funeral oration for HW 530–31
Hafiz 112, 160, 162n, 163, 166n, 450
Hagedorn, Friedrich von 157n
Halévy, Jacques: *La Juive* (*Die Jüdin*) 534
Halle University 17, 274
Halm, August 45n, **485**
    'Das taube Mütterlein' 205, 544
Halpern, Martin: *The Scaffolding* 266
Hamburg xxvii, 182–4, 197n, 496
Hamelin 13
Hammer-Purgstall, Joseph, Freiherr von 112, 450
Handel, George Frideric: *Messiah* 112
Hanslick, Eduard xxxi, 417n, 453, 527n
Harrach, Countess 349n, 351
Harrow 8
Härtel, August: *Deutsches Liederlexicon...* 397n
Hartlaub, Wilhelm 332, 334, 335, 340, 363, 365n, 366n, 383n, 384n, 386n, 393n
Hartmann, Heinrich 295
Harz mountains 17, 191n
Hasselriis, Louis 203n
Hauff, Wilhelm 332
Hauffe, Friederike 291
Hauptmann, Gerhart
    Hannele 535
    Die versunkene Glocke 536
Hausegger, Friedrich von 3, 117, 117n, 301, 304, 304n, 305
Haydn, Joseph xxix, 333
    'Lob der Faulheit' 152n
    masses 112
Hebbel, Friedrich xlvii, 4, 174–80, **174–5**, 336, 345
    Agnes Bernauer 175
    'Dem Schmerz sein Recht' 175
    Gedichte 175
    Gedichte von Friedrich Hebbel 175
    Genoveva 174, 432
    Gyges und sein Ring 175, 178, 536

GENERAL INDEX

Herodes und Mariamne 174
Judith 174, 175, 177
Julia 175, 176
'Das Kind am Brunnen' 175
'Knabentod' 175
Maria Magdalene 174
Michel Angelo 174
Mutter und Kind 174
Neue Gedichte 175
Die Nibelungen 174
'Schön Hedwig' 175
Tagebücher 175
'Das Vöglein' 175
Hebe 171n
Heckel, Emil xxiii, 485
Heckel, Karl **485–6**
   correspondence xliii, 10–11, 323, 487, 537
   Buddha 535
   Prospero (libretto) 486
   see also Karl Heckel Verlag
Hegel, Georg Wilhelm Friedrich 332
Heide 174
Heidelbach, Paul 54
Heidelberg xxxvii, 18, 337
   University 17, 276, 422
Heilbronn 422, 499
Heiligenkreuz monastery 239n
Heine, Amalie (Molly) xxvii, 182–4, 197n
Heine, Heinrich xxvii, xxx, xlv, xlvii,
   xlviii, xlix, 11, 14, 15, 175, 181–204, **181–7**,
   276, 340, 341, 422, 434, 469, 489
   Almansor 185
   'Belsatzar' xxvi
   Das Buch der Lieder 182, 186, 188, 189,
     190, 339
   Deutschland: Ein Wintermärchen 187
   'Du bist wie eine Blume' 205
   'Es blasen die blauen Husaren' 189
   Geständnisse 181
   Die Harzreise 190, 191–2, 191–2n
   Die Heimkehr 186, 189, 195, 196, 197, 198,
     200
   'Ich mache die kleinen Lieder' 199n
   Ideen. Das Buch Le Grand 204n
   Junge Leiden 185
   Letzte Gedichte . . . 203n
   Lyrisches Intermezzo 185–6, 197, 198, 199,
     200
   'Mädchen mit dem roten Mündchen'
     205
   'Mein Wagen rollet langsam' 522
   Neue Gedichte 187, 190, 201, 202, 202, 203
   Die Nordsee 187
   Prinzessin Ilse 535
   Reisebilder 186–7, 191–2, 191–2n, 424
   Die romantische Schule 14
   Romanzen und vermischte Gedichte 203n
   Romanzero 195
   'Die Rose, die Lilie, die Taube, die
     Sonne' 185
   'Seraphine' 201
   'Sie haben heut' abend Gesellschaft'
     xxvii
   Der Schwabenspiegel 341
   Schwanengesang (6 Heine poems from
     Schubert's cycle) 186
   *Tragödien nebst einem Lyrischen
     Intermezzo* 185
   Verschiedene 201
   William Ratcliff 185
   'Zum Polterabend' 199n
Heine, Salomon 182, 197n
Heine, Therese 183–4, 196n, 197n
Heißenstamm (playwright) 300
Helbing, C. (editor) 277
Helgoland 321
Hellmer, Edmund 12n, 322
   Hugo Wolf. Erlebtes und Erlauschtes 12n,
     162n
Helm, Theodor 37n, 291, **486**
   correspondence xl, 292
Henckell, Karl 497
Henschel, Georg
   'Du bist wie eine Blume' 196
   'Es war ein alter König' 201
   'Morgenstimmung' 445
Hensel, Fanny Mendelssohn 54, 209, 451
   'Der Fischer' 124
   'Die Nacht' 50
   'Erster Verlust' 126
   'Harfenspieler I' 130
   'Kennst du das Land' 139

'Nur wer die Sehnsucht kennt' 134
'Sehnsucht' 123
'Stille wird's im Walde' 310
'There be none of Beauty's daughters' 11
'Traurige Wege' 310
'Wanderers Nachtlied' 130
'Wenn ich in deine Augen seh' 197
Hercules 169n
Hercules (ship) 8
Herd, David 143n
Herder, Johann Gottfried 110, 316
   'Das Lied vom Fischer' 124n
   'Radoslaus' 370n
   Stimmen der Völker in Liedern 56, 124n, 143n
   Volkslieder 370n
Herloßsohn, Karl xlvii, 55, **205-6**
   'Agathe' 205
   Buch der Liebe . . . 205
   Das Buch der Lieder . . . 205
Hermann, Landgraf of Thüringen 461n
Herrick, Robert xxvi, 335
Hertz, Henrik: *Svend Dyrings Huus* 266
Hertz, Wilhelm (publishing house), *see* Wilhelm Hertz
Hervé (Florimond Ronger) 527-8n
   Mam'zelle Nitouche 527-8n
Herwegh, Georg 340
Herzfeld, Victor von 293, 293n
Herzlieb, Wilhelmine 112
Herzog, Emilie 358-9, 358n
Herzogenburg, Elisabet von 278
Hesse, Hermann
   'Im Presselschen Gartenhaus' 340, 341
   Unterm Rad 332
Hetsch, Ludwig 334, 341
   'Agnes' 381
   'Elfenlied' 383
   'Erstes Liebeslied eines Mädchens' 406
   'Der Feuerreiter' 409
   'Jägerlied' 371
   'Der Knabe und das Immlein' 369
   'Lied eines Verliebten' 406
   'Das verlassene Mägdlein' 373
Hetzendorf 510

Heuberger, Richard 471
   'Ein Ständchen Euch zu bringen kam ich her' 207, 244
Heubner, Konrad:
   'Als ich auf dem Euphrat schiffte' 116
Heyse, Ernst 210
Heyse, Margarethe 210
Heyse, Marianne 210
Heyse, Paul 52-106, 207-58, **209-12**, 316, 336, 340, 345, 422, 448
   as Don Luis el Chico 102n
   'An Emanuel Geibel' 211
   'Auf dem grünen Balcon' 78n
   'Auf die Nacht in der Spinnstub'n' 54
   Gedichte 211
   Italienisches Liederbuch 210-13
   'Liebe mir im Busen zündet' 90
   Meinen Todten 210
   La Rabbiata 210
   Skizzenbuch 211
   Spanisches Liederbuch, see Geibel, Emanuel, and Paul Heyse
   Zwölf Dichterprofile 212
Heyse, Wilfried 210
Hietzing 492
Hiller, Ferdinand 184
   'Agnes' 381
   'Bedeckt mich mit Blumen' 97
   'Es war ein alter König' 201
   'Klinge, klinge, mein Pandero' 75
   'Um Mitternacht' 386
   'Und schläfst du, mein Mädchen' 98
Hilmar, Ernst xxiii
   Hugo Wolf Enzyklopädie xxiii
Himburg, Christian Friedrich 274
Himmel, Friedrich 397n
Hindemith, Paul 315
Hirsch, Richard 26, 26n
Hirschfeld, M.
   'Mit Mädchen sich vertragen' 147n
Hobhouse, John Cam 9
Hoch-Osterwitz 377n
Hoefer, Edmund xlvi, 259-60, **259**
   Altermann 259
   Aus alter und neuer Zeit 259
   Bewegtes Leben 259

Deutsche Herzen 259
Gedichte von Edmund Hoefer 259
Der große Baron 259
Norien. Erinnerungen einer alten Frau 259
Tolleneck 259
Unter der Fremdherrschaft 259
Vergangene Tage 259
Wie das Volk spricht 259
Hoernes, Moriz 63, 63n, 486
　Manuel Venegas (libretto) 270, 535
Hoffmann, Franz: *Der böse Geist* 421n
Hoffmann von Fallersleben, August Heinrich xxxviii, xlvii, 261–5, **261–2**, 276, 341
　correspondence 263
　'Alle Vögel sind schon da' 262
　Des fahrenden Schülers Liebe und Leiden 264n
　'Deutschland, Deutschland über alles' 261
　Fünfzig Kinderlieder 262
　Fünfzig neue Kinderlieder 262
　Gedichte 262
　Hundert Schullieder 262
　In beiden Welten 262
　'Kuckuck, Kuckuck ruft aus dem Wald' 262
　Unpolitische Lieder 261
　'Wer hat die schönsten Schäfchen' 262
　'Winter, ade!' 262
Hofmann, Friedrich 502
Hofmannsthal, Hugo von 110, 380n, 477, 478, 536
Hogarth, William 393n
Hohenschild, Fräulein (Vienna) 357
Holbrooke, Joseph 11
　'There be none of Beauty's daughters' 11
Hölderlin, Friedrich 212, 276, 290, 332, 341, 357, 407n
　'Patmos' 382n
Höll, Hartmut 535
Hollanda, Francisco de 321
Hölty, Ludwig 29, 450
　'Am Mummelsee' 411n

　'Mailied' 544
　'Trinklied im Mai' 544
Horace: *Odes* 376
Housman, A. E. 182
Huber, Hans: 'Wie lange schon war immer mein Verlangen' 207, 237
Huber, Victor Aimé 54
Hucknall Torkard 9
Hugo Wolf Gramophone Record Society xxii
Hugo Wolf Society xxii, xxiii, 130n
Humperdinck, Engelbert xli, 24, **487**, 509
　correspondence 27, 61, 269
　Hänsel und Gretel 487, 520
Hungary 505
Hüsch, Gerhard xxiii

Ibsen, Henrik xx, liv, 266–73, **266–7**, 538
　Gildet paa Solhoug (*Das Fest auf Solhaug*) xxxiii, 266–73, 535, 537, 540
　Hedda Gabler 266
　The Master Builder 266
　Peer Gynt 266
　The Vikings at Helgeland 266
Ilm, River 159n
Immermann, Karl Leberecht 424
　'Tristan und Isolde' 370n
Internationale Hugo Wolf-Gesellschaft xxiii
Iran 166n
Iris (periodical) 274
Ischl 44n, 122, 299
Istria 540n
Italy 111, 134n, 145n, 210, 424, 432, 448, 457
　Austrian Occupation 231
Ives, Charles 9, 182
　'Du bist wie eine Blume' 196

Jacobi, Johann Georg xlvi, 116, 118n, 274–5, **274**, 303n
Jäger, Ferdinand xxxii, 37n, 61, 375n, 433, 433n, 434, 444, 502, 504
Jäger, Ferdinand, jnr xxiii
Jahn, Ludwig 19
James, Henry 453–4n
　The Aspern Papers 453–4n

Jancik, Hans 307n
Janssen, Herbert xxii, 130n
Jena 205, 469
Jensen, Adolf 54, 212, 448
  'Dereinst, dereinst, Gedanke mein' 95
  'In dem Schatten meiner Locken' 76
  'Klinge, klinge, mein Pandero' 75
  'Sie blasen zum Abmarsch' 99
  'Und schläfst du, mein Mädchen' 98
  'Wenn du zu den Blumen gehst' 80
Jestremski, Margret xxiv, 3, 541
  Hugo Wolf. Skizzen und Fragmente 541
  Hugo-Wolf-Werkverzeichnis xxiv, xlv, 3, 455n
Johann (Joh.) André (publisher) xxx, xlv, 3, 4, 190, 301, 304
Johanna, Queen of Bohemia 150n
John of the Cross, St
  'En una noche oscura' 57
John of Nepomuk, St 150–51n
Johnson, Graham xxiv, 385n, 397n
  Franz Schubert: The Complete Songs xviii
Jong, Jeanette de 466
Josephine (Scheer) 339, 374n, 380n, 399n
Jung, Marianne, *see* Willemer, Marianne
Junius bookshop, Leipzig 315

Kafka, Franz 20
Kahn, Robert
  'Auf ein altes Bild' 389
  'Denk' es, o Seele!' 403
  'Er ist's' 372
  'Der Gärtner' 384
  'Gebet' 393
  'Jägerlied' 371
  'Der Knabe und das Immlein' 369
  'Ein Stündlein wohl vor Tag' 370
  'Zum neuen Jahr' 392
Kalbeck, Max 209–10, 526–7n
  Johannes Brahms 526n
Kammler, Johannes 397n
Kapp, Johanna 277
Karadjordjević, Prince Božidar 56, 63
Karg-Elert, Sigfrid: 'Sun of the sleepless' 12
Karl August, Duke 110

Karl Heckel Verlag (publishing house) xxxiii, xxxiv, 190, 194, 267, 444, 465, 485–6, 509–10
Karlsruhe xxxiii, xxxvii, 356, 500
Kasinoverein 302n
Kastner, Emerich, 304, 304n
Katzer, Anton: *Mr. Wolf in Amerika, Golddollars gewinnend* 514
Kauffmann, Emil xxxiii, 25, 30, 41n, 337, 341, 344, 355–6, 359, 360, 376n, 405n, 410n, 478, 485, **487–90**, 505, 520
  correspondence ix, xx, xl, xli, xlii, xliii, 27–9, 121, 212, 214, 218, 219, 221, 225, 227, 228, 326, 355, 357, 360, 386n, 433, 434, 460, 466, 497–8, 526, 537, 538, 539
  'Eduard Mörike und Hugo Wolf' 488, 489
  'An eine Äolsharfe' 377, 490
  'An den Schlaf' 394, 490
  'Auf ein altes Bild' 389, 490
  'Denk' es, o Seele!' 403, 490
  'Du bist Orplid, mein Land' 490
  'Früh im Wagen' 490
  'Gebet' 393
  'Gesang Weylas' 411
  'Heimweh' 400, 490
  'Lebe wohl' 400, 490
  'Mausfallen-Sprüchlein' 365, 490
  'Seufzer' 389, 490
  'Wo find' ich Trost?' 395, 490
Kauffmann, Ernst Friedrich 333, 334, 341, 355n, 356, 383n, 405n, 487, 489–90
  'Agnes' 381
  'Begegnung' 374, 490
  'Er ist's' 372
  'Der Feuerreiter' 409, 489
  'Der Frühling' 489
  'Der Gärtner' 383n, 384, 384n, 489
  'In der Frühe' 390, 490
  'Jägerlied' 490
  'Kirchengesang zu einer Trauung' 490
  'Der König bei der Krönung' 367, 490
  'Lammwirts Klagelied' 490
  'Lied vom Winde' 402, 489
  'Peregrina I' 397n, 490
  'Rosenzeit, wie schnell vorbei' 489

'Schön Rohtraut' 489
'Die Schwestern' 490
'Ein Stündlein wohl vor Tag' 370, 489
'Die Soldatenbraut' 489
'Die traurige Krönung' 489
'Um Mitternacht' 386, 489
Kayser, Philipp Christoph 110, 111, 129n
  'Wanderers Nachtlied' 130
Keats, John 363n
Keller, Gottfried lii, 20, 212, 276–89, **276–8**, 324, 324n, 332, 337, 345, 457, 497
  Der grüne Heinrich 276–9, 283, 324n
  Die Leute von Seldwyla 276
  Gesammelte Briefe 277
  Neuere Gedichte 278, 286n, 287n, 288n, 289n
  Romeo und Julia auf dem Dorfe 279
  Von Weibern 277, 278, 286n, 287n, 288n, 289n
Kerner, Justinus xxxi, xxxv, xlix, 18, 290–94, **290–91**, 299, 336, 340, 345, 377n
  'An Anna' 291
  Bilderbuch aus meiner Kindheit 291
  'Der schwere Traum' 291
  Dichtungen 291
  Die Seherin von Prevorst 290–91
  Gedichte 291
  Kleksographien... 291
  König Eginhart 411n
  Der letzte Blumenstrauß 291
  Lyrische Gedichte 291
  Magikon 407n
  Nachspiel der zweiten Schattenreihe... 291
  Reiseschatten 291, 411n
  Winterblüthen von Justinus Kerner 291
  'Zur Ruh, zur Ruh!' 129n, 291–2, 530–31n
Kerner, Theobald 290
  Das Kernerhaus und seine Gäste 290
Kerr, Alfred 282n, 509
  Krämerspiegel 453n, 509
Kersting, Georg Friedrich 295
  Auf Vorposten (*At the Sentry Post*) 19, 295
  Die Kranzwinderin 295
Kiel 496

Kienzl, Wilhelm
  'So wahr die Sonne scheinet' 454
Kinkel, Johanna
  'Als ich auf dem Euphrat schiffte' 116, 165
  'So wahr die Sonne scheinet' 454
Kipnis, Alexander xxii
Kistner Verlag (publishing house) xxxi, 190
Klagenfurt xxix, 517, 534
Klaiber, Julius 384n, 422
Klein, Bernhard: 'Gretchen vor dem Andachtsbild der Mater Dolorosa' 128
Klein, Joseph 187
  'Wenn ich in deine Augen seh' 197
Kleist, Heinrich von 18, 217–18, 217n, 284n, 507
  Amphitryon 536
  Penthesilea 507, 540
  Der Prinz von Homburg 191–2, 191–2n, 507, 540
  Der zerbrochene Krug 192, 192n, 507
Kleist, Ulrike von 217n
Klinckerfuß, Margarethe 116
  Aufklänge aus versunkener Zeit 116
Klindworth, Karl xxxi, 193, 193n
Klingenfeld, Emma 267
Klopstock, Friedrich Gottlieb 316
  'Die Genesung' 368n
Knab, Arnim
  'Die Bekehrte' 155
  'Blumengruß' 153
  'Der neue Amadis' 153
  'Der Schäfer' 152
  'Die Spröde' 154
Köchert, Heinrich xx, xxxi, 217n
Köchert, Hilde 149n
Köchert, Ilse 149n
  correspondence xl, 280
Köchert, Ermina 149n
Köchert, Heinrich 490–91, 494
Köchert, Hilde, *see* Wittgenstein-Köchert, Hilde
Köchert, Ilse 490–91
  correspondence 280
Köchert, Irmina 490–91

Köchert, Melanie xx, xxiii, xxx, xxxiii,
    39n, 56, 58, 105n, 149n, 171n, 245n, 255n,
    299, 300, 371n, 373n, 484, 486, **490–92**,
    493, 494, 515–16, 520–22
  correspondence xvii, xl, xli, xlii, xliii, 59,
    60–62, 120, 157n, 211, 216, 219, 228, 229,
    230, 246n, 251n, 255n, 270, 280, 281, 282,
    283, 284, 355, 359, 360, 361, 392n, 433,
    464, 466, 483, 486, 488, 508, 522, 525,
    539
  travels with HW xxxiv, 492, 516, 540n
  visits HW in asylum xxi, 484, 492
Köchert, Theodor 494
Köchert family xxi, xxxi, xxxii, xxxiv,
    xxxvii, 58, 216n, 301, 491, 521
Kodály, Zoltán 109
Kohl, Helmut 43n
Kohler, Andreas 337
Köhler, Louis 334
Komet, Der (journal) 205
Köngen 335
Königsberg 20
Kopisch, August: *Agrumi* 211
Koran 160n
Körner, Theodor xlvii, 4, 19, 34n, 261, **295–7**
  Alboin und Rosamunde 421n, 535
  Alfred der Große 296
  Knospen 295
  Leyer und Schwert . . . 19, 261, 295
  Rosamunde 296
  Vermischte Gedichte 295
Korngold, Erich Wolfgang 235n
  'Das Ständchen' 39–40
Köstritz 469
Kotzebue, Otto von 14
Kövecses 505
Krais (publisher) 366n
Krämer, August 502
Krämer-Wild, Marie 502
Kraus, Karl 477
Krauss, Rudolf 360–61
  Mörike als Gelegenheitsdichter . . . 360,
    360n
Krebs, Carl August 432
Krek, Gojmir: 'Hugo Wolf in Slovenci'
    126n

Krenek, Ernst: 'Der neue Amadis' 153
Kreutzer, Conradin: 'Nur wer die
    Sehnsucht kennt' 134
Krokodile, Die 54
Krotoschin 448
Krüdener, Julia von 337
Krufft, Nikolaus von 316
Kücken, Friedrich Wilhelm 432
Kugler, Franz 210, 211, 212, 332, 431, 432,
    448, 457
Kuh, Emil 175, 176
  Friedrich Hebbel 176n
Kunersdorf 13
Kunst und Altertum 143n
Kürnberger, Ferdinand
  Der Amerika-Müde 301
Kurtz, V. C. (artist) 337
Kurz, Hermann 336, 417n

Lachner, Franz
  'Aus meinen großen Schmerzen' 199
  'Du bist wie eine Blume' 196
  'Er ist's' 372
  'Harfenspieler III' 131
  'Ich stand in dunkeln Träumen' 198
  'Klinge, klinge, mein Pandero' 75
  'Lebe wohl' 400
  'Mädchen mit dem roten Mündchen'
    195
  'Mir träumte von einem Königskind'
    199
  'Sie haben heut' abend Gesellschaft' 197
  'Ein Stündlein wohl vor Tag' 370
  'Um Mitternacht' 386
  'Das verlassene Mägdlein' 373
  'Wenn ich in deine Augen seh' 197
Lachner, Ignaz 336
  Die Regenbrüder 336
Lackhner, Bertha von 318n, 365n, **492–3**,
    511
  correspondence xxxix, xl, 318, 345, 349,
    365n
Lacom (publisher), see C. Lacom
Lahn, River 126n
Laibach 504
Lang, Anton 243n

GENERAL INDEX 581

Lang, Edmund xxviii, xxxi, xxxv, 24, 374n, **493**, 494–5
  correspondence xl, 188, 291, 292, 345, 346, 347, 349, 350, 352, 536
Lang, Henriette xxxi, xxxix, 33n, **493–4**, 505
  correspondence 192, 243n, 492
Lang, Josefine 316
Lang, Marie **494–5**, 505, 540
  correspondence xl, 25, 348, 491
  'Hugo Wolfs Entwicklungszeit' 494
Lang, Melanie, *see* Köchert, Melanie
Lang family 493, 535
Lange, Fräulein 63
Langgaard, Rued Immanuel
  'Blumengruß' 153
Lanner, Joseph 418n
  'Hoffnungs-Strahlen' 418n
Larisch, Aloysia (Louise) von 18, 19, 20
Larisch, Rudolf von 281, **495–6**
  correspondence xl, 120, 280
  Unterricht in ornamentaler Schrift 495
Lassen, Eduard 54
  'Lebe wohl' 400
  'Mein Liebchen, wir saßen zusammen' 199
  'Ständchen' 443
  'Verborgenheit' 378
  'Das verlassene Mägdlein' 373
Lauter, River 396n
Lauterbach & Kuhn (publisher) 30, 190
Lavant valley 534
Lavater, Johann Kaspar 126n
Lawrence, D. H. xxvii
  The Collected Poems xxvii
  Lady Chatterley's Lover xxvi, 384n
Lechner Wald 314
Legge, Walter xxii–xxiii, 33n, 105n, 491
Leghorn 8
Leibnitz 508
Leidesdorf Psychiatric Clinic 490
Leigh, Augusta 8
Leipzig xxviii, 192, 205, 315, 489
  Conservatoire 117
  University 295, 315
Leipziger Zeitung 315

Lemnitz, Tiana xxii
Lenau, Nikolaus xlv, xlvi, xlvii, xlviii, 4, 116, 190, 212, 290, **298–313**, 298–301, 431, 473–4, 483, 490
  'An*' 300, 473–4
  Die Albingenser 301
  'Die Stimme des Kindes' 205
  Don Juan 301
  Faust 301
  Gedichte 300
  'Meerstille' 117
  'Meine Rose' 300
  Savonarola 301
  Schilflieder 299
  'Stimme der Glocken' 307n
  'Stimme des Regens' 307n
  'Stimme des Windes' 307n
  Stimmen 307n
  Tagebuchblätter 299
Lensing, Elise 174
Lepanto 9
Lessing, Gotthold Ephraim 157n
Leuthold, Heinrich 55–6, 210
Levetzow, Ulrike von 112
Levi, Hermann 120–21, 120n
Levy family 209
Liberation, War(s) of 18, 295, 340
Lichtenberg, Georg Christoph 393n
Liebknecht, Sonja 152n
Liliencron, Detlev von xv, xxxiii, 120–21, 344, 357, 359n, **496–7**
  correspondence xli, 218, 283
  Adjutantenritte 497
  'An Hugo Wolf' xvii, 344, 357, **525–9**
  'An M. G. Conrad' 527n
  'Auf dem Kirchhofe' 497
  Der Haidegänger 357, 497, 526
  Kampf und Spiele 497, 527n
  Leben und Lüge 496
  'Maienkätzchen' 497
  'Die Musik kommt' 497
Limousin 101n
Lindpaintner, Peter Josef von 432
Lingg, Hermann 210, 212
  'Immer leiser wird mein Schlummer' 54
  'Julinacht' 484

Lipperheide, Franz Josef von xxxvii, 497–8
Lipperheide, Frida von xxxvii, **497–8**
  correspondence xliii, 230, 520
Lipperheide family xxxiii
Lisbon 146n
Liszt, Franz xv, xxxi, 9, 54, 174, 175, 182,
    184, 193n, 209, 262, 301, 333, 380n, 455n,
    477
  'Du bist wie eine Blume' 196
  'Die Glocken von Marling' 175
  'Harfenspieler III' 131
  'Kennst du das Land' 137n, 139
  Tasso 9
  'Wanderers Nachtlied' 130
Litzmann, Carl Conrad Theodor 53
Lodi, battle of 346n
Loeben, Otto Heinrich, Graf von 18, 37n
Loewe, Carl xvi, 9, 116, 143n, 210, 295, 315,
    316, 451
  'Archibald Douglas' xviii
  'Dank des Paria' 157
  'Des Paria Gebet' 157n
  'Edward' xvi
  'Erlkönig' xviii
  Frauenliebe 14
  'Frühling übers Jahr' 156
  'Ganymed' 172
  'Gretchen vor dem Andachtsbild der
    Mater Dolorosa' 128
  'Gutmann und Gutweib' 144
  'Heinrich der Vogler' xvi
  'Legende' 157n
  'Nur wer die Sehnsucht kennt'
    ('Sehnsucht') 134
  'Der Pilgrim vor St. Just' 424
  'Der Sänger' 140
  'Die Sonne der Schlaflosen' 12, 12n
  'Die Spinnerin' 455n, 456
  'There be none of Beauty's daughters'
    11
  'Der verliebte Maikäfer' 433
  'Wanderers Nachtlied' 130
Lohbauer, Rudolf 337, 407n
London 146n, 187
London Lieder Club xxii
Loninger (professor) 117

Loos, Adolf 477
Lope de Vega 57
  'No lloreis ojuelos' 100
  Los Pastores de Bélen 68n
  'Pues andais en las palmas' 68
López de Ubeda
  'Los ojos del niño' 70
Lorenzi, Lenz xlvi, **314**
Lortzing, Albert
  Der Waffenschmied 512n, 534
  Zar und Zimmermann 534
Louis-Philippe I, King of France 184
Lovrana 492
Löwe, Ferdinand 26, 26n, 464
Löwenthal, Max von 299
Löwenthal, Sophie von 299–300, 313n
Lubowitz, Schloß 17, 19
Lucerne xv, xxi, 539–40
Ludwigsburg 332, 337, 338, 355–6, 376n
Luise, Duchess 129n
Luise, Princess, von Anhalt-Dessau 316, 317
Lussin 492
Lützow, Adolf von 295
Lützowsches Freikorps 18–19, 45n, 295
Luxemburg, Rosa 152n

M. Simions Verlag (publisher) 259
McCormack, John xxii
MacCunn, Hamish
  'There be none of Beauty's daughters' 11
MacDowell, Edward 182
  'Mein Liebchen, wir saßen
    zusammen' 200
McFarlane, James Walter, and Graham
  Orton: *The Oxford Ibsen* 267
Mackenzie, Compton xxii
Macpherson, James 56
  Fragments of Ancient Poetry . . . 56
Madrid 146n
Magdeburg 316, 471
Magazin für Litteratur 507
Magikon (periodical) 336
Mahler, Alma xxx
  Erinnerungen an Gustav Mahler xxx
Mahler, Gustav xv, xxi, xxix, xxx, xxxiv,
    380n, 451, 458, 477, 513

Des Knaben Wunderhorn 39n
Symphony No. 1 458
Symphony No. 4 289n
Mahlmann, August xlvi, **315**
  Der Hausbau 315
  'Gottvertrauen' 259
  Herodes vor Bethlehem 315
Mährlen, Johannes 333, 335, 379n, 380n
Maierling xxix, **xxxvii**, xxxviii, xxxix, 190, 239n, 318n, 365n, 376n, 483, 492, 511, 518
  Marienhof xxxvii, 365n, 483, 492, 511
Main, River 159n
Mainz xxxi, xxxvii, xli, 207, 221n, 283, 425, 509, 520, 521
Makart, Hans 477
Malborghet 514
Malsburg, Ernst Otto von der 53
Malsburg, Kammerherr von der 53
Malta 146n
Manchester Guardian xxii
Mann, Thomas 14
  Doktor Faustus 535
  Die Entstehung des Doktor Faustus 535
Mannheim xxxiii, xxxiv, xxxvii, xli, 190, 425, 465, 479, 484, 500, 534
Marbach am Neckar 337
Marburg (now Maribor) 54, 116
  Gymnasium xxix
  University 54
Marchant, Leslie A. 11n
Marcoaldi, Oreste 231
  Canti popolari inediti Umbri Liguri Piceni Piemontesi Latini 211–12, 215, 232, 234, 252n
Marischka, Hubert 235n
Marschner, Heinrich 432
  'Es war ein alter König' 201
  'Harfenspieler III' 131
  'Liebchen, wo bist du?' 440
  Der Vampyr 534
Marx, Joseph 212, 215
  'Wanderers Nachtlied' 130
Marx, Karl Julius 54
Massenet, Jules: *Werther* 225n
Matthisson, Friedrich von xlvii, 4, **316–19**, 316–18

'Adelaide' 316–17
'Andenken' 317
Das Stammbuch Friedrich von Matthissons 316
Flora, Teutschlands Töchtern geweiht 317
Literarischer Nachlaß 318
Schriften 318
'Todtenkranz für ein Kind' 316
Matthisson, Ludwig von 316
Matzen **xxxvii**, xlii, 376n, 497–8, 500
Matzen, Schloß xxxiii
  Jägerhäusl 497
Mauthner, Fritz 507
Mavrocordato, Alexander 8–9
Maximilian II, King 210
Mayer, Friederike 62, 62n, 502, 506
Mayr, Karl 479, **499**
  correspondence xv, xvi, xliii, 11, 63, 285, 378n, 436
Mayrhofer, Johann 295
Mayreder, Karl 498, 503
Mayreder, Rosa (Rosa Meyreder-Obermayer) 477, 503, 516, 534, 539
  Die Bernsteinhexe 536
  Der Corregidor (libretto) xxxiii, 477, 495, 534
  Eldas Untergang 536
  Erinnerungen an Hugo Wolf xix
  Mein Pantheon 477
Mayreder family 535
Mayser, Edwin xliii, 215, **499**
  correspondence 363
Medtner, Nicolas
  'Die Bekehrte' 155
  'Erster Verlust' 126
  'Geistesgruß' 126
  'Harfenspieler II' 130
  'Mailied' 127
  'Nur wer die Sehnsucht kennt' 134
  'Die Spröde' 154
  'Wanderers Nachtlied' 130
Meibom, Heinrich 393n
Meidling xxx
Meilhac, Henri, and Albert Millaud
  Mam'zelle Nitouche (libretto) 527n

Meinhold, Wilhelm
Maria Schweidler, die Bernsteinhexe 536
Mémoires du maréchal de Bassompierre 142n
Mendelssohn, Felix xiii, 3, 5, 9, 12, 54, 182, 209, 262, 305, 316
'Andenken' 317, 319
'Auf dem Teich, dem regungslosen' 299
'Erster Verlust' 126
'Die Liebende schreibt' 112
'Liebesglück' 47–8
Lieder ohne Worte 334
Lobgesang 395n
'Mein Liebchen, wir saßen zusammen' 199
piano music 501
'Schlafloser Augen Leuchte' 12n
'So lang man nüchtern ist' 162
'Sun of the sleepless' 12
'There be none of Beauty's daughters' 11
'Todtenkranz für ein Kind' 316
Mendelssohn family 209
Menzel, Adolph von 54, 210, 448
Merckel, Friedrich 186
Mergenthaler (brewery owner) 337
Merz, Oskar 120, 120n
Metternich, Klemens von 169n
Meyer, Conrad Ferdinand 497
Meyer, Helena 337
Meyer, Herbert (ed.)
Eduard Mörike. Zeichnungen 389n
Meyer, Maria xxvii, 334, 337–9, 355–7, 373n, 378n, 380n, 393n, 395n, 397n
Meyerbeer, Giacomo 182, 184
L'Africaine (*Die Afrikanerin*) 534
Les Huguenots (*Die Hugenotten*) 534
Le Prophète (*Der Prophet*) 534
'Schillerlied' 422
Michelangelo Buonarroti **320–29**, 501
Canti de' Morti 322
'Chiunche nascie a morte arriva' 322
'D'altrui pietoso e sol di sé spietato' 321
'I' ho già fatto un gozzo in questo stento' 321
'Io crederrei, se tu fussi di sasso' 322
'Non so se s'è la desiata luce' 322
'Un uomo in una donna' 321
Mieding, Johann Martin 110
Milbanke, Annabella 8
Millaud, Albert, *see* Meilhac, Henri
Minnesota Opera 266
Miramare 492
Mirat, Crescencia Eugénie 184
Mirjam (Gnesin) 196n
Mitchell, Donald 458
Mittwochsgesellschaft 431
Möhringen 335
Moldau, River 150n
Moniuszko, Stanisław
'Kennst du das Land' 139
Montañés, Juan Martínez 57
Montefeltro, Federigo da 321
Monthly Musical Record xxiii
Moor, Karel: *Hjördis* 266
Moore, Gerald xxii, 130n
Moravia 17
Morgenstern, Christian 267–8
Galgenlieder 268
Palmström 268
Mörike, August 334
Mörike, Charlotte 332, 335, 336, 338
Mörike, Eduard xvii, xxvii, xxxi, xxxii, xxxiii, xlviii, xlix, l, lii, liii, liv, lv, 4, 55, 175, 188, 202n, 211, 212, 215, 276, 290, **330–418**, 422, 448, 487, 489, 497, 505, 507, 509, 525, 527
'Abschied' 340, 417n
'Agnes' 339, 342
'An eine Äolsharfe' 332, 334, 376n
'An die Geliebte' 335, 342, 396n, 399n
'An Longus' 488
'An Moritz von Schwind' 333
Anakreon und die sogenannten Anakreontischen Lieder 157n
'Auf eine Christblume I' 381n, 386n
'Auf einer Wanderung' 333, 381n, 382n
'Auf zwei Sängerinnen' 381n
'Auftrag' 340
Ausgabe letzter Hand 337, 393n
'Begegnung' 339, 369n, 374n
'Besuch in der Kartause' 211, 337

'Besuch in Urach' 376n
'Denk es, o Seele!' 336, 402n
'Dünkt euch die Schöne' 339
'Die Elemente' 341, 364
'Elfenlied' 342. 410n
'Er ist's' 342, 372n, 373n
'Erinna an Sappho' 157n, 337
'Erinnerung' 334
'Erstes Liebeslied eines Mädchens' 339, 355, 369n, 374n, 399n
'Der Feuerreiter' 214, 341, 342, 357, 364, 407n
'Der Fluß' 369n
'Frage und Antwort' 339, 374n, 400n
'Der Gärtner' xxvi, 339, 369n, 384n
'Gebet' 339, 341, 342, 374n, 380n, 385n, 394n
Gedichte 332, 341, 342, 363, 372n, 385n, 388n, 393n, 400n, 401n, 402n, 407n, 417n
'Die Geister am Mummelsee' 342
'Gesang Weylas' 339
'Grabgedanken' 402n
'Heimweh' 400n
'Im Frühling' 339, 342
'In ein freundliches Städtchen tret' ich ein' 343
'Der Jäger' 339, 342
'Joseph Haydn' 333
'Karwoche' 335, 342
Klassische Blumenlese (ed.) 336
'Der Knabe und das Immlein' 339, 369n
'Der König bei der Krönung' 129n
'Lebe wohl' 335, 339, 399n, 400n
'Die Leier' 157n
'Der letzte König von Orplid' 411n
'Die Liebe zum Vaterlande' 340
'Liebesvorzeichen' 141–2n, 339
'Lied eines Verliebten' 339
'Lied vom Winde' 339, 342, 369n
Maler Nolten 20, 333, 337–40, 342, 367n, 372n, 373n, 379n, 380n, 382n, 388–9n, 391n, 393n, 394n, 395n, 396n, 397n, 401n, 403n, 407n, 410n, 411n, 422
'Mausfallen-Sprüchlein' xxxvii, 336, 340
'Mein Fluß' 339

Mozart auf der Reise nach Prag 333–4, 336, 340, 402n
'Muse und Dichter' 337
'Nachklang' 334
'Nächtliche Fahrt' 339
'Neue Liebe' 219n, 342, 394n
'Nimmersatte Liebe' 339, 348, 369n, 374n, 399n
Peregrina poems 338–9, 342, 355–7, 395n, 397–8n
Die Regenbrüder (libretto) 336
'Romanze vom wahnsinnigen Feuerreiter' 407–8n
'Schlafendes Jesuskind' 337
'Selbstgeständnis' 340
'Seufzer' 342, 395n
'Storchenbotschaft' 339, 340
'Ein Stündlein wohl vor Tag' 339
'Suschens Vogel' 339
'Der Tambour' 371n
'Die Tochter der Heide' 339, 366n
'Die traurige Krönung' 366n
'Verborgenheit' 339, 374n, 385n, 394n
'Das verlassene Mägdlein' 339, 342
'Vicia faba minor' 334
'Wo find' ich Trost?' xxvii, 342, 388n, 395n
'Zitronenfalter im April' 339
'Zur Warnung' 340
Mörike, Karl 333, 336, 339, 340, 341, 381n, 388–9n
'Die Geister am Mummelsee' 411n
Mörike, Karl Friedrich 332
Mörike, Klara 335, 336–7, 340, 381n, 386n
Mörike, Luise xxvii, 334–6, 395n, 397n
Mörike, Marie 333, 381n
Mosen, Julius 290
Moser, Moses xxvii, 183, 185, 187, 197n
Motte, Countess Jeanne de la 146n
Mottl, Felix xxx, 451, 452–3, **500**, 509
correspondence xl, 453
Mozart, Constanze 402n
Mozart, Wolfgang Amadeus xxix, 109, 318n, 333, 337, 358n, 402n, 488, 541
'Die Alte' 404n
'An Chloe' 274

La clemenza di Tito 333
'Dans un bois solitaire' 47n
Don Giovanni 110, 258n, 334, 534
Die Entführung aus dem Serail 110, 534
masses 112
Le nozze di Figaro (*Figaros Hochzeit*) 110, 125n, 534
operas 17, 110
Requiem 388n
'Das Veilchen' 110
'Der Zauberer' 246n
Die Zauberflöte 110
Müller, Hans Udo xxii
Müller, Paul xxxi, xxxiv, 322, **500–501**
   correspondence xliii, 63, 122, 228, 322–3, 325, 435
   'Erinnerungen an Hugo Wolf' 501
Müller, Wilhelm 185–6, 290, 316
   Egeria 211
   'Fastnachtslied von den goldenen Zöpfen' 195n
   Die schöne Müllerin 185–6
   Sieben und siebzig Gedichte . . . 185
   Die Winterreise 454n
Mummelsee 411n
Münchener Allgemeine Zeitung 504
Münchner Dichterkreis 54, 210
Munich xxxii, xxxiii, xxxvii, xli, 54, 120n, 121, 174, 209, 210–11, 276, 285, 359, 424, 448, 457, 483, 488, 499, 522, 523, 525–6, 529n
Murau xxxii, 376n, 508
Murray, John 363n
Musenalmanac 13
Music & Letters xxiii
Music Review xxiii
Musical Times xxiii
Musik, Die xxii, 501
Musikalisches Wochenblatt 489
Musikbuch aus Österreich 526n
Mussorgsky, Modest 9, 182
   'Harfenspieler II' 130
Mystes 376n

Naples 146n, 174
Napoleon Bonaparte 13, 45n, 188, 295, 340, 346n, 424
Napoleonic Wars 14
Nash, Ogden 197n
Nathan, Isaac 9
   'Sun of the sleepless' 12
Naturalismus movement 525
Nessler, Victor
   Der Trompeter von Säkkingen 458, 534
Netherlands 13
Netzer, Osnat
   'Der Schwalben Heimkehr' 206
Neue Freie Presse 491
Neue musikalische Presse 479
Neue Pariser Modelblätter 174
Neuenstadt 381n, 386n
Neues Wiener Tagblatt xxii, 527n
Neueste Nachrichten (Munich) 120n
Neuffer, Christian Ludwig
   'Lindamor an Cölinen' 399n
Neuffer, Klärchen 334, 339
Neuried 126n
New German School 21
New Philharmonia Orchestra 458
Newman, Ernest xvi
   Hugo Wolf xxii, 535
Newstead Abbey 8, 9
Nicolai, Otto 262
Nicolai, Philipp: 'Wie schön leucht' uns der Morgenstern' 390n
Nicolovius, Alfred 274
Niederösterreichische Landesirrenanstalt xxvii, xxxiv, xlvi, 32n, 326n, 479, 484, 492, 496, 504, 513, 515, 516, 540n
Nietzsche, Friedrich 9, 54, 230, 284n, 341, 362–3, 362n, 380n, 477
   Der Antichrist 230n
   Manfred-Meditation 9
   Nachgelassene Fragmente 362n
   'Sun of the sleepless' 12
Nikisch, Arthur 122, 122n, 425
Nobel Prize for Literature 212
Nölting, Henriette 54
Norderney 203n

Norway 182, 266
　language 271
Norwegian National Theatre 266
Nottebohm, Gustav 526n
Novalis 134n
Novi Akordi 126n
Nuñez, Nicolás
　'O Virgen que á Dios pariste' 66
Nuremberg 18, 358n
Nürtingen 388n
Nußdorf 482

Ober-Döbling xli, xlii, 300, 301, 490
Öblarn 508
Obrist, Dr 326
Ocaña 68n
　'Caminad esposa' 66-7
Ochs, Siegfried xlii, 62, 149n, **501-2**
　correspondence 223-4, 358
　Geschehenes, Gesehenes 501-2
　'Persönliche Erinnerungen' 501
Ochsenwang 335
Oder valley 17
Offenbach am Main 301, 304
Offenbach-am-Rhein 3
Orff, Carl
　'Mir träumte von einem Königskind' 199
Orr, C. W. 182
Orton, Graham, *see* McFarlane, James Walter
Orvieto 213
Ossian 56
Ostade, Adriaen von 143n
Österreichische Nationalbibliothek 342, 541
Otlingen 335
Otto, Ernst Julius 433
Ovid: *Metamorphoses* 468n
Owen 335
Oxus, River 165n

Paër, Ferdinando 110
Paisiello, Giovanni 110
Palestrina, Giovanni Pierluigi da 488
Palgrave, Francis Turner xxvi
Papier, Rosa xxxii, 4, 291, 486

Paris 13, 18, 19, 25, 146n, 183, 184, 187, 224n, 422, 471, 480, 483
　Montmartre Cemetery 203n
　Saint-Eustache 528n
　Théâtre des Variétés 527n
Park, Agnes 521
Parodiarum horatianarum libri III ... 393n
Parry, Hubert
　'There be none of Beauty's daughters' 11
Partisan Review 541
Paul, Jean 356, 356n
　Der Titan 356n, 478
Paumgartner, Hans 354, 354n
Pausanias: *Descriptions of Greece* 156n
Peitl, Paul xlvii, **419-21**
　pseudonyms 419, 420n
　König Alboin 419
Pepping, Ernst
　'Epiphanias' 150
　'Wanderers Nachtlied' 130
Perchtoldsdorf xxxi, xxxii, xxxiii, xxxiv, **xxxviii**, xl, xlii, xliii, 58, 195, 325, 326n, 342, 365n, 376n, 461n, 477, 495, 511, 527n
　Brunnergasse 26 xxxviii, 368n, 493, 511-12
　Häuslein Windebang xxxviii, 343, 361, 361n, 368-9n, 512
　Hugo-Wolf-Haus xxxviii, 511
　Siebenbrunnengasse 477
Peter, St 289n
Peter Lang Verlag (publisher) 211
Petersen, Wilhelm 31
　'Einkehr' 31
　'Die Spröde' 154
Petrarchism 320
Petrich, Franz 354n
Pfau, Ludwig xlvi, 422-3, **422**
　'Badisches Wiegenlied' 422
　Gedichte 422, 423n
　'Herr Biedermeier' 422
　'Die deutschen Flüchtlinge' 422
　'Im stillen Friedhof' 205, 519
　Lieder vom Herzen 423n
　'O Blätter, dürre Blätter!' 422
　'O Sterne, goldene Sterne' 422
　'Schillerlied' 422

'Sonette für das deutsche Volk auf das Jahr 1850' 422
'Zum 18, März 1848' 422
Pfenniger, J. C. 129n
Pfitzner, Hans 54, 175, 182, 276, 301, 451, 497
  Das Fest auf Solhaug (incidental music) 266
  'Denk' es, o Seele!' 403
  'Kuriose Geschichte' 433
  'Du milchjunger Knabe' 287
  'Sie haben heut' abend Gesellschaft' 188, 197
  'Singt mein Schatz wie ein Fink' 287
  'Tragische Geschichte' 14
  'Tretet ein, hoher Krieger' 278, 286
  'Das verlassene Mägdlein' 373
  'Wanderers Nachtlied' 130
  'Wandl' ich in dem Morgentau' 278, 288
Pflummern 335
Philharmonia Chorus xxii
Philip Augustus, King of France 462n
Philippsburg xxxiii, xxxvii
Phöbus Apollo (Anon.) 536
Piaste, Antonie 14
Pierpont Morgan Library 203n
Pigot, Elizabeth 12n
Pirano 492
Pirc, Father Sales 534
Platen, Karl August Georg Maximilian, Graf von Platen-Hallermünde (August von Platen) lii, 424–9, **424–5**, 451
  'Christnacht' xix
  Ghaselen 425
  'Die Liebe hat gelogen' 424
  'Du liebst much nicht' 424
  Lyrische Blätter 424
  'Der Pilgrim vor St. Just' 424
  Der romantische Oedipus 424
  Sonette aus Venedig 425
  'Der Strom, der neben mir verrauschte' 424
  Tagebuch 424
  'Wie rafft' ich mich auf in der Nacht' 424
Plattenhardt 335, 399n
Pleyer, Joseph 112

Plön 497
Plüddemann, Martin 486
Pöch, Alexander
  correspondence xxxix, 116–18
Poe, Edgar Allan
  'How to write a Blackwood article' 96n
Polish insurrection (1830) 478
Polko, Elise 469
  see also *Dichtergrüße* . . .
Ponchielli, Amilcare: *La Gioconda* 534
Porges, Heinrich 121, 121n
Portorosa 492
Posen 448
Potpeschnigg, Heinrich xxxiii, 327n, 354n, 500, **502–4**, 511
  correspondence xxi, xlii, xliii, xliv, xlvi, 10, 64, 228, 229, 284, 326, 406n, 498, 535, 536, 539
Pozo Morena, Sierra del 98n
Prague 150n, 205, 358n, 402n
Pressel, Gustav 341
Preussische Jahrbücher 113
Prey, Hermann 43n, 46n
Preyss, Therese 492
Preyss, Victor 492
Preyss family 365n, 511
Prill-Quartett 351n
Prokrajinski Archive, Maribor 544
Prometheus 169n
Provençal 101n
Prussia 261
  army 13, 496
  Civil Service 19
  court 13
Prussia, King of 372n
Pushkin, Alexander 9
  Eugene Onegin 9
Putnam, Samuel 96n
Pyrenees 184
Pyrker, Johann Ladislaus
  'Das Heimweh' 462n

Quilter, Roger
  'There be none of Beauty's daughters' 11

Rachmaninov, Sergei
   'Du bist wie eine Blume' 196
Ratibor, Duke of 262
Raphael 333
Rau, Franz 215
Rau, Luise 335, 377n, 391n, 396–7n, 399–400n
Rauchberg, Heinrich 425
Raucheisen, Michael xxii, 130n
Ravenna 363n
Reclam (publisher) 539
Reger, Max 30, 32n, 54, 175, 425, 448, 451
   12 *Lieder für eine Singstimme* 371n
   arrangements of Wolf settings 64n, 371n, 375n
   'Auf ein altes Bild' 389
   'Begegnung' 374
   'Er ist's' 372
   'Ergebung' 32
   'In der Frühe' 390
   'Der König bei der Krönung' 367
Reichardt, Johann Friedrich 109, 110, 111, 116, 316, 397n
   'Cophtisches Lied I' 146
   'Cophtisches Lied II' 147
   'Erster Verlust' 126
   'Der Fischer' 124
   'Frech und froh I' 147
   'Ganymed' 172
   'Geistesgruß' 126
   'Harfenspieler I' 130
   'Harfenspieler II' 130
   'Harfenspieler III' 131
   'Heiß mich nicht reden' 133
   'Kennst du das Land' 137n, 139
   'Der neue Amadis' 153
   'Nur wer die Sehnsucht kennt' 134
   'Prometheus' 171
   'Ritter Kurts Brautfahrt' 142
   'Der Sänger' 140
   'Der Schäfer' 152
   'Sehnsucht' 123
   'Singet nicht in Trauertönen' 137
   'So laßt mich scheinen' 136
   'Wanderers Nachtlied' 130
Reichmann, Theodor xvi

Reid, Paul
   The Beethoven Song Companion xviii
Reimann, Aribert 21
   Nachtstück II 21
   'Was ist mir denn so wehe?' 21
Reinhold, Albert 3
Reinick, Robert xxxi, xxxiii, xlviii, xlix, lii, liv, lvii, 34n, 174–5, 332, 415n, **430–47**, 457, 460, 504
   Drei Umrisse... 431
   'Gefährliche Nachbarschaft' 431
   Illustriertes ABC-Buch... 432
   'Im Sommer' 437n
   'Im Winter' 438n
   'In dem Himmel ruht die Erde. Ständchen' 441n
   'Komm in die stille Nacht! Ständchen' 442n
   Lieder und Fabeln für die Jugend 432
   Lieder eines Malers... 431
   Lieder von Robert Reinick 432
   Liederbuch für deutsche Künstler 431
   'Morgenlied' 436
   Ritter, Tod und Teufel... 431
   'Sonntags am Rheine' 431
   Vier Wiegenlieder 437n, 438n
Reinicke, Carl
   'Das verlassene Mägdlein' 373
Reissiger, Carl Gottlieb 262, 433
Reitzes, Joseph xxxvii, 365n, 483
Rembrandt van Rijn 171n
Rethberg, Elisabeth xxii
Rettenbach 44n
Reuss 469
Reutlingen 355–6
Révfy, Elise von 291
Rheinberger, Josef Gabriel: 'Die Nacht' 50
Rhine, River 8, 126n, 130n, 159n
Richard I 462n
Richter, Hans xxx, 118n, 302–3, 354n
Richter, Ludwig 345
Rickelt, Karl 360, 360n
Riedl, Jakob 19
Riedl, Oberbergrat 515
Ries, Ferdinand 316
Ries & Erler (publisher) 464, 466

Rieter, Luise 277
Rietz, Julius 433
Rihm, Wolfgang
  'Phänomen' 159
  'Sehnsucht' 123
  'Wo wird einst' 204
Rilke, Rainer Maria 373n
  'Der Panther' 373n
  Neue Gedichte 373n
Rimsky-Korsakov, Nikolai 9
  'Sun of the sleepless' 12
  'Wenn ich in deine Augen seh' 197
Rinnbach am Traunsee xxxi, xli, 216n, 376n, 490, 505
Ritterbund 118n, 302–3
Robert-tornow, Walter 321–2, 325n, 327, 328n, 329n
Röhr, Hugo 485
Rohrbach 17
Rolandseck 43
Rome 146n, 174, 210, 321, 432
  San Silvestro 321
  Sistine Chapel 321
Ropartz, Joseph
  'Mein Liebchen, wir saßen zusammen' 200
  'Wo ich bin, mich rings umdunkelt' 200
Roquette, Otto xlvi, 55, **448–9**
  Liederbuch von Otto Roquette 448
  'Perlenfischer' 205
  'Der Tunnel über der Spree' 448
Rorem, Ned: 'Sun of the sleepless' 12
Rosé-Quartett xxxii
Roskosch 480, 482
Rosner, Ernst (Elsa Bernstein-Porges)
  Königskinder 536
Rossini, Gioachino 534
  Il barbiere di Siviglia (Der Barbier von Sevilla) 534
  Guillaume Tell (Wilhelm Tell) 534
Roswaenge, Helge xxii
Roth, Ludwig 365n
Rovigno 492
Royal Academy of Music 534
Royal Opera House, Covent Garden xxii, 225n

Rubinstein, Anton 54
  'Bedeckt mich mit Blumen' 97
  'Du bist wie eine Blume' 196
  'Es war ein alter König' 201
  'Heiß mich nicht reden' 133
  'Kennst du das Land' 137n, 139
  'Klinge, klinge, mein Pandero' 75
  'Singet nicht in Trauertönen' 137
Rückert, Ernst 450
Rückert, Friedrich xlvii, 4, 210, 212, 316, 341, 424, **450–56**
  Deutsche Gedichte 450
  Geharnischte Sonette 450
  Gesammelte Gedichte 450
  Ghaselen 450
  Herodes der Große 451
  Kindertotenlieder 450
  Kranz der Zeit 450
  Liebesfrühling 451
  Östliche Rosen 450
  Saul und David 451
  'So wahr die Sonne scheinet' 454n
  'Die Spinnerin' 205
  Weisheit des Brahmanen . . . 450
Rückert, Luise 450
Rudorff, Ernst 501
Ruiz, Juan 65
Ruppert, Anton: *Baumeister Solness* 266
Russia 182, 315
Rütli, Das 448

Sæverud, Harald: *Gildet paa Solhoug* 266
St Paul 376n
St Paul's Cathedral 9
St Petersburg 146n
Säkkingen 457
Saladin 462n
Salieri, Antonio
  'Andenken' 317, 319
  Axur, Re d'Ormus 392n
Salis-Seewis, Johann Gaudenz von 316
Sallet, Friedrich von: 'Der Morgen' 544
Salomon, Josef 515
Salomon, Käthe, *see* Wolf, Käthe
Salzburg xxxi, xxxvii, 22, 516
  Königliches Nationaltheater xxxi

GENERAL INDEX

Salzer, Marcell 529n
Salzkammergut xxxviii
Sams, Eric xxiv, 93n, 193n, 256n
   The Songs of Hugo Wolf xviii, xxiv
   The Songs of Johannes Brahms xviii
Sand, Georges 184
Sankt Paul, Konvikt of, Carinthia xxix, 534
Sappho of Lesbos 156n
Savonarola, Girolamo 321, 328n
Saxe-Weimar-Eisenach 124n
Schack, Adolf Friedrich, Graf von 54, 210
   'Mach auf, mach auf! doch leise, mein Kind' 54
Schadow, Gottfried 431
Schaffhausen 337
Schalk, Franz 24, 26, 26n, 121, 121n, 437, 504–5
   correspondence xl, 348, 349, 350
Schalk, Joseph xxxii, 24, 37n, 351n, 483, **504–5**, 535
   correspondence 25–6
   'Neue Lieder, neues Leben' 483, 488, 504, 525
Schaumann, Franz 471, 506
Schebest, Agnes 383n
Scheer 339, 380n, 399n
Scheffel, Joseph Victor von xxxii, xlix, lvi, 212, 332, **457–62**
   'Alt-Heidelberg, du feine' 457, 458
   'Behüt dich Gott, es wär zu schön gewesen' 458
   'Biterolf' 129n, 458, 462n
   Ekkehard 457
   Frau Aventiure... 457, 458–9, 461n
   Gaudeamus... 457
   Hugideo 457
   Der Trompeter von Säkkingen 457
   'Wächterlied auf der Wartburg' 129n, 458
   Waldeinsamkeit 457
   Wartburglieder 461n
   Werke 457
Scheffel, Josephine von 457
Scheibner, Johann xxi
Schelling, Friedrich Wilhelm Joseph 332
Scherer, Georg 359, 359n
   Deutsche Volkslieder 359n
   Die schönsten deutschen Volkslieder 359n
Scherzer, Otto 341
Schey, Joseph von xli, 494, **505**
   correspondence 537
Schey, Witold xxiii
Schikaneder, Emanuel 110–11
Schiller, Friedrich von 290, 295, 316, 360n
   Demetrius 175
   'Der Geisterseher' 146n
   Musenalmanach 146n
   Wilhelm Tell 370n, 448
Schiller National Museum 337
Schillings, Max von
   'Erschaffen und Beleben' 160
Schinkel, Karl Friedrich 432
Schladebach, Julius 433
Schlegel, August Wilhelm 13, 14, 185–6, 467, 468
Schlegel, Dorothea 18
Schlegel, Friedrich 18, 290
Schmid, Wilhelm xli, 376n, 489, **505–6**, 512n
   correspondence 268
Schmidt, Hans 3
Schmied, Alfred 526
Schmoll, Maler 126n
Schnezler, August
   Mummelsee-Balladen 411n
Schoeck, Othmar 21, 175, 276, 301, 338, 339, 341, 397n
   'An die Lützowschen Jäger' 18
   'Einkehr' 31
   'Er ist's' 372
   'Frage nicht' 313
   Gaselen 276
   'Gebet' 393
   'Herbstentschluß' 312
   Das holde Bescheiden 341, 393n
   'In der Fremde' 33
   Lebendig begraben 276
   'Liebesfrühling' 307
   'Nachruf' 29–30
   'Resignation' 31–2
   'Stille Sicherheit' 308

    Unter Sternen 276
    'Von fern die Uhren schlagen' 21
    'Wo wird einst' 204
Schoenberg, Arnold 212, 422
    'Mailied' 127
Schönaich, Gustav 191, 191n
Schönemann, Anna Elisabeth (Lili) 111, 124n
Schönfield, Clementine 285, 289n, 499
Schopenhauer, Arthur 284n, 518
Schoppe, Amalia 174
Schorr, Friedrich xxii
Schott's, *see* B. Schott's Söhne
Schreckenberger, Waldemar 43n
Schreker, Franz 212
Schröter, Corona 149n
    'Erlkönig' 149n
    'Der neue Amadis' 153
Schubart, Anna 210
Schubart, Christian 316
Schubert, Franz ix, xv, xvii, xviii, xix, xxi, xxxv, 19, 55, 142n, 169n, 182, 186, 187, 193n, 295, 334, 351, 354n, 433n, 450, 451, 513
    'Am Tage aller Seelen' 274
    'An die Leier' 157n
    'An den Mond' 111
    'Andenken' 317, 319
    'Auf dem Wasser zu singen' xv, 199n
    'Ave Maria' xv
    Claudine von Villa Bella 110
    'Du bist die Ruh' xv
    'Du liebst mich nicht' 424
    'Erlkönig' xv, xviii, 109, 110, 384
    'Erster Verlust' 126
    'Es rauschet das Wasser' 151n
    'Der Fischer' 109, 124
    Die Fischerin 110
    'Die Forelle' xv
    'Frech und froh I' 147
    'Freiwilliges Versinken' 396n
    'Frühlingsglaube' xv
    'Ganymed' 116, 121, 171n, 172, 172n
    'Geistesgruß' 126
    Gesänge des Harfners xvi
    Goethe settings xvi, 109, 110, 112, 114, 116, 120–21, 172n, 343

    'Der Gott und die Bayadere' 157n
    'Grenzen der Menschheit' 116, 172n, 173
    'Gretchen am Spinnrade' xv, 109, 127n, 155n, 300
    'Gretchens Bitte' 128
    'Harfenspieler I' 130, 172n, 501
    'Harfenspieler II' 130, 172n, 501
    'Harfenspieler III' 131, 172n, 501
    'Das Heimweh' 463n
    Heine settings 186, 187
    'Heiß mich nicht reden' 133, 172n
    'Ich stand in dunkeln Träumen' 189, 198
    Jery und Bätely 110, 151n
    'Die junge Nonne' xv
    'Kennst du das Land' 137n, 139, 172n
    'Der Leiermann' xvi
    'Die Liebe hat gelogen' 424
    'Liebe schwärmt auf allen Wegen' 110
    Liszt transcriptions xv
    'Meeres Stille' xv, 109
    'Nacht und Träume' 385n
    'Nur wer die Sehnsucht kennt' 134, 134n, 172n
    'Prometheus' 116, 121, 171, 172n
    'Rastlose Liebe' xv
    'Der Rattenfänger' 141n, 142
    'Der Sänger' 140
    Die schöne Müllerin xv, 367
    Schwanengesang xv, 186, 189, 201n
    'Sehnsucht' 123
    'So laßt mich scheinen' 135n, 136
    'Die Stadt' 201n
    'Suleika 1' 112
    'Suleika 2' 112
    'Sun of the sleepless' 12
    'Todtenkranz für ein Kind' 316
    Der vierjährige Posten 295
    'Der Wanderer' 300
    'Wanderers Nachtlied' 130
    'Wandrers Nachtlieder' 111
    'Willkommen und Abschied' 111
    Winterreise xv, 63n
    'Wonne der Wehmut' 112
Schulhof, Hilda 50n
Schulze, Ernst 450

Schumann, Clara 19, 54, 291, 451
   'Ich stand in dunkeln Träumen' 189, 198
Schumann, Ludwig 432
Schumann, Robert ix, xv, xix, xxxv, xlv,
   5, 9, 12, 15, 19, 21, 22, 23, 24, 54, 55, 56,
   174–5, 182, 194, 212, 262, 301, 305, 315,
   341, 342, 345, 351, 352, 431–2, 433, 451, 513
   correspondence 263
   'Alle gingen, Herz, zur Ruh' 94
   'An Anna' 291
   'Bedeckt mich mit Blumen' 97
   'Belsatzar' xxvi
   'Du bist wie eine Blume' 196
   'Dunkler Sichtglanz' 82n
   'Der Einsiedler' 22
   'Dereinst, dereinst, Gedanke mein' 95
   Dichterliebe 182, 188, 189
   'Ein Jüngling liebt ein Mädchen' 188
   'Er ist's' 372
   'Der Fischer' 124
   Frauenliebe und -leben 14, 188
   'Frühlingsglocken' 442
   'Frühlingsnacht' 155n
   'Der Gärtner' 384
   Genoveva 174–5, 432
   'Das Glück' 176, 179
   Goethe settings xvi, 114, 116, 120–21
   'Harfenspieler I' 130
   'Harfenspieler II' 130
   'Harfenspieler III' 131
   Heine settings 187, 343
   'Heiß mich nicht reden' 133
   'Der Hidalgo' 53, 59n
   'Ich hab' im Traum geweinet' 189
   'Intermezzo' 19
   'Jägerlied' 371
   'Ein Jüngling liebt ein Mädchen' 482
   'Kennst du das Land' 137n, 139
   Kerner-Lieder 188, 336
   'Klinge, klinge, mein Pandero' 75
   'Liebesbotschaft' 443
   Liederalbum für die Jugend 176
   Liederkreis, Op. 24 182, 188
   Liederkreis, Op. 39 19, 21, 23, 188, 189
   Manfred 9
   'Mein Wagen rollet langsam' 194, 194n
   'Meine Rose' 300
   'Mögen alle bösen Zungen' 87
   Myrthen 196n
   'Nachtlied', Op. 108 175
   'Nur wer die Sehnsucht kennt' 134, 134n
   'Der Nußbaum' 290
   'O wie lieblich ist das Mädchen' 98n
   'Der Page' 53
   postludes 188, 256n
   'Resignation' 31–2
   'Der Sänger' 140
   Sechs Gedichte von N. Lenau xvi
   Sechs Lieder nach R. Reinick 431
   'Singet nicht in Trauertönen' 136n, 137
   'So laßt mich scheinen' 136
   'So wahr die Sonne scheinet' 454
   'Soldatenlied' 263n
   Spanische Liebeslieder 56, 98n
   Spanisches Liederspiel 56, 98n
   'Ständchen' 443
   'Die Stille' 19
   'Tamburinschlägerin' 75n
   'Tief im Herzen trag' ich Pein' 95
   'Und schläfst du, mein Mädchen' 98, 98n
   'Das verlassene Mägdlein' 373, 373n
   'Von dem Rosenbusch, o Mutter' 98n
   'Waldmädchen' 50–51
   'Weh, wie zornig ist das Mädchen' 98n
   'Wenn ich in deine Augen seh' 197
   'Wer nie sein Brot mit Tränen aß' xvi
   'Zwielicht' 22, 189
   Zwölf Gedichte aus F. Rückert's Liebesfrühling für Gesang und Pianoforte xvi
   Zwölf Gedichte von Justinus Kerner xvi, 291
Schur, Gustav 351n, 464, **506–7**
   correspondence xl, xli, 61, 215–16, 279, 280, 465, 509, 526, 537
   Erinnerungen an Hugo Wolf… xviii, 172n, 507
Schütz, Heinrich 488
Schwab, Gustav 14, 290, 299, 431
Schwäbische Kronik 485, 488

Schwarz-Schilling, Reinhard 38
  Der wandernde Musikant 38n
  'Der Musikant' 38
Schwarzkopf, Elisabeth xxiii, 385n
Schwerin 261
Schwind, Moritz von 142n, 157n, 333, 340, 345
Scribe, Eugène: *Actéon* 535
'Se davno mrači, moj'ga pobča še ni' 126n
Seckendorff, Siegmund von
  'Der Fischer' 124
Sethe, Christian 182-4, 186, 203n
Shakespeare, William xxxii, xxxiii, xxxviii, lii, lv, 11, 30, 284n, 321, **463-8**, 486, 489
  Antony and Cleopatra 464
  Hamlet 136n, 464
  King Lear 172n
  A Midsummer Night's Dream (*Ein Sommernachtstraum*) xix, 194, 464-6, 467n, 468n, 535
  The Tempest (*Der Sturm*) xxxiii, 464, 465, 486, 496, 535, 535n
Shelley, Mary 8
Shelley, Percy Bysshe 8
  'To Constantia singing' 11n
Siebold, Agathe von 523
Siena 213
Silcher, Friedrich 54, 291, 341
  'Wohin mit der Freud'? 439
Silesia 17
Simrock (publisher) 451, 453-4
Sipek, Karl 461n
Sirnach 338
Sitwell, Mrs 317
Sleeman, Margaret G., and Gareth A. Davies: 'The *Spanisches Liederbuch* of Emanuel Geibel...' 71n, 78n, 102n
Slovenia xxxviii
  Volksschule xxxviii
Solomon, Julie 209
Sorrento 210
Spain 54-6
Speeth, Margarethe von 336-7
Spender, Stephen
  'The Making of a Poem' 541

Spitzer, Leopold xxiii-xxiv
  Hugo Wolf: Briefe xxiii, xxxiv
Spitzweg, Carl 333
  The Poor Poet 335
Spohr, Louis 54, 262, 291, 315, 433
  'Frühlingsglocken' 442
  'Kennst du das Land' 137n, 139
Spontini, Gaspare 110
  'Kennst du das Land' 139
Spurny, Fräulein (singer) 228
Staël, Madame de 13
Stanford, Charles Villiers
  'There be none of Beauty's daughters' 11
  'Ernst ist der Frühling' 202
  'Sterne mit den goldnen Füßchen' 203
  'Wie des Mondes Abbild zittert' 202
Stephan, Rudi 175
Stein, Charlotte von 111, 117, 125n, 130n, 133n, 152n, 158n, 335
Steinebach, Friedrich 3
  'Das Lied der Waise' 544
Steiner, Rudolf 477, 494
Steinitzer, Max 458
Stenhammar, Wilhelm
  The Feast at Solhaug 266
Stern, Julius 433
Sterne, Laurence
  Tristram Shandy 284n, 478
Sternfeld, Richard xxxiii, xlii, 142n, 375n, **507-8**
  correspondence 358, 460
  'Ein neuer Liederfrühling' 507
  'Zum Gedächtnis eines Meisters...' 508
Stevenson, Robert Louis 317
Stifter, Adalbert 284n
  Bunte Steine xx
Stockhausen, Julius 487, 520
Stockholm 266
Stolberg, Friedrich 316
Storm, Theodor 21, 212, 340, 345, 448, 496, 497
Strasbourg xxxiv, 109, 146n
Strasser, Josef xxxii, 455n, **508**, 516
  correspondence ix, xix, xl, 59, 293, 351, 475, 496, 537

Strasser, Modesta (HW's sister) xxxii,
    xxxiv, 455n, 484, 503, 508, 513, 514, **516**,
    517
  correspondence xl, 293
Straus, Oscar 497
  'Die Musik kommt' 497
Strauss, Richard xv, xxxiii, 14, 54, 55, 110,
    182, 295, 301, 451, 478, 483, 487, 497
  Acht Gedichte aus Letzte Blätter von
    Hermann von Gilm xiii
  'Erschaffen und Beleben' 160
  'Der Fischer' 124
  'Gefunden' 111, 156n
  Krämerspiegel 282n, 453n, 509
  Eine Nacht in Venedig 235n
  'Unser Feind ist, großer Gott' 282n
  'Waldesfahrt' 194n
  'Wo ich bin, mich rings umdunkelt' 200
Stravinsky, Igor
  'Herr, was trägt der Boden hier'
    (orchestral arrangement) 73n
  'Wunden trägst du, mein Geliebter'
    (orchestral arrangement) 74n
Strecker, Ludwig xxxiii, 27, 27n, 30, 61, 282,
    282n, 425, 464–5, 487, **509–10**, 534
  correspondence xxxix, 221–2, 224n, 452
  wife 28, 61, 282, 509
Strodtmann, Adolf 203n
Sturm, Julius xlvii, 190, **469–70**
  Fromme Lieder 469
  'Über Nacht' 469
Stuttgart xxxiii, xxxiv, xxxvii, xli, xliii,
    299, 326, 332, 336, 338, 358–9, 358n,
    360n, 392n, 402n, 422, 434–5, 478–9,
    488, 499, 520
  Gymnasium 332
  Hofkapelle 488
  Hoftheater 334
  Hugo-Wolf-Verein 479, 499, 535
  Karlsgymnasium 499
  Katharinenstift 336
  Liederkranz 434, 435
  Musikhochschule 365n
  Polytechniker-Liederkranz 488
  Schwäbisch Hall 336
Styria 426, 508, 515

Sunday Times xxii
Svetlin, Dr xxxiv, 131n, 252n, 322, 325n,
    445n, 484, 489, 492, 496, 504, 515, 540n
Swabia 341, 361, 372n
Sweden 315
Swift, Jonathan: Gulliver's Travels 284n
Swiss Mining Board and Forestry
    Commission 471
Switzerland 8, 13, 261, 338, 448, 471, 472n,
    480
Symonds, John Addington 320
Syracuse 425
Szell, George xv

Tauber, Richard 235n
Taubert, Karl 433
  'Wenn du zu den Blumen gehst'
    80
Tchaikovsky, Pyotr Ilyich 9, 182
  'Heiß mich nicht reden' 133
  'Kennst du das Land' 137n, 139
  'Nur wer die Sehnsucht kennt' 134,
    134n
Tendering, Betty 277
Teos 156n
Thatcher, David, see Gooch, Bryan N. S.
Theremin, Franz 12n
Thomas, Ambroise: Hamlet 534
Thomas, Eugen 30
Thomson, James: The Seasons 138–9n
Thoresen, Johan 267
Thoresen, Magdalene 267
Thoresen, Suzannah 267
Thouret, Georg 322
Thrun (composer) 433
Thuille, Ludwig: 'Ein Stündlein wohl vor
    Tag' 370
Thuringia 130n
Tieck, Ludwig 14
  Leben und Tod der heiligen Genoveva
    432
Tiehsen, Otto 433
Tigri, Giuseppe 213, 231
  Canti popolari toscani 212, 213, 215, 233,
    235, 237, 240–43, 247–8, 252–3, 252n,
    254, 256, 258

Tillier, Claude
   Mon Oncle Benjamin 284n, 422, 478
Tiroler Jägerkompagnie 18
Tirso de Molina
   El burlador de Sevilla 56
   Marta la piadosa 56
Tomášek, Václav
   'Die Bekehrte' 155
   'Erster Verlust' 126
   'Der Fischer' 124
   'Geistesgruß' 126
   'Heiß mich nicht reden' 133
   'Kennst du das Land' 139
   'Nur wer die Sehnsucht kennt' 134
   'Der Rattenfänger' 141n, 142
   'Singet nicht in Trauertönen' 137
   'Die Spröde' 154
   'Wanderers Nachtlied' 130
Tommaseo, Niccolò 231
   Canti popolari toscani corsi illirici greci 211, 215, 231, 234–8, 240–42, 244–5, 247–51, 252n, 253, 255, 257
Toscanini, Arturo 130n
Traunkirchen xxiii, xxxiv, **xxxviii**, xli, xlii, xliv, 491, 494, 505
   Pfarrhof xxxviii
Traunsee xxi, xxxiv, xxxviii, xlvi
Trieste xxxiv, 492, 516
Trinity College, Cambridge 8
Trunk, Richard 33, 40, 42
   'In der Fremde' 33
   'Nachtzauber' 42
   'Das Ständchen' 39–40
   'Um Mitternacht' 386
Tübingen xxxiii, xxxvii, 227, 334, 338, 340, 355–7, 364, 388n, 393n, 478, 479, 485, 488, 489, 505, 520
   Akademische Musiktafel 488
   University 290
Tübinger Chronik 505–6
Tunnel über der Spree 210
Turgenev, Ivan 333, 515
Twain, Mark 380n, 477
   The Adventures of Huckleberry Finn 284n, 478
Tyrol xxxvii, 479, 497

Überbrettl 529n
Uhland, Ludwig 174, 175, 186, 290, 291, 299, 345
Umlauft, Friedrich
   correspondence xxxviii
Unger, Karoline 300
Universal (publisher) 537
Unterach xxxii, **xxxviii**, xl, xli, 477
   Höllengebirge xxviii
   Hugo-Wolf-Weg xxxviii
Urach 340, 376n
   Klosterschule 332
Urania ... 454n
USA 182
Uz, Johann Peter 157n

Valdivielso, José de
   'Feridas teneis mi vida' 73
Valerius Maximus 156n
Valgius Rufus 376n
Varnhagen, Rahel 196n, 290
Vasari, Giorgio 320
   Le Vite (*Lives*) 321
Vatican Library 210
Veit, Philipp 18
Verdi, Giuseppe xxiii
   Aida 534
   Il Corsaro 9
   I due Foscari 9
   'Gretchen vor dem Andachtsbild der Mater Dolorosa' 128
   Harold en Italie 9
   Il trovatore (*Der Troubador*) 534
Verlaine, Paul 182
Vesque von Püttlingen, Johann 182, 186, 187
   'Du bist wie eine Blume' 196
   'Es blasen die blauen Husaren' 200
   'Es war ein alter König' 201
   'Der Fischer' 124
   'Ich stand in dunkeln Träumen' 198
   'Mädchen mit dem roten Mündchen' 195
   'Mir träumte von einem Königskind' 199
   'Sie haben heut' abend Gesellschaft' 197
   'Wo ich bin, mich rings umdunkelt' 200

GENERAL INDEX

Viardot, Pauline 333
　'Agnes' 381
　'Er ist's' 372
　'Der Gärtner' 384
　'In der Frühe' 390
　'Nixe Binsefuß' 409
　'Das verlassene Mägdlein' 373
Vicente, Gil
　'Mal haya quien los envuelve' 104
　'Si dormis doncella' 98, 98n
Victoria, Tomás Luis de 55
Viehoff, Heinrich
Vienna xxiii, xxxi, xxxii, xxxiv, xxxvii, xxxviii, xxxix, xl, xli, xlii, xliii, 18, 19, 26n, 58, 119n, 122n, 169n, 190, 205, 227, 295, 296, 300, 30 n1, 304, 349, 351, 358n, 362n, 419, 434, 451, 479, 480, 482, 490, 491, 494, 495, 514, 515, 517, 521, 526, 527, 533
　Alleegasse 18 419, 420
　Burgtheater (Hofburgtheater) xxxiii, 174, 267–9, 295, 464, 537
　Conservatoire xxii, xxx, 117, 471, 473, 504, 510
　Hirschengasse xxxvii
　Hofoper xxi, xxxiv, 225n, 303, 513, 534
　Hotel Imperial xxx
　Hugo-Wolf-Verein xxi, xxxiv, 267, 479, 484, 495, 511
　Jordanstraße 504
　Kumpfgasse 495
　Margaretenstraße 7 510
　Mayergasse 14 510
　Mehlmarkt xxxii, 490, 492, 494
　Musikverein xxx
　Mühlgasse 22 xxxiv, 492
　National History Museum 484
　Prater 418n
　Ring-Theater 500
　Saal Bösendorfer 4, 37n, 291, 406n, 486, 503, 521
　Schwindgasse 3 xxxiv, 479, 492, 495, 499, 501, 503, 511, 534
　Stadt- und Landesbibliothek 22, 513, 541
　Theater an der Wien 235n
　University 493

Votivkirche xxxv
Wagner-Verein xxxii, 25n, 45–6n, 477, 500, 504–5, 506, 516
Wienbibliothek (City Library) 22, 473
　Nachlaß Hugo Wolf 45n
Zentralfriedhof xix, xxvii, xxxv, 292, 484
Viennese Secession 495
Vignoles, Roger 397n
Vinzenzberg, Anna 510
　correspondence xxxix, 296
Vinzenzberg, Ida 510
Vinzenzberg, Katharina **510**
Vogl, Johann Michael 300, 433n
Volkspartei 422
Vondung, Anke 258n
Voss, Johann Heinrich 29
Vulpius, Christian 125n
　Der Directeur in der Klemme 154n
Vulpius, Christiane 111–12

Wagner, Richard xviii, 19, 21, 121, 191n, 193n, 210, 225n, 284, 296n, 303, 333–4, 345, 354n, 362–3, 380n, 395n, 417n, 453, 477, 479, 495, 500, 506, 507, 511, 518
　death 23, 32n, 294n, 509
　Der fliegende Holländer 334, 534
　Fünf Gedichte für eine Frauenstimme xvi
　'Gretchen vor dem Andachtsbild der Mater Dolorosa' 128m
　Lohengrin xxviii, 225n, 334, 534
　Die Meistersinger von Nürnberg xxxi, xxxii, xlv, 358n, 435n, 444n, 492, 501, 509, 534
　Parsifal xxxi, 120n, 225n, 395n, 411n, 433n, 453, 490, 492, 509, 523
　Religion und Kunst 318
　Das Rheingold 534
　'The Ride of the Valkyries' 193
　Rienzi 302–3
　Der Ring des Nibelungen 492, 500
　Siegfried Idyll 484, 509
　Tannhäuser xxx, 296, 334, 461n, 462n, 534
　Tristan und Isolde xxxii, 354–5, 492, 534
　Die Walküre xxxi, xlv, 225n, 372n, 514, 521

Während 482
Waiblinger, Wilhelm 341, 382n
Waidhofen an der Ybbs **xxxviii**, xxxix, 176n, 190
   Gasthaus Zum goldenen Pflug xxxviii
Walker, Frank xxiii, 3, 143n, 294n, 455n, 491, 499, 514
   Hugo Wolf: A Biography xxiii, 3, 314, 386n, 469, 482, 491
Walter, Bruno 485
   'Der Soldat' 40
Ward, Robert: *Claudia Legare* 266
Weber, Carl Maria von 295, 316, 319
   Euryanthe 534
   Der Freischütz 534
   Oberon 534
Weber, Ludwig xxii
Webern, Anton: 'Blumengruß' 153
Wedekind, Frank 529n
Weilheim 335
Weimar 110–11, 146n, 148n, 154n, 156n, 172n, 174, 262
   court 111, 130n, 145n, 149n
   Hoftheater 110
Weimar, Duke of 139n
Weingartner, Felix 60–61, 60n, 62, 121, 425, 483
   'An die Geliebte' 60n, 397
   'Er ist's' 60n, 372
   'Gebet' 393
   'Jägerlied' 60n, 371
   Mörike settings 60n
   'Ein Stündlein wohl vor Tag' 60n, 370
   'Zitronenfalter im April' 385n
   'Zum neuen Jahr' 60n, 392
Weinsberg 290
Weißenbach 44n
Welzheim 290
Wenceslas IV, King of Bohemia 150n
Werner, Anton von 458
Werner, Heinrich 326n, 365n, 483, 484, 507, 511–12, 535
   Hugo Wolf in Maierling: Eine Idylle xviii, xxxi, 483, 512
   Hugo Wolf in Perchtoldsdorf 368n, 511

Hugo Wolf und der Wiener akademische Wagner-Verein 512
'Hugo Wolf. Zur zwanzigsten Wiederkehr des Todestags' 527n
Werner, Hugo, jr 365n, 511
Werner, Hugo, sr 511
Werner, Marie 365n, 511
Werner, Mitzi 342, 345, 365n, 493, 511
Werner family xxxi, xxxii, xxxviii, 58, 343, 346, **511–12**
Wesselburen 174
Westminster Abbey 9
Westphalia 262
Wette, Hermann 487
Wetzler, Emil xxxii, 292
   see also Emil Wetzler (publisher)
White, Maude Valérie 182
   'There be none of Beauty's daughters' 11
Widmann, Maria 422
Wiener a cappella Chorverein 32n
Wiener akademischer Wagner-Verein 351, 351n, 354n
Wiener Philharmoniker xxxii
Wiener Salonblatt xx, xxx, xxxi, xxxii, xlv, 486, 490, 526n, 534
Wiener Werkstätte 495
Wiener Zeitung 354n
   Abendpost 354
Wiesbaden xxvii, 46n, 113, 158n
Wiethaus, Luise 451
Wigmore, Richard xviii
Wildbach 290
Wilferth, Ferdinand 469
Wilhelm Hertz (publisher) 283
Willemer, Geheimrat Johann Jakob von 112, 113
Willemer, Marianne von xxvii, 112, 113, 158n, 163, 164n, 167n, 169n
   'Ach, um deine feuchten Schwingen' 163
   'Als ich auf dem Euphrat schiffte' 163
   'Hochbeglückt in deiner Liebe' 113, 163
   'Nimmer will ich dich verlieren!' (attrib.) 169n
   'Was bedeutet die Bewegung?' 163
   'Wie mit innigstem Behagen' 163
Willemer family 166n

GENERAL INDEX

Windischgraz (now Slovenj Gradec, Slovenia) xxix, xxxi, **xxxviii**, xxxix, xl, 5, 118n, 190, 302n, 304, 314, 421n, 513, 515
  Wolf Museum 514
Winnenthal 300
Winterthur 338
Wittgenstein-Köchert, Hilde xxiii, 22n, 490–91
Wolf, Adrienne (died in infancy; HW's sister) 513, 514
Wolf, Adrienne ('Jenny'; HW's sister) **513**, 514, 515, 517
  correspondence 513, 539
  daughters 513
Wolf, Cornelia 514
Wolf, Gilbert (HW's brother) xxiii, **513–14**, 517
WOLF, HUGO
  as accompanist xxx, xxxii, 37n, 45n, 224, 303, 406n, 407n, 479, 484, 490, 503, 504, 511
  anonymous texts, settings of **3–4**
  appearance 240n, 507
  arrangements xxxiv
  at asylum xxi, xxxiv, 479–80, 484, 493, 511, 514, 515–16
    see also Niederösterreichische Landesirrenanstalt and Dr Svetlin
  audience response xv–xviii, 25n, 25–6, 43n, 45n, 62, 121, 122, 304, 488–9
  'Bilder aus und um Maierling' xxxvii
  birth xxix
  Bruder Maxens Höllenfahrt 516
  Byron settings xxxiii, xxxiv, **9**, 11–12, 194–5, 489
  and chamber music xxix, xxx, xxxi
  Chamisso settings **14–15**, 22
  characterisation xviii
  chromaticism xvi
  coffee addiction 12n, 518–19
  as correspondent xix, xxiii–xxiv, xxvii, **xxxvii–xliv**
  creative inertia xviv–xx, xxxiii, xxxviii, xlv, xlvi, 24, 212, 367, 368n, 451, 532
  as critic 526–7n, 534
  and dance music xxx
  Daten aus meinem Leben xxxi, 22
  death xl, 5n, 484, 527n
  delusions of grandeur xxi
  depression xxxiv, xxxviii, xlv, 25, 129n, 212, 217–18, 475, 495
  dissonance xvi
  early life xxix, 426, 517
  Eichendorff settings xviii, xxxi, xxxii, xxxiv, xlv, xlvi, 16–51, **21–5**, 354n, 483, 509, 542
  extremes of mood ix, xix, xxi, xxxi, xxxv, 25, 216–18, 267, 351, 502
  finances 175, 176n, 191n, 226, 267, 268, 270, 281, 302, 349n, 351n, 419n, 420, 477, 479, 483, 484, 486, 489, 496, 497–8, 506, 514, 518
  funeral service and burial xxi, xxxv, 26n, 32n, 292, 484, **530–31**
  Geibel settings 52–106, **55–8**
  Gesamtausgabe 307n
  Goethe settings xvi, xvii, xviii, xxiii, xxxii, xxxiii, xlv, **107–73**, 214, 303n, 354n, 473, 509, 527, 542
  Halm settings **205**
  health xxxiv, 58, 118, 220, 228–9, 279, 446n, 508
    syphilis xxi, xxx, xxxi, xxxiv, 131n, 212–13, 301, 445n, 503, 523
  Hebbel settings 174–80, **175–6**, 190
  Heine settings xxx, xxxi, xxxiv, xlv, 11, 181–204, **188–91**, 205, 482–3, 489, 542
  Hoefer setting 259–60, **259**, 543
  Hoffmann von Fallersleben settings 261–5, **262**
  humour in music xviii, 24, 27, 360, 375n
  Ibsen settings xlvi, 266–73, **267–8**
  incidental music xx, xxxi
  insomnia 12n, 94n, 390n
  Italienisches Liederbuch settings xv, xvii, xviii, xx, xxiii, xxvi, xxxiii, xxxiv, 207–58, **212–58**, 543
  Jacobi setting 274–5, **303**
  juvenilia 55, 116, 306n
  as Kapellmeister xxxi

Keller settings 276–89, **278–9**
Kerner settings xxxi, xxxv, 129n, 290–94, **291–2**
Körner settings 34n, 295–7, **296**
Lenau settings xlv, 3, 190, 205, 298–313, **301–2**, 473, 483, 543
'Lodi in song' 346–7
Loewe, influence of xviii
Lorenzi setting **314**
love affairs xxiii, xxx, xxxiii, 39n, 105n, 171n, 176, 190, 301–2, 305–6, 312n, 313n, 480–83, 490–92, 493–4, 520–24
Mahlmann setting **315**
Matthisson setting 316–19, **318**, 543
and melody xv, xvii
Michelangelo settings xxxiv, 320–29, **322**
Mörike settings xv, xvii, xviii, xx, xxvi, xxxi, xxxii, xxxiii, xlv, 24, 129n, 154–5n, 158n, 188, 202n, 214, 330–418, **342–5**, 507, 509, 525, 527, 543
as music critic xvi, xx, xxx, xlv 23
nicknames xxix, 350n, 421n
nomadic nature xxxvii, 38n, 362n, 419n, 420, 508
and opera xxi, xxix, xxxi, xxxiii, 25, 27, 55, 190, 218, 223, 224n, 267, 269, 296, 346, 419, 421, 464–5, 471, 478, 485–6, 487, 496, 506–7, 510, 513, 532, **534–40**
orchestrations xx, xxxii, xxxiii, xxxviii, xlv, xlvi, lii, liii, liv, lv, lvi, lvii, 64n, 169n, 322, 326, 355, 532–3
and organ xxix
paralysis xxxiv
Peitl settings 419–21, **419**
Pfau settings 205, 424–5, **425**
piano paraphrases xxxi
piano playing xxxiv, 193–4, 223, 296, 425, 484, 487, 492, 526
piano studies xxix, 223, 500, 517
as piano teacher xx, xxxviii, 224, 302, 349n, 490, 493–4
piano tuning 477, 517
piano writing xvi
pictorial elements 48n, 150n, 241n, 246n, 256n, 390n, 396n, 404n, 414n

Platen settings 424–9, **425**, 543
postludes 24, 45n, 188
prosody xviii, 93n, 232n, 383n
and publishers xxi, xxx, xxxiii, xxxiv, xxxvii, xlv, 10–11, 21, 23, 30, 58, 60–61, 194–5, 212, 221–7, 267, 268, 281–3, 292, 301, 304, 353, 354, 367, 425, 451–4, 459, 464–6, 485–6, 487, 493, 500, 506, 508, 509–10
Reinick settings xxxi, xxxiii, xxxiv, xlv, 34n, 430–47, **432–3**, 544
and religion 239n, 344
repetition of text xvii–xix, xxvi, 58, 88n, 94n
Roquette settings 205, **448–9**
Rückert settings 205, 450–56, **451**
Scheffel settings xxxii, 129n, 457–62, **458–9**, 544
Shakespeare settings xxxiv, xxxviii, 11, 194, 463–8, **464–5**, 489
as singing teacher 365n
sketches and fragments **541–4**
social awkwardness 84–5n
Spanisches Liederbuch settings xxxiv, 52–106, **55–8**, 544
as student xxix
Sturm settings 190, 469–70, **469**
suicide attempt and thoughts xxi, xxxiv, xxxviii, xlvi, 326n, 371n
swearing 350n
tonality xvi, xvii
tours xxxiii
vegetarianism xxxi, 318n, 518–19
violin studies xxix, 517
and Wagner xvi, xxx, xxxi, 23, 296, 318n, 345, 381n, 395n, 417n, 492–3, 494–5, 511, 518
Zschokke settings 471–2, **471**
Zusner settings 473–4, **473**
Wolf, Käthe (HW's sister) xxiii, 22, 211, 423, 513, 514, **515–16**, 517, 519
correspondence xli, xlii, 61, 225, 421, 521
travels with hw xxxiv, 492
Wolf, Katharina (née Nußbaumer; HW's mother) xxix, xxxiv, 3, 4, 22, 116, 129n,

190, 226, 230, 291, 292, 459, 510, 513,
514–15, 517
  correspondence xxxviii, xxxix, xl, xli,
    xlii, xliii, 4–5, 15, 118–19, 176–7, 220,
    230, 239n, 268, 270, 283, 302, 304, 305,
    354, 357, 452, 453, 489, 514, 520, 526n,
    536
Wolf, Max (HW's brother) 22, **516**
  correspondence xxxix, 22, 25
Wolf, Modesta, see Strasser, Modesta xxxii
Wolf, Philipp (HW's father) xxix, xxx, 3, 22,
    116, 117, 129n, 190, 291, 292, 354n, 423,
    459, 510, 513, 514, **517–19**, 534
  correspondence xxxix, xl, 4–5, 10,
    118–19, 176–7, 191, 239n, 263, 302, 304,
    305, 419, 452, 453, 473, 523, 526n, 536
  death xxxii, xlv, 24, 129n, 368n, 514, 519
Wolf-Ferrari, Ermanno 215
  4 Rispetti, Opp. 11 and 12 215
  'Alza la bionda testa, e non dormire'
    241
  'La casa del mi' amor vada in profondo'
    257
  'Facciam la pace, caro bene mio' 235
  Italienisches Liederbuch 215
  'M'è stato detto che tua madre 'n
    vuole' 243
  'Sia benedetto chi fece lo mondo' 233
Wolfsbach 514
Württemberg 335, 399n, 422
Württemberg, Duke of 317
Würzburg 13, 424

Youens, Susan xxiv
  Hugo Wolf and his Mörike Songs xxiv,
    338, 342, 368–9n
  Hugo Wolf: The Vocal Music xxiv, 146n,
    202n

Zangger, Fritz
  Das ewige Feuer im fernen Land 514
Zeisl, Erich
  'Der Schäfer' 152
  'Ein Stündlein wohl vor Tag' 370
Zeit, Die 494
Zeitung für die elegante Welt 315

Zelter, Carl Friedrich 109, 111, 116, 158, 316,
    317
  'Beherzigung' 148
  'Die Bekehrte' 155
  'Epiphanias' 150
  'Erschaffen und Beleben' 116, 160
  'Erster Verlust' 126
  'Der Fischer' 124
  'Geistesgruß' 126
  'Genialisch Treiben' 151
  'Harfenspieler I' 130
  'Harfenspieler II' 130
  'Harfenspieler III' 131
  'Heiß mich nicht reden' 133
  'Kennst du das Land' 138n, 139
  'Mailied' 127
  'Nur wer die Sehnsucht kennt' 134
  'Ritter Kurts Brautfahrt' 142
  'St. Nepomuks Vorabend' 150
  'Der Sänger' 140
  'So lang man nüchtern ist' 162
  'Die Spröde' 154
  'Wanderers Nachtlied' 130
  'Willkommen dem 28. August 1749' 153,
    153n
Zemlinsky, Alexander von 212, 473
  'Es war ein alter König' 201
  'Mailied' 127
  'O Blätter, dürre Blätter!' 422
  'O Sterne, goldene Sterne' 422
Zerny, Frieda (née Zimmer) xxiii, xxxiii,
    33n, 105n, 136n, 149n, 165n, 171n, 194,
    300, 371n, 406n, 479, 484, 489, 491, 503,
    514, **520–24**
  correspondence xlii, 194, 414n, 459,
    522–3
  'In memoriam' 524
Zeus 171n
Zilcher, Hermann
  'Resignation' 31–2
  'St. Nepomuks Vorabend' 150
Zillig, Winfried
  'Beherzigung' 148
  'Wanderers Nachtlied' 130
Zimmermann, Johann Georg 130n
  Über die Einsamkeit 130n

Zois von Edelstein, Hans Freiherr 293, 293n
Zschokke, Heinrich xlvi, 55, 116, **471–2**
 Abenteuer einer Neujahrsnacht 471
 Feldblumen ... 471
 Das Goldmacherdorf 471
 'Heimweh nach der Schweiz' 471
 'Nacht und Grab' 471, 472n
Zum schwarzen Adler (Gasthaus) 343

Zumsteeg, Johann Rudolf 315, 316, 397n
 'Andenken' 319
 'Heiß mich nicht reden' 133
Zurich 20, 277, 278
Zurich, Lake 124n
Zusner, Vincenz xlvi, 55, **473–4**
 'Das Abendglöcklein' 473, 474n
 Gedichte von Vincenz Zusner 472
Zweybrück, Franz 55
Zwickau 56